Critical Economic Implications of Global Demographic Changes

Bryan Christiansen
https://orcid.org/0000-0001-7282-8497
Southern New Hampshire University, USA

John D. Branch
https://orcid.org/0000-0002-5201-125X
University of Michigan, USA

IGI Global Scientific Publishing
Publishing Tomorrow's Research Today

Vice President of Editorial — Melissa Wagner
Director of Acquisitions — Mikaela Felty
Director of Book Development — Jocelynn Hessler
Production Manager — Mike Brehm
Cover Design — Jose Rosado

Published in the United States of America by
IGI Global Scientific Publishing
701 East Chocolate Avenue
Hershey, PA, 17033, USA
Tel: 717-533-8845 | Fax: 717-533-7115
Website: https://www.igi-global.com E-mail: cust@igi-global.com

Library of Congress Cataloging-in-Publication Data

Names: Christiansen, Bryan, 1960- editor | Branch, John D., 1967- editor
Title: Critical economic implications of global demographic changes / edited by: Bryan Christiansen, John D. Branch.
Description: Hershey, PA : IGI Global Scientific Publishing, [2026] | Includes bibliographical references and index. | Summary: "This book examines in-depth how rapidly changing global demographics are affecting national economies and businesses in an era of increasing hyper competition worldwide"-- Provided by publisher.
Identifiers: LCCN 2025013504 (print) | LCCN 2025013505 (ebook) | ISBN 9798337325507 hardcover | ISBN 9798337325514 paperback | ISBN 9798337325521 ebook
Subjects: LCSH: Population--Economic aspects | Demography--Economic aspects | Demographic transition
Classification: LCC HB849.41 .C75 2026 (print) | LCC HB849.41 (ebook) | DDC 304.6--dc23/eng/20250929
LC record available at https://lccn.loc.gov/2025013504
LC ebook record available at https://lccn.loc.gov/2025013505

British Cataloguing in Publication Data
A Cataloguing in Publication record for this book is available from the British Library.

Table of Contents

Detailed Table of Contents

perspective, this chapter critically examines the role of the old-age population in enhancing economic growth and sustainable development of society. It also proposes specific policy suggestions for achieving the UN Decade of Healthy Aging objectives (2021-2030) that align with the SDGs.

Population aging poses multifaceted challenges to sustainable economic development, particularly within the financial services industry and the broader economy. Despite the growing body of research on demographic shifts and finance, the relationship between an aging population and sustainable finance remains underexplored. This study seeks to contribute to filling this research gap by employing bibliometric perspective and content analysis with the aim of mapping the existing research landscape. Our findings reveal a recent increase in focus on green finance (since 2024), highlighting the need for more integrated approaches to explore how sustainable finance can mitigate the economic (and social) pressures related to an aging society. This work contributes to the literature by laying the foundation for future studies, and promoting insights for policymakers, practitioners, and researchers seeking to align sustainable finance initiatives with the specific needs of aging populations.

The aging of the population in European countries is causing structural shifts in consumption patterns. Declining fertility rates and rising life expectancy are transforming not only total consumption levels but also the sectoral composition of demand across countries. Household expenditure data and demographic projections demonstrate that consumption preferences vary significantly by age. While older individuals allocate more spending to housing, healthcare and basic needs, younger populations prioritize transportation, entertainment, and education. Cluster analyses classify countries based on similarities in their age-related consumption profiles. Projections for 2100 suggest that population aging will lead to a permanent restructuring of consumption baskets. These sectoral shifts are expected to generate employment in healthcare, care services, and age-friendly industries, while contraction

while youth-dense nations struggle with underemployment and the need for large-scale skilling. The study reveals a significant policy gap in adapting automation strategies to demographic realities, risking increased inequality and social instability. The findings underscore the urgency for differentiated, forward-looking labor and education policies tailored to each demographic context. This research aligns with SDGs 8, 4, 10, and 9, offering insights for sustainable economic planning amid global demographic upheavals.

Aging economies—characterized by declining birth rates, increasing life expectancy, and shrinking labor forces—face unprecedented challenges in sustaining economic productivity. As traditional workforces contract, automation and artificial intelligence (AI) are increasingly seen as crucial solutions for maintaining economic stability and supporting aging populations. Technologies such as robotic process automation (RPA), machine learning, and autonomous systems are transforming industries, reshaping the future of work, and redefining economic structures in aging societies. This article explores the impact of automation on labor markets in aging economies, focusing on both challenges and opportunities. It examines how automation affects employment trends, economic productivity, healthcare, and workforce dynamics, while also addressing policy considerations, social implications, and ethical concerns.

Disability insurance is essential for providing financial security, facilitating meaningful employment participation, and helping people with disabilities. The importance of disability insurance is discussed in this chapter with an emphasis on its advantages, drawbacks, and effects on workforce growth. It looks at how disability insurance helps people with disabilities maintain their financial stability and participate in work-related activities by offering vocational rehabilitation, income replacement, and other support services. The chapter also covers the challenges that people with impairments encounter while trying to obtain and make use of disability insurance, such as difficult qualifying standards, intricate administrative procedures, and social stigma. In addition, it examines how disability insurance affects employment results and rates of workforce participation, emphasizing how it helps to advance sustainable workforce development.

This empirical investigation employs a multivariate time series framework utilizing the Vector Error Correction Model (VECM) to unravel the intricate long-run equilibrium and short-run dynamics among GDP, youth population, and youth literacy in India for the time- period 1990 to 2024, revealing through Johansen cointegration test the existence of two statistically significant cointegrating vectors, with normalized equations underscoring the pivotal elasticity-driven relationships between economic growth and demographic-literacy indicators, while adjustment coefficients demonstrate the system's endogenous correction mechanism toward long-run equilibrium, and the impulse response and variance decomposition analyses substantiate the dominance of literacy shocks in driving GDP variability over extended horizons, thereby yielding profound macroeconomic implications for policy formulation directed at enhancing human capital and ensuring sustainable developmental trajectories.

Africa undergoes a profound demographic transition as the number of its youth exhibits a significantly rapid rise. In this context, entrepreneurship serves as a major opportunity to harness this demographic dividend and to foster economic development. This chapter explores the role of youthful populations in driving economic growth in Africa. It presents the conceptual framework of youth entrepreneurship and

corresponding migration patterns. Findings suggest that countries with secular or culturally open societies show higher net immigration, whereas those with more conservative or religious homogeneous environments tend to face high emigration rates. This study underscores the nuanced but significant role that cultural and religious factors play in shaping global human mobility.

Preface

The world stands at a demographic crossroads. Never before in history have global populations shifted so dramatically and so unevenly across regions. While some nations grapple with rapidly aging populations and declining fertility rates, others are experiencing a surge in youthful demographics eager to contribute to their nations' economic and social development. These demographic transitions, shaped by fertility, mortality, migration, and urbanization, are redefining the foundations of global economic systems, reshaping labor markets, altering patterns of consumption, and challenging public policies across the world.

This edited volume, *Critical Economic Implications of Global Demographic Changes*, explores the profound ways in which population dynamics influence economic structures and outcomes. The chapters assembled in this book offer an interdisciplinary examination of how demographic change intersects with economics, public policy, and business strategy in the 21st century. The contributions analyze issues such as aging workforces and pension sustainability, the economic potential of youthful populations in developing nations, the role of migration in balancing global labor markets, and the complex interplay between urbanization, infrastructure development, and economic growth.

CHAPTER OVERVIEW

Chapter 1 explores the intricate relationship between population growth and economic stability in the South Asian Association for Regional Cooperation (SAARC) nations. By analyzing demographic data from 1960 to 2023 using mathematical modeling and statistical methods, this study uncovers how population acceleration and deceleration vary across countries such as India, Bangladesh, Pakistan, and Sri Lanka. The chapter provides valuable comparative insights into how these variations influence economic structures, resource distribution, and long-term growth trajectories, offering an empirical foundation for understanding the demographic shifts shaping South Asia's economic future.

Chapter 2 addresses the growing global concern of population aging and its implications for sustainable development. It examines the shifting balance among youth, working-age, and elderly populations over the last century and assesses the economic contributions of older generations. This chapter not only highlights the challenges of declining fertility rates and rising longevity but also proposes policy directions aligned with the United Nations Decade of Healthy Aging and the Sustainable Development Goals (SDGs). Its insights encourage policymakers to view aging populations as a resource for growth rather than merely a demographic burden.

Chapter 3 presents a bibliometric analysis of the emerging intersection between population aging and sustainable finance. It maps global research trends and identifies increasing attention to green finance initiatives since 2024. The analysis underscores the necessity of integrating demographic insights into sustainable finance strategies to address the fiscal and social pressures of aging societies. This chapter serves as an important contribution to future policymaking and research, demonstrating how financial innovation can help maintain economic resilience amid demographic transformation.

Chapter 4 analyzes how population aging reshapes sectoral consumption patterns in European economies. Using data-driven cluster analyses, it reveals how demographic shifts alter consumer priorities, with older populations emphasizing healthcare, housing, and basic needs, while younger groups focus more on leisure and education. The projections suggest a long-term restructuring of economic activity across sectors, with growth in age-friendly industries and contraction in others. This work provides a crucial perspective on how evolving demographics will redefine future market demand and employment trends.

Chapter 5 highlights how global demographic shifts influence agricultural markets and food security. Population growth in developing regions, coupled with urbanization and changing dietary patterns, is transforming food production and distribution systems. This chapter assesses the pressures on agricultural sustainability, trade flows, and innovation in food systems. It underscores that ensuring food security in the face of demographic and environmental change requires integrated strategies that align agricultural productivity with sustainability and equitable resource access.

Chapter 6 investigates the interaction between demographic transitions, automation, and policy adaptation in the global economy. It contrasts aging societies facing shrinking workforces with youth-dense regions grappling with underemployment. The chapter demonstrates how automation reshapes productivity and labor markets, emphasizing the risks of policy inertia. It calls for differentiated strategies tailored to each demographic context, advocating education, training, and technology alignment to promote inclusive and sustainable economic growth.

Chapter 7 continues the exploration of automation by focusing specifically on its role in aging economies. It analyzes how technologies such as artificial intelligence, robotics, and automation compensate for declining labor forces while transforming employment structures. The chapter discusses both the opportunities and ethical dilemmas that automation presents, offering insights into how governments and industries can foster technological adoption without exacerbating social inequality.

Chapter 8 focuses on the critical role of disability insurance in fostering sustainable workforce development. It examines how such insurance provides financial stability, rehabilitation, and inclusion for individuals with disabilities. The chapter also identifies persistent barriers such as social stigma, complex eligibility procedures, and limited accessibility. By framing disability insurance as an integral element of inclusive growth, this contribution reinforces the broader economic and moral imperative of building equitable labor systems.

Chapter 9 delves into the dynamics between human resource development and economic growth, particularly in the context of India's youthful population. Through advanced econometric analysis, it reveals how youth literacy and education levels directly influence GDP growth and long-term development. The findings emphasize the transformative power of human capital investment, highlighting literacy as a key driver of economic stability and a cornerstone of sustainable national progress.

Chapter 10 examines youth entrepreneurship in Africa as a vital catalyst for economic transformation. As the continent's young population expands rapidly, entrepreneurship emerges as a means to harness its demographic potential. Through comparative case studies, the chapter evaluates policy initiatives and identifies barriers to entrepreneurial success, including limited financing and regulatory challenges. It advocates for inclusive policies and educational programs that empower young innovators, fostering resilience and self-sustaining growth across African economies.

Chapter 11 explores the pivotal role of women in shaping demographic and economic outcomes. It examines women's participation in the labor market, entrepreneurship, and leadership while addressing systemic barriers such as wage inequality and unpaid care work. Drawing from global case studies, the chapter demonstrates that gender-inclusive policies and organizational reforms not only promote equality but also drive economic growth and sustainability. It reinforces the idea that empowering women is essential to achieving balanced demographic and economic progress.

Chapter 12 investigates how cultural and religious factors influence global migration trends. By employing cluster analysis across nations, the chapter reveals how societal openness, secularism, and cultural homogeneity affect migration patterns. It finds that more inclusive societies attract immigrants, while conservative or restrictive cultural environments tend to experience emigration. These insights emphasize the deep interconnections between culture, religion, and the economic dimensions of human mobility in the globalized world.

As editors, we believe that understanding these shifts is crucial for academics, policymakers, and business leaders alike. The global economy is increasingly characterized by hyper competition, where nations and corporations must adapt to the demographic realities that shape their human capital, innovation capacity, and long-term competitiveness. The economic opportunities associated with a youthful population, particularly in Africa, South Asia, and Latin America, can yield a demographic dividend, but only if accompanied by strategic investments in education, healthcare, and employment. Conversely, aging populations in advanced economies present both fiscal challenges and new market opportunities, particularly in healthcare innovation, automation, and eldercare industries.

Our goal with this publication is to provide a comprehensive reference source that captures both the challenges and the possibilities of global demographic transformation. The book's diverse chapters address questions that are at the forefront of economic and policy debates: How can nations mitigate the economic strain of aging populations? What policies best leverage youthful populations for sustainable growth? How will migration and urbanization reshape global labor and real estate markets? And how can technology bridge the widening demographic and economic divides across nations?

This volume is intended for a wide readership, including scholars, practitioners, and graduate students, who seek a deeper understanding of how demographic trends shape economic realities in both developed and emerging economies. By bringing together global perspectives, theoretical insights, and empirical case studies, this reference work serves as both a foundation for academic inquiry and a practical guide for policymakers navigating an era of unprecedented demographic transformation.

We extend our gratitude to the contributing authors for their rigorous scholarship and thoughtful analysis, and to the readers who continue to engage in the essential dialogue about how demographic change will define the world's economic future.

Bryan Christiansen
Southern New Hampshire University, United States

John Branch
University of Michigan, United States

Chapter 1
Exploring Population Growth and Economic Stability in SAARC Nations:
A Cross-National Examination

Vishnu Achutha Menon
https://orcid.org/0000-0003-4028-3685
Institute for Educational and Developmental Studies, Noida, India

T. K. Sateesh Kumar
https://orcid.org/0000-0002-8406-409X
Kristu Jayanti College, India

Juby Thomas
https://orcid.org/0000-0003-2167-0620
Kristu Jayanti College, India

K. G. Suresh
Apeejay Institute of Mass Communication, India

Lijo P. Thomas
Kristu Jayanti College, India

ABSTRACT

This study investigates the population growth patterns in South Asian countries by examining key population statistics from 1960 to 2023. This study applies mathematical derivatives to analyze the rate of change in both first and second-order

DOI: 10.4018/979-8-3373-2550-7.ch001

trends for countries including Afghanistan, Bangladesh, Bhutan, India, Maldives, Nepal, Pakistan, and Sri Lanka. The analysis involves calculating the mean and standard deviation of the first and second derivatives, which provides insights into population growth acceleration and deceleration over time. The research employs a quantitative approach to understand the long-term trends in population dynamics, aiming to identify and compare the population growth patterns of these countries. The results show distinct differences in the rates of growth and acceleration between countries, highlighting key periods of demographic shifts.

INTRODUCTION

The South Asian Association for Regional Cooperation (SAARC) is an intergovernmental organization established in 1985 to promote economic and regional integration among its member states. The organization comprises Afghanistan, Bangladesh, Bhutan, India, Maldives, Nepal, Pakistan, and Sri Lanka. These nations collectively represent a significant proportion of the global population and are characterized by diverse demographic trends, economic conditions, and social structures. The SAARC region is home to over 1.8 billion people, making it one of the most densely populated regions in the world. Understanding the dynamics of population growth within these countries is crucial for evaluating their socio-economic development, resource allocation, and long-term sustainability. The study of population growth in SAARC nations is important due to its impact on economic development, public policy, and social welfare. Population growth influences labor force participation, economic productivity, healthcare systems, education infrastructure, and environmental sustainability. Countries experiencing rapid population growth, such as India, Pakistan, and Bangladesh, encounter challenges related to employment generation, urbanization, and resource distribution, while nations with slower population growth, such as Bhutan and the Maldives, may face issues related to an aging population and workforce shortages. Examining these trends helps policymakers develop strategies that support economic stability, social development, and environmental sustainability.

The differences in population growth among SAARC nations reflect variations in fertility rates, mortality rates, migration patterns, and government policies. While some countries have implemented successful population control measures, others continue to experience high birth rates, leading to demographic expansion. Analyzing these variations allows for a comparative approach in identifying best practices and developing policies tailored to each country's demographic structure. Population growth has economic implications for the SAARC region, influencing GDP growth, income distribution, and human capital development. A growing population can create a demographic dividend, leading to a large and youthful workforce that contributes to economic expansion. If population growth outpaces investments in education, healthcare, and job creation, it may result in unemployment, poverty, and socio-economic disparities. Examining population growth trends helps align economic development strategies with demographic changes to promote inclusive and sustainable growth. Environmental sustainability is closely linked to population growth in SAARC countries. Increasing demand for natural resources, food, water, and energy places pressure on the environment, contributing to deforestation, water scarcity, pollution, and climate change. Many SAARC nations are already facing environmental challenges due to high population densities and rapid urbanization. Understanding population growth dynamics helps governments design sustainable development policies that balance economic growth with environmental conservation, ensuring resilience against climate-related risks.

REVIEW OF LITERATURE

Population growth, urban population growth, and rural population growth exert a negative and statistically significant influence on the long-term growth of GDP per capita. Over an extended period, these demographic factors contribute to economic challenges, impeding sustained improvements in income levels across nations. The statistical evidence underscores that as the population increases, particularly in urban and rural areas, the strain on resources, infrastructure, and employment opportunities negatively affects economic expansion.

There exists a one-way causal relationship in which population growth and rural population growth drive changes in GDP per capita. However, urban population growth does not exhibit a direct causal impact on GDP per capita, suggesting that economic transformations are primarily shaped by overall population dynamics and rural development patterns rather than urbanization alone (Asim et al., 2022). This finding indicates that policies focusing solely on urban growth without addressing rural population expansion may not yield the anticipated economic benefits. The concept of demographic dividend plays a crucial role in influencing economic growth, particularly in the SAARC countries, including Bangladesh, India, Nepal, Sri Lanka, and Pakistan. The demographic dividend, which refers to the economic advantages arising from shifts in population age structure, has been found to positively contribute to economic expansion in these nations. This impact is evident not only when considering the SAARC region as a whole but also when examining each country individually. The presence of a working-age population that surpasses the dependent population creates an environment conducive to increased productivity and economic progress.

The growth of gross capital formation stands out as a significantly influential factor in promoting economic growth within the SAARC region. Investments in capital assets, including infrastructure, machinery, and technology, contribute directly to higher levels of productivity and efficiency, fostering an environment where economies can experience sustained development. The availability of capital resources ensures that businesses and industries can expand, generate employment, and contribute to the overall economic well-being of the region (Jafrin et al., 2021). Given these economic dynamics, there is an urgent necessity to enhance research and publication efforts within the SAARC region. Researchers, institutions, and governments must prioritize publishing their findings in reputable, high-impact journals. Ensuring that valuable research reaches the global academic community is essential for knowledge dissemination and policy formulation. It is equally important to prevent research from being left unpublished or appearing in predatory journals, which can undermine the credibility and reach of scholarly contributions.

A particular need has been identified for more specialized journals within the disciplines of orthopedics and sports medicine in the SAARC region. Establishing such journals can facilitate advancements in medical research and clinical practices. Moreover, collaborations between national and international institutions can enhance the quality and impact of research publications. These partnerships can lead to higher research standards, greater knowledge exchange, and improved visibility of studies originating from the SAARC countries (Vaishya & Vaish, 2023). The COVID-19 pandemic has also been an area of extensive research, with predictive models being used to analyze infection trends. The logistic model has been particularly effective in describing the upward trend of COVID-19 cases in SAARC countries, yielding an R^2 value greater than 0.96. This high degree of accuracy demonstrates the model's reliability in forecasting infection patterns and aiding policymakers in making informed decisions. Projections indicate that the final number of infections during the second wave was highest in India, reaching an estimated 19.8 million cases. In contrast, Afghanistan experienced the lowest predicted infection count, with approximately 0.041 million cases. A distinct variation in the timing of the pandemic's peak was observed among SAARC countries, with Bangladesh reaching its peak 14 days earlier than other nations in the region. These findings emphasize the importance of timely interventions and country-specific strategies in managing pandemic outbreaks effectively (Lamichhane et al., 2022).

The rate of COVID-19 infection has been found to be highest among the young, working-age population in SAARC countries. This demographic group constitutes more than 80% of the total population, making them the most affected by the virus. Given their active social interactions, mobility, and work-related exposures, individuals in this age group are more likely to come into contact with the virus, increasing the overall transmission rate in the region. Despite the widespread belief that hot and humid weather may slow the spread of COVID-19, research suggests that the slower transmission observed in SAARC countries is not due to climatic conditions. Instead, various factors, including diverse lifestyles, immunity levels, and genetic predispositions, have contributed to the patterns of disease spread in these countries. These factors differentiate the SAARC region from other parts of the world, emphasizing the need for localized strategies to manage the outbreak. In the absence of a specific treatment or an available vaccine at the time of the study, preventive measures remained the only viable option to protect the population. Timely interventions such as social distancing, mask mandates, and lockdowns were essential in mitigating the spread of the virus. Without these measures, the consequences of the pandemic could have been significantly more severe in the region (Sultana & Reza, 2020).

A separate study investigated the relationship between economic growth and carbon emissions in SAARC countries. The findings confirmed the existence of a unidirectional causal relationship, where economic growth influences carbon emissions, but not vice versa. This suggests that as economies expand, the level of carbon emissions increases, reinforcing concerns about environmental sustainability. The study further established a positive association between economic growth and carbon emissions, lending support to the environmental Kuznets curve (EKC) hypothesis. According to this hypothesis, carbon emissions tend to rise as economic development progresses, but after reaching a certain level of prosperity, emissions begin to decline due to increased environmental awareness and the adoption of cleaner technologies. The study also identified a causal link between urban population growth and energy consumption with carbon emissions. Additionally, domestic capital and inflation rate were found to have a causal relationship with economic growth, indicating the interconnected nature of these economic and environmental factors (Latief et al., 2021). In an effort to assess the early-stage spread of COVID-19, researchers estimated the basic reproduction number (R_0) of SARS-CoV-2 in SAARC countries for the first 60 days of the outbreak. The findings indicated that the initial growth of infections was exponential. The R_0 values varied across the region, with the highest value recorded in Bangladesh (3.86), suggesting that the epidemic was most severe there during the initial phase. Conversely, Bhutan recorded the lowest R_0 value (1.31), indicating a slower rate of infection. For the remaining SAARC countries, the estimated R_0 values were as follows: India (2.07), Maldives (3.22), Nepal (1.75), Pakistan (1.43), Afghanistan (1.47), and Sri Lanka (2.39). These differences in transmission rates highlight variations in public health responses, population density, and intervention effectiveness across the region (Uddin et al., 2020).

Another study examined the correlation between COVID-19-related deaths and health expenditure as a percentage of GDP in SAARC countries. The analysis revealed a significant positive correlation, suggesting that higher healthcare spending was associated with an increased number of reported COVID-19 deaths. This could be due to the fact that countries with better healthcare infrastructure may have recorded and reported cases more accurately, rather than the spending itself contributing to a higher fatality rate. Interestingly, factors such as population density, literacy rate, percentage of the adult population, and poverty levels were not significantly correlated with the number of COVID-19 cases and deaths. This challenges assumptions that these socio-economic factors directly influence pandemic outcomes, suggesting that other elements, such as government responses, healthcare accessibility, and testing capacity, play a more decisive role in determining case and death rates. The study also found that India had the highest initial real-time reproductive number (R) among SAARC countries, followed by Bangladesh. This indicates that the rate at which the virus was spreading in these countries was initially higher compared to others in the region, reinforcing the importance of early interventions and stringent public health measures (Malik et al., 2021).

The Environmental Kuznets Curve (EKC) hypothesis, which suggests that environmental degradation initially worsens with economic growth before improving at higher income levels, does not hold in the SAARC region. Instead, a U-shaped quadratic relationship has been identified between GDP and environmental pollution. This implies that environmental degradation decreases at lower GDP levels, worsens as economic growth accelerates, and then improves only at significantly high income levels. The unique economic and environmental dynamics of the SAARC region indicate that pollution reduction does not naturally follow rising prosperity. The primary source of environmental pollution in SAARC countries is the reliance on fossil fuels. The use of coal, oil, and natural gas has significantly contributed to the worsening environmental conditions in the region. However, a transition toward renewable energy sources and nuclear power could help reduce pollution in the long run. The findings suggest that economic progress alone is insufficient to address environmental challenges in SAARC countries. Policymakers need to implement targeted environmental regulations and promote clean energy adoption to achieve sustainable development (Voumik et al., 2023).

A separate study examined the factors influencing life expectancy at birth in SAARC countries. The findings indicate that an increase in the average years of schooling and improved sanitation services are positively associated with higher life expectancy. Access to education plays a crucial role in shaping health awareness and hygiene practices, while better sanitation reduces the prevalence of communicable diseases, leading to longer life expectancy. Factors such as a higher total fertility rate, increasing urban population, and rising CO_2 emissions were negatively associated with life expectancy. Rapid urbanization often leads to overcrowding, inadequate healthcare facilities, and increased exposure to pollutants, all of which contribute to adverse health outcomes. A higher total fertility rate may strain healthcare resources, making it difficult to provide adequate medical services. Surprisingly, the study found that higher health expenditure had a significant but negative impact on life expectancy. This unexpected result suggests that increased spending on healthcare may not always translate into better health outcomes, potentially due to inefficiencies in the healthcare system, misallocation of resources, or rising medical costs without corresponding improvements in service quality (Jafrin, Masud, et al., 2021).

Financial inclusion has been identified as an important factor in supporting economic growth in SAARC countries. A study found a long-term relationship between financial inclusion and economic growth, suggesting that increasing access to financial services contributes to overall economic development. Financial inclusion allows individuals and businesses to participate more actively in the economy, leading to increased savings, investments, and entrepreneurship. The study identified a bi-directional causal relationship between financial inclusion and economic growth. This indicates that not only does financial inclusion promote economic growth, but economic expansion also drives further advancements in financial services. As economies grow, access to banking, credit, and insurance services improves, creating a cycle that reinforces economic stability and development (Singh & Stakic, 2020).

Another study explored the relationship between demographic structure, industrial growth, and environmental indicators in SAARC countries. The findings revealed evidence of cross-sectional dependence and panel heterogeneity among these variables, indicating that the relationships are complex and vary across different nations. These results highlight the need for country-specific policies rather than a one-size-fits-all approach to addressing environmental challenges. The study supports the Environmental Kuznets Curve hypothesis, showing that industrial growth initially worsens environmental quality before leading to improvements in the long run. As industries expand, pollution and environmental degradation tend to increase. However, with higher levels of economic development, technological advancements, regulatory measures, and environmental awareness contribute to reducing the negative impact of industrial activities. Despite this long-term improvement, certain factors remain detrimental to environmental quality in SAARC countries. A growing working-age population, rapid urbanization, and increasing trade activities have been identified as major contributors to environmental degradation. These factors often lead to increased consumption, higher energy demand, and greater waste generation, all of which strain environmental resources. Addressing these challenges requires sustainable urban planning, investment in green technologies, and stricter environmental policies to balance economic growth with environmental conservation (Khan et al., 2021).

The role of renewable energy sources in driving economic growth has been examined in the context of SAARC countries. Findings indicate that all three renewable energy sources—geothermal, hydro, and wind—had a positive and significant impact on economic growth. The expansion of renewable energy infrastructure has contributed to increased energy availability, reduced reliance on fossil fuels, and enhanced industrial productivity. Among the three renewable energy sources, hydropower was found to have the strongest effect on economic growth. The significant contribution of hydropower can be attributed to its large-scale energy generation capacity, reliability, and cost-effectiveness compared to geothermal and wind energy. Given the abundance of water resources in certain SAARC nations, hydropower has emerged as a key driver of sustainable economic progress in the region (Li et al., 2021).

In response to the COVID-19 pandemic, countries that effectively controlled the spread of the virus did so by implementing early and strict non-pharmaceutical interventions. Measures such as nationwide lockdowns, social distancing mandates, and travel restrictions played a crucial role in slowing down transmission rates. These actions helped prevent healthcare systems from being overwhelmed and allowed authorities to manage the crisis more effectively. India, the largest nation within the SAARC bloc, emerged as the epicenter of the COVID-19 pandemic in the region. With rising infection rates and an increasing death toll, urgent and effective measures were necessary to curb the spread of the virus. Delayed responses or ineffective containment strategies could result in severe public health and economic consequences. To combat the challenges posed by the pandemic, SAARC authorities were urged to take swift, coordinated, and decisive actions. Strengthening regional collaboration, sharing resources, and implementing joint strategies were crucial steps in addressing the crisis. A united effort among SAARC nations could improve pandemic management and enhance preparedness for future health emergencies (Shohan et al., 2020).

The environmental consequences of economic activities have been widely studied in South Asian countries. Research indicates that economic growth, urbanization, and industrialization have led to increased carbon dioxide emissions in the region. As cities expand and industries develop, energy consumption rises, contributing to higher levels of air pollution and greenhouse gas emissions. However, certain factors have played a role in mitigating carbon dioxide emissions. Population growth, natural resource rents, and increased electrification have contributed to a reduction in emissions. The relationship between population growth and lower emissions may be attributed to increased investments in cleaner energy solutions and more efficient resource utilization. Revenue generated from natural resources has been used to support environmental initiatives and energy-efficient technologies. Among these factors, urbanization has been identified as having the most severe negative impact on the environment. Rapid urban expansion often leads to deforestation, waste accumulation, and increased fossil fuel consumption, exacerbating environmental degradation. On the other hand, natural resource rents have been more effective than electrification in preventing environmental damage, suggesting that revenue from resource extraction has been utilized for sustainable development efforts (Voumik, Mimi, et al., 2023).

The influence of information and communication technology (ICT) on economic growth has also been analyzed in SAARC countries. Findings indicate that ICT has had a positive and statistically significant impact on economic growth in the region. Digital transformation, improvements in telecommunication infrastructure, and the widespread adoption of internet-based services have contributed to enhanced productivity and economic development. The impact of ICT on economic growth has been the highest in India, followed by Sri Lanka, Bangladesh, and Pakistan. India's strong ICT sector, supported by its extensive software and technology industries, has played a crucial role in driving economic expansion. As digital connectivity continues to improve across the region, ICT is expected to further contribute to economic progress by fostering innovation, facilitating business operations, and increasing access to global markets (Tripathi & Inani, 2020).

The relationship between renewable energy consumption and carbon dioxide (CO_2) emissions in SAARC countries shows that an increase in renewable energy use significantly reduces CO_2 emissions. This effect is most noticeable in countries with higher pollution levels, where the shift to renewable energy sources helps lower overall emissions. Reducing reliance on fossil fuels is a necessary step toward addressing environmental concerns and improving air quality. Urbanization has a strong positive impact on economic growth in SAARC countries. As cities expand, they become centers of business, industry, and employment, leading to higher GDP. At the same time, natural resource rents—revenues generated from extracting natural resources—contribute to economic growth. However, resource extraction is also linked to higher CO_2 emissions, indicating that economic activities dependent on natural resources come with significant environmental costs.

Broad money, which measures the total money supply in an economy, affects GDP in different ways depending on economic conditions. In lower-income groups, broad money increases GDP by making more capital available for investment and business activities. However, in higher-income groups, excess money supply has a negative impact, possibly due to inflationary pressures or inefficient use of capital (Khan et al., 2023). India's economic growth and trade activities have had a positive impact on neighboring South Asian countries, including Bangladesh, Sri Lanka, Nepal, and Bhutan. As the largest economy in the region, India plays an important role in shaping trade relationships, supply chains, and investment flows. Economic expansion in India creates opportunities for trade and business across SAARC nations, supporting regional development. To achieve balanced economic development, increasing trade openness within the region is necessary. Reducing trade barriers, improving infrastructure, and encouraging cross-border trade would help strengthen economic ties between SAARC nations. India, given its economic position, can contribute significantly to regional development by engaging in political and economic cooperation through the South Asian Association for Regional Cooperation (SAARC) (Kumar, 2019).

Agriculture, forestry, and fishing (AFF) play an essential role in economic growth across SAARC countries. Research shows that fisheries production, aquaculture, and agriculture all have a positive and significant impact on the economy. These sectors provide jobs, ensure food security, and contribute to exports. Modernizing agricultural practices, improving fisheries management, and developing aquaculture industries would support further economic progress (Alharthi & Hanif, 2020). Among SAARC nations, India has the highest CO_2 emissions. Industrialization, urban expansion, and energy consumption contribute to this trend. However, increasing the use of renewable energy and implementing environmental management systems such as ISO 14001 certification have been linked to lower emissions. Expanding clean energy production and adopting better environmental policies can help reduce the environmental impact of economic growth. The results of these studies provide useful insights for policymakers and businesses seeking to lower CO_2 emissions and improve environmental sustainability. Investing in renewable energy and encouraging industries to adopt environmental standards can help reduce pollution and support long-term environmental goals (Ikram et al., 2020).

Research on microplastics in SAARC countries is still limited, with India leading in studies on this issue. Other countries in the region have conducted little to no research on microplastic pollution. There is also a lack of studies on airborne microplastics and their presence in agricultural and forest soils, leaving important environmental concerns unaddressed. In addition, little research has been done on the effectiveness of wastewater treatment plants in removing microplastics in SAARC countries. Understanding how well these facilities filter out microplastics is necessary for preventing contamination of freshwater and marine ecosystems. Expanding research and implementing policies to manage microplastic pollution would help protect both the environment and public health in the region (Amrutha et al., 2021).

A study developed a modified Susceptible-Infected-Recovered (M-SIR) predictive model to analyze the epidemic trend of COVID-19 in SAARC countries. This model was designed to provide a more accurate forecast of infection, recovery, and active case trends in the region, considering variations in healthcare responses, policy interventions, and population dynamics. Using the M-SIR model, the study estimated COVID-19 trends over different time frames: short-term (20 days), mid-term (90 days), and long-term (180 days). These estimates provided valuable insights into the expected progression of the epidemic, helping policymakers make informed decisions regarding containment strategies, resource allocation, and healthcare system preparedness. The findings indicate that India, Bangladesh, Sri Lanka, and Pakistan have been gradually increasing their recovery rates and reducing the number of active cases. This suggests that healthcare interventions and preventive measures in these countries have contributed to improving patient outcomes. In contrast, Afghanistan, Nepal, and Bhutan are projected to experience a steep increase in active cases over the long term, highlighting the need for stronger mitigation efforts in these nations to control the spread of the virus (Dey et al., 2020).

The challenges faced by women entrepreneurs vary across different regions, shaped by unique social and cultural factors. Developing countries, including those in the SAARC region, present a distinct set of conditions compared to developed economies, influencing the opportunities and obstacles encountered by women in business. The study emphasizes the importance of conducting more in-depth qualitative and quantitative research to gain a comprehensive understanding of the experiences of women entrepreneurs in emerging economies. By analyzing both structural and cultural barriers, future research can offer solutions tailored to the specific needs of female entrepreneurs in these regions. The paper presents a systematic literature review on women entrepreneurship in emerging economies, with a particular focus on the SAARC region. It identifies significant gaps in the existing research and calls for further studies to address these areas, ensuring that policy recommendations and support mechanisms are evidence-based and effective (Rashid & Ratten, 2020).

Bangladesh has a unique trade pattern within the SAARC region, exporting more to member countries than it imports from them. However, despite its higher export volume, Bangladesh continues to experience a negative trade balance overall. This trade deficit indicates that while Bangladesh benefits from regional trade, it still relies heavily on imports from non-SAARC countries to meet domestic demand. One of the key trade imbalances exists in its economic relationship with India. Bangladesh has a large trade deficit with India, which should be addressed by focusing on increasing exports to other SAARC nations with greater export potential. Diversifying its export markets within the region would help reduce dependency on a single trading partner and create more balanced trade dynamics. Bangladesh needs to work toward reducing its overall import dependence, both within SAARC and globally. Strengthening domestic industries, promoting local production, and exploring alternative trade partners could contribute to a more sustainable and resilient economic structure (Gazi et al., 2022).

In the financial sector, research suggests that loan growth can contribute to increased bank risk in the South Asian economic region. While expanding credit availability supports economic growth, excessive loan growth without proper risk management mechanisms can lead to financial instability. The study found that bank solvency and profitability are significantly correlated with bank risk. This suggests that financial institutions must maintain a careful balance between profitability and risk exposure to ensure long-term stability. A stronger regulatory framework and risk assessment measures are essential to mitigate potential banking crises in the region. To evaluate bank risk, the researchers used the ZSCORE as an alternative measure, allowing for a more robust analysis of financial stability. The findings highlight the importance of prudent lending practices and effective regulatory oversight to safeguard the banking sector against financial volatility (Bhowmik & Sarker, 2021).

Air quality in South Asia has significantly deteriorated over the past three decades, with large increases in carbon dioxide (CO_2) emissions, greenhouse gas emissions, methane emissions, and nitrous oxide emissions. Rapid industrialization, urbanization, and increased energy consumption have contributed to worsening environmental conditions across the region. These rising emissions pose serious risks to public health, climate stability, and overall environmental sustainability. In addition to greenhouse gas emissions, ambient air pollution has also risen sharply in many South Asian countries, as indicated by increasing concentrations of fine particulate matter (PM2.5). The highest levels of PM2.5 pollution have been recorded in Nepal, India, and Bangladesh, where urbanization, vehicular emissions, and industrial activities have intensified air quality concerns. Prolonged exposure to PM2.5 is associated with respiratory diseases, cardiovascular problems, and reduced life expectancy, making air pollution a major public health issue in the region. Sustainability indicators such as access to safe drinking water, sanitation services, and electricity remain low in many South Asian countries compared to high-income nations. Limited access to these basic services highlights disparities in infrastructure development and the need for greater investments in public health, sanitation, and energy accessibility to improve living standards across the region (Jabbar et al., 2022).

Economic growth in South Asia is influenced by several key factors, including CO_2 emissions and population density. Studies indicate that both CO_2 emissions and population density positively contribute to economic growth, with population density having a greater impact. Densely populated regions benefit from higher labor availability, increased consumer demand, and greater economic activity, which collectively support economic expansion. However, trade openness has been found to have a negative impact on economic growth in South Asia. While open trade policies can enhance market access and boost exports, they may also expose domestic industries to increased competition, affecting local production and employment. The study also found bidirectional causality between economic growth and CO_2 emissions, as well as between trade openness and CO_2 emissions. Additionally, there is a one-way causal relationship from trade openness to economic growth, from population density to CO_2 emissions, and from labor to both economic growth and population density. These findings highlight the complex interactions between environmental, economic, and trade factors in the region (Rahman et al., 2020).

The relationship between macroeconomic factors and stock market returns in South Asia has also been analyzed. The Granger Causality test revealed that GDP growth rate and exchange rate have a causal relationship with stock market returns, indicating that fluctuations in economic growth and currency value directly impact financial markets. Several other economic indicators play a role in shaping stock market performance. Inflation rate and foreign currency reserve growth rate have a significant impact on stock returns, while GDP growth rate, foreign currency reserve growth rate, and fiscal deficit contribute positively to stock market growth. In contrast, interest rates, inflation rate, foreign direct investment (FDI) to GDP ratio, and exchange rate negatively influence stock market returns. These findings suggest that economic stability, monetary policy, and foreign investment trends are key determinants of financial market behavior in South Asia (Alam et al., 2020).

Early marriage (EM) and early childbearing (ECB) remain widespread in South Asia, though their prevalence varies across countries and subnational regions. Despite continued challenges, the rates of decline in EM and ECB over the past decade have differed significantly among nations, with India experiencing the most substantial and fastest reductions. This progress is largely attributed to policy interventions, educational improvements, and shifting social norms regarding marriage and family planning. One of the main drivers behind the decline in early marriage across South Asia has been the improvement in women's education and increased household wealth. Higher education levels provide women with greater economic independence, career opportunities, and awareness of their rights, reducing the likelihood of early marriage. Similarly, improved financial conditions in marital households contribute to delayed marriages by enabling families to prioritize education and personal development over early family formation. These findings emphasize the role of education and economic development in addressing gender-based social challenges in South Asia (Scott et al., 2020).

The frequency and extent of drought events are projected to increase significantly in the near-term and mid-term periods compared to the long-term period. Climate models suggest that the impact of drought will be more intense in the coming decades, affecting water availability, agricultural productivity, and livelihoods across the region. These projections highlight the urgency of implementing adaptive measures to mitigate the consequences of climate variability. The number of people exposed to drought conditions is also expected to rise significantly. Projections indicate that population exposure to drought will increase by more than 1.5 times in the near-term and mid-term periods before declining in the long-term. This pattern suggests that while climate change will worsen drought conditions in the short to medium term, long-term adaptation strategies, policy interventions, and shifts in settlement patterns may help reduce exposure. Among various climate scenarios, the largest increase in population exposure to drought is expected under the SSP3-7.0 scenario during the mid-term period, with a projected 2.3-fold rise. This scenario assumes high population growth, regional conflicts, and slow technological advancements, leading to greater vulnerability to extreme weather events. These findings highlight the need for proactive policies to address water scarcity and enhance resilience to climate change in SAARC countries (Mondal et al., 2021).

Economic growth in SAARC countries is influenced by multiple demographic and economic factors. In the long run, the real stock of capital, fertility rate, and life expectancy all have a positive relationship with economic growth. Higher capital investment leads to greater industrial and technological advancements, while longer life expectancy contributes to a healthier and more productive workforce. However, the young dependency ratio—representing the proportion of non-working young individuals to the working-age population—has a negative impact on economic growth. A high young dependency ratio places pressure on resources, requiring higher social expenditures on education and healthcare while limiting immediate economic productivity. In the short run, the young dependency ratio continues to have a significant negative impact on economic growth, whereas life expectancy has a significant positive effect. The study also found a unidirectional causal relationship from the young dependency ratio and fertility rate to GDP per capita in the short run, suggesting that demographic changes play a crucial role in shaping economic outcomes over time (Munir & Shahid, 2020).

The relationship between carbon emissions and macroeconomic factors in SAARC countries has been analyzed over the period from 1990 to 2018. The study identified a long-term cointegration relationship between consumption-based CO_2 emissions and five key macroeconomic determinants: GDP growth, energy consumption, foreign direct investment (FDI), trade openness, and urbanization. The findings confirm the presence of an N-shaped Environmental Kuznets Curve (EKC) for the SAARC region. This means that CO_2 emissions initially rise with economic growth, then decline after reaching a certain level of development, but subsequently increase again at higher income levels. The N-shaped curve suggests that while economic advancement can lead to cleaner technologies and regulatory improvements, rapid industrialization and urban expansion can later reverse these gains. In the long run, energy consumption and urbanization have been found to increase CO_2 emissions, as higher energy demands and expanding cities contribute to pollution. However, FDI and trade openness have a reducing effect on emissions, contradicting the pollution-haven hypothesis. This finding suggests that foreign investments and open trade policies in SAARC countries are associated with cleaner production methods rather than the outsourcing of polluting industries from developed nations (Shekhawat et al., 2021).

Economic growth has also been linked to environmental performance in SAARC countries. Research indicates that higher levels of economic growth have had a positive impact on environmental performance, suggesting that as countries develop, they invest more in pollution control, cleaner technologies, and regulatory enforcement. On the other hand, population density has had a significant negative impact on environmental performance. Densely populated areas tend to experience greater environmental degradation due to higher resource consumption, increased waste generation, and greater pressure on natural ecosystems. Managing urban expansion and promoting sustainable development are essential to mitigating these environmental challenges. Interestingly, regulatory quality was not found to have a significant impact on environmental performance in SAARC countries. This suggests that while regulations exist, their enforcement and effectiveness may be limited. Strengthening institutional frameworks, improving governance, and ensuring compliance with environmental policies will be crucial for achieving long-term sustainability goals in the region (Bose et al., 2024).

Research Questions

1. How does the population growth rate vary across SAARC countries from 1960 to 2023?
2. Is the demographic composition – male, female impact on the rate of change of GDP growth over the years for the SAARC countries?

METHODOLOGY

This study conducts a time-series analysis of population data for eight South Asian countries that are part of the South Asian Association for Regional Cooperation (SAARC). The countries included in this analysis are Afghanistan, Bangladesh, Bhutan, India, Maldives, Nepal, Pakistan, and Sri Lanka. The dataset covers the years 1960 to 2023 and consists of annual population statistics. It includes key demographic indicators such as male and female population percentages, total population, and other relevant measures that help in understanding population trends in the region. The population data was collected from reliable demographic sources and formatted for analysis. Since datasets spanning long time periods often contain missing values, appropriate imputation methods were used to fill in the gaps. This step ensured that the data remained consistent and suitable for further calculations. To study population growth patterns, derivative-based calculations were applied. The first derivative of the population data was calculated to measure the rate of change in population growth per year. This provided information on whether the population was increasing or decreasing at a steady rate. The second derivative was then computed to examine the acceleration or deceleration in the rate of growth. These calculations helped in identifying periods of rapid or slowing growth in different countries. The mean and standard deviation of both the first and second derivatives were determined for each country. The mean values provided an average growth rate, while the standard deviation measured how much the growth rate varied over time. These calculations allowed for a comparison of population trends across the SAARC countries, showing periods of steady growth, fluctuations, or decline.

RESULTS

The calculus is used develop finite derivative for the analysis with

1. First Derivative (Rate of Change):

$$f'(x) = \frac{y_{t+1} - y_t}{t + 1 - t}$$

where Y_t is the population at time t.

a f is function and x gives the rate at which the function is changing at any given point.

2. Second Derivative (Acceleration of Rate of Change):

$$f''(x) = \frac{f'(t+1) - f'(t)}{(t+1) - t}$$

The summary of the computed metrics for each country, showing the mean and standard deviation of the first and second derivatives, which represent the population growth acceleration and its changes over time.

Table 1. Summary Statistics of Population Growth Trends in SAARC Countries

Country	*Mean First Derivative*	*Std First Derivative*	*Mean Second Derivative*	*Std Second Derivative*
Afghanistan	514598.70	522123.23	5145986984126984.00	5221232333966073.00
Bangladesh	1899021.11	382677.99	18990211111111112.00	3826779937749525.00
Bhutan	8925.41	7143.20	89254126984126.98	71432014756510.62
India	15906019.97	3066191.19	159060199682539648.00	30661911912780352.00
Maldives	6901.67	3940.33	69016666666666.66	39403345398220.05

continued on following page

Table 1. Continued

Country	Mean First Derivative	Std First Derivative	Mean Second Derivative	Std Second Derivative
Nepal	310650.10	139713.83	3106500952380952.50	1397138311926582.75
Pakistan	3203098.17	1077011.87	32030981746031748.00	10770118671733268.00
Sri Lanka	196438.27	131893.73	1964382698412698.50	1318937256636384.50

The Table 1, shows the mean and standard deviation of the first and second derivatives of population data for several South Asian countries (SAARC). The first derivative represents the rate of population change, while the second derivative reflects the change in that rate. India has the highest mean first derivative (15,906,019.97), indicating the largest average annual population increase, followed by Pakistan (3,203,098.17) and Bangladesh (1,899,021.11). Bhutan and Maldives have significantly smaller mean first derivatives, suggesting slower population growth. The extremely large values for the mean and standard deviation of the second derivatives across all countries, such as India's mean of 159,060,199,682,539,648, indicate substantial fluctuations in the *rate* of population growth, although the sheer magnitude of these numbers makes direct interpretation difficult.

The analysis suggests considerable variation in population growth dynamics across South Asia. India, Pakistan, and Bangladesh are experiencing rapid population growth, while Bhutan and Maldives have much slower growth rates. The high second derivative values across all countries indicate volatility in the *change* of population growth rate, likely due to factors like fluctuating birth rates, migration, and mortality. The results clearly show significant variation in population growth rates across South Asia. India, Pakistan, and Bangladesh exhibit much higher mean first derivatives, indicating faster growth, compared to Bhutan and the Maldives, which have considerably smaller values. The standard deviations of the first derivative also highlight differences in the consistency of growth, with some countries showing more variability than others. Thus, addressing the research question (RQ1) – rate of change of population differs over the period of years among the SAARC.

In the Second phase, the researcher analysed the demographic composition, viz., RQ2 with visual representation.

Figure 1. First Derivative (Year-on-Year Change in GDP)

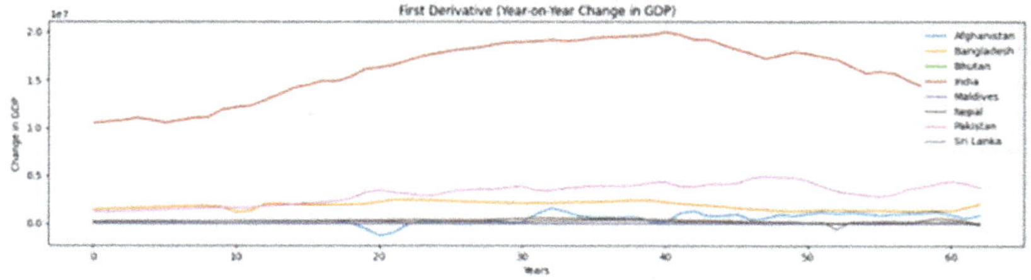

The figure 1 represents the first derivative of GDP, which measures the year-on-year change in GDP for eight SAARC countries over time. This helps in understanding how the rate of GDP growth has evolved across different nations. India, shown in red, has the highest and most consistent GDP growth over time. The curve shows an upward trend for most of the period, indicating steady economic expansion. However, towards the later years, there is a decline, suggesting that the rate of economic growth has slowed down. Nepal, represented in pink, exhibits moderate growth with some fluctuations. The GDP change increases gradually, though with some periods of slowing growth. This suggests that while Nepal's economy has expanded over time, it has not followed a consistent growth pattern. Bangladesh and Pakistan, shown in orange and purple, respectively, maintain steady but moderate GDP growth. Their year-on-year GDP changes do not show extreme fluctuations, indicating consistent but smaller-scale economic development compared to India. Afghanistan, Bhutan, Maldives, and Sri Lanka have relatively small changes in GDP compared to the larger economies. Their growth rates remain low, with occasional dips and fluctuations. Afghanistan, in particular, shows negative values at certain points, which could indicate economic contractions during certain periods. These dips may be associated with political instability, conflicts, or external economic shocks.

Figure 2. Second Derivative (Change of GDP based on Gender Composition)

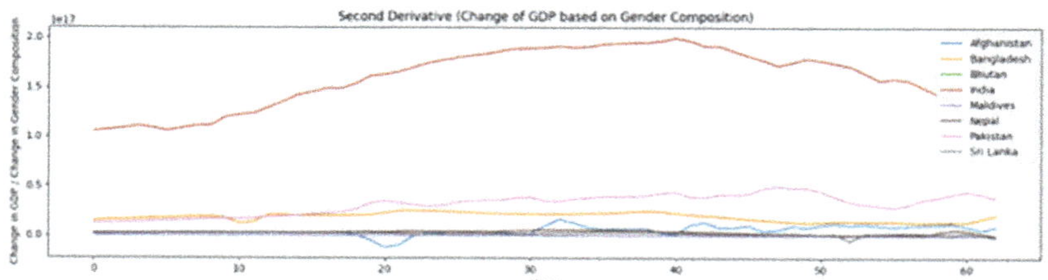

The figure 2 represents the first derivative of GDP for eight SAARC countries, illustrating the year-on-year change in GDP over time. This measure helps in understanding how GDP growth has evolved and whether economies are expanding or contracting at different points in time. India, represented by the red line, shows the highest and most consistent GDP growth among all SAARC nations. The GDP change follows an upward trend for most of the period, peaking towards the later years before experiencing a slight decline. This pattern suggests that India's economic growth was strong and stable over time, with some signs of a slowdown towards the end. Nepal, shown in pink, also exhibits a gradual increase in GDP growth, though at a much lower scale compared to India. The changes in GDP appear more fluctuating, indicating that while Nepal's economy has grown over time, it has also experienced periods of slower growth or minor downturns. Bangladesh and Pakistan demonstrate a steady but smaller GDP growth rate compared to India. Their year-on-year GDP changes remain relatively stable, without significant spikes or dips. This suggests that both economies have maintained moderate and consistent growth over the years. Afghanistan, Bhutan, Maldives, and Sri Lanka, represented by blue, brown, and gray lines, show relatively small changes in GDP compared to the larger economies. These countries exhibit low growth rates with occasional fluctuations, and some, like Afghanistan, even show negative values at certain points. Negative values indicate a possible GDP contraction, which could be due to economic crises, conflicts, or external shocks affecting their economies. The graph indicates that India has been the driving force behind GDP growth in the SAARC region, while other countries have experienced moderate to low growth. Some countries, particularly Afghanistan and Bhutan, have unstable growth trends, reflecting potential economic challenges.

CONCLUSION

This study examined population growth trends in South Asian Association for Regional Cooperation (SAARC) countries using calculus-based analysis, focusing on the first and second derivatives of population data. The first derivative measured the rate of population change over time, while the second derivative provided insights into acceleration or deceleration in growth. These metrics allowed for a comparative assessment of population trends across the region. India, Pakistan, and Bangladesh experience rapid population growth, with India showing the highest average annual increase. Bhutan and the Maldives have much lower growth rates. The second derivative values across all countries show changes in growth acceleration, likely due to birth rates, migration patterns, and mortality rates. The standard deviation of the first derivative indicates differences in population growth consistency, with Afghanistan and Bangladesh showing more variation, while Bhutan and Sri Lanka have more stable trends. Beyond population growth, the study examined the relationship between GDP and demographic changes. Over the past six decades, India has maintained strong and steady GDP growth, outpacing other SAARC countries. Bangladesh and Pakistan show moderate but fluctuating growth, while Afghanistan, Bhutan, Maldives, Nepal, and Sri Lanka experience lower but more stable GDP trends. Differences in government policies, resource distribution, and demographic patterns influence these economic trends. India's GDP expansion is closely linked to its large population, urbanization, and global market integration. The study also analyzed gender composition's role in GDP growth. India shows a strong connection between workforce participation by gender and economic expansion. This suggests that an increase in female workforce participation has played a role in India's economic progress. Other South Asian nations show little change in GDP related to gender composition, which may indicate lower female labor force participation or gender disparities in employment opportunities. India and Pakistan experience the highest population growth rates, while Bhutan and the Maldives have the lowest. Countries with rapid population growth have also seen shifts in growth acceleration, especially in the latter half of the 20th century. The GDP analysis shows India's economic strength and steady growth, while other nations face more uncertain economic conditions. Gender participation in the workforce plays a greater role in India's economic development, while its impact remains less visible in other South Asian countries.

REFERENCES

Alam, Q., Nur, Q., & Lecturer, A. (2020). Impacts of macroeconomic variables on the stock market returns of South Asian Region. *Canadian Journal of Business and Information Studies*, 24–34. DOI: 10.34104/cjbis.020.24034

Alharthi, M., & Hanif, I. (2020). Impact of blue economy factors on economic growth in the SAARC countries. *Maritime Business Review*, *5*(3), 253–269. DOI: 10.1108/MABR-01-2020-0006

Amrutha, K., Unnikrishnan, V., Shajikumar, S., & Warrier, A. K. (2021). Current State of Microplastics Research in SAARC Countries—A Review. In *Sustainable textiles* (pp. 27–63). DOI: 10.1007/978-981-16-0297-9_2

Asim, M., Jaffry, S. S., Rehman, Z., Scholar, M., & Jaffry, S. (2022). Population Dynamics and Economic Growth; Empirical Evidence from SAARC Countries. *Global Journal of Humanities and Social Sciences Research*, *1*(2), 28–42. DOI: 10.59129/gjhssr/v1i2.3

Bhowmik, P. K., & Sarker, N. (2021). Loan growth and bank risk: Empirical evidence from SAARC countries. *Heliyon*, *7*(5), e07036. DOI: 10.1016/j.heliyon.2021.e07036 PMID: 34036201

Bose, S., Hoque, A., & Weber, O. (2024). Enhancing environmental performance: Evidence from SAARC Countries. *Contemporary South Asia*, •••, 1–24. DOI: 10.1080/09584935.2024.2371782

Dey, S. K., Rahman, M. M., Shibly, K. H., Siddiqi, U. R., & Howlader, A. (2020). Epidemic trend analysis of SARS-COV-2 in SAARC countries using Modified SIR (M-SIR) Predictive model. medRxiv *(Cold Spring Harbor Laboratory)*. DOI: 10.1101/2020.06.29.20142513

Gazi, M. I., Masud, A. A., Shuvro, R. A., Hossain, A. I., & Rahman, M. K. (2022). Bangladesh and SAARC countries: Bilateral trade and flaring of economic cooperation. *ETIKONOMI*, *21*(2), 251–268. DOI: 10.15408/etk.v21i2.24353

Ikram, M., Zhang, Q., Sroufe, R., & Shah, S. Z. A. (2020). Towards a sustainable environment: The nexus between ISO 14001, renewable energy consumption, access to electricity, agriculture and CO2 emissions in SAARC countries. *Sustainable Production and Consumption*, *22*, 218–230. DOI: 10.1016/j.spc.2020.03.011

Jabbar, S. A., Qadar, L. T., Ghafoor, S., Rasheed, L., Sarfraz, Z., Sarfraz, A., Sarfraz, M., Felix, M., & Cherrez-Ojeda, I. (2022). Air Quality, Pollution and Sustainability Trends in South Asia: A Population-Based Study. *International Journal of Environmental Research and Public Health, 19*(12), 7534. DOI: 10.3390/ijerph19127534 PMID: 35742785

Jafrin, N., Mahi, M., Masud, M. M., & Ghosh, D. (2021). Demographic dividend and economic growth in emerging economies: Fresh evidence from the SAARC countries. *International Journal of Social Economics, 48*(8), 1159–1174. DOI: 10.1108/IJSE-08-2020-0588

Jafrin, N., Masud, M. M., Saif, A. N. M., Mahi, M., & Khanam, M. (2021). A panel data estimation of the determinants of life expectancy in selected SAARC countries. *Badania Operacyjne I Decyzje/Operations Research and Decisions, 31*(4). DOI: 10.37190/ord210404

Khan, A., Sicen, L., Khan, B., & Salman, N. (2021). On the influence of demographic structure and industrial growth on environmental quality. *Journal of Environmental Management, 288*, 112453. DOI: 10.1016/j.jenvman.2021.112453 PMID: 33827026

Khan, I., Muhammad, I., Sharif, A., Khan, I., & Ji, X. (2023). Unlocking the potential of renewable energy and natural resources for sustainable economic growth and carbon neutrality: A novel panel quantile regression approach. *Renewable Energy, 221*, 119779. DOI: 10.1016/j.renene.2023.119779

Kumar, R. (2019). India & South Asia: Geopolitics, regional trade and economic growth spillovers. *The Journal of International Trade & Economic Development, 29*(1), 69–88. DOI: 10.1080/09638199.2019.1636121

Lamichhane, T. R., Ghimire, M. P., Bhatt, S., & Joshi, R. K. (2022). The epidemic trend of COVID-19 in SAARC countries: A predictive modelling and analysis. *TheScientificWorldJournal, 15*(15), 113–119. DOI: 10.3126/sw.v15i15.45669

Latief, R., Kong, Y., Javeed, S. A., & Sattar, U. (2021). Carbon Emissions in the SAARC Countries with Causal Effects of FDI, Economic Growth and Other Economic Factors: Evidence from Dynamic Simultaneous Equation Models. *International Journal of Environmental Research and Public Health, 18*(9), 4605. DOI: 10.3390/ijerph18094605 PMID: 33925274

Li, Q., Cherian, J., Shabbir, M. S., Sial, M. S., Li, J., Mester, I., & Badulescu, A. (2021). Exploring the Relationship between Renewable Energy Sources and Economic Growth. The Case of SAARC Countries. *Energies, 14*(3), 520. DOI: 10.3390/en14030520

Malik, Y. S., Rajendran, V. O., Ma, I., Pande, T., Ravichandran, K., Jaganathasamy, N., Ganesh, B., Santhakumar, A., Tazerji, S. S., Rahman, M. T., Safdar, M., Dubal, Z. B., & Dhama, K. (2021). Responses to COVID-19 in South Asian Association for Regional Cooperation (SAARC) countries in 2020, a data analysis during a world of crises. *Chaos, Solitons, and Fractals*, *152*, 111311. DOI: 10.1016/j.chaos.2021.111311 PMID: 34376927

Mondal, S. K., Huang, J., Wang, Y., Su, B., Zhai, J., Tao, H., Wang, G., Fischer, T., Wen, S., & Jiang, T. (2021). Doubling of the population exposed to drought over South Asia: CMIP6 multi-model-based analysis. *The Science of the Total Environment*, *771*, 145186. DOI: 10.1016/j.scitotenv.2021.145186 PMID: 33736148

Munir, K., & Shahid, F. S. U. (2020). Role of demographic factors in economic growth of South Asian countries. *Journal of Economic Studies (Glasgow, Scotland)*, *48*(3), 557–570. DOI: 10.1108/JES-08-2019-0373

Rahman, M. M., Saidi, K., & Mbarek, M. B. (2020). Economic growth in South Asia: The role of CO2 emissions, population density and trade openness. *Heliyon*, *6*(5), e03903. DOI: 10.1016/j.heliyon.2020.e03903 PMID: 32420481

Rashid, S., & Ratten, V. (2020). A Systematic Literature review on women entrepreneurship in emerging economies while reflecting specifically on SAARC countries. In *Contributions to management science* (pp. 37–88). DOI: 10.1007/978-3-030-35415-2_4

Scott, S., Nguyen, P. H., Neupane, S., Pramanik, P., Nanda, P., Bhutta, Z. A., Afsana, K., & Menon, P. (2020). Early marriage and early childbearing in South Asia: Trends, inequalities, and drivers from 2005 to 2018. *Annals of the New York Academy of Sciences*, *1491*(1), 60–73. DOI: 10.1111/nyas.14531 PMID: 33258141

Shekhawat, K. K., Yadav, A. K., Sanu, M. S., & Kumar, P. (2021). Key drivers of consumption-based carbon emissions: Empirical evidence from SAARC countries. *Environmental Science and Pollution Research International*, *29*(16), 23206–23224. DOI: 10.1007/s11356-021-17413-6 PMID: 34800276

Shohan, M. U. S., Alam, A. S. M. R. U., Rakhi, N. N., Kabir, M., Siam, M. K. S., Hasan, M. M., Sheriff, R., Karim, M. A., Rahman, A., Moni, M. A., & Khan, M. A. (2020). Onset, transmission, impact, and management of COVID-19 epidemic at early stage in SAARC countries. *Authorea (Authorea)*. DOI: 10.22541/au.159775079.90952648

Singh, D., & Stakic, N. (2020). Financial inclusion and economic growth nexus: Evidence from SAARC countries. *South Asia Research*, *41*(2), 238–258. DOI: 10.1177/0262728020964605

Sultana, F., & Reza, H. M. (2020). Are SAARC countries prepared to combat COVID-19 to save young, working-age population? *AIMS Public Health*, *7*(3), 440–449. DOI: 10.3934/publichealth.2020036 PMID: 32968669

Tripathi, M., & Inani, S. K. (2020). Does information and communications technology affect economic growth? Empirical evidence from SAARC countries. *Information Technology for Development*, *26*(4), 773–787. DOI: 10.1080/02681102.2020.1785827

Uddin, M. N., Karim, A. R., & Parvez, S. M. (2020). Estimation of the SARS-CoV-2 specific reproduction number in SAARC countries: A 60-days Data-driven analysis. *Journal of Applied and Natural Science*, *12*(4), 628–634. DOI: 10.31018/jans.v12i4.2397

Vaishya, R., & Vaish, A. (2023). Orthopedic research output from SAARC countries in the last 25 years: 1996-2021. *Journal of Bone and Joint Diseases*, *38*(2), 131–133. DOI: 10.4103/jbjd.jbjd_19_23

Voumik, L. C., Hossain, M. I., Rahman, M. H., Sultana, R., Dey, R., & Esquivias, M. A. (2023). Impact of Renewable and Non-Renewable Energy on EKC in SAARC Countries: Augmented Mean Group approach. *Energies*, *16*(6), 2789. DOI: 10.3390/en16062789

Voumik, L. C., Mimi, M. B., & Raihan, A. (2023). Nexus between urbanization, industrialization, natural resources rent, and anthropogenic carbon emissions in South Asia: CS-ARDL approach. *Anthropocene Science*, *2*(1), 48–61. DOI: 10.1007/s44177-023-00047-3

Chapter 2
Aging Populations, Economic Growth, and Sustainable Development:
A Policy Perspective

Jipson Joseph
https://orcid.org/0009-0005-1795-5051
Christ University, India

ABSTRACT

Over the last century (from 1925 to 2025), there has been a 311% growth in global population (from 2 billion to 8.22 billion). Scientific and technological advancements, increased educational and healthcare facilities, and active involvement of women in the labor market have contributed to this significant change. However, the globe faces an imbalance between the percentages of youth, working, and old-age populations. The decline in the fertility rate and an increase in longevity have contributed to the disproportionate growth of the old-age population. Although the increased life expectancy can be credited as a substantial achievement of society, there are complex discussions on the contributions of older people to economic growth. From this perspective, this chapter critically examines the role of the old-age population in enhancing economic growth and sustainable development of society. It also proposes specific policy suggestions for achieving the UN Decade of Healthy Aging objectives (2021-2030) that align with the SDGs.

DOI: 10.4018/979-8-3373-2550-7.ch002

1 INTRODUCTION

As of 19 June 2025, the total global population is almost 8.22 billion. India is leading with nearly 1.46 billion, and China is just behind with 1.41 billion (Worldometer, 2025). In 1925, the global population was just 2 billion. However, factors like scientific and technological advancements that reduced child mortality rate, economic development that provided bare essentials to the maximum number of people, and prioritization of human rights that facilitated education and healthcare facilities increased the population rate. Accordingly, the last century witnessed an overwhelming rise in the global population. The UN projects that the world population will reach 10 billion by 2060 (Worldometer, 2025). This is mainly due to the increase in life expectancy at birth, which has reached 73.3 years in 2024 (UNDESA, 2024). However, the population of developed countries is not increasing along with the global population. The latest data affirms that the population upsurge occurs primarily in underdeveloped countries (Statista, 2025). Along with an increase in population, the percentage of the old-age population is increasing rapidly. It underlines that the globe is aging, and the transition toward an aging society has become a global phenomenon (Temsumrit, 2023; Trong et al., 2024). Population aging is understood by evaluating its proxy, the old-age population (Lee & Shin, 2019). The UNFPA (2025) states that the global share of the old-age population has almost doubled from 5.5% to 10.3% between 1974 and 2024. It also predicts that between 2024 and 2074, it will double again to reach 20.7%. The percentage of aging populations is comparatively high in developed countries (Nagarajan et al., 2016; Wei, 2025). However, the latest trends show that low- and middle-income countries have started to experience it in significant numbers (WHO, 2024b).

The aging population's happiness and standard of living indicate the state's efficient functioning for its citizens' protection and meaningful existence. Most developed countries have such facilities that prioritize the well-being of their aged population (Sekher & Gupta, 2024). In some other parts, where the state does not offer such support systems, the families of older people are willing to take care of them. Countries like India, China, and Bangladesh have a tradition of showing tremendous respect and concern for the elderly members (Mamun et al., 2020). The majority of them stay together with their children and grandchildren. It gives them physical, psychological, emotional, and financial support, enhancing their longevity. As a result, the aging population is rising all over the world. The presence of an aging population benefits society, as their experience can guide future generations. However, some researchers claim that the old-age population's economic contributions will be minimal (Eggertson et al., 2017; Lee & Shin, 2019; Maestas et al., 2023). Some others do not agree with this claim and affirm that their experience and expertise will fortify the economy (Achemoglu & Restrepo, 2017; Gao et al., 2023; Trong et al., 2024).

The aging population may not be able to contribute to society's economic development like the working-age population. The older people's financial activities are significantly less. They are also forced to depend on social security schemes like pensions, insurance, and other benefits for survival. When the percentage of the aging population increases, the state's financial burden also increases. Since their contribution to the economy is significantly less, it adversely affects the country's economic development. This forces those states to open their borders to migrant workers, as happens in many developed countries. The chapter does not argue that migration is bad, but it says that it is a serious concern for any state if it is due to the increased aging population.

From this perspective, this chapter critically examines the present scenario of the aging population in the context of economic development. It is often said that there is a negative correlation between the aging population and a country's economic growth, and the chapter critically studies this argument. After examining the problem statement under the title 'significance of the study,' the chapter provides a brief theoretical framework based on the literature review. It then critically examines the interplay between the aging population and economic growth. The chapter then puts forward some required changes for an inclusive approach toward the elderly.

2 SIGNIFICANCE OF THE STUDY

The WHO (2024b) states that the whole globe is witnessing an unprecedented increase in the size and proportion of the old-age population. The latest trends show that population aging has become a dominant field of discussion and interaction (Trong et al., 2024). The significant scientific and technological advancements in almost all fields of human interaction have caused this positive situation, where people living in their 60s and 70s have become so common. In 2020, the number of people aged 60 years and above was 1 billion worldwide, projected to reach 1.4 billion by 2030 and 2.1 billion by 2050. That is, 16% of the global population will be older than 65 years by 2050 (Xu et al., 2022). While this notable change in the distribution of a country's population started with high-income countries, the latest trends show that it is swiftly moving towards low- and middle-income countries. Currently, 30% of Japan's population is already above 60 years of age. However, the statistics predict that by 2050, two-thirds of the global population over 60 will live in low- and middle-income countries. SDG3 states that the globe is responsible for ensuring healthy lives and promoting well-being for all people, regardless of age differences. The health and well-being of the aged people are thus a crucial concern for all. The increased healthcare facilities and social security schemes have improved people's longevity.

Realizing the importance of securing the lives of older people, the UN has declared 2021-2030 as the Decade of Healthy Aging, intending to improve their lives, their families, and the communities in which they live. The WHO (2023, p.2) states, "While the proportion and absolute number of older people globally are increasing rapidly, too little has been given to how older populations live, the contributions they can make, and the services and support they require." Although global life expectancy rose by almost 10 years between 1990 and 2024 to reach 73.3 years (UNDESA, 2024), little attention is given to the concerns, opportunities, and contributions of the aged people. Accordingly, this chapter focuses on the possibilities of the economic contributions that aged people can provide to society. They can contribute significantly to society's social and environmental sustainability. However, Lee and Shin (2019) note that many countries have experienced the adverse effects of the aging population on economic growth in recent years. Trong et al. (2024) state that although population aging poses significant financial pressures, it simultaneously provides meaningful opportunities to expand society's resources. From such a perspective, practical thinking and policy-making should be used to examine how the financial contributions of the old-age population could be increased. Accordingly, this chapter concentrates on their role in improving economic sustainability since the majority think that older people contribute nothing to society but receive many financial benefits from society.

3 CONCEPTUAL FRAMEWORK

People have a significant role in the economic development of any country. However, its role in economic growth also depends on the nature of the age groups. Different age groups have various productivity levels, demands, and concerns (Pham & Vo, 2021). Demographic changes refer to the variations in the size, age structure, and population distribution over time. These changes can happen due to low or high birth rates, death rates, or migration patterns (Samir, 2013). When the death rate in a society is low due to better healthcare, social security facilities, and a low birth rate, it increases longevity and the size of the old-age population. Society's growing number of older people underlines the development in many vital areas. At the same time, it also shows that when the aging population increases, it adversely affects the economic development of a country as its contributions to the GDP are less than those of the working-age population. While the working-age population significantly contributes to the GDP, the old-age population is at the receiving end. It may create an imbalance in society. However, if longevity is coupled with adequate physical, psychological, and emotional well-being, they can continue to contribute to society in many ways.

3.1 Demographic Changes

Demographic changes refer to the variations in the size of a society's population due to changes in mortality and fertility rates (Samir, 2013). For instance, the US population started to age due to a sharp decline in the birth rate, which began in the 1960s, and a long-running decline in mortality rates (Maestas et al., 2023). The current society witnesses an unprecedented increase in longevity, which increases the average age of a population. If there had been a comparative increase in the fertility rate, it would have balanced the rhythm of society with young, working-age, and old-age populations. Since the fertility rate is comparatively very low in many countries, it affects the societal equilibrium. It underlines that, more than the aging population, the low fertility rate has become society's most complicated issue. Developed countries' uncontrollable increase in the aging population is primarily due to an irrepressible decrease in the fertility rate.

The active participation of women in higher education and the labor market has also determined the changes in the fertility rates. In the previous centuries, women were primarily engaged in household and agricultural activities. They were less educated and rarely employed in other sectors. Besides, contraceptive pills and other reproductive methods were neither invented nor popularized. However, in the second half of the 20th century, women gained the freedom and capacity to decide on their pregnancies due to the immense growth in women's rights and the medical field (Trong et al., 2024). Whether or not to have a child has become a choice of women rather than the choice of the family and society. All these broadened the horizon of women's inclusion in societal life. However, it caused a decrease in the fertility rate. Nagarajan et al. (2016) underline that the involvement of women in the labor market has increased human capital in the short term. However, since it diminishes the fertility rate, it will reduce the strength of human capital in the long run.

Alders and Broer (2004) suggest that the fertility rate can increase if the couple advocates altruistic behavior. However, how far can this altruistic behavior be promoted in a world where one's employment may not be suitable for looking after a whole family? Some countries, like South Korea and Italy, provide families with financial and other support systems to intensify the fertility rate. It may increase the government's financial burden in the short term, but balancing society in the long run would be beneficial. If society cannot stabilize its fertility rate with that of the aging population, it will create severe drawbacks to a global sustainable future (Wei, 2025). Baldanzi et al. (2019) thus stated that declining fertility was the leading cause of the aging population rather than the rising life expectancy. Maestas et al.

(2023) suggest that although immigration can be seen as a substitute for population aging, it cannot be considered a perfect solution as it will create imbalances in global sustainability.

Demographic changes due to a lower fertility rate create a situation where the working-age population will have fewer children to succeed them (Alam & Mitra, 2012). The discussions on demographic changes and their impact on economic growth should prioritize the population's replacement level. The ideal replacement level is calculated as 2.1 children/woman. Almost all developed countries, including the US (1.62), the UK (1.56), Germany (1.44), and Japan (1.21), and developing countries like Russia (1.45), India (1.98), and China (1.0), are below the replacement level (Ritchie, 2024; Minzner, 2024). When the replacement level goes below the required percentage, it affects the global march towards sustainability. A reduction in the fertility rate is a serious concern. However, it alone will not lead a country to an aging population. Factors like increased life expectancy and decreased mortality also cause these changes (Nagarajan et al., 2016). The world is radically shifting toward an aging population as all three factors have come together notably. While developed countries have already started to experience the plight of this change, most developing countries now feel relieved as they somehow manage to reduce the birth rate. However, within a short period, they, too, will experience the same plight.

Demographic changes can have three types of effects on the economy: positive, negative, and neutral (Mamun et al., 2020). When society changes from a youth-age to a working-age population, it positively influences economic growth as they actively contribute to labor and productivity. Historically, demographic changes benefited society by increasing the working-age population (Lee et al., 2011). However, when there is a crucial change from the working-age to the old-age population, it can cause negative impacts. Many countries experience it as the working-age population has become smaller than the retired population (Bell & Rutherford, 2013). Many developed countries face the issue of a larger non-working old-age population than the working-age population (Nagarajan et al., 2016). When the working-age population is smaller than the other two categories of dependent populations, it increases their financial burden and limits their contributions to society. However, if this change is only nominal without rising beyond 10% of the country's total population, it will only neutralize economic growth (Lee & Shin, 2019).

3.2 Aging Population

Aging is an unavoidable factor in human life. It results from molecular and cellular damage in human systems over the years. Such damages decrease an individual's physical and mental capacity and the immune system, leading to diseases and, finally, to death. Although it cannot be said that these changes always happen with a person's age in years, they mostly happen with older age. Aging is also associated with other factors like retirement, relocation to a more comfortable housing where special care is given to older people, and the death of partners and friends (WHO, 2024b). Such a situation creates a feeling of loneliness, depression, and emotional imbalance among the elderly. They tend to show geriatric syndromes. They also face the risk of falling, which sometimes causes injuries and affects their confidence and quality of life (Xu et al., 2022). The UN has fixed the cut-off point for the old-age population as 60. However, the WHO (2002) states that life expectancy in developed countries is comparatively higher than in developing countries. Accordingly, it fixes 65 as the cut-off point for measuring the old-age population in the developed world (Mamun et al., 2020).

Population aging occurs when the percentage of people aged 60 or 65 and above increases in an area or a nation. A society is considered an aging society if the total percentage of its aging population exceeds 7% of its total population (Meng & Yu, 2024). Pham and Vo (2021) note that while the average fertility reduced from 4.77 to 2.54 during 1970-2015, life expectancy rose from 58.65 to 71.89. Such an imbalance will continue to increase in the coming years. The aging population has become one of the most crucial problems in developed and developing countries (Trong et al., 2024). Nagarajan et al. (2016) thus insist that there should be efficient empirical studies across the globe to understand the real picture of the aging population and its influence on various areas of human life. Although developed countries have initiated multiple programs and policies to address the aging population issue, developing countries have not yet engaged in such activities. However, developing countries will face this issue more severely within a few decades than developed countries (Pham & Vo, 2021). The disproportionate increase of the old-age population in contrast to the working-age population can cause issues in economic growth if not adequately addressed.

Population aging can happen due to many factors. The predominant factors among them are increased life expectancy and improved healthcare facilities. The living standards of people have increased substantially, providing more scope for longevity (Meng & Yu, 2024). Increased life expectancy and decreased mortality rates are laudable factors. With these increases, if society had an increased fertility rate, it would not have had unfavorable effects. However, the many factors (some of which are already explained in the previous point) that contributed to the low fertility rate created a rapid increase in the old-age population compared to the working-age population (Trong et al., 2024). Accordingly, the UNDESA (2022) affirms that the global population is aging, and almost all countries have already started to experience it.

Older age in the present context is more associated with retirement. Many people think retirement is a new beginning in such a way that they neglect responsibilities, avoid initiatives, and prefer a dependent life. Del Webb, an American developer, introduced and associated retirement with age-restricted communities in the 1960s (Keeler & Bernstein, 2021). Retired people choose to live in a community where they engage in interrelational activities among themselves. This idea circulated across the globe. It gives them a friendly and sympathetic social environment. However, I believe they should continue living in the same place where they have lived for years. Freedman and Nicolle (2020) claim that social isolation is a primary concern of older people. To overcome such a complex framework, the conditions where they are born, live, and age have a unique role. It can help them to engage in various social, political, religious, and environmental activities. It can also encourage them to contribute significantly to the country's GDP. Analyzing the US Scenario, Keeler and Bernstein (2021) also state that older people and their caretakers face indignities and insecurities. If this were the situation in the US, what would the problem be in many developing and underdeveloped countries with minimal resources? Society should prioritize awareness-building so that the other sections of society have a positive approach towards the elderly. For instance, giving preference for seats in a public transport system, prioritizing them in a queue, or assisting them in carrying something. Most importantly, the old-age population and others must see aging as an opportunity (Chatterjee, 2019) rather than a drag (Donorfio et al., 2023).

The WHO (2022) states that elder abuse is growing in the present society. The abuse of older people involves all single or repeated commissions and omissions by a caregiver or another person, breaching the expectation of trust and causing harm to an adult aged 60 years and above. This comes under the broader ambit of violence against aged people. It can also happen even if there is no expectation of trust in a relationship, as in the case of a stranger harming an older person. Violence against older people can happen in community or institutional settings in many forms, including physical, psychological, emotional, material, and sexual. Neglecting their concerns and interests, abandoning them, and harming their dignity and respect by their family members, caretakers, and others are also areas of abuse (WHO, 2024a). When they face severe violence and abuse, it increases their mortality rate, physical injuries, depression, emotional imbalances, poverty, and other vulnerabilities (WHO, 2022). Society should respect the elderly, as they were the prime contributors to building up its culture and economy in the past.

3.3 Economic Development

People's economic interests change with their age. Usually, when people advance in age, especially after 60 and 65, they prioritize a happier retired life without much involvement in the labor market and savings. They prefer good healthcare and social security systems rather than actively contributing to society. When the life expectancy increases, it affects their saving and forces them to depend heavily on governmental or family support. However, their expectations of living longer than the previous generation may sometimes induce them to remain in the workforce longer than the already fixed retirement age. They will also be interested in increasing their savings even at a later age. Such changes also affect the country's economic characteristics (Bloom et al., 2010). Gao et al. (2023) state that population aging has become a significant global concern due to its impact on labor, finance, production and consumption, environment, housing, public expenditure, and social security. All these factors are vital in the discussions on economic development. If any of these areas are negatively affected, it will obscure the global economy.

Economic development and demographic changes are closely related. During the 1970s and 1980s, many East-Asian countries experienced an enormous increase in the working-age population. This shift from a youth-age population to a high working-age population contributed to the noteworthy economic growth of those countries (Bloom & Williamson, 1998). The productivity, economic output, and GDP growth depend on the contributions of the working-age population. However, East-Asian countries are now experiencing another shift from the working-age population to an old-age population, jeopardizing their economic development in the years to come. For instance, Japan's old-age population increased from 5.6% in 1960 to 26.6% in 2016 (Lee & Shin, 2019).

Many factors are responsible for the slow or reverse economic growth rate due to the larger old-age population. Compared to the working-age population, the elderly cannot fully and actively participate in the labor force due to their physical and mental incapacities. Their productivity is less vibrant than that of the working-age population (Aiyar et al., 2016). They also save less as they have more or less completed their responsibilities and might be thinking of living their final years without being burdened by further responsibilities (Horioka & Niimi, 2017). When they are more employed, the country's economic growth will be affected, as their contributions will be limited (Lee & Shin, 2019). However, there are also studies like Bloom et al. (2008), Lee et al. (2013), and Acemoglu and Restrepo (2017) affirm that the active involvement of older people in the various employment sectors of a country does not hold back its economic growth. At the same time, some recent studies like Lee et al. (2017), Eggertson et al. (2017), and Maestas et al. (2023) underline that the aging population adversely affects both short- and long-term economic growth. It harms the GDP per capita of any country. Eggertson et al. (2017) argue that compared to 1990-2008, the correlation between economic growth as reflected through GDP and population aging has become negative during 2008-2015.

Lee and Shin (2019) claim that a nominal increase in the old-age population will not affect the percentage of the working-age population and economic growth. However, if the old-age population and old-age dependency increase beyond a specific limit, it will affect the working-age population and economic growth. For instance, the old-age population and dependency share of the Republic of Korea was around 5% in 1960, which became 10-12% in 2013. Until the old-age population share reached 11.5% in 2013, it did not adversely affect the percentage of the working-age population. It steadily increased from 53.4% in 1960 to 73.4% in 2013. However, from 2014 onwards, the percentage of the working-age population started to decline. It shows that if the old-age population is around 10%, it will not affect the percentage and contributions of the working-age population. Maestas et al. (2023) argue that if the percentage of the old-age population increases by more than 10%, GDP per capita will decrease by 5.5%. Economic growth will reverse when the working-age population declines and the old-age population and their dependency increase. Just as there is a positive linear relationship between the working-age population and economic growth, there is a nonlinear relationship between the increased old-age population and economic growth.

4 INTERPLAY BETWEEN AGING POPULATIONS AND ECONOMIC GROWTH: A CRITIQUE

The aging population is one of society's crucial concerns. When a society's young, working-age, and old-age populations fail to balance in size, it causes many issues with sustainable economic growth and human security. The gradually growing aged population will be forced to depend on relatively fewer working adults or the country's social security schemes, adversely affecting economic development. To reduce this dilemma, working adults should systematically accumulate capital for the benefit of their retirement. The basic idea behind this system is to save something when one has a low dependency for the benefit of a high-dependency period (Weil, 2025). Without such a capital accumulation, people's well-being and countries' economic stability would be in danger. Sløk (2024) notes that while the working-age population is shrinking in Europe and Japan, the US, the UK, and Canada show significant progress in the size of the same population category. This does not mean that their aged population ratio is decreasing. For instance, 17% of the Canadian population was 65 and older in 2017, which is expected to be more than double in the coming 20 years (Freedman & Nicolle, 2020). It shows that the increase in the working-age population might be mainly due to increased immigration. When the size of the working-age population decreases in developed countries, they will be forced to invest more in developing countries, besides favoring migration. For instance, India's working-age population shows an increase of 1.8% per year between 2000 and 2025, whereas Japan's same category of population shrinks at an annual rate of 0.6%. Accordingly, there is every possibility of having more investment from Japan to India (Weil, 2025). This process benefits both countries by providing employment opportunities to the growing working-age populations of developing and underdeveloped countries and enhancing the economic interactions of developed countries.

Maestas et al. (2023) argue that the rapid growth of the aged population reduces economic growth and increases the government's burden. Without government assistance, many older people will be living in poverty. It is explicit in many developing countries. When the old-age population of rural areas faces a lack of income compared to their counterparts in urban areas, the gap between urban and rural areas is widened. They also face insecurities compared to the older population of the metropolitan regions if there is no perfect health insurance system (Chen et al., 2015). Besides, many young people from rural areas migrate to cities for employment. The typical pattern of rural life was that older people depended on the other two generations, who happily supported them physically, financially, and emotionally. However, the migration of the young population to the cities causes a vacuum in the lives of older people. All these affirm that older people in the rural areas of developing countries experience poverty and other insecurities in large numbers. Keeler and Bernstein (2021) state that 3 times more older adults live in poverty than in age-restricted communities in the US. It points to a precarious situation where older people are not adequately cared for. However, they state that labor force participation and productivity growth differ.

Scientific and technological advancements have somehow managed to reduce the importance of human capital in the production process. Labor productivity thus may not be affected much with the increase in aging population. However, the labor force's strength will be negatively impacted (Achemoglu & Restrepo, 2017). Lee and Shin (2019) state that most studies do not even consider the variations in the level of the aging population while discussing the correlation between the aging population and economic growth. Population aging may negatively influence economic growth only when the aging population reaches a certain high level. However, this has become a reality in many developed countries and emerging economies. It demands a more progressive and visionary approach toward the issues of the old-age population in connection with economic interactions.

Baldanzi et al. (2019) explain that the correlation between the old-age population and economic growth will differ in developed and developing countries. Applying the same methodology to both of them will not work effectively. Most developing countries, especially the less developed, have not yet experienced the severity of demographic changes. When the life expectancy in those countries increases, it causes an increase in their overall population. Such an increase leads to capital dilution and decreases economic growth. On the other hand, the developed world has already experienced demographic changes. An increase in life expectancy in developed countries will not cause a significant increase in population, as their fertility rate would have been lower. Their economic outcome is higher compared to the size of their population. Since their population growth and capital dilution are lower, they experience substantial economic growth.

Mamun et al. (2020, pp.14-15) state that population aging can change the economy in many ways: "economic growth, savings, investment, consumption, labor markets, pensions, taxation, and the transfer of wealth and property from one generation to another." Older people cannot effectively promote savings. They mainly spend from their savings to meet their daily needs. Since savings are the only source of income, continuous spending weakens their saving and future lives (Davies & Robert III, 2006). Their consumption choices are mainly dependent on their savings. It endangers the overall consumption level of the country if the percentage of the aged population is higher. A diminution in consumption patterns also reduces production and economic growth (Hock & Weil, 2012). Pham and Vo (2021) state that the consumption level of high-income countries increases along with an increase in age. The consumption level of older people is higher in high-income countries, as they can easily rely on social security schemes for their survival and medical care. However, in low and low-middle-income countries, they spend very little as they prioritize saving something for the future. It affects their choices and consumption preferences.

Nagarajan et al. (2016) make some surprising observations. According to them, the household consumption level of the old-age population would be very low. Labor markets, taxation, and GDP growth are affected when individual and household consumption levels decrease. Besides, their primary consumption spending is related to medical care. When a society spends more on medical care than education and other vital activities, it complicates economic growth (Mamun et al., 2020). De Meijer et al. (2013) inform that when the percentage of the old-age population increases, the government will be forced to spend more on social security systems and medical care, negatively impacting its spending on other vital productive areas. On the one hand, governmental spending has increased along with the old-age population. Conversely, the government's income is reduced as the percentage of the working-age population, consumption patterns, and taxation from the old-age population decreases. When an imbalance occurs between the income and expenditure of a government, it affects the state's infrastructure development and economic growth.

4.1 Positive Correlation

Most people desire a healthy and meaningful long life. When people grow in age, they also accumulate a lot of experience. Some aged people think they are a burden to their family and society, as they do not substantially contribute to society. However, if they are positive, they can bring many opportunities and benefits to their family and society through active involvement in various fields. Many find a rhythm in pursuing further education, a different career, and a long-neglected passion like music, painting, reading, writing, etc. Although all these depend primarily on their health, without which they cannot persevere in their dreams, their positive and progressive attitude is also a significant concern (WHO, 2024b).

Baldanzi et al. (2019) claim that aging benefits economic growth in many ways. According to them, aging increases aggregate savings, innovation initiatives, scientific and technological advancements, focus on the R&D sector, and long-term economic growth. Rising longevity has the potential to expand the expected working life, which encourages people and society to invest more in education and infrastructure development. Such progressive measures increase productivity and economic growth. An analysis of the situations of developed countries affirms that technological and innovative developments and implementations occur rapidly in so-called aging countries like Germany, Japan, and South Korea. Realizing the importance of automation technology in benefiting the old-age population, they prioritize R&D and technological developments. The initiatives to implement the latest technologies strengthen economic growth (Gao et al., 2023). Since most older people are experienced in evaluating market changes, they can make better investments that enhance economic growth.

4.2 Negative Correlation

Meng and Yu (2024) state that the aging population has many undesirable consequences on economic growth. When a society ages, its labor force participation is severely affected, leading to economic slowdowns. Studies claim that Japan faced a 'lost decade' in the 1990s due to the disproportion between labor force demands and the working-age population. When Japan's old-age population increased, it failed to ensure human capital in the industrial sector. Besides, since the old-age population primarily depends on government funding, it causes an increase in the government's fiscal deficit. Lee and Mason (2007) argue that the escalation in the old-age population in any society affects the per capita income of all three generations: youth-age, working-age, and old-age populations. The family's consumption patterns are also affected when the per capita income is reduced. It will create an over-dependency on the working-age population, forcing them to lower fertility rates (Hock & Weil, 2012). Their choice of goods and services will be minimal. Such limited demand will affect the production of goods and services, adversely affecting the productivity and GDP of the country (Nagarajan et al., 2016).

4.3 Increase in Dependency Ratio

The growing number of older people states that a particular society's dependency ratio will be higher. We cannot neglect that people above a certain age may not have the physical and mental capacities to produce more compared to other sections of society. They consume more than what they produce and contribute to society (Temsumrit, 2023). Any society can be divided into three groups: dependent children, working adults, and dependent elderly. Both children and older people depend on working adults for meaningful survival (Weil, 2025). However, the consumption patterns of the first and third categories would be more complex than the second, as they require the support of working adults for education, healthcare, and daily needs. The dependent youth-age population is not seen as a burden but a hope. They are the future of society. Investments in the youth-age population are always regarded as assets.

Old-age dependency means the dependence of people aged 65 years and above on those between the ages of 20 and 64 (Pham & Vo, 2021). Taking the example of Bangladesh, Mamun et al. (2020) argue that the increasing share of the old-age population can increase the dependency ratio. Hock and Weil (2012) note that when a country's fertility rate is decreased, the dependency burden on the working-age population is reduced as the number of children is lower. This will create economic advantages in the short term. However, in the long run, it complicates the issue as the reduction in fertility increases the old-age ratio. When the old-age population is forced to depend on the working-age population, it creates more confusion than the children's dependency (Nagarajan et al., 2016). If the fertility and old-age ratios are almost equal, there will be a perfect synergy between the different population levels. According to the proportion of an increase in the old-age population, society also needs fertility rates for smooth functioning.

From 1960 to 2016, there has been a notable increase in the percentage of the old-age population in Japan. The old-age dependency also increased from 8.8% to 43.9% during the same period (Lee & Shin, 2019). The UNDESA (2015) states that the old-age dependency ratio in Europe is projected to double between 2015 and 2050. Such an increase causes an average increase in public expenditure. Both pension systems and healthcare demands cause severe concerns about the intensification of public spending (Pham & Vo, 2021). Although old-age dependency brings some financial burdens to society, it is society's responsibility to find suitable means to respond to such needs. The old-age population is the pillar of any society. Responding to older people's needs should be considered a responsibility and an expression of gratitude. Besides, each society should design its progressive methods to reduce the dependency ratio through adequate policies and programs.

4.4 Question of Social Security Schemes

Demographic changes pose various social, economic, environmental, and health challenges. Many older people are not financially and socially equipped to address these challenges. This is evident in developing countries (Sekher & Gupta, 2024). In most developed countries, the older population depends on government transfer programs and social security schemes for a meaningful life. It is estimated that 65% of the income of Germany's older people depends on government transfers (Maestas et al., 2023). The US and other developed countries face the same scenario. Although social security schemes and government transfer programs are not so effective in developing countries, they face financial challenges with the aging population.

Regardless of the developmental scenario of a country, older people depend primarily on social welfare schemes to ensure a peaceful life. Most governments design social security schemes to increase the quality of life of the vulnerable, including the elderly (Sekher & Gupta, 2024). As the name suggests, social security schemes guarantee security and protection to the weaker sections of society. The old-age population of those countries where the social welfare schemes function properly experiences security compared to other countries. However, the functioning of social security schemes is not without any drawbacks. Some countries design and implement them as part of their political strategy to win elections without prioritizing the genuine concerns of older people. Some others have designed them, but without an effective implementation mechanism. Besides, they cause a financial burden to many developing countries, affecting the revenue and increasing government expenditure. When the governmental revenue is reduced, taxes increase, negatively impacting and burdening the working-age population. Social welfare schemes should be efficiently designed not to burden anyone but to benefit the weaker sections of society.

4.5 Impact on Long-Term Economic Growth

Compared to developed countries, most developing countries have not yet seriously felt the aging population issue and its impact on economic growth. Many of these countries still have a low proportion of the old-age population and a high proportion of the working-age population. When the working-age population outnumbers the old-age population, it will not disturb economic growth (Temsumrit, 2023). Besides, many of these countries have just started to experience low fertility rates due to improved education and healthcare facilities, more involvement of women in the workforce, and governmental population control initiatives. However, within a few decades, these countries will experience an imbalance between the old and working-age populations, affecting their economic growth. Since these countries also experience an uncontrollable increase in migration to developed countries in addition to the low fertility rates, it will complicate the equilibrium between the old and working-age populations in the long run (Pham & Vo, 2021).

The rising old-age population points to a decrease in human capital. The mass of the working-age population will be significantly reduced, causing alarming insecurities in the labor market (Alam & Mitra, 2012). Authors like Elgin and Tumen (2010) argue that when the human capital is less, there is a tendency to prioritize machines for production. The latest advancements even prefer AI-supported machines over human capital to increase the quality and efficiency of production and augment the investors' profit. The amplified use of machines, AI, and other technological advancements benefits the economy. However, if they are highly incorporated into the industrial and other sectors, it reduces human involvement. Although it may increase the GDP due to increased productivity, it will not effectively ensure human security, as many will not have employment. It demands more effective policy-making concerning balancing the economy, incorporating the concerns that evolved from technological advancements, the future of the working-age and youth-age populations, and economic growth.

5 REQUIRED CHANGES IN POLICY PERSPECTIVES

Aging and its related complexities adversely affect millions of people. However, the global community has not yet designed effective policy frameworks supporting the concerns and interests of aged people. They require an inclusive and participatory approach that values their experiences and future problems. A human rights-based public health approach is also essential as it will provide them with appropriate security and revolve around them as rights-holders (WHO, 2022). The current global life expectancy at birth is 73.5 years for both sexes. In 2010, Bloom et al. (2010) projected that the life expectancy would be 75 years in 2050. However, looking at the current pace of scientific and technological advancements in healthcare and other facilities, there is every possibility that life expectancy might be increased further. This necessitates that the globe be prepared systematically to address the concerns of old age. It has to prudently design policies and programs to ensure an inclusive approach toward the problems and insecurities of the old-age population. International institutions, national governments, multinational and transnational actors, NGOs, and civil society should collaborate to devise plans to incorporate the increasing old-age population into society's socioeconomic, cultural, and political life.

5.1 Increase the Retirement Age

Countries across the globe have different retirement ages. It is estimated that the UAE has one of the lowest retirement ages, i.e., 49 for its citizens. Iceland, Israel, and Norway rank among the countries with the highest retirement age (67 years). Retirement age specifies an initiative of the government to provide employment opportunities to the younger generation and ensure a dignified life for older people who have enormously contributed to society's welfare in various ways. For countries with fast-growing younger generations, it would be an essential requirement. However, where the youth-age population is less, they can practice a higher retirement age, as it would support many older people in responding positively to the various concerns of life. We cannot always claim that advancement in age is a restriction on actively contributing to society. For instance, Donald Trump, the President of the USA, is 79 years old; Narendra Modi, the Prime Minister of India, is 74 years old; Xi Jinping, the President of China, is 72 years old; and Vladimir Putin, the President of Russia, is 72 years old. The retirement age in these countries is 67, 60-65, 50-60, and 60-65, respectively. Suppose the heads of these states can perform such significant responsibilities in their old age. In that case, those with physical and mental capacities and a willingness to work and contribute to society even in their old age should be promoted.

Bloom et al. (2010) affirm that older people are growing in numbers and becoming substantially healthier. The increased awareness of the importance of diet, exercise, and proper healthcare has contributed to this positive situation. It helps them to live in old age without many health issues. Suppose they remain healthier and active even after the currently fixed retirement age. In that case, the retirement age can be extended to incorporate them as contributors to economic growth. The problem with the decrease in human capital can be effectively managed if there is robust and systematic coordination to promote immigration and increase the retirement age. Some older people are forcefully retired and would have continued to work if there had been a choice. It is high time for many countries to rethink their retirement age and devise plans to provide choice-making powers to workers concerning the continuation of work.

Regardless of developed and developing countries, the globe witnesses a gradual decrease in fertility rates, as stated above. The global fertility rate dropped from 3.2 births/woman in 1990 to 2.5/woman in 2019. Sub-Saharan Africa has the highest fertility rate in the world. Even then, it faced a significant decrease in fertility rates, dropping from 6.3 births/woman in 1990 to 4.6/woman in 2019 (UNDESA, 2020). Female participation in higher education and the labor market has also affected the fertility rate (Temsumrit, 2023). However, the life expectancy increased from 65 years during 1990-1995 to 71 years between 2010 and 2015 (UNDESA, 2017).

The advances in healthcare facilities have helped significantly to increase people's life expectancy (Temsumrit, 2023). Both have contributed to an increasing number of the old-age population across the globe. Such a scenario necessitates that the retirement age be increased further, depending on the unique circumstances of each country. The same parameter cannot be applied to the whole world. Nevertheless, there is a crucial need to increase the retirement age to increase economic growth.

There can be arguments claiming that scientific and technological advancements have provided a situation where economic growth can be easily achieved without human capital. Technology-driven economic growth that neglects human capital increases the country's GDP but will not ensure human security concerns. People's financial security can be guaranteed only by more employment opportunities. Bloom et al. (2010) state that if healthier older people are given employment, their experience can contribute to economic growth and reduce their dependence on public funding. Multinational and transnational corporations, business firms, and other employment providers should seriously consider incorporating the experience and expertise of older people to improve their productivity. They also suggest that firms reconsider moving their pay patterns from seniority-based to performance-based. Many firms regard older workers as a burden. However, their expertise and knowledge add value to productivity. Realizing this positivity, they should provide them with flexible roles and schedules. In sum, the economic sector should switch from traditional production prioritizing young workers to human capital-oriented production emphasizing incorporating older people into the workforce (Nagarajan et al., 2016).

5.2 Encourage Lifelong Learning

Scientific and technological advancements like AI, machine learning, and block-chain have broadened the global vision towards interrelationality. People actively interact in virtual and real worlds, enhancing their positivity and connectivity. Social media platforms, entertainment sites, and other virtual banking, e-commerce, and communication platforms provide many opportunities to people. There are also disadvantages to the broader use of AI, as it will reduce human capital requirements (Chu et al., 2022). Keeler and Bernstein (2021, p.11) state that the awareness and the capacity to use innovative technologies will provide "independence, mobility and remote access to work, continued education, socialization, and recreation" to older people living in 2050. However, the problem is that many older adults are unaware of these platforms that can benefit them in many ways. Such a scenario necessitates that they should be given adequate training to benefit from these mechanisms.

Lifelong learning should be encouraged to align with these latest technological advancements. Governments must invest more in educating older people to provide them with effective awareness about the latest technologies (Gao et al., 2023). Many older people actively engage in a few certificate courses on Coursera and other online learning platforms. Such engagement and continuous learning broaden their thinking and increase quality and confidence. As stated above, healthy older people can be given various employment opportunities to utilize their expertise for the benefit of society. When incorporated into the labor market, it would be better to provide them with ongoing training to support them in mastering new skills as the economy changes (Bloom et al., 2010). Such training would help them to feel accustomed to the changing circumstances.

5.3 People-Centered Sustainable Development

Sustainable development is the ultimate objective of the international community in the present century. It aims at people-centered development without neglecting anyone from the global developmental agenda. This insists that society is responsible for providing a supportive physical and social environment to the marginalized sections of society, including older people. When they lose physical and mental capacities, society should support them with those essentials for their meaningful survival. For instance, safe and accessible public buildings and transport facilities support them in becoming socially active. Many countries have reserved seats in public transport systems for aged people to ensure they are cared for (WHO, 2024b). The UN has declared the decade 2021-2030 as the Decade of Healthy Aging to ensure people-centered sustainable development of the old-age population. The discussions on the interconnection between SDGs and the old-age population mainly revolve around SDG1 (no poverty), SDG3 (good health and well-being), SDG10 (reduced inequalities), and SDG11 (sustainable cities and communities) (Shevelkova, 2023).

Older people have every tendency to become victims of poverty, as their income is minimal compared to the growing expenses. Although most countries provide some social welfare support systems, they are inadequate in many countries. Those who have worked in the unorganized sector cannot rely on their pension, as it will also be minimal (Keeler & Bernstein, 2021). For instance, the Indian central government, with the assistance of state governments, has ensured a monthly pension for all senior citizens. But mostly, it is not sufficient for them to meet their needs. SDG1 should cover the concerns and worries of the old-age population to ensure they are also valued members of society. Older people prefer good health care and income security. In most developing countries, these essentials were provided by family members. However, the increased migration and the active engagement of women in the workforce have changed this scenario. Accordingly, older people cannot wholly rely on their family members for survival. As a result, they look for governmental support (Bloom et al., 2010). This necessitates that the countries increase and update their social protection policies and programs, ensuring an appropriate income for older people and providing them with good healthcare facilities (SDG3). For instance, under the Ayushman Bharat-Pradhan Mantri Jan Arogya Yojana, the government has provided the possibility to get free medical treatment to senior citizens above the age of 70 up to 5 lakh. They also face severe inequalities and marginalization due to their old age. A society cannot grow if it does not respect older people. It should show a preferential option to the old-age population to ensure that they are always treated well in various walks of life (SDG10). Besides, it should also prioritize designing societies and communities sustainably to accommodate and incorporate the old-age population (SDG11). The apartments, parks, shopping complexes, public transport facilities, hospitals, and other facility centers should be designed in such a way as to accommodate the elderly without giving them any burden.

6 CONCLUSION

Population aging is a serious problem that the globe is facing in this era. An increase in the percentage of the old-age population poses many societal concerns. It also challenges many governmental policies and programs, as the governments will be forced to spend more on older people's healthcare and social security. This is evident in developed countries, but developing countries have not yet fully realized the pressure of the demands of the old-age population. Surprisingly, they have not started addressing this complicated issue in the policies and programs, thinking they are still predominantly a working-age population. However, the whole global society is swiftly moving towards an aging population. There are debates concerning the economic contributions of the aging population. Some people claim that they contribute nothing to society and the economy. They regard older people as a burden to society since public expenditure is growing due to their healthcare necessities and other requirements. However, others affirm that their experience and expertise should be utilized appropriately. In such a way, they can contribute to society in many ways.

Longevity has significantly increased in almost all societies due to scientific and technological advancements, improved healthcare facilities, and other vital infrastructural advancements. It should be seen as one of the most significant advantages of human flourishing. However, the question is, how can the old-age population be incorporated into the active life of society? Since most present-day older people are healthier and the working-age population is smaller in many countries, they can be included in the labor market if the retirement age is increased. They can continue to contribute and lead a satisfactory and engaged life. Online learning portals like Coursera can be used to enhance their continuous learning possibilities. Since the world is fast-growing with new knowledge and scientific advancements, older people should be provided with practical learning possibilities. It will help them to become more active and confident. Furthermore, international institutions and national governments should devise appropriate policies, strategies, and programs that prioritize a people-centered development revolving around the human rights framework to enhance the rights and security of the old-age population. The UN Decade of Healthy Aging (2021-2030) will become meaningful only if it perfectly aligns with the demands of SDGs. The globe has five more years to realize this objective. If the world fails to address the concerns of its aging population, it will become a severe setback to realizing the SDGs.

REFERENCES

Achemoglu, D., & Restrepo, P. (2017). Secular Stagnation? The Effects of Aging on Economic Growth in the Age of Automation. *The American Economic Review, 107*(5), 174–179. https://www.aeaweb.org/articles?id=10.1257/aer.p20171101. DOI: 10.1257/aer.p20171101

Aiyar, S., Ebeke, C., & Shao, X. (2016). The Impact of Workforce Aging on European Productivity. *IMF Working Paper, WP/16/238.*

Alam, M., & Mitra, A. (2012). Labor Market Vulnerabilities and Health Outcomes: Older Workers in India. *Journal of Population Ageing, 5*(4), 241–256. https://link.springer.com/article/10.1007/s12062-012-9070-z. DOI: 10.1007/s12062-012-9070-z

Alders, P., & Broer, D. P. (2004). Aging, Fertility, and Growth. *Journal of Public Economics, 89*(5-6), 1075–1095. DOI: 10.1016/j.jpubeco.2004.06.001

Baldanzi, A., Prettner, K., & Tscheuschner, P. (2019). Longevity-Induced Vertical Innovation and the Tradeoff between Life and Growth. *Journal of Population Economics, 32*(4), 1293–1313. https://link.springer.com/article/10.1007/s00148-018-0724-x. DOI: 10.1007/s00148-018-0724-x

Bell, D. N. F., & Rutherford, A. C. (2013). Older Workers and Working Time. *The Journal of the Economics of Ageing, 1-2*, 28–34. DOI: 10.1016/j.jeoa.2013.08.001

Bloom, D. E., Canning, D., & Fink, G. (2010). Implications of Population Aging for Economic Growth. *Oxford Review of Economic Policy, 26*(4), 583–612. DOI: 10.1093/oxrep/grq038

Bloom, D. E., Canning, D., & Finlay, J. E. (2008). Population Aging and Economic Growth in Asia. *PGDA Working Paper No. 40*. Harvard School of Public Health. https://content.sph.harvard.edu/wwwhsph/sites/1288/2013/10/PGDA_WP_40.pdf

Bloom, D. E., & Williamson, J. G. (1998). Demographic Transitions and Economic Miracles in Emerging Asia. *The World Bank Economic Review, 12*(30), 419–455. https://academic.oup.com/wber/article-abstract/12/3/419/1632238?redirectedFrom=fulltext. DOI: 10.1093/wber/12.3.419

Chen, J., Wang, Y., Wen, J., Fang, F., & Song, M. (2015). The Influences of Aging Population and Economic Growth on Chinese Rural Poverty. *Journal of Rural Studies, 30*, 1–12. https://www.sciencedirect.com/science/article/abs/pii/S0743016715300383?via%3Dihub

Davies, R. B., & Robert, R. R., III. (2006). Population Aging, Foreign Direct Investment, and Tax Competition. https://scholarsbank.uoregon.edu/server/api/core/bitstreams/40f97ad4-b9ce-4aa7-94d9-9b6b53742d7f/content

de Meijer, C., Wouterse, B., Polder, J., & Koopmanschap, M. (2013). The Effect of Population Aging on Health Expenditure Growth: A Critical Review. *European Journal of Ageing*, *10*(4), 353–361. https://link.springer.com/article/10.1007/s10433-013-0280-x. DOI: 10.1007/s10433-013-0280-x PMID: 28804308

Eggertson, G., Lancastre, M., & Summers, L. H. (2017). Aging, Output Per Capita, and Secular Stagnation. Institute for New Economic Thinking. https://www.ineteconomics.org/research/research-papers/aging-output-per-capita-and-secular-stagnation

Elgin, C., & Tumen, S. (2010). Can Sustained Economic Growth and Declining Population Co-exist? Barro-Becker Children Meet Lucas. *Economic Modelling*, *29*(5), 1899–1908. DOI: 10.1016/j.econmod.2012.06.004

Freedman, A., & Nicolle, J. (2020). Social Isolation and Loneliness: The New Geriatric Giants. *Canadian Family Physician Médecin de Famille Canadien*, *66*, 176–182. https://www.cfp.ca/content/66/3/176.short PMID: 32165464

Gao, W., Chen, Y., Xu, S., Lyulyov, O., & Pimonenko, T. (2023). The Role of Population Aging in High-Quality Economic Development: Mediating Role of Technological Innovation. *SAGE Open*, *13*(4), 1–15. https://journals.sagepub.com/doi/10.1177/21582440231202385. DOI: 10.1177/21582440231202385

Hock, H., & Weil, D. N. (2012). On the Dynamics of the Age Structure, Dependency, and Consumption. *Journal of Population Economics*, *25*(3), 1019–1043. https://link.springer.com/article/10.1007/s00148-011-0372-x. DOI: 10.1007/s00148-011-0372-x PMID: 24353374

Horioka, C. Y., & Niimi, Y. (2017). Saving Behavior of the Japanese Middle-Aged and the Elderly. ESRI *International Conference on Empirical Analysis on Population Decline and Aging in the Japanese Economy*. ESRI.

Keeler, L. W., & Bernstein, M. J. (2021). The Future of Aging in Smart Environments: Four Scenarios of the United States in 2050. *Futures*, *133*, 102830. https://www.sciencedirect.com/science/article/pii/S0016328721001312. DOI: 10.1016/j.futures.2021.102830

Lee, H.-H., Huh, H.-s., Lee, Y.-Y., & Lim, J.-Y. (2013). Effects of Population Aging on Economic Growth: A Panel Analysis. *Seoul Journal of Economics*, *26*(4), 401–432. https://www.sje.ac.kr/xml/26454/26454.pdf

Lee, H.-H., & Shin, K. (2019). Nonlinear Effects of Population Aging on Economic Growth. *Japan and the World Economy*, *51*, 100963. DOI: 10.1016/j.japwor.2019.100963

Lee, H.-H., Shin, K., & Park, D. (2017). Population Aging and Its Impact on Economic Growth: Implications for Korea. *Economic Analysis*, ESRI 196, 159-178. https://www.esri.cao.go.jp/jp/esri/archive/bun/bun196/bun196h_1.pdf

Lee, S.-H., & Mason, A. (2007). Who Gains from the Demographic Dividend? Forecasting Income by Age. *International Journal of Forecasting*, *23*(4), 603–619. https://pubmed.ncbi.nlm.nih.gov/18443647/. DOI: 10.1016/j.ijforecast.2007.07.004 PMID: 18443647

Lee, S.-H., Mason, A., & Park, D. (2011). Why Does Population Aging Matter so Much for Asia? Population Aging, Economic Security, and Economic Growth in Asia. *ADB Economics Working Paper Series No. 284*. https://www.adb.org/sites/default/files/publication/30454/economics-wp284.pdf

Maestas, N., Mullen, K. J., & Powell, D. (2023). The Effect of Population Aging on Economic Growth, the Labor Force, and Productivity. *American Economic Journal. Macroeconomics*, *15*(2), 306–332. https://www.aeaweb.org/articles?id=10.1257/mac.20190196. DOI: 10.1257/mac.20190196

Mamun, S. A. K., Rahman, M. M., & Khanam, R. (2020). The Relation between an Aging Population and Economic Growth in Bangladesh: Evidence from an Endogenous Growth Model. *Economic Analysis and Policy*, *66*, 14–25. DOI: 10.1016/j.eap.2020.02.001

Meng, Q., & Yu, W. (2024). The Impact of Population Aging on Economic Growth. *Advances in Economics, Management, and Political Sciences*, 140, 109-116. https://www.ewadirect.com/proceedings/aemps/article/view/18557

Minzner, C. (2024). China's Population Decline Continues. *Council on Foreign Relations*. https://www.cfr.org/blog/chinas-population-decline-continues

Nagarajan, N. R., Teixeira, A. A., & Silva, S. T. (2016). The Impact of an Aging Population on Economic Growth: An Exploratory Review of the Main Mechanisms. *Analise Social*, *51*(218), 4–35. https://www.jstor.org/stable/43755167

Pham, T. N., & Vo, D. H. (2021). Aging Population and Economic Growth in Developing Countries: A Quantile Regression Approach. *Emerging Markets Finance & Trade*, *57*(1), 108–122. https://www.tandfonline.com/doi/full/10.1080/1540496X.2019.1698418. DOI: 10.1080/1540496X.2019.1698418

Ritchie, H. (2024). Which Countries have Fertility Rates Above or below the "Replacement Level"? *Our World in Data*. https://ourworldindata.org/data-insights/which-countries-have-fertility-rates-above-or-below-the-replacement-level

Samir, K. C. (2013). Population Stabilization, Human. In Levin, S. A. (Ed.), *Encyclopedia of Biodiversity* (2nd ed., pp. 199–209). Elsevier., https://www.sciencedirect.com/science/article/abs/pii/B9780123847195004135

Sekher, T. V., & Gupta, S. (2024). Social Security Schemes for the Elderly in India: Awareness, Utilization, and Barriers. In James, K. S., & Sekher, T. V. (Eds.), *India Population Report* (pp. 199–245). Cambridge University Press.

Shevelkova, V., Mattocks, C., & Lafortune, L. (2023). Efforts to Address the Sustainable Development Goals in Older Populations: A Scoping Review. *BMC Public Health*, *23*(1), 456. DOI: 10.1186/s12889-023-15308-4 PMID: 36890447

Sløk, T. (2024). Working-Age Population Growth in the G-7. *Apollo*. https://www.apolloacademy.com/working-age-population-growth-in-the-g7/

Temsumrit, N. (2023). Can Aging Population Affect Economic Growth through the Channel of Government Spending? *Heliyon*, *9*(9), e19521. DOI: 10.1016/j.heliyon.2023.e19521 PMID: 37809751

Trong, N. T., Dong, N. T., & Ly, P. T. (2024). Population Aging and Economic Growth: Evidence from ASEAN Countries. *Cogent Business & Management*, *11*(1), 2298055. https://www.tandfonline.com/doi/full/10.1080/23311975.2023.2298055. DOI: 10.1080/23311975.2023.2298055

UNDESA. (2015). World Population Aging 2015. *ST/ESA/SER.A/390*. https://www.un.org/en/development/desa/population/publications/pdf/ageing/WPA2015_Report.pdf

UNDESA. (2017). World Population Prospects: the 2017 Revision. *Working Paper No. ESA/P/WP/248*. https://desapublications.un.org/publications/world-population-prospects-2017-revision

UNDESA. (2020). World Fertility and Family Planning 2020: Highlights. ST/ESA/SER.A/440. https://www.un.org/development/desa/pd/content/world-fertility-and-family-planning-2020-highlights

UNDESA. (2022). Aging. https://social.desa.un.org/issues/ageing

UNDESA. (2024). World Population Prospects 2024: Summary of Results. *UNDESA/POP/2024/TR/No.9*. https://desapublications.un.org/publications/world-population-prospects-2024-summary-results

UNFPA. (2025). Aging. https://www.unfpa.org/ageing

Wei, W. (2025). Population Aging. In Yinxing, H. (Ed.), *Dictionary of Contemporary Chinese Economics* (pp. 525–529). Springer., https://link.springer.com/rwe/10.1007/978-981-97-4036-9_219 DOI: 10.1007/978-981-97-4036-9_219

WHO. (2022). Tackling Abuse of Older People: Five Priorities for the United Nations Decade of Healthy Aging (2021-2030). https://iris.who.int/bitstream/handle/10665/356151/9789240052550-eng.pdf?sequence=1

WHO. (2023). Progress Report on the United Nations Decade of Healthy Aging, 2021-2023. *Decade of Healthy Aging*. https://iris.who.int/bitstream/handle/10665/374192/9789240079694-eng.pdf?sequence=1

WHO. (2024a). Abuse of Older People. https://www.who.int/news-room/fact-sheets/detail/abuse-of-older-people

WHO. (2024b). Aging and Health. https://www.who.int/news-room/fact-sheets/detail/ageing-and-health

Worldometer. (2025). Current World Population. https://www.worldometers.info/world-population/

Xu, Q., Ou, X., & Li, J. (2022). The Risk of Falls among the Aging Population: A Systematic Review and Meta-analysis. *Frontiers in Public Health*, *10*, 902599. https://www.frontiersin.org/journals/public-health/articles/10.3389/fpubh.2022.902599/full. DOI: 10.3389/fpubh.2022.902599 PMID: 36324472

KEY TERMS AND DEFINITIONS

Demographic Changes: Demographic changes refer to the changes in the essential nature of the population over time due to low/high fertility rate, low/high mortality rate, increased percentage of working-age or old-age population, and the like.

Economic Growth: Economic growth refers to a country's increased income and wealth, which is examined through its GDP rate.

Human Rights: Human rights are the basic entitlements of people evolving from their human nature and dignity, regardless of any differentiating parameters.

Human Security: Human Security is a UNDP-designed policy perspective that advances a people-centered development for security, well-being, and dignity.

Non-Discrimination: Non-discrimination is an ethical principle affirming that no individual should be discriminated against or marginalized in society for any reason or differentiating parameters.

Social Welfare Schemes: Social welfare schemes are the support systems provided by the state to ensure an adequate standard of living for specific groups like the disabled, widows, unemployed, and older people of its population.

Sustainable Development: Sustainable development is the UN-proposed policy perspective, which demands balancing the developmental and environmental needs of the present and future generations for a sustainable future.

Chapter 3
Exploring the Interplay Between Population Aging and Sustainable Finance:
A Bibliometric Analysis

Eugenia Strano
https://orcid.org/0009-0005-8318-2704
Department of Law, Economics, and Sociology, University Magna Græcia, Catanzaro, Italy

Shikha Daga
https://orcid.org/0000-0003-4620-5282
PGDAV College, University of Delhi, India

Kiran Yadav
PGDAV College, University of Delhi, India

ABSTRACT

Population aging poses multifaceted challenges to sustainable economic development, particularly within the financial services industry and the broader economy. Despite the growing body of research on demographic shifts and finance, the relationship between an aging population and sustainable finance remains underexplored. This study seeks to contribute to filling this research gap by employing bibliometric perspective and content analysis with the aim of mapping the existing research landscape. Our findings reveal a recent increase in focus on green finance (since 2024), highlighting the need for more integrated approaches to explore how sustainable finance can mitigate the economic (and social) pressures related to an aging society.

DOI: 10.4018/979-8-3373-2550-7.ch003

This work contributes to the literature by laying the foundation for future studies, and promoting insights for policymakers, practitioners, and researchers seeking to align sustainable finance initiatives with the specific needs of aging populations.

1. INTRODUCTION

The issue of ageing population is one of the pertinent issues in the transit towards sustainable development. This demographic shift has widespread implications for economic growth, putting pressure on the sustainability and the (continual) enhancement of innovation capabilities (Wang, Liang &Wang, 2024). At the same time, the transition to an aging society places greater strain on social welfare systems, elderly care services, and pension expenditures (Yan et al., 2022; Dashjamts et al., 2024), leading severe financial challenges. In this vein, financial institutions try to adapt their products and services to meet the needs of an aging population (Fang, 2023; Jane Osareme et al., 2024), providing more elderly care financial products and insurance products (as regards health, longevity, and pension), as well as tailored risk management approaches to manage life-stage risks (e.g., Mitchell, 2018; Ba, 2022; Jakovljevic et al., 2023; Haward, 2024). Additionally, financial consultation, financial literacy, and financial education are key drivers in improving financial security, allowing older people to better manage their wealth accumulation, savings behaviors, retirement savings, and investment plans (e.g., Pan et al., 2022; Fang, 2023; Cai et al., 2025).

It is worth noting that in recent years, most of the existing literature has been carried out to investigate and understand the growth of academic trends in the research of the finance landscape and aging population concerns, focusing on individual economic indicators (e.g., Wang, Liang &Wang, 2024). Particularly, the most prominent studies explore the impact of aging population issues on 1. the financial services industry, such as the changes in the savings and investment market and the transformation and development of the insurance industry (e.g., Liu, 2024; Kim et al., 2024); and 2. the economic development, including the labor market, the social security system, and the consumption structure (Li et al., 2022; Yu et al., 2022; Dumiter et al., 2024). In addition, it is necessary to specify that the works largely carried out in the most recent years were independently made. At the moment, there is a lack of a unified vision of the different results that each work has produced, as well as a comparison between the various studies performed, and the topic of sustainable finance in the context of an aging population appears unexplored.

As ageing is populaton increasing, personalized elderly sustainable long-term care financial services become more critical (Fang, 2023). A recent study underlined the deep intertwining between population aging and green finance, asserting how important green finance is in promoting green growth (Wang, Liang & Wang, 2024; Wang, Zhang, Wang et al., 2024). Nonetheless, impact of the same on sustainable finance field is overlooked, and scholars call for further qualitative research to explore the correlation (Wang, Liang &Wang, 2024).

In response to this call, our work aims to provide a comprehensive map of research landscape of the sustainable finance in the context of population aging, seeking to answer the following research questions:

R1. What is the publications trend for sustainable finance research in the transition to an aging society?
R2. Which articles have influenced the most academic research related to sustainable finance in the context of population aging?.
R3. Which are the main themes and emerging topics related to sustainable finance in the context of population aging?.
R4. Which are the research gaps and future research directions?

Given that the relationship between the demographic shift and the sustainable economic development under the lens of green (or sustainable) finance is a nascent theme (Wang, Liang &Wang, 2024), this study intends to map the broader landscape of sustainable finance in the context of population aging to better understand the intricate linkages between sustainability, sustainable finance, and population aging. To this end, the work adopts the systematic literature review methodology (Tranfield et al., 2003). To guarantee more broader coverage of topics, the research analyzes studies published until 2024 and sourced from the Scopus database. Additionally, this study uses a bibliometric analysis that, recently, has seen a noteworthy growth in the finance landscape (e.g., Bahoo et al., 2020; Kahn et al., 2022; Trotta et al., 2024) in order to identify key themes, current trends, emerging challenges, and frontier areas.

To the best of our knowledge, this study is the first to apply a bibliometric approach to a sample of scientific publications on this topic. Findings are useful to academics, practitioners, and policymakers who seek to better understand key characteristics, challenges, and opportunities related to sustainable finance in the transition to an aging society. Finally, our findings offers new insights into the literature about sustainable finance, providing the basis for a research agenda.

2. THEORETICAL BACKGROUND AND CONCEPTUAL FRAMEWORK

Population ageing is on the verge of becoming one of the most significant demographic changes in the 21st century, with significant implications for economies, financial systems, and sustainability programs. Theoretically, this link finds its roots at the point where demographic transition theory, lifecycle hypothesis, and sustainable development theory overlap. As nations transition demographically characterized by declining fertility rates and rising life expectancies, more of the population reaches post-retirement age. This changing population in turn affects consumption habits, savings patterns, healthcare needs, and eventually investment choices, thereby changing the financial outlook. The life-cycle hypothesis (Modigliani & Brumberg, 1954) states that in one's working period, wealth is accumulated and dissaved in retirement, which means that ageing population can decrease aggregate savings and change long-term investment products demand.

From a sustainability perspective, the United Nations' Sustainable Development Goals (SDGs) SDG 3 (Good Health and Well-being), SDG 8 (Decent Work and Economic Growth), and SDG 13 (Climate Action) highlight the importance of inclusive and forward-looking financial systems. Sustainable finance, comprising ESG investing, green bonds, and social impact investing, has emerged as a strategic means of directing financial flows towards environmentally and socially beneficial initiatives. But population aging brings new complexity. Short- to medium-term income security may take precedence in aging societies over long-term environmental outcomes, presenting the risk of misalignment between demographic fact and sustainable investment requirement. By contrast, older populations particularly in developed countries have huge financial assets and can shape sustainable finance agendas through pension funds, retirement schemes, and ethical investment choices.

Institutional theory also offers a perspective for examining how policy frameworks, market structures, and societal norms mediate the aging-sustainable finance nexus. In certain countries, progressive regulations (e.g., mandatory ESG disclosures or green pension overhauls) build facilitating environments for sustainable financial behaviors even in aging society. Additionally, behavioral finance proposes that cognitive biases among aging investors—risk aversion or status quo bias are likely to affect the uptake of innovative sustainable instruments.

Bibliometric analysis presents a holistic window through which to investigate the evolution of scholarly discussion on such interlinked topics. Plotting the intellectual landscape of available literature may show prevailing schools of thought, methodological streams, country-level evidence, and thematic developments. In addition, it enables the finding of untapped linkages like the influence of intergenerational wealth transfer, gendered aspects of aging, or fintech-driven sustainable retirement solutions. With the world shifting towards a global gray economy, comprehending these dynamics is imperative not merely for scholarly enrichment but also for informing evidence-based policymaking.

In these regards, the current research has the objective of identifying the outlines of scholarly research on population aging and sustainable finance using bibliometric analysis. In so doing, it hopes to synthesize a conceptual framework bridging demographic economics and sustainable financial systems. The resulting insights will be used to guide future research agendas, identify policy lacunae, and enhance the understanding of how aging populations can make the global economy more sustainable.

2.1 Methodology and Data

2.1.1 Methods and Software

Inspired by the methodological framework adopted by Alshater et al. (2023), this study utilizes a hybrid review strategy that integrates bibliometric techniques with qualitative content analysis. Such an approach has gained prominence in contemporary business and finance research, as evidenced in recent studies (e.g., Khan et al., 2020; Hassan et al., 2021). There are two main technique categories for bibliometric analysis: performance analysis and science mapping (Donthu et al. 2021). Among the most important measures, it is worth mentioning both the number of publications and citations per year or constituents (e.g., Baker et al. 2021). On the other hand, science mapping represents the relationships between research constituents. We use RStudio with the "Bibliometrix" package for performance analysis (Aria & Cuccurullo, 2017) and VOSviewer (Van Eck & Waltman, 2010).

2.1.2. Sample Selection Process

As shown in Figure 1, the sample selection process involves three step process. For this review, we select the *Scopus* database where we extracted the relevant literature using keywords. Firstly, since the primary objective of this study is to shed light on the interplay of the aging population and sustainable finance, we use very generic keywords i.e. 'aging population'; 'financ*'; and 'sustainable financ*'. It gave a total of 487 documents. We carry out the keyword analysis by adoping VOSviewer. Secondly, we then search the keywords (obteined from keyword analysis) i.e. 'aging population,' 'sustainable financ*', and 'green finance', and combine them with 'financ*' by adopting the Boolean operators "AND" and "OR". We search the aforementioned keywords in the title, abstract, and keywords of the publications until 2024, which yields us a total of 785 articles.

To clean the data, we applied the following filters: 1. the subject areas was limited to Economics, Econometrics and Finance; and Business, Management and Accounting; 2. we selected publications in the form of articles published only in the English language; 3. we excluded articles published in 2025 as these papers still need citations for authentication. The search string was as follows: *(TITLE-ABS-KEY ("population aging") AND ("financ*") OR ("sustainab* financ*" OR "greenfinanc*"))AND PUBYEAR > 1979AND PUBYEAR < 2025AND(LIMIT-TO (SUBJAREA, "BUSI") OR LIMIT-TO (SUBJAREA, "ECON")) AND (LIMIT-TO (DOCTYPE, "ar")) AND (LIMIT-TO (LANGUAGE, "English")).*

During the third step, a careful examination of the sample was conducted by three independent researchers to confirm the relevance of each article. We rejected the "irrelevant" articles, as well as the articles discussing the topic of sustainable finance and aging population in a trivial and marginal way We are finally left with a total of 94 articles extracted from the *Scopus* database.

3. ANALYSIS OF DATA AND TREND

3.1. Publication Trend

Figure1 shows that the sustainable finance research in the transition to an aging society has been increasing in the last years. During the years 2001 to 2015, publication was stable in this field, whereas researchers have intensified their interest in aging populations since 2015, with a significant increase in 2023 and 2024. However, 10 and 22 articles were published in year in 2023 and 2024 10 and 22, respectively.

Figure 1. Articles per year

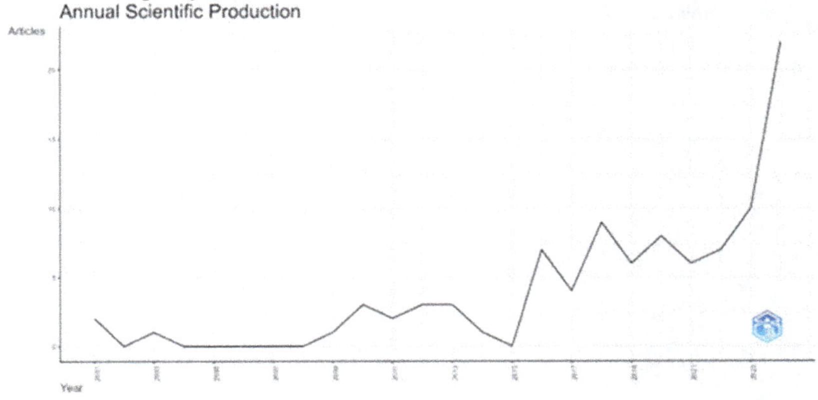

3.2. Influential Countries

While early studies mainly focused on developed markets (e.g., USA), there has been a more recent shift towards emerging markets (e.g., China). As noted in Figure2, most studies are conducted by research groups from the USA, especially in the initial phase (until 2014). Instead, starting in 2015, researchers from China one of the largest developing markets led the top list, especially in recent years. As most of these studies are based in USA and China, they have received a high number of citations, as reported in Figure3. However, Japan led the list and represents the most influential country. Researchers from Germany, Denmark, and Canada are the least cited in the field, to date.

Table 1. Countries with highest and lowest papers production.

Country	Articles
USA	127
China	122
Spain	96
Germany	81
Australia	40
Korea	35

Source: Authors' elaboration.

Figure 2. Country production over time

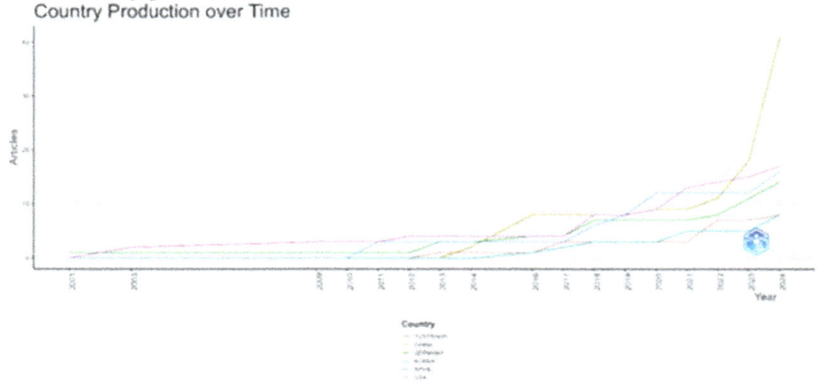

Figure 3. Top influential country over time

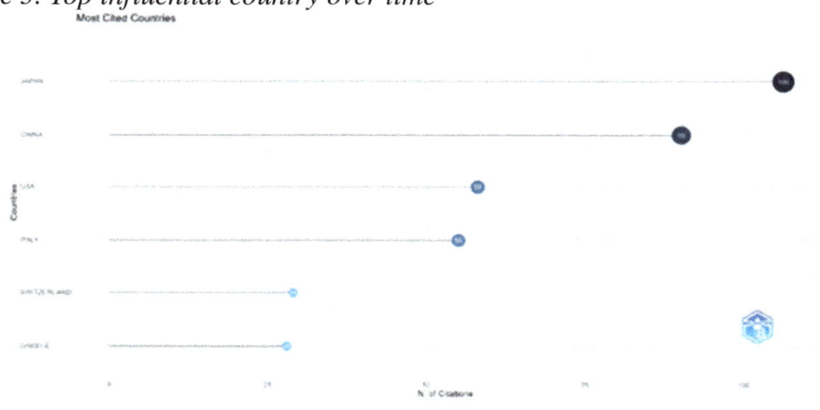

3.3. Influential Journals and Authors

Table 2 presents the most productive and influential journals, based on the total number of articles. Most journals fall broadly within the domain of economics, followed by finance. More specifically, "*Journal of the Economics of Ageing*" led the top list with 7 articles, followed by "*Finance Research Letters*" with 5 articles published. At the last place, there were "*Applied Economics*", "*Insurance: Mathematics And Economics*", And "*International Review of Financial Analysis*" with 2 publications, respectively. On the other hand, as regards the most influential journals, "*Journal of the Economics of Ageing*" continues to led the top list, which is a journal specialized on the interaction between demographic change and the economy. Other notable influential journal is "*Japan and the World Economy*", confirming the role of Japan as influential country (see Figure3) and, emphasizing that population aging is an important feature of Japan's economy. Additionally, "*Finance Research Letters*" appears also among the main influential journals.

Table 3 display the most productive and influential authors. Notably, Horioka, C.Y. appears at the top of the lists. It is worth noting that the authors are all academics, emphasizing the lack of interdisciplinary and transdisciplinary perspectives among researchers of a different matrix from the university, such as non-university research bodies. Nevertheless, these results become interesting if we look at them from the relationship between authors, keywords, and sources, the so-called "Three-field plot" (see Figure4). The "*Asian Development Bank Economics Working Paper Series*" presents the highest weights, whose aim is to stimulate discussion on research and policy studies dealing with economic and development problems and issues in the Asia and Pacific region. Particularly, the "*Asian Development Bank Economics Working Paper Series*" is a professional journal that supports projects in developing member countries, like the Asian region. This result is not surprising, as the Asia and Pacific regions represent the major emerging and frontier economies that address the main challenges related to the social issue of aging populations.

Figure 4 shows keyword correlations across authors, revealing key topics and research domains within the literature. Three-Field Plot, we can observe several authors with relatively high weights, including Härtl, K.; Leite, D.N.; and Börsch-Supan, A. Notably, most researchers focus on topics such as population aging, pension reform, China, and labor supply. These prominent research directions likely mirror the current open issues in the fields of sustainable finance, providing valuable guidance for future research.

Table 2. Most relevant and influential sources

Relevant sources	Articles	Influential sources	Total citation
Journal of the Economics of Ageing	7	Journal of the Economics of Ageing	108
Finance Research Letters	5	Japan and the World Economy	98
Applied Economics Letters	4	Finance Research Letters	28
Risks	4	Insurance: Mathematics and Economics	26
ADB Economics Working Paper Series	3	Risks	18
Economic and Political Studies	3	International Review of Financial Analysis	17
Journal of Public Economics	3	Journal of Public Economics	15
Applied Economics	2	ADB Economics Working Paper Series	14

continued on following page

Table 2. Continued

Relevant sources	Articles	Influential sources	Total citation
Insurance: Mathematics and Economics	2	Applied Economics	10
International Review of Financial Analysis	2	Economic and Political Studies	5

Source: Authors' elaboration.

Table 3. Most relevant and influential authors

Relevant authors	Articles	Influential authors	Total citation
Börsch-Supan, A.	3	Horioka, C.Y.	82
Horioka, C.Y.	3	Terada-Hagiwara, A.	63
Wang, X.	3	Grable, J.E.	54
Flici, F.	2	Joo, S.H.	54
Härtl, K.	2	Lyons, A.C.	54
Leite, D.N.	2	Faruqee, H.	44
Park, D.	2	Mühleisen, M.	44
Terada-Hagiwara, A.	2	Park, D.	27
Wagner, J.	2	Wagner, J.	26
Wang, H.	2	Cipriani, G.P.	26

Source: Authors' elaboration.

Figure 4. Three-Field Plot.

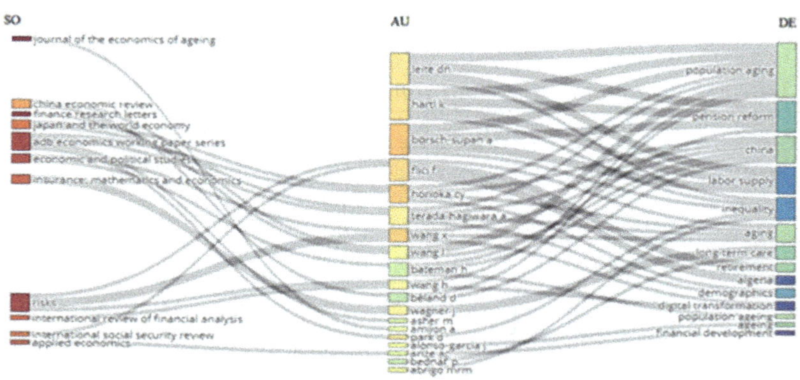

3.4. Relevant Institutions

Table 3 shows the research institutions that have published papers on aging population in (sustainable) finance field. Examining Table 3, we see that all the most institutions are from China, emphasizing how the topic of aging population in finance is pursued mainly by academics in the developing country of China. This result confirms that China's aging population is more serious and complicated than that of other developed countries and regions in the globe.

Table 3. Most relevant institutions

Relevant institutions	Articles
Henan University of Economics and Law, China	4
Macao Polytechnic University, Denmark	4
Renmin University of China, China	4
University of Lausanne, Swiss	4
University of Macau, China	4
"Vasile Goldi " Western University of Arad, Romania	4
Henan University, China	3
Nicolaus Copernicus University, Poland	3
Shangqiu Normal University, China	3
The Danish Center For Social Science Research, Denmark	3

Source: Authors' elaboration.

3.5. Influential Articles

Influential and tranding article, based on total citation shown in Table 4, is the demographic shift in the (sustainable) finance. However, Lyons et al. (2018) and Horiokaet al. (2012) with 54 citations are by far the most cited papers, following by Faruqee et al. (2003) with 44 citation, with more recent article Liu et al. (2023) having the lowest number of citations (19).

Table 4. Most influential articles

Authors (year)	Title	Source	Total citation
Lyons et al. (2018)	A cross-country analysis of population aging and financial security	Journal of the Economics of Ageing	54
Horioka & Terada-Hagiwara (2012)	The determinants and long-term projections of saving rates in Developing Asia	Japan and the World Economy	54
Faruqee & Mühleisen (2003)	Population aging in Japan: Demographic shock and fiscal sustainability	Japan and the world economy	44
Cipriani (2018)	Aging, retirement, and pay-as-you-go pensions	Macroeconomic Dynamics	26
Fuino & Wagner (2018)	Long-term care models and dependence probability tables by acuity level: New empirical evidence from Switzerland	Insurance: Mathematics and Economics	23
Abrigo et al. (2018)	Human Capital Spending, Inequality, and Growth in Middle-Income Asia	Emerging Markets Finance and Trade	22
Wang et al. (2014)	Pension financing in China: Is there a looming crisis?	China Economic Review	21
Amilon et al. (2020)	Willingness to pay for long-term home care services: Evidence from a stated preferences analysis	The Journal of the Economics of Ageing,	21
Bravo (2019)	Funding for longer lives. Retirement wallet and risk-sharing annuities	Ekonomiaz	20
Liu et al. (2023)	Research on the impact of population aging and endowment insurance on household financial asset allocation- Evidence on CFPS data	Finance Research Letters	19

Source: Authors' elaboration.

4. INTELLECTUAL STRUCTURE (CO-CITATION ANALYSIS AND BIBLIOGRAPHIC COUPLING)

4.1. Keyword Analysis

4.1.1. Most Used Frequently Words

Tree map shown in Fig 5, in this analysis a total of 388 author keywords are retrieved, out of which 50 of the most frequently encountered words are displayed on the tree map in Figure5. The most used words are 'aging population', 'pension system', 'financial system' and 'sustainability', followed by 'savings', 'Asia', 'financial market', 'capital market', 'China' and 'elderly are'.

Figure 5. Tree map

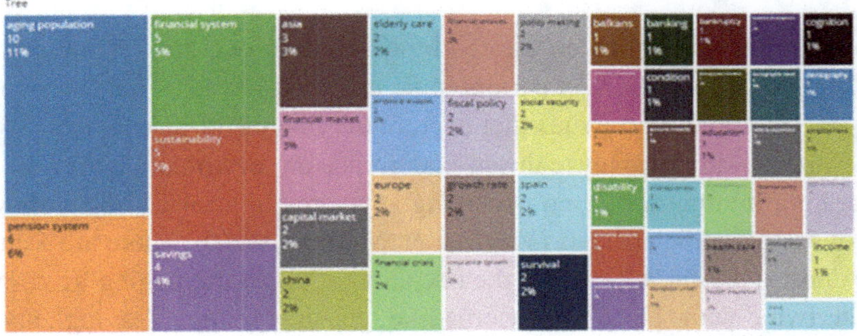

4.1.2. Trend topics and words' frequency over time

In the above analysis, the top 10 most cited words, we noted shifts in their usage over time. The production period shown in Figure6 ranges from 2001 to 2024. Many words exhibit a consistent increase in keyword frequency from the beginning. The other words (such as 'savings,' 'sustainability,' and 'financial system') appear later but grow faster. Figure6 shows 'aging population', followed by 'sustainability', 'financial system', and 'pension system' are trending topics in this research field.

Figure 6. Words' frequency over time

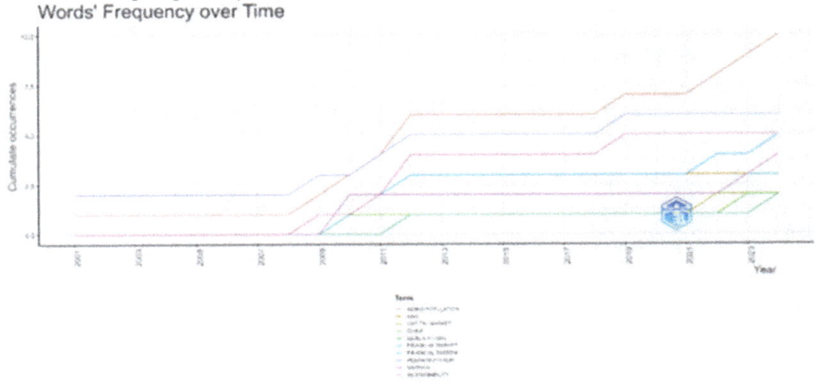

4.1. Cartographic Analysis

A map of keywords that are created based on their occurrence in the selected article sample is done through cartographic analysis. It allows for the identification of the key topics and issues that capture the interest of researchers. We used VOSviewer software to analyze the co-occurrence of keywords. Figure7, obtained considering a minimum of 3 co-occurring keywords in a total of 388, shows the results of cartographic analysis (Van Eck & Waltman, 2010). There are 5 clusters.

The densest cluster is certainly the one around 'population aging' (red), whose links intertwine with financial concerns like 'pension system', 'saving', and 'sustainability'. In contrast, the less dense (violet), containing the keyword with the latest number of co-occurrences (5) is the one around 'long-term care'. The cluster in green contains the 'sustainability' term, representing the main keyword linked to 'aging population' (total link: 20). There are also two marginal clusters that concern targets such as 'fiscal policy' (yellow cluster) or 'financial system' (blue cluster).

Regarding the occurrences of co-authorship over time, Figure 8 depicts how many countries were added to the pioneer Japan and Italy, such as the United States, which have the major links among the other countries. China, on the other hand, appears as a country that has recently invested in the topic.

Figure 7. Cartography with 3 minimum co-occurring keywords.

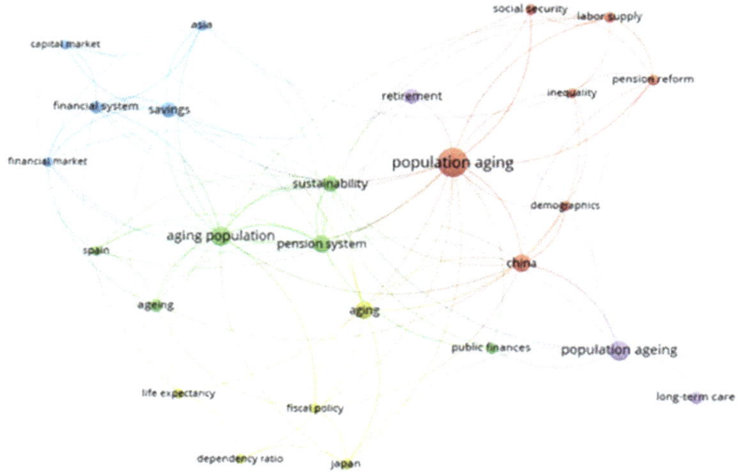

Source: VOSviewer.

Figure 8. Co-authorship cartography with 3 minimum co-occurring of keywords.

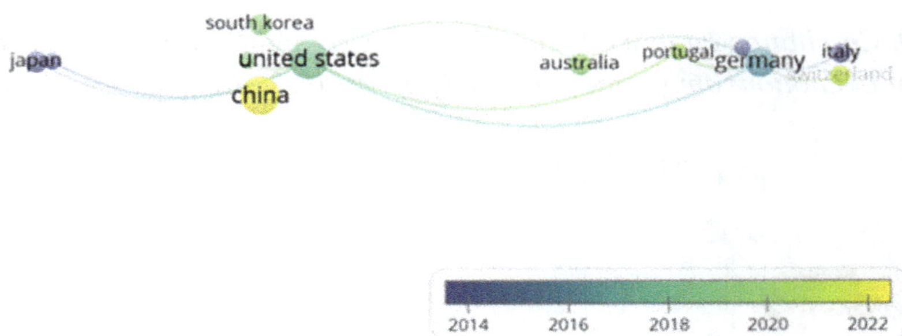

Source: VOSviewer.

4.2. Co-Citation Analysis

The objective of employing co-citation analysis is to reveal 'hidden' patterns of relationships between researchers based on their publications(Yadav et al., 2022). The frequency of author co-citation is represented by multiple lines emanating from each node. The thickness of the nodes indicates the strength of co-citation links, while the proximity between researchers is reflected in the closeness of their connections. Co-citation analysis, as shown in Figure 9, is grounded on the number of citations an article receives and the total link strength of the article.

Co-citation analysis conducted using VOSviewer outputs a diagram that shows the streams in different colors, in this case, red, green, and blue. As represented in Figure 9, the red cluster (Horioka and Terada-Hagiwara, 2012; Abrigo et al., 2018; Cheng and Lee, 2022) identifies articles outlining the impact of population aging both on investing behavior, including the long-term projections of saving rate, and on human capital investments. Additionally, this cluster gathers papers focusing on specific geographic areas like Asia. The green cluster, on the other hand, encompasses articles centered on the issues related to the aging in Europe area. In this vein, it is worth noting Börsch-Supan and Brugiavini (2001)—the first article searched out from literature—emphasizing how the public pensions in the provision of retirement income appear hardly sustainable in the light of population aging. Finally, the blue cluster encompasses studies proposing changes to the measurement of population aging—globally and for East Asian countries—outlining critical policy paths to address population aging successfully, and exploring the implications of population aging for the selection of an old-age financial protection system (e.g., Holzmann, 2013).

Figure 9. Co-citation analysis. Figure illustrates co-citation analysis based on the minimum 11 citations among the published papers 2001–2024. Source: VOSviewer.

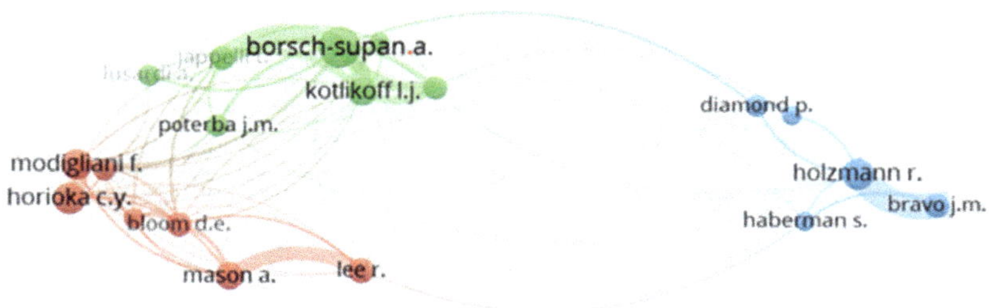

5. A Review of the Research Streams: Open Issues and Emerging Frontiers

We carry out an in-depht content analysis of the 95 articles included in our sample to better explore the different domains that constitute the aging population literature thought the lens of sustainable finance. From content analysis, we identify five main research streams, and such partitioning is confirmed by cartographic analysis (see Figure 7).

The first research stream (cluster in red) we label "The impact of an aging population on (sustainable) economic growth: a focus on the labor market" because it includes contributions dealing with the (shortage of) labor supply due to the severe supply-demand imbalance with the aging population and the pressure on the social security system, especially in areas such as pensions, thereby affecting the long-term development prospects of the economy. The second research stream (cluster in blue) gathers the impact of the aging population on the financial services industry. This cluster encompasses articles focused on changes in the savings and investment market and the innovation in financial service methods (such as, customized savings and investment plans for more senior people)(Daga et al., 2024). This stream is linked to cluster in violet, exploring a specific subtopic, that is, retirement planning services. The interplay between (un)sustainability and aging population emerges, especially in the context of fiscal policy. This research stream is denoted in green in Figure

7. Instead, the economic and fiscal changes of demographic shift are included in the yellow cluster.

5.1. The Impact of an Aging Population on (Sustainable) Economic Growth: a Focus on the Labor Market

The aging population is widely recognized as one of the most pressing social challenges of the twenty-first century, with implications for nearly all sectors of society, including the labor and financial markets, the demand for goods and services, social protection, as well as family structures and intergenerational ties (Daved, 2021). The effect of this demographic shift on the economy is especially evident in the labor market, where an increasing shortage in labor supply results in a decline in productivity, which in turn affects potential (sustainable) economic growth. This supply-demand imbalance has been extensively explored in the literature, and the relevance of these characteristics is also explored through cartographic analysis, reported in Figure 7, highlighting keywords such as 'social pressure,' 'labor supply,' and 'inequality'.

Most contributions are in the form of case studies. Asia and China are the main studied geographical areas, as these regions undergo rapid demographic transitions that significantly influence human capital investments, equity, and public finances. Along this line, Abrigo et al. (2018) empirically analyze the effect of human capital investment in Asian countries on economic growth, inequality, and fiscal balance, suggesting that human capital investments have a positive effect on labor productivity and fiscal balance. This positive effect is particularly pronounced for poorer and rural households, which helps to enhance equity (Abrigo et al., 2018; Cuéllar-Fernández et al., 2024). Contrary to the "conventional" view of aging as a purely negative force, these findings suggest that an aging population may present opportunities for firms to improve labor investment efficiency, challenging the traditional narrative of aging as solely a threat (Jian et al., 2024).

An aging population also places considerable pressure on public finances. Specifically, it reduces government tax revenue, particularly in labor-intensive sectors, where low-cost labor is a significant component of economic activity. Gao and Tian (2023) use mediation effect analysis to explore how the aging population decreases government tax revenue, hindering the transformation of low-cost labor sectors. However, the authors also note that increased healthcare spending has a positive effect on the economy, highlighting the complex interplay between aging, government spending, and tax revenue (Lim, 2016).

Another critical sub-theme in this research stream involves the debate around the (un)sustainability of "pay-as-you-go" social security programs, particularly in many OECD countries. These programs, while designed to support retirees, are facing significant financial challenges due to demographic shifts (Thøgersen, 2010). In this vein, several studies highlight the need to shift towards funded security programs, which could permanently enhance welfare for future generations.

In this context, alternative funding strategies, such as increased government asset accumulation and the adoption of actuarial supplementary pensions, are proposed to improve future welfare outcomes. Thus, these strategies are expected to generate substantial welfare gains and reduce future tax distortions (Thøgersen, 2010; Yang, 2020). To do so, a well-designed multi-pillar pension scheme can yield positive results across several performance indicators without causing excessive transition costs. On the other hand, maintaining the current "pay-go" scheme would lead to a gradual decrease in real pensions, lower pension-to-wage ratios, higher budget deficits, or any combination thereof (Štěpánek, 2019), ultimately increasing elderly poverty (Jun, 2020). As a result, older workers may have an incentive to remain in the labor market, which, however, is not advantageous for older wage earners. For this reason, many studies call for policies aimed at ensuring pension stability while minimizing elderly poverty (Jun, 2020; Cousins, 2021).

To effectively address these challenges, a significant shift in societal mindsets and policies is necessary, particularly in the way retirement income schemes are structured (Holzman, 2013). Additionally, the concerns surrounding social welfare and inequality are paramount in the debate on pension reform, as the absence of "social sustainability" may undermine the long-term financial sustainability of pension systems (Börsch Supan et al., 2023; Ghosh, 2023).

Moreover, the postponement of the introduction of changes, which leads to the adjustment of the total pension transfers to younger cohorts, can create pressure for more rapid reforms and higher variability of pension incomes between cohorts in the future (Chłoń-Domińczak et al., 2020). To avoid substantial increases in contributions and maintain both financial sustainability and social adequacy, risk-sharing and automatic balancing mechanisms need to be implemented within pension schemes (Morsomme et al., 2024). Along this line, sustainable finance appears vital in directing capital towards sustainable projects, enhancing the economy's resilience to social pressures, and boosting long-term economic stability and growth.

5.2. The Impact of Aging on Financial Behavior

The aging population has led to a growing demand for savings mechanisms, such as pension plans, insurance, and retirement savings, emphasizing the increasing prioritization of financial security during this demographic transition (Ha and Hoa, 2020; Doerr et al., 2024). In this vein, Lyons et al. (2018) have shown that older individuals are more inclined to save for retirement, particularly in countries with larger aging populations. This investment behavior is typically associated with a decrease in the proportion of risky assets allocated to households (Brunetti and Torricelli, 2010; Liu et al., 2023; Wang, Yao, & Zhao, 2024), including housing loans (Foo and Witkowska, 2021; Sever, 2023). As stated by Foo and Witkowska (2021, p. 73), "*savings and investment behavior for retirement associated with the aging population in advanced countries tends to follow the Life-Cycle Investment Hypothesis, first put forth by Modigliani and Brumberg in in1954 and the Life-Cycle Risk Aversion Hypothesis*". As a result, the population variable is a notable determinant of the savings rate (Xie et al., 2023; Rezaei, 2022).

On the other hand, vulnerable groups—such as women and low-income populations—face greater financial insecurity, particularly in developing countries. For these vulnerable groups, financial development is relevant for the aging-saving nexus, and clarifying the consequence of population aging on saving is critical as saving represents the predominant source of capital accumulation and economic growth (Kim et al., 2024).

The disparity between developing and developed countries differed according to the financial inclusion status of older people. Developed countries generally have well-established campaigns and policies to promote financial inclusion, encouraging private savings and asset building (Lyons et al., 2018). Instead, in many developing countries, aging populations are linked to a decrease in savings rates due to the growing number of retirees. Thus, financial sector development, along with rising income levels, has the potential to moderate these effects (Horioka & Terada-Hagiwara, 2012).

The literature also points to an urban-rural divide in how old-age insurance influences asset allocation (Liu et al., 2023). Differences in financial literacy among older individuals may account for this disparity, as higher financial literacy tends to boost confidence in a secure retirement, which is particularly important in the context of aging populations and declining pension systems (Gu et al., 2020; Cheung et al., 2023). Along this line, Yang et al. (2024) argue that population aging can inhibit pension financial asset allocation, with older individuals' risk behavior and financial literacy acting as a mediating role in the decision-making process. It is not surprising that in developed countries, characterized by high financial literacy, increasing the caps on tax-favored retirement contributions leads to a significant rise in retirement savings, largely funded by increased earned income (Chan et al., 2022).

Within this research stream, Asia is the main case-study area, in line with results from Figure 7. According to Horioka (2010), the aging population in Asia significantly impacts household, private, government, and national saving rates due to the reduction in saving rates and the increase in the elderly dependency ratio. Both youth and elderly dependency ratios negatively impact national saving rates, and countries with higher proportions of elderly individuals are likely to decline in household savings (Pitoňáková, 2019). Along this line, Mahalik et al. (2022) found that changes in young age dependency have a significant impact on changes in financial development in India. However, the aging population does not appear to have the same impact on financial development. By admission of the authors, the government and regulators should protect the health, longevity, and working conditions of younger generations in order to encourage better financial development in India.

In contrast, in China, a paradigm shift occurs: while demographic factors like old dependency (the ratio of elderly to working-age population) negatively affect saving rates, the effect is offset by the demographic shift due to the one-child policy and the subsequent decline in the young dependency ratio (Gu et al., 2020). In this context, voluntary pension schemes emerge as an alternative to supplement the public pension pillar (Castro-González et al., 2020).

However, the demographic transition has broader implications beyond household savings and pensions. Butler and Yi (2022) discuss the impact of aging on municipal credit markets, noting that the decline in income tax revenue, alongside increased pension liabilities and higher healthcare spending, has led to higher bond spreads. This study reveals that municipal borrowing is more expensive, further emphasizing the shift toward sustainability-oriented municipal bonds to face the financial and social challenges of an aging population.

5.3. Toward a (Tailored) Long-Term Care Services to an Aging Population

The aging population is contributing to a growing demand for long-term care (LTC) services, particularly among individuals aged 80 and older, thereby placing increasing pressure on public finances (Colombier, 2018). OECD countries exhibit diverse approaches to the provision and financing of LTC. More in detail, Nordic countries allocate a larger proportion of GDP to publicly funded care, while nations, such as Germany and Switzerland, rely on a combination of public and private resources.

To address the funding gap, there is a need for sustainable financing models that strike a balance between public and private funding sources (Halásková et al., 2017; Wouterse and Smid, 2017). At the same time, the increasing pressure on LTC systems is exacerbated by the financial behavior of younger generations. The financial behavior of young people, characterized by low retirement savings, worsens the challenge of LTC financing.

As emerged from Börsch-Supan et al. (2018), public pension reforms, such as abolishing earnings tests, may increase labor supply but also lead to earlier pension claims, especially if pension systems are not adjusted to maintain neutrality. Without adequate retirement savings, younger generations will face greater financial burdens as they age, further increasing future LTC costs. Along this line, some studies call for policymakers to take into account the various dimensions of older adults' health status and recognize their heterogeneity in care expectations when estimating future demand for benefit claims in public LTC schemes (Fong and Piggott, 2024). To this end, Vanella et al. (2024) suggested a novel approach for long-term forecasting of LTC schemes, incorporating demographic and epidemiological trends and different care definitions. Starting from the premise that the population continues to age, the demand for LTC insurance will rise significantly. In response, financial institutions must develop and promote more comprehensive, tailored insurance products that meet the evolving risk management needs of older people.

5.4. The Interplay Between (Un) Sustainability and Aging Population

Many studies reveals the financial unsustainability of retirement system (Guerard et al., 2012; Cousins, 2021; Cho and Kim, 2021; Gawthorpe, 2022; Flici, 2023), from the perspectives of labour supply, population aging, and demographic changes (Dumiter et al., 2024).

Wang, Liang and Wang (2024) explore the impact of population aging on sustainable economic development, emphasizing the moderating role of green finance in shaping the effects of demographic transitions. This study demonstrates that population aging has a significant negative impact on sustainable economic growth, primarily due to the decline in the labor force and changes in consumption patterns, leading to reduced demand and rising labor costs.

In this context, green finance is identified as a crucial moderating factor, mitigating the adverse effects of aging by fostering investments in green technologies, clean energy, and sustainable infrastructure, supporting economic growth even in aging societies. However, by admission of the authors (Wang, Liang and Wang, 2024), much of the existing literature is centered on individual economic indicators (such as labor markets and pension costs) and lacks a holistic analysis of the broader implications of aging on sustainable development, particularly with regard to the role of green finance in promoting sustainable development in a demographic transition. Along this line, Vukmirović et al. (2024) investigate the impact of sociodemographic factors on the growth of green finance, revealing a positive impact of the aging population. First, older populations tend to prioritize long-term, stable investments, making green finance products more appealing as they align with concerns for environmental (and social) sustainability and economic stability. Second, aging populations can prompt governments to invest in green research and development, as they have greater fiscal capacity due to a productive working-age population, supporting green economic transition.

Green finance is a key component of the broader concept of sustainable finance (Migliorelli, 2021; La Torre, 2022), which is aimed at integrating environmental, social, and governance (ESG) information into the decision-making processes of companies and financial institutions. Along this line, a recent study (Wang, Zhang, Wang et al., 2024) explores the interplay between corporate social responsibility (CSR) strategies of companies and occupational pensions.

This work emphasizes the role of CSR in enhancing organizational resilience, as companies facing higher occupational pension costs tend to increase the (two) social (internal and external) dimensions by reinforcing strategic CSR (focused on long-term business goals and stakeholder engagement). By admission of the authors (Wang, Zhang, Wang et al., 2024), the results of the study should be taken into consideration by both policymakers in comprehending and evaluating the extent of the impact of the occupational pension system and corporate managers in relation to more effective strategic decision-making when faced with labor costs.

5.5. Aging in Japan: Challenges in Fiscal Policy

The research stream entitled "Aging in Japan: challenges in fiscal policy" stands out as a niche topic, primarily because it delves into the specific socio-economic dynamics of an aging population within a country with one of the highest life expectancies and lowest infant mortality rates in the world. These factors combine to create a unique set of challenges, particularly in fiscal and social policy areas, which is not commonly addressed in broader, more generalized studies of aging populations across other nations.

The pressure of aging population in Japan has become a focal point of policy debate, especially concerning the reforms of insurance benefits and tax financing tools (Peng, 2024).

Within this search stream, a key ("outdate") study by Faruqee and Mühleisen (2003) remains highly relevant as it effectively predicted the ongoing demographic trend in Japan area. The authors stated that "*by 2025, one elderly person will depend on roughly two working-age individuals, significantly raising the elderly dependency ratio*" (Faruqee and Mühleisen, 2003, p. 186). As a solution, the authors suggest a gradual reform approach that involves intergenerational redistribution, which might be easier to implement politically than drastic, immediate changes. Finally, a recent study (Peng, 2024) adds another dimension to this ongoing debate. The author highlights the potential benefits of retirees returning to the workforce, particularly as Japan faces a shrinking labor force.

6. CONCLUSION

This study has tried to investigate the existing literature that has considered aging population and sustainable finance areas by using a bibliometric perspective and content analysis.

Our work has led us to the conclusion that studies in these fields started increasing in number in the last years (see Figure 1). In particular, studies focusing on the interplay between green finance, aging populations and sustainable developments goals (SDGs) appear in 2024 (see refs. Wang, Liang & Wang, 2024; Vukmirović et al., 2024; Zhang et al., 2024; Wang, Zhang, Wang et al., 2024).

Along this line, Yao et al. (2025) reveal that the ageing population is significant individual mediator through which green finance contributes to human well-being improvement. However, the literature related to the aging population and sustainable finance domain, according to the number of published works regarding the cluster in green, is still relatively scarce. This can be justified by the fact that the literature is immature, and this finding align with results of cartography analysis (Figure 7), in which terms like 'sustainable finance' and/or 'green finance' are lacking.

While the connection of the 'sustainability' node in the green cluster appears relatively good with the finance field (cluster in blue), the evidence that emerged from content analysis indicated that relationships between keywords in these clusters and between (green and blue) clusters are still weak, emphasizing a need for further and more collaborative research worldwide (Figure 7). As a results, these results confirm that the research is in a nascent phase and align with very few studies performed. We believe that the academia on the topics will evolve and strengthen in the coming years.

As shown in Table 2, the majority of the articles are from the "*Journal of the Economics of Ageing*", which is at the top of the list of both influential and productive sources, confirming that the majority of literature delves into the demographic change topic from both microeconomic and macroeconomic perspectives to discuss related topics, including labor, health, family economics, social security, income distribution, economic growth, and development.

Additionally, our analysis reveals that the research field of sustainable finance and aging populations is evolving to (re)consider the role of green and/or sustainable finance in facing up to social pressures like aging populations. This result highlights the fact that, to date, sustainable finance has mainly tried to respond to the growing climate change issues (see, for example, Singhania et al., 2024), overlooking the issues related to the demographic shift. In this regard, we encourage a reshaping of sustainable investing towards not only the green economy but also the silver economy to promote more financial and social inclusion.

From policy/practitioner and academic perspectives, four main conclusions may be drawn from this work: 1. Global challenges, such as an aging population and climate change, are increasingly interconnected with the growing silver economy. Therefore, proactive strategies and policies that enhance the efficiency of sustainable finance are essential, including through tailored fiscal policies. 2. Rethinking strategies for fostering green and silver economies, including considerations of which (sustainable) financial models may be fostered and supported. 3. Governments must address the specific needs of aging populations when designing and establishing sustainable finance programs, ensuring that public projects and trade activities align with sustainability principles. 4. Given the positive impact of green finance on well-being in demographic transitions, it is crucial to develop a new perspective on economic, environmental, and social sustainability in aging societies. This could attract foreign direct investment into sustainable projects to further support these objectives.

REFERENCES

Abrigo, M. R., Lee, S. H., & Park, D. (2018). Human capital spending, inequality, and growth in middle-income Asia. *Emerging Markets Finance & Trade*, *54*(6), 1285–1303. DOI: 10.1080/1540496X.2017.1422721

Alshater, M. M., Khan, A., Hassan, M. K., & Paltrinieri, A. (2023). Islamic banking: Past, present and future. *Journal of College of Sharia and Islamic Studies*, *41*(1), 193–221. DOI: 10.29117/jcsis.2023.0351

Amilon, A., Ladenburg, J., Siren, A., & Østergaard, S. V. (2020). Willingness to pay for long-term home care services: Evidence from a stated preferences analysis. *The Journal of the Economics of Ageing*, *17*, 100238. DOI: 10.1016/j.jeoa.2020.100238

Aria, M. and Cuccurullo, C. (2017), "Bibliometrix: An R-tool for comprehensive science mapping

Ba, S. (2022). Influence of Aging Population on China's Financial System: A Look into Pace of Population Aging in China Against Background of the World. In *The New Cycle and New Finance in China* (pp. 243–249). Springer Nature Singapore. DOI: 10.1007/978-981-16-8209-4_30

Bahoo, S., Alon, I., & Paltrinieri, A. (2020). Sovereign wealth funds: Past, present and future. *International Review of Financial Analysis*, *67*, 101418. DOI: 10.1016/j.irfa.2019.101418

Baker, H.K., Kumar, S., & Pandey, N.: (2021). Forty years of the *Journal of Futures Markets*: a bibliometric

Börsch-Supan, A., & Brugiavini, A. (2001). Savings: The policy debate in Europe. *Oxford Review of Economic Policy*, *17*(1), 116–143. DOI: 10.1093/oxrep/17.1.116

Börsch-Supan, A., Härtl, K., & Leite, D. N. (2018). Earnings test, non-actuarial adjustments and flexible retirement. *Economics Letters*, *173*, 78–83. DOI: 10.1016/j.econlet.2018.09.020

Bravo, J. M. (2019). Funding for longer lives. Retirement wallet and risk-sharing annuities. *Ekonomiaz: Revista vasca de economía*, (96), 268-291.

Brunetti, M., & Torricelli, C. (2010). Population age structure and household portfolio choices in Italy. *European Journal of Finance*, *16*(6), 481–502. DOI: 10.1080/13518470903075961

Butler, A. W., & Yi, H. (2022). Aging and public financing costs: Evidence from US municipal bond markets. *Journal of Public Economics*, *211*, 104665. DOI: 10.1016/j.jpubeco.2022.104665

Cai, S., Zheng, Y., Li, J., Tu, D., & Liu, H. (2025). Research on the impact mechanism of financial fraud risk among urban elderly in the context of population aging: Empirical data from China aging finance forum. *Finance Research Letters*, *77*, 107068. DOI: 10.1016/j.frl.2025.107068

Castro-González, S., Rey-Ares, L., Fernández-López, S., & Daoudi, D. (2020). The effect of self-control upon participation in voluntary pension schemes. *Economics & Sociology (Ternopil)*, *13*(1), 11–23. DOI: 10.14254/2071-789X.2020/13-1/1

Chan, M. K., Morris, T., Polidano, C., & Vu, H. (2022). Income and saving responses to tax incentives for private retirement savings. *Journal of Public Economics*, *206*, 104598. DOI: 10.1016/j.jpubeco.2021.104598

Cheng, M. C., & Lee, C. C. (2022). The impact of demographic aging on the investing behavior: The case of Taiwan stock market. *Review of Pacific Basin Financial Markets and Policies*, *25*(04), 2250026. DOI: 10.1142/S0219091522500266

Cheung, Y. L., Mak, B. S., Shu, H., & Tan, W. (2023). Impact of financial investment on confidence in a happy future retirement. *International Review of Financial Analysis*, *89*, 102784. DOI: 10.1016/j.irfa.2023.102784

Chłoń-Domińczak, A., Strzelecki, P., & Łątkowski, W. (2020). Pension reforms or consequences of the economic crisis? Measuring the changes of pension incomes in selected EU countries using APC approach. *The Journal of the Economics of Ageing*, *17*, 100131. DOI: 10.1016/j.jeoa.2017.09.002

Cho, S., & Kim, J. R. (2021). Population aging in Korea: Implications for fiscal sustainability. *Seoul Journal of Economics*, *34*(2), 237–264.

Cipriani, G. P. (2018). Aging, retirement, and pay-as-you-go pensions. *Macroeconomic Dynamics*, *22*(5), 1173–1183. DOI: 10.1017/S1365100516000651

Colombier, C., & Braendle, T. (2018). Healthcare expenditure and fiscal sustainability: Evidence from Switzerland. *Public Sector Economics*, *42*(3), 279–301. DOI: 10.3326/pse.42.3.3

Cousins, M. (2021). The sustainability of China's Urban Employees' Pension Programme: A case of getting old before getting rich? *International Social Security Review*, *74*(1), 59–77. DOI: 10.1111/issr.12257

Cousins, M. (2021). The sustainability of China's Urban Employees' Pension Programme: A case of getting old before getting rich? *International Social Security Review*, *74*(1), 59–77. DOI: 10.1111/issr.12257

Cuéllar-Fernández, B., Fuertes-Callén, Y., & Serrano-Magdalena, A. (2024). Factors behind the resilience of rural startups. *Technological Forecasting and Social Change*, *206*, 123521. DOI: 10.1016/j.techfore.2024.123521

Daga, S., Pahuja, S., & Yadav, K. (2024). BOARD GENDER DIVERSITY AND CSR SPENDING ON GENDER EQUALITY AND WOMEN EMPOWERMENT: DO EMPOWERED WOMEN WORK FOR WOMEN EMPOWERMENT? *Corporate Governance*, *6*(2). https://grfcg.in/wp-content/uploads/journal/published_paper/volume-6/issue-2/YwD6spQg.pdf

Dashjamts, A. E., Bayaraa, S. O., & Budjav, U. (2024). The Impact of Population Aging Trends on Mongolia's Pension Insurance Fund. *Journal of Human Resource and Sustainability Studies*, *12*(4), 878–886. DOI: 10.4236/jhrss.2024.124046

Daved, F. (2021). Towards A Productive Ageing Thai Society: Are Senior Citizens A Silver Lining For The Shrinking Labor Market. *Academy of Entrepreneurship Journal*, *27*, 5–6.

Doerr, S., Kabaş, G., & Ongena, S. (2024). Population aging and bank risk-taking. *Journal of Financial and Quantitative Analysis*, *59*(7), 3037–3061. DOI: 10.1017/S0022109023001011

Donthu, N., Kumar, S., Mukherjee, D., Pandey, N., & Lim, W. M. (2021). How to conduct a bibliometric analysis: An overview and guidelines. *Journal of Business Research*, *133*, 285–296. DOI: 10.1016/j.jbusres.2021.04.070

Dumiter, F. C., Schebesch, K. B., Nicoară, . A., & Ben e, C. (2024). The impact of social features on the financial sustainability of pension systems in Central and Eastern Europe and Baltic States. *Technological and Economic Development of Economy*, *30*(6), 1920–1949. DOI: 10.3846/tede.2024.22835

Fang, H. (2023). The Impact of Population Aging on Financial Services and Economic Development. *Available at SSRN* 4574199.

Faruqee, H., & Mühleisen, M. (2003). Population aging in Japan: Demographic shock and fiscal sustainability. *Japan and the World Economy*, *15*(2), 185–210. DOI: 10.1016/S0922-1425(02)00017-8

Flici, F. (2023). The limits of parametric reforms in sustaining the Algerian retirement system in a context of population ageing. *International Social Security Review*, *76*(3), 47–67. DOI: 10.1111/issr.12335

Fong, J. H., & Piggott, J. (2024). Accessing long-term care social insurance benefits in South Korea and its correlates. *The Japanese Economic Review*, *75*(4), 1–24. DOI: 10.1007/s42973-024-00177-2

Foo, J., & Witkowska, D. (2021). Savings Behavior, Asset Investment Choices and Institutional Pension Capital Market Performance. *International Journal of Business*, *26*(3), 72–104.

Fuino, M., & Wagner, J. (2018). Long-term care models and dependence probability tables by acuity level: New empirical evidence from Switzerland. *Insurance, Mathematics & Economics*, *81*, 51–70. DOI: 10.1016/j.insmatheco.2018.05.002

Gao, K., & Tian, Z. (2023). How ageing affects manufacturing transformation: Empirical evidence from China. *Applied Economics Letters*, *30*(10), 1358–1362. DOI: 10.1080/13504851.2022.2053650

Gawthorpe, K. (2022). Population ageing and sustainable fiscal policy in Czechia. *eastern. Journal of European Studies*, *13*(1), 81–105.

Ghosh, D. (2023). Social Support System and Old Age Vulnerability: An Investigation in India. *Studies in Microeconomics*, 23210222231171495.

Gu, X., Tam, P. S., Li, G., & Zhao, Q. (2020). An alternative explanation for high saving in China: Rising inequality. *International Review of Economics & Finance*, *69*, 1082–1094. DOI: 10.1016/j.iref.2018.12.004

Guerard, Y., Asher, M., Park, D., & Estrada, G. B. (2012). *Reducing Disparities and Enhancing Sustainability in Asian Pension Systems* (No. 313). ADB Economics Working Paper Series.

Ha, N. T. T., & Hoa, L. B. (2020). The relationship between population ageing and private savings in Vietnam. *Malaysian Journal of Consumer and Family Economics*, *24*, 1–32.

Hálásková, R., Bednář, P., & Hálásková, M. (2017). Forms of providing and financing long-term care in OECD countries. *Review of Economic Perspectives*.

Hassan, M. K., Alshater, M. M., Hasan, R., & Bhuiyan, A. B. (2021). Islamic microfinance: A Bibliometric review. *Global Finance Journal*, *49*, 100651. Advance online publication. DOI: 10.1016/j.gfj.2021.100651

Haward, V. (2024). Impact of Japan's aging population on healthcare costs and the Long-term care insurance system. *Studies in Social Science & Humanities*, *3*(2), 39–44. DOI: 10.56397/SSSH.2024.02.06

Holzmann, R. (2013). An optimistic perspective on population ageing and old-age financial protection. *Malaysian Journal of Economic Studies: Journal of the Malaysian Economic Association and the Faculty of Economics and Administration, University of Malaya*, *50*(2), 107–137.

Horioka, C. Y. (2010). Aging and saving in Asia. *Pacific Economic Review*, *15*(1), 46–55. DOI: 10.1111/j.1468-0106.2009.00489.x

Horioka, C. Y., & Terada-Hagiwara, A. (2012). The determinants and long-term projections of saving rates in developing Asia. *Japan and the World Economy*, *24*(2), 128–137. DOI: 10.1016/j.japwor.2012.01.006

Jakovljevic, M., Kumagai, N., & Ogura, S. (2023). Global population aging–Health care, social and economic consequences, volume II. *Frontiers in Public Health*, *11*, 1184950. DOI: 10.3389/fpubh.2023.1184950

Jane Osareme, O., Muonde, M., Maduka, C. P., Olorunsogo, T. O., & Omotayo, O. (2024). Demographic shifts and healthcare: A review of aging populations and systemic challenges. *Int. J. Sci. Res. Arch*, *11*(1), 383–395. DOI: 10.30574/ijsra.2024.11.1.0067

Jun, H. (2020). Social security and retirement in fast-aging middle-income countries: Evidence from Korea. *The Journal of the Economics of Ageing*, *17*, 100284. DOI: 10.1016/j.jeoa.2020.100284

Khan, A., Hassan, M. K., Paltrinieri, A., Dreassi, A., & Bahoo, S. (2020). A bibliometric review of takaful literature. *International Review of Economics & Finance*, *69*, 389–405. DOI: 10.1016/j.iref.2020.05.013

Kim, D. H., Liu, P., & Lin, S. C. (2024). Population aging and saving: Evidence from China. *Review of Development Economics*, *28*(4), 1494–1521. DOI: 10.1111/rode.13111

Kim, D. H., Liu, P., & Lin, S. C. (2024). The moderating role of financial development in the nexus between population aging and saving. *Economic Change and Restructuring*, *57*(2), 72. DOI: 10.1007/s10644-024-09670-5

La Torre, M. (2022). Banche e finanza sostenibile: per un business model Esg-oriented. *Bancaria, 5*(Contributi), 2-19.

Li, H., Zhou, X., Tang, M., & Guo, L. (2022). Impact of population aging and renewable energy consumption on agricultural green total factor productivity in rural China: Evidence from panel var approach. *Agriculture*, *12*(5), 715. DOI: 10.3390/agriculture12050715

Lim, T. (2016). Population aging in Korea: Macroeconomic impacts and financing national health insurance. *Korean Economic Review*, *32*(2), 355–382.

Liu, S., Zhu, M., & Ling, W. (2023). Research on the impact of population aging and endowment insurance on household financial asset allocation-Evidence on CFPS data. *Finance Research Letters*, *54*, 103719. DOI: 10.1016/j.frl.2023.103719

Liu, Y. (2024). Population Ageing and Economic Growth: An Analysis of Central and Eastern Europe.

Lyons, A. C., Grable, J. E., & Joo, S. H. (2018). A cross-country analysis of population aging and financial security. *The Journal of the Economics of Ageing*, *12*, 96–117. DOI: 10.1016/j.jeoa.2018.03.001

Mahalik, M. K., Inekwe, J. N., Das, K. K., Dash, U., & Arize, A. C. (2022). Does the pattern of age dependency matter in the promotion of financial development in an emerging economy? *Applied Economics*, *54*(48), 5622–5637. DOI: 10.1080/00036846.2022.2047605

Migliorelli, M. (2021). What do we mean by sustainable finance? Assessing existing frameworks and policy risks. *Sustainability (Basel)*, *13*(2), 975. DOI: 10.3390/su13020975

Mitchell, O. S. (2018). Enhancing risk management for an aging world. *The Geneva Risk and Insurance Review*, *43*(2), 115–136. DOI: 10.1057/s10713-018-0027-x

Morsomme, H., Alonso-Garcia, J., & Devolder, P. (2024). Intergenerational risk sharing in pay-as-you-go pension schemes. *Scandinavian Actuarial Journal*, •••, 1–29.

Pan, F., Zhu, K., & Wang, L. (2022). Impact analysis of population aging on public education financial expenditure in China. *Sustainability (Basel)*, *14*(23), 15521. DOI: 10.3390/su142315521

Peng, T. C. (2024). The effect of demographic shift on property values in Japan. *International Journal of Housing Markets and Analysis*.

Pitoňáková, R. (2019). Modelling impact of economic and demographic factors on personal saving rate in the euro area. *International Journal of Trade and Global Markets*, *12*(3-4), 333–344. DOI: 10.1504/IJTGM.2019.101556

Rezaei, E. (2022). Demographic changes and savings behavior: The experience of a developing country. *Journal of Economic Studies (Glasgow, Scotland)*, *49*(4), 603–622. DOI: 10.1108/JES-01-2021-0021

Sever, C. (2023). Population aging and convergence of household credit. *The B.E. Journal of Macroeconomics*, *23*(1), 497–520. DOI: 10.1515/bejm-2022-0048

Singhania, M., Chadha, G., & Prasad, R. (2024). Sustainable finance research: Review and agenda. *International Journal of Finance & Economics*, *29*(4), 4010–4045. DOI: 10.1002/ijfe.2854

Štěpánek, M. (2019). Pension reforms and adverse demographics: Options for the Czech Republic. *Finance a Uver*, *69*(2), 174–210.

Thøgersen, Ø. (2010). Reforming social security: Assessing the effects of alternative funding strategies. *Applied Economics*, *33*(12), 1531–1540. DOI: 10.1080/00036840010014436

Tranfield, D., Denyer, D., & Smart, P. (2003). Towards a methodology for developing evidence-informed management knowledge by means of systematic review. *British Journal of Management*, *14*(3), 207–222. DOI: 10.1111/1467-8551.00375

Trotta, A., Rania, F., Scalise, L., & Strano, E. (2024). Civic crowdfunding for local governments: Trends and perspectives from a bibliometric analysis. *Public Money & Management*, •••, 1–13.

Trotta, A., Rania, F., & Strano, E. (2024). Exploring the linkages between FinTech and ESG: A bibliometric perspective. *Research in International Business and Finance*, *69*, 102200. DOI: 10.1016/j.ribaf.2023.102200

Van Eck, N. J., & Waltman, L. (2010). Software survey: VOSviewer, a computer program for Bibliometric mapping. *Scientometrics*, *84*(2), 523–538. DOI: 10.1007/s11192-009-0146-3

Vanella, P., Wilke, C. B., & Heß, M. (2024). Long-Term Care in Germany in the Context of the Demographic Transition—An Outlook for the Expenses of Long-Term Care Insurance through 2050. *Ekonometria*, *12*(4), 28.

Vukmirović, V., Kojić, M., Spasenić, Ž., & Milosavljević, M. (2024). How do socio-demographic factors affect green finance growth? *Stanovnistvo*, *62*(2), 211–230. DOI: 10.59954/stnv.647

Wang, H., Zhang, T., Wang, X., & Zheng, J. (2024). Relationship between Occupational Pension, Corporate Social Responsibility (CSR), and Organizational Resilience: A Study on Listed Chinese Companies. *Risks*, *12*(4), 65. DOI: 10.3390/risks12040065

Wang, L., Liang, J., & Wang, B. (2024). Population aging and sustainable economic development: An analysis based on the role of green finance. *Finance Research Letters*, *70*, 106239. DOI: 10.1016/j.frl.2024.106239

Wang, Z., Yao, Q., & Zhao, G. (2024). Population ageing and household risk aversion. *Applied Economics Letters*, •••, 1–10.

Wouterse, B., & Smid, B. (2017). How to finance the rising costs of long-term care: Four alternatives for the Netherlands. *Fiscal Studies*, *38*(3), 369–391. DOI: 10.1111/j.1475-5890.2017.12137

Xie, X., Osińska, M., & Szczepaniak, M. (2023). Do young generations save for retirement? Ensuring financial security of Gen Z and Gen Y. *Journal of Policy Modeling*, *45*(3), 644–668. DOI: 10.1016/j.jpolmod.2023.05.003

Yadav, K., Daga, S., & Yadav, B. (2022). Behavioral Finance and Future Research Agenda: A Bibliometric Analysis. *IUP Journal of Applied Finance, 28*(4).

Yadav, K., Daga, S., & Yadav, B. (2022). Behavioral Finance and Future Research Agenda: A Bibliometric Analysis. *IUP Journal of Applied Finance, 28*(4). https://search.ebscohost.com/login.aspx?direct=true&profile=ehost&scope=site&authtype=crawler&jrnl=09725105&AN=161241617&h=W0oev3aMOvAvZlUR%2BOkmdrf9JTYXDTgo6WhfVN0eV7ehkSfPQr7ftd93T5CoW42s7EcOFImL0qRIYOIis1qbVA%3D%3D&crl=c

Yan, S., Zhou, Y., & Zhang, Y. (2022). Analysis of balance of income and expenditure and optimal retirement age of pension insurance co-ordination account based on improved machine learning algorithm. *Computational Intelligence and Neuroscience*, *2022*(1), 5870893. DOI: 10.1155/2022/5870893

Yang, C., Wang, J., & Liu, X. (2024). What affects the financial asset allocation of the elderly? From the perspective of financial literacy and risk attitude. *Finance Research Letters*, *63*, 105327. DOI: 10.1016/j.frl.2024.105327

Yang, T. T. (2020). The effect of workplace pensions on household saving: Evidence from a natural experiment in Taiwan. *The Journal of Risk and Insurance*, *87*(1), 173–194. DOI: 10.1111/jori.12254

Yao, Y., Wang, Z., & Lei, C. K. (2025). How does green finance affect human well-being in the context of aging populations? Evidences from China. *Sustainability Accounting. Management and Policy Journal*, *16*(1), 259–291.

Yu, M., Meng, B., & Li, R. (2022). Analysis of China's urban household indirect carbon emissions drivers under the background of population aging. *Structural Change and Economic Dynamics*, *60*, 114–125. DOI: 10.1016/j.strueco.2021.11.013

Zhang, C., Liu, S., Chen, G., & Harper, S. (2024). Green finance and the silver economy: Catalyzing China's low-carbon development. *Frontiers in Environmental Science*, *12*, 1406812. DOI: 10.3389/fenvs.2024.1406812

Zhang, G. (2023). The heterogeneous role of green finance on industrial structure upgrading-Based on spatial spillover perspective. *Finance Research Letters*, *58*, 104596. DOI: 10.1016/j.frl.2023.104596

Chapter 4
How Population Aging Reshapes Sectors?
Evidence From EU Consumption Data and Future Projections

Volkan Kaymaz
https://orcid.org/0000-0001-7556-9507
Istanbul Yeni Yuzyil University, Turkey

ABSTRACT

The aging of the population in European countries is causing structural shifts in consumption patterns. Declining fertility rates and rising life expectancy are transforming not only total consumption levels but also the sectoral composition of demand across countries. Household expenditure data and demographic projections demonstrate that consumption preferences vary significantly by age. While older individuals allocate more spending to housing, healthcare and basic needs, younger populations prioritize transportation, entertainment, and education. Cluster analyses classify countries based on similarities in their age-related consumption profiles. Projections for 2100 suggest that population aging will lead to a permanent restructuring of consumption baskets. These sectoral shifts are expected to generate employment in healthcare, care services, and age-friendly industries, while contraction may occur in sectors like transport, education, and leisure, ultimately affecting macroeconomic balances.

INTRODUCTION

The European Union, with a population of over 448 million, accounts for 5.6% of the world's population, and more than 21% of its population is over 65 years of

DOI: 10.4018/979-8-3373-2550-7.ch004

age (Eurosat, 2025). Declining birth rates and increasing life expectancy are causing the European population to age and reducing the share of the productive population in the total population. The proportion of elderly populations is increasing rapidly in developed countries. In developing countries with relatively young populations, the decline in fertility rates makes the increase in the elderly population on a global scale inevitable in the long term. The increase in the elderly population and the decrease in birth rates cause potential economic and social problems. The decrease in the productive population can cause a contraction in the labor market. The retired elderly population causes an increase in public expenditures, and the increasing number of retirees per employee causes an increase in the retirement premiums paid per employee. As individuals age, they need more healthcare services, which creates the danger that the healthcare sector will not be able to meet increasing demands.

Consumption refers to the demand of individuals for goods and services in order to meet their needs. Consumption expenditures, which are one of the basic determinants of economic volume, are divided into subcategories according to purpose and quality. The change in the size of expenditures for consumption categories, which are generally based on the Classification of Individual Consumption by Purpose (COICOP), can affect many dynamics such as economic growth, sectoral productivity, general price level, and social policies.

The increase in the elderly and retired population, changing consumption patterns and changing demand also cause sectoral transformations. The potential effects of demographic aging also cause consumption patterns to change. Changing consumption patterns are important for both macroeconomics and welfare. The silver economy refers to economic activities that include goods and services oriented to the demands and preferences of the elderly population and that grow rapidly with demographic transformation. The silver economy, which encompasses a wide range of sectors from health services to financial products, housing to entertainment and tourism, creates new opportunities and challenges for both the public and private sectors. While this transformation leads to the emergence of new sectors and business models that will respond to the increasing demands of the elderly population, it also leads to relative declines in the total market share of some traditional sectors. The silver economy in the European Union has created a market worth 5 trillion Euros, and is expected to reach a volume of 20 trillion dollars worldwide by 2030 (European Commission, 2018). This growth is not limited to the expansion of economic volume; it also paves the way for the emergence of innovative products and services in many sectors such as healthcare, long-term care, financial products, tourism, housing and technology-focused solutions. It also brings pressures for the transformation of employment structure, changing education and skill requirements and restructuring public expenditures. Demographic aging shapes consumption patterns by differentiating needs, tastes, preferences and expectations.

The change in consumption patterns is not only due to demographic characteristics. Today, the increasing use of social media and the ease of access to information have expanded the scope of Duesenberry's (1948) Hypothesis that consumption patterns will be shaped according to the social class and environment to which one belongs, and global trends and fashion approaches have paved the way for consumption expenditures to be affected by new factors. Changes in consumer behavior and the effects of this change are among the most frequently studied topics by academics in recent years; however, studies in the literature focus on changes in consumption patterns after retirement or after the age of 60, and do not make comparisons with lower age categories. In addition, studies focus on a single country and do not examine differences in consumption patterns between countries.

This study examines how consumption patterns differ depending on age in European countries on a country basis. It also draws conclusions on how sectoral transformations will occur as consumption patterns change in line with population projections. Thus, it aims to fill an important gap in the literature on the relationship between ageing and consumption. In this context, the study systematically compares consumption patterns based on age groups in European countries using Eurostat data; empirically analyzes the long-term sectoral and macroeconomic effects of ageing through cluster analyses and demographic projections for the year 2100. Thus, it provides insights for policy makers and the private sector on the potential transformations that ageing societies will face.

CONCEPTUAL AND THEORETICAL FRAMEWORKS OF CONSUMPTION

Consumption is affected by many factors; however, income and wealth are the most important of these factors. Although income and wealth growth are positively related to consumption expenditures, the increase in both affects consumption and expenditures on consumption categories differently. Macroeconomic variables specific to countries and global developments also affect consumption. Variables such as inflation, interest rates, unemployment rates, public expenditures, tax policies, asset prices, exchange rates, consumer confidence, expectations and uncertainty are also used to explain consumption expenditures. On the other hand, in addition to economic factors, variables specific to countries such as demographic structure, education, the ratio of urban to rural population, culture and psychological factors also play a role in consumption. There are basic theories in the literature used to explain the effects of demographic change on consumption. In this section, consumption theories are briefly explained and the factors that cause changes in age-related consumption patterns are discussed.

In classical economics literature, consumption expenditures have generally been considered as a function of income. In his Absolute Income Hypothesis, which he put forward in 1936, John Maynard Keynes argued that consumption depends on current income and that the marginal propensity to consume relative to income decreases as income increases. However, later studies criticized this assumption. Simon Kuznets' study based on historical data in 1946 revealed that the average propensity to consume, which shows how much of the income is allocated to consumption in the long term, has remained fairly constant over the years. This situation, called the Kuznets paradox, paved the way for new theoretical approaches by indicating that consumption behavior observed in the short term differs from long-term trends. Irving Fisher (1930), on the other hand, developed a model before Keynes that explained consumption as an intertemporal choice within the framework of lifetime income and interest rates. This Intertemporal Choice Theory put forward by Fisher later formed the basis for approaches such as Milton Friedman's Permanent Income Hypothesis and Modigliani's Life Cycle Theory; these approaches were used to explain short-term and long-term consumption differences by suggesting that individuals adjust their consumption according to their lifetime income expectations, in line with Kuznets' findings.

According to the Life Cycle Theory developed by Modigliani and Brumberg (1954), individuals try to distribute their income and expenses in a balanced way throughout their lives. Individuals who generally get into debt in their youth allocate a portion of their income to savings when they enter business life and reach middle age. Individuals who aim to make consumption smoothing use the savings they make during retirement to finance their current consumption expenditures. Thus, individuals aim to maintain their standard of living throughout their lives and ensure the continuity of their current quality of life despite their decreasing income during retirement. Individuals who have to save during their working life are forced to increase their consumption expenditures in proportion to their income during retirement. To sustain their consumption standards, individuals often convert their financial assets into liquid resources, a behavior that is also documented in empirical studies (Banks, Blundell, & Tanner, 1998; Bernheim, Skinner, & Weinberg, 2001; Aguila, Attanasio, & Meghir, 2010). However, this theory does not fully take into account the bequest motivation, heterogeneity among individuals, and changing consumption patterns. Decreasing socialization with age, decreasing transportation expenses as a result of the end of work life, increasing health needs, and changing life expectancies differentiate both the total consumption expenditures of individuals and the consumption categories in which the expenditures are made. In addition, not every individual makes consumption smoothing, and cannot save enough during their working life. For these reasons, the theory has been criticized and expanded in both theoretical and empirical literature.

Consumption does not change only according to immediate income. Individuals can change their expenditures by taking into account temporary and permanent income while engaging in consumption behavior. According to the Permanent Income Hypothesis developed by Friedman (1957), households' consumption decisions are not based on current income levels, but on permanent income, which is the long-term income expectation. According to this approach, individuals do not take temporary income fluctuations into account in their consumption decisions because it is assumed that such income changes are not permanent and do not reflect the long-term level of disposable income. Therefore, consumption remains relatively insensitive to temporary increases and decreases in current income. Individuals try to maintain their standard of living in a stable manner by smoothing their consumption. In this context, changes observed in consumption are mostly associated with fluctuations in permanent income. The decreasing permanent income during retirement is the most important factor determining consumption, and if pensions are insufficient to maintain living standards or if they cannot maintain purchasing power in the face of inflation, the elderly are forced to reduce their spending. Therefore, just like in the Life Cycle Theory, individuals are expected to save throughout their working lives in anticipation of the decrease in their income during retirement. However, many individuals fail to take future needs into account when making intertemporal choices and tend to overweight short-term benefits. Time preference biases, which systematically underestimate future well-being in favor of present consumption, prevent individuals from making optimal long-term consumption plans.

Life Cycle and Permanent Income Theories assume that individuals have rational expectations and can make excellent plans for their consumption decisions; however, they do not take into account people's psychological biases. The Behavioral approach, which examines the effects of individuals' emotions, habits, mental calculations and social norms on economic behavior in recent years, indicates that consumption can be affected by many factors.

While traditional Life Cycle and Permanent Income Theories assume that individuals act fully rationally, the Behavioral Life Cycle Hypothesis developed by Shefrin and Thaler (1988) argues that individuals act with various cognitive and psychological biases in their savings and consumption decisions. Within the framework of this model, individuals segment their wealth into separate mental accounts (e.g., current income, savings, pension funds, inheritance), rather than perceiving their total wealth as a unified pool. Each account is associated with varying marginal propensities to consume, with liquid wage income being more easily spent compared to long-term investment assets, which are perceived as less accessible for current consumption. For example, while liquid salary incomes are more easily consumed, long-term investments are seen as less spendable. Another important contribution of the behavioral approach is that it emphasizes self-control problems. Individuals may ignore their future consumption needs in the face of today's short-term benefits and may not be able to save enough. While short-term consumption preferences are emphasized, especially due to hyperbolic discount behavior, consumption needs during retirement may be neglected. This situation may lead individuals to encounter lower consumption levels than expected during retirement.

In addition, within the framework of behavioral, social norms, status consumption and comparative consumption behaviors also explain age-related differences in consumption patterns. Spending on clothing and technology at a young age, housing and savings-oriented preferences at a middle age, and increased health and care expenses at an older age are considered as a natural result of these behavioral patterns. The decreases observed in consumption in the post-retirement period are not only related to income decline, but also to uncertainty, health risks and precautionary savings tendencies. Especially factors such as long life risk, uncertainty in health expenses and care costs lead individuals to cautious consumption behavior. On the other hand, Thorstein Veblen brought a sociological perspective to economics and drew attention to the role of social status and ostentation elements in consumption behavior. The concept of "conspicuous consumption", which he defined in his famous work dated 1899, suggests that individuals make consumption choices not only for benefit but also to display their social status. This perspective has made an important contribution to traditional theories by emphasizing that consumption decisions can be shaped by social norms, cultural values, and the motivation to "compare with others."

In conclusion, consumption behavior cannot be fully explained without considering individuals' intertemporal preferences, income expectations, psychological biases, and social norms. While the Life-Cycle and Permanent Income Hypotheses emphasize rational income-smoothing behavior, the Behavioral Life-Cycle Approach incorporates individuals' irrational tendencies and decision-making biases, thereby providing more realistic explanations. These diverse theoretical perspectives offer an important framework for understanding the effects of demographic aging on consumption patterns.

LITERATURE REVIEW ON DEMOGRAPHICS AND CONSUMPTION

In recent years, the effects of demographic change on consumption patterns along with the aging population have become an increasingly important area of research for both academics and policy makers. The literature mainly focuses on consumption theories and savings behaviors of individuals; however, the sectoral and macroeconomic effects of the transformation in age-related consumption patterns have not yet been systematically addressed.

A household is considered sufficiently prepared for retirement if its wealth accumulated before retirement is sufficient to maintain its current consumption level until the end of its life (Yuh et al., 1998). This view, which briefly summarizes the Life Cycle Hypothesis, cannot be confirmed by empirical studies, and many people reduce their consumption during retirement. Many empirical studies testing the hypothesis conclude that individuals cannot smooth out their consumption and that their consumption expenditures decrease after retirement. Aguiar and Hurst (2007) reached conclusions supporting that there is a decrease in consumption expenditures after retirement due to loss of income and increase in health expenditures. Using Consumer Expenditure Survey data, Danziger et al. (1982) reach conclusions supporting that Americans reduce their consumption and service expenditures during retirement and that individuals cannot smooth out their consumption.

Numerous academic studies reveal the negative effects of retirement on consumption expenditures (Blau, 2008; Aguiar and Hurst, 2005). According to Erlandsen (2003), the age group between 50-66 has high income and low household size. This age group, whose needs decrease and income increases over time, increases their savings. The results of another study using the American Consumption Expenditure Survey data also support the conclusions that total consumption decreases and expenditure categories change as age increases; the only exception to these categories is household maintenance expenditures (Lee, 2001). According to Börsch-Supan (1992), who examined consumption expenditures after retirement using the German Income and Consumption Survey, savings rates fall to their lowest level 5-10 years after retirement, and individuals increase their savings rates after age 70. Net savings reach their highest level at ages 80 and above. The increase in the retirement age in Germany has also caused savings rates to increase in later years. This situation, which contradicts the hypothesis, is explained by the change in consumption patterns of elderly individuals and the fact that their health expenses are covered by compulsory health insurance. The research reveals that only the housing expenses of elderly people have not changed, because although the number of households has decreased, retired individuals do not want to give up their current homes, while there are slight increases in health expenses. There is a decrease in other consumption expenses, especially food consumption, clothing and durable consumer goods. According to the researchers, the benefit obtained from consumption decreases with age, therefore elderly individuals voluntarily reduce their consumption expenses.

The aging population is causing countries to increase the legal retirement age in order to keep their retirement systems working. The increasing retirement age, in turn, causes individuals to shorten their retirement years and work longer to retire.

The idea that longer working hours will increase lifetime wealth causes individuals to reduce their savings rates (Feldstein, 1976). Another study using the German Income and Consumption Survey also finds results that support the negative effect of increasing the retirement age on savings (Etgeton et al. 2023); however, the strength of this effect varies according to many factors such as marriage, education, age, gender, etc.

The change in consumption patterns along with the increase in the elderly population also has an impact on the economic sectors of the country. Changing demand due to factors other than income causes investments to shift to different sectors. Laitner and Silverman (2012) examined the relationship between retirement and consumption using US consumption expenditure, retirement age and income data and concluded that retirement reduces consumption expenditure by 8.3%. In addition, consumption growth slows down after the age of 50. According to Ong et. al (2008), goods and services aimed at elderly consumers, called the Silver Market, will become more important in the future. According to Szmigin and Carrigan, (2001), markets aimed at elderly consumers do not receive enough attention; however, changing physical, social and psychological needs due to aging reshape consumption patterns.

Using data from the Thai National Statistical Office's Household Socio-Economic Survey, Mananjit et al. (2020) examined consumption patterns and analyzed the effects of socio-econometric factors on expenditures through cluster analysis and logistic regression. According to their findings, elderly individuals allocate a substantial portion of their consumption expenditures to food and housing. Transportation expenditures are negatively correlated with age. Although increasing age reduces general consumption expenditures, the increase in time spent at home causes expenditures to increase in some consumption categories. Zhu and Lin (2022) examine the effects of retirement on energy consumption using the Fuzzy Regression Discontinuity method with data from China Family Panel Studies (CFPS) between 2010 and 2018. The results show that electricity consumption increases between 20% and 32% after retirement, and the increase varies according to lifestyle habits, income, education, and health status. Abrigo and Ortiz (2024) also conclude that the aging population causes an increase in electricity demand in the Philippines. Chen et al. (2024) using the China Family Tracking Survey data show that the increase in age dependency ratio has a decreasing effect on tourism expenditure; however, factors such as wage increase and social media slow down these decreasing effects. According to the researchers, the increase in leisure time is offset by care and health services, thus decreasing tourism expenditure.

Generational differences lead to the emergence of new behavioral dynamics in consumption patterns. Johnson-Hillery et al. (1997) emphasize that older individuals attach more importance to shopping based on customer experience and face-to-face interaction. In contrast, it is stated that younger generations (generations Y and Z) prefer consumption models based on access rather than ownership (sharing economy, subscription systems, digital products); and they also tend to seek short-term satisfaction with the rising "doom spending" trend in the post-pandemic period (Belk, 2014; Vogels, 2023).

According to the study examining the relationship between age and consumption volume and pattern using the 2007 Serbian Household Budget Survey data, income peaks in the 50-54 age range, while consumption levels decline rapidly after the age of 60. In Serbia, consumption expenditures account for the highest share of consumption expenditures at 40%. While clothing and communication expenditures are in the first place between the ages of 25-29, the share of education expenditures in total expenditures decreases as expected after the age of 50. Restaurant, entertainment and cultural expenditures also peak in the 40s and then gradually decrease (Radivojević and Vasić, 2012). According to the researchers, newborn babies may have an impact on the transformation of consumption in middle-aged families.

In Malaysia, where the elderly population is not yet as large as European countries, but the average age is increasing, a study examining the spending patterns of individuals over the age of 55 shows that increasing age increases healthcare spending and decreases spending such as entertainment and eating out. According to the results, 67% of the total spending of Malaysians over the age of 55 consists of food, rent, fuel and energy categories. The largest category is food spending with a share of 39%. (Ong, et al. 2008). Using data from the Korean Family Income and Expenditure Survey, Lee and Huh (2004) examined differences in consumption and saving behaviors between two cohorts in Korea: those born between 1953-1960 and those born between 1961-1968. Based on their Ordinary Least Squares regression estimates, younger boomers tend to spend more on dining out, communication, entertainment, and technology-related goods and services, whereas older boomers allocate a larger share of their expenditures to their children's education.

In studies conducted at the macroeconomic level, the OECD (2020) emphasizes that the aging population creates long-term pressures on public budgets and changes the composition of public expenditures. According to the IMF (2021) report, aging increases the weight of health and food expenditures and causes absolute demand reductions in some sectors such as education and transportation. In general, the literature reveals that demographic aging creates multidimensional and complex effects on consumption patterns. Individuals' income status, health conditions and life expectancy, as well as generational values, social norms and behavioral factors, are among the determinants of this transformation. In the following sections of this study, consumption patterns by age groups in European countries will be analyzed in detail in the light of the theoretical and empirical literature in question.

DATA AND METHODOLOGY

The consumption data used in this study were obtained from the European Statistical Office (Eurostat) database. Household consumption expenditures were used as data categorized according to the Classification of Individual Consumption by Purpose (COICOP) standard according to expenditure types. The COICOP consumption classification includes 12 consumption categories: Food and non-alcoholic beverages, Clothing and footwear, Housing, water, electricity, gas and other fuels, Furnishings, household equipment and routine household maintenance, Health, Transport, Communications, Recreation and culture, Education, Restaurants and hotels, Miscellaneous goods and services. In order to monitor the changes in consumption expenditures according to age categories, four age categories are considered for ease of comparison: Less than 30 years, From 30 to 44 years, From 45 to 59 years, 60 years or over.

In order to identify similarities and differences in consumption patterns, k-means clustering analysis was applied to the data. The k-means method allows grouping data points (in this case countries or consumer age groups) into several clusters according to similar expenditure profiles. In our analysis, similar countries were grouped together in the same cluster based on the distribution of consumption expenditures according to COICOP categories. This clustering result revealed groups of countries representing different consumption patterns and allowed the examination of the relationships between these patterns and demographic composition.

After the cluster analysis, ANOVA (one-way analysis of variance) test was applied to test whether the differences between the obtained clusters were statistically significant. ANOVA enables comparison of means between multiple groups. In this study, the means of the groups formed by clustering were compared in terms of certain consumption indicators and the significance of the differences between the clusters was evaluated. Thus, it was tested whether the consumption differences observed between the groups were random or not and it was shown that the different consumption patterns defined by clustering were statistically significantly separated.

Finally, population projections were used to evaluate the effect of the change in the population structure in the future period analyses. Population projections are based on Eurostat's 2100 estimates and are based primarily on the cohort-component method. In this method, each age cohort is carried forward to the next period under certain fertility, mortality and migration assumptions; thus, the change in the age composition of the total population over time is calculated. Thus, consumption projections for future periods are made in a way that is consistent with the changes in the age distribution. The obtained estimates allow the future assessment of the impact of the ageing process on consumption categories.

AVERAGE SPENDING BY CATEGORY

In this section, household consumption expenditure data obtained from the Eurostat database are used to reveal the structural characteristics of consumption patterns by age groups. The data are divided into 12 main consumption categories within the framework of the Classification of Individual Consumption by Purpose (COICOP). For each age group, category-based expenditure levels in countries were directly taken and average expenditure levels for each age group were calculated using these values. In the calculation process, the category-based values of countries for each age group were combined by arithmetic average. Thus, average profiles representing category-based expenditure levels within total consumption were obtained for each age group. Figure 1 and Figure 2 visualize the consumption structures of age groups and the weights between categories using these average values.

The relationship between age and consumption varies considerably in some categories. Food expenditures increase positively with age. The increase in the time spent at home by elderly individuals with retirement and the decrease in eating habits outside are possible factors that can explain this situation. Elderly individuals generally prefer a more controlled and home-centered diet for health reasons. Alcohol and tobacco expenditures are different from other expenditure categories. Although alcohol and tobacco consumption is quite high in the young age group, expenditures decrease in the 30-44 age group, reaching a peak in the 45-59 age category and decreasing again after the age of 60. This category is related to both the physical health and social environment of the individual. These consumption items, which are part of entertainment and socialization in young age groups, decrease in later ages due to both health reasons and the decrease in social activity levels. At the same time, this decrease can be associated with the increasing health awareness of elderly individuals.

In the clothing category, the young and 30-44 age groups have high spending averages; however, clothing spending decreases as age increases. Withdrawal from work life, the decrease in pressure to conform to social norms and the decrease in interest in fashion that begins with age reduce spending. There is a rapid increase in housing spending, especially in the 60 years or over; this age group spends the most in housing among other spending categories. The time spent at home increases consumption by increasing heating, water and electricity needs. In addition, since the possibility of elderly individuals changing homes is low, their investment tendencies for their current homes are high. Furniture spending is similar in all age categories; however, the 30-44 age group may spend more in this category compared to other age groups due to moving into their own homes or getting married. There is a significant increase in spending in the health category as age increases. This situation is related to both the increase in the incidence of chronic diseases and the fact that elderly individuals access health services more frequently.

Figure 1. Average Expenditures by Age Groups and Consumption Categories

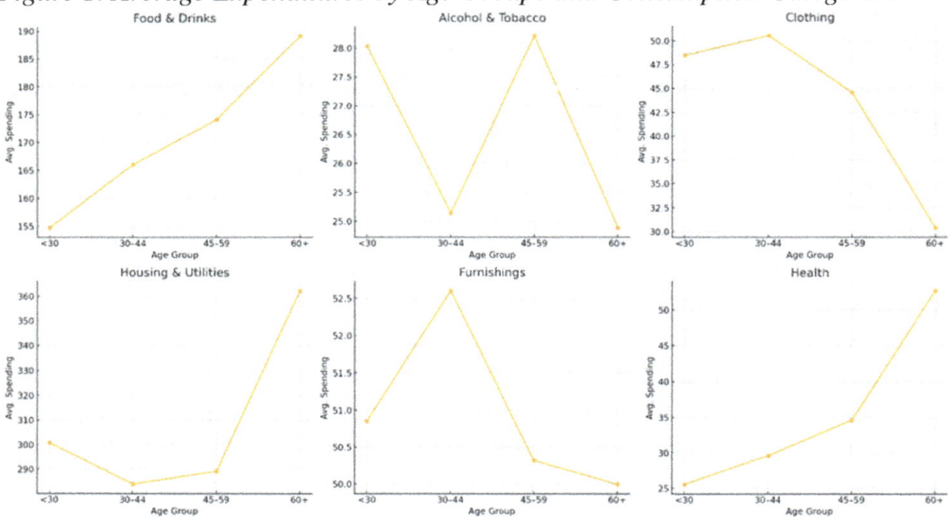

The change in transportation expenditures can also be explained by retirement and socialization. Travel expenditures are low in the 60 years or over group, who travel and socialize less and reduce long trips due to health concerns; however, other age groups spend at similar levels. A similar situation applies to communication. The difficulty of older age groups to adapt to technology is one of the factors that reduce the expenditures of older individuals for communication. Expenditures in the entertainment category reach their highest between the ages of 30-44. The limited income of younger ages and the decrease in social activities of the elderly show that entertainment expenditures decrease with age. One of the categories in which the 60 years or over group differs most from the other three age categories is education expenditures. Although education expenditures are similar in all age groups, the 60 years or over group almost does not spend on education, services and materials. This shows that participation in formal education ends with age. Unlike food expenditures, restaurant and hotel expenditures are quite low in the elderly group. When all categories are examined, the average expenditures of the 60 years or over group are clearly different from the others in this category. This differentiation is closely related not only to the decrease in income but also to life expectancy, health status, social environment and habits. Analyses show that the consumption of older individuals is directed more towards mandatory categories and they reduce discretionary expenditures.

Figure 2. Average Expenditures by Age Groups and Consumption Categories

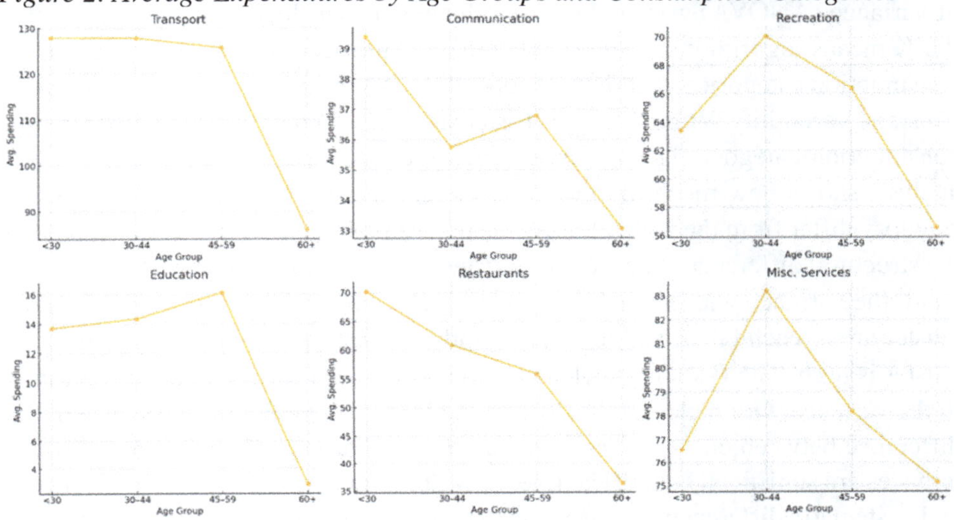

Overall, expenditure categories exhibit significant variations across age groups. While discretionary spending (such as clothing, transportation, and entertainment) is more prominent among younger individuals, the share of essential and health-related expenditures increases with age. This differentiation shapes the sectoral implications of consumption patterns amid demographic transformation and provides important insights for policymakers in anticipating future trends.

CLUSTER ANALYSIS

In this section, cluster analysis was performed to systematically classify the structural similarities and differences observed in the consumption patterns of countries according to age groups. The K-means clustering algorithm was applied by considering the consumption levels of countries on a category basis for each age group. The K-means algorithm groups the observations in a way that maximizes the variance between clusters and minimizes the variance within clusters, thus grouping countries with similar consumption profiles under the same cluster. In this way, systematic patterns in age-related consumption compositions can be identified and the effects of demographic structure on consumption patterns can be analyzed in detail.

The number of clusters in the analysis was determined as 3 in order to avoid excessive separation and to ensure interpretability of the results. One-way analysis of variance (ANOVA) was applied to evaluate whether the clusters obtained after the K-means algorithm contained statistically significant differences in terms of consumption categories. Within the scope of the ANOVA test, Variability Between Clusters, Variability Within Clusters, F-statistic and p-value were calculated for each consumption category. The variance between clusters calculated in the ANOVA analysis shows how much the means of the clusters in the relevant consumption category differ from the general mean; as this value increases, it is understood that the structural differences between the clusters become more apparent. On the other hand, the variance within clusters indicates how similar the countries in the same cluster are to each other, and low values indicate that the homogeneity within the cluster is high. The F-statistic calculates the ratio of the variance between clusters to the variance within clusters, reflecting the level of statistical significance of the difference between clusters. The p-values obtained test whether the observed differences are statistically significant; low p-values indicate that there are significant and systematic differences between clusters in the relevant consumption category.

The results of the ANOVA-based variance analysis conducted for the under 30 and 30-44 age groups are shown in Table 1. The results show that consumption patterns differ considerably by country. The most important category separating the clusters from each other in the under 30 age category is "Food and non-alcoholic beverages". In the categories of "Clothing and footwear", "Housing, water, electricity, gas and other fuels" and "Furniture, household equipment and home maintenance", the Variability Between Clusters and Variability Within Clusters are quite low and the results are statistically significant. Therefore, the difference between countries in these categories is quite low and consumption expenditures have a more homogeneous structure. In categories where Variability Between Clusters is greater than Variability Within Clusters, more separating results are obtained for the clusters. In this respect, there is a difference in the transportation category in addition to food expenditures in the under 30 age category. In summary, similar consumption expenditures, other than basic needs, are distributed homogeneously across countries in the young age category.

Table 1. The results of the analysis of variance for clustering - Less than 30 years and From 30 to 44 years

	Less than 30 years				From 30 to 44 years			
Category	**Variability Between Clusters**	**Variability Within Clusters**	**F-statistic**	**p-value**	**Variability Between Clusters**	**Variability Within Clusters**	**F-statistic**	**p-value**
Food	26544.67	6103.33	10.873	0.0151	10324.17	6321.83	4.083	0.0889
Alcohol	2117.54	1143.33	4.63	0.0728	474.17	195.33	6.069	0.046
Clothing	50.04	589.83	0.212	0.8158	75.33	854.67	0.22	0.8096
Housing	750.83	7201.17	0.261	0.7804	125.67	25615.83	0.012	0.9878
Furnishings	391.21	844.67	1.158	0.3862	384.17	33.33	28.812	0.0018
Health	220.83	508.67	1.085	0.406	369.38	736.5	1.254	0.362
Transport	6847.71	2631.17	6.506	0.0406	4093.67	1105.83	9.255	0.0209
Communications	294.0	72.0	10.208	0.0172	300.33	131.17	5.724	0.0509
Recreation	5864.33	5433.17	2.698	0.1604	1509.54	1895.33	1.991	0.2312
Education	569.71	247.17	5.762	0.0504	279.71	519.17	1.347	0.3405
Restaurants	154.83	4112.67	0.094	0.9117	1953.33	1412.67	3.457	0.1141
Miscellaneous	3819.33	5506.67	1.734	0.2679	2373.33	484.67	12.242	0.0118

There are larger and statistically significant differences in the upper age category by country. The results indicate a large difference in expenditures on furniture and maintenance. There are significant differences in the "Alcoholic beverages, tobacco and drugs" category by country. This situation potentially explains that home ownership and house prices in the current age category vary greatly by country, while in some countries the 30-44 age group continues to live with their family, and therefore their expenditures do not increase. The difference in the alcoholic beverages category is an important indicator that consumption habits can vary by country and culture. There is a significance level of 10% in the "Food and non-alcoholic beverages" category. The results obtained in categories such as "Transportation", "Health", "Education", "Restaurants and hotels" show that consumption trends in these categories do not change much and that the 30-44 age group has similar expenditures in the selected countries. In summary, the differences in the countries occur in the "Alcoholic beverages, tobacco and drugs" and "Furnishings, household equipment and routine household maintenance" categories. These differences are explained by income level, culture, social policy and purchasing power. In addition, country-specific policies can increase home ownership or the increase in the number of permanent tourists and immigrants makes it difficult for the 30-44 age group to buy a house.

Table 2. The results of the analysis of variance for clustering - From 45 to 59 years and 60 years or over

	From 45 to 59 years				60 years or over			
Category	**Variability Between Clusters**	**Variability Within Clusters**	**F-statistic**	**p-value**	**Variability Between Clusters**	**Variability Within Clusters**	**F-statistic**	**p-value**
Food	7704.67	9597.33	2.408	0.1707	19490.54	10367.33	4.7	0.071
Alcohol	110.89	219.33	1.517	0.293	217.21	574.67	0.945	0.4486
Clothing	370.89	1149.33	0.968	0.4321	97.04	309.83	0.783	0.506
Housing	3277.56	55014.67	0.179	0.8406	19535.71	17669.17	2.764	0.1554
Furnishings	101.56	1038.67	0.293	0.7559	326.83	360.67	2.265	0.1993
Health	456.22	604.67	2.264	0.1852	1942.71	2127.17	2.283	0.1975
Transport	1198.22	12365.33	0.291	0.7577	8349.38	452.5	46.129	0.0006
Communications	468.22	270.0	5.202	0.0489	172.17	141.33	3.045	0.1365
Recreation	54.22	2770.0	0.059	0.9435	6733.33	1994.67	8.439	0.025
Education	50.67	529.33	0.287	0.7602	4.21	2.67	3.945	0.0937
Restaurants	1692.67	689.33	7.367	0.0242	1174.17	633.83	4.631	0.0728
Miscellaneous	4554.67	973.33	14.038	0.0055	15546.83	633.83	8.257	0.026

The variance analysis results for the 45-59 and over 60 age categories are presented in Table 2. The variance results for the 45-59 age group show that the expenditure categories are not at high levels among country clusters, and therefore there are no significant differences between clusters. The results obtained in categories such as "Alcoholic beverages, tobacco and drugs", "Clothing and footwear", and "Furniture, household equipment and home maintenance" are statistically insignificant. This situation shows that there are no significant differences between clusters. Similarly, in the "Housing, water, electricity, gas and other fuels" category, although the variance between clusters is high, the p-value reveals that the results are insignificant. This shows that the structure of housing expenditures between countries is quite scattered and cannot be sufficiently explained by clusters. In the analysis for the 45-59 age group, the differences between clusters are statistically weak. A more homogeneous appearance is exhibited in the expenditure structures, and there are no strong structural differences between the consumption patterns of countries in this age group.

In the over 60 age group, consumption patterns differ significantly and typical effects of demographic aging are strongly observed. In this group, the share of food, housing and health expenditures in total consumption increases, while flexible consumption categories such as transportation, clothing, entertainment and education decrease significantly. This situation reflects the transition to a consumption composition focused on mandatory and basic needs, together with the new lifestyle brought about by increased leisure time and decreased labor force participation. In addition, the increase in access to health services and care expenditures emerges as a reflection of the efforts of the elderly population to maintain their quality of life. Although it varies among countries, in some economies, the over 60 age group's housing dependency (tendency not to downsize) also increases domestic consumption and energy use. These findings indicate that the demand for health, housing, care and home services in particular will tend to increase in the long term within the scope of the silver economy.

The cluster analysis results reveal that there are systematic and predictable differences in the consumption patterns of different age groups. While discretionary expenditures gain weight in younger age groups, it is observed that the share of expenditures for mandatory and basic needs increases with age. In particular, health, food and housing expenditures come to the fore in the consumption basket of the elderly population, whereas expenditures in categories such as transportation, entertainment, clothing and education decrease. The findings show that demographic transformation reshapes not only the total amount of consumption but also the demand structure between sectors; indicating that this transformation may have long-term effects in terms of economic and social policy.

SPENDING PROFILES OF CLUSTERS

As a result of the K-means clustering analysis applied to analyze whether there are structural similarities among countries according to the consumption patterns of individuals under the age of 30, three separate clusters were obtained. Each cluster consists of profiles with different priorities and distributions in consumption categories. The determined clusters reflect the effect of age categories on consumption behaviors and show the determinants of country-specific socioeconomic conditions and public policies on lifestyle and therefore consumption patterns.

The radar chart in Figure 3 shows consumption expenditures in 12 categories for the specified clusters and thus contributes to the understanding of the differences in consumption patterns between the clusters. In addition, the radar charts drawn for 4 different age categories are a very useful display method for policy makers to understand which areas need development.

In the under 30 age category, the first cluster generally consists of Lithuania, Bulgaria, Slovakia, Estonia, Romania, Greece, Poland, Italy, Serbia and Hungary. This cluster group, which generally consists of Eastern European and Balkan countries, is a lower income group and relatively new EU member and developing countries. In this group of countries, expenditures on basic needs are high compared to others. In the countries in this cluster, young individuals allocate a large share of their budgets to consumption categories such as food and housing. Therefore, expenditures such as restaurants, entertainment, cultural events and education remain low compared to other clusters. The second cluster obtained in this age category consists of Norway, Finland, Portugal, Austria, Netherlands, Belgium, France, Spain, Ireland, Germany, Denmark, Czechia and Luxembourg. The countries in this cluster consist of Western and Northern European countries with higher per capita income and welfare compared to other countries. Individuals under the age of 30 in this cluster have a service and experience-oriented consumption profile. Expenditures on Recreation and culture and Miscellaneous goods and services categories are higher compared to other clusters. In these countries, the young population is active in socializing, seeking experience and cultural activities. The third cluster is more heterogeneous compared to the other clusters and consists of Malta, Latvia, Cyprus, Slovenia and Turkiye. In these countries with a low proportion of elderly population, young individuals distribute their total expenditures more equally.

Although the clusters determined according to the consumption patterns of individuals in the 30-44 age group are similar to the clusters of young individuals, some countries are in different clusters. The first cluster consists of Belgium, Norway, Finland, Denmark, Germany, Ireland, Spain, France, Portugal, Austria, Netherlands and Luxembourg. This cluster consists of countries with high per capita income, developed social welfare systems, but high elderly population rates. The majority of the expenditures of the 30-44 age group in the first cluster are made in the categories of housing, transportation, restaurants and entertainment. The high housing prices and transportation in these countries increase the cost of living. The second cluster consists of Slovakia, Romania, Poland, Lithuania, Serbia, Estonia, Bulgaria, Hungary, which are in the transition process and developed but frequently affected by economic crises, and Italy and Greece. Individuals in this cluster have a consumption profile focused on services and socialization. The categories with the highest expenditures are restaurants, hotels, entertainment and cultural expenditures. Compared to the first cluster, the spending patterns of this cluster, which is more experience and socially focused, show that consumption expenditures are not only dependent on income, but also on many social and cultural factors. The third cluster, consisting of Malta, Latvia, Cyprus, Slovenia and Czechia and Turkiye, has a more balanced consumption structure, as in the under 30 category. The spending of the 30-44 age group in this country is more homogeneously distributed according to their categories.

Figure 3. Spending Profiles of Clusters

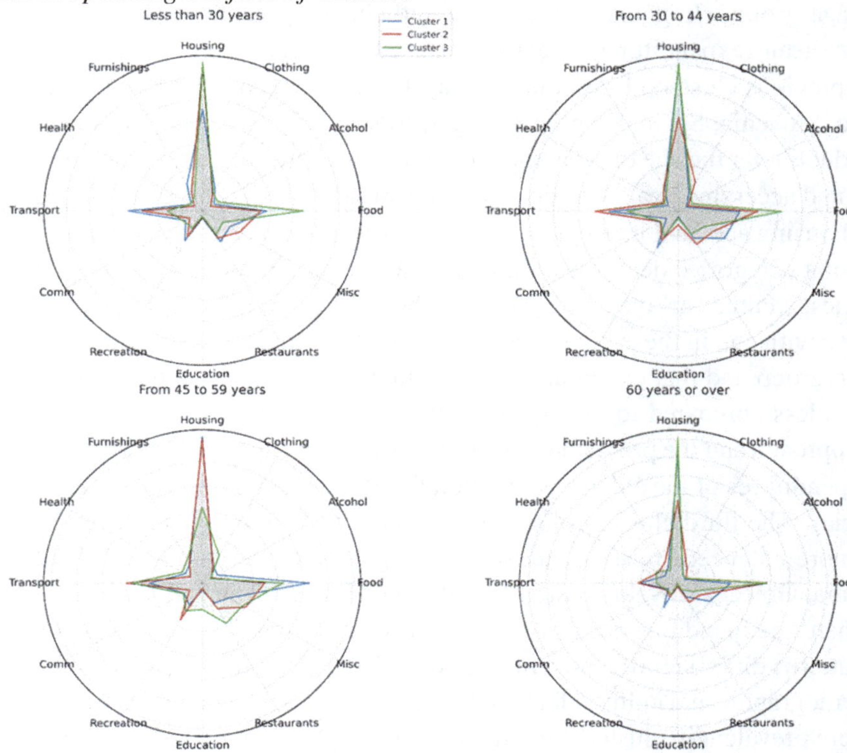

The increasing health needs in the 45-59 age group, the effects of work life and lifestyle, and the approaching retirement show the impact of not only income but also lifestyle and social protection needs on expenditures. The first cluster includes Belgium, Slovakia, Romania, Poland, Hungary, Serbia, Latvia, Italy, Lithuania, Greece, Estonia, Bulgaria and Spain. In these countries, the expenditures of the 45-59 age group are concentrated in housing, health and transportation categories. The second cluster shows a different consumption pattern compared to the first cluster in terms of consumption pattern. Discretionary consumption expenditures, restaurant, cultural event and entertainment expenditures are higher than other cluster groups. This cluster consists of France, Norway, Finland, Slovenia, Portugal, Denmark, Austria, Germany, Luxembourg, Ireland and the Netherlands. In these countries, the higher economic welfare compared to other countries, urbanization and high level of education make it easier for individuals to make choices to increase their quality of life. The third cluster consists only of Malta, Czechia, Cyprus and Turkiye. Again, individuals in the countries included in this cluster try to balance their consumption expenditures with mandatory and discretionary expenditures.

The consumption patterns of the 60 and above age group are quite different from other age groups. In general, retirement and changing needs with increasing age increase health expenditures. The first cluster consists of developed countries similar to the previous clusters: Belgium, Norway, Czechia, Denmark, Germany, Finland, Ireland, Slovenia, Spain, France, Portugal, Austria, Netherlands and Luxembourg. Individuals over the age of 60 in these countries prioritize maintaining their quality of life and accessing health services. For this reason, expenditures are concentrated in the housing and health categories. Expenditures for education, entertainment and restaurant categories decrease with age. The second cluster consists of only three countries: Malta, Turkiye and Cyprus. Although health and housing expenditures increase with age in these countries, it is understood that there is a more social upper age group and that expenditures for restaurants, culture and entertainment are reduced less compared to the countries in the first cluster. In addition, the social state approach and the provision of health expenditures by the state can also explain the expenditures of the elderly population for other expenditure categories in these countries. The third cluster consists of Eastern and Southern European countries with more balanced spending across 12 categories: Serbia, Latvia, Poland, Italy, Romania, Greece, Slovakia, Estonia, Bulgaria, Hungary and Lithuania.

When the expenditure profiles of the clusters are examined, it is seen that consumption patterns differ significantly among countries depending on both income levels and demographic and cultural factors. While food, housing and health expenditures are more prevalent in clusters with high mandatory expenditures, in some clusters, discretionary expenditures such as entertainment, restaurants, transportation and communication are more prevalent. The findings show that different consumption structures are formed in line with the economic development level of the countries, social security systems, lifestyles and demographic weights of age groups. These differences point to the potential of demographic transformation to shape future sectoral demands and public policies.

PROJECTIONS for 2100

In this section, a forecast study based on demographic projections was conducted to assess the long-term effects of the ageing population on consumption patterns in European countries. The transformation in the age composition of the population provides important indicators of how the balance between basic needs and discretionary expenditures will change in the future. With low fertility rates and increasing life expectancy, the proportion of elderly people in Europe is projected to increase significantly in the coming years. This demographic change has the potential to structurally transform not only the level of total consumption but also the sectoral composition of consumption.

In the analysis, consumption patterns of current age groups were determined based on category-based average expenditure levels obtained from the Eurostat dataset and separated according to the COICOP classification. Demographic projections for the year 2100 were obtained using age-based population estimates produced by Eurostat using the cohort-component method. In the estimation process, average consumption expenditure of each age group by category was multiplied by the total population size of that age group in the projection, and total expected consumption amounts were calculated at the country and category level. The total consumption values obtained were then normalized, and the percentage shares of consumption categories in the total for each country were derived. Thanks to this method, the impact of demographic aging on consumption composition was quantitatively assessed in terms of structural and relative change dynamics. With this approach, the long-term effects of demographic aging on sectoral demand structure and macroeconomic resource allocation are quantitatively assessed, contributing to the development of foresight for policy makers.

The changing consumption patterns by age groups will change permanently with the aging of the whole continent of Europe. The changing demand for consumption categories causes structural transformations by changing the volume and employment of sectors. The changes in consumption expenditures calculated with estimated data for 2100 compared to 2025 are shown in Figure 4. The estimates show that the share of the elderly population in the total population in Europe will increase significantly. This structural demographic transformation also creates significant changes in consumption patterns. Similar to the changes in consumption patterns by age groups, expenditures in the categories of housing, health and food increase with the aging of the average European population. The share of housing, water, electricity and fuel expenditures in total consumption increases by 1.6%, and the share of health expenditures increases by 0.37%; however, in many categories, the demand for social activities, transportation and tourism decreases with increasing age.

The findings reveal that with the increase in the elderly population, there has been a significant increase in the share of housing and health expenditures in total consumption. This increase in housing expenditures is consistent with the increasing demands of elderly individuals for safe, accessible and comfortable living spaces. The increase observed in health expenditures is directly related to the chronic diseases, treatment processes and needs for care services that aging brings. The increase observed in food expenditures can be interpreted as a result of a more sedentary lifestyle; elderly individuals tend to prefer eating at home rather than eating out.

In contrast, a significant decrease was observed in transportation expenditures. This can be explained by the decrease in mobility levels of older individuals, the decrease in the frequency of travel, and their lower dependence on motor vehicles compared to younger individuals. Similarly, there was a decrease in areas where younger age groups spend heavily, such as restaurants and hotels, clothing, recreation, and education. These findings support the observation that older individuals tend to live more introverted, calm, and sedentary lives. Such lifestyle changes also necessitate the restructuring of economic sectors.

Marginal changes were observed in some categories – such as alcohol, household goods, communication, and various services – indicating that spending flexibility in these categories is low. Stability in these areas indicates that certain basic spending items are maintained regardless of age.

Figure 4. Structural Change Forecast of Consumption (2100)

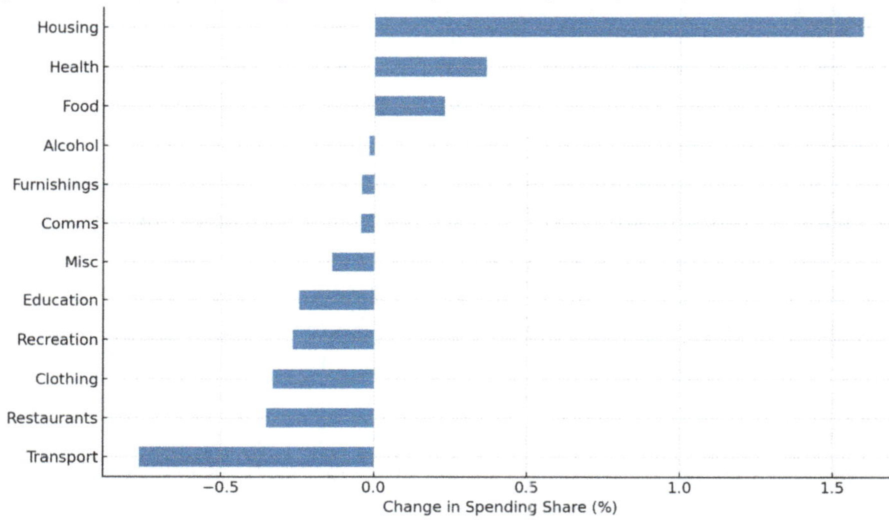

In order to calculate the changes that the aging population may cause in the consumption composition in the future, the current average consumption expenditures of age groups were associated with the age group populations in the projections. The average consumption per capita of each age group was multiplied by the projected population size of the relevant age group to estimate total category expenditures. Thus, the effect of the transformation in the population structure on consumption patterns was calculated quantitatively for countries and periods. These total expenditures obtained were normalized for each year and the percentage shares of consumption categories in the total were calculated. Thus, the structural changes that demographic aging may cause in the composition of the consumption basket were evaluated quantitatively on a country basis.

The analysis results are visualized in Figure 5 and the relative change rates expected to occur in consumption categories throughout the period are presented. The findings reveal that the effect of demographic aging on consumption patterns is not homogeneous among European countries. Both the aging rates and the initial levels of current demographic structures differ among countries; accordingly, the magnitude and direction of changes in consumption composition exhibit significant differences among countries.

The first group includes countries where demographic ageing is expected to lead to strong structural shifts in the consumption basket. Bulgaria, Latvia, Lithuania and Romania are included in this group. In these countries, long-standing low fertility rates and increasing life expectancy are causing the proportion of the young population to decline rapidly and the weight of the elderly population in the total population to increase sharply. At the same time, net labor migration in these countries is accelerating the decline of the young population, thus further accelerating the increase in the average age. This demographic change is creating a significant shift in consumption patterns. In particular, the shares of discretionary expenditures such as education, clothing, transportation and entertainment in total consumption are expected to shrink significantly. In contrast, the weight of expenditures on health services, care and housing is expected to increase significantly in parallel with the increase in the elderly population. The expansion in these categories brings about a transformation that will affect both individual welfare preferences and the distribution of public resources in the long term in these countries.

Similarly, Italy and Germany are among the countries that will experience certain structural changes, but the change is more controlled in terms of speed and intensity compared to the first group. Low fertility rates have been continuing in Italy for many years, and while a decrease is observed in the relative shares of expenditures in the education and transportation categories, an increase is expected in the health, housing and basic food categories. In Germany, demographic aging is more gradual due to the size of the current population structure and balanced labor migration policies. Despite this, by 2100, the weight of health and housing expenditures in Germany is also expected to increase, while education, restaurant and transportation expenditures are expected to decrease relatively. This limited but significant change in Germany is emerging together with the country's strong social state structure and balancing migration policies.

Figure 5. Consumption Pattern Analysis Based on Demographic Projections by Country

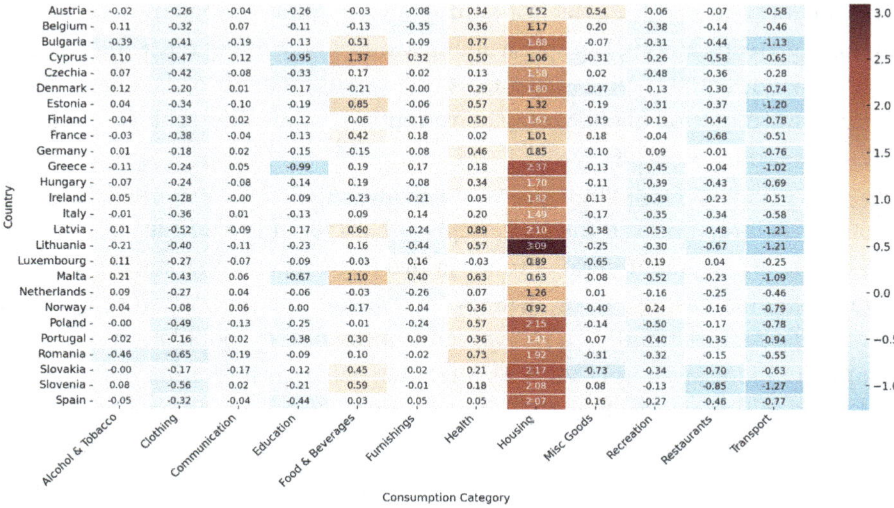

The second group includes countries where demographic transformation will have relatively limited effects on consumption patterns. Austria, the Netherlands, Luxembourg and Norway stand out among the countries in this group. The common feature of these countries is that both fertility rates are relatively stable and the proportions of young and old populations develop in a balanced manner. In addition, the positive course of net migration flows contributes to the stability of the demographic structure by supporting the continuity of the young workforce. In Luxembourg, the small population structure and high income level together with the strong capacity to receive migration allow the young population rate to be preserved, which leads to very limited structural changes in the consumption pattern. While some increases are expected in health, housing and communication expenditures in Austria and the Netherlands, the weights of discretionary expenditures such as education, entertainment and transportation in the total remain largely constant. In Norway, a fairly stable structure continues in consumption patterns thanks to balanced fertility rates and the protection of the young population. The low-level structural shifts observed in these countries are closely related to the strong functioning of social state mechanisms, the flexibility of retirement and health systems and the success of long-term demographic planning.

The results generally indicate that a broad consensus emerges that demographic aging in European countries will increase the weight of expenditures on basic food, health, care and housing in consumption patterns; on the other hand, there will be relative contractions in flexible expenditure items such as education, transportation, entertainment and restaurants. However, the heterogeneity between countries in terms of the speed and intensity of this structural transformation will continue to be significant. The findings reveal the importance of policy makers to design long-term policies by taking into account demographic projections not only in terms of population growth rate but also the sectoral effects it will create on consumption composition and resource allocation requirements. In particular, considering the effects of demographic transformation on consumption composition in social security systems, retirement reforms, health service infrastructure and sectoral employment plans will be one of the fundamental determinants of the economic and social policy-making process in the coming years.

POLICY RECOMMENDATIONS

The demographic aging process creates multidimensional effects on individuals' income levels, consumption patterns and service demands; therefore, it necessitates policy makers to develop multi-layered intervention areas.

First of all, it is necessary to maintain the level of income after retirement for the continuity of total consumption expenditures. It is of great importance to prevent sharp declines in retirement incomes for elderly individuals to maintain their living standards. Keeping retirement incomes close to working-period income is necessary not only for social justice, but also for keeping total demand alive. In this context, practices such as tax advantages, automatic enrollment systems and state contributions that encourage participation in individual retirement systems can support income security. At the same time, although regulations to increase the retirement age are on the agenda, as in many European countries, these policies remain controversial in terms of social support. Therefore, it is important for policy makers to balance the system with inflation indexing and income support mechanisms that will protect the purchasing power of retirement salaries.

Increasing health and care needs with aging lead to significant changes in consumption patterns. The increase in average life expectancy significantly increases the share of health expenditures in the Gross Domestic Product (Kallestrup-Lamb et al., 2024). In this context, the expansion of models such as long-term care insurance, national care services, and publicly supported care funds will facilitate individuals' budget allocation for other consumption categories by limiting their health and care expenses in advanced ages. For example, the Pflegeversicherung system, which was implemented in Germany in 1995, provides financial security for long-term care needs. The increasing number of elderly individuals living alone along with changing family structures necessitates the strengthening of institutional capacity in care services and the development of flexible service models. In addition, encouraging digitalization in health services—for example, telemedicine applications, home health monitoring systems, and smart elderly care technologies—can increase the efficiency of health expenditures and reduce the pressure on the public budget.

The expansion of social policies that support the active participation of elderly individuals in social life is necessary for both individuals and consumption expenditures. In order to reduce the risk of social isolation of elderly individuals, practices that encourage active aging such as social centers, volunteer programs, cultural and sports activities should be expanded. Such social integration programs both increase individual well-being and can limit the long-term pressures of health and care expenditures.

The issue of taxation of goods and services consumed intensively by the elderly population is one of the central issues of policy discussions. In some countries, special subsidies are provided to elderly individuals for basic consumption items and energy expenses related to housing; support programs are implemented for fixed expenses such as electricity, water and heating. Discounted or free transportation rights in transportation services are also among the important mechanisms that encourage participation in social life.

Finally, new consumption demands arising from aging also open the door to new economic opportunities. Sectors within the scope of the silver economy—such as elderly-friendly housing and architectural projects, nursing homes, smart home systems, care and health insurance, personalized financial products—have the potential for both growth and employment creation. Health tourism, cultural travel programs and elderly-friendly tourism packages in particular are creating rapidly growing markets for retired individuals who want to make use of their increasing free time. Indeed, some countries, such as Poland and Italy, position themselves as attractive living centers for retirees in order to attract silver economy investments. Such practices support not only economic growth but also the quality of life and social participation of elderly individuals.

As a result, demographic ageing should not only be considered as a cost element, but also as a multidimensional transformation process that offers significant social and economic opportunities when guided by strategic planning and innovation.

CONCLUSION

This study examines the effects of the ageing population on consumption patterns in Europe in the light of empirical data, revealing the long-term reflections of demographic transformation on economic structures. Bringing together demographic projections with household consumption data disaggregated by age groups has made it possible to see the shifts in the consumption components of ageing societies in detail.

The findings reveal that consumption shows significant changes not only in quantity but also in composition with age. While younger age groups focus on flexible spending categories such as clothing, transportation, entertainment and education, the spending of older individuals is directed towards mandatory consumption categories such as housing, healthcare, food and basic services. These structural changes are compatible with both traditional life cycle theories and the behavioral life cycle approach. In particular, behavioral factors such as prudent saving tendencies, self-control problems and mental calculations play an important role in shaping the consumption decisions of the elderly population.

The cluster analyses conducted in the study show that there are significant regional differences in consumption patterns among countries. It has been observed that consumption expenditures are concentrated on basic needs in Eastern and Southern European countries; while more diversified consumption patterns emerge in Western and Northern European countries due to income level, social welfare structure and health systems. Consumption categories that differ with age reflect not only individual preferences but also the influence of institutional structures, cultural norms and public policies.

Projections for 2100 show that the weight of health, care and housing expenditures will increase in a large part of Europe due to aging; on the other hand, the share of categories focused on the young population such as education, transportation and social activities will decrease. This transformation process, in which radical changes will be experienced in resource allocation at the sectoral level, will also be decisive on macroeconomic balances.

This study also provides an important basis for a more comprehensive study of the effects of demographic change on consumption and sectors. The additional effects of factors such as technological advances, migration movements, intergenerational wealth transfers and changing family structures on this transformation can be addressed in more detail in future studies. In-depth country analyses, especially on micro data sets, will contribute to a more precise estimation of the sectoral and macroeconomic effects of demographic transformation.

REFERENCES

Abrigo, M. R., & Ortiz, M. K. P. (2024). Residential electricity consumption over the demographic transition in the Philippines. *The Journal of the Economics of Ageing*, *27*, 100503. DOI: 10.1016/j.jeoa.2024.100503

Aguiar, M., & Hurst, E. (2007). Life-cycle prices and production. *The American Economic Review*, *97*(5), 1533–1559. DOI: 10.1257/aer.97.5.1533

Aguila, E., Attanasio, O., & Meghir, C. (2010). Changes in consumption at retirement: Evidence from panel data. *The Review of Economics and Statistics*, *93*(3), 1094–1099. DOI: 10.1162/REST_a_00140

Banks, J., Blundell, R., & Tanner, S. (1998). Is there a retirement-savings puzzle? *The American Economic Review*, *88*(4), 769–788.

Belk, R. (2014). You are what you can access: Sharing and collaborative consumption online. *Journal of Business Research*, *67*(8), 1595–1600. DOI: 10.1016/j.jbusres.2013.10.001

Bernheim, B. D., Skinner, J., & Weinberg, S. (2001). What accounts for the variation in retirement wealth among US households? *The American Economic Review*, *91*(4), 832–857. DOI: 10.1257/aer.91.4.832

Börsch-Supan, A. (1992). Saving and consumption patterns of the elderly: The German case. *Journal of Population Economics*, *5*(4), 289–303. DOI: 10.1007/BF00163062

Chen, F., Mao, S., & Huang, R. (2024). Age structure of the population and household consumption expenditure on tourism. *Finance Research Letters*, *60*, 104896. DOI: 10.1016/j.frl.2023.104896

Danziger, S., Van Der Gaag, J., Smolensky, E., & Taussig, M. K. (1982). The life-cycle hypothesis and the consumption behavior of the elderly. *Journal of Post Keynesian Economics*, *5*(2), 208–227. DOI: 10.1080/01603477.1982.11489357

Duesenberry, J. S. (1948). *The consumption function: A study of relations between income and consumer expenditures*. University of Michigan.

Erlandsen, S. K. (2003). *Age structure effects and consumption in Norway, 1968 (3)-1998 (4)* (No. 2003/1). Working Paper.

Etgeton, S., Fischer, B., & Ye, H. (2023). The effect of increasing retirement age on households' savings and consumption expenditure. *Journal of Public Economics*, *221*, 104845. DOI: 10.1016/j.jpubeco.2023.104845

European Commission. (2018). *The Silver Economy*. Retrieved from https://ec.europa.eu/docsroom/documents/33163

Eurostat. (2024). *Ageing Europe – statistics on pensions, income and expenditure*. European Commission. https://ec.europa.eu/eurostat/statistics-explained/index.php?title=Ageing_Europe_-_statistics_on_pensions,_income_and_expenditure

Eurostat (2025). *Population structure and ageing*. Retrieved May 13, 2025, from https://european-union.europa.eu/principles-countries-history/facts-and-figures-european-union_en

Feldstein, M. (1976). Social security and the distribution of wealth. *Journal of the American Statistical Association*, *71*(356), 800–807. DOI: 10.1080/01621459.1976.10480950

Fisher, I. (1930). *The theory of interest: As determined by impatience to spend income and opportunity to invest it*. Macmillan.

Friedman, M. (1957). The permanent income hypothesis. In *A theory of the consumption function* (pp. 20–37). Princeton University Press. DOI: 10.1515/9780691188485-005

IMF. (2021). *Demographic Change and Economic Well-Being*. International Monetary Fund. Retrieved from https://www.elibrary.imf.org/display/book/9781498344753/9781498344753.xml

Johnson-Hillery, J., Kang, J., & Tuan, W. J. (1997). The difference between elderly consumers' satisfaction levels and retail sales personnel's perceptions. *International Journal of Retail & Distribution Management*, *25*(4), 126–137. DOI: 10.1108/09590559710166304

Kallestrup-Lamb, M., Marin, A. O., Menon, S., & Søgaard, J. (2024). Aging populations and expenditures on health. *The Journal of the Economics of Ageing*, *29*, 100518. DOI: 10.1016/j.jeoa.2024.100518

Keynes, J. M. (1936). *The General Theory of Employment, Interest and Money*. Macmillan.

Kuznets, S., Epstein, L., & Jenks, E. (1946). *National product since 1869*. NBER Books.

Laitner, J., & Silverman, D. (2012). Consumption, retirement and social security: Evaluating the efficiency of reform that encourages longer careers. *Journal of Public Economics*, *96*(7-8), 615–634. DOI: 10.1016/j.jpubeco.2012.02.005

Lee, H. (2001). Factors influencing the consumption expenditures of retired elderly households: Focused on the factor of wealth components. *International Journal of Human Ecology*, *2*(1), 17–38.

Lee, Y. G., & Huh, E. (2004). Consumption and saving behavior of older and younger baby boomers in Korea. *Journal of Family and Economic Issues*, *25*, 507–526.

Modigliani, F., & Brumberg, R. (1954). Utility analysis and the consumption function: An interpretation of cross-section data. *Franco Modigliani*, *1*(1), 388–436.

OECD. (2020). *Ageing and Fiscal Challenges across Levels of Government*. OECD Publishing. Retrieved from https://www.oecd.org/content/dam/oecd/en/publications/reports/2020/10/ageing-and-fiscal-challenges-across-levels-of-government_f565f895/2bbfbda8-en.pdf

Radivojević, B., & Vasić, P. (2012). Household age structure and consumption in Serbia. *Economic annals, 57*(195), 79-101.

Shefrin, H. M., & Thaler, R. H. (1988). The behavioral life-cycle hypothesis. *Economic Inquiry*, *26*(4), 609–643. DOI: 10.1111/j.1465-7295.1988.tb01520.x

Sim Ong, F., Kitchen, J. P., & Jama, A. T. (2008). Consumption patterns and silver marketing: An analysis of older consumers in Malaysia. *Marketing Intelligence & Planning*, *26*(7), 682–698. DOI: 10.1108/02634500810916663

Szmigin, I., & Carrigan, M. (2001). Learning to love the older consumer. *Journal of Consumer Behaviour*, *1*(1), 22–34. DOI: 10.1002/cb.51

Veblen, T. (1899). Mr. Cummings's Strictures on" The Theory of the Leisure Class. *Journal of Political Economy*, *8*(1), 106–117. DOI: 10.1086/250640

Vogels, E. A. (2023). Americans are worried about inflation — but many are still spending big. *Pew Research Center.* Retrieved from https://www.pewresearch.org/

Yuh, Y., Montalto, C. P., & Hanna, S. D. (1998). Are Americans prepared for retirement? *Financial Counseling and Planning*, *9*(1).

Zhu, P., & Lin, B. (2022). Do the elderly consume more energy? Evidence from the retirement policy in urban China. *Energy Policy*, *165*, 112928. DOI: 10.1016/j.enpol.2022.112928

ADDITIONAL READING

Bloom, D. E., Canning, D., & Fink, G. (2010). *The greying of the global population and its macroeconomic consequences*. Twenty-First Century Society. DOI: 10.1080/17450144.2010.480826

Lee, R. D., & Mason, A. (Eds.). (2011). *Population aging and the generational economy: A global perspective*. Edward Elgar Publishing. DOI: 10.4337/9780857930583

Maestas, N., Mullen, K. J., & Powell, D. (2023). The effect of population aging on economic growth, the labor force, and productivity. *American Economic Journal. Macroeconomics*, *15*(2), 306–332. DOI: 10.1257/mac.20190196

Mason, A., & Lee, R. (2007). Transfers, capital and consumption over the demographic transition. In *Population aging, intergenerational transfers and the macroeconomy*. Edward Elgar Publishing. DOI: 10.4337/9781847208583.00014

Schulz, J. H. (2000). *The economics of aging*. Bloomsbury Publishing USA. DOI: 10.5040/9798400643651

KEY TERMS and DEFINITIONS

Cluster Analysis: A statistical method used to group countries or individuals based on the similarity of their characteristics—in this study, consumption expenditure profiles—allowing for the identification of distinct consumption behavior patterns across populations.

Consumption Patterns: The distribution of household expenditures across various goods and services, which varies significantly across different age groups due to income levels, preferences, and life cycle stages.

Demographic Aging: The process by which the proportion of elderly individuals in a population increases over time due to declining fertility rates and rising life expectancy, leading to significant economic, social, and policy implications.

Sectoral Transformation: The process by which shifts in demographic structure, such as aging populations, alter the relative size, employment, and resource allocation across different sectors of the economy, including healthcare, housing, transportation, and leisure.

Silver Economy: The economic activities, products, and services designed to meet the needs and preferences of the aging population, covering sectors such as healthcare, housing, financial services, tourism, and assistive technologies.

Chapter 5
Impact of Global Demographic Shifts on Agricultural Markets and Food Security

M. U. Vinod Krishna
https://orcid.org/0009-0009-5150-3701
Dayananda Sagar College of Engineering, India

R. A. Ayyapparajan
https://orcid.org/0000-0002-5352-9712
Nehru Institute of Information Technology and Management, India

Nilesh Anute
https://orcid.org/0000-0001-6599-813X
Sri Balaji University, India

Ganesh Pandit Pathak
https://orcid.org/0000-0003-0427-2145
Sri Balaji University, India

Ann Mary Cherian
https://orcid.org/0009-0002-1452-8941
Christ College, Irinjalakuda, India

P. Selvakumar
https://orcid.org/0000-0002-3650-4548
Department of Science and Humanities, Nehru Institute of Technology, Coimbatore, India

T. C. Manjunath
https://orcid.org/0000-0003-2545-9160
Rajarajeswari College of Engineering, India

ABSTRACT

Demographic changes have long been a driving force in shaping economies, societies, and markets. In the 21st century, shifting population dynamics—marked by growth, aging populations, urbanization, migration, and changing consumer preferences—are significantly influencing agricultural markets and food security worldwide. As populations grow in some regions while stagnating or declining in

DOI: 10.4018/979-8-3373-2550-7.ch005

others, the demand for food, the structure of agricultural production, and global trade patterns are all undergoing profound transformations. Population Growth and Agricultural Demand: One of the most fundamental demographic changes is global population growth. According to projections, reach will occur in developing regions, particularly in Africa and South Asia, where food insecurity remains a pressing challenge. Increases, placing greater agricultural systems expand production while maintaining sustainability. However, food demand is not just about population size but also about income growth and dietary changes.

INTRODUCTION TO GLOBAL DEMOGRAPHIC SHIFTS AND THEIR IMPACT ON AGRICULTURAL MARKETS

Demographic changes have long been a driving force in shaping economies, societies, and markets. In the 21st century, shifting population dynamics—marked by growth, aging populations, urbanization, migration, and changing consumer preferences—are significantly influencing agricultural markets and food security worldwide. As populations grow in some regions while stagnating or declining in others, the demand for food, the structure of agricultural production, and global trade patterns are all undergoing profound transformations. Population Growth and Agricultural Demand: One of the most fundamental demographic changes is global population growth. According to projections, reach will occur in developing regions, particularly in Africa and South Asia, where food insecurity remains a pressing challenge. Increases, placing greater agricultural systems expand production while maintaining sustainability. However, food demand is not just about population size but also about income growth and dietary changes. As incomes rise, especially in emerging economies, consumers tend to shift from staple grains to more protein-rich diets, including meat, dairy, and processed foods. This shift has major implications for agriculture, as livestock production requires more land, water, and feed crops such as soy and corn, further straining resources. Aging Populations and Agricultural Workforce Challenges: While some regions experience rapid population growth, others face an aging demographic profile, particularly in developed economies and parts of East Asia. The aging population has a direct impact on agricultural production, as it leads to labor shortages in farming communities. Many young people are leaving behind an aging farming workforce with fewer successors. The implications of this trend include a decline in smallholder farming, increased farm consolidation, and a growing reliance on mechanization and agricultural technology to compensate for labor shortages. Governments and agricultural organizations are increasingly promoting policies to attract younger generations into farming through subsidies, education, and technology-driven solutions.

THE CHANGING GLOBAL DEMOGRAPHICS: POPULATION GROWTH, URBANIZATION, AND AGING

Demographic changes have always affected crucial economies and global markets. In the 21st century, shifts in population growth, urbanization, and aging are profoundly influencing social structures, economic development, and resource distribution. These trends vary significantly across regions, with some countries experiencing rapid population expansion while others face declining birth rates and aging populations. Meanwhile, urbanization continues to transform lifestyles, labor markets, and consumption patterns. Shifts businesses, communities adapt and plan for the future effectively. Population Growth: A Divided Trend: Global Population Growth Patterns: The world's population has been growing rapidly for decades, reaching over 8 billion in recent years. However, while some southern countries continue to have high birth rates, others, including much of Europe, East Asia, and North America, are seeing stagnation or even decline in population numbers. According to projections by the United Nations, Africa is projected to be the main driver of such a significant change (Gu D., et al, 2021). On the other hand, countries like Japan, Italy, and South Korea face declining birth rates, leading to shrinking and aging populations. Impacts of Population Growth: effects are multifaceted. Regions there is increasing water, housing, healthcare, education, and employment. Rapid population growth can place immense pressure on governments and infrastructure, particularly in developing nations where resources are already strained. However, a growing population also presents economic opportunities by expanding labor markets and consumer bases, potentially driving economic growth if managed effectively. In contrast, countries experiencing population decline face challenges related to labor shortages, economic stagnation, and a shrinking tax base. Fewer young workers mean that fewer people are contributing to economic productivity while an increasing proportion of the population is dependent on pensions and healthcare services. This demographic imbalance necessitates policy adjustments, such as immigration incentives, automation in industries, and reforms in pension and healthcare systems. Urbanization: The Shift to Cities: The Rise of Urban Populations Urbanization is one of the most significant demographic trends of the modern era. As of today, 56% expected (Osareme O J., et al, 2024).

Another significant challenge is ensuring that elderly populations maintain a high quality of life. Issues such as elder care, social isolation, and healthcare accessibility become increasingly important. Many governments are promoting policies that encourage active aging, such as lifelong learning programs, flexible work arrangements for older adults, and investments in elderly-friendly infrastructure (Wang Q., et al, 2022). The Intersection of Population Growth, Urbanization, and Aging: Demographic trends occur in many ways. For example, urbanization often accelerates aging in rural areas, as younger generations move to cities, leaving behind older populations. This can lead to declining rural economies and challenges in providing healthcare and social services in remote areas. Additionally, urban areas with rapidly growing populations must prepare for the future implications of aging. As urban populations age, cities will need to adapt their infrastructure, healthcare systems, and public services to accommodate an older demographic. Housing, transportation, and community services will all need to be designed with accessibility and inclusivity in mind. Furthermore, countries with aging populations may turn to immigration as a solution to labor shortages. Policies encouraging skilled migration can help offset workforce declines, but they also require integration strategies to ensure social cohesion and economic benefits (Mason A., et al, 2022).

THE IMPORTANCE OF AGRICULTURAL MARKETS AND FOOD SECURITY IN THE FACE OF GLOBAL DEMOGRAPHIC SHIFTS

These demographic shifts create new challenges and opportunities for food production, distribution, and consumption. Addressing these changes in agriculture and technology to maintain shifting demand resource constraints. The Role of Agricultural Markets in a Changing World: Defining Agricultural Markets: Agricultural markets encompass the linking, suppliers, traders, and consumers across local, national, and international economies. Efficient agricultural markets provide fair compensation to producers. How Demographic Shifts Impact Agricultural Markets: Demographic trends influence agricultural markets in several ways. Population Growth and Rising Food Demand: Food will rise significantly. This growth will put pressure on agricultural systems, minimizing impact. And will need to expand agricultural production and enhance distribution networks to prevent food shortages (Barrett C B., et al, 2021). Urbanization and Changing Consumer Preferences: Food supply chains evolve to meet urban demand. Urban consumers often prefer processed and convenience foods, leading to increased demand for packaged and frozen goods, dairy, meat, and fresh produce. Urbanization also drives the expansion of supermarkets and e-commerce food delivery services, transforming how food is bought and sold. Aging Populations and Labor Challenges: In many countries, an aging workforce is leading to labor shortages in agriculture. Fewer young people are taking up farming, resulting in the need for mechanization and technology-driven solutions. Policies encouraging youth participation in agriculture and investments in smart farming technologies can help address these challenges (Aryal J P., et al, 2022).

Food Waste: portion due to poor storage, transportation inefficiencies, and consumer habits. Reducing food waste can improve food availability and lower production pressure on agricultural systems (Wang X., et al, 2023). Conflict and

Political Instability: War leading to shortages and price spikes. Investment in resilient agricultural infrastructure and emergency food aid programs can help mitigate food security risks in conflict-affected areas. Strategies for Strengthening Agricultural Markets and Food Security: Improving Agricultural Productivity: Investing in Technology: Precision farming, AI-driven monitoring, and automated irrigation systems can enhance yields and efficiency. Promoting Sustainable Farming: Crop rotation, soil conservation, and organic farming can improve long-term food production. Enhancing Food Supply Chains: Building Better Infrastructure: Roads, cold storage, and transport networks are essential for efficient food distribution. Supporting Local and Global Trade: Balanced trade policies can ensure that food reaches where it is needed most. Strengthening Policy and Governance: Government Support for Farmers: Subsidies, credit access, and training programs can help farmers adapt to changing demands. Food Security Programs: School feeding programs, food assistance, and nutrition education can combat hunger (Stavi I., et al, 2022). Encouraging Sustainable Consumption: Reducing Food Waste: Public awareness campaigns and improved storage solutions can reduce food loss. Shifting to Alternative Proteins: Lab-grown meat, plant-based diets, and insect proteins offer sustainable food options. As global demographics continue to shift, agricultural markets and food security remain critical to sustaining economic stability and human well-being. Population growth, urbanization, and aging will reshape food demand, requiring innovative solutions in food production, distribution, and consumption. Strengthening agricultural systems through technology, infrastructure, and policy reforms. Addressing challenges proactively, governments, businesses, and communities face demographic pressures and environmental changes. Sustainable and inclusive agricultural markets are key to securing a stable and prosperous future for all.

THE IMPACT OF POPULATION GROWTH ON AGRICULTURAL MARKETS: INCREASING DEMAND FOR FOOD AND RESOURCES

As food demand rises, agricultural markets must evolve to meet these challenges through improved productivity, sustainable resource management, and enhanced supply chain efficiencies. Understanding these dynamics agribusinesses, consumers coming decades. The Rising Demand for Food: Projected Growth in Food Consumption: As global population numbers surge, food consumption is expected to increase significantly (Hemathilake D., et al, 2022). At least needs and increasingly affluent demand is not just for more food but also greater diversity in dietary options, influenced by rising incomes and urbanization. The challenge is that while the global population grows, the amount of available farmland remains relatively fixed. In many regions, agricultural expansion is limited due to urbanization, desertification, deforestation, and land degradation (Norton G W., et al, 2021). To meet food production needs, farmers are forced to adopt more intensive agricultural practices, including higher crop yields per hectare and precision farming techniques. However, excessive land use and deforestation pose environmental risks, including increased. Sustainable food production is critical for balancing food production with environmental protection. Water Scarcity and Irrigation Challenges: an essential yet in many parts of the world. Population growth increases the demand for fresh water for drinking, sanitation, and industrial use, creating competition between agricultural and non-agricultural sectors. Agriculture currently accounts for about 70% of global freshwater withdrawals. Rapid South Asia and are already experiencing water stress, which threatens agricultural productivity.

Innovations in animal breeding, feed optimization, and disease prevention are making livestock production environmentally friendly. Digital Agriculture and Smart Farming: Big data in agriculture is revolutionizing food production. Drones provide management and waste. AI-Driven Pest Control: AI-powered monitoring systems help farmers detect and respond to pest infestations quickly, reducing crop losses (Jie H., et al, 2023). Automated Machinery: Robotics and automation in planting, harvesting, and sorting streamline agricultural operations, addressing labor shortages and increasing efficiency. Global Trade and Market Adjustments: Shifts in Agricultural Trade: As food demand rises, global agricultural trade patterns are evolving. Countries with surplus food production, such as the United States, Brazil, and Canada, export grains, meat, and dairy to food-deficient regions. Trade policies, tariffs, and geopolitical tensions significantly impact agricultural markets, influencing food prices and availability. For developing countries, improving trade infrastructure—such as transportation networks, storage facilities, and port operations—is critical for efficient food distribution. Additionally, diversifying food sources and strengthening local agricultural production can enhance food security in regions that rely heavily on imports. Supply Chain Resilience: Disruptions in food supply chains due to population growth-related pressures, climate change, or global conflicts can have severe economic and social consequences. Strengthening supply chain resilience through diversification, regional food hubs, and digital tracking systems can help mitigate risks and ensure stable food access. Food Security Implications: Addressing Malnutrition and Hunger: Despite increased food production, hunger and malnutrition remain significant global challenges. 700 worldwide suffer from food insecurity. Population growth exacerbates this issue, particularly in regions with weak food distribution systems and economic instability (Daszkiewicz T., et al, 2022).

URBANIZATION AND CHANGING DIETARY PREFERENCES: IMPLICATIONS FOR AGRICULTURAL MARKETS

Policymakers, businesses involved in food production and distribution. Urbanization and Its Impact on Food Demand: The Shift from Traditional Diets to Processed and Convenient Foods: Urban populations typically experience lifestyle changes that affect food consumption (Zhang Y., et al, 2022). These include: Higher Incomes and Diversified Diets: Urban dwellers generally have higher disposable incomes, enabling them to purchase a wider variety of foods. Diets in urban areas shift from staple grains to high-protein and nutrient-rich foods, including meat, dairy, fruits, and vegetables. Greater Consumption of Processed and Packaged Foods: Due to time constraints and busy lifestyles, urban consumers rely more on processed, ready-to-eat, and fast foods. This increases the demand for food processing industries and packaged goods, affecting supply chains and raw material sourcing. Increased Demand for Meat and Dairy Products: As incomes rise in urban areas, meat and dairy consumption increases significantly. This drives higher demand for livestock farming, animal feed production, and water-intensive agricultural practices. Rising Popularity of International and Specialty Foods: Urban areas, especially in globalized economies, see a growing demand for diverse cuisines and imported foods (Ramakrishnan T. et al. 2022). The rise of supermarkets, restaurants, and online food delivery services fuels international food trade and supply chain expansion. E-Commerce and Online Food Delivery: Digital platforms such as grocery delivery apps and meal-kit services have become dominant in urban food markets. This has altered traditional food supply chains, requiring new logistics strategies and cold storage solutions (Casari S., et al, 2022). Pressure on Smallholder Farmers: Traditional often struggle meet volume, consistency demands urban food markets. Larger agribusinesses and commercial farms are better positioned to supply urban retailers, potentially marginalizing small farmers.

Supply Chain Adaptations and Challenges: Need for Cold Storage and Efficient Logistics: Perishable food items, such as dairy and fresh produce, require improved storage and distribution systems. Investment in cold chain logistics (refrigerated transport and warehouses) is crucial to prevent food spoilage. Increase in Food Imports and Global Trade: Urban food preferences have expanded the international trade of food products. Countries with high urbanization rates increasingly depend on imported food items, raising concerns about food security and trade balance. Food Waste and Sustainability Issues: Urban food systems generate higher levels of food waste due to inefficient distribution, consumer behavior, and packaging waste. Governments and businesses must implement strategies to reduce food waste and promote sustainable consumption. Environmental and Sustainability Implications: Impact on Land and Water Resources: Urban food demand drives agricultural expansion and resource use in several ways. Deforestation for Agricultural Expansion: Increased livestock and crop production often leads to deforestation and biodiversity loss. Water Scarcity: Intensive agriculture to meet urban demand strains water resources, particularly in regions with high meat and dairy consumption. Carbon Footprint of Urban Food Systems: Longer Supply Chains Increase Carbon Emissions Transporting food over long distances from rural areas to cities contributes to higher greenhouse gas emissions. Urban-driven food imports further add to the carbon footprint of the global food system. High Energy Use in Food Processing and Packaging: Urban demand for processed and packaged foods increases energy consumption in manufacturing and packaging industries (De Bruin S., et al, 2021). Cities are investing in food waste reduction programs, including composting, food recovery networks, and sustainable packaging solutions. Policy and Market Responses: Government Regulations and Support: Encouraging Sustainable Agriculture: Policies promoting organic farming, regenerative agriculture, and sustainable livestock management can help balance food demand with environmental concerns. Investing in Food Infrastructure: Governments must support the development of efficient food supply chains, cold storage facilities, and food processing industries (Ren Y., et al, 2021).

THE IMPACT OF AGING POPULATIONS ON AGRICULTURAL MARKETS: LABOR SHORTAGES AND CHANGING CONSUMER PREFERENCES

This discussion explores how labor shortages and changing consumer preferences, driven by demographic shifts, are influencing agricultural markets worldwide. Labor Shortages and Their Impact on Agricultural Production: Labor Force Decline in Agriculture: As populations age, fewer young people are entering the agricultural workforce. Agriculture, especially in developed countries, is increasingly becoming an industry with an older workforce, which presents serious challenges for agricultural productivity. In many advanced economies, farming is seen as a low-status, physically demanding profession, and young workers are willing to enter the field (Moschis G P., et al, 2022). The combination of an aging workforce and the reluctance of younger generations to pursue farming is contributing to labor shortages, which can result in higher production costs, reduced output, and less flexibility in responding to changing market conditions. In countries like Japan, Italy, and Germany, where the aging population is particularly pronounced, the agricultural sector is facing acute labor shortages. As elderly farmers retire, there are insufficient replacements to take on their responsibilities. This creates a productivity gap and can lead to decreased agricultural output, particularly in labor-intensive sectors like crop farming, dairy production, and horticulture. Impact on Rural Communities and Farm Labor

Availability: Rural communities, where agriculture is often the mainstay of the economy, are feeling the effects of this labor shortage most acutely. Young people are migrating to urban centers for better job opportunities, and many of those who remain in rural areas are older and nearing retirement. This migration results in a loss of vital labor and intellectual capital, further exacerbating the challenges facing the agricultural industry. Moreover, the scarcity of labor in rural areas can lead to higher wages for farmworkers, driving up the cost of production. These rising labor costs can reduce the profitability of farming and make it less competitive, especially when compared to regions with abundant labor or mechanized farming solutions (Mahadev Madgule, et al. 2023). Technological Innovations and Automation: One solution to the labor shortage is the increasing use of technology and automation in agriculture. However, capital and those with limited access to financing. In addition, there are concerns about the potential displacement of workers, particularly in regions where technology cannot fully replace the labor required for specific tasks (Addessi W., et al, 2024).

Changing Consumer Preferences and Their Impact on Food Demand: As populations age, consumer preferences are shifting in ways that impact agricultural markets. Older consumers tend to have different dietary needs, health considerations, and purchasing behaviors compared to younger populations. Farmers are increasingly focusing on high-quality, nutrient-dense crops, as well as offering food options that cater to the growing demand for health and wellness products (Christiaensen L., et al, 2021). Moreover, older consumers may prefer smaller portion sizes or ready-to-eat meals due to limited cooking ability or time constraints. Convenient, pre-packaged foods, ready meals, and meal kits. Agricultural markets must adapt to these changing preferences by offering value-added products that cater to the aging population's need for convenience, nutrition, and ease of preparation. Preference for Local and Sustainable Foods: Older consumers are also showing a preference for locally produced, sustainable, and environmentally friendly foods. Supporting local farmers, practices, and products that have minimal environmental impact. This shift reflects a broader societal concern about food sustainability and the environmental footprint of agriculture. Simultaneously, there is a growing interest in alternative proteins, or lab-grown meats, as consumers seek healthier and more sustainable food options (Mehrotra S., et al, 2021). Agricultural markets are responding by investing in the production of alternative protein sources and exploring the potential of cellular agriculture and other innovative food technologies. The aging population agricultural markets. The labor shortages, reduced workforce participation, and changing consumer preferences create pressure on agricultural production and supply chains.

THE IMPACT OF DEMOGRAPHIC SHIFTS ON FOOD SECURITY: CHALLENGES AND OPPORTUNITIES

Global demographic shifts—characterized by population growth, aging populations, urbanization, and migration—are reshaping the landscape of and demographics evolve, systems are confronted with both challenges and opportunities that will impact their ability to and changing concept food security multi-faceted, only United Nations defines as existing “when all people, at all times, have physical, social, and economic access to sufficient, safe, and nutritious food that meets their dietary needs and food preferences for an active and healthy life.” Achieving this ideal amidst demographic shifts requires addressing a variety of challenges, including labor shortages, resource scarcity, environmental pressures, and evolving consumer needs, while also seizing the opportunities that these changes bring, such as technological advancements, improved efficiency, and more sustainable food systems. Challenges to Food Security Amid Demographic Shifts: Population Growth and Increased Demand for Food: The most obvious and pressing demographic shift is the continued growth of the global population. much of this. The increase in population translates directly into higher demand for food (Aschemann-Witzel J., et al, 2021). the world by 2050.This increased demand for food presents a major challenge, particularly as agricultural land and water resources are already under significant pressure. few, arable land has steadily declined due to urbanization, deforestation, and land degradation. Additionally, precipitation further complicating efforts expansion urban areas conversion agricultural land for other purposes only intensifies the strain on available resources, leaving food producers with limited options to meet rising demand. Labor Shortages and Workforce Challenges: As discussed in previous sections, demographic shifts also affect the availability of labor in the agricultural sector. Aging populations, particularly in developed nations, have decreased the number of young people entering agriculture. At the same time, the physical demands and low status of agricultural work discourage younger generations from pursuing farming as a profession. This has resulted in labor shortages in rural areas, which are especially problematic in developing countries where agriculture still plays a dominant role in the economy. In many cases, aging farmers are either retiring without replacements or continuing to work beyond the typical retirement age, which can negatively affect productivity. Labor shortages are particularly challenging in labor-intensive sectors such as vegetable farming, fruit picking, and livestock care (Johri S., et al. 2025). The reduction in available workers directly impacts food production, as fewer people are available to maintain and harvest crops, manage livestock, or process food. The aging of the global population, particularly in high-income countries, introduces a range of challenges related to food preferences and nutritional needs. As people age, they tend to consume fewer calories and require foods that are more easily digestible, lower in salt, sugar, and fat, and higher in nutrients that support aging bodies, such as calcium, fiber, and antioxidants (Erenstein O., et al, 2022).

Opportunities for Food Security Amid Demographic Shifts: Technological Innovation in Agriculture: One of the most promising opportunities to address the challenges posed by demographic shifts is the rapid advancement of agricultural technologies. Innovations (GM), vertical farming, and agroecology offer ways to increase food production sustainably while reducing resource usage. Precision farming techniques, for example, drones, sensor technologies, water fertilizer usage, and minimizing environmental impact. These technologies help maximize the efficiency of existing agricultural systems in smaller spaces. Additionally, biotechnology and genetically modified crops can help address issues, making food systems more resilient to climate change and population growth. Lab-grown meat can also provide sustainable food options for a growing population. The commercialization and scaling of these innovations hold enhance face both growing demand and environmental challenges. Improved Food Distribution Systems: As urbanization continues to reshape food security, there are opportunities to develop more resilient, efficient, and equitable food distribution systems. Digital platforms for food present opportunities to reach underserved populations, reduce food waste, and increase fresh food (Wendimu G Y., et al, 2021). Policy Responses and Global Cooperation: food security amid demographic changes. Policy interventions that focus on improving agricultural productivity, ensuring fair trade practices, and investing in sustainable food systems can provide a foundation for long-term food security (Kubatko O., et al, 2023).

FOOD AVAILABILITY, ACCESS, AND UTILIZATION: HOW DEMOGRAPHIC SHIFTS AFFECT FOOD SECURITY

This discussion explores how demographic changes impact the three key areas and examines potential implications for global food systems. Food Availability: Challenges and Opportunities: Increased Demand for Food Production: Grow. Availability is one of the most pressing challenges for food security. much of it occurring in urban areas of developing countries. This population increase directly translates into an increased demand, putting immense pressure on the growing system (Molotoks A., et al, 2021). Growing. The challenges to food availability are compounded by arable land, water, and other agricultural inputs. In many parts of the world, the amount of arable land per capita has been decreasing due to urban expansion, land degradation, and deforestation. Furthermore, resource scarcity, rainfall droughts, floods, and rising temperatures negatively impact crop yields. These environmental pressures, combined with growing food demand, create a significant challenge for ensuring food availability. However, technological innovations offer opportunities to increase food availability in the face of demographic shifts. analytics, sensors, and drones increase crop yields. Additionally, stressors enhance growing in city environments and also present solutions to urban food insecurity by increasing the local production of fresh, nutritious food. Supply Chain Efficiency and Food Storage: efficiency food distribution and storage ensuring food availability. As urbanization accelerates, more food must be transported from rural areas to cities, where a growing proportion of the population resides. However, lengthy supply chains can lead to food losses due to spoilage, especially for perishable foods (Affoh R., et al, 2022). Economic inequality is compounded by limited access to social safety nets, which are often made unaffordable or inaccessible, leading to hunger and malnutrition. In high-income countries, rising income inequality can also limit access to healthy food (Debnath P., et al. 2025).

As demographic shifts alter the structure of populations, they also influence dietary preferences and nutritional needs. For example, as populations age, the dietary needs of individuals change (Owoo N S., et al, 2021). Older adults often require diets that are lower in sodium, sugar, and fat and higher in fiber, vitamins, and minerals to support their changing metabolism. At the same time, dietary patterns are shifting globally due to factors such as urbanization, globalization, and changing consumer preferences. In many developing countries, for example, there is a growing demand for processed, calorie-dense foods as urban populations adopt Western-style diets. This shift toward higher consumption of meats, sugary beverages, and packaged foods is causing diabetes, hypertension, and. In addition, as more people in urban areas join the middle class, there is a greater demand for high-protein foods, especially animal-based products, leading to increased pressure on food systems. However, this shift in dietary preferences may not align with local agricultural capabilities, particularly in countries that face resource constraints, environmental degradation, and climate change-related challenges. In response, we see protein, which offers a sustainable way to meet the changing nutritional demands of populations. Cultural Preferences and Food Traditions: Cultural factors also play a key role in food utilization, as individuals' food choices are often shaped by cultural preferences, beliefs, and traditions. For example, dietary habits vary widely across regions, with certain populations prioritizing vegetarianism, others focusing on meat-heavy diets, and still others relying heavily on grains, legumes, and vegetables (Walker R J., et al, 2021).

THE ROLE OF SUSTAINABLE AGRICULTURE IN ENSURING FOOD SECURITY IN THE FACE OF DEMOGRAPHIC SHIFTS

Increasing Food Production through Sustainable Practices Sustainable agriculture addresses the increasing demand for food driven by demographic shifts through efficient and innovative farming practices. As populations grow, pressing nutritional requirements (Mrabet R., et al, 2023). However, this must be done without further degrading the environment or exhausting natural resources. Conventional farming methods and resources improve yields while minimizing environmental impact. Agroecology, tillage, and enhancing resilience food systems by preserving soil health, reducing improving water-use efficiency. For example, crop rotation and intercropping, which are fundamental components of sustainable agriculture, help incidence leading to more stable yields over time. Additionally, the restoration of organic matter enhances water retention, which agroforestry, another sustainable practice, integrates landscapes, which biodiversity, carbon sequestration, and enhanced soil quality. By utilizing these approaches, sustainable agriculture can increase food production without the need to expand agricultural land, helping to preserve natural ecosystems and mitigate deforestation, a key contributor to biodiversity loss and climate change (Viana C M., et al, 2022). Moreover, sustainable agriculture can help ensure food availability through innovations in farming. Drones and soil sensors inform farmers about crops and the application of fertilizers.

Furthermore, it can contribute to the alleviation of insecurity by improving the economic viability of smallholder farming (Toromade A S., et al, 2024). Smallholder farmers, particularly in developing countries, are often at the forefront of the fight against hunger. By promoting agroecological practices, offering access to better markets, and providing training to smallholder farmers, these efforts improve the livelihoods of rural populations and increase their ability to access and afford healthy food. Social Equity and Food Sovereignty: Sustainable agriculture-only food systems are equitable and inclusive. One of the central tenets of sustainable agriculture is rights own control the production and distribution of food. This approach prioritizes local knowledge, social justice, and the equitable distribution of resources, ensuring that food systems benefit all people, particularly marginalized and vulnerable groups. In the face of demographic shifts, particularly allows retain over reducing may By their food production consumption, agriculture helps people culturally appropriate, and affordable food. Sustainable Agriculture and Food Utilization: Enhancing Nutritional Quality Sustainable agriculture improves utilization, ensuring that the food produced is not only available but also nutritious and safe for consumption. As the global population ages and dietary needs evolve, the food system must adapt to provide healthier, more nutrient-dense foods. Agroecology focuses on producing food that is high in nutrients and free from harmful chemicals, improving the overall nutritional quality of the food supply (Vijayakumar G, et al. 2024). Moreover, it can also promote traditional, culturally appropriate diets that are nutrient-dense and aligned with local food preferences (Liang X., et al, 2022).

REGIONAL IMPACTS OF DEMOGRAPHIC SHIFTS ON AGRICULTURAL MARKETS AND FOOD SECURITY: A COMPARATIVE ANALYSIS

As global demographic shifts—such as population growth, urbanization, aging populations, and migration—reshape societies, the implications for agricultural markets and food security vary significantly across regions. While the broad patterns of demographic change affect all countries, the specific impacts are shaped by regional contexts, including economic development, climate conditions, political stability, and local agricultural practices. These shifts influence food availability, access, and utilization in different ways, leading to region-specific challenges and opportunities for addressing food security. his demographic growth, combined with a rising urban population, presents both significant challenges and opportunities for agricultural markets and food security. As rural-to-urban migration accelerates, there is increasing pressure on food systems to supply growing cities, often resulting in greater dependence on food imports (Van Dijk M., et al, 2021). The promotion of sustainable farming practices, improved irrigation, and better training for will also help ensure that agricultural markets are able (Devaux A., et al, 2021). Asia: Aging Populations, Urbanization, and Food Security Challenges: over and its demographic trends reflect a mix of population growth, aging populations, and rapid urbanization. response to these challenges, many Asian countries are focusing on increasing agricultural productivity through technological innovation, such as precision agriculture, and improving food distribution networks to ensure that food reaches urban populations (Sreenivasulu A., et al. 2022). Sustainable agricultural practices are also being promoted to mitigate environmental degradation, with an emphasis on water-efficient farming and soil conservation. rural areas and low-income urban populations facing challenges in accessing nutritious food.The aging agricultural workforce is a major issue, as many farmers are approaching retirement without sufficient younger generations to replace them. This demographic trend raises sustainability in the region (Rehman A., et al, 2022). Migration, particularly from Eastern Europe, is reshaping food security dynamics in Europe. The Aging population in North America is leading to labor shortages in agriculture, as fewer young people are entering farming as a profession. In addition, the growing demand for food, particularly plant-based and sustainably produced food, is driving changes in agricultural practices (Junaid M D., et al, 2024). To ensure global sustainability, regional policies must address the area while promoting collaboration and knowledge sharing across borders.

COUNTRY-SPECIFIC IMPACTS OF DEMOGRAPHIC SHIFTS ON AGRICULTURAL MARKETS AND FOOD SECURITY: CASE STUDIES

Challenges: India's agricultural sector, which employs around 50% of the workforce, faces numerous challenges exacerbated by demographic changes. Rapid urbanization has led to a reduction in arable land, as cities expand and agricultural areas are converted for housing and infrastructure (Iannotti L., et al, 2024). To address the challenges of urbanization, India is also promoting urban farming initiatives and the development of farmers' markets in cities, which can help shorten supply chains and improve food access in urban areas (Djeufack Dongmo A., et al, 2024). This shortage has led to a reliance on older farming techniques, which are less efficient and less sustainable. Additionally, Japan imports a significant portion of its food, which makes its food system vulnerable to global supply chain disruptions (Aragani, V M., et al. 2025). The aging population also changes dietary preferences, with older individuals typically consuming fewer calories and preferring softer, easier-to-eat foods, which affects the types of food produced and consumed in Japan. By adopting climate-resilient farming techniques and integrating more sustainable practices, Brazil can mitigate the environmental impacts of its agricultural sector and ensure long-term food security (Fayad D., et al, 2023). The government and civil society organizations are also working to improve food access through which provides nutritious children in schools. government has implemented programs to promote through weather events. Kenya is also encouraging urban farming and vertical farming in cities and improving access in urban areas (Pickson R B., et al, 2022).

THE IMPACT OF DEMOGRAPHIC SHIFTS ON AGRICULTURAL MARKETS AND FOOD SECURITY IN DEVELOPING COUNTRIES

Population growth is one of the most significant demographic trends impacting agricultural markets and United Nations, population global South more than people between 2020 and sub-Saharan This rapid population increase places immense pressure on agricultural systems to produce more food, often with limited access to resources like land, water, and capital. For instance, the rising demand for grains, fruits, vegetables, and animal-based products is changing the structure of agricultural production. often adapt to these shifts due to modern farming technologies and insufficient access to markets (Musa S F P D., et al, 2021). This creates logistical challenges in terms of food supply chains, distribution infrastructure, and market access for smallholder farmers. Moreover, urbanization creates a divide between rural and urban food systems, leading to disparities in food access (Mutale-Joan C., et al, 2023). Although developing countries are generally characterized by younger populations compared to developed countries, certain regions are beginning to experience demographic shifts related to aging. For example, in East Asia, increasing life expectancy coupled with declining fertility rates are leading to older populations (Sugumaran K M D., et al. 2024). On the other hand, migration can also offer opportunities for remittances to support rural households and local economies, especially in countries where migrants send money back to their families (Smyth S J., et al, 2021). CSA practices such as crop diversification, agroforestry, improved irrigation techniques, and seeds while reducing environmental impacts (Sundram P., et al, 2023). In addition, investments in refrigeration and storage are improving food distribution and reducing waste. Can key financial support technical assistance to and food systems.

POLICY RESPONSES TO DEMOGRAPHIC SHIFTS: IMPLICATIONS FOR AGRICULTURAL MARKETS AND FOOD SECURITY

Demographic shifts, rapid aging populations, and migration present significant challenges to agricultural markets and food security, particularly. However, shifts reforming agricultural policies are improving food systems to meet the evolving needs of societies. Policies should support smallholder farmers, who are the backbone of food production in many developing countries, through access to modern farming technologies, high-quality inputs, extension services, and financial support (Mustafa M A., et al, 2021). One key policy approach is to promote urban agriculture (Shende A D., et al. 2025). As populations age, there is a reduction in the available labor force for agriculture, leading to potential labor shortages in rural areas. This challenge is compounded by the fact that older populations often have different dietary needs and preferences, requiring a shift in food production to meet their needs for more easily digestible foods, smaller portions, and nutrient-dense diets. One important policy response is to address labor shortages in agriculture (Tamasiga P., et al, 2023). Climate Change, Demographic Shifts, and Policy Synergies: in context of demographic shifts (World Health Organization, 2022). Policies must prioritize the inclusion of these groups in agricultural development, food systems, and decision-making processes (Farooq A., et al, 2023). Empowering women equally to land, resources, and technology is essential in improving agricultural productivity and food security. Including assistance and hunger malnutrition among vulnerable populations.

INNOVATIVE PRACTICES IN AGRICULTURE: HOW TO ADDRESS THE CHALLENGES OF DEMOGRAPHIC SHIFTS

Precision agriculture tools, remote sensing, drones, gather crop, soil conditions, environmental factors. Planting, fertilization, pest control, harvesting. Particularly relevant context of demographic shifts, as these technologies help increase productivity and reduce waste, and labor, critical inputs that are becoming increasingly scarce as population growth and climate change strain natural resources (Xia L., et al, 2022). For example, soil farmers irrigate crops more efficiently, reducing water usage and minimizing the risk of drought-related crop failures. In water resources such as arid regions in Africa and Asia, which face both increasing populations and worsening climate conditions. Moreover, agroecological practices contribute to carbon sequestration, making them an effective strategy for mitigating the impact of climate change, which disproportionately affects regions with high levels of food insecurity. In regions experiencing rapid urbanization, agroecological practices can also support urban farming initiatives, such as community gardens and rooftop farming, which help increase access to fresh, local food in cities (Von Cramon-Taubadel S., et al, 2022).

Vertical Farming and Controlled-Environment Agriculture: address and scarcity. These technologies enable food production areas to grow rapidly. Often, this allows for high-density food production in small spaces, such as warehouses, rooftops, or abandoned buildings. CEA takes this concept further by creating optimal growing conditions for crops through the use of climate-regulated systems that control temperature, humidity, light, and CO2 levels. This method produce food external farming and CEA significantly increase food production in cities, reduce reliance on rural contribute local urban areas. Key advantages vertical farming and CEA include reduced water usage (since these systems typically use recirculating water systems), minimized land use, and the ability to grow a variety of crops in diverse climates. This approach also helps Furthermore, vertical farming provides opportunities for urban communities to engage in fresh, nutritious food in deserts or underserved areas (Galanakis C M., et al, 2024). Smart Irrigation Systems: Smart irrigation systems have become essential in addressing agricultural water use. Automated irrigation controls ensure that crops receive the necessary hydration while conserving water, which is critical in regions experiencing water scarcity. In regions experiencing rapid population growth, where urbanization and agricultural expansion put additional strain on water supplies, irrigation helps ensure that agricultural systems remain sustainable and resilient. Furthermore, these systems can support the efficient use of water in both rural and urban farming practices, helping food populations. Blockchain and Traceability in Food Supply Chains: The adoption of blockchain and traceability in food supply chains is another innovative practice that addresses challenges in agricultural markets, particularly in the context of urbanization and demand. Blockchain provides tracking movement food products through quality, safety food. Blockchain technology can improve food security by reducing fraud, increasing the efficiency of supply chains, and preventing foodborne illnesses (Du M., et al, 2025).

THE ROLE OF INTERNATIONAL COOPERATION IN ADDRESSING THE IMPACTS OF DEMOGRAPHIC SHIFTS ON AGRICULTURAL MARKETS AND FOOD SECURITY

International organizations play key roles in facilitating cooperation between countries. These organizations help identify and disseminate successful agricultural precision farming that can enhance food production while minimizing environmental impact. By sharing best practices from regions that have successfully dealt with similar demographic challenges, countries can avoid costly trial-and-error processes and accelerate the adoption of sustainable agricultural techniques that enhance food security (Erenstein O., et al, 2022). Moreover, global agricultural research centers that new improving soil health, increasing productivity in smallholder farming systems, provide invaluable contributions to international efforts aimed at addressing food insecurity. However, international trade policies must be carefully designed to ensure that they do not undermine local agricultural production or exacerbate food insecurity in vulnerable regions. Trade liberalization, if not properly managed, can lead to market disruptions, price volatility, and reduced agricultural incomes for smallholder farmers. Therefore, it is essential to engage in fair trade agreements that prioritize the interests of both producers and consumers and include safeguards for food security (Giller K E., et al, 2021).

Global cooperation on labor migration can help facilitate the movement of agricultural workers between countries, ensuring that agricultural labor shortages are addressed while also protecting migrant workers' rights (Abay K A., et al, 2023). Decent work must be a priority in international agreements on labor migration. Additionally, countries can collaborate to provide training programs for migrant workers they need to improve agricultural productivity. Moreover, degradation, and creating sustainable livelihoods in rural areas. International cooperation can support initiatives aimed at improving rural development, enhancing local food systems, and creating economic opportunities in rural communities, thereby reducing the pressure on agricultural labor markets and improving food security. Global Governance and Policy Coordination: Multifaceted demographic shifts on coordinated governance policy frameworks are essential. International organizations, such as the WTO, play crucial roles in facilitating dialogue, setting international standards, and promoting policy coordination among countries (Gruère G P., et al, 2021). The complexity and interdependence of these challenges require coordinated global efforts that foster knowledge sharing, improve trade systems, provide humanitarian assistance, address climate change, and manage migration. By working together, countries can create a changing global population while promoting sustainability and equity. Through collective action and collaboration, international cooperation can ensure that the world's agricultural markets and food systems remain capable of providing sufficient, nutritious, and accessible food for all, now and in the future.

THE IMPACT OF GLOBAL DEMOGRAPHIC SHIFTS ON AGRICULTURAL MARKETS AND FOOD SECURITY - A CALL TO ACTION

The demographic shifts occurring in the 21st century, including rapid population growth, urbanization, aging populations, migration, and evolving dietary preferences, markets These shifts present both challenges and opportunities for countries around the world, particularly in how they adapt their agricultural systems changing while addressing environmental sustainability, resource constraints, and socio-economic inequalities. The agricultural sector must rise to the challenge of ensuring and promoting equitable nutrition and safeguarding resilience. This shift complicates supply chain logistics, making food access more tenuous in cities that rely on long-distance transportation from rural regions. Moreover, the impact of climate change exacerbates these demographic shifts, as erratic weather patterns, droughts, and floods threaten agricultural productivity, further straining global food systems. Consequently, the challenge is not simply one of feeding more people but doing so sustainably and equitably, ensuring that food systems remain resilient, adaptive, and capable of diversity (Dietrich S., et al, 2022).

FUTURE DIRECTIONS: PREPARING FOR THE CHALLENGES AND OPPORTUNITIES OF DEMOGRAPHIC SHIFTS IN AGRICULTURAL MARKETS AND FOOD SECURITY

This necessitates rapid adoption of cutting-edge technologies that can. Precision agriculture and robotics are at the forefront of a revolution, enabling optimal use, thus increasing efficiency and reducing waste. Technologies like gene editing (e.g., CRISPR) hold yields, disease resistance, and drought tolerance, which are crucial as climate change continues to affect agricultural outputs (Hassan Z U., et al, 2023). Agencies and investors fund and implement large-scale climate-adaptation programs, including infrastructure improvements, early warning systems for weather-related disasters, and programs to assist farmers in transitioning to sustainable and climate-resilient farming techniques (Kraklow V., et al, 2024). Governments and organizations must invest in programs that promote healthier diets, especially in low-income and rural communities, where access to nutritious food may be limited (Erenstein O., et al, 2022). As demographic shifts lead to greater disparities in food access and wealth, the future of agricultural markets and food security will depend on creating more inclusive and equitable food systems. Ensuring that marginalized populations, including smallholder farmers, women, indigenous communities, and the resources, technology, and markets necessary thrive is critical to addressing food insecurity (Giller K E., et al, 2021). Future strategies must prioritize equity, agricultural innovation, and sustainable practices fairly. Through targeted investments, such as funding for infrastructure development, climate adaptation programs, and agricultural research, international cooperation can help sustainably counter the pressures of demographic shifts (Jiuhardi J., et al, 2022).

CONCLUSION

Another opportunity lies in addressing the aging workforce through technological innovation. Automated machinery and robotics in the agricultural sector reduce the reliance on manual labor and enable older farmers or those with fewer labor resources to remain productive. By improving efficiencies and reducing labor costs, these innovations can help mitigate the effects of labor shortages, particularly in aging rural populations. Finally, international cooperation in sharing knowledge, technology, and financial resources offers the possibility of addressing many of the structural inequalities in food production systems. Global partnerships, such as those between international organizations, research institutions, and actors, are pivotal in equipping farmers in countries with skills demographic. Policymakers must prioritize agricultural sustainability, equitable access to resources, and resilience to demographic pressures in their agendas. This includes supporting policies that promote innovation in agriculture, strengthen rural economies, and ensure the equitable distribution of food. Governments must invest to encourage food production and distribution. Moreover, policies that promote the integration of environmental sustainability and climate change adaptation into agricultural practices are crucial. Supporting the transition to agroecology, climate-smart agriculture will not only help but also in the face of demographic challenges. At the same time, governments need to prioritize policies that ensure food accessibility and affordability for all populations, particularly the most vulnerable. This includes expanding social safety nets, investing in food distribution infrastructure, and supporting urban and peri-urban farming initiatives. Addressing the demographic shifts that markets food security requires, the global community must collaborate to foster an agricultural environment that is not only productive but also sustainable, equitable, and resilient. Global partnerships, investments in technology and infrastructure, and innovative policy frameworks are all essential to addressing the complex, interconnected challenges of population growth, urbanization, aging populations, and shifting dietary patterns. The urgency of this call to action cannot be overstated. Pressures on agricultural systems intensify, and the need for innovation, sustainability, and collaboration in agricultural markets becomes more critical than ever. By coming together to address the impacts of demographic shifts, we can ensure that agricultural systems remain capable of growing while safeguarding resources. Food security in a rapidly changing world will require bold actions, sustained investment, and a shared commitment to a food system that works for all. The time to act is now.

REFERENCES

Abay, K. A., Breisinger, C., Glauber, J., & Kurdi, S. (2023). The Russia-Ukraine war: Implications for global and regional food security and potential policy responses. *Food Security*, *15*(2), 257–276. DOI: 10.1007/s12571-023-01311-6

Addessi, W., & Sallusti, F. (2024). *Consumer preferences and changes in the labour market*. Handbook on Labour Markets in Transition, Elgar Online. DOI: 10.4337/9781839106958.00016

Affoh, R., Zheng, H., Dangui, K., & Dissani, B. M. (2022). The impact of climate variability and change on food security in sub-Saharan Africa: Perspective from panel data analysis. *Sustainability (Basel)*, *14*(11), 6556. DOI: 10.3390/su14020759

Aragani, V. M., Anumolu, V. R., & Selvakumar, P. (2025). Democratization in the Age of Algorithms: Navigating Opportunities and Challenges. In Wongmahesak, K., Wekke, I., Seftyono, C., & Nurdin, N. (Eds.), *Democracy and Democratization in the Age of AI* (pp. 39–56). IGI Global Scientific Publishing., DOI: 10.4018/979-8-3693-8749-8.ch003

Aryal, J. P., Manchanda, N., & Sonobe, T. (2022). Expectations for household food security in the coming decades: A global scenario. *Future Foods: a Dedicated Journal for Sustainability in Food Science*, *4*, 100093. DOI: 10.1016/j.fufo.2022.100093

Aschemann-Witzel, J., Gantriis, R. F., & Fraga, P. (2021). Plant-based food and protein trend from a business perspective: Markets, consumers, and the challenges and opportunities in the future. *Trends in Food Science & Technology*, *116*, 95–106. DOI: 10.1016/j.tifs.2021.06.038 PMID: 32654499

Barrett, C. B. (2021). Overcoming global food security challenges through science and solidarity. *American Journal of Agricultural Economics*, *103*(3), 1071–1084. DOI: 10.1111/ajae.12160

Casari, S., Di Paola, M., Banci, E., Diallo, S., Scarallo, L., Renzo, S., Gori, A., Renzi, S., Paci, M., de Mast, Q., Pecht, T., Derra, K., Kaboré, B., Tinto, H., Cavalieri, D., & Lionetti, P. (2022). Changing dietary habits: The impact of urbanization and rising socio-economic status in families from Burkina Faso in Sub-Saharan Africa. *Nutrients*, *14*(11), 2216. DOI: 10.3390/nu14091782 PMID: 35565752

Christiaensen, L., Rutledge, Z., & Taylor, J. E. (2021). The future of work in agri-food. *Food Policy*, *101*, 102043. DOI: 10.1016/j.foodpol.2021.102043 PMID: 33071436

Daszkiewicz, T. (2022). Food production in the context of global developmental challenges. *Agriculture*, *12*(11), 1863. DOI: 10.3390/agriculture12060832

De Bruin, S., Dengerink, J., & van Vliet, J. (2021). Urbanisation as driver of food system transformation and opportunities for rural livelihoods. *Food Security*, *13*(5), 1031–1044. DOI: 10.1007/s12571-021-01182-8 PMID: 34221191

Debnath, P., Deshmukh, S. M., Laroia, M., Selvakumar, P., Manjunath, T. C., & Bhattacharya, S. (2025). Challenges Faced by Countries in Renewable Energy Adoption. In Özsungur, F., Chaychi Semsari, M., & Küçük Bayraktar, H. (Eds.), *Geopolitical Landscapes of Renewable Energy and Urban Growth* (pp. 295–320). IGI Global Scientific Publishing., DOI: 10.4018/979-8-3693-8814-3.ch010

Devaux, A., Goffart, J. P., Kromann, P., Andrade-Piedra, J. L., Polar, V., & Hareau, G. (2021). The potato of the future: Opportunities and challenges in sustainable agri-food systems. *Potato Research*, *64*(2), 257–276. DOI: 10.1007/s11540-021-09501-4 PMID: 34334803

Dietrich, S., Giuffrida, V., & Martorano, B. (2022). COVID-19 policy responses, mobility, and food prices. *Journal of Agricultural Economics*, *73*(2), 257–276. DOI: 10.1111/1477-9552.12453

Djeufack Dongmo, A., & Avom, D. (2024). Urbanization, civil conflict, and the severity of food insecurity in Africa. *Politics & Policy*, *52*(2), 257–276. DOI: 10.1111/polp.12572

Du, M., Lei, J., & Li, S. (2025). Navigating the Path to Food Security in China: Challenges, Policies, and Future Directions. *Foods*, *14*(1), 151. DOI: 10.3390/foods14040644 PMID: 40002086

Erenstein O, Jaleta M, Mottaleb K A. (2022). "Global trends in wheat production, consumption and trade". Food Security in a Changing Climate, 257-276.

Erenstein, O., Jaleta, M., Sonder, K., Mottaleb, K. A., & Prasanna, B. M. (2022). Global maize production, consumption and trade: Trends and R&D implications. *Food Security*, *14*(2), 357–373. DOI: 10.1007/s12571-022-01288-7

Farooq, A., Farooq, N., Akbar, H., Hassan, Z. U., & Gheewala, S. H. (2023). A critical review of climate change impact at a global scale on cereal crop production. *Agronomy (Basel)*, *13*(1), 151. DOI: 10.3390/agronomy13010162

Fayad D. (2023). "Food insecurity and climate shocks in Madagascar: Republic of Madagascar".

Galanakis, C. M. (2024). The future of food. *Foods*, *13*(2), 332. DOI: 10.3390/foods13020332 PMID: 38397483

Giller, K. E., Delaune, T., Silva, J. V., Descheemaeker, K., van de Ven, G., Schut, A. G. T., van Wijk, M., Hammond, J., Hochman, Z., Taulya, G., Chikowo, R., Narayanan, S., Kishore, A., Bresciani, F., Teixeira, H. M., Andersson, J. A., & van Ittersum, M. K. (2021). The future of farming: Who will produce our food? *Food Security*, *13*(5), 1031–1044. DOI: 10.1007/s12571-021-01184-6

Giller, K. E., Delaune, T., Silva, J. V., van Wijk, M., Hammond, J., Descheemaeker, K., van de Ven, G., Schut, A. G. T., Taulya, G., Chikowo, R., & Andersson, J. A. (2021). Small farms and development in sub-Saharan Africa: Farming for food, for income or for lack of better options? *Food Security*, *13*(5), 1031–1044. DOI: 10.1007/s12571-021-01209-0

Gruère, G. P., & Brooks, J. (2021). Characterising early agricultural and food policy responses to the outbreak of COVID-19. *Food Policy*, *101*, 102043. DOI: 10.1016/j.foodpol.2020.102017 PMID: 33390644

Gu, D., Andreev, K., & Dupre, M. E. (2021). Major trends in population growth around the world. *China CDC Weekly*, *3*(2), 33–36. DOI: 10.46234/ccdcw2021.160 PMID: 34594946

Hemathilake, D., & Gunathilake, D. (2022). Agricultural productivity and food supply to meet increased demands. *Future Foods: a Dedicated Journal for Sustainability in Food Science*, *4*, 100094. DOI: 10.1016/j.fufo.2022.100094

Iannotti, L., Kleban, E., & Fracassi, P. (2024). Evidence for policies and practices to address global food insecurity. *Annual Review of Nutrition*, *44*, 19–40. DOI: 10.1146/annurev-nutr-122221-014648 PMID: 38166503

Jie, H., Khan, I., Alharthi, M., Zafar, M. W., & Saeed, A. (2023). Energy policy, socio-economic development, and ecological footprint: The economic significance of natural resources, population growth, and industrial development. *Utilities Policy*, *79*, 101094. DOI: 10.1016/j.jup.2023.101490

Jiuhardi J, Hasid Z, Darma S. (2022). "Sustaining agricultural growth: traps of socio–demographics in emerging markets".

Johri, S., Selvakumar, P., Satyanarayana, P., Das, A., Gupta, S., & Bhattacharya, S. (2025). Urbanization and Energy: The Nexus of Global Challenges. In Özsungur, F., Chaychi Semsari, M., & Küçük Bayraktar, H. (Eds.), *Geopolitical Landscapes of Renewable Energy and Urban Growth* (pp. 453–478). IGI Global Scientific Publishing., DOI: 10.4018/979-8-3693-8814-3.ch016

Junaid, M. D., & Gokce, A. F. (2024). Global agricultural losses and their causes. *Journal of Biological and Allied Sciences Research*, *13*(1), 1–12.

Kraklow V, Paff K, Comeau D, Solander K, Pitts T. (2024). "Impact of Drought on Global Food Security by 2050".

Kubatko O, Merritt R, Duane S. (2023). "The impact of the COVID-19 pandemic on global food system resilience". Mechanism of an Action, 1-14.

Liang, X., Jin, X., Han, B., Sun, R., Xu, W., Li, H., He, J., & Li, J. (2022). China's food security situation and key questions in the new era: A perspective of farmland protection. *Journal of Geographical Sciences*, *32*(8), 1285–1303. DOI: 10.1007/s11442-022-1982-9

Mahadev Madgule, N. (2023). Vinayaka, Yeshwant M. Sonkhaskar, Dhiren Ramanbhai Patel, R. Karthikeyan, P. Selvakumar, (2023). Mechanical properties and microstructure of activated TIG welded similar joints of Inconel alloys by desirability approaches. *Materials Today: Proceedings*, *77*, 528–533. DOI: 10.1016/j.matpr.2022.12.250

March, A., & Failler, P. (2022). Small-scale fisheries development in Africa: Lessons learned and best practices for enhancing food security and livelihoods. *Marine Policy*, *136*, 104824. DOI: 10.1016/j.marpol.2021.104925

Mason, A., Lee, R., & Network, N. T. A. (2022). Six ways population change will affect the global economy. *Population and Development Review*, *48*(2), 257–276. DOI: 10.1111/padr.12469

Mehrotra, S., & Parida, J. K. (2021). Stalled structural change brings an employment crisis in India. *The Indian Journal of Labour Economics : the Quarterly Journal of the Indian Society of Labour Economics*, *64*(2), 257–276. DOI: 10.1007/s41027-021-00317-x PMID: 34092956

Molotoks, A., Smith, P., & Dawson, T. P. (2021). Impacts of land use, population, and climate change on global food security. *Food and Energy Security*, *10*(2), e261. DOI: 10.1002/fes3.261

Moschis, G. P. (2022). "Marketing to the aging population". Management for Professionals, Springer. DOI: 10.1007/978-3-031-13097-7

Mrabet R. (2023). "Sustainable agriculture for food and nutritional security". Sustainable Agriculture and the Environment, 157-174.

Musa, S F P. D., & Basir, K. H. (2021). Smart farming: Towards a sustainable agri-food system. *British Food Journal*, *123*(10), 257–276. DOI: 10.1108/BFJ-03-2021-0325

Mustafa M A, Mabhaudhi T, Avvari M V. (2021). "Transition toward sustainable food systems: A holistic pathway toward sustainable development". Food Security and Sustainability, 257-276.

Mutale-Joan, C., Sbabou, L., & Hicham, E. A. (2023). Microalgae and cyanobacteria: How exploiting these microbial resources can address the underlying challenges related to food sources and sustainable agriculture. *Journal of Plant Growth Regulation*, *42*(2), 257–276. DOI: 10.1007/s00344-021-10534-9

Norton, G. W., Alwang, J., & Masters, W. A. (2021). *Economics of agricultural development: world food systems and resource use*. Taylor & Francis. DOI: 10.4324/9780429316999

Oruma, S. O., Misra, S., & Fernandez-Sanz, L. (2021). Agriculture 4.0: An implementation framework for food security attainment in Nigeria's post-Covid-19 era. *IEEE Access : Practical Innovations, Open Solutions*, *9*, 257–276. DOI: 10.1109/ACCESS.2021.3086453

Osareme, O. J., & Muonde, M. (2024). Demographic shifts and healthcare: A review of aging populations and systemic challenges. *International Journal of Scientific Research*, *13*(1), 1–10. DOI: 10.2139/ssrn.3849678

Owoo, N. S. (2021). Demographic considerations and food security in Nigeria. *Journal of Social and Economic Development*, *23*(2), 257–276. DOI: 10.1007/s40847-020-00116-y

Pickson, R. B., & Boateng, E. (2022). Climate change: A friend or foe to food security in Africa? *Environment, Development and Sustainability*, *24*(5), 257–276. DOI: 10.1007/s10668-021-01621-8 PMID: 34276245

Ramakrishnan, T., Mohan Gift, M. D., Chitradevi, S., Jegan, R., & Subha Hency Jose, P. Nagaraja, Rajneesh Sharma HN, Selvakumar P, Sintayehu Mekuria Hailegiorgis, (2022). "Study of Numerous Resins Used in Polymer Matrix Composite Materials", Advances in Materials Science and Engineering, vol. 2022, Article ID 1088926, 8 pages, 2022. https://doi.org/DOI: 10.1155/2022/1088926

Rehman, A., Farooq, M., Lee, D. J., & Siddique, K. H. M. (2022). Sustainable agricultural practices for food security and ecosystem services. *Environmental Science and Pollution Research International*, *29*(10), 15311–15325. DOI: 10.1007/s11356-022-23635-z PMID: 36258111

Ren, Y., Castro Campos, B., Peng, Y., & Glauben, T. (2021). Nutrition transition with accelerating urbanization? Empirical evidence from rural China. *Nutrients*, *13*(15), 2632. DOI: 10.3390/nu13030921 PMID: 33809126

Ruben, R., Cavatassi, R., Lipper, L., Smaling, E., & Winters, P. (2021). Towards food systems transformation—Five paradigm shifts for healthy, inclusive and sustainable food systems. *Food Security*, *13*(5), 1031–1044. DOI: 10.1007/s12571-021-01221-4 PMID: 34667484

Shende, A. D., Tekade, S. A., Deshmukh, A. A., Tembhurkar, S. P., & Selvakumar, P. (2025). Water Quality Monitoring and Control With AI. In Ruiz-Vanoye, J., & Díaz-Parra, O. (Eds.), *Smart Water Technology for Sustainable Management in Modern Cities* (pp. 51–80). IGI Global Scientific Publishing., DOI: 10.4018/979-8-3693-8074-1.ch003

Smyth, S. J., Webb, S. R., & Phillips, P. W. B. (2021). The role of public-private partnerships in improving global food security. *Global Food Security*, *28*, 100494. DOI: 10.1016/j.gfs.2021.100588

Somoye, O. A., Mar'I, M., & Olowu, G. (2025). Does carbon dioxide emission influence food security in the United States amidst economic expansion, population growth, and inflation? A QARDL and Wavelet approach. *Natural Resources Forum*, *49*(1), 257–276. DOI: 10.1111/1477-8947.12422

Sreenivasulu, A., & Manimozhi, T. Satheesh kumar P, Selvakumar P. and Singh P, (2022). "The Model of Smart Sensing Device For Sensitive Nanoclusters Modification in Sensing Properties," 2022 2nd International Conference on Advance Computing and Innovative Technologies in Engineering (ICACITE), Greater Noida, India, 2022, pp. 1043-1047, DOI: 10.1109/ICACITE53722.2022.9823846

Stavi, I., & Roque de Pinho, J. (2022). Food security among dryland pastoralists and agropastoralists: The climate, land-use change, and population dynamics nexus. *Anthropocene*, *37*, 100313. DOI: 10.1016/j.ancene.2022.100313

Sugumaran K M D, Pandiyarajan V Y B S, Selvakumar P. and M. S, (2024). "Analysis of Electromyography Signals for Control of Mechanical Prosthesis using Machine Learning Techniques," 2024 2nd International Conference on Intelligent Data Communication Technologies and Internet of Things (IDCIoT), Bengaluru, India, 2024, pp. 1059-1067, .DOI: 10.1109/IDCIoT59759.2024.10467707

Sundram, P. (2023). Food security in ASEAN: Progress, challenges and future. *Frontiers in Sustainable Food Systems*, *7*, 1095313. DOI: 10.3389/fsufs.2023.1095313

Tamasiga, P., Onyeaka, H., Akinsemolu, A., & Bakwena, M. (2023). The interrelationship between climate change, inequality, poverty and food security in Africa: A bibliometric review and content analysis approach. *Sustainability (Basel)*, *15*(11), 6556. DOI: 10.3390/su15075628

Toromade, A. S., Soyombo, D. A., & Kupa, E. (2024). Reviewing the impact of climate change on global food security: Challenges and solutions. *International Journal of Environmental Sciences and Development*, *15*(1), 1–12.

Van Dijk, M., Morley, T., Rau, M. L., & Saghai, Y. (2021). A meta-analysis of projected global food demand and population at risk of hunger for the period 2010–2050. *Nature Food*, *2*(7), 533–542. DOI: 10.1038/s43016-021-00322-9 PMID: 37117684

Viana, C. M., Freire, D., Abrantes, P., Rocha, J., & Pereira, P. (2022). Agricultural land systems importance for supporting food security and sustainable development goals: A systematic review. *The Science of the Total Environment*, *806*, 150737. DOI: 10.1016/j.scitotenv.2021.150718 PMID: 34606855

Vijayakumar, G. (2024). Muniyandi Rajkumar, Rajiv Chandar N, Selvakumar P and Ramesh Duraisamy, (2024). Environmentally friendly TDS removal from wastewater by electrochemical ion exchange batch-type recirculation (EIR) technique. *Environmental Science. Water Research & Technology*, *10*, 826–835. DOI: 10.1039/D3EW00793F

Von Cramon-Taubadel, S. (2022). Russia's invasion of Ukraine–implications for grain markets and food security. *German Journal of Agricultural Economics*, *71*(2, Supplement), 57–64. DOI: 10.30430/71.2022.5.Apol

Walker, R. J., Garacci, E., Dawson, A. Z., Williams, J. S., Ozieh, M., & Egede, L. E. (2021). Trends in food insecurity in the United States from 2011–2017: Disparities by age, sex, race/ethnicity, and income. *Population Health Management*, *24*(3), 257–266. DOI: 10.1089/pop.2020.0123 PMID: 32941115

Wang, Q., Wang, X., & Li, R. (2022). Does population aging reduce environmental pressures from urbanization in 156 countries? *The Science of the Total Environment*, *807*, 150788. DOI: 10.1016/j.scitotenv.2022.157330 PMID: 35842167

Wang, X., Ma, L., Yan, S., Chen, X., & Growe, A. (2023). Trade for food security: The stability of global agricultural trade networks. *Foods*, *12*(11), 2211. DOI: 10.3390/foods12020271 PMID: 36673361

Wendimu, G. Y. (2021). The challenges and prospects of Ethiopian agriculture. *Cogent Food & Agriculture*, *7*(1), 1907553. DOI: 10.1080/23311932.2021.1907553

World Health Organization. (2022). "WHO global strategy for food safety 2022-2030: towards stronger food safety systems and global cooperation".

Xia, L., Robock, A., Scherrer, K., Harrison, C. S., Bodirsky, B. L., Weindl, I., Jägermeyr, J., Bardeen, C. G., Toon, O. B., & Heneghan, R. (2022). Global food insecurity and famine from reduced crop, marine fishery and livestock production due to climate disruption from nuclear war soot injection. *Nature Food*, *3*(7), 533–542. DOI: 10.1038/s43016-022-00573-0 PMID: 37118594

Zhang, Y., Li, S., Jin, L., & Wu, F. (2022). How will the global food landscape accommodate developing countries' dietary change under urbanization? *Foods*, *11*(15), 2311. DOI: 10.3390/foods11223598 PMID: 36429189

Chapter 6

Economic Impact of Demographic Shifts Amid Labor Automation and Policy Inertia:

Aging vs. Youth in an Automated Global Economy

Namrata Singh
Noida Institute of Engineering and Technology, India

Sabina Sehajpal
https://orcid.org/0009-0004-6655-6279
Chandigarh University, India

ABSTRACT

This study investigates the intricate economic implications arising from global demographic transitions, particularly the dual emergence of aging societies and youth-dense economies, through the lens of labor automation and policy inertia. By analyzing time-series data on robot density and demographic trends across countries, the research explores how rising automation interacts with shifting age structures to reshape labor markets, productivity, and fiscal sustainability. Aging economies face mounting pressures from shrinking workforces and rising dependency ratios, while youth-dense nations struggle with underemployment and the need for large-scale skilling. The study reveals a significant policy gap in adapting automation strategies to demographic realities, risking increased inequality and social instability. The findings underscore the urgency for differentiated, forward-looking labor and

DOI: 10.4018/979-8-3373-2550-7.ch006

education policies tailored to each demographic context. This research aligns with SDGs 8, 4, 10, and 9, offering insights for sustainable economic planning amid global demographic upheavals.

INTRODUCTION

The global economic landscape is undergoing a profound metamorphosis, driven not merely by the forces of financial globalization or technological disruption, but increasingly by the tectonic shifts in demographic compositions across regions. At the heart of this evolving paradigm lies an unprecedented divergence: while advanced economies are grappling with rapidly aging populations and shrinking labor forces, several emerging economies remain ensnared in the paradox of youth bulges, large, underutilized cohorts of working-age individuals confronted with structural unemployment, educational mismatches, and fragile institutional scaffolding (Larsson & Teigland, 2019). This asymmetrical demographic trajectory poses complex implications for global macroeconomic stability, productivity dynamics, labor market equilibrium, fiscal sustainability, and intergenerational equity. Yet, extant literature has seldom synthesized these disparate transitions within a unified analytical framework, often privileging regional or unilateral explorations over systemic global perspectives (K. A. Aksyonov et al., 2016).

Demographic evolution, while ostensibly a slow-moving variable, exerts inexorable pressure on both microeconomic behavior and macroeconomic aggregates. In aging economies such as Japan, Germany, and South Korea, fertility decline and longevity expansion have precipitated a contraction in the economically active population, thus inducing distortions in labor supply, consumption patterns, savings behavior, and public expenditure commitments, particularly in pensions and healthcare (Vakhnin et al., 2018). Conversely, countries in South Asia, Sub-Saharan Africa, and parts of Latin America find themselves at the cusp of a potentially transformative demographic dividend, contingent on their ability to productively absorb burgeoning cohorts of youth into gainful employment. This dichotomy, of labor scarcity in the Global North juxtaposed against labor surplus in the Global South, necessitates a reconceptualization of how demographic shifts interact with economic structures in a globally integrated world (Pai et al., 2025).

What complicates this demographic-economic interface further is the concurrent acceleration of automation and artificial intelligence (AI) technologies, which threatens to reconfigure the very nature of work and human capital relevance. While automation offers productivity enhancements and cost efficiency, it disproportionately displaces routine-intensive jobs, which often constitute the entry points for younger labor market participants in emerging economies. Simultaneously, in aging societies, technological substitution could partially offset the diminishing workforce, yet exacerbate skill-biased inequality and social displacement if not accompanied by robust policy buffers (Markova et al., 2021). This intersection of demography and automation represents a critical, yet under-theorized, inflection point in economic development narratives. The promise of a demographic dividend or the peril of demographic drag is increasingly contingent not on population metrics alone, but on the capacity of institutions to align human capital development with rapidly evolving techno-economic paradigms (Millar, 2021).

Further exacerbating these dynamics is the widespread inertia in policy adaptation. Fiscal frameworks, labor laws, education systems, and immigration protocols remain largely path-dependent, designed for demographic realities of the mid-20th century. For instance, pay-as-you-go pension systems are increasingly untenable in societies with old-age dependency ratios exceeding sustainable thresholds (Trovato et al., 2021). Likewise, youth-heavy economies continue to rely on static curricula and outdated skill-building infrastructures, failing to anticipate the demands of digitally mediated labor markets. This institutional lag, termed here as "policy inertia", magnifies the economic volatility induced by demographic shocks. It also perpetuates allocative inefficiencies in public investment, with ageing economies overburdening future generations through unfunded liabilities, and youth-rich economies squandering potential productivity by underinvesting in early-stage human capital formation (Bonab et al., 2021).

Another dimension that remains inadequately explored is the global redistribution of demographic dividends via channels of trade, capital flows, and migration. As aging economies seek to outsource labor-intensive production and increasingly rely on imported services or care labor, they engage in transnational demographic arbitrage. Similarly, cross-border remittances from youthful migrant workers contribute significantly to the economic resilience of sending countries (Niederer et al., 1980). However, such transfers are inherently volatile and dependent on the political economy of immigration policies, often shaped more by populist sentiment than long-term strategic rationality (Miglani, Taneja, et al., 2025). Furthermore, the demographic disequilibrium between regions may reshape global consumption geographies, with younger populations in Asia and Africa emerging as future demand anchors, thereby altering supply chain configurations and multinational investment strategies.

While numerous econometric models have attempted to forecast the macroeconomic impact of aging or youth surpluses, these approaches often operate in silos, failing to capture the interconnectivity and spillovers inherent in an open global economy. Moreover, the treatment of automation in demographic-economic discourse remains underdeveloped, often confined to either speculative dystopias or narrowly focused productivity analyses (Fischer, 2020). There is a compelling need, therefore, to construct a more integrative theoretical framework that situates demographic transitions within the broader contours of technological change, policy adaptability, and global interdependence.

This research seeks to bridge this critical lacuna by systematically analyzing how divergent demographic trajectories, in both aging and youth-dense economies, mediate their respective economic futures when filtered through the lenses of labor automation and policy inertia. Employing a comparative, cross-regional methodology, the study will investigate the mechanisms through which demographic variables interact with labor-replacing technologies and institutional responsiveness to shape national and global economic outcomes (Otoiu et al., 2022). Particular attention will be paid to labor force participation, wage stagnation, skill polarization, fiscal strain, and capital-labor substitution, as well as the role of migration and international cooperation in mitigating demographic asymmetries.

By integrating demography with automation and governance variables, the study endeavors to contribute both empirically and theoretically to the field of political economy and development studies. It challenges the static assumptions of demographic determinism and instead posits a dynamic, contingent relationship between population structure and economic vitality. The outcomes of this inquiry are not merely of academic interest but bear profound implications for policy architects seeking to future-proof their economies. Whether it is recalibrating pension entitlements in graying societies or revamping vocational ecosystems in youth-dense regions, understanding the economic consequences of demographic change through a multidimensional prism is imperative for sustainable growth and social cohesion in the 21st century.

Table 1. Theoretical Framework

Name of Theory	Explanation of Theory	Relevance to Present Research	Source
Demographic Transition Theory	Describes the shift from high birth/death rates to low rates as countries develop.	Explains how different stages of demographic transition lead to aging or youth-heavy populations, influencing economic outcomes.	(Rust & Huang, 2012)
Dependency Theory	Economic imbalances between core and periphery nations are perpetuated by structural dependencies.	Highlights how youth-dense economies remain trapped in low-skill, low-growth trajectories despite demographic potential.	(Pai et al., 2025)
Solow Growth Model (with demographic extension)	Economic growth is driven by labor, capital, and technology, with population as an exogenous factor.	Serves as a baseline to analyze how demographic shifts impact long-run output through changes in labor and productivity.	(Nesterov, 2023)

continued on following page

Table 1. Continued

Name of Theory	Explanation of Theory	Relevance to Present Research	Source
Lewis Dual Sector Model	Surplus labor from traditional sectors can be transferred to modern sectors to spur growth.	Applied to youth-dense economies, this theory helps explain underutilized labor and the need for structural transformation.	(Sheriyarji, 2019)
Human Capital Theory	Investment in education and skills enhances individual productivity and economic growth.	Justifies the role of policy in converting demographic dividends into economic gains via education and reskilling.	(K. A. Aksyonov et al., 2016)
Skill-Biased Technological Change (SBTC)	Technological change disproportionately benefits skilled workers, widening wage inequality.	Helps analyze how automation affects employment differently in aging vs. youth-rich economies.	(Celentano, 2024)
Institutional Theory	Economic outcomes are shaped by the quality and adaptability of institutions.	Frames the concept of "policy inertia", lagging institutional reforms worsen the impact of demographic shocks.	(Kumar et al., 2025; Miglani, Bhatnagar, et al., 2025; Sharma et al., 2025)
Life-Cycle Hypothesis (LCH)	Individuals plan consumption and savings behavior based on expected lifetime income.	Explains changing consumption/ savings trends in aging societies and their macroeconomic implications.	(Dixit & Bhatnagar, 2025)

Table 1 encapsulates a curated compendium of seminal theoretical frameworks that collectively scaffold the analytical bedrock for understanding the multidimensional ramifications of global demographic asymmetries, particularly the dualistic phenomenon of aging and youth-dense economies. Each theory incorporated within this schema offers a nuanced ontological lens, enabling a layered dissection of structural, economic, institutional, and labor-market dynamics that underpin contemporary demographic shifts.

The **Demographic Transition Theory**, as outlined in *Table 1*, serves as the foundational narrative arc, offering a longitudinal comprehension of how socioeconomic maturation invariably catalyzes transformations in fertility and mortality regimes. The theory situates economies within a continuum of demographic evolution—from high fertility-high mortality equilibria toward low fertility-low mortality plateaus—thereby elucidating the emergent bifurcation between aged, post-transition societies and youth-heavy, pre- or mid-transition polities. This dichotomy is not merely demographic but deeply economic, influencing consumption patterns, labor market composition, and macrostructural policy exigencies. Moving beyond demographic determinism, **Dependency Theory** posits that global economic stratification is perpetuated through historically entrenched asymmetries between the global core and periphery. Within the current context, youth-dense economies—despite harboring abundant demographic capital—remain structurally subservient to the core due to techno-financial dependencies, limited value-chain integration, and epistemic capture in development paradigms. Thus, the mere possession of a favorable age structure is rendered inert without systemic recalibration of institutional and technological architectures. The **Solow Growth Model**, especially when expanded to incorporate demographic variables, is indispensable in framing the exogenous infusion of population dynamics into long-run growth trajectories. A surge in the working-age cohort augments potential output only conditionally—if accompanied by proportional increases in capital deepening and technological absorption. Inversely, in aging societies, stagnating labor force participation, absent compensatory automation or productivity spikes, precipitates secular stagnation. The **Lewis Dual Sector Model** operationalizes labor reallocation from subsistence economies to industrialized enclaves as a conduit for transformation. Youth-abundant nations, however, often struggle with a demographic surplus that lacks effective structural absorption mechanisms. This theoretical framing accentuates the paradox of demographic advantage coexisting with chronic underemployment—a failure of productive transition rather than population excess. **Human Capital Theory** augments this discourse by centering the transformative potential of education, health, and skill augmentation. The theory elucidates how demographic dividends remain unrealized in the absence of concerted investments in cognitive and non-cognitive capabilities that render labor globally competitive. This dovetails with **Skill-Biased Technological Change**, which problematizes automation by demonstrating its asymmetric utility: in aging societies, automation compensates for labor shortages; in youth-heavy contexts, it potentially displaces surplus labor, exacerbating jobless growth and intensifying socioeconomic bifurcation.

Institutional Theory furnishes an endogenous critique, highlighting how governance regimes, policy elasticity, and regulatory agility mediate the translation of demographic realities into macroeconomic trajectories. Institutional sclerosis, path dependency, and lagging reform cycles thus amplify demographic vulnerabilities rather than attenuating them. Lastly, the **Life-Cycle Hypothesis** situates demographic change within behavioral economics, spotlighting the macro-implications of shifting consumption-savings patterns. As aged societies exhibit higher savings propensities and diminished consumption elasticity, demand-side dynamics wane, aggravating deflationary pressures and complicating monetary transmission. In summation, *Table 1* demonstrates that demographic phenomena are not isolated population statistics but deeply embedded within economic systems, requiring a multiplex of theoretical interrogations to unpack their full implications. This necessitates integrative, inter-disciplinary approaches that are attuned to both structural constraints and endogenous capabilities.

In conclusion, demographic change is neither a monolith nor a destiny; it is a variable whose economic salience is magnified or mitigated through the mediating forces of technology and institutional agility. As the global economy tiptoes through the contradictions of labor shortages and youth unemployment, skill surpluses and employment deficits, savings gluts and consumption scarcities, a new paradigm of growth must emerge, one that is not merely reactive to population trends but strategically adaptive to their implications. It is this intellectual and policy imperative that this research seeks to engage with and illuminate.

RESEARCH GAP

The extant body of scholarship, while voluminous in its treatment of demographic transition, automation, and institutional dynamics, remains profoundly fragmented, privileging region-specific, siloed analyses that either isolate aging economies from youth-dense counterparts or examine technological substitution devoid of demographic contextualization. What is conspicuously absent is a coherent, integrative framework that simultaneously interrogates the dialectical interplay between divergent demographic trajectories, labor-displacing automation, and the inertia of policy architectures across heterogeneous national contexts. Existing econometric and theoretical models inadequately capture the cross-regional spillovers, temporal asynchronies, and institutional rigidities that mediate whether demographic asymmetries culminate in dividend or drag. Furthermore, the literature seldom addresses the paradox whereby automation offsets labor scarcity in aging societies even as it exacerbates structural unemployment in youth-heavy economies, thereby generating asymmetric vulnerabilities and uneven developmental pathways. This lacuna underscores the need for a multidimensional, comparative approach that situates demographic change within techno-economic paradigms, institutional elasticity, and global interdependence, thereby moving beyond static determinisms toward a dynamic theorization of demographic-economic futures.

LITERATURE REVIEW

Table 2 synthesizes a compendium of empirical research methodologies and their associated findings that collectively provide a multidimensional understanding of the economic implications of global demographic transitions. The interpretative analysis of this table reveals a consistent and nuanced narrative: demographic dynamics—whether of aging or youth-dense populations—generate deeply variegated economic outcomes, contingent not only on the inherent demographic structure but critically on the mediating role of institutions, technology, and policy responsiveness.

Panel regression analyses across OECD and G20 countries disclose the stark fiscal ramifications of population aging. A salient finding is the inverse relationship between aging and labor force participation, exacerbated in policy environments constrained by static retirement norms and inflexible pension systems (Balabanova et al., 2021). The economic drag manifests not solely through diminished productivity but also via ballooning fiscal outlays, pressuring public finances and compromising intergenerational equity. The temporal inflexibility of welfare institutions appears ill-equipped to adjust to these evolving demographic pressures.

Time-series econometric modeling reveals that youth-dense economies, despite their perceived demographic dividend, are no less vulnerable. Without strategic investment in human capital formation and public education, the demographic surplus transmutes into a liability marked by high structural unemployment (Nielsen et al., 2014). This suggests a fragile equilibrium wherein labor abundance, unaccompanied by absorptive economic structures and social mobility pathways, culminates in socio-economic volatility. Public education expenditure emerges not just as a fiscal allocation but as a strategic lever to convert demographic inertia into economic momentum.

Agent-based simulation models illuminate the disruptive potential of automation as both a compensatory and destabilizing force. In aging societies, automation provides a technological antidote to shrinking labor pools, mitigating productivity declines. However, its uneven deployment across economies with varying skill endowments and education systems engenders widening disparities, polarizing income and employment landscapes. In youth-heavy regions, automation without targeted upskilling programs magnifies existing inequalities and relegates vast segments of the population to technological obsolescence.

The structural equation modeling approach introduces an institutional lens, foregrounding the inertia embedded in policy architectures. Countries that delay reforms in social protection and fiscal adaptability incur cumulative structural deficits. The velocity of demographic transition outpaces institutional response, creating governance disequilibrium that perpetuates stagnation rather than structural transformation. Institutional dynamism, therefore, is not ancillary but central to demographic resilience.

Comparative case studies contrast Japan's aging-automation equilibrium with India’s youth-demographic paradox. The former illustrates how institutional and technological alignment can generate stability in the face of demographic decline, while the latter exemplifies the underutilization of labor due to inadequate employment elasticity and low productivity absorption. The lesson is clear: demographic potential is inert without systemic capacity to integrate human resources into productive paradigms.

Furthermore, CGE models and pooled ARDL analyses reaffirm the importance of labor mobility, foreign investment, and governance architecture. While migration can reallocate demographic pressures, it simultaneously introduces asymmetries in capital flows and social tensions. The African context demonstrates that even with technological penetration, the absence of institutional reform nullifies its potential in addressing youth unemployment.

The overarching synthesis from Table 2 is unequivocal: demographic shifts, in isolation, are neither destiny nor determinism. It is the interplay between human capital, institutional agility, and technological absorption that ultimately determines whether such transitions culminate in economic vitality or vulnerability.

Table 2. Theoretical Framework

Methodology	Variables	Findings	Source
Cross-country panel regression (OECD and G20 countries)	Aging population, labor force participation, pension expenditure, GDP growth	Aging populations are significantly associated with declining labor participation and increased fiscal burden, especially in countries with rigid retirement systems.	(Akbar et al., 2016)
Time-series econometric modeling (ARIMA + VAR)	Youth population ratio, unemployment rate, human capital index, public education expenditure	Countries with youth bulges experience higher unemployment unless accompanied by increased public investment in skill-building and education reforms.	(Knesl, 2023)
Machine learning–based scenario simulations (agent-based modeling)	Automation intensity, median age, dependency ratio, income inequality	Automation can offset aging-induced labor shortages but also exacerbates income and skill inequality in the absence of reskilling programs.	(Bochko et al., 2022)
Structural equation modeling (SEM)	Policy responsiveness, demographic transition speed, fiscal adaptability, social protection coverage	Delays in institutional reforms magnify negative effects of demographic shocks; high policy inertia correlates with long-term economic stagnation.	(Larsson, 2019b)
Comparative case study (Japan vs. India)	Demographic dividend, automation adoption, employment elasticity, productivity growth	Japan's aging and automation equilibrium offers stability, whereas India's demographic dividend remains underutilized due to poor labor absorption capacity.	(Lordos & De Weck, 2018)
Computable General Equilibrium (CGE) modeling	Population structure, labor migration, capital inflows, trade dynamics	Interregional migration partially offsets demographic disequilibrium but leads to uneven capital accumulation and political tensions in host nations.	(K. Aksyonov et al., 2016)

continued on following page

Table 2. Continued

Methodology	Variables	Findings	Source
Pooled Mean Group ARDL analysis (selected African economies)	Youth employment rate, FDI inflows, ICT penetration, institutional quality	Technological development alone does not reduce youth unemployment without accompanying governance improvements and targeted labor policies.	(Tokunova et al., 2023)
Meta-analysis of 35 empirical studies	Aging index, social spending, productivity change, automation resilience	There is no uniform effect of aging on economic decline, policy design, technological adaptation, and institutional capacity mediate outcomes.	(Lin et al., 2024)

METHODOLOGY

The present study adopts a comparative, mixed-methods research design to investigate the asymmetric economic consequences of demographic transitions, namely population aging and youth bulges, across advanced and emerging economies. By integrating quantitative econometric techniques with qualitative institutional diagnostics, the research aims to uncover not only measurable economic outcomes but also the underlying structural and policy-oriented dynamics that mediate the demographic-economy nexus.

At the quantitative level, the study utilizes panel data regression across a dataset comprising select OECD, G20, and Global South economies over a 25-year period (2000–2025). Variables such as old-age dependency ratio, youth population share, labor force participation rate, GDP per capita growth, and public social expenditure are drawn from reputable global datasets including the World Bank, UNDESA, ILO, and IMF. Fixed-effects and random-effects models are applied to control for country-specific heterogeneity. Additionally, Pooled Mean Group (PMG) ARDL models are employed for sub-regional time series estimations to distinguish between short-run volatility and long-run equilibrium relationships.

To examine causality and interdependence among variables such as human capital investment, technological advancement, and demographic structure, Vector Autoregression (VAR) and Impulse Response Function (IRF) analyses are performed. These models help in visualizing the dynamic response of economic output to demographic shocks over time, capturing the lagged effects of policy inertia and technological absorption capacity. For aging economies, Life-Cycle Hypothesis (LCH)-based modeling is incorporated to assess shifts in aggregate consumption and savings behavior. Meanwhile, for youth-dense economies, Lewis-type surplus labor models are adapted to capture labor transfer constraints.

Recognizing the limitations of purely econometric approaches in addressing institutional and political dimensions, the study incorporates a comparative case study framework, with Japan and India as the anchor cases. This dyad was selected due to their starkly contrasting demographic profiles and policy approaches: Japan exemplifies an aging society with high technological penetration, while India represents a youth-majority nation grappling with labor market rigidity and skill gaps. The case studies rely on secondary document analysis, national policy reviews, and development reports to analyze the effectiveness of demographic governance mechanisms in each context.

In addition, the research applies scenario-based simulations using agent-based modeling (ABM) techniques to forecast the economic impacts of demographic transitions under varying policy conditions. These simulations are calibrated using assumptions drawn from the Solow Growth Model (augmented with demographic inputs) and Skill-Biased Technological Change (SBTC) theory, thus allowing for nuanced projections under automation-heavy and automation-light futures.

Finally, to contextualize the quantitative findings within a global theoretical framework, a meta-synthesis of 35 empirical studies is conducted. This step involves coding published literature across multiple regions and economic contexts to triangulate evidence on the mediating role of institutions, education policy, and technological change in shaping demographic outcomes.

Through this robust, triangulated methodological approach, the study endeavors to produce not only statistically significant results but also policy-relevant insights that are sensitive to contextual, institutional, and temporal variances.

ANALYSIS

Table 3. Labour automation worldwide

Year	Global Robot Density (robots per 10 000 employees in manufacturing)	Estimated Operational Stock (millions of robots)	Notes	Source
2013	~74 (doubled within 7 years by 2020)	—	IFR World Robotics trends; 2013 baseline from 2020 comparison	(Larsson, 2019a)
2014	~80 (extrapolated from CAGR)	—	Continuous rise implied between 2013 and 2016	(Zubkova et al., 2019)
2015	~90	—	IFR reports 66 in 2015 rising to 126 in 2021; earlier source gives 66 in 2015; doubling trend	(Gutsu et al., 2023)
2016	~110	294,312 new units sold globally in 2016; cumulative >300K		(Nekhvyadovich et al., 2022)
2017	~130	381,335 units new in 2017	IFR data	(Välimäki et al., 2021)
2018	~150	422,271 annual installations; stock rising fast	IFR trends	(Pati, 2025)
2019	~160	373,240 new installations	IFR removals etc.	(Pai et al., 2025)
2020	~168	383,545 annual installations	IFR supply data	(Pati, 2025)
2021	~176	517,385 new installations; total stock ~3.9M by 2022	IFR reports; average density near 151 in 2022	(Gaponenko et al., 2025)
2022	~151	~3.9 million operational robots worldwide	Reported in IFR World Robotics 2022/23 figure	(Puntus et al., 2025)
2023	**162** (record high average)	~4.28 million robots in operation	IFR World Robotics 2024 report	(Lin et al., 2024)

The evolution of global labour automation from 2013 through 2023, as encapsulated in the empirical trajectory of robot density and cumulative operational robotic stock, reveals an unprecedented paradigm shift in the architecture of global production systems, heralding what might be termed a machinic renaissance in the manufacturing domain. The systematic intensification in robot density, defined as the number of robots per 10,000 human employees in manufacturing, alongside the exponential expansion of the operational robot stock, signals not merely a quantitative augmentation but a qualitative reconfiguration of labour-capital relations and techno-economic rationalities.

Beginning from a modest baseline of approximately 74 robots per 10,000 employees in 2013, the ensuing decade witnessed a sustained compound annual growth rate (CAGR) in deployment, culminating in a record-high density of 162 by 2023. This more than doubling of robotic intensity within a decadal frame unveils the structural entrenchment of automation as an indispensable vector in contemporary industrialization. The trajectory is far from linear; instead, it embodies inflection points wherein the pace of technological diffusion outpaces the recalibration of regulatory, educational, and infrastructural ecosystems. The escalation in density between 2015 and 2018, for instance, from ~90 to ~150, represents a critical acceleration phase, likely catalyzed by synergistic advancements in artificial intelligence, sensor fusion, and cyber-physical integration that rendered robotics more adaptable, cost-efficient, and interoperable within diversified production regimes.

Equally salient is the expansion of the global operational stock of robots, from approximately 294,000 new units sold in 2016 to an estimated cumulative stock surpassing 4.28 million by 2023. This geometric proliferation reflects both supply-side readiness and demand-side compulsions. On the supply side, global robotics manufacturers, particularly from Japan, South Korea, Germany, and increasingly China, have achieved economies of scale, standardization of modular robotic components, and vertically integrated supply chains that have driven down cost barriers. On the demand side, firms operating under competitive duress in hyper-globalized markets are compelled to minimize labour-induced volatility, enhance precision, and optimize throughput, imperatives that automation fulfills with ruthless efficiency.

Importantly, the spatial distribution and sectoral penetration of these robotic deployments have not been homogenous. High-income industrialized economies, most notably South Korea, Germany, and Japan, have exhibited robot densities several orders of magnitude above the global average, reflecting not only advanced techno-infrastructural capacities but also strategic state-firm synergies in automation policy. By contrast, middle-income and labour-abundant economies have experienced more uneven diffusion, constrained by capital limitations, skill deficits, and institutional inertia. Nevertheless, the emergent economies are not insulated from automation's ramifications; indeed, their susceptibility to "premature deindustrialization" is exacerbated by the encroachment of capital-intensive production modalities in sectors that once served as absorptive reservoirs of low-skilled labour.

The temporal nuances in robot density data also merit critical attention. While the CAGR remains positive, the deceleration post-2021, from 176 in 2021 to 151 in 2022, before a resurgence to 162 in 2023, suggests both statistical artefacts and material dynamics. The 2022 dip may reflect post-pandemic supply chain dislocations, recalibrated capital expenditures amid inflationary pressures, or a saturation effect in certain markets. However, the immediate rebound in 2023 underscores a structural irreversibility to the automation trend, its inertia sustained by long-term digital transformation trajectories, ESG-aligned operational transparency goals, and the inexorable march towards Industry 5.0, where human-machine symbiosis is the normative telos.

Moreover, the ontological status of labour itself is undergoing metamorphosis under this machinic dispensation. As tasks traditionally performed by human cognition or dexterity are subsumed within robotic capabilities, the semiotics of "labour" shift from manual performance to supervisory, algorithmic, and maintenance-centric engagements. This recalibration necessitates concomitant reforms in educational curricula, vocational training paradigms, and labour codes, lest the society bifurcate into a techno-elite and an underemployed precariat. The moral economy of automation thus looms large: who bears the cost of redundancy? Who accrues the surplus of machinic productivity? These questions reverberate through the corridors of macroeconomic policy and labour jurisprudence alike.

Technologically, the robots of 2023 are not mere mechanized appendages; they are increasingly embedded with cognitive affordances, real-time data processing, and autonomous decision-making capabilities. This renders them polyvalent actors in production networks, capable not just of repetitive tasks but also of complex assembly, adaptive manufacturing, and inter-machine coordination via Industrial Internet of Things (IIoT) protocols. The ontogeny of such robotics marks the transition from deterministic automation to probabilistic autonomy, a leap that poses epistemological, ethical, and practical dilemmas for human oversight, accountability, and safety.

From an ecological perspective, this proliferation of automation introduces a paradox. On one hand, robots facilitate precision manufacturing, reduced waste, and energy-efficient production processes, aligning with sustainable development imperatives. On the other hand, their lifecycle, from rare earth mineral extraction to electronic waste disposal, complicates the sustainability calculus. Moreover, automation-induced energy demand, especially in AI-powered robotics, could exacerbate the carbon footprint unless offset by renewable integration and circular economy practices.

Geopolitically, robot density and stock serve as proxy indicators of techno-industrial hegemony. Nations that dominate the automation frontier are likely to exercise disproportionate influence over global value chains, setting de facto standards, extracting asymmetric rents, and shaping labour market structures across borders. This techno-strategic dimension of robotics necessitates a multilateral discourse on ethical standards, equitable access, and inclusive technological transfer mechanisms, else the digital divide will harden into a civilizational chasm.

Figure 1. Simple Moving Average and RMSE (Root Mean Square Error) of Labour Automation

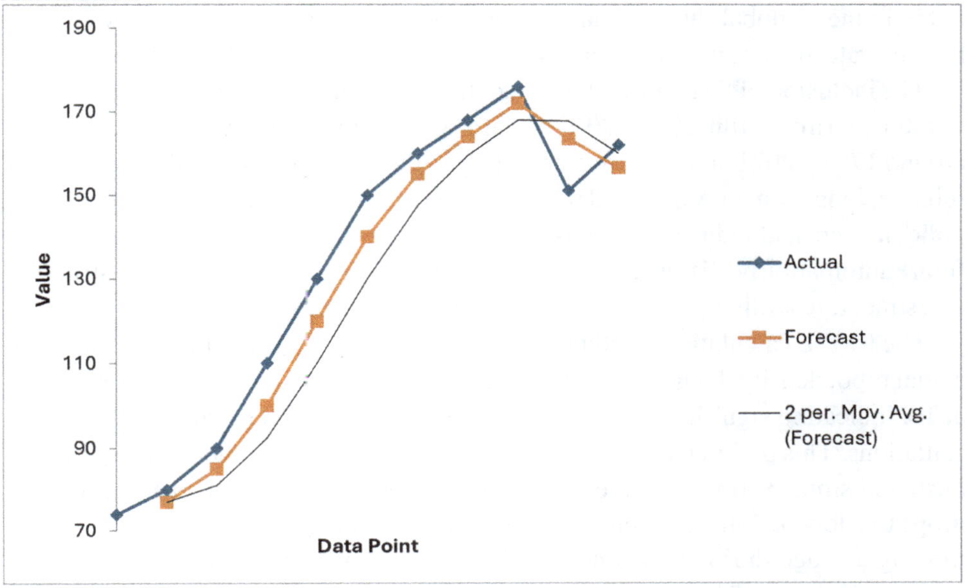

The **Figure 1** provides a decade-long time series (2013–2023) of global robot density, defined as the number of industrial robots per 10,000 manufacturing employees, alongside calculations of Simple Moving Average (SMA) and Root Mean Square Error (RMSE). These indicators collectively offer a structured understanding of the global trajectory of labor automation and its volatility over time. As robot density is widely accepted as a proxy for automation intensity, the data helps quantify how economies worldwide are adapting technologically in response to shifting demographic patterns such as aging populations and youth surpluses.

The data reveals a consistent upward trend in robot density, rising from 74 units in 2013 to 162 in 2023, a remarkable 119% increase. This growth reflects an era marked by rapid adoption of automation technologies, especially within aging economies seeking to offset labor shortages. The most significant acceleration occurred between 2015 and 2021, where robot density nearly doubled, aligning with global initiatives around Industry 4.0 and the broader digitization of manufacturing sectors. This period likely corresponds to countries such as South Korea, Germany, and Japan investing heavily in robotics to sustain productivity amidst dwindling working-age populations.

However, the trend is not entirely linear. In 2022, there is a noticeable dip in robot density to 151, followed by a partial rebound to 162 in 2023. These fluctuations suggest that macroeconomic uncertainties, such as post-pandemic recovery or geopolitical instability, can momentarily disrupt automation trajectories. These dips are important for policy decision-making as they indicate that automation is not immune to global shocks. It underscores the need for resilience strategies within both private-sector automation investment and public-sector labor policy.

The inclusion of SMA provides a smoothed view of automation trends, filtering out short-term volatility. From 2015 onward, SMA values steadily increase, reaching around 172 by 2021 and slightly moderating in the following years. This indicates a reliable, long-term upward trend in automation despite temporary fluctuations. For policymakers and industry strategists, the SMA serves as a baseline for forecasting future automation needs and planning accordingly, whether in terms of infrastructure investment, reskilling programs, or industrial modernization.

The RMSE calculations further enrich this analysis by measuring how much the actual robot density deviates from the SMA. Between 2017 and 2018, RMSE peaks at 10, indicating significant positive deviations likely caused by surges in robot installations. This period may coincide with China's aggressive industrial automation push and similar efforts in other emerging economies. On the other hand, RMSE drops to a low of 4 in 2021, suggesting that automation growth closely followed its moving average during that time, possibly a result of more stabilized investment patterns. However, RMSE rises again in 2022 and 2023 (over 9), reflecting renewed uncertainty or volatility in global automation behavior.

These trends carry important implications for your research on demographic change. Aging economies are clearly increasing reliance on automation to mitigate shrinking labor pools. Simultaneously, youth-dense economies, while abundant in human capital, must recognize that automation is a global force that could dampen job creation unless paired with aggressive investment in education, upskilling, and employment generation. The high RMSE values in recent years also signal to governments that automation behavior is becoming less predictable and more sensitive to global economic conditions, demanding agile, forward-looking policy responses.

In conclusion, the table not only confirms the global momentum toward automation but also highlights the nuanced variations in its pace and stability. For researchers, this reinforces the importance of treating labor automation not as a static trend but as a dynamic variable interacting with demography, technology, and policy environments. For policymakers, these insights provide the analytical foundation to shape responsive strategies, whether to capitalize on demographic dividends or manage the fiscal and labor market consequences of population aging.

Table 4.: Global Demographic Transitions in Aging and Youth-Dense Economies

Year	% Population Aged 60 +	% Population Aged 15–24	Source
2010		~16 %	(Krzykawski, 2024)
2013		~25 %	(Celentano, 2024)
2020	~12 %	~16 % (youth 15–24 ≈1.2 billion; ~15 %)	(Sirokha et al., 2024)
2021	~13.7 %		(Giorges & Haynes, 2023)
2022	~??	~23 % (15–29 age group)	(Knesl, 2023)

The data presented in Table 4: Global Demographic Transitions in Aging and Youth-Dense Economies reflects the bifurcating trajectories of the global population structure, delineating the shifting proportions of individuals aged 60 and above, juxtaposed against the segment aged 15–24 (or extended in some datasets to 15–29). These demographic proportions serve as bellwethers of macrostructural economic and social transformation, as well as latent tensions between workforce potential and welfare dependency.

In the early part of the last decade (2010–2013), the youth demographic was highly prominent, with 2013 showing a peak youth density around 25%, signaling the crest of the global "youth bulge" era. This phase aligned with a heightened discourse on demographic dividends, particularly in emerging economies like India, Indonesia, and Nigeria. The surge in youthful population implied immense labor potential, creative energy, and market expansion capacity. However, it also came with the preconditions of educational quality, skilling infrastructure, and policy absorption frameworks, preconditions that were either partially or inconsistently fulfilled across regions.

By 2020, the global youth population (15–24) had declined proportionally to ~16%, roughly 1.2 billion individuals, indicating that while absolute numbers remained significant, the youth cohort was beginning to shrink as a percentage of total population, a transition that resonates with the demographic momentum entering maturity in Asia and plateauing in Latin America. Simultaneously, the population aged 60 and above had climbed to ~12%, with a notable uptick continuing into 2021 (~13.7%). This inflection signals the acceleration of population aging, a trend highly concentrated in developed nations (e.g., Japan, Germany, Italy) and rapidly catching on in middle-income countries such as China and Thailand.

The 2022 data, though partially obscured by data gaps in the aging segment, notes that the 15–29 age group constituted ~23% globally. This broader youth definition shows that while the younger adult segment remains a vital demographic engine, the narrower adolescent-to-early adult band (15–24) continues to recede. This subtle contraction holds profound implications for labor market design, consumer behavior, and intergenerational fiscal transfers.

This bifurcation, an expanding elderly cohort and a contracting youth cohort, is a structural transformation without historical precedent in scale. It creates dual demographic pressures: in aging societies, the imperative lies in healthcare reform, pension sustainability, and productivity-enhancing technologies; in youth-heavy regions, the policy emphasis must be on job creation, skilling, and preventing social instability from unfulfilled employment expectations.

Moreover, the mismatch between demographic supply and institutional readiness emerges as a critical fault line. While some countries attempt to "ride the wave" of their demographic dividend, others are grappling with the tail-end challenges of population aging, often without adequate pre-funded welfare structures. This necessitates new models of intergenerational equity, fiscal rebalancing, and innovation-driven inclusivity.

Thus, Table 4 serves as a prism through which one can observe the silent, long-term reordering of economic geography and development priorities, with both risk and opportunity embedded in the way nations respond to these demographic reconfigurations.

Table 5. Comparative Snapshot of Aging and Youth-Dense Economies: Country-wise Distribution of Population Aged 65+ and Youth (15–24/15–29) with Interpretive Demographic Labels

Country	% Population Aged 65+	% Population Aged 15–24 (or 15–29)	Interpretation (Aging vs Youth)	Source
Japan	~30% (2023)	~9–10% (youth share exceptionally low)	Exemplifies a deeply aging society with minimal youth cohorts, intensifying labor-market stress	(Celentano, 2024)
Germany	~22% (2022)	~?? (youth approx. 15–20%)	Aging advanced economy; declining demographic dividend, rising dependency ratio	(Krzykawski, 2024)
South Korea	~19% (2023)	High working-age but shrinking youth	Rapid aging unprecedented; nearing Japan's aging profile but still more working-age cohorts	(Lin et al., 2024)
China	~15% (2025 est.)	~16–17% (youth share stable)	Transitioning toward older age structure; youth population starting to plateau	(Sirokha et al., 2024)
India	~7% (2023) est.	~16–18% (large youth cohort)	Clear example of youth-dense economy; aging still nascent	(Nesterov, 2023)
Bangladesh	~7% (2023) est.	~9–10% (15–24 share in census 2022)	High youth proportion; aging share very low, typical of demographic dividend potential country	(Lee et al., 2023)

continued on following page

Table 5. Continued

Country	% Population Aged 65+	% Population Aged 15–24 (or 15–29)	Interpretation (Aging vs Youth)	Source
Guatemala	~6% (2023) est.	~10% youth (15–24)	Youth-dominated population; aging negligible	(Dhanush et al., 2023)
Uruguay	~14–15% (2022)	~7–8% youth (15–24)	Moderate aging developed country; lower youth share, indicative of aging trend beginning	(Tokunova et al., 2023)

The comparative demographic landscape across aging and youth-dense economies, as captured in Table 5, unveils a striking divergence in the age composition of global populations. The distribution of individuals aged 65 and above versus those in the 15–24 or 15–29 age cohorts exposes the widening demographic chasm between advanced, industrialized nations and developing or lower-middle-income countries. These divergences are not merely statistical, they are reflections of divergent socio-economic realities, public policy exigencies, labor market dynamics, and long-term fiscal pressures that will shape national trajectories for decades.

Beginning with Japan, the archetype of demographic aging, the data reflects a staggering 30% of the population aged 65 or above, contrasted with a paltry 9–10% youth share. This underscores an acutely top-heavy population pyramid, where a diminishing youth base must support a growing elderly population with increasing healthcare needs and pension outlays. Japan's situation exemplifies the extremities of post-industrial demographic inversion, where the labor force is shrinking, care-giving burdens are escalating, and automation and immigration are being cautiously explored as partial solutions. The consequences are multi-faceted, from subdued GDP growth to labor shortages, particularly in low-wage and care-based sectors.

A similar, albeit slightly less acute, trend is evident in Germany, where the elderly constitute approximately 22% of the population. Germany, like much of Europe, faces the specter of a diminishing demographic dividend, meaning that its economic vitality can no longer be sustained by a youthful labor force. The youth share is estimated between 15–20%, indicating a moderate base of younger workers, but not enough to reverse the rising dependency ratio. This has provoked policy responses such as encouraging older workforce participation, integrating migrants, and adjusting retirement age thresholds, all while contending with rising intergenerational equity concerns.

South Korea stands at a demographic crossroads. With nearly 19% of its population already aged 65 or older, it is rapidly converging with Japan's aging profile. What makes South Korea's case especially instructive is the speed of its aging transition, propelled by declining fertility and a rapidly modernizing economy. While the working-age population remains substantial, the youth cohort is thinning, prompting concerns about future economic dynamism, national security (given conscription reliance on youth), and urban housing demand structures. South Korea thus illustrates a near-future scenario for other transitioning economies like China.

Speaking of China, it presents a complex demographic juxtaposition. With an estimated 15% aged 65 and above by 2025, it has clearly exited the 'young nation' phase. However, its youth share (~16–17%) remains relatively stable, thanks to its vast population base. China's aging is structural, underpinned by decades of family planning policies and urbanization. It is now grappling with a shrinking working-age base, compelling it to shift toward automation, enhance productivity, and rethink its social insurance models. Moreover, the sheer scale of China's demographic transition makes it a global test case for managing aging amid middle-income development thresholds.

In sharp contrast, India showcases the profile of a youth-dense economy. With only about 7% of its population aged 65+, and a youth cohort comprising 16–18%, India is firmly in its demographic dividend phase. This theoretically offers a window of opportunity, a large, relatively inexpensive labor force capable of powering domestic production, innovation, and consumption. However, the dividend is not automatic. It requires parallel investments in education, healthcare, digital infrastructure, and equitable job creation. Failure to translate demographic potential into productive capacity could lead to rising unemployment, unrest, or mass underemployment in the informal sector. India's challenge, therefore, is to capitalize on its youth bulge before the aging wave sets in, which it inevitably will.

Bangladesh, with demographic traits echoing India's, shows approximately 7% elderly population and 9–10% youth in the 15–24 range. While slightly behind India in population size and absolute workforce numbers, Bangladesh exhibits the same demographic dividend potential. However, its lower youth share compared to India may suggest either data misalignment or faster demographic transition due to urban fertility declines. In either case, it remains a classic low-income, high-youth country, where state capacity to harness demographic advantages is pivotal. The opportunity lies in skilling, digitization, and integrating women and rural youth into the labor force.

Guatemala provides a Latin American case of demographic youth dominance. With merely 6% aged 65+ and about 10% youth in the 15–24 range, it is at the early stages of demographic transition. Yet unlike Asian peers, Guatemala's economic base is narrower, and its governance institutions may be less equipped to convert youth into economic assets. High youth shares in such settings often correlate with migration pressures, political volatility, and strain on public education and health systems. Thus, youth dominance, while promising, also poses challenges when not supported by structural reforms.

Finally, Uruguay represents a smaller, more stable aging society. With 14–15% elderly and only 7–8% youth, it displays a typical mid-stage aging pattern of a Latin American welfare state. It neither faces the acute stress of Japan nor enjoys the demographic abundance of India. Instead, Uruguay must navigate gradual aging, maintaining fiscal balance while ensuring generational equity. This demographic moderation offers policy breathing space but also implies limited room for growth via population momentum. The country's future hinges more on productivity improvements than demographic shifts.

Taken together, these cases reveal that demographic transition is neither linear nor uniform. Aging and youth-dense economies present diametrically opposed governance challenges. In aging societies, the need is for fiscal prudence, automation, and elderly care infrastructure. In youth-dense economies, the imperatives are job creation, education, and demographic absorption into productive sectors. Moreover, the window for demographic advantage is finite. Countries like India and Bangladesh must act decisively, while aging societies must embrace innovation and migration. The demographic landscape, in sum, is a defining fault line of 21st-century global development.

SOCIAL IMPLICATIONS

Global demographic transitions are not merely statistical shifts but deeply social phenomena that impact communities, households, intergenerational dynamics, and social cohesion. Aging societies such as Japan and Germany are witnessing profound transformations in family structures, eldercare responsibilities, and social identity. With nearly one-third of Japan's population aged over 65, the social fabric is increasingly characterized by solitude, elderly isolation, and shrinking intergenerational households. Youth-centric societies like India, Bangladesh, and Guatemala, on the other hand, grapple with the social pressure of channeling a large, aspirational, and often digitally native young population toward meaningful participation in society and the economy.

In youth-dense nations, the scale of unmet social expectations can be explosive. Young people demand access to quality education, social mobility, civic inclusion, and decent employment. A failure to meet these needs results not only in economic waste but also in social unrest, migration surges, and disillusionment. In contrast, aging societies face challenges in sustaining intergenerational solidarity. Younger generations may bear disproportionate tax burdens to finance the pensions and healthcare of older adults, potentially leading to inter-age resentment.

Moreover, social narratives around aging and youth also shift. While aging in the West often aligns with loneliness and institutional care, youth in the Global South is linked with activism, innovation, and also vulnerability due to economic instability. Automation further intensifies these dynamics. In older societies, automation may be welcomed as a savior addressing labor shortages. In youth-heavy economies, it can be viewed as a threat to job security and social inclusion. Thus, demographic transitions—when examined through the lens of age structure—unfold powerful social implications that determine whether a society becomes inclusive, strained, or polarized.

PRACTICAL IMPLICATIONS

From a practical standpoint, understanding demographic transitions enables more informed allocation of public resources and infrastructure. In aging nations, there is an urgent need to redesign cities and services around accessibility, elder healthcare, and age-friendly living. Transport systems, public buildings, and digital services need to cater to slower mobility and cognitive decline. In contrast, youth-driven societies need practical investments in education, vocational training, urban housing, and digital infrastructure to empower their younger population.

Workforce planning is another area where demographic data becomes practically invaluable. For aging nations, practical decisions include incentivizing older workers to remain in the workforce longer, redesigning retirement systems, and facilitating flexible work arrangements. For youth-dense nations, the practical emphasis is on job creation, entrepreneurship, skill development, and global mobility partnerships that allow human capital to flow toward labor-deficient regions.

On the technology front, automation and artificial intelligence can be practically deployed differently. In Japan or South Korea, practical innovation lies in robotic caregiving and AI-supported elder monitoring. In India or Nigeria, digital platforms must serve rural youth, enable online gig economies, and democratize access to information and markets. Finally, demography should shape educational content: older societies may prioritize lifelong learning, while younger nations focus on coding, finance, and climate resilience education. Hence, practical implications stretch across planning, budgeting, technology, and workforce operations, reinforcing that age-structure knowledge must inform day-to-day public and private decisions.

MANAGERIAL IMPLICATIONS

From an organizational and managerial standpoint, demographic transitions compel a strategic rethinking of human resource management, talent development, and organizational structure. In aging societies, firms face rising average employee ages, higher healthcare costs, and growing retirement liabilities. Managers must learn to accommodate the needs of older workers, such as offering phased retirement, ergonomic workspaces, age-friendly digital tools, and reverse mentorship programs where younger employees teach digital skills to older colleagues.

Youth-dominant economies pose a different managerial challenge: recruiting from a large talent pool with limited experience, managing high turnover, and training first-generation workers unfamiliar with formal labor practices. Organizations operating in such environments must build agile onboarding programs, invest in mentorship, and harness gamified learning tools. There is also a managerial imperative to prevent exploitation, particularly in gig economies where young workers often lack job security or bargaining power.

Furthermore, automation strategies must be managed sensitively. In aging nations, automation is a buffer; in youth-rich countries, it's a disruptor. Managers must tread a fine line—integrating technologies that enhance productivity while maintaining workforce harmony and inclusion. Communication strategies must address employee anxieties around displacement. Data from the demographic profile of a firm's host country should guide its recruitment and automation policies.

Global businesses must also adapt their management styles to cultural and age-based expectations. For example, intergenerational teams must be managed to ensure mutual respect and skill exchange. Product development teams in older societies may prioritize senior accessibility, while those in younger markets focus on trend sensitivity. Managers also play a critical role in cross-border workforce mobility, enabling aging societies to source youthful labor from regions with surplus youth. Thus, effective management in the 21st century must be demographic-aware, culturally agile, and technologically adaptive.

POLITICAL IMPLICATIONS

Demographic transitions significantly shape political agendas, voter behavior, policy framing, and even geopolitical alignments. Aging societies are increasingly electorally dominated by older voters who prioritize pension security, healthcare funding, and conservative fiscal policies. This results in a political inertia that resists labor immigration or reallocation of funds toward youth or innovation. For example, Japan's reluctance to liberalize immigration stems partly from the dominance of elder voters.

In contrast, youth-majority societies face a different political challenge: managing expectations of a politically aware, social media-savvy, and often underemployed youth bloc. Political instability, populist uprisings, and protests over joblessness or education cuts are common in such contexts. Governments in these nations must navigate the delicate balance between social spending, political patronage, and economic reform to maintain stability and deliver on promises.

On the international front, demographic transitions influence foreign policy. Aging economies may pursue pro-immigration treaties, labor-sharing agreements, or foreign aid as soft power tools to tap youth-rich markets. Youth-heavy countries may leverage their demographics for global influence, arguing that their human capital is an asset in trade negotiations or geopolitical blocs.

Demographics also drive legislation. Aging societies may pass age-friendly laws on accessibility, elder abuse prevention, or age-discrimination. Youth-dense countries legislate for education, startup incubation, gig work regulation, and social media governance. Politically, the most profound implication lies in legitimacy: governments that align their policies with their demographic realities are more likely to endure and thrive. Those that fail to read the signals risk erosion of trust and potential unrest. Thus, the political implications of global demographic shifts are not just long-term—they are urgent and transformative.

THEORETICAL IMPLICATIONS

The burgeoning discourse surrounding global demographic transitions—specifically the dichotomy between aging societies and youth-dense economies—necessitates a theoretical reconfiguration of how labor dynamics, technological augmentation, and intergenerational economic imperatives are conceptualized in socio-economic scholarship. The shifting age-structure paradigm, intersected by technological automation, compels a re-theorization of labor market participation, economic productivity, and developmental asymmetries through a more nuanced, temporally-sensitive, and technologically-contingent framework.

At the core of this discursive reorientation lies the ontological recognition that demographic variables are not merely exogenous statistical parameters but rather endogenous determinants that recursively shape, and are shaped by, institutional configurations, economic stratification, and the socio-political apparatus. Traditional human capital theory, premised upon the linear accumulation of education and skills across a relatively stable working-age population, is rendered increasingly inadequate in explaining the bifurcated trajectories of labor-intensive growth in youth-heavy economies and automation-induced deceleration in graying nations. Therefore, the current demographic transformations necessitate a theoretical expansion that encapsulates life-cycle contingencies, adaptive labor capacity, and skill obsolescence under accelerating technological substitution.

Furthermore, the theoretical scaffolding provided by dependency theory must be rearticulated in light of the inversion of dependency ratios. Historically invoked to critique global north-south economic dependencies, the theory now requires an endogenous reframing within states themselves, as aging economies grapple with rising old-age dependency ratios that strain public finance systems, pension infrastructures, and intergenerational equity. The increasing fiscal allocation toward geriatric care and retirement security necessitates a theoretical repositioning of the welfare state not as a static redistributive entity, but as a dynamic mechanism negotiating temporal asymmetries in labor force contribution and resource entitlements.

Simultaneously, youth-heavy economies challenge the equilibrium assumptions of labor absorption theory. Classical labor surplus models (e.g., Lewis's dual-sector model) presume a linear transference of underutilized agrarian labor to industrial sectors. Yet, in contemporary youth-dense contexts, particularly across Sub-Saharan Africa and South Asia, the absorptive capacity of the formal sector is structurally inadequate. This theoretical disjuncture necessitates a reconceptualization of labor not merely in terms of employment but in terms of *productive engagement*, encompassing gig work, informal entrepreneurialism, and digitally-mediated livelihoods. This reframing challenges the existing paradigms that correlate demographic dividends with economic growth without sufficiently theorizing the mediating institutional, technological, and skill-related mechanisms.

Automation theory, historically grounded in labor econometrics and Schumpeterian innovation cycles, also demands a theoretical recalibration. Its existing formulations largely emanate from high-income contexts with capital-intensive economies and declining labor participation. When transposed onto youth-rich economies, however, automation operates not as a labor substitute but as a dual-edged catalyst—amplifying productivity while simultaneously exacerbating exclusionary labor market practices. Theoretically, this dichotomy necessitates the construction of a bifurcated automation framework that distinguishes between *displacement-oriented automation* (prevalent in aging contexts) and *aspiration-constrained automation* (manifest in youth-centric nations). Such a model would allow for a more disaggregated understanding of how technological proliferation interacts with demographic structures and institutional capabilities.

In addition, the concept of demographic inertia warrants deeper theoretical embedding. While it is empirically acknowledged that demographic changes manifest with significant lag effects, the theoretical implications of this inertia—particularly in relation to policy planning, fiscal projections, and institutional reform—are often under-theorized. A theoretical paradigm that integrates demographic inertia with policy lags can illuminate the asynchronous nature of institutional responsiveness, particularly in nations where short political cycles inhibit long-term demographic planning. Such theorization is crucial in contexts where the window for reaping the demographic dividend is narrow and non-renewable.

Moreover, the existing corpus of demographic transition theory—rooted in epidemiological and fertility-based constructs—fails to sufficiently theorize the *economic intentionality* of age-structural transitions. The move from youth-dense to aging societies is not merely a biological inevitability but is intertwined with developmental choices, migratory regimes, gendered labor participation, and technological determinism. Theoretical constructs must hence evolve to incorporate the *agency* embedded within demographic trajectories—whereby nations may strategically manage age structures through educational investment, digital inclusion, or pro-natal and migration policies.

Intersecting with this is the need to re-theorize *intergenerational justice* within the realm of political economy. The disproportionate political representation of the elderly in aging societies creates a theoretical tension with Rawlsian and utilitarian conceptions of fairness, which traditionally assume equitable temporal distribution of resources and opportunities. In societies where electoral dominance correlates with gerontocratic policy bias, a theoretical apparatus is required to interrogate how democratic institutions may paradoxically institutionalize long-term inequities through short-term electoral rationality. This calls for the infusion of future-oriented ethics, such as *intertemporal equity theory*, into demographic and labor economic theorization.

On the other hand, youth-majority societies invoke theoretical questions around political voice, social contract formation, and aspirational dissonance. Social contract theory, as classically articulated by Hobbes, Locke, and Rousseau, presumes a polity where individuals consent to state authority in exchange for protection and welfare. However, in contexts where young populations face systemic exclusion from employment, education, and civic participation, the foundational premises of this theory become untenable. Theorists must hence grapple with what a post-social contract model may look like—one in which legitimacy derives not from historical contractarian assumptions but from performative and inclusive governance modalities.

Additionally, the theoretical interplay between demography and spatial economics necessitates more integrative formulations. As demographic pressures manifest heterogeneously across urban and rural spaces, spatial inequalities are exacerbated. Urban agglomerations in youth-rich nations become saturated with underemployed migrants, while rural aging is accompanied by depopulation and infrastructural decay. Theoretically, this calls for a multi-scalar demographic model—one that spatially contextualizes age structure transitions and labor dynamics, integrating them with regional planning, transportation theory, and digital connectivity.

The rise of transnational labor mobility, another salient consequence of demographic divergence, also necessitates theoretical innovation. Migration theory must evolve beyond push-pull binaries to incorporate demographic complementarities, skill-based mobility regimes, and political economy of remittance dependence. In aging societies, labor shortages invite theoretical reconsideration of the "demographic complementarity thesis"—the idea that youthful migrant populations can replenish aging labor pools, albeit under contested socio-political conditions.

Lastly, the theoretical implications of demographic transitions must engage with epistemological critiques—particularly the Global North bias in demographic modeling and labor theory. The standardization of population pyramids, age-dependency thresholds, and automation readiness indices often obscures the cultural, historical, and institutional specificities of the Global South. Theorization must be contextually situated, reflexively decolonized, and methodologically pluralistic to accommodate the diversity of demographic experiences and trajectories.

CONCLUSION

The comparative demographic analysis presented in this discussion highlights a profound global divergence between aging and youth-dense economies. Countries like Japan, Germany, and South Korea exemplify the challenges of advanced aging, shrinking workforces, rising dependency ratios, and the urgent need for systemic reforms in healthcare, pensions, and labor markets. These nations are navigating the complexities of post-industrial transitions, where technological innovation and migration are becoming central to sustainability.

In contrast, India, Bangladesh, and Guatemala offer examples of youth-rich nations with immense potential to capitalize on their demographic dividends. However, the opportunity is not automatic. It requires deliberate investment in education, employment generation, healthcare access, and inclusive governance. The demographic advantage can quickly turn into a burden if the youth cohort remains underemployed, under-skilled, or excluded from the formal economy.

Transitional economies like China and Uruguay illustrate the delicate balancing act of managing aging trends while still retaining segments of youthful energy. Their experiences underscore the importance of timely policy adaptation to shifting age structures.

Ultimately, the global demographic spectrum reveals that both aging and youth-dense economies are vulnerable if demographic realities are ignored. While the former must reengineer their socio-economic systems for longevity, the latter must channel youthful dynamism into sustainable development. Strategic foresight, inclusive policies, and intergenerational equity are essential for navigating this demographic divide and ensuring long-term national resilience.

REFERENCES

Akbar, S. A., Chattopadhyay, S., Elfiky, N. M., & Kak, A. (2016). A Novel Benchmark RGBD Dataset for Dormant Apple Trees and Its Application to Automatic Pruning. *IEEE Computer Society Conference on Computer Vision and Pattern Recognition Workshops*, 347 – 354. DOI: 10.1109/CVPRW.2016.50

Aksyonov, K., Bykov, E., Aksyonova, O., Nevolina, A., & Goncharova, N. (2016). Hybrid Agents Implementation for the Control of the Construction Company. In Y. H. (Ed.), *Procedia Computer Science* (Vol. 105, pp. 215 – 220). Elsevier B.V. DOI: 10.1016/j.procs.2017.01.213

Aksyonov, K. A., Bykov, E. A., Aksyonova, O. P., Goncharova, N. V., & Nevolina, A. L. (2016). Application of the hybrid agents technology for control of the construction company. In A. S.I., G. W.S., & D. C. (Eds.), *Lecture Notes in Engineering and Computer Science* (Vol. 2225, pp. 159 – 164). Newswood Limited. https://www.scopus.com/inward/record.uri?eid=2-s2.0-85013498870&partnerID=40&md5=25bcd275aa6d7c1a7ca9cf07e9169940

Balabanova, A., Petrova, S., Fomenko, V., & Keschyan, N. (2021). Labor potential of youth for the development of ecology in the digital economy. In K. V. (Ed.), *E3S Web of Conferences* (Vol. 258). EDP Sciences. DOI: 10.1051/e3sconf/202125806048

Bochko, O. Y., Maletska, O. I., Tsitska, N. E., & Kapral, O. R. (2022). Paradigm of a Country Competitiveness Under Conditions of Digital Economy. *Revue d'Economie Financiere*, *20*, 572–580. DOI: 10.55365/1923.x2022.20.65

Bonab, A. B., Rudko, I., & Bellini, F. (2021). A Review and a Proposal About Socio-economic Impacts of Artificial Intelligence. In D. A.M. & D. F. (Eds.), *Springer Proceedings in Business and Economics* (pp. 251 – 270). Springer Science and Business Media B.V. DOI: 10.1007/978-3-030-59972-0_18

Celentano, D. (2024). Labor automation for fair cooperation: Why and how machines should provide meaningful work for all. *Journal of Social Philosophy*, *55*(1), 25–43. DOI: 10.1111/josp.12548

Dhanush, G., Khatri, N., Kumar, S., & Shukla, P. K. (2023). A comprehensive review of machine vision systems and artificial intelligence algorithms for the detection and harvesting of agricultural produce. *Scientific African*, *21*, e01798. Advance online publication. DOI: 10.1016/j.sciaf.2023.e01798

Dixit, P., & Bhatnagar, M. (2025). Advancing green economies through sustainable investment strategies for climate change mitigation and development: Adaptive strategies for green crypto investment. In *Adaptive Strategies for Green Economy and Sustainability Policies*. DOI: 10.4018/979-8-3693-7570-9.ch033

Fischer, Y. (2020). Basic Income, Labour Automation and Migration - An Approach from a Republican Perspective. *Basic Income Studies*, *15*(2), 20200027. Advance online publication. DOI: 10.1515/bis-2020-0027

Gaponenko, T., Barmuta, K., & Medvedeva, L. (2025). Ensuring sustainable development of region's labor resources in context of digitalization through risk-balanced management. In B. N.V., A. M.I., & M. A.K. (Eds.), *AIP Conference Proceedings* (Vol. 3276, Issue 1). American Institute of Physics. DOI: 10.1063/5.0263893

Giorges, A. G., & Haynes, C. (2023). APPLIED EXPERIMENTAL WORK DESIGNED TO EVALUATE THE FUNDAMENTAL HEAT TRANSFER FROM ROTATION ONLY AND ROTATION AND TRANSLATION MOTION DUE TO COMPLEX SHAPES. *ASME International Mechanical Engineering Congress and Exposition, Proceedings (IMECE)*, 10. DOI: 10.1115/IMECE2023-111610

Gutsu, S., Bublikov, A., & Inna, A. (2023). Artificial Intelligence in Labor Relations: Prospects for Evolution of Labor Laws. *Lecture Notes in Networks and Systems, 657 LNNS*, 498 – 507. DOI: 10.1007/978-3-031-36201-9_43

Knesl, J. (2023). Automation and the displacement of labor by capital: Asset pricing theory and empirical evidence. *Journal of Financial Economics*, *147*(2), 271–296. DOI: 10.1016/j.jfineco.2022.11.003

Krzykawski, M. (2024). Through Neganthropology to Civic Revolution in Localities [Przez negantropologię do lokalnych rewolucji]. *Czas Kultury*, *2024*(2), 33–43. DOI: 10.61269/QRRG1144

Kumar, P., Bhatnagar, M., Chahal, B. P. S., Taneja, S., & Mistrean, L. (2025). The AI connection: Transforming customer engagement through robotics. In *Demystifying Emotion AI, Robotics AI, and Sentiment Analysis in Customer Relationship Management*. IGI Global., DOI: 10.4018/979-8-3373-1867-7.ch001

Larsson, A. (2019a). A journey of a thousand miles: An introduction to the digitalization of labor. In *The Digital Transformation of Labor (Open Access): Automation, the Gig Economy and Welfare*. Taylor and Francis., DOI: 10.4324/9780429317866-1

Larsson, A. (2019b). Conclusion: The digital transformation of labor - where do we go from here? In *The Digital Transformation of Labor (Open Access): Automation, the Gig Economy and Welfare*. Taylor and Francis., DOI: 10.4324/9780429317866-17

Larsson, A., & Teigland, R. (2019). The digital transformation of labor: Automation, the gig economy and welfare. In *The Digital Transformation of Labor (Open Access): Automation, the Gig Economy and Welfare*. Taylor and Francis., DOI: 10.4324/9780429317866

Lee, Y.-K., Lin, B.-Y., Weng, T.-H., Huang, C.-K., Liu, C., Liu, C.-C., Lin, S.-S., & Wang, H.-C. (2023). Counting and measuring the size and stomach fullness levels for an intelligent shrimp farming system. *Connection Science*, *35*(1), 2268878. Advance online publication. DOI: 10.1080/09540091.2023.2268878

Lin, H., Xu, N., Xing, G., Shang, Y., Wang, X., & Lin, L. (2024). Microfluidic chip-based microbial metabolism-indexed BOD sensor for rapid determination of biochemical oxygen demand. *Sensors and Actuators. B, Chemical*, *400*, 134868. Advance online publication. DOI: 10.1016/j.snb.2023.134868

Lordos, G. C., & De Weck, O. L. (2018). Evaluating the sustainability of long term manned Mars campaigns using a physical economics framework. *Proceedings of the International Astronautical Congress, IAC, 2018-October*. https://www.scopus.com/inward/record.uri?eid=2-s2.0-85065747763&partnerID=40&md5=ff4062ae6f43c7ede0fe169a36c8e12c

Markova, S. M., Tsyplakova, S. A., Sedhyh, E. P., Filatova, O. N., & Khizhnyi, A. V. (2021). University modernization in the conditions of industrialization of production and intelligent machines. *Lecture Notes in Networks and Systems*, *200*, 940–947. DOI: 10.1007/978-3-030-69421-0_104

Miglani, M., Bhatnagar, M., & Rajaram, R. (2025). Managing human capital in renewable energy amid geopolitical uncertainty: A financial outlook. In *Geopolitical Landscapes of Renewable Energy and Urban Growth*. IGI Global., DOI: 10.4018/979-8-3693-8814-3.ch011

Miglani, M., Taneja, S., Bhatnagar, M., & Johri, A. (2025). Transforming Financial Services: Ethical Pathways of Workforce Automation towards Achieving SDG 9. *International Research Journal of Multidisciplinary Scope*, *6*(2), 1298–1308. DOI: 10.47857/irjms.2025.v06i02.03963

Millar, G. (2021). Ambition and ambivalence: Reconsidering positive peace as a trans-scalar peace system. *Journal of Peace Research*, *58*(4), 640–654. DOI: 10.1177/0022343320941909

Nekhvyadovich, L. I., Adarina, R. T., & Robets, D. S. (2022). Environmental Factors for Measuring Service Performance. In *Geo-Economy of the Future: Sustainable Agriculture and Alternative Energy: Volume II*. (Vol. 2). Springer International Publishing. DOI: 10.1007/978-3-030-92303-7_4

Nesterov, O. G. (2023). Post-working Society: Synthetic Freedom and Work Ethics. *Voprosy Filosofii*, *2023*(2), 79–88. DOI: 10.21146/0042-8744-2023-2-79-88

Niederer, R., Richter, W., & Keller, H. (1980). Ion - selective Electrodes for Determination of Urine Electrolytes [Ionen-selektive Elektroden zur Bestimmung von Urin-Elektrolyten]. *Biomedizinische Technik*, *25*(3), 42–47. DOI: 10.1515/bmte.1980.25.3.42 PMID: 7448299

Nielsen, J. U., Madsen, N. T., & Clarke, R. (2014). Slaughter line operation. In *Encyclopedia of Meat Sciences*. Elsevier Inc., DOI: 10.1016/B978-0-12-384731-7.00150-1

Otoiu, A., Titan, E., Paraschiv, D. M., Dinu, V., & Manea, D. I. (2022). Analysing Labour-Based Estimates of Automation and Their Implications. A Comparative Approach from an Economic Competitiveness Perspective. *Journal of Competitiveness*, *14*(3), 133–152. DOI: 10.7441/joc.2022.03.08

Pai, S.-L., Hsia, K.-H., & Ho, C.-C. (2025). Quality Inspection of PVC Shoe Chopsticks: A Research Study. In J. Y., I. T., & L. J.-J. (Eds.), *Proceedings of International Conference on Artificial Life and Robotics* (pp. 200 – 203). ALife Robotics Corporation Ltd. https://www.scopus.com/inward/record.uri?eid=2-s2.0-85219532146&partnerID=40&md5=5f996c93592269ab43fc07cee8a84461

Pati, A. K. (2025). *Agentic AI: A Comprehensive Survey of Technologies, Applications, and Societal Implications*. IEEE., DOI: 10.1109/ACCESS.2025.3585609

Puntus, D. A., Yaroshenko, O. M., Chanysheva, H. I., Klemparskyi, M. M., & Yakovlyev, O. A. (2025). Social Insurance in the Context of Growing Labor Automation: New Challenges and Solutions. *Perspectives on Global Development and Technology*, *24*(3–4), 540–557. DOI: 10.1163/15691497-12341722

Rust, R. T., & Huang, M.-H. (2012). Optimizing service productivity. *Journal of Marketing*, *76*(2), 47–66. DOI: 10.1509/jm.10.0441

Sharma, R., Bhatnagar, M., & Ozen, E. (2025). The role of intellectual capital in combatting deepfake threats to corporate reputation and trust. In *Mastering Deepfake Technology: Strategies for Ethical Management and Security*. River Publishers. https://www.scopus.com/inward/record.uri?eid=2-s2.0-105007657679&partnerID=40&md5=f313a80a3279f91fbedf7fd10c6a4f7a

Sheriyarji, J. (2019). Braverman's legacy degraded labour, automation and information technology in the era of globalisation. *Economic and Political Weekly*, *54*(29), 92–99. https://www.scopus.com/inward/record.uri?eid=2-s2.0-85069716936&partnerID=40&md5=81431795676394a8b92d58f62b1b6698

Sirokha, D., Volynets, V., Kovalenko, R., Pohorielova, O., & Tkachuk, A. (2024). Labor Protection in the Perspective of Artificial Intelligence: New Challenges for the EU and the ILO. *Adam Mickiewicz University Law Review*, *16*, 67–98. DOI: 10.14746/ppuam.2024.16.03

Tokunova, A., Zvonar, V., Polozhentsev, D., Pavlova, V., & Teres, Y. (2023). Economic Consequences of Artificial Intelligence and Labor Automation: Employment Recovery, Transformation of Labor Markets, and Dynamics of Social Structure in the Context of Digital Transformation. *Economic Affairs (New Delhi)*, *68*(4), 2035–2046. DOI: 10.46852/0424-2513.4.2023.15

Trovato, G., Mavridis, N., Huerta-Mercado, A., & Chellali, R. (2021). Cross-Cultural Timeline of the History of Thought of the Artificial. *Lecture Notes in Computer Science (Including Subseries Lecture Notes in Artificial Intelligence and Lecture Notes in Bioinformatics), 13086 LNAI*, 14 – 23. DOI: 10.1007/978-3-030-90525-5_2

Vakhnin, N. A., Vakhnina, E. G., & Smirnova, N. N. (2018). Role of physical education in competitive specialist training process. *Teoriya i Praktika Fizicheskoy Kultury, 4*, 23 – 24. https://www.scopus.com/inward/record.uri?eid=2-s2.0-85044468438&partnerID=40&md5=96c01120fffb014edae47094332dddaa

Välimäki, S., Hazubska-Przybył, T., Ratajczak, E., Tikkinen, M., Varis, S., & Aronen, T. (2021). Somatic Embryo Yield and Quality From Norway Spruce Embryogenic Tissue Proliferated in Suspension Culture. *Frontiers in Plant Science*, *12*, 791549. Advance online publication. DOI: 10.3389/fpls.2021.791549 PMID: 34987536

Zubkova, L. D., Dyachkov, S. M., & Maksimov, I. B. (2019). An Indicator of Financial Condition in Industry Investment Analysis. In K. M., I. T., & M. G.A. (Eds.), *Springer Proceedings in Business and Economics* (pp. 243 – 250). Springer Science and Business Media B.V. DOI: 10.1007/978-3-030-26284-6_22

Chapter 7
Automation and the Future of Work in Aging Economies

M. U. Vinod Krishna
https://orcid.org/0009-0009-5150-3701
Dayananda Sagar College of Engineering, India

Shashank M. Hiremath
https://orcid.org/0009-0004-4082-3375
Presidency Business School, Presidency College, India

M. Arul Raja
https://orcid.org/0000-0003-1766-5650
Kongu Arts and Science College, India

Ravi Kishor Agrawal
https://orcid.org/0009-0001-2768-4946
MATS University, India

Sourabh Singh Roy
Gopal Narayan Singh University, India

P. Selvakumar
https://orcid.org/0000-0002-3650-4548
Department of Science and Humanities, Nehru Institute of Technology, Coimbatore, India

T. C. Manjunath
https://orcid.org/0000-0003-2545-9160
Rajarajeswari College of Engineering, India

ABSTRACT

Aging economies—characterized by declining birth rates, increasing life expectancy, and shrinking labor forces—face unprecedented challenges in sustaining economic productivity. As traditional workforces contract, automation and artificial intelligence (AI) are increasingly seen as crucial solutions for maintaining economic stability and supporting aging populations. Technologies such as robotic process automation (RPA), machine learning, and autonomous systems are transforming industries, reshaping the future of work, and redefining economic structures in aging societies.

DOI: 10.4018/979-8-3373-2550-7.ch007

This article explores the impact of automation on labor markets in aging economies, focusing on both challenges and opportunities. It examines how automation affects employment trends, economic productivity, healthcare, and workforce dynamics, while also addressing policy considerations, social implications, and ethical concerns.

INTRODUCTION TO AUTOMATION AND THE FUTURE OF WORK IN AGING ECONOMIES

Aging economies—characterized by declining birth rates, increasing life expectancy, and shrinking labor forces—face unprecedented challenges in sustaining economic productivity. As traditional workforces contract, automation and artificial intelligence (AI) are increasingly seen as crucial solutions for maintaining economic stability and supporting aging populations. Technologies such as robotic process automation (RPA), machine learning, and autonomous systems are transforming industries, reshaping the future of work, and redefining economic structures in aging societies. This article explores the impact of automation on labor markets in aging economies, focusing on both challenges and opportunities. It examines how automation affects employment trends, economic productivity, healthcare, and workforce dynamics, while also addressing policy considerations, social implications, and ethical concerns. The Impact of Automation on Aging Economies: The Demographic Shift in Aging Economies: Aging economies, primarily found in countries like Japan, Germany, South Korea, and Italy, face labor shortages due to low birth rates and a growing elderly population. These demographic changes create economic pressures, including declining workforce participation, leading to reduced economic output. Increased dependency ratios, where fewer working-age individuals support a larger retired population. Rising healthcare and pension costs, placing strain on public and private sector resources. Automation is seen as a potential solution to compensate for labor shortages by augmenting or replacing human workers in critical sectors. Automation's Role in Economic Productivity: Automation can enhance economic resilience in aging economies by increasing efficiency. Robots and AI-driven systems can boost productivity in manufacturing, logistics, and services. Reducing labor shortages: Automation fills gaps left by retiring workers, ensuring the continuity of economic activities.

Lowering operational costs: Automated systems reduce reliance on human labor, improving cost efficiency in businesses. For instance, Japan has invested heavily in robotics for elderly care, using humanoid robots to assist in nursing homes and reduce the burden on human caregivers. Industry-Specific Impacts of Automation: Manufacturing and Industrial Automation: Smart factories, powered by the Internet of Things (IoT) and AI, enhance production with minimal human intervention.

Cobots (collaborative robots) are used in aging economies to assist older workers in industrial settings, extending their ability to work. Healthcare and Elderly Care Automation: AI-driven diagnostics and robotic surgery improve healthcare outcomes. Automated elderly care solutions, such as robotic companions and AI-assisted monitoring, address shortages in healthcare workers. Service and Knowledge-Based Industries: AI chatbots and virtual assistants replace human customer service roles. Automation in finance and law streamlines data processing, fraud detection, and compliance management. Challenges of Automation in Aging Economies: Job Displacement and Workforce Transition: While automation fills labor gaps, it also displaces traditional jobs, leading to Structural unemployment, where workers lack the skills for new AI-driven roles. Resistance to technological adoption, especially among older workers unfamiliar with automation technologies.

THE AGING ECONOMY: DEMOGRAPHIC TRENDS AND IMPLICATIONS FOR THE LABOR MARKET

The global economy is undergoing a profound transformation due to population aging, a trend driven by increasing life expectancy and declining birth rates. This shift is especially pronounced in developed economies such as Japan, Germany, South Korea, Italy, and China, where the proportion of elderly citizens is rising rapidly. As a result, labor markets in these countries face significant challenges, including shrinking workforces, increased dependency ratios, and evolving employment dynamics. Understanding the demographic trends in aging economies is crucial for policymakers, businesses, and society at large. The implications of an aging population extend far beyond workforce availability; they impact economic growth, productivity, healthcare, pension systems, and technological innovation. This discussion explores the key demographic trends, their consequences for the labor market, and potential strategies for mitigating the challenges of an aging workforce. Key Demographic Trends in Aging Economies: Declining Birth Rates and Population Shrinkage: One of the most defining characteristics of aging economies is the declining fertility rate, which leads to population shrinkage and labor shortages. Key trends include: Fertility rates below replacement level (2.1 children per woman) in most developed economies (Maestas N., et al, 2023). Aging workforce composition, with older workers (aged 55+) making up a growing share of the labor market. As fewer young people enter the workforce, businesses struggle to find talent, and governments face difficulties in sustaining economic growth. Increasing Life Expectancy and Rising Dependency Ratios: Advancements in healthcare and living standards have led to longer life expectancies, resulting in Higher old-age dependency ratios, meaning fewer workers are supporting a growing number of retirees. Rising pension and healthcare costs, placing pressure on government budgets. Delayed retirement trends, as older workers stay employed longer to compensate for inadequate pensions. For example, in Germany, the proportion of people aged 65 and older is expected to reach nearly 30% by 2050, significantly impacting the labor market.

Shifts in Workforce Participation and Employment Patterns: With fewer young workers entering the job market, employment structures are shifting, including Increased workforce participation among older workers, often in part-time or flexible roles. A rise in automation and AI-driven jobs replacing traditional labor-intensive roles (Domash & Summers, 2022). Greater reliance on immigration to supplement labor shortages, though this approach varies by country due to political and social challenges. These changes demand adaptive workforce policies to support aging employees while ensuring economic stability. Implications for the Labor Market: Labor Shortages and Productivity Challenges: Aging economies face severe labor shortages, leading to reduced economic growth, as fewer workers contribute to national productivity. Skill gaps, as industries struggle to replace retiring professionals with younger, skilled workers. Greater reliance on automation, AI, and robotics to fill workforce gaps in key sectors such as manufacturing, healthcare, and services.

Alternative workforce solutions, such as cross-border digital labor and outsourcing. Canada and Australia have implemented successful immigration policies to attract skilled talent, setting an example for other aging economies. Strategies for Addressing the Challenges of an Aging Workforce: Workforce Reskilling and Lifelong Learning: To adapt to an aging workforce, businesses and governments must invest in: Upskilling programs for older workers to transition into emerging job roles (Osareme O J., et al, 2024). Lifelong learning initiatives to keep employees productive beyond traditional retirement age. Incentives for businesses to retain experienced workers through flexible work arrangements. Leveraging Automation and AI: Technology can help mitigate labor shortages by integrating AI and robotics in key industries such as manufacturing, healthcare, and logistics. Implementing AI-driven workforce management tools to enhance productivity. To counter labor shortages, countries should explore International talent exchange programs, promoting knowledge-sharing (Albanesi & Kim, 2021). Remote and digital work solutions allow businesses to access global talent pools. Policies that balance immigration needs with social and economic stability.

THE RISE OF AUTOMATION: TECHNOLOGICAL ADVANCEMENTS AND THEIR IMPACT ON WORK

Automation is transforming the global workforce at an unprecedented pace. Driven by advancements in artificial intelligence (AI), robotics, machine learning (ML), and the Internet of Things (IoT), automation is reshaping industries, redefining job roles, and altering economic landscapes. While automation has long been a part of industrial progress, recent breakthroughs in intelligent systems, data analytics, and autonomous machines are accelerating its adoption across nearly every sector. As businesses strive for efficiency, cost reduction, and competitiveness, automation is replacing or augmenting traditional human labor in fields such as manufacturing, logistics, finance, healthcare, and customer service. While these innovations offer significant benefits—including increased productivity, improved safety, and lower operational costs—they also present challenges related to job displacement, workforce adaptation, and ethical considerations. This discussion explores the key technological advancements driving automation, their impact on various industries, the benefits and challenges of automation in the workforce, and strategies to ensure a balanced transition into an increasingly automated world (Loku, 2025). Technological Advancements in Automation: Artificial Intelligence and Machine Learning: AI and ML are at the heart of modern automation, enabling machines to analyze vast amounts of data and make decisions without human intervention. Recognize patterns and optimize processes, improving efficiency and reducing errors. Continuously learn and improve performance over time. Examples include AI-powered chatbots in customer service. Predictive analytics in finance and healthcare. AI-driven automation in logistics, optimizing supply chain management. Robotics and Autonomous Systems: Industrial and service robots are increasingly replacing manual labor, particularly in repetitive, dangerous, or precision-required tasks. Advancements include Collaborative robots (cobots) that work alongside humans in manufacturing.

Autonomous drones are used in agriculture, security, and logistics. Self-driving vehicles are revolutionizing transportation and delivery services. The IoT connects machines, devices, and systems through the internet, enabling Smart factories that optimize production lines with real-time data. Automated home systems enhance convenience and energy efficiency. Predictive maintenance, reducing downtime and costs in industrial settings. Cloud Computing and Edge Computing: The rise of cloud-based automation has transformed industries by enabling remote work through virtual collaboration tools. Facilitating large-scale automation with AI-driven decision-making in real time (Khogali & Mekid, 2023). Allowing seamless data storage and retrieval and improving operational efficiency.\Automation is also transforming transactions and contracts through Blockchain-powered smart contracts, reducing reliance on human intermediaries. Decentralized finance (DeFi) automation, enhancing security and efficiency in banking. Supply chain automation, ensuring transparency and traceability in logistics. \Workforce Displacement and Job Transformation: While automation eliminates some jobs, it also creates new roles that require higher skill levels. Key trends include the decline of repetitive, manual jobs in manufacturing, retail, and data processing. Growth in AI-related roles, such as AI ethics specialists, machine learning engineers, and automation strategists. Emergence of hybrid human-AI jobs, where workers use AI tools to enhance productivity.

Changes in Employment Across Industries: Manufacturing and Industrial Automation: Traditional assembly line jobs are being replaced by robots. Human workers are shifting to oversight roles, managing robotic systems, 3D printing, and AI-driven production, which are reducing material waste and increasing efficiency. Healthcare and Medical Automation: AI-assisted diagnostics improve accuracy in disease detection. Surgical robots enhance precision in complex procedures. Automated administrative systems reduce paperwork and improve hospital efficiency. Financial Services and Banking: AI-driven trading algorithms optimize stock market decisions. Chatbots and virtual assistants handle customer inquiries. Automated fraud detection enhances security. Retail and E-Commerce: Self-checkout kiosks reduce cashier dependency, and AI-driven recommendation systems enhance customer experience. Automated warehouses streamline inventory management. Transportation and Logistics: Autonomous delivery vehicles reduce reliance on drivers. AI-powered route optimization improves supply chain efficiency. Smart traffic management reduces congestion and fuel consumption (Tschang F T., et al, 2021). The Benefits of Automation in the Workforce: Automation offers numerous advantages, including Increased efficiency, reduced time, and lower labor costs. Improved workplace safety, as hazardous tasks are automated. Higher productivity, allowing businesses to scale faster. Better job quality, as routine work is replaced by higher-value tasks. Challenges and Ethical Considerations: Despite its benefits, automation presents challenges such as Job displacement, particularly for low-skilled workers. Skills gap, requiring retraining and upskilling efforts. Bias in AI algorithms leads to ethical concerns in hiring and decision-making. Economic inequality, as automation benefits higher-skilled workers disproportionately. Strategies for Managing the Impact of Automation: Workforce Reskilling and Education: To mitigate job displacement, businesses and governments must: Invest in lifelong learning programs, ensuring workers remain employable. Promote STEM education, preparing younger generations for AI-driven jobs. Encourage public-private partnerships and funding reskilling initiatives. Human-AI Collaboration: Rather than replacing workers, AI can enhance human productivity through AI-assisted decision-making in healthcare, finance, and engineering. Collaborative robots that support human workers in factories. Augmented intelligence tools help professionals analyze complex data. Ethical AI and Automation Policies: Governments must establish ethical AI guidelines, ensuring fairness and accountability. Regulate automated decision-making, preventing bias and discrimination. Create safety nets, such as universal basic income (UBI) for displaced workers (Parry E., et al, 2023).

JOB DISPLACEMENT AND CREATION: THE DUAL EFFECTS OF AUTOMATION ON EMPLOYMENT

Automation is reshaping the global workforce, bringing both opportunities and challenges. While it enhances efficiency, productivity, and innovation, it also disrupts traditional job structures. The replacement of human labor with machines, artificial intelligence (AI), and robotics has raised concerns about job displacement, especially in sectors reliant on repetitive tasks. At the same time, automation is creating new industries, job roles, and economic opportunities, requiring workers to adapt, upskill, and embrace new technologies. The debate over automation's impact on employment is complex. Some fear mass unemployment due to machines taking over jobs, while others argue that automation, as with past industrial revolutions, will ultimately lead to net job creation. This discussion explores the dual effects of automation on employment, examining both job displacement and job creation, as well as strategies to manage workforce transitions in an increasingly automated world (Parker S K., et al, 2022). Job Displacement Due to Automation: Understanding Job Loss in an Automated Economy: Job displacement occurs when technology replaces human labor, reducing the demand for certain occupations. This happens in industries where Tasks are repetitive, predictable, and routine, making them easy to automate. Efficiency gains from automation outweigh the costs of human labor. AI and robotics outperform humans in speed, accuracy, and cost-effectiveness. The most vulnerable sectors include manufacturing, retail, logistics, finance, and customer service, where automation is already eliminating traditional roles. Industries Most Affected by Job Displacement: Manufacturing and Industrial Automation: Factory jobs are being replaced by robots and automated assembly lines. 3D printing is reducing the need for traditional manufacturing processes. AI-powered quality control systems are minimizing human inspection roles. Example: Foxconn, Apple's supplier, replaced 60,000 factory workers with robots in China, increasing efficiency while reducing human employment. Retail and E-Commerce: Self-checkout kiosks are replacing cashiers, and AI-driven inventory management reduces the need for stock clerks. Online shopping is disrupting traditional retail jobs. Example: Amazon's cashier-less "Just Walk Out" stores eliminate the need for checkout workers, transforming the retail experience. Transportation and Logistics: Autonomous vehicles and delivery drones are reducing the need for drivers. AI-driven route optimization minimizes human decision-making in logistics (Cazzaniga M., et al, 2024). Warehouse automation, such as robotic picking systems, replaces manual labor.

Job Creation Through Automation: How Automation Creates New Jobs. While automation eliminates certain jobs, it also generates demand for new skills and professions. Drives growth in technology-related industries. Creates opportunities in fields that support automation, such as AI development and robotics maintenance.

Industries Benefiting from Automation-Driven Job Growth: Technology and AI Development: Machine learning engineers and AI specialists develop and refine automation technologies. Data scientists and analysts interpret automation-driven insights. Cybersecurity experts protect AI-driven systems from cyber threats. Example: The AI and robotics industry is expected to create millions of high-tech jobs globally. Healthcare and Biotechnology: AI-assisted diagnostics and medical imaging create demand for AI-trained healthcare professionals. Robot-assisted surgeries require specialized engineers and technicians. Elderly care robots are leading to new roles in health robotics maintenance and programming (Sugumaran K M D., et al. 2024). Example: The healthcare sector is increasingly using AI for medical research, patient care, and diagnostics, leading to new job opportunities. Green Energy and Sustainability: Hybrid jobs combine human expertise with AI assistance, such as AI-assisted doctors and nurses using machine learning to diagnose diseases. Financial analysts using AI-powered risk assessment tools. Customer service agents supported by AI chatbots handle complex inquiries, while automation manages routine tasks (Rodrik D., 2022). To prevent economic inequality, policymakers should Explore Universal Basic Income (UBI) models to support displaced workers. Reform taxation policies, ensuring that automation-driven profits benefit society. Strengthen worker protections, balancing automation adoption with fair employment practices (Konstantis K., et al, 2024). Encouraging Innovation and Entrepreneurship: Automation opens doors for new startups leveraging AI and robotics. Job creation in digital and remote work environments. Expansion of creative industries, which are less prone to automation. Navigating the Future of Work in an Automated Economy: The dual effects of automation—job displacement and job creation—will define the future of work.

THE CHANGING NATURE OF WORK: FROM ROUTINE TO NON-ROUTINE TASKS

The nature of work has been transforming at an unprecedented pace, driven by technological advancements, automation, artificial intelligence (AI), and shifts in economic structures. Over the past few decades, there has been a noticeable shift from routine-based tasks to non-routine tasks, fundamentally altering the skills required in the labor market. While routine jobs, particularly those that involve repetitive and predictable processes, were once the backbone of the industrial economy, modern workplaces are increasingly demanding cognitive, creative, and interpersonal skills that machines cannot easily replicate. This shift has profound implications for employment patterns, income distribution, job security, and workforce development. As routine tasks become automated, employees must adapt by developing problem-solving abilities, critical thinking, and technological literacy to remain relevant in the labor market (Priyadarshi P., et al, 2022). This discussion explores the differences between routine and non-routine tasks, the impact of automation, and how workers and organizations can adapt to the changing landscape of work. Due to their predictability, routine tasks are the most susceptible to automation, AI, and robotic process automation (RPA). What Are Non-Routine Tasks? Non-routine tasks, in contrast, require human judgment, creativity, social interaction, problem-solving, and adaptability. These tasks do not follow a strict set of rules and often require workers to respond to dynamic and unpredictable situations (Johri S., et al. 2025).

These require physical effort but also judgment and adaptability, such as construction work, emergency response, skilled trades, and healthcare. As industries move toward a more knowledge-based economy, non-routine tasks are becoming increasingly valuable and in demand. Automation and the Decline of Routine Tasks: How Automation Replaces Routine Jobs: Technological advancements, particularly in AI, robotics, and machine learning, have enabled machines to perform routine tasks more efficiently, accurately, and cost-effectively than humans. The most affected industries include Manufacturing. Industrial robots now perform repetitive assembly-line tasks with precision (Salimgereyev N., et al, 2024). Retail and Customer Service: Self-checkout kiosks and AI chatbots reduce the need for human cashiers and customer service agents. To remain relevant, workers must learn digital and technical skills to work alongside AI (Okubo T., 2024). Shaping Policy for an Automated Future: Governments and institutions must implement policies that support workforce transitions (e.g., unemployment benefits, retraining programs). Encourage job creation in non-routine fields through innovation and investment. Promote universal access to education and upskilling opportunities (Frank K., et al, 2021).

THE SKILLS GAP: PREPARING WORKERS FOR AN AUTOMATED ECONOMY

Understanding the Skills Gap in an Automated Economy: As automation, artificial intelligence (AI), and robotics continue to reshape industries, the global workforce faces an unprecedented skills gap. The demand for highly skilled workers is increasing, while routine-based jobs are being replaced by machines. This creates a discrepancy between the skills workers possess and those required by employers, making it difficult for many individuals to find stable employment in the evolving job market. The skills gap is particularly evident in industries undergoing rapid digital transformation, such as manufacturing, finance, healthcare, logistics, and customer service (Afonso & Forte, 2024). Companies struggle to fill positions requiring technical expertise, problem-solving, creativity, and adaptability, while many workers lack the necessary training to transition into these roles. Addressing this skills gap is crucial for economic growth, job security, and societal stability. Changing Employer Expectations: Employers increasingly seek workers with a mix of technical and soft skills, such as adaptability, emotional intelligence, and digital literacy (Ramakrishnan T. et al. 2022). The lack of skilled workers in critical industries like AI, cybersecurity, and engineering slows down innovation and economic progress. Widening Inequality: High-skilled workers in technology and automation fields enjoy rising wages and job security, while low-skilled workers experience stagnant wages and job instability (Al Saad & Blomqvist, 2024). This deepens economic and social inequalities, as well-paid jobs become concentrated among those with access to advanced education and training. Providing career counseling and job placement services for workers affected by automation. Example: Singapore's Skills Future program offers financial incentives for workers to reskill in high-demand fields. Encouraging Lifelong Learning and Micro-Credentials: Online platforms like Coursera, Udemy, and edX provide flexible, affordable learning options (Adepoju & Aigbavboa, 2021). Companies should encourage employees to experiment with new technologies (Bukartaite & Hooper, 2023). Governments should promote entrepreneurship and innovation in emerging fields. Example: Estonia's digital-first economy invests in workforce digital literacy to prepare citizens for automation.

AGING ECONOMIES AND AUTOMATION: A PERFECT STORM?

This discussion explores how aging economies and automation are converging, the potential risks, and strategies for managing the transition. The Demographic Challenge: Aging Populations and Workforce Decline: The Growing Share of Older Populations: Many developed nations are experiencing a decline in working-age populations, meaning fewer workers supporting more retirees (Deschacht N., 2021). Supporting elderly care through robotics, AI-driven diagnostics, and automated assistance. Which Jobs Are Most Affected? Automation is more likely to replace routine manual and cognitive tasks, while non-routine jobs requiring creativity, decision-making, and social intelligence remain relatively safe. High-risk jobs: Manufacturing and assembly-line work (robots and automated production).Retail and customer service (self-checkout, chatbots, AI-driven support).Clerical and administrative roles (automated bookkeeping, data entry, and HR processing) (Glover & Mustre-del-Río, 2024). Low-risk jobs: Healthcare and elder care (nurses, caregivers, therapists).Creative and strategic roles (scientists, designers, entrepreneurs).Skilled trades (electricians, plumbers, repair technicians).

Governments and businesses must invest in lifelong learning programs to help workers adapt to AI-driven industries (Lee I., 2023). Older workers should receive training in digital literacy, problem-solving, and emerging technologies. Flexible work arrangements and hybrid jobs can help older employees stay in the workforce longer. Strategies for Managing Automation in Aging Economies: Policy Reforms for Workforce Adaptation: Incentivizing continuous learning through tax benefits, subsidies, and employer-sponsored training. Encouraging later retirement ages while ensuring flexible, lower-intensity jobs for older workers. Introducing universal basic income (UBI) or wage subsidies for displaced workers. Strengthening Social Safety Nets: Expanding pension and healthcare support for aging populations. Implementing AI-driven job-matching platforms to help displaced workers transition to new roles. Investing in AI-Augmented Workforces: Encouraging businesses to adopt "cobots" (collaborative robots) that work alongside humans rather than replace them. Redesigning job roles to integrate automation while preserving meaningful employment. Fostering Public-Private Collaboration: Governments should partner with tech companies, universities, and businesses to create tailored workforce training programs (Grinin L., et al, 2024). Multinational cooperation can ensure equitable access to AI-driven economic benefits. A Double-Edged Sword: The intersection of aging economies and automation presents both significant risks and transformative opportunities. If managed effectively, automation can boost productivity, support elder care, and create new career paths for workers of all ages. However, without proactive policies, it could exacerbate job displacement, economic inequality, and workforce instability.

THE IMPACT OF AUTOMATION ON AGING WORKERS: CHALLENGES AND OPPORTUNITIES

The Intersection of Aging and Automation: The global workforce is undergoing a fundamental On the other hand, automation offers opportunities for older workers to extend their careers by reducing physical labor, enabling flexible work arrangements, and improving workplace efficiency. This discussion explores the challenges older workers face due to automation, the opportunities it presents, and potential strategies for ensuring a smooth transition into an increasingly automated economy (Keeler & Bernstein, 2021). Challenges Faced by Aging Workers in an Automated World: Higher Risk of Job Displacement: Automation is particularly disruptive to routine-based jobs, which tend to have a higher proportion of older workers. Jobs in manufacturing, administration, retail, and transportation—fields heavily occupied by older workers—are among the most vulnerable to automation. Older workers who lose jobs due to automation face greater challenges in finding new employment compared to younger workers. Difficulty Adapting to New Technologies: Many older workers lack digital skills needed for emerging industries. Resistance to change or fear of technology can make adaptation more difficult. On-the-job training programs often focus on younger employees, leaving older workers with fewer opportunities to reskill (Debnath P., et al. 2025). Pension and Financial Security Risks: Job loss due to automation can disrupt retirement plans, forcing older workers to delay retirement or take lower-paying jobs (Alcover C M., et al, 2021).

The Adoption of AI-powered tools, exoskeletons, and automation that support rather than replace older workers (Acemoglu & Restrepo, 2022). Development of workplace modifications that make jobs more accessible for aging employees. Social Safety Net Strengthening: Adjusting pension systems to reflect longer work lives and support displaced older workers. Exploring policies like Universal Basic Income (UBI) to support workers impacted by automation. Case Studies: How Aging Workers Are Adapting to Automation: Japan: Integrating Robots to Support an Aging Workforce: Japan, facing one of the world's oldest populations, is using collaborative robots ("cobots") to assist aging workers in factories. Companies like Toyota and Panasonic have introduced automation tools that reduce physical strain, allowing older workers to extend their careers. Germany: Reskilling Older Workers for a Digital Economy: Germany's lifelong learning initiatives provide free training for older workers to develop AI, cybersecurity, and software skills. The German government encourages public-private partnerships to help older employees transition into automation-driven roles (Nagarajan N R., et al, 2023). United States: Remote Work and AI-Powered Job Matching: The shift to remote and gig economy jobs has allowed older workers in the U.S. to remain employed longer.

DESIGNING AGE-FRIENDLY WORKPLACES IN AN AUTOMATED ECONOMY

This discussion explores strategies for designing age-friendly workplaces in an automated economy, addressing physical and cognitive adaptations, technological solutions, policy considerations, and real-world case studies (Chu CH., et al, 2022). Challenges Faced by Older Workers in Automated Workplaces: Digital and Automation Skill Gaps: Many older workers lack experience with digital tools and automation systems. Lack of retraining opportunities forces many older workers into early retirement. Mental Well-Being and Workplace Inclusion: Older employees may experience isolation or anxiety when working in high-tech environments. Intergenerational work conflicts may arise if younger workers are perceived as more tech-savvy (Aragani, V M., et al. 2025). Wearable devices and exoskeletons to reduce physical strain in industries like manufacturing and logistics. Digital Inclusion and Training Programs: Bridging the digital divide is key to empowering older workers (Da Silva, 2025). Lifelong learning programs should include AI and automation training tailored to older employees. Funding for lifelong learning initiatives. Stronger legal protections against age discrimination in automated workplaces. Case Studies: Companies Implementing Age-Friendly Automation: Toyota (Japan): Robotics for Aging Workers: Toyota uses "cobots" (collaborative robots) to assist older employees in factories. Exoskeletons and automation tools reduce the physical strain on older workers (Wissemann A K., et al, 2022). BMW (Germany): Adapting Workstations for an Older Workforce: BMW redesigned assembly lines with adjustable-height workbenches, softer floors, and AI-powered monitoring to help older workers. Productivity increased after these changes were implemented. AT&T (USA): Digital Reskilling for Older Workers: AT&T launched a company-wide upskilling initiative to train employees in AI and digital skills. Older employees were given access to online courses and flexible training schedules. The Future of Age-Friendly Workplaces in an Automated Economy: Automation is not inherently a threat to older workers—it can be a tool for inclusion and empowerment if implemented thoughtfully (Segkouli S., et al, 2023).

POLICY RESPONSES TO AUTOMATION IN AGING ECONOMIES: A REVIEW OF INTERNATIONAL APPROACHES

The Intersection of Automation and Aging Economies: As automation and artificial intelligence (AI) reshape industries, aging economies face unique challenges and opportunities. Many developed nations, including Japan, Germany, South Korea, and the United States, are experiencing shrinking labor forces due to low birth rates and increasing life expectancy. At the same time, rapid advancements in automation and robotics are transforming manufacturing, healthcare, and service industries, altering the demand for labor. Governments worldwide are adopting policy responses to mitigate job displacement, support older workers, and maximize the economic benefits of automation. This review explores international approaches to automation in aging economies, focusing on workforce adaptation, social protections, economic incentives, and regulatory frameworks. Key Policy Challenges in Automation and Aging Economies: Shrinking Labor Forces and Productivity Gaps: As retirement rates exceed workforce entry rates, automation is seen as a tool to maintain productivity despite a declining working-age population. The challenge lies in balancing automation with job retention, ensuring that automation supplements rather than replaces human labor (McGinley C., et al, 2022). Workforce Adaptation and Reskilling Initiatives: Japan: Lifelong Learning and Digital Retraining Programs: Japan, the world's oldest major economy, has introduced government-funded retraining programs to equip older workers with digital skills (Shende A D., et al. 2025). Workforce development subsidies encourage businesses to retrain workers rather than replace them (Koch T., 2024). Social Protection and Singapore: Government Grants for Senior-Friendly Automation: Singapore provides financial incentives to companies that invest in age-inclusive automation, such as AI-driven assistance tools and ergonomic workplace technologies. The government also co-funds retraining programs for companies that retain and upskill older employees.

Figure 1. Types of Automation

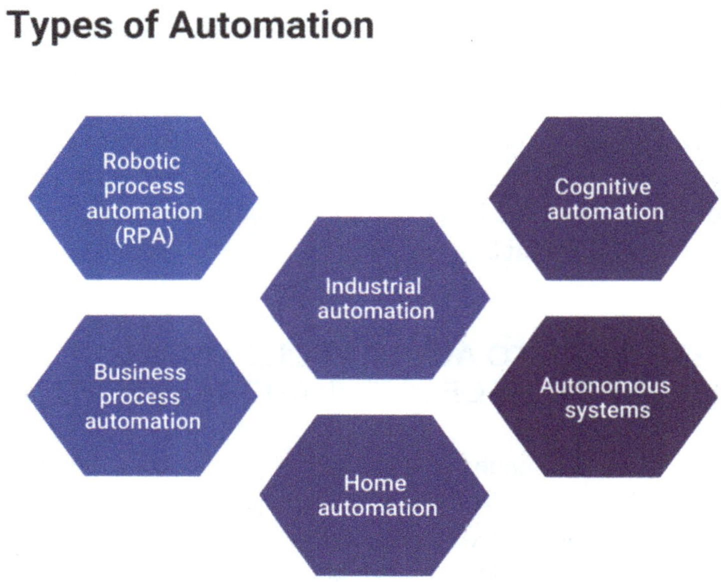

Labor Market Regulations and Anti-Age Discrimination Policies: United States: Age Discrimination in Employment Act (ADEA): The ADEA prohibits age discrimination in hiring, training, and promotions, ensuring older workers have equal opportunities in an automated workforce. However, enforcement challenges remain, requiring continuous policy refinement. European Union: Digital Inclusion Strategies for Older Workers: The EU has adopted the Digital Skills and Jobs Coalition, promoting intergenerational mentoring and AI-assisted learning tools for older employees. Legal frameworks ensure that automation adoption does not disproportionately disadvantage aging workers. Policy Recommendations for Automation in Aging Economies: Based on international best practices, governments should adopt a multi-pronged approach to managing automation's impact on aging economies (Ho M T., et al, 2022). Automation tax revenues could be redirected toward pension funds and reskilling programs. Strengthen Anti-Age Discrimination Policies:

Stricter enforcement of age discrimination laws in hiring and training. AI-driven bias detection tools can help ensure fair recruitment and promotion practices. The Future of Automation Policy in Aging Economies: Automation poses both risks and opportunities for aging economies. While automation can help sustain economic growth despite a declining workforce, it also creates workforce disruptions that disproportionately affect older employees (Mansour H., 2022).

UPSKILLING AND RESKILLING: STRATEGIES FOR WORKERS IN AN AUTOMATED ECONOMY

Understanding Upskilling and Reskilling: What is Upskilling? Upskilling refers to enhancing existing skills or learning new advanced skills to improve job performance and career progression within the same or a related field (Horoshko O I., et al, 2021). Example: A manufacturing worker learning data analysis and robotics programming to operate automated systems. Boosts economic resilience: Enables industries to adapt to technological disruptions without massive layoffs. Enhances job satisfaction and security: Workers feel more confident and secure in their careers. Strategies for Upskilling and Reskilling Workers in an Automated Economy: Employer-Led Training Programs Businesses play a crucial role in workforce development by providing on-the-job training, digital learning platforms, and career transition support (Costa I., et al, 2024). Example 1: Amazon's Upskilling 2025 Initiative (United States) Amazon is investing $1.2 billion to train 300,000 employees in high-demand fields such as cloud computing, AI, and cybersecurity. Offers free certifications and technical courses to transition warehouse workers into IT and data roles. Example 2: Siemens' Lifelong Learning Programs (Germany)Siemens integrates AI-powered training platforms into its workforce strategy. Employees receive continuous learning opportunities through online courses, workshops, and mentorship programs. Employer-Led Training Strategies: Partnerships with universities and tech companies for skill certification programs (Mahadev Madgule et al., 2023).

Reskilling traditional banking staff in fintech and blockchain technology and AI-powered customer service training for support agents working with chatbots and virtual assistants. Online Learning Platforms and Digital Training: Online platforms provide affordable, flexible, and scalable ways for workers to upskill. Popular Digital Training Platforms for Upskilling: Coursera, Udacity, and edX – They offer AI, machine learning, and automation-related courses. LinkedIn Learning – Focuses on business, technology, and leadership skills. Google Career Certificates – These provide industry-recognized credentials in IT, data analysis, and cybersecurity (Morandini S., et al, 2023). As automation handles repetitive tasks, upskilling will emphasize creativity, problem-solving, and emotional intelligence. Public-Private

Collaboration for Large-Scale Reskilling: Stronger government-business partnerships will ensure that training programs align with industry needs (Ekuma K., 2023). Building a Future-Ready Workforce: The shift to an automated economy presents challenges and opportunities. Workers must be proactively upskilled and reskilled to remain competitive.

SOCIAL PROTECTION AND SAFETY NETS: SUPPORTING WORKERS IN AN AUTOMATED ECONOMY

This discussion explores key strategies for designing robust social protection systems that support workers in an increasingly automated economy. Understanding Social Protection and Safety Nets in an Automated World: What Are Social Protection and Safety Nets? Social protection refers to government and employer-provided policies and programs that help individuals cope with economic shocks, job losses, health issues, and financial instability (Li L., 2024). Safety nets are targeted social assistance programs designed to support vulnerable populations (Sreenivasulu A., et al. 2022). Why Are They Essential in an Automated Economy? Automation replaces low-skilled jobs: Many routine jobs in manufacturing, retail, and logistics are at risk of automation, increasing unemployment rates. Link unemployment benefits with mandatory reskilling programs. Provide wage subsidies to encourage companies to retain employees (Spasova S., et al, 2023). Universal Basic Income (UBI): A Potential Safety Net? With automation reducing the demand for human labor, UBI is being considered as a way to ensure economic stability. Example 1: Finland's UBI Pilot Program (2017-2018) Provided €560/month to unemployed individuals without conditions. Improved mental well-being and job-seeking motivation but had limited impact on employment rates. Test regional pilot programs to measure the effectiveness of automation-driven job losses. The European Union's Platform Work Directive ensures gig workers have basic social protections, including minimum wage and sick leave (Gentilini U., 2022). Key Strategies: Establish portable benefits that move with gig workers between jobs. Implement minimum wage protections for digital labor platforms. Introduce AI-driven monitoring to prevent algorithmic bias in gig work assignments. Hybrid Models Combining UBI and Workforce Training: Future policies may merge UBI with mandatory training programs to ensure productivity (Busemeyer & Sahm, 2022). Global Collaboration on Social Protection Standards: Governments will work together to set international labor protections for automation-driven economies.

CASE STUDY: AUTOMATION AND AGING WORKERS IN THE MANUFACTURING SECTOR

Aging workers, defined as those aged 50 and older, represent a significant portion of the manufacturing workforce in developed economies such as the United States, Germany, Japan, and South Korea. Many have spent decades in physically intensive roles, relying on manual skills rather than digital proficiency (McKay & Reis, 2021). The manufacturing sector has one of the oldest workforces in the global economy: United States: The average age of a manufacturing worker is 44 years, with nearly 25% over 55. Germany: Over 30% of manufacturing workers are over the age of 50 (Vijayakumar G, et al. 2024). Japan: Due to low birth rates, nearly 40% of manufacturing workers are over 50, prompting major workforce shortages. Many of these workers have deep industry experience but limited digital skills, making automation a disruptive force in their careers. Automation in Manufacturing: Key Technologies: Automation in manufacturing includes: Industrial Robotics – Machines performing repetitive tasks with high precision & Machine Learning – Smart systems optimizing workflows and predicting equipment failures. Collaborative Robots (Cobots) – Robots that assist rather than replace human workers. Digital Twin Technology – Virtual simulations that allow remote monitoring and training. As automation spreads, aging workers must adapt to new roles that require technical proficiency rather than manual labor (Lowe B D., et al, 2023). Companies investing in upskilling aging workers see productivity gains. Examples include Siemens' Industry 4.0 Training Program, which provides VR-based automation training tailored for older employees. Toyota's AI-Augmented Apprenticeship Model – Pairs younger engineers with senior workers to transfer technical knowledge while upskilling in automation. Redesigning Work Environments for Aging Employees Ergonomic workstations reduce physical strain. Wearable assistive devices support mobility and vision, and AI-driven adaptive work schedules accommodate age-related limitations (De Felice F., et al, 2022). Global Case Studies: Successful Custom AI training modules are designed for older workers. Flexible automation policies that balance human-machine collaboration (Olurin J O., et al, 2024). Outcome: 85% of aging workers successfully transitioned into new roles.

EXAMPLE OF A SUCCESSFUL AGE-FRIENDLY WORKPLACE INITIATIVE IN AN AUTOMATED ECONOMY

A Model for Age-Inclusive Automation Background on Siemens and the Aging Workforce Challenge Siemens, a global leader in industrial automation and digital manufacturing, employs thousands of workers across multiple industries, including energy, healthcare, transportation, and manufacturing. As 40% of its workforce in Europe and North America is over the age of 50, Siemens recognized the need to create a sustainable, age-inclusive workforce strategy that aligns with its shift toward Industry 4.0, smart factories, and AI-driven automation. To address this, Siemens launched the "Lifelong@Siemens" initiative, focusing on Workplace Adaptation: Designing ergonomic, AI-assisted workstations for aging employees. Reskilling & Upskilling: Providing digital training programs tailored to older workers (Ward P., 2023). Collaborative Robotics (Cobots): Assisting aging employees in physical tasks. Flexible Work Policies: We offer part-time, remote, and hybrid roles for older employees. Key Components of the Lifelong@Siemens Initiative: Workplace Adaptation: Age-Friendly Smart Factories: One of the core aspects of the initiative was transforming Siemens' factories into "Smart Factories" where aging employees could continue working in automation-driven environments. Siemens implemented Collaborative Robots (Cobots): Cobots assist older workers by handling repetitive or physically demanding tasks, allowing them to focus on supervision and quality control. Ergonomic Workstations: AI-driven adjustable desks, wearable exoskeletons, and fatigue-monitoring systems reduce physical strain for older employees. Voice-Activated Machines: Instead of requiring manual input, Siemens introduced voice-controlled automation systems, making it easier for older employees to operate machinery without extensive retraining. Outcome: Workplace injuries among older employees decreased by 30%, and job satisfaction improved significantly. Reskilling and Upskilling: AI-Enhanced Training for Older Employees: Many aging workers at Siemens lacked digital literacy, which created a barrier to adapting to new automation-driven workflows (Ghosh M., 2024). A Shift in Industry Standards: Other companies, including Bosch, General Electric, and Toyota, have adopted similar strategies (Chen & Feng, 2024). Government Recognition: The German government included Lifelong@Siemens in its Industry 4.0 policy, providing tax incentives for companies investing in age-friendly automation strategies. AI-powered training programs should be personalized for aging employees (Emery-Tiburcio E E., 2024). Mentorship models (reverse mentorship, peer learning) create knowledge-sharing opportunities..

LESSONS FROM JAPAN: ADDRESSING THE CHALLENGES OF AN AGING WORKFORCE IN AN AUTOMATED ECONOMY

Japan as a Global Case Study for an Aging Workforce in an Automated Economy Japan is one of the most rapidly aging countries in the world, with over 28% of its population aged 65 and older. Productivity Concerns and Automation Resistance: While automation can help compensate for a reduced workforce, older employees may face technological barriers, digital illiteracy, and resistance to change (Czaplicka M., et al, 2024). Automation to Assist, Not Replace, Aging Workers: Japan has pioneered the development of collaborative robots (cobots), AI tools, and ergonomic workplace solutions to help aging workers stay productive: Robotic Assistance in Manufacturing: Companies like Fanuc, Honda, and Panasonic use cobots that work alongside aging employees to reduce physical strain. AI-Driven Workplace Assistance: AI-powered voice recognition, gesture-based controls, and augmented reality (AR) tools help older workers interact with technology without extensive retraining. Wearable Robotics for Physical Support: Exoskeletons, such as those developed by Cyberdyne, help aging workers lift heavy objects and maintain mobility (Schaede U., et al, 2022). Example: Toyota's factories use smart manufacturing systems that allow senior employees to supervise automated assembly lines rather than perform physically demanding tasks. Upskilling and Reskilling Older Workers for Automation-Driven Jobs: Japan has invested heavily in lifelong learning programs to ensure that older workers can transition into automation-friendly roles.

The Robot Care Subsidy supports businesses investing in robotic solutions that help elderly employees. Reforming Social Security to Encourage Longer Careers: The pension system rewards workers who stay employed beyond 65 with increased payouts. "Silver Human Resources Centers" offer part-time job matching services for retired professionals. International Collaboration on Automation and Aging: Japan has partnered with Germany, Singapore, and South Korea to share best practices on automation and aging workforce policies (Trencher G., et al, 2024). Wearable robotics and assistive AI help older employees perform physically demanding jobs (Nagarajan N R., et al, 2023). A Blueprint for Aging Workforces in an Automated Future: Japan's approach to managing an aging workforce in an automated economy provides a practical roadmap for other nations facing similar challenges. By implementing flexible retirement policies, automation-assisted workplaces, continuous upskilling, and industry-specific innovations, Japan has demonstrated that an aging workforce can thrive alongside automation rather than be displaced by it. As automation reshapes the global labor market, countries with aging populations must proactively adapt, ensuring that their economies remain competitive, inclusive, and sustainable. The Japanese model offers critical insights into how to balance technological advancements with human capital preservation, creating a future where automation empowers workers of all ages rather than rendering them obsolete.

AUTOMATION AND THE FUTURE OF WORK IN AGING ECONOMIES – A CALL TO ACTION

This conclusion serves as a call to action for governments, businesses, educators, and workers to collaboratively build a future where automation complements rather than displaces human labor (Miranda A E R., 2021). Key Findings: The Interplay Between Automation and Aging Workforces: Demographic Shifts Will Reshape Labor Markets: The aging population is growing rapidly across major economies, including Japan, Germany, the U.S., and South Korea. Declining birth rates and a shrinking working-age population will create severe labor shortages, requiring automation as a compensatory workforce solution. Longer life expectancy and improved healthcare mean that older workers must remain in the workforce longer, necessitating reskilling programs, flexible work models, and age-inclusive policies. Automation Presents Both Threats and Opportunities: Job displacement is inevitable in sectors heavily reliant on routine, repetitive tasks (e.g., manufacturing, logistics, retail). However, automation also creates new roles in AI oversight, robotics maintenance, data analysis, and digital services, providing opportunities for upskilling and career transitions. Industry-specific solutions, such as collaborative robots (cobots) and AI-powered customer service, demonstrate that automation can augment rather than replace human labor. The Nature of Work is Changing: Shift from Routine to Non-Routine Tasks: The demand for cognitive, creative, and interpersonal skills is increasing, while routine manual labor is being automated (Nissim G., et al, 2021). Hybrid work models, where humans and machines collaborate, will become the norm, requiring a workforce skilled in AI-human interaction. Develop ethical AI policies to ensure fairness, transparency, and accountability in automated workplaces. Businesses: Designing Workplaces that Integrate Automation and Aging Workers: Shift from replacement-based automation to augmentation-based automation, ensuring that AI and robotics assist rather than replace human workers. Redesign age-friendly workplaces with ergonomic technology, AI-driven training programs, and flexible work options (Howcroft & Taylor, 2023). Automation and human labor will coexist rather than compete, with AI handling repetitive tasks while humans focus on higher-order functions. Expansion of Lifelong Learning Ecosystems: Education will no longer be confined to early life stages; continuous skill acquisition will be essential (Mindell D A., et al, 2023).

FUTURE DIRECTIONS: PREPARING FOR AN AUTOMATED ECONOMY WITH AN AGING WORKFORCE

The Urgency of Preparing for an Automated Economy: The global economy is undergoing a profound transformation driven by automation, artificial intelligence (AI), robotics, and digital technologies. At the same time, many nations face an aging workforce, with declining birth rates and increasing life expectancy reshaping labor markets. By 2050, nearly one in six people worldwide will be over 65, and many advanced economies will experience significant labor shortages. This convergence of demographic and technological change presents both challenges and opportunities. Aging workers, who have traditionally played a crucial role in economic growth, must now adapt to a rapidly evolving work environment where automation is becoming an integral part of industries. The question is no longer whether automation will reshape work but how societies can proactively prepare for this shift to ensure economic resilience, social inclusion, and workforce sustainability (Assaad & El-Adaway, 2021). The future direction of workforce preparation in an automated economy with an aging population will depend on four key pillars: Policy and Regulatory Adaptation – Governments must implement policies that support older workers, encourage workforce participation, and promote lifelong learning. Education and Workforce Training – A continuous learning model must be established to help workers of all ages adapt to automation (Frey & Osborne, 2023). Business Strategies and Workplace Innovation – Companies must design age-friendly, automation-integrated workplaces to retain and upskill aging employees. Social Protection and Inclusive Economic Models – Social safety nets must evolve to support displaced workers and ensure a just transition. This discussion outlines the critical future directions needed to prepare for an automated economy while ensuring that aging workers are empowered, rather than marginalized, in the workforce of tomorrow. Public-private partnerships should be encouraged to develop worker transition programs that help aging employees move into new roles (Liu Z., et al, 2021). Digital and Technological Literacy for Aging Workers: Many older workers face technological literacy challenges, limiting their ability to adapt to automation-driven roles. Governments and businesses must invest in digital training programs focused on AI, robotics, data analytics, and automation technologies.

CONCLUSION

Mentorship programs where younger, tech-savvy employees guide older workers in using automation tools can enhance digital inclusion. Industry-Specific Reskilling Initiatives: Different industries will experience automation in unique ways, requiring sector-specific reskilling strategies. Manufacturing: Training aging workers in collaborative robotics (cobots) to work alongside AI-driven machines. Healthcare: Upskilling older healthcare professionals in telemedicine and AI-driven diagnostics. Retail and Customer Service: Training employees in AI-assisted customer service and e-commerce platforms. Business Strategies and Workplace Innovation: Designing Age-Friendly Automation: Rethinking Workplace Design: Companies must create age-inclusive workplaces with ergonomic tools, automation-assisted workflows, and flexible job roles. Human-centric automation should be prioritized, where machines support rather than replace older workers. AI-driven workload optimization systems can reduce physical strain while maintaining productivity. Promoting Intergenerational Collaboration: Businesses should encourage mentorship programs where older employees share industry knowledge while younger workers help with technology adaptation. A multigenerational workforce fosters knowledge transfer, innovation, and smoother digital transformation. Implementing Hybrid Work Models: Remote and flexible work arrangements should be expanded to accommodate older workers who may prefer reduced commuting and flexible hours (Dwivedi Y K., et al, 2023). AI-driven project management and collaboration tools can enable seamless remote work for aging employees. Social Protection and Inclusive Economic Models: Redesigning Social Safety Nets: With automation displacing certain job categories, enhanced social protection policies must support aging workers. Universal Basic Income (UBI), wage subsidies, and retraining grants should be explored to ensure economic security during job transitions. Ensuring Fairness and Equity in AI-Driven Workplaces: AI systems must be designed to avoid biases against aging workers, ensuring fair hiring, promotion, and job assignment practices. Transparency in AI decision-making and regular audits of automated systems can prevent discrimination. Encouraging Public-Private Partnerships for Sustainable Workforce Growth: Collaborations between governments, businesses, and educational institutions will be key to developing a cohesive, forward-looking workforce strategy. Cross-industry initiatives can share best practices, create scalable training solutions, and foster innovation. The Future of Work: What Lies Ahead? Looking forward, the successful integration of automation into aging economies will depend on proactive, coordinated efforts across multiple stakeholders. Key future trends include: AI-Augmented Workforces – Older workers will increasingly collaborate with AI-powered tools to enhance productivity. Personalized Learning Ecosystems – AI-driven education platforms will provide adaptive, on-demand training for workers at all career stages. New Employment Models – Hybrid work, gig opportunities, and fractional employment will redefine workforce participation. Ethical AI and Workforce Policies – Governments will need to implement strong AI governance frameworks to prevent labor market inequalities. A Call to Action for a Sustainable Automated Economy: The future of work in aging economies is not about replacing human labor with machines but about strategically integrating automation to enhance workforce sustainability. By embracing lifelong learning, adaptive policies, inclusive workplace design, and robust social protections, societies can turn automation into a tool for empowerment rather than exclusion. This transformation requires immediate action from policymakers, businesses, educators, and workers alike. The time to prepare for an automated economy with an aging workforce is now—the choices made today will define whether automation serves as a catalyst for progress or a source of inequality in the decades to come.

REFERENCES

Acemoglu, D., & Restrepo, P. (2022). Demographics and automation. *The Review of Economic Studies*, *89*(1), 1–44. Advance online publication. DOI: 10.1093/restud/rdab031

Adepoju, O. O., & Aigbavboa, C. O. (2021). Assessing knowledge and skills gap for construction 4.0 in a developing economy. *Journal of Public Affairs*, *21*(3), e2264. Advance online publication. DOI: 10.1002/pa.2264

Afonso, Ó., & Forte, R. (2024). Routine and non-routine sectors, tasks automation and wage polarization. *Applied Economics*, *56*(55), 7262–7285. Advance online publication. DOI: 10.1080/00036846.2023.2280461

Al Saad, N., & Blomqvist, E. (2024). "Mind the gap–Automation skills gap in SMEs in Sweden" DOI: DOI: 10.18160/DIVA-108811

Albanesi, S., & Kim, J. (2021). Effects of the COVID-19 recession on the US labor market: Occupation, family, and gender. *The Journal of Economic Perspectives*, *35*(3), 3–24. Advance online publication. DOI: 10.1257/jep.35.3.3

Alcover, C. M., Guglielmi, D., Depolo, M., & Fraboni, F. (2021). *"Aging-and-Tech Job Vulnerability": A proposed framework on the dual impact of aging and AI, robotics, and automation among older workers*. Organizational., DOI: 10.1177/13505084211029231

Aragani, V. M., Anumolu, V. R., & Selvakumar, P. (2025). Democratization in the Age of Algorithms: Navigating Opportunities and Challenges. In Wongmahesak, K., Wekke, I., Seftyono, C., & Nurdin, N. (Eds.), *Democracy and Democratization in the Age of AI* (pp. 39–56). IGI Global Scientific Publishing., DOI: 10.4018/979-8-3693-8749-8.ch003

Assaad, R., & El-Adaway, I. H. (2021). Guidelines for responding to COVID-19 pandemic: Best practices, impacts, and future research directions. *Journal of Management Engineering*, *37*(3), 06021001. Advance online publication. DOI: 10.1061/(ASCE)ME.1943-5479.0000906

Bukartaite, R., & Hooper, D. (2023). Automation, artificial intelligence and future skills needs: An Irish perspective. *European Journal of Training and Development*, *47*(10), 163–185. Advance online publication. DOI: 10.1108/EJTD-03-2023-0045

Busemeyer, M. R., & Sahm, A. H. J. (2022). Social investment, redistribution or basic income? Exploring the association between automation risk and welfare state attitudes in Europe. *Journal of Social Policy*, *51*(4), 751–770. Advance online publication. DOI: 10.1017/S0047279421000519

Cazzaniga M, Jaumotte F, Li L, Melina MG, (2024). "Gen-AI: Artificial intelligence and the future of work"

Chen, X., & Feng, S. (2024). Age-Friendly Transportation Policies and Practices in the US and China: A Comparative Study. *Sustainability*. Advance online publication. DOI: 10.3390/su16074439

Chu, C. H., Nyrup, R., Leslie, K., Shi, J., Bianchi, A., & Regini, O. (2022). Digital ageism: Challenges and opportunities in artificial intelligence for older adults. *The Gerontologist*, *62*(7), 947–955. Advance online publication. DOI: 10.1093/geront/gnab167 PMID: 35048111

Costa, I., Machado, C. S., & Conceição, O. (2024). "Automation and the Importance of Reskilling Workers: A Case Study in the Automotive Industry" *Proceedings of the 19*th. DOI: 10.34190/ecmlg.20.1.2923

Czaplicka, M., Dudzińska, M., Dawidowicz, A., & Marszałek, A. (2024). Concept of Assessment of Age-Friendly Residential Areas (AFRA): A Case Study of Gdańsk, Poland. *Sustainability (Basel)*, *16*(14), 6000. Advance online publication. DOI: 10.3390/su16146000

Da Silva, T. M. H. R. (2025). *Designing for Longevity: Economic Perspectives on Age-Friendly Housing and Urban Development*. Perspectives on the Economics of Aging.

De Felice, F., Longo, F., Padovano, A., Falcone, D., & Baffo, I. (2022). Proposal of a multidimensional risk assessment methodology to assess ageing workforce in a manufacturing industry: A pilot case study. *Safety Science*, *149*, 105681. Advance online publication. DOI: 10.1016/j.ssci.2022.105681

Debnath, P., Deshmukh, S. M., Laroia, M., Selvakumar, P., Manjunath, T. C., & Bhattacharya, S. (2025). Challenges Faced by Countries in Renewable Energy Adoption. In Özsungur, F., Chaychi Semsari, M., & Küçük Bayraktar, H. (Eds.), *Geopolitical Landscapes of Renewable Energy and Urban Growth* (pp. 295–320). IGI Global Scientific Publishing., DOI: 10.4018/979-8-3693-8814-3.ch010

Deschacht, N. (2021). *"The digital revolution and the labour economics of automation: A review" The Journal of the Automated Economy*. DESCHACHT., DOI: 10.46763/JAE.N

Domash, A., & Summers, L. H. (2022). *How tight are US labor markets?* National Bureau of Economic Research., DOI: 10.3386/w29739

Dwivedi, Y. K., Sharma, A., Rana, N. P., Giannakis, M., & Hughes, L. (2023). Evolution of artificial intelligence research in Technological Forecasting and Social Change: Research topics, trends, and future directions. *Technological Forecasting and Social Change*, *192*, 122579. Advance online publication. DOI: 10.1016/j.techfore.2023.122579

Ekuma, K. (2023). "Rethinking Upskilling and Reskilling in the Age of AI and Automation: A fsQCA Approach" *Preprints*. DOI: DOI: 10.20944/preprints202307.0401.v1

Emery-Tiburcio, E. E. (2024). Age-friendly mental health systems: A step toward geriatric competency. *The American Psychologist*, *79*(9), 1422–1430. Advance online publication. DOI: 10.1037/amp0001446 PMID: 39715398

Frank, K., Yang, Z., & Frenette, M. (2021). "The changing nature of work in Canada amid recent advances in automation technology" ResearchGate. DOI: DOI: 10.13140/RG.2.2.14143.57120

Frey, C. B., & Osborne, M. (2023). Generative AI and the future of work: A reappraisal. *The Brown Journal of World Affairs*.

Gentilini, U. (2022). *Social protection and jobs responses to COVID-19: A real-time review of country measures*. Social Protection and Jobs Responses.

Ghosh M, (2024). "Case Studies of Effective Age-Friendly Digital Initiatives" India's Silver Surfers: Transforming the Digital. DOI: .DOI: 10.1007/978-981-19-6563-6_12

Glover A, & Mustre-del-Río J, (2024). "Aging and growth: can automation outpace falling labor supply, reduced dynamism, and fewer innovations?" Handbook on Labour Markets in Emerging Economies. DOI: .DOI: 10.4337/9781800887476.00025

Grinin, L., Grinin, A., & Korotayev, A. (2024). *Cybernetic Revolution and Global Aging*. Springer., DOI: 10.1007/978-3-031-56764-3

Ho, M. T., Mantello, P., Ghotbi, N., Nguyen, M. H., & Hollier, S. (2022). Rethinking technological acceptance in the age of emotional AI: Surveying Gen Z (Zoomer) attitudes toward non-conscious data collection. *Technology in Society*, *70*, 102011. Advance online publication. DOI: 10.1016/j.techsoc.2022.102011

Horoshko, O. I., Horoshko, A., Bilyuga, S., & Yurchyshena, S. (2021). *Theoretical and methodological bases of the study of the impact of digital economy on world policy in 21 century*. Forecasting and Social Change., DOI: 10.1016/j.techfore.2021.120640

Howcroft, D., & Taylor, P. (2023). Automation and the future of work: A social shaping of technology approach. *New Technology, Work and Employment*, *38*(2), 351–370. Advance online publication. DOI: 10.1111/ntwe.12240

Johri, S., Selvakumar, P., Satyanarayana, P., Das, A., Gupta, S., & Bhattacharya, S. (2025). Urbanization and Energy: The Nexus of Global Challenges. In Özsungur, F., Chaychi Semsari, M., & Küçük Bayraktar, H. (Eds.), *Geopolitical Landscapes of Renewable Energy and Urban Growth* (pp. 453–478). IGI Global Scientific Publishing., DOI: 10.4018/979-8-3693-8814-3.ch016

Keeler, L. W., & Bernstein, M. J. (2021). The future of aging in smart environments: Four scenarios of the United States in 2050. *Futures*, *133*, 102830. Advance online publication. DOI: 10.1016/j.futures.2021.102830

Khogali, H. O., & Mekid, S. (2023). The blended future of automation and AI: Examining some long-term societal and ethical impact features. *Technology in Society*, *73*, 102232. Advance online publication. DOI: 10.1016/j.techsoc.2023.102232

Koch T, (2024). "The Economic Consequences of Population Aging: A Global Perspective on Policies and Responses" Journal of Economic Science Research.

Konstantis, K., Georgas, A., Faras, A., Georgas, K., & Tympas, A. (2024). Ethical considerations in working with ChatGPT on a questionnaire about the future of work with ChatGPT. *AI and Ethics*, *4*(4), 1335–1344. Advance online publication. DOI: 10.1007/s43681-023-00312-6

Lee, I. (2023). "Economic Effects of Industrial Automation in Aging Workforces" Intersect: The Stanford Journal of Science, Technology. DOI: DOI: 10.25740/ij1137.124906

Li, L. (2024). Reskilling and upskilling the future-ready workforce for industry 4.0 and beyond. *Information Systems Frontiers*. Advance online publication. DOI: 10.1007/s10796-023-10463-6 PMID: 35855776

Liu, Z., Liu, J., & Osmani, M. (2021). Integration of digital economy and circular economy: Current status and future directions. *Sustainability (Basel)*, *13*(13), 7217. Advance online publication. DOI: 10.3390/su13137217

Loku, A., & Loku, N. (2025). "Globalization, Automation, and the Future of Work: Examining the Impact of Technological Advancements on the Workforce" Quality-Access to Success. DOI: DOI: 10.35115/qas.v15i2.678

Lowe B D, Hayden M, Albers J, Wurzelbacher S, (2023). "Case studies of robots and automation as health/safety interventions in small manufacturing enterprises" Journal of Manufacturing & Services Management. DOI: .DOI: 10.1002/jams.1057

Maestas, N., Mullen, K. J., & Powell, D. (2023). *The effect of population aging on economic growth, the labor force, and productivity*. American Economic Journal., DOI: 10.1257/aer.20221741

Madgule, M., Vinayaka, N., Sonkhaskar, Y. M., Patel, D. R., Karthikeyan, R., & Selvakumar, P. (2023). Mechanical properties and microstructure of activated TIG welded similar joints of Inconel alloys by desirability approaches. Materials Today: Proceedings, 77, 528-533.

Mansour, H. (2022). How successful countries are in promoting digital transactions during COVID-19. *Journal of Economic Studies (Glasgow, Scotland)*, *49*(3), 435–452. Advance online publication. DOI: 10.1108/JES-10-2020-0489

McGinley, C., Myerson, J., Briscoe, G., & Carroll, S. (2022). Towards an age-friendly design lens. *Journal of Population Ageing*, *15*(2), 541–556. Advance online publication. DOI: 10.1007/s12062-022-09367-5

McKay, A., & Reis, R. (2021). Optimal automatic stabilizers. *The Review of Economic Studies*, *88*(5), 2375–2406. Advance online publication. DOI: 10.1093/restud/rdaa038

Mindell, D. A., & Reynolds, E. (2023). *The work of the future: Building better jobs in an age of intelligent machines*. MIT Press.

Miranda, A. E. R. (2021). *Finding opportunities in Japan's aging population*. FSI Insights and Commentaries.

Morandini S, Fraboni F, De Angelis M, Puzzo G, Giusino D, Pietrantoni L, (2023). "The impact of artificial intelligence on workers' skills: Upskilling and reskilling in organisations" Informing Science: The International Journal of an Emerging Transdiscipline, 26, 039-068.

Nagarajan, N. R., & Sixsmith, A. (2023). Policy initiatives to address the challenges of an older population in the workforce. *Ageing International*, *48*(1), 41–77. Advance online publication. DOI: 10.1007/s12126-021-09442-w PMID: 34465930

Nagarajan, N. R., & Sixsmith, A. (2023). Policy initiatives to address the challenges of an older population in the workforce. *Ageing International*, *48*(1), 41–77. Advance online publication. DOI: 10.1007/s12126-021-09442-w PMID: 34465930

Nissim, G., & Simon, T. (2021). The future of labor unions in the age of automation and at the dawn of AI. *Technology in Society*, *67*, 101732. Advance online publication. DOI: 10.1016/j.techsoc.2021.101732

Okubo, T. (2024). Non-routine tasks and ICT tools in telework. *Labour*, *38*(2), 177–202. Advance online publication. DOI: 10.1111/labr.12262

Olurin, J. O., Okonkwo, F., Eleogu, T., & Nwobodo, C. C. (2024). Strategic HR management in the manufacturing industry: Balancing automation and workforce development. *International Journal of Innovation and Scientific Research*, *X*(XII), 380–401. DOI: 10.51244/IJRSI.2023.1012030

Osareme, O. J., Muonde, M., Adeyemi, O. A., & Afolabi, A. O. (2024). Demographic shifts and healthcare: A review of aging populations and systemic challenges. *International Journal of Scientific Research.* Advance online publication. DOI: 10.29322/IJSR.15.2.2024.001

Parker, S. K., & Grote, G. (2022). Automation, algorithms, and beyond: Why work design matters more than ever in a digital world. *Applied Psychology*, *71*(4), 1171–1204. Advance online publication. DOI: 10.1111/apps.12241

Parry, E., & Battista, V. (2023). The impact of emerging technologies on work: A review of the evidence and implications for the human resource function. *Emerald Open Research*, *1*(4). Advance online publication. DOI: 10.1108/EOR-04-2023-0001

Priyadarshi, P., & Premchandran, R. (2022). Insecurity and turnover as robots take charge: Impact of neuroticism and change-related uncertainty. *Personnel Review*, *51*(1), 21–39. Advance online publication. DOI: 10.1108/PR-06-2019-0310

Ramakrishnan, T., Mohan Gift, M. D., Chitradevi, S., Jegan, R., & Subha Hency Jose, P. Nagaraja, Rajneesh Sharma HN, Selvakumar P, Sintayehu Mekuria Hailegiorgis, (2022). "Study of Numerous Resins Used in Polymer Matrix Composite Materials", Advances in Materials Science and Engineering, vol. 2022, Article ID 1088926, 8 pages, 2022. DOI: 10.1155/2022/1088926

Rodrik, D. (2022). An industrial policy for good jobs. In *Hamilton Project—Policy proposal*. OECD Publishing., DOI: 10.1787/3c3f1559-

Salimgereyev, N., & Mukhamediyev, B. (2024). Measuring the routine and non-routine task contents: A comparative study between state and industrial sector employees. *International Journal (Toronto, Ont.).*

Schaede, U., & Shimizu, K. (2022). *The digital transformation and Japan's political economy*. Cambridge University Press., DOI: 10.1017/9781009084115

Segkouli, S., Giakoumis, D., Votis, K., & Tzovaras, D. (2023). Smart Workplaces for older adults: Coping 'ethically'with technology pervasiveness. *Universal Access in the Information Society*, *22*(1), 37–49. Advance online publication. DOI: 10.1007/s10209-021-00829-9 PMID: 34305502

Shende, A. D., Tekade, S. A., Deshmukh, A. A., Tembhurkar, S. P., & Selvakumar, P. (2025). Water Quality Monitoring and Control With AI. In Ruiz-Vanoye, J., & Díaz-Parra, O. (Eds.), *Smart Water Technology for Sustainable Management in Modern Cities* (pp. 51–80). IGI Global Scientific Publishing., DOI: 10.4018/979-8-3693-8074-1.ch003

Spasova, S., Atanasova, A., Sabato, S., & Bouget, D. (2023). *Making access to social protection for workers and the self-employed more transparent through information and simplification*. Social Policy Network.

Sreenivasulu, A., & Manimozhi, T. Satheesh kumar P, Selvakumar P. and Singh P, (2022). "The Model of Smart Sensing Device For Sensitive Nanoclusters Modification in Sensing Properties," 2022 2nd International Conference on Advance Computing and Innovative Technologies in Engineering (ICACITE), Greater Noida, India, 2022, pp. 1043-1047, DOI: 10.1109/ICACITE53722.2022.9823846

Sugumaran K M D, Pandiyarajan V Y B S, Selvakumar P. and M. S, (2024). "Analysis of Electromyography Signals for Control of Mechanical Prosthesis using Machine Learning Techniques," 2024 2nd International Conference on Intelligent Data Communication Technologies and Internet of Things (IDCIoT), Bengaluru, India, 2024, pp. 1059-1067, .DOI: 10.1109/IDCIoT59759.2024.10467707

Trencher, G., Yarime, M., & Yu, J. (2024). Using emerging technologies to tackle mobility challenges caused by population ageing: Experiences from Japan. *Technological Forecasting and Social Change*, *208*, 123729. Advance online publication. DOI: 10.1016/j.techfore.2024.123729

Tschang, F. T., & Almirall, E. (2021). Artificial intelligence as augmenting automation: Implications for employment. *The Academy of Management Perspectives*, *35*(4), 642–659. Advance online publication. DOI: 10.5465/amp.2019.0062

Vijayakumar, G. (2024). Muniyandi Rajkumar, Rajiv Chandar N, Selvakumar P and Ramesh Duraisamy, (2024). Environmentally friendly TDS removal from wastewater by electrochemical ion exchange batch-type recirculation (EIR) technique. *Environmental Science. Water Research & Technology*, *10*, 826–835. DOI: 10.1039/D3EW00793F

Ward, P. (2023). *Welfare politics in Mexico: Papering over the crack*. Routledge. DOI: 10.4324/9781003431725

Wissemann, A. K., Pit, S. W., Serafin, P., & Bollwerk, E. (2022). Strategic guidance and technological solutions for human resources management to sustain an aging workforce: Review of international standards, research, and use cases. *JMIR Human Factors*, *9*(3), e27250. Advance online publication. DOI: 10.2196/27250 PMID: 35862177

Chapter 8
A Study on the Importance of Disability Insurance for Sustainable Workforce Development

Amir Ahmad Dar
https://orcid.org/0000-0002-0379-2272
Lovely Professional University, India

Akshat Jain
Lovely Professional University, India

Bashir Ahmad Dar
Lovely Professional University, India

Birendri
https://orcid.org/0000-0003-0933-3103
Lovely Professional University, India

ABSTRACT

Disability insurance is essential for providing financial security, facilitating meaningful employment participation, and helping people with disabilities. The importance of disability insurance is discussed in this chapter with an emphasis on its advantages, drawbacks, and effects on workforce growth. It looks at how disability insurance helps people with disabilities maintain their financial stability and participate in work-related activities by offering vocational rehabilitation, income replacement, and other support services. The chapter also covers the challenges that people with impairments encounter while trying to obtain and make use of disability insurance,

DOI: 10.4018/979-8-3373-2550-7.ch008

such as difficult qualifying standards, intricate administrative procedures, and social stigma. In addition, it examines how disability insurance affects employment results and rates of workforce participation, emphasizing how it helps to advance sustainable workforce development.

1. INTRODUCTION

An effective social security system must include disability insurance, which offers essential help to those with disabilities who are unable to work. It guarantees that people with disabilities can preserve financial stability and engage meaningfully in the workforce, which makes it extremely important in the context of workforce development. Handicap insurance helps people avoid the financial difficulty that frequently follows a handicap by providing income replacement and other support services. This allows people to concentrate on their rehabilitation and recovery. In addition to benefiting the individual, this financial stability also serves the larger workforce by preserving a talented and varied pool of workers. Moreover, by reducing constraints on employment for people with disabilities, disability insurance is essential in creating inclusion in the workforce (Burkhauser & Daly, 2011).

Several important aspects will be explored in the review of the significance of disability insurance for workforce development. First, a study of the different disability insurance benefits—like income replacement, vocational rehabilitation, and other support services—will be conducted. It will examine how these advantages affect the financial security and employment status of people with impairments. The evaluation will also look at the challenges and obstacles that people with impairments have when trying to get and use disability insurance. This covers problems including difficult qualifying standards, bureaucratic roadblocks, and social shame. Developing solutions to increase the efficacy and accessibility of disability insurance programs requires understanding these obstacles (Rupp et al., 2008).

Thirdly, the test will evaluate how disability insurance affects the development of the labor force. The impact of disability insurance policies and programs on the job outcomes and labor force participation rates of people with disabilities will be examined. The review will demonstrate how disability insurance contributes to sustainable workforce development by looking at the empirical data. Finally, the evaluation will offer policy recommendations meant to improve disability insurance's usability and efficacy (Campolieti & Goldenberg, 2007). The enhancement of eligibility requirements, the simplification of administrative procedures, and raising public knowledge of disability insurance will be the main goals of these recommendations. The assessment will also include recommendations for how employers can make their workplaces more inclusive of people with disabilities.

2. LITERATURE REVIEW

Disability insurance is essential for determining how people with disabilities participate in the job market and for guaranteeing their financial stability. Recent years have seen a significant increase in research on this subject, with a particular emphasis on the efficacy of vocational rehabilitation, income replacement, and comparative policy frameworks across nations.

Disability insurance has a major impact on employment participation, according to studies. Overly lavish benefits may deter labor market involvement, according to some early research, although more recent data have complicated this view. According to a study, eliminating disability payments improved temporary employment but had detrimental long-term consequences on people's well-being and financial security, highlighting the significance of well-balanced program design (Autor & Duggan, 2003). According to a different investigation, people who had access to organized disability insurance schemes were more likely than those who did not to return to work following an illness or accident. This lends credence to the idea that, when designed appropriately, disability insurance acts as a transitional measure to gainful employment rather than a permanent departure from the labour market (Brucker & Scally, 2015).

Labor results have also been demonstrated to be improved by vocational rehabilitation (VR) services included in disability insurance plans. Job training, counseling, and placement are some of the services that assist people in regaining their employability and functionality. Increased productivity and higher return-to-work rates were observed by employee benefit systems that included virtual reality, according to a systematic review (Li, 2023). Another study indicated that early and targeted treatments were the most successful ways to use VR. Virtual reality (VR) has been shown to enhance economic productivity and organizational diversity in addition to providing benefits to employees in both European and North American contexts (Mamun et al., 2011).

The disparate effects of disability insurance policies are further illustrated by cross-national comparisons. To prevent total labor exit, Nordic nations like Sweden and Norway use early-intervention approaches and partial rewards. Canada, on the other hand, has a structured adjudication procedure but offers substantial return-to-work assistance; it has been demonstrated that rejecting disability claims dramatically lowers labor force participation (Lewis & Dijkema, 2022). Australia has a hybrid strategy, combining financial assistance with active labor market requirements for those with partial disabilities. Incorporating disability insurance into inclusive labor policies promotes equity and long-term worker development, according to international organizations (OECD, 2022).

3. BACKGROUND

3.1 Definition and Importance

Disability insurance is a type of policy that protects people financially if they become incapable of working because of a disability (Burkhauser & Daly, 2011). Usually, this insurance pays a percentage of the person's pre-disability income to assist with living costs and other financial commitments. The understanding that disabilities can occur suddenly and significantly affect the ability of an individual to make a living is the foundation of the concept of disability insurance. Disability insurance acts as a safety net, reducing the financial risks that come with being disabled and enabling people to maintain a basic quality of living even when they cannot work. One of the main functions of disability insurance is to give disabled workers a backup source of income. This is particularly crucial for employees without access to other income protection sources, such as savings accounts or other insurance policies. In the absence of disability insurance, disabled workers could find it difficult to fulfill their financial commitments, which could result in long-term financial instability and suffering. By offering a steady income stream to replace lost wages, disability insurance helps to prevent this and helps people and their families maintain financial security during trying times.

Disability insurance is essential for helping workers with disabilities continue working or reenter the workforce, in addition to replacing lost income. Access to vocational rehabilitation services, including job training, education programs, and help finding employment, is frequently made possible by disability insurance (Rupp et al., 2008). These programs assist people with impairments in obtaining the knowledge and assistance necessary to go back to work and keep a job that pays well. Disability insurance helps people with disabilities reintegrate into employment, which is a crucial component of a more inclusive and diversified labor force for the long-term viability of the workforce. Moreover, disability insurance reduces the financial strain that hiring people with disabilities places on firms. Disability insurance helps reduce the costs of accommodating disabilities in the workplace by offering financial support to workers with disabilities. Employers may find it more financially possible to hire and retain individuals with disabilities as a result, which may lead to a workforce that is more inclusive and long-lasting in general (Campolieti & Goldenberg, 2007). Disability insurance is essential for helping employees who become disabled to maintain their employment or reenter the workforce by protecting their finances. Disability insurance serves to ensure that people with disabilities can maintain their financial stability and fully participate in society by offering income replacement and access to vocational rehabilitation programs. Disability insurance ultimately helps to sustain the workforce by encouraging people with disabilities to enter the workforce and making sure they can use their skills and talents to benefit the economy.

3.2 Theoretical Framework

The importance of disability insurance in workforce development can be better understood by applying a number of theoretical frameworks that describe how policy interventions affect individual well-being, inclusion, and labor market participation. The conventional wisdom that physical or medical impairments are the only cause of disability is contested by the Social Model of Disability. Rather, it contends that institutional attitudes, environmental impediments, and social structures are the main causes of exclusion (Shakespeare, 2006). This concept views disability insurance as a corrective instrument that lowers social barriers to equal workforce participation, rather than just a welfare mechanism.

According to human capital theory, investments in people's health, education, and training increase their economic contribution and productivity. This idea is supported by disability insurance programs that offer vocational rehabilitation and return-to-work assistance, which assist individuals with disabilities in gaining or retaining the skills necessary for reentering the workforce (Becker, 1964). Through these approaches, individuals with disabilities are treated as assets capable of significant economic involvement rather than as dependents. Amartya Sen's Capability Approach builds on inclusiveness by emphasizing people's capacities, or what they can accomplish and be. Disability insurance helps people with disabilities enjoy more independence by giving them the tools and assistance they need to live fulfilling lives, such as full employment (Sen, 1999).

4. BENEFITS OF DISABILITY INSURANCE

Disability insurance offers people with disabilities several important benefits that support their capacity to remain financially independent and participate in society. Replacing income is one of the main advantages of disability insurance. Disability insurance pays a percentage of a person's pre-disability income if they become disabled and are unable to work. With the support of this income replacement, people with disabilities may pay for daily necessities like food, housing, and medical care without having to rely entirely on savings or other types of financial aid. Occupational rehabilitation is one of disability insurance's key advantages. Access to vocational rehabilitation services, which can assist people with disabilities in re-entering employment, is frequently provided by disability insurance (Burkhauser & Daly, 2011).

These services could include help with job placement, education programs, and job training. Vocational rehabilitation helps people with disabilities preserve their economic independence and make a contribution to society by giving them the tools and assistance they need to go back to work. Access to additional support services, like personal care services and assistive technologies, can also be made possible by disability insurance (Rupp et al., 2008). With the aid of these programs, people with disabilities can live freely and actively engage in their communities. For instance, personal care services can help with chores like bathing, clothing, and meal preparation, while assistive technologies like wheelchairs or hearing aids can help people with disabilities accomplish everyday tasks and communicate effectively (Campolieti & Goldenberg, 2007).

Overall, the advantages offered by disability insurance support people with disabilities in maintaining their financial independence and making multiple contributions to the labor market. First and foremost, income replacement guarantees that people with disabilities can continue to live up to a specified quality of life and meet their fundamental needs even in the event that they are unable to work. This stability in finances helps keep disabled people out of poverty and allows them to concentrate on their healing and rehabilitation. Second, assistance for vocational rehabilitation assists people with problems in returning to the workforce and keeping productive employment. Vocational rehabilitation programs help people with disabilities gain the skills necessary to compete in the workforce and find fulfilling jobs by offering job training, education, and aid with job placement. This helps the workers individually as well as making the workforce more inclusive and varied in general (Li, 2023). Disability insurance also covers various services that enable people with disabilities to live independently and fully engage in their communities, like personal care and assistive technology.

These support services help people with disabilities contribute their skills and talents to the workforce and society at large by reducing barriers to involvement. Disability insurance helps people with disabilities be financially independent and participate in the workforce by offering several advantages. Support services such as vocational rehabilitation, income replacement, and others are essential in enabling people with disabilities to live freely, engage fully in their communities, and realize their full potential. Disability insurance contributes to sustainability and inclusion in the workforce and society by offering these advantages (Bíró et al., 2023).

5. CHALLENGES AND BARRIERS

It can be difficult for people with problems to obtain and use disability insurance, which can have a big influence on their ability to get the money they require. The intricate eligibility requirements are one of the main obstacles. People with disability insurance frequently have to fulfill rigorous requirements to be eligible for benefits, such as proving the extent and length of their impairment. People with disabilities may find this difficult to understand or meet the requirements, particularly if their disabilities are less obvious or poorly understood. Another major obstacle to obtaining disability insurance is administrative complexity (Rupp et al., 2008). Disability insurance applications can be difficult and time-consuming to complete, needing a lot of paperwork and supporting medical records. People with impairments may already be coping with the difficulties posed by their handicap, so this complexity may be overwhelming.

The challenges that people with disabilities have in obtaining the benefits to which they are legally entitled can often be made worse by administrative mistakes or delays. Accessing and utilizing disability insurance is also significantly hampered by the stigma attached to disabilities. It may be difficult for people with impairments to obtain disability insurance or feel comfortable using it because of prejudice or unfavorable attitudes from insurers, employers, or society at large. The perception of disability insurance benefits may also be impacted by this stigma, as some people may feel embarrassed or humiliated to apply for or receive benefits. It's also possible that the possibilities for disability insurance may be limited, particularly for people with high-risk disabilities or pre-existing diseases. For those who need it most, this may further limit their access to disability insurance (Gruber, 2000).

Acquiring disability insurance is fraught with difficulties for those with disabilities. Among these difficulties are the intricate qualifying requirements, bureaucratic roadblocks, and the stigma attached to disability. To guarantee that people with disabilities may obtain the financial assistance they require to preserve their freedom and quality of life, these obstacles must be addressed (Marie & Castello, 2012).

6. IMPACT OF WORKFORCE DEVELOPMENT

The employment outcomes and rates of involvement in the workforce for people with impairments are significantly influenced by disability insurance. Research has indicated that having access to disability insurance can have a positive impact on the employment rates of people with disabilities. For instance, a study conducted in 2015 by Livermore, Stapleton, and O'Toole discovered that those who had access to disability insurance had a higher propensity than people without such insurance to continue working or reenter the workforce after becoming disabled. This implies that disability insurance acts as an essential safety net, allowing disabled people to continue working or go back to it after a period of disability (Autor & Duggan, 2003).

Disability insurance can also help people with disabilities obtain labor, which is another benefit of it. Disability insurance helps people with disabilities overcome financial obstacles and gain the skills required to find and keep a job by replacing lost income and giving access to vocational rehabilitation programs. This helps the workers individually as well as making the workforce more inclusive and varied in general. Disability insurance policies and programs can be developed to better meet the requirements of people with disabilities, hence supporting workforce development goals. Policies can be modified, for instance, to offer extra assistance to people with disabilities who encounter obstacles in entering the workforce, such as those with low levels of education or skill (Bound & Burkhauser, 1999).

Disability insurance plans can also be combined with other workforce development activities, such as job placement and training programs, to offer people with disabilities who are looking for work a comprehensive support network. Furthermore, disability insurance plans can be created to provide companies with incentives to recruit and keep disabled workers. Employers might be given tax breaks or other financial incentives, for instance, if they recruit people with disabilities or provide accommodations for them. Policies for disability insurance can contribute to the creation of a more welcoming and encouraging work environment for people with disabilities by coordinating with workforce development objectives (Burkhauser & Daly, 2012).

Disability insurance significantly affects the employment outcomes and rates of involvement in the workforce for people with disabilities. Disability insurance facilitates the attainment of economic independence and helps people with disabilities overcome obstacles to employment by offering income replacement and access to vocational rehabilitation programs. Policymakers can contribute to the creation of a more inclusive and long-lasting workforce for people with disabilities by developing disability insurance policies and programs that better complement workforce development objectives (Vornholt et al., 2018).

6.1 International Comparisons

The welfare models, labor laws, and cultural views on disability have influenced the various methods of disability insurance that different nations have taken. Experiences from other countries offer important insights for enhancing the social protection and employment results for individuals with impairments.

6.1.1 Sweden: Early Intervention and Partial Capacity Benefits

Early intervention and assessments of partial work capacity are key components of Sweden's strategy. Based on their residual abilities, people can get benefits while working part-time. By reducing reliance, this "graded" system promotes flexible re-entry into the workforce (Authority, 2020). To guarantee prompt rehabilitation and return-to-work initiatives, the Swedish Social Insurance Agency also works closely with employers and healthcare providers. According to evaluations, this paradigm benefits individuals with episodic or chronic disabilities by increasing their partial workforce engagement and decreasing long-term exclusion (Barr et al., 2016).

6.1.2 Canada: Integrated Disability and Employment Supports

The Canada Pension Plan Disability (CPP-D) and provincial employment programs that provide case management, retraining, and incentives for returning to work are part of Canada's system. Programs like WorkBC and the Opportunities Fund for Persons with Disabilities offer integrated support for employment and skill development, despite the fact that eligibility requirements can be stringent (Government of Canada, 2021). According to research, people in Canada who are denied disability payments have a far lower chance of staying employed, particularly if they do not receive additional job supports (Lewis & Dijkema, 2022).

6.1.3 Australia: Conditional Support and Workforce Activation

Workplace adjustments, job matching, and continuous post-placement support are provided by Disability Employment Services (DES), which supplements Australia's Disability Support Pension (DSP). Many applicants are required to participate in job-seeking or retraining, and Australia's system is increasingly based on work capacity assessments rather than just medical diagnoses. Reducing welfare dependency and improving labor market inclusion are the goals of this strategy. The National Disability Insurance Scheme (NDIS) provides tailored care and employment planning to promote long-term functional independence and workforce participation (Mavromaras et al., 2018).

These international models highlight how crucial it is to combine proactive workforce engagement tactics with financial assistance in order to establish more inclusive labor markets. While Canada's model places more focus on vocational rehabilitation and targeted job support, Australia places more emphasis on conditional participation, which encourages participants to stay connected to career paths. Slow reintegration is made possible by Sweden's flexible benefits and early intervention policies, which allow for limited job capacity. Every strategy provides useful advice for striking a balance between labor market activation and social protection. These tactics can be used by policymakers to create disability insurance programs that enable people with disabilities to find fulfilling, long-term work in addition to offering financial stability.

7. POLICY RECOMMENDATIONS

A multifaceted strategy involving politicians, employers, and other stakeholders is needed to improve disability insurance's accessibility and efficacy. Simplifying the requirements and application process for disability insurance is a crucial suggestion for legislators. This can lessen the administrative load on applicants and insurance companies while facilitating easier access to benefits for people with disabilities. Furthermore, authorities want to think about broadening the range of coverage options to accommodate more disabled people, especially those with less severe disabilities who might not be eligible for benefits at the moment(Burkhauser & Daly, 2012). Organizations can also be very important in encouraging the employment of people with disabilities. Using inclusive employment strategies, such as focused recruitment campaigns and accommodations for people with disabilities, is one tactic.

To give employees with disabilities the tools and resources they need to succeed at work, employers can also offer training and support. Employers can assist people with disabilities to feel valued and supported by fostering a more inclusive work environment, which will improve employment outcomes and retention rates. Additionally, companies and politicians must collaborate to encourage the use of vocational rehabilitation programs by people with impairments. This may entail offering incentives to people to engage in vocational rehabilitation programs and making certain that these initiatives are customized to meet the requirements of people with disabilities (Mamun et al., 2011). Encouraging policymakers and businesses to assist people with disabilities in obtaining the necessary skills and assistance to return to the workforce can enhance the overall efficacy of disability insurance schemes.

One further important suggestion is to deal with the stigma attached to disability. Public awareness campaigns and educational programs that aim to lessen preconceptions and advance an inclusive society can help achieve this. Policymakers and employers can foster a more inclusive work environment for people with disabilities by modifying their attitudes towards these persons. Policymakers, companies, and other stakeholders must work together to improve the usability and efficacy of disability insurance (Schimmel Hyde & Stapleton, 2017). Policymakers and businesses can support the participation of people with disabilities in the workforce and increase the overall efficacy of disability insurance programs by streamlining qualifying requirements, encouraging inclusive hiring practices, and eliminating stigma.

7.1 Economic Implications

Enhancing disability insurance offers substantial long-term financial advantages. Disability insurance lowers reliance on long-term social aid by assisting people in finding new employment, which expands the revenue base. Additionally, a more diverse workforce reduces employer expenses related to absenteeism and turnover while increasing overall productivity.

Even though early intervention and vocational rehabilitation may need short-term support, they eventually save money by reducing long-term unemployment, medical expenses, and reliance on supplementary benefits (Bíró et al., 2023). Research indicates that nations with disability payments and aggressive labor market policies have greater rates of economic engagement and workforce reintegration (Lewis & Dijkema, 2022).

7.2 Social and Organizational Impact

From a social standpoint, disability insurance schemes that are modernized and expanded promote more inclusion and equity. People with disabilities are able to participate in significant roles in society, which enhances their feeling of purpose, psychological health, and self-sufficiency (Li, 2023). Diversity, creativity, and social cohesiveness are all enhanced by inclusive recruiting and retention strategies in businesses. Higher employee morale, improved company reputation, and adherence to national legislative requirements for equality and workplace rights are all common reports from disability-inclusive workplaces (Vornholt et al., 2018).

By integrating disability insurance benefits into a larger human resources strategy, a business can recruit top talent and socially conscious customers by showcasing its dedication to equality and social responsibility.

Sweden, the Netherlands, and Australia are among the many OECD nations that have embraced hybrid disability insurance plans that prioritize integrated vocational routes, early intervention, and partial payments. These models, which serve as global best practices, show that increasing the workforce engagement of individuals with disabilities is possible without sacrificing social protection objectives (OECD, 2022). To increase the impact, sustainability, and accessibility of their own disability insurance schemes, policymakers in other countries should learn from these systems (Lewis & Dijkema, 2022).

8. CASE STUDY AND EXAMPLE

8.1 Methodology

In order to determine the importance of disability insurance for long-term workforce development, we carried out a case study in study. As part of our methodology, we used data from Kaggle, namely the 2018 American Community Survey that we downloaded from Census.gov. This dataset provides gender-specific statistics as well as detailed insights into the prevalence and distribution of people with disabilities in the United States across a range of age groups, demographics, and geographic regions. Our approach involved utilising the Python programming language to perform data manipulation and analysis in order to derive significant insights from the dataset. This made it possible for us to investigate the connection between the sustainability of the workforce and the prevalence of disabilities, which highlighted the role that disability insurance plays in supporting a resilient and diverse workforce. After collecting the first set of data and preprocessing it, we looked at the disability percentage distribution by race. We calculated the proportion of people with disabilities to the overall population for each racial category using Pandas in Python. In order to ensure consistency in data types for accurate computation, this required converting the pertinent DataFrames into NumPy arrays. The resulting percentage distribution was then arranged into a new data frame, in which each column denotes a demographic category (such as age groups or gender) and each row represents a particular racial group. After calculating the percentage distribution of disability by race, we used a bar plot to display the results. We made a bar plot using the Matplotlib Python library, in which each bar represents a race category, and the height of the bars shows the percentage of people with disabilities of the total population for each race. After analysing the disability distribution by race, we looked at the disability percentage distribution by gender. Within each gender category, we calculated the proportion of people with disabilities to the total population using the same methodologies as before. The percentage distribution of disability among males and females was obtained by converting pertinent DataFrames into NumPy arrays and making sure that data types were consistent for accurate computation. This information is organised in the resulting DataFrame, where each row denotes a particular gender category and each column denotes a demographic variable (such as age groups). After calculating the disability percentage distribution by gender, we used a bar plot to display the results. With the use of the Python Matplotlib library, we produced a bar plot in which the height of the bars indicates the percentage of people with disabilities in relation to the total population for each gender group, and each bar represents a gender category.

8.2 Results and Analysis

In Table 1, the percentage of people with disabilities in the US across various racial groups is displayed.

Table 1. Percentage of people with disabilities for different ages and ethnicities

Age	<18	18-64	>65	Total
White	0.041392	0.102563	0.334527	0.131760
Black	0.050315	0.129501	0.379779	0.138443
American Indian / Alaska Native	0.054486	0.166196	0.488566	0.169317
Asian	0.021996	0.042500	0.284209	0.069452
Pacific Islander / Native Hawaiian	0.030030	0.097348	0.413215	0.110588
Other	0.038708	0.076840	0.372522	0.083947
Two or More Races	0.050547	0.127628	0.408231	0.107229
White - Not Hispanic or Latino	0.041577	0.107077	0.331751	0.139882
Hispanic or Latino	0.041433	0.081418	0.372477	0.090152

Among the various racial groups in the US, we found significant differences in the prevalence of disabilities by race. The group with the highest percentage of disabilities was the Native American population, with about 17% of members of this group reporting disabilities. On the other hand, Asian Americans had the lowest disability rate of any racial group, at 7%, suggesting a notable difference in the prevalence of disabilities between racial groups. It's interesting to note that although the overall disability rate for White people was 13%, the rate for Hispanic or Latino people was lower at 9%, below the average. This presents a nuanced picture of the prevalence of disabilities in particular racial communities, emphasising the need for intersectional factors to be taken into account when analysing workforce dynamics and the requirement for customised support systems, like disability insurance, in order to guarantee inclusivity and long-term workforce development. To show it, the bar plot is shown in Figure 1:

Figure 1. Percentage of people with disabilities

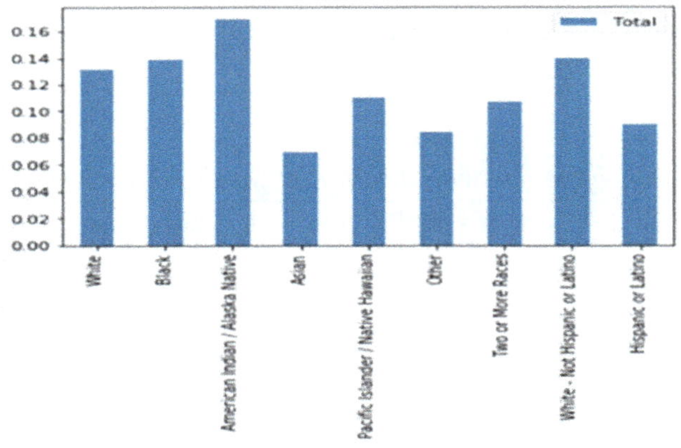

This graph provides a clear visual of the differences in the prevalence of disabilities among the various racial groups, which makes it easier to comprehend the demographic factors that affect the sustainability of the workforce and the critical role disability insurance plays in promoting equity and inclusivity in the workplace.

The analysis of disability prevalence by gender showed significant trends in the prevalence of disabilities in both genders and age groups, as shown in Table 2:

Table 2. Percentage of people with disabilities for different ages and genders

Age	Male	Female	Total
<5	0.008071	0.006609	0.007357
5-17	0.068007	0.041541	0.055073
18-34	0.068910	0.059357	0.064134
35-64	0.123786	0.126009	0.124927
65-74	0.261626	0.229441	0.244444
>75	0.461762	0.485180	0.475403
Total	0.124844	0.127314	0.126107

Important patterns in the number of disabilities by gender and age groups were found by the analysis. When it came to disabilities, the average population percentage was about 13%. The prevalence of disabilities also showed a notable age trend, rising from 6% of people in their 18–34 years to 49% of people in their 75+ years. This pattern emphasizes how age-related impairments are more likely to occur. Apart from that, the analysis also showed that about 12% of people would get a disability before they retired, which underscores the need for disability insurance and other support systems to guarantee an inclusive society and sustainable workforce development. The results were then displayed using a bar plot as shown in Figure 2:

Figure 2. Percentage of people with disabilities

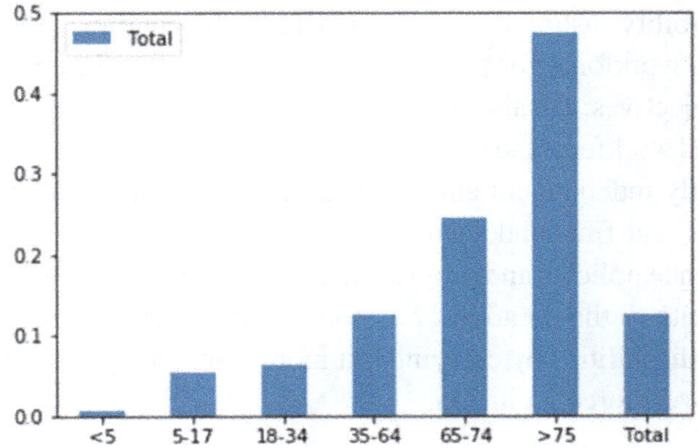

9. CONCLUSION

In summary, the significance of disability insurance for long-term workforce development has been emphasized by this review. Disability insurance is essential for helping those who become disabled to maintain their employment or reenter the workforce by protecting their finances. Disability insurance helps people stay financially independent and participate in the workforce by offering vocational rehabilitation, income replacement, and other support services. The case studies included in this analysis highlight the benefits of disability insurance for both workers and individuals, demonstrating how it can help people overcome obstacles related to money and keep working in spite of their disabilities. However, there are still areas in need of study and policy improvement, even if disability insurance is a crucial instrument for encouraging sustainability and workforce inclusion. The effect of disability insurance on employment outcomes and workforce participation rates for people with disabilities is an important subject for further study. To better understand how disability insurance can be used to support people with disabilities achieve their career objectives and encourage workforce inclusion, more research is required. Further investigation is required to examine the efficacy of various disability insurance policies and programmes in accomplishing these objectives.

The establishment of disability insurance policies and programs to better support workforce development objectives is another topic that needs more investigation. Stakeholders and policymakers should think about methods to lessen administrative red tape, ease the stigma attached to disabilities, and streamline qualifying requirements. Policymakers should also look for ways to provide financial incentives, such as tax breaks, to encourage firms to hire and keep people with disabilities. Policies for disability insurance can contribute to the creation of a more inclusive and long-lasting workforce for people with disabilities by aligning with workforce development objectives. Disability insurance is a vital instrument for encouraging sustainability and workforce participation. Disability insurance helps disabled people stay economically independent and participate in the workforce by offering them support services and financial security. To increase the usability and efficacy of disability insurance policies and programs, more work needs to be done. Policymakers may contribute to the creation of a more inclusive and long-lasting workforce for people with disabilities by carrying out more research and formulating policies that encourage workforce inclusion.

REFERENCES

Autor, D. H., & Duggan, M. G. (2003). The rise in the disability rolls and the decline in unemployment. *The Quarterly Journal of Economics, 118*(1), 157–206. DOI: 10.1162/003355303360535171

Barr, B., Taylor-Robinson, D., Stuckler, D., Loopstra, R., Reeves, A., Wickham, S., & Whitehead, M. (2016). Fit-for-work or fit-for-unemployment? Does the reassessment of disability benefit claimants using a tougher work capability assessment help people into work? *Journal of Epidemiology and Community Health, 70*(5), 452–458. DOI: 10.1136/jech-2015-206333 PMID: 26646692

Becker, G. S. (1964). *Human capital: a theoretical and empirical analysis, with special reference to education* (Vol. 3). University of Chicago Press.

Bíró, A., Hornok, C., Krekó, J., Prinz, D., & Scharle, Á. (2023). *The labor market effects of disability benefit loss* (No. 2256). Kiel Working Paper.

Bound, J., & Burkhauser, R. V. (1999). Economic analysis of transfer programs targeted on people with disabilities. Handbook of labor economics, 3, 3417-3528. DOI: 10.1016/S1573-4463(99)30042-0

Brucker, D. L., & Scally, C. P. (2015). Linking public housing, employment, and disability benefits for working-age people with disabilities. *Housing and Society, 42*(2), 126–147. DOI: 10 1080/08882746.2015.1076130

Burkhauser, R. V., & Daly, M. (2011). *The declining work and welfare of people with disabilities: What went wrong and a strategy for change.* AEI Press.

Burkhauser, R. V., & Daly, M. C. (2012). Social Security Disability Insurance: Time for fundamental change. Journal of Policy Analysis and Management, 454-461. Authority, E. P. (2020). Swedish Social Insurance Agency Certification Practices Statement. *Changes (Hove, England), 1*, 6.

Campolieti, M., & Goldenberg, J. (2007). Disability insurance denial rates and the labor force participation of older men and women in Canada. *Atlantic Economic Journal, 35*(1), 59–75. DOI: 10.1007/s11293-006-9061-7

Campolieti, M., & Goldenberg, J. (2007). Disability insurance denial rates and the labor force participation of older men and women in Canada. *Atlantic Economic Journal, 35*(1), 59–75. DOI: 10.1007/s11293-006-9061-7

Government of Canada. (2021). *Opportunities Fund for Persons with Disabilities – Overview*. Retrieved from https://www.canada.ca/en/employment-social-development/services/funding/disability-opportunity-national-regional.html

Gruber, J. (2000). Disability insurance benefits and labor supply. *Journal of Political Economy, 108*(6), 1162–1183. DOI: 10.1086/317682

Lewis, J., & Dijkema, B. (2022). *Breaking Down Work Barriers for People with Disabilities*. Centre for Cultural Renewal.

Li, X. (2023). Employee benefits and its impacts on business performance-a systematic review. In *SHS Web of Conferences* (Vol. 170, p. 03021). EDP Sciences. DOI: 10.1051/shsconf/202317003021

Mamun, A., O'Leary, P., Wittenburg, D. C., & Gregory, J. (2011). Employment among Social Security disability program beneficiaries, 1996-2007. *Soc. Sec. Bull., 71*, 11. Lewis, J., & Dijkema, B. (2022). *Breaking Down Work Barriers for People with Disabilities*. Centre for Cultural Renewal.

Marie, O., & Castello, J. V. (2012). Measuring the (income) effect of disability insurance generosity on labour market participation. *Journal of Public Economics, 96*(1-2), 198–210. DOI: 10.1016/j.jpubeco.2011.10.004

Mavromaras, K., Moskos, M., Mahuteau, S., & Isherwood, L. (2018). *Evaluation of the NDIS, final report*. National Institute of Labour Studies, Flinders University. Website., https://www.dss.gov.au/disability-and-carers/programs-services/for-people-with-disability/national-disability-insurance-scheme/ndis-evaluation-consolidated-report

Organisation for Economic Co-operation and Development. (2022). *Disability, Work and Inclusion: Mainstreaming in All Policies and Practices*. OECD Publishing.

Rupp, K., Davies, P. S., & Strand, A. (2008). Disability benefit coverage and program interactions in the working-age population. *Social Security Bulletin, 68*, 1. PMID: 18837269

Schimmel Hyde, J., & Stapleton, D. C. (2017, December). Using the health and retirement study for disability policy research: A review. [). De Gruyter.]. *Forum for Health Economics & Policy, 20*(2), 20170002. DOI: 10.1515/fhep-2017-0002 PMID: 31419905

Sen, A. (1999). Development as Freedom Oxford University Press Shaw TM & Heard. *The Politics of Africa: Dependence and Development*.

Shakespeare, T. (2006). *Disability rights and wrongs*. Routledge. DOI: 10.4324/9780203640098

Vornholt, K., Villotti, P., Muschalla, B., Bauer, J., Colella, A., Zijlstra, F., Van Ruitenbeek, G., Uitdewilligen, S., & Corbière, M. (2018). Disability and employment–overview and highlights. *European Journal of Work and Organizational Psychology*, *27*(1), 40–55. DOI: 10.1080/1359432X.2017.1387536

Chapter 9
Human Resource Development and Economic Growth: Leveraging India's Youthful Population

Pragti Dixit
https://orcid.org/0009-0002-4034-4572
Chandigarh University, India

Varsha Sharma
https://orcid.org/0000-0001-5462-4693
Chandigarh University, India

Manisha Seth
https://orcid.org/0009-0009-4570-1218
Noida Institute of Engineering and Technology, India

Mukul Bhatnagar
https://orcid.org/0000-0002-7773-5641
Graphic Era University, India

Nikhil Varghese
Christ University, India

ABSTRACT

This empirical investigation employs a multivariate time series framework utilizing the Vector Error Correction Model (VECM) to unravel the intricate long-run equilibrium and short-run dynamics among GDP, youth population, and youth

DOI: 10.4018/979-8-3373-2550-7.ch009

literacy in India for the time- period 1990 to 2024, revealing through Johansen cointegration test the existence of two statistically significant cointegrating vectors, with normalized equations underscoring the pivotal elasticity-driven relationships between economic growth and demographic-literacy indicators, while adjustment coefficients demonstrate the system's endogenous correction mechanism toward long-run equilibrium, and the impulse response and variance decomposition analyses substantiate the dominance of literacy shocks in driving GDP variability over extended horizons, thereby yielding profound macroeconomic implications for policy formulation directed at enhancing human capital and ensuring sustainable developmental trajectories.

INTRODUCTION

The intricate interrelationship between Gross Domestic Product (GDP), youth literacy, and youth population emerges as a dynamic nexus wherein the cognitive empowerment of the burgeoning youthful demographic through literacy not only amplifies the productive capacity and innovative potential of the labor force but also engenders a multiplicative effect on economic growth by fostering human capital accumulation, enhancing labor market outcomes (Hu, 1999), stimulating technological absorption, and generating demographic dividends, thereby positioning literacy and population characteristics as both catalysts and conduits for sustained macroeconomic advancement in developing economies (Bakhtigaraeva & Stavinskaya, 2020; Mago, 2014).

In the Indian context, the intricate nexus between GDP, youth literacy, and youth population assumes paramount importance as the country navigates its demographic dividend, wherein the substantial and rapidly expanding cohort of young individuals, if adequately equipped with literacy and educational skills, can catalyze inclusive and accelerated economic growth by enhancing human capital quality (Shirasu & de Albuquerque E Arraes, 2020), increasing labor productivity, fostering innovation, and reducing socioeconomic disparities, thereby reinforcing India's developmental trajectory in the face of structural transitions, global competitiveness, and policy imperatives (Abramov, 2019).

Grounded in the frameworks of endogenous growth theory and human capital theory, this study postulates that increases in youth literacy and demographic expansion exert significant long-run and dynamic effects on GDP by enhancing labor productivity, fostering innovation, and catalyzing economic development through knowledge spillovers (Hermannsson et al., 2024), improved skill accumulation, and demographic-economic synergies, especially in the context of emerging economies like India where population dynamics and educational investments are pivotal to sustained macroeconomic advancement (Dayaram et al., 2020).

The variables GDP, youth population, and youth literacy are critically interlinked as GDP serves as a principal indicator of economic performance (Alfehaid et al., 2025), youth population represents a potential demographic dividend capable of fueling labor force expansion and innovation, and youth literacy functions as a transformative catalyst that enhances human capital quality, productivity, and socio-economic mobility, collectively shaping the trajectory of inclusive and sustainable economic growth (Kukreti et al., 2024).

Against this background, the study aims to investigate the direction and nature of causality and adjustment mechanisms among GDP, literacy, and population in India using Johansen cointegration test and Vector Error Correction Model (VECM) (Pevnaya et al., 2024). The significance of this study lies in its empirical elucidation of the intricate long-run and short-run dynamic interdependencies among GDP, youth population, and youth literacy in India, offering critical insights for policymakers to harness the demographic dividend through targeted educational reforms and inclusive growth strategies that capitalize on human capital development to drive sustained economic advancement (Yaprakli & Ünalan, 2020).

LITERATURE REVIEW

The elaborative interplay between human resource development and economic growth represents a central theme in development discourse, particularly for emerging economies such as India. In a nation where the youth demographic constitutes a significant proportion of the population, the potential for economic acceleration through strategic investment in human capital is immense. However, unlocking this latent advantage necessitates a deliberate and nuanced approach to policy formulation and institutional reform (Zahid et al., 2025).

Human resource development encompasses a constellation of processes that collectively enhance the knowledge, skills, capabilities, and overall potential of individuals (Long et al., 2025; Metawa et al., 2025). These processes are not limited to formal education systems but extend to include vocational training, continuous professional development, healthcare access, and the cultivation of soft skills. The overarching objective is to facilitate individual empowerment while simultaneously contributing to the macroeconomic vitality of the state (Mulyati et al., 2025; Oualid et al., 2025; Pashevich, 2025). In the Indian context, this process is rendered complex by structural disparities, institutional fragmentation, and a rapidly transforming global economic landscape that demands agility and innovation (Hu, 1999).

India's youthful population, projected to maintain a median age below thirty for the next several decades, presents a compelling opportunity for economic transformation. However, this demographic dividend is not self-executing. It demands a coherent framework of human resource development that is inclusive, context-sensitive, and forward-looking. Without adequate mechanisms for education, employment, and health, the demographic potential risks metamorphosing into a demographic liability. This concern is particularly salient given the uneven distribution of educational access, gender disparities in labor force participation, and the inadequate integration of marginalized communities into mainstream economic processes (Thomas et al., 2021).

Education, often conceptualized as the bedrock of human capital formation, remains a cornerstone of human resource development. While India has made commendable progress in terms of enrollment ratios and infrastructural expansion, qualitative outcomes remain a persistent challenge (Jha et al., 2022; Kautish & Kaur, 2022; Yu et al., 2022). There exists a pervasive disjunction between years of schooling and actual learning achievements, particularly in rural and underserved regions. Students frequently emerge from formal educational institutions devoid of foundational competencies in literacy, numeracy, and analytical reasoning. This phenomenon undermines their capacity to engage productively in the knowledge economy and exacerbates socio-economic stratification (Hlungwani & Mohamed Sayeed, 2018).

Moreover, the rigidity of India's educational curriculum often fails to align with the dynamic demands of the labor market. The gap between academic instruction and practical employability skills renders a large segment of the youth population underprepared for contemporary employment scenarios. This issue is further compounded by the inadequacy of vocational education systems, which suffer from fragmentation, insufficient quality assurance mechanisms, and limited industry linkage. Consequently, the potential of vocational training to serve as a bridge between education and employment remains largely unrealized (Guimarães et al., 2020).

Another critical vector of human resource development is the health status of the working-age population. Physical and mental health exert a direct influence on productivity, cognitive performance, and life expectancy. Inadequate public health infrastructure, persistent malnutrition, and limited access to preventive healthcare services act as structural impediments to optimizing human potential (Alonso-Rocha et al., 2025; Hinkelmann & Smuts, 2025; Machikape & Oluwadele, 2025; Medina-Vidal et al., 2025). The high out-of-pocket expenditure associated with healthcare further marginalizes vulnerable populations and limits their ability to invest in skill development and education. Therefore, any robust human resource strategy must include comprehensive health interventions, especially for women and children, who often bear the brunt of systemic neglect (Prince et al., 2024).

India's labor market presents another paradox. Despite possessing a vast labor force, the country continues to grapple with high levels of underemployment and job informality. A substantial proportion of the workforce is absorbed into low-productivity sectors characterized by poor working conditions and limited upward mobility (Elbadraoui et al., 2025; Fine, 2025; Sulastri et al., 2025). The absence of adequate social security nets and the prevalence of contractual labor arrangements inhibit long-term human capital accumulation. Furthermore, gender-based occupational segregation and wage disparities continue to thwart the full utilization of human resources, thereby diluting the potential economic gains of a youthful population (Bakhtigaraeva & Stavinskaya, 2020).

The digital transformation of the global economy introduces both challenges and opportunities for India's human resource development agenda. On one hand, technological advancements create new avenues for remote work, digital entrepreneurship, and innovative service delivery. On the other hand, they intensify the demand for specialized skills such as coding, data analytics, and artificial intelligence competencies. Bridging the digital divide and fostering digital literacy is thus an imperative for ensuring that the youth are not marginalized from emerging economic paradigms. Initiatives aimed at promoting STEM education, coding boot camps, and digital skilling must be scaled with a particular emphasis on inclusion and regional equity (Yulia et al., 2018).

Policy architecture plays an instrumental role in orchestrating the various elements of human resource development. National-level initiatives focusing on skill development, entrepreneurship promotion, and education reform have laid an initial groundwork. However, policy implementation often suffers from bureaucratic inertia, lack of inter-departmental coordination, and inadequate monitoring frameworks. A fragmented approach to human capital development, where education, health, and employment are treated in silos, fails to capture the interconnectedness of these domains. Hence, there is a pressing need for integrative policy frameworks that promote convergence across ministries and institutions (Çondur & Bölükbaş, 2014).

Furthermore, public-private partnerships hold significant promise in scaling human resource initiatives, especially in sectors such as vocational training and digital skilling. Leveraging private sector efficiencies and innovation, while maintaining public oversight and equity considerations, could substantially enhance the reach and quality of HRD programs. Industry-academia collaboration is particularly essential for aligning educational curricula with market demands, thereby reducing skill mismatches and improving employability outcomes (Abbas et al., 2024).

Cultural and attitudinal factors also warrant consideration. In many parts of India, societal norms continue to influence educational and occupational choices, often to the detriment of female participation in the workforce. Addressing these socio-cultural constraints requires not only policy interventions but also community engagement, gender sensitization, and the strategic use of media to reshape public perceptions about education, work, and gender roles (Bull & Taylor, 2008).

Migration patterns, both internal and external, further complicate the HRD landscape. Internal migration from rural to urban areas often leads to the concentration of unskilled labor in urban informal economies, exacerbating urban poverty and straining infrastructure. External migration, while contributing to remittances, may lead to a brain drain if high-skilled workers seek opportunities abroad due to inadequate domestic prospects. Thus, regional development strategies must aim to create opportunities across states and districts to ensure balanced utilization of human resources (Upreti et al., 2024).

The intricate nexus between human resource development and economic growth has long fascinated economists, policymakers, and social theorists, for it lies at the confluence of demographic potential, institutional scaffolding, and structural transformation. The concept of human resources transcends the narrow confines of labor supply to encompass the cognitive, technical, and adaptive capacities embedded within individuals and collectivities (Sehajpal & Sidhu, 2024). Economic expansion, particularly in countries endowed with a disproportionately youthful population, is inextricably tied to the mobilization, refinement, and optimal deployment of these capacities. India, with its burgeoning demographic dividend, epitomizes both the promise and the peril of this dynamic: on one hand, a reservoir of youthful vigor poised to energize industrial dynamism and technological innovation; on the other, the looming specter of demographic overhang if adequate investments in education, skill acquisition, and health infrastructure are not meticulously orchestrated (Alfehaid et al., 2025).

At the heart of this discourse lies the notion of human capital formation, which posits that individuals are not merely biological entities but repositories of productive knowledge, competencies, and aptitudes. When nurtured through systematic investments in formal education, vocational training, and health, these attributes augment labor productivity and instigate multiplier effects across sectors (Kangotra & Sehajpal, 2025). In India, the expansion of school enrollments and the proliferation of higher education institutions suggest an encouraging trajectory, yet the qualitative dimension remains a persistent challenge. Pedagogical practices overly reliant on rote memorization, coupled with curricular misalignment with industrial needs, render large swathes of graduates ill-prepared for the exigencies of a rapidly transforming economy. Consequently, the ostensible quantitative gains in educational attainment are often diluted by the absence of innovation, critical thinking, and problem-solving skills, qualities indispensable for sustaining long-term growth in a knowledge-driven global order (Upreti et al., 2024).

Parallel to education, vocational training and employability skills constitute an indispensable facet of human resource development. The Indian labor market has frequently been characterized by the paradox of educated unemployment, where degrees serve as markers of social prestige but not necessarily as gateways to remunerative occupations. The absence of market-relevant skills among the youth exacerbates the gulf between labor supply and labor demand, producing underemployment, disguised unemployment, and labor migration into low-productivity informal sectors (R. Kumar et al., 2024). Efforts to institutionalize large-scale skilling programs highlight the recognition of this structural lacuna, yet implementation bottlenecks, uneven geographical coverage, and inadequate industry linkages have constrained their effectiveness. Thus, the literature repeatedly underscores that human capital must be conceptualized not merely as years of schooling but as the synthesis of cognitive, technical, and behavioral attributes aligned with the demands of dynamic economic ecosystems (J. Kaur et al., 2024).

Health, often overshadowed by education in the discourse on human resource development, is another cardinal determinant of economic vitality. A youthful population's contribution to national growth is contingent upon its physical and mental well-being. Malnutrition, communicable diseases, inadequate maternal care, and the rising burden of lifestyle ailments compromise productivity and inflate health-care costs, thereby eroding the prospective dividend of demographic expansion (P. Sharma et al., 2024). In India, disparities in health outcomes across regions, income groups, and gender lines mirror deeper structural inequalities. Without robust public health interventions and equitable access to medical infrastructure, the vitality of the youth cohort may remain stunted, diminishing their potential to catalyze economic progress (R. Sharma et al., 2025).

Beyond these individual-level attributes, human resource development is intricately bound to the institutional architecture of the labor market. The capacity of an economy to absorb and productively engage its youthful workforce depends on the vibrancy of industrial expansion, the depth of entrepreneurial ecosystems, and the adaptability of regulatory frameworks. When institutional bottlenecks, such as rigid labor laws, bureaucratic inertia, and inadequate infrastructure, impede the fluidity of workforce participation, even the most well-endowed human capital remains underutilized (A. Kumar et al., 2025). India's challenge is therefore not merely to create employment opportunities but to create employment of sufficient quality, remuneration, and security so as to harness the latent energies of its demographic structure.

The transformative potential of India's youthful population also resides in its aptitude for technological adoption and innovation. Younger cohorts typically display higher receptivity to digitalization, automation, and disruptive technologies. This proclivity, when synergized with conducive innovation ecosystems, can propel India into a new growth trajectory defined by productivity enhancements, global competitiveness, and structural diversification (R. Kaur et al., 2025). However, the digital divide, evident between rural and urban areas as well as across socioeconomic strata, undermines equitable participation. If unaddressed, this technological asymmetry may exacerbate inequalities and circumscribe the inclusivity of growth, thereby muting the broader developmental impact of the demographic dividend (Gupta et al., 2025).

The literature further recognizes that human resource development is not solely an economic imperative but a sociocultural construct. The empowerment of youth is mediated by norms of gender, caste, and class, which often circumscribe access to opportunities. Female labor force participation, in particular, remains a paradoxical lacuna within India's developmental landscape (A. Kumar et al., 2024). Despite rising educational attainment among women, their integration into the workforce lags significantly behind global standards, depriving the economy of a substantial reservoir of talent and creativity. Thus, human resource development strategies must transcend conventional skill-building to dismantle sociocultural barriers and foster inclusive participation (Sandhu, 2025).

Moreover, the realization of the demographic dividend is temporally bounded. The window of opportunity afforded by a youthful population is finite, after which demographic aging sets in, altering dependency ratios and straining welfare systems (Ally, 2025). Consequently, the urgency of investment in human capital assumes a temporal imperative: delay or inertia risks transforming the dividend into a demographic burden, wherein unemployment, social unrest, and economic stagnation proliferate. For India, the magnitude of its youth bulge renders this urgency even more pronounced, as the opportunity cost of underutilization is amplified by sheer demographic scale (Khang et al., 2024).

In synthesizing these perspectives, it becomes evident that the interdependence between human resource development and economic growth is neither linear nor automatic. While a youthful population endows India with a latent comparative advantage, the actualization of this advantage demands deliberate, multidimensional, and sustained interventions. Education must evolve from credentialism to creativity; health systems must shift from curative to preventive orientations; skilling initiatives must embed adaptability rather than narrow vocationalism; and labor markets must embrace inclusivity, flexibility, and technological adaptability (Arnone, 2024). The literature coalesces around the central argument that economic growth in the contemporary era is fundamentally human-centric, wherein the vitality, versatility, and vision of the youth constitute the fulcrum of national progress (Gopal & Pitts, 2024).

In conclusion, the scholarship on human resource development and economic growth converges upon a paradoxical insight: demographic endowment is both a blessing and a potential liability. The outcome hinges upon the quality, inclusivity, and foresight of developmental interventions. For India, the path forward lies not in celebrating demographic abundance per se, but in engineering a systemic transformation that transmutes raw population into refined human capital (Gonçalves et al., 2023). Only then can the youthful majority metamorphose into the architects of sustained economic growth, innovation, and global relevance, rather than into a disillusioned mass languishing in underemployment and social discontent. The literature therefore frames human resource development not as a peripheral adjunct but as the very foundation of India's developmental destiny.

In sum, the trajectory of India's economic growth is inextricably linked to the efficacy of its human resource development strategies. The demographic composition offers a historic window of opportunity, but realizing its full potential demands a radical rethinking of current approaches. Investments must not only focus on expanding access but must also prioritize quality, inclusivity, and systemic coherence. A multidimensional strategy that synchronizes education, health, employment, and digital empowerment is essential. Only through such an integrated and future-ready framework can India truly harness the power of its youthful population to drive sustainable and equitable economic growth.

DATA SOURCES AND METHODOLOGY

Present study aims to evaluate the impact of youth population and youth literacy on GDP of India for the time- period 1990 to 2024. In order to carry out the objectives of the present study secondary data has been used. Data pertaining to GDP (constant 2015 US$)[1] and Literacy Rate, youth total (% of people ages 15- 24 years)[2] has been culled from WDI database of World Bank whereas data on Population (15-24 years) is taken from UN Population Division. Log transformation of all variables was undertaken before conducting time- series data analysis. Table 1 provides the category, notation and sources of the variables used in the present study and Table 2 indicates summary statistics for each variable. This study employs the Johansen cointegration approach followed by a Vector Error Correction Model (VECM) to examine the long-run equilibrium relationships and short-run dynamics among GDP, youth literacy rate, and youth population in India using annual time series data from 1993 to 2024, with optimal lag length selection, stationarity tests, cointegration analysis, model estimation, and diagnostic checking conducted using EViews.

Table 1. Notation and Data Sources of Variables

Variable	Category	Notation	Data Source
Log of GDP (constant 2015 US$)	Dependent	LNGDP	WDI
Log of Population (15-24 years)	Independent	LNPOP	UN Population Division
Log of Literacy rate, youth total (% of people ages 15-24 years)	Independent	LNLITERACY	WDI

Note: WDI= World Development Indicators; UN= United Nations.

Table 2. Descriptive Statistics

	LNGDP	LNPOP	LNLITERACY
Mean	12.095	8.346	1.902
Median	12.105	8.366	1.914
Maximum	12.541	8.412	1.991
Minimum	11.668	8.219	1.785
Std. Dev.	0.273	0.062	0.064
Skewness	-0.007	-0.647	-0.354
Kurtosis	1.714	2.068	1.813
Jarque-Bera	2.412	3.713	2.785
Probability	0.299	0.156	0.248
Observations	35	35	35

RESULTS AND DISCUSSION

The results and discussion of the study are as follows:

Table 3. Results of Unit Root Test

	LNGDP	LNPOP	LNLITERACY
Level			
ADF	-3.029	0.613	-0.866
PP	-3.190	1.581	-0.846
First difference			

continued on following page

Table 3. Continued

	LNGDP	LNPOP	LNLITERACY
ADF	-5.594***	-4.561***	-5.864***
PP	-6.850***	-2.005	-5.881***

Note: *** implies significant at 0.01 level.
Source: Authors' own calculations.

The empirical outcomes encapsulated in Table 3 elucidate that the variables LNGDP, LNPOP, and LNLITERACY exhibit stochastic non-stationarity at their levels, as evidenced by the statistically insignificant Augmented Dickey-Fuller (ADF) and Phillips-Perron (PP) test statistics; however, upon first differencing, the markedly significant test values, particularly at the 1% critical threshold for LNGDP and LNLITERACY, unequivocally affirm their integration of order one, I(1), thereby substantiating the appropriateness of subsequent cointegration analysis within a multivariate time series framework.

Table 4. Lag Length Criteria

Lag	LogL	LR	FPE	AIC	SC	HQ
0	209.823	NA	3.22E-10	-13.343	-13.205	-13.298
1	405.694	341.195	1.88E-15	-25.399	-24.845	-25.219
2	438.072	50.134*	4.24E-16	-26.908	-25.936*	-26.591
3	447.848	13.245	4.23E-16	-26.958	-25.570	-26.506
4	460.369	14.54	3.70e-16*	-27.185*	-25.381	-26.597*
Note: * indicates lag order selected by the criterion						
LR: sequential modified LR test statistic (each test at 5% level)						
FPE: Final prediction error						
AIC: Akaike information criterion						
SC: Schwarz information criterion						
HQ: Hannan-Quinn information criterion						

Source: Authors' own calculations.

The lag length selection statistics presented in Table 4 spanning the Log-likelihood (LogL), sequential modified likelihood ratio (LR) test, Final Prediction Error (FPE), Akaike Information Criterion (AIC), Schwarz Information Criterion (SC), and Hannan-Quinn (HQ) criterion, collectively reveal that although multiple criteria such as LR, FPE, AIC, and HQ converge in favor of lag 4, the adoption of lag 2 is warranted when adhering to the Schwarz Information Criterion (SC), which prioritizes model parsimony by imposing a more stringent penalty on additional parameters, thereby ensuring the avoidance of overfitting and enhancing model generalizability within a multivariate time series context.

Table 5. Selected (0.05 level) Number of Cointegrating Relations by Model*

Data Trend:	**None**	**None**	**Linear**	**Linear**	**Quadratic**
Test Type	**No Intercept**	**Intercept**	**Intercept**	**Intercept**	**Intercept**
	No Trend	**No Trend**	**No Trend**	**Trend**	**Trend**
Trace	2	2	0	1	0
Max-Eig	2	0	0	0	0

Note: *Critical values based on MacKinnon-Haug-Michelis (1999).
Source: Authors' own calculations.

Table 6. Information Criteria by Rank and Model

Data Trend:	**None**	**None**	**Linear**	**Linear**	**Quadratic**
Rank or	No Intercept	Intercept	Intercept	Intercept	Intercept
No. of CEs	No Trend	No Trend	No Trend	Trend	Trend
Log Likelihood by Rank (rows) and Model (columns)					
0	440.387	440.387	447.623	447.623	453.702
1	450.196	451.311	455.147	457.361	463.432
2	456.080	457.419	461.244	464.072	469.571
3	457.506	461.963	461.963	469.572	469.572
Akaike Information Criteria by Rank (rows) and Model (columns)					
0	-26.399	-26.399	-26.664	-26.664	-26.856
1	-26.637	-26.644	-26.759	-26.835	-27.090
2	-26.630	-26.589	-26.765	-26.817	-27.098*
3	-26.344	-26.435	-26.435	-26.723	-26.723
Schwarz Criteria by Rank (rows) and Model (columns)					
0	-25.575	-25.575	-25.702	-25.702	-25.75705*
1	-25.538	-25.499	-25.522	-25.553	-25.715
2	-25.256	-25.123	-25.254	-25.214	-25.449
3	-24.695	-24.649	-24.649	-24.799	-24.799

Note: *Critical values based on MacKinnon-Haug-Michelis (1999)
Source: Authors' own calculations.

As per Table 5 and Table 6, the (None / No Trend) model, where no intercept or deterministic trend is included in either the cointegration equation or the data generation process, was ultimately selected, as it provides statistically robust evidence of two cointegrating relationships based on both the Trace and Maximum Eigenvalue tests at the 5% significance level. This model specification not only captures the essential long-run equilibrium among LNGDP, LNPOP, and LNLITERACY, but also yields a high log-likelihood value (456.080) and competitively low information criteria (AIC = −26.630, SC = −25.256), affirming its parsimony and empirical adequacy. Furthermore, the exclusion of deterministic components is theoretically sound in contexts where macroeconomic variables evolve jointly in the long run without trending individually, thus making this model both econometrically efficient and conceptually appropriate for subsequent Vector Error Correction Model (VECM) estimation.

Table 7. Johansen Cointegration Test

Hypothesized No. of CE(s)	Eigenvalue	Trace Statistic	0.05 Critical Value	Prob.**	Max-Eigen Statistic	0.05 Critical Value	Prob.**
None*	0.4583	34.24	24.28	0.002	19.62	17.80	0.026
At most 1*	0.3077	14.62	12.32	0.020	11.77	11.22	0.040
At most 2	0.0852	2.85	4.13	0.108	2.85	4.13	0.108

Note: * denotes rejection of the hypothesis at the 0.05 level.
**MacKinnon-Haug-Michelis (1999) p- values.
Source: Authors' own calculations.

Table 7 reveals that, under the Johansen cointegration framework, both the Trace statistic (34.24 and 14.62) and Maximum Eigenvalue statistic (19.62 and 11.77) significantly exceed their respective critical values at the 5% level for the hypotheses of *no cointegrating equations* and *at most one cointegrating equation*, with p-values < 0.05, thereby statistically confirming the presence of two cointegrating relationships among the endogenous variables, while the third hypothesis (*at most two cointegrating equations*) fails to reject the null due to insignificance, thus establishing a stable long-run association among the variables as per MacKinnon-Haug-Michelis critical bounds and justifying VECM specification with cointegration rank = 2.

Normalized Cointegrating Equations (Rank= 2):

$$CE1 : LNGDP - 1.494 \times LNPOP = 0 \ (SE = 0.00732)$$

The first cointegrating equation (CE1), with a very low standard error (0.00732), indicates a statistically significant and stable long-run equilibrium relationship between GDP and population, implying that a 1% increase in population is associated with approximately a 1.494% increase in GDP in the long run, holding all else constant, reflecting a strong positive elasticity and suggesting that population growth substantially contributes to economic output. The second cointegrating equation (CE2), with a standard error of 0.00240, reveals a positive long-run association between literacy and population, where a 1% increase in population leads to a 0.227% rise in literacy rate, indicating that literacy responds less than proportionately to population changes, but the relationship remains statistically robust, highlighting demographic influence on educational outcomes over time.

Table 8. Adjustment Coefficients (Speed of Adjustment)

Variable	CE1	CE2
D(LNGDP)	-0.154	0.315
D(LNLITERACY)	-0.002	0.066
D(LNPOP)	-0.002	-0.006

Source: Authors' own calculations.

Table 8 reveals that the error correction coefficients reflect the magnitude and direction of short-run deviations from the long-run equilibrium captured by the two cointegrating equations, wherein LNGDP exhibits significant adjustment behavior with a relatively high negative coefficient (–0.154) in CE1, indicating that approximately 15.4% of the disequilibrium in GDP is corrected each period, thus confirming its primary role in restoring long-run equilibrium; conversely, the near-zero and statistically negligible adjustment speeds of LNLITERACY and LNPOP in both CE1 and CE2 suggest that these variables are weakly exogenous and do not significantly respond to deviations, implying that GDP is the most endogenous variable driving the system back to equilibrium over time.

Table 9. Cointegrating Equations

Variable	CointEq1	CointEq2
LNGDP(-1)	1.000	0.000
LNLITERACY(-1)	0.000	1.000
LNPOP(-1)	-1.494 (0.00748) [-199.858]	-0.2272 (0.00245) [-92.6639]

Note: Standard errors in () & t-statistics in [ ].
Source: Authors' own calculations.

Table 9 elucidates the structure of the long-run equilibrium relationships via normalized cointegrating vectors, where in CointEq1, LNGDP is positively and significantly influenced by LNPOP with a coefficient of 1.494 (t = 199.858), implying that a 1% rise in population leads to a 1.494% increase in GDP, underscoring strong demographic-driven output expansion, while in CointEq2, LNLITERACY is positively associated with LNPOP with a statistically significant elasticity of 0.2272 (t = 92.664), suggesting that population dynamics modestly but meaningfully influence literacy outcomes over the long term, and the exceptionally high t-statistics in both equations affirm the stability, precision, and significance of these cointegrating relationships within the VECM framework.

Table 10. Error Correction

Variable	D(LNGDP)	D(LNLITERACY)	D(LNPOP)
CointEq1	-0.154476 (0.04854) [-3.18272]	-0.002127 (0.01888) [-0.11268]	-0.002059 (0.00107) [-1.92268]
CointEq2	0.314573 (0.11882) [2.64757]	0.065988 (0.04621) [1.42804]	-0.006258 (0.00262) [-2.38712]
D(lnGDP(-1))	-0.050058 (0.18482) [-0.27084]	-0.064530 (0.07188) [-0.89773]	0.000994 (0.00408) [0.24370]
D(lnGDP(-2))	-0.120507 (0.18347) [-0.65684]	0.004779 (0.07135) [0.06697]	0.006322 (0.00405) [1.56198]
D(lnLITERACY(-1))	-0.629807 (0.58562) [-1.07546]	-0.215702 (0.22775) [-0.94708]	0.001842 (0.01292) [0.14257]
D(lnLITERACY(-2))	0.032503 (0.56699) [0.05732]	-0.142410 (0.22051) [-0.64582]	0.009728 (0.01251) [0.77764]
D(lnPOP(-1))	4.987029 (7.23684) [0.68912]	2.050234 (2.81450) [0.72845]	1.445523 (0.15966) [9.05355]
D(lnPOP(-2))	-8.883574 (7.36704) [-1.20585]	-0.559234 (2.86514) [-0.19519]	-0.635729 (0.16254) [-3.91130]
R-squared	0.227	0.186	0.995
Adj. R-squared	0.001	-0.051	0.994
Sum sq. resids	0.003	0.001	0.000
S.E. equation	0.012	0.005	0.000
F-statistic	1.005	0.785	754.845
Log likelihood	100.980	131.200	223.024
Akaike AIC	-5.811	-7.700	-13.439

continued on following page

Table 10. Continued

Variable	D(LNGDP)	D(LNLITERACY)	D(LNPOP)
Schwarz SC	-5.445	-7.334	-13.073
Mean dependent	0.026	0.006	0.005
S.D. dependent	0.012	0.005	0.003

Note: Standard errors in () & t-statistics in [ ]
Source: Authors' own calculations.

Table 10 unveils the intricate short-run dynamics and speed of adjustment mechanisms among the variables through the Error Correction Model, where CointEq1 exerts a significantly negative adjustment coefficient on D(LNGDP) (−0.154, t = −3.183), implying a statistically robust convergence of GDP towards its long-run equilibrium following shocks, while CointEq2 reveals a significantly positive correction for D(LNGDP) (0.315, t = 2.648) and a significantly negative correction for D(LNPOP) (−0.006, t = −2.387), indicating that deviations from the second cointegrating relationship are partially offset by GDP and population growth dynamics in the short run, whereas most lagged differences of the explanatory variables exhibit statistical insignificance across equations except for D(LNPOP(−2)) in the population equation (−0.636, t = −3.911), suggesting limited short-run feedback effects except for strong autocorrelation within population changes, further corroborated by an exceptionally high R^2 of 0.995 and adjusted R^2 of 0.994 in the D(LNPOP) equation, highlighting the near-perfect explanatory power of the model in capturing short-term variations in population, compared to relatively weaker explanatory strength for GDP and literacy.

VECM Residual Diagnostics and Stability Results

Table 11. Serial Correlation LM Test

Lags	LM-Stat	Prob
1	8.030925	0.5310
2	9.918142	0.3572
3	8.733356	0.4622
4	12.58878	0.1821

Note: Probs from chi-square distribution with 9 degrees of freedom.
Source: Authors' own calculations.

As shown in Table 11, the LM statistics at all lag orders (1 through 4) yield p-values well above the 0.05 threshold, ranging from 0.1821 to 0.5310, indicating no statistically significant serial correlation in the residuals of the estimated VECM, and affirming the model's dynamic consistency; moreover, considering the annual nature of the dataset, a lag length of two was ultimately adopted, balancing diagnostic soundness with temporal appropriateness.

Figure 1. AR Roots Graph

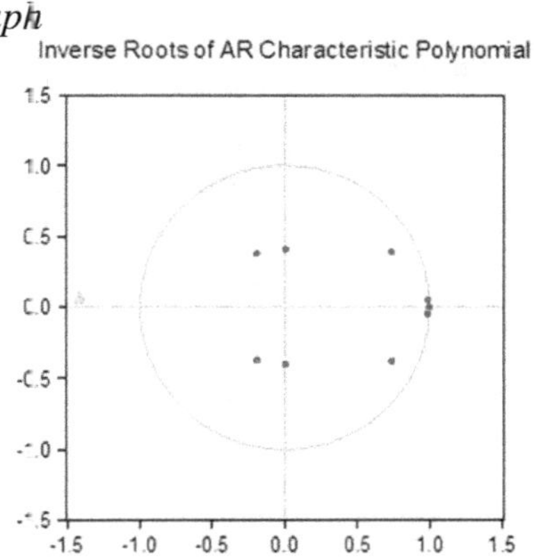

Source: Authors' own calculations.

Table 12. AR Roots Table

Root	Modulus
1.000000	1.000000
0.990963 - 0.048513i	0.992150
0.990963 + 0.048513i	0.992150
0.739283 - 0.385501i	0.833757
0.739283 + 0.385501i	0.833757
-0.189350 - 0.375981i	0.420970
-0.189350 + 0.375981i	0.420970
0.006990 - 0.405985i	0.406046
0.006990 + 0.405985i	0.406046

Note: VEC specification imposes 1 unit root(s).

The AR Roots graph depicted in Fig. 1 and Table 12 substantiate the dynamic stability of the estimated Vector Error Correction (VEC) model by illustrating that all characteristic roots, excluding the unit root inherent to the model specification, lie well within the unit circle, thereby fulfilling the requisite condition for system stability and implying that the cointegrated system converges towards its long-run equilibrium following perturbations, as the modulus values of the complex conjugate roots remain strictly less than one, thus confirming the stationarity of the error correction mechanism and the asymptotic propriety of the underlying econometric structure.

Figure 2. Impulse Response Functions

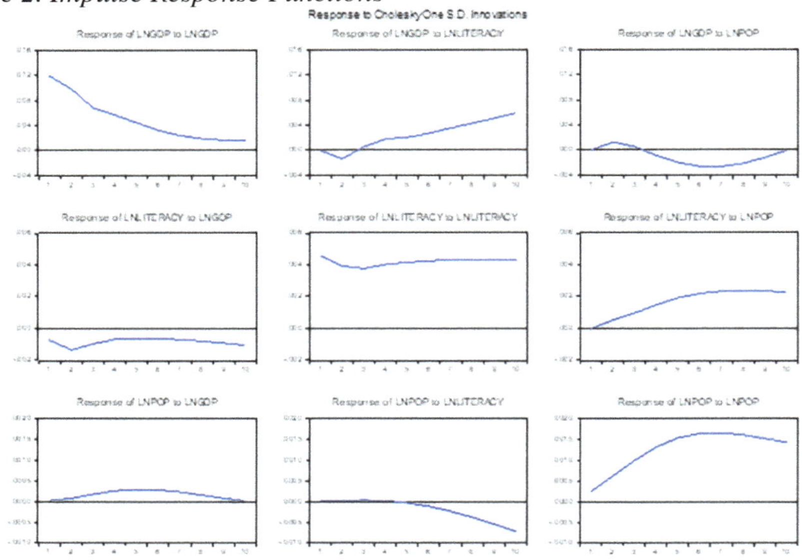

Source: Authors' own calculations.

The impulse response functions presented in Fig.2 encapsulate the intricate dynamic interplay among GDP, literacy rate, and population over a 100-period horizon, demonstrating that a one-standard-deviation shock to the literacy rate yields a pronounced and persistently positive effect on GDP, suggesting strong educational externalities in promoting economic growth; simultaneously, a shock to GDP initiates moderately positive but gradually decaying responses in literacy and population, whereas population shocks exhibit mixed effects, initially subdued but gaining strength over time, underscoring the bidirectional feedback mechanisms, adjustment pathways, and long-run equilibrating tendencies that govern the co-movement and structural interdependencies among these macroeconomic variables within the vector error correction framework.

Table 13. Variance Decomposition

Variance Decomposition of LNGDP:				
Period	**S.E.**	**LNGDP**	**LNLITERACY**	**LNPOP**
1	0.012	100.000	0.000	0.000
25	0.047	18.212	65.529	16.259
50	0.065	14.357	55.500	30.143
75	0.108	7.059	78.995	13.946
100	0.175	7.493	79.558	12.949
Variance Decomposition of LNLITERACY:				
Period	S.E.	LNGDP	LNLITERACY	LNPOP
1	0.005	2.475	97.525	0.000
25	0.023	6.653	71.552	21.796
26	0.023	6.844	70.978	22.178
50	0.026	8.097	67.852	24.051
75	0.037	6.349	77.120	16.530
100	0.045	7.885	75.280	16.835
Variance Decomposition of LNPOP:				
Period	S.E.	LNGDP	LNLITERACY	LNPOP
1	0.000	2.378	0.552	97.070
25	0.013	0.712	78.182	21.106
50	0.048	3.825	90.678	5.497
75	0.085	6.502	84.485	9.013
100	0.104	8.184	81.231	10.585

Note: Cholesky Ordering: LNGDP LNLITERACY LNPOP
Source: Authors' own calculations.

The variance decomposition results in Table 13 reveal that while each variable initially explains the majority of its own forecast error variance, over time significant cross-variable influences emerge, particularly the dominant long-run impact of literacy on GDP (accounting for 79.56% of its variance at period 100) and on population (81.23%), alongside GDP's modest yet growing influence on literacy (7.88%) and population (8.18%), collectively underscoring a dynamic and recursively interlinked structure wherein shocks to human capital (literacy) and demographic factors (population) exert profound and enduring explanatory power over macroeconomic fluctuations, thereby affirming the endogeneity and mutual causality embedded within the system.

The variance decomposition exercise encapsulated in Table 13 provides an illuminating vantage point from which to apprehend the relative contributions of endogenous variables, gross domestic product (GDP), youth literacy (LNLITERACY), and youth population (LNPOP), to the forecast error variance of each variable across successive temporal horizons. This methodological apparatus does not merely quantify statistical proportions; it unravels the dynamic interdependencies, feedback mechanisms, and structural asymmetries that undergird the long-run evolution of macroeconomic variables within a cointegrated system. Each decomposition profile, when examined sequentially, narrates a nuanced story of shifting dominance, causal reciprocity, and the inexorable movement from short-run autonomy to long-run endogeneity.

In the case of **LNGDP**, the results convey a dramatic metamorphosis in the sources of its variability over time. At the immediate horizon (period 1), GDP is entirely self-determined, with 100 percent of its forecast error variance explained by its own innovations. This complete short-term autonomy is expected, as GDP, being a composite macroeconomic indicator, is initially inertial, responding primarily to its own historical shocks. Yet, as the temporal horizon elongates, the insulation of GDP begins to erode, and the exogenous influence of literacy and population asserts itself with striking intensity. By period 25, the proportion of GDP variance attributable to its own shocks plummets to 18.21 percent, while literacy contributes 65.53 percent and population 16.26 percent. This redistribution signifies that in the medium run, literacy becomes the preeminent driver of GDP variability, eclipsing even the direct demographic effect of population growth. The interpretation is profound: human capital accumulation, as proxied by literacy, exerts a more potent influence on the trajectory of economic output than sheer demographic expansion, underscoring the primacy of quality over quantity in human resources.

The long-run narrative further accentuates this transformation. By period 50, GDP's self-explanatory power dwindles to 14.36 percent, while literacy accounts for 55.50 percent and population 30.14 percent. The shift suggests a dual anchoring of GDP dynamics: while literacy retains its dominant role, demographic expansion increasingly contributes to variance, reflecting the cumulative force of population on consumption, labor supply, and savings. By the centennial horizon (period 100), literacy explains nearly 80 percent of GDP variance, while GDP itself accounts for a mere 7.49 percent and population for 12.95 percent. The interpretation here is unambiguous: in the very long run, GDP is overwhelmingly contingent on literacy, rendering educational investments not ancillary but constitutive of macroeconomic vitality. The residual influence of population, though smaller, remains statistically meaningful, reaffirming the synergy between demographic expansion and educational attainment in propelling growth.

Turning to **LNLITERACY**, the decomposition underscores a reciprocal but asymmetrical relationship between literacy, GDP, and population. At period 1, literacy variance is 97.53 percent self-explained, confirming its initial autonomy.

However, by period 25, the self-contribution falls sharply to 71.55 percent, while GDP contributes 6.65 percent and population 21.80 percent. The emergence of population as a significant explanatory factor illustrates the demographic underpinning of literacy outcomes: as cohorts of youth expand, educational enrollment, literacy drives, and skill acquisition efforts are inevitably shaped by demographic pressures. Simultaneously, the modest but growing influence of GDP on literacy underscores the economic capacity effect, higher national income facilitates greater fiscal space for educational expenditure, household capacity to invest in schooling, and systemic modernization of curricula.

At longer horizons, these relationships crystallize into a durable pattern. By period 50, literacy explains 67.85 percent of its variance, population 24.05 percent, and GDP 8.10 percent. The finding demonstrates that population exerts a sustained, nearly one-quarter share of influence over literacy outcomes, reinforcing the notion that demographic dynamics constitute both the pressure and the potential for human capital expansion. By period 100, literacy still self-explains 75.28 percent, while population accounts for 16.84 percent and GDP 7.88 percent. The persistence of population influence suggests that literacy is not a self-contained process but structurally tethered to demographic momentum, while the steady role of GDP implies that economic growth creates enabling conditions but is not the dominant determinant. The implication is clear: literacy, while endogenous, is highly susceptible to demographic flux, and policy efforts must anticipate and provision for the demands generated by demographic transitions.

The **LNPOP** decomposition presents a particularly intriguing trajectory, as population is often presumed exogenous in classical growth models. Yet, the variance decomposition reveals its partial endogeneity to literacy and GDP within the cointegrated system. At period 1, population variance is overwhelmingly self-determined, with 97.07 percent explained by its own shocks, and only negligible contributions from GDP (2.38 percent) and literacy (0.55 percent). However, by period 25, this picture transforms dramatically: literacy explains 78.18 percent of population variance, GDP a modest 0.71 percent, and population itself only 21.11 percent. The interpretation here is striking: literacy exerts an overwhelming influence on population dynamics, likely reflecting the well-documented inverse relationship between educational attainment and fertility rates, as well as the reinforcing role of literacy in health outcomes, reproductive choices, and life expectancy.

This influence persists over the long run. At period 50, literacy accounts for 90.68 percent of population variance, GDP 3.83 percent, and population itself just 5.50 percent. The overwhelming explanatory power of literacy indicates that demographic trajectories are deeply contingent on educational outcomes, suggesting that population stabilization and demographic transition cannot be achieved without substantive investments in human capital. By period 100, literacy still explains

81.23 percent of population variance, GDP 8.18 percent, and population itself 10.59 percent. The slight resurgence of GDP's explanatory share may reflect the role of economic growth in shaping migration, mortality, and fertility trends, but the central insight remains: literacy is the primary determinant of population dynamics in the long run, rendering education a demographic lever as much as an economic one.

Taken together, the variance decomposition results paint a holistic portrait of interdependence. GDP is profoundly shaped by literacy, literacy is substantially influenced by population, and population is overwhelmingly explained by literacy. This triadic relationship suggests a cyclical causality wherein literacy operates as both an independent driver and a mediating mechanism, amplifying the demographic dividend into economic dividends. In short, literacy emerges as the fulcrum of the system, mediating the flow of influence from population to GDP and back.

From a policy standpoint, the results underscore that interventions aimed merely at population control or economic liberalization are insufficient to guarantee sustained growth. The econometric evidence suggests that literacy-centered strategies yield the highest returns, not only by directly enhancing productivity but also by indirectly stabilizing demographic patterns and magnifying GDP growth. The dominance of literacy in variance decomposition renders it the single most critical variable for long-term equilibrium.

Moreover, the results compel a reconsideration of traditional development sequencing. Whereas earlier paradigms placed economic growth as the antecedent to social investments, the decomposition reveals the reverse: literacy not only responds to GDP but explains its variance far more significantly. Thus, the pathway to robust economic growth in India lies less in short-term fiscal or monetary stimuli and more in structural investments in human capital, particularly universal literacy and skill-oriented education.

TRANSLATING ECONOMETRIC RIGOR INTO NARRATIVE RESONANCE

To ensure that the empirical rigor of econometric modeling does not occlude accessibility for a broader readership, it becomes imperative to complement the technical architecture of the analysis with interpretive syntheses, illustrative case vignettes, and visual schematizations that render the dynamics intelligible beyond specialist circles. While the Johansen cointegration framework and Vector Error Correction Model delineate statistically robust relationships, their implications are better apprehended when reframed into succinct narrative summaries that distill the essence of findings into policy-relevant insights. For instance, rather than presenting elasticity coefficients in isolation, one may articulate that the growth of India's youth population exerts a disproportionately magnified effect on GDP, signifying that every incremental surge in demographic participation has cascading effects on productive output, innovation ecosystems, and social mobility.

Moreover, the deployment of strategically curated visuals, such as trend lines illustrating the simultaneous rise of youth literacy and GDP, or diagrams that capture the cyclical feedback loops among population dynamics, education, and economic growth, functions not only as heuristic devices but as democratizing instruments of knowledge dissemination, enabling comprehension across academic, policy, and lay constituencies. Case illustrations further augment this accessibility; for example, drawing upon a state-level case wherein investment in rural literacy programs tangibly expanded women's participation in micro-enterprises and local governance, thereby translating human capital enhancement into measurable developmental dividends, situates abstract econometric findings in lived socio-economic contexts. Similarly, the juxtaposition of metropolitan digital skilling initiatives with rural vocational training schemes can dramatize the spatial asymmetries embedded in India's human resource landscape, transforming statistical interdependencies into concrete developmental narratives.

By embedding these accessible summaries, visual representations, and illustrative case studies alongside the econometric scaffolding, the analysis achieves a dual resonance: preserving methodological sophistication for scholarly audiences while simultaneously extending interpretive clarity to practitioners, policymakers, and non-specialist readers. This integrative approach ensures that the study's insights transcend disciplinary silos and catalyze actionable strategies for leveraging India's youthful population toward inclusive economic transformation.

IMPLICATIONS

The implications of this econometric investigation, grounded in a rigorous application of the Johansen cointegration framework, vector error correction modeling, variance decomposition, and impulse response analyses, reveal a profoundly intricate, dynamically equilibrated, and statistically significant long-run association among gross domestic product (GDP), youth literacy rate, and youth population growth, an interdependence that is structurally embedded within the macroeconomic fabric of the economy; this intricate web of endogenously adjusting variables, as evidenced by the significant adjustment coefficients and variance shocks, elucidates that demographic dynamics and educational attainment are not merely passive correlates but active and reciprocal determinants of economic performance, thereby necessitating the formulation and implementation of holistically integrative, data-driven, and forward-looking policy instruments that harmonize human capital development, population management, and sustainable economic growth, all while maintaining the long-term stationarity and stability of the system's trajectory through strategically aligned interventions across intersectoral domains.

While much of the extant discourse emphasizes education, skills, and health as the core axes of human resource development, a more nuanced interrogation reveals that the trajectory of India's demographic dividend is inextricably conditioned by neglected but crucial dimensions such as entrenched gender asymmetries, stark rural–urban dichotomies, and the structural dynamics of labor market absorption. The underrepresentation of women in the workforce, despite rising educational attainment, exemplifies the paradox of latent talent rendered economically inert by patriarchal norms, occupational segregation, and pervasive wage differentials, thereby truncating the aggregate productive potential of the youthful cohort. Simultaneously, spatial disparities manifest in the unequal distribution of educational infrastructure, healthcare facilities, and vocational opportunities between urban centers and rural hinterlands, where deficiencies in digital connectivity, transportation, and institutional presence curtail the capacity of rural youth to access and leverage developmental initiatives. This geographic unevenness exacerbates migratory flows from agrarian landscapes to metropolitan enclaves, intensifying informalization of labor, depressing wage structures, and generating precarious employment conditions that undermine the promise of human capital investments. Furthermore, the absorptive capacity of India's labor market remains a decisive bottleneck, as the proliferation of low-quality, insecure, and non-remunerative jobs fails to match the quantitative expansion of the working-age population, engendering a scenario where human capital accumulation does not seamlessly translate into upward mobility or sustained productivity growth. In this sense, the demographic dividend risks devolving into a demographic burden unless gender parity is institutionally engineered, rural capacities are systematically fortified, and labor market mechanisms are recalibrated to prioritize quality employment over mere numerical expansion, thereby ensuring that the latent energies of India's youth are transformed into a structural engine of inclusive and durable economic growth.

POLICY LINKAGES AND ACTIONABLE RECOMMENDATIONS

The econometric revelations derived from cointegration and error-correction frameworks, while intellectually rigorous, acquire practical gravitas only when tethered to ongoing policy discourses and developmental interventions. For a study situated within the Indian socio-economic milieu, the imperative extends beyond academic precision to include an explicit mapping of results onto the scaffolding of national strategies, flagship programs, and regulatory architectures that seek to transform the demographic dividend into an engine of inclusive growth. To that end, the evidence indicating robust long-run complementarities between youth literacy, population dynamics, and GDP growth necessitates a deliberate alignment with India's multifaceted policy ecosystem, ranging from educational reforms to labor market restructuring, from digital skilling missions to gender mainstreaming initiatives.

At the forefront lies the National Education Policy (NEP) 2020, which seeks to reconfigure India's educational architecture by emphasizing multidisciplinary learning, digital integration, and experiential pedagogy. The cointegration analysis, by demonstrating the significant elasticity between youth literacy and GDP, underscores the economic rationale for rapid operationalization of NEP's objectives. Yet, the policy's transformative potential hinges on bridging the chasm between intent and execution: without calibrated investments in teacher training, localized curricular adaptation, and rural digital infrastructure, the policy's promise may dissipate into rhetorical abstraction. Thus, an actionable recommendation is the establishment of district-level literacy accelerators that fuse NEP's vision with region-specific learning strategies, thereby ensuring that gains in literacy translate into measurable macroeconomic dividends.

Complementary to educational reforms is the Skill India Mission, designed to recalibrate employability through vocational training and industry-linked skilling modules. The empirical finding that GDP responds significantly to population expansions implies that sheer labor force growth, absent concurrent skill alignment, risks engendering structural unemployment. Skill India's current emphasis on numerical targets, millions trained annually, must evolve toward qualitative calibration, wherein training curricula are co-designed with industry clusters, ensuring congruence with emergent demands in renewable energy, digital finance, artificial intelligence, and sustainable infrastructure. Accordingly, a concrete policy recommendation entails the institutionalization of Industry–Academia Skilling Consortia at the state level, wherein firms articulate competency requirements and training institutes align modules dynamically, thereby embedding adaptability within the skilling ecosystem.

The econometric evidence also reinforces the centrality of health interventions, a domain frequently relegated to secondary status in growth discourses but indispensable for optimizing human resource development. Initiatives such as Ayushman Bharat, with its twin pillars of health insurance coverage and the establishment of Health and Wellness Centres, directly intersect with the study's findings that demographic and literacy improvements sustain GDP trajectories only when mediated by health security. The actionable implication here is the need to expand Ayushman Bharat's ambit beyond curative paradigms toward preventive health literacy campaigns, targeting malnutrition, adolescent health, and mental well-being, especially within rural and marginalized populations. This expansion would ensure that the youthful demographic is not merely numerically robust but physically and cognitively capable of sustaining productivity over the long run.

The labor market, as illuminated by the error-correction dynamics, emerges as the primary adjustment mechanism restoring equilibrium after exogenous shocks. Yet, India's labor absorption capacity remains compromised by informality, under-employment, and gender exclusion. Here, linkage with the Pradhan Mantri Kaushal Vikas Yojana (PMKVY) and Start-up India Mission becomes pivotal. PMKVY's certification-based skilling programs, while commendable, must incorporate mobility-linked outcomes, ensuring that certifications are portable across states and recognized by diverse industry sectors. Start-up India, on the other hand, provides a fertile avenue for channeling youthful entrepreneurial energy; however, without integration into mainstream labor policies, entrepreneurial ventures remain urban-centric and exclusionary. Therefore, an actionable recommendation entails creating Rural Start-up Incubation Hubs, leveraging local resources and aligning them with state-specific comparative advantages, such as eco-tourism in Uttarakhand or agro-processing in Madhya Pradesh, thereby decentralizing entrepreneurship and reducing migratory pressures on urban economies.

Another critical policy architecture intersecting with the study's findings is Digital India, which aspires to democratize digital access and foster e-governance. The econometric demonstration of literacy's long-run impact on GDP can be magnified through digital literacy, which functions as a multiplier by enabling access to e-commerce, fintech, telemedicine, and e-learning platforms. Yet, the persistent digital divide, manifest in rural–urban disparities, undermines inclusive growth. A nuanced recommendation would be to institute Digital Literacy Vouchers for low-income households, redeemable across accredited training centers, thereby fostering equitable digital capacity-building. Such an intervention not only reinforces the statistical nexus between literacy and GDP but also broadens the inclusivity of India's digital transformation.

The gendered dimensions of human capital development, often underemphasized in macroeconomic models, acquire renewed salience when aligned with flagship programs like Beti Bachao Beti Padhao and Mahila Shakti Kendras. The study's insights, when contextualized against female labor force participation rates, reveal that failure to harness women's productive capacity dilutes the elasticity of demographic growth on GDP. Actionable strategies here involve transcending symbolic interventions and embedding Gender Mainstreaming Audits across all skill and education programs, ensuring that at least a fixed proportion of resources, training seats, and entrepreneurial incentives are mandatorily allocated to women. Additionally, incentivizing firms through gender-responsive tax rebates for employing women in high-skill sectors can counteract occupational segregation and recalibrate the labor market toward inclusivity.

Migration dynamics, both internal and external, also warrant integration with the study's econometric insights. Programs such as the Atmanirbhar Bharat Abhiyan, aimed at enhancing domestic self-reliance, must internalize the reality that rural–urban migration is not merely a labor market phenomenon but a structural response to spatially unequal opportunities. The actionable recommendation is the formulation of Regional Balanced Development Clusters, wherein infrastructural investments, skill training, and employment generation are regionally synchronized to stem distress migration. Externally, migration policies must pivot toward creating pathways for circular migration, wherein remittances, skills, and experiences of overseas workers are reinvested domestically through structured reintegration programs.

In the macroeconomic sphere, fiscal and monetary policies must also be reframed in light of the econometric findings. The evidence of significant GDP responsiveness to youth population and literacy justifies a countercyclical public investment strategy directed explicitly toward human capital sectors. During economic downturns, fiscal stimulus should privilege education, skilling, and health, ensuring that demographic potential does not stagnate due to cyclical shocks. Moreover, the Reserve Bank of India's credit facilitation frameworks should prioritize low-interest credit lines for youth-led enterprises, thereby directly translating demographic dynamism into productive capital formation.

In synthesizing these policy linkages, it becomes clear that the empirical findings of this study are not isolated statistical curiosities but embedded within a larger tapestry of developmental strategies. The actionable recommendations, from district literacy accelerators to gender mainstreaming audits, from rural start-up hubs to digital literacy vouchers, coalesce into a comprehensive agenda that recognizes the temporally bounded nature of the demographic dividend. If operationalized with coherence, coordination, and political will, these interventions can ensure that India's youthful population metamorphoses into a structural engine of innovation, productivity, and inclusive prosperity. Conversely, inertia or fragmented implementation risks transforming demographic potential into socio-economic volatility. The urgency is therefore unambiguous: India's human capital development strategies must now shift from incremental reform to transformative execution, guided by the dual imperatives of empirical evidence and policy foresight.

CONCLUSION

In summation, the empirical findings of this study, meticulously derived through the integration of Johansen cointegration analysis, vector error correction modeling, and dynamic forecasting tools such as impulse response functions and variance decomposition, unequivocally substantiate the existence of a statistically robust and economically meaningful long-run equilibrium relationship among GDP, youth literacy, and youth population, thereby accentuating the imperative of recognizing literacy enhancement and demographic regulation not merely as auxiliary developmental parameters but as intrinsically interwoven, bidirectionally causative forces within the structural architecture of macroeconomic growth, ultimately reinforcing the exigency for strategically synchronized, evidence-based policy interventions that can perpetuate sustainable economic advancement within an evolving socio-demographic milieu.

REFERENCES

Abbas, M., Alharthi, M., & Arshad, Z. (2024). Population dependency ratios and economic growth in SAARC nations: Insights on aging and youth dynamics. *Journal of Infrastructure. Policy and Development*, *8*(8), 4875. Advance online publication. DOI: 10.24294/jipd.v8i8.4875

Abramov, R. A. (2019). Socio-economic importance of state support for youth innovative entrepreneurship in the economic development of the state. *Academy of Entrepreneurship Journal, 25*(Special Issue 1).

Alfehaid, M. M. A., Johri, A., Sehajpal, S., & Jain, A. (2025). Exploring the Synergies Between SDG 9 and SDG 3: The Role of Innovation and Infrastructure in Enhancing Public Health. *International Journal of Sustainable Development and Planning*, *20*(6), 2293–2315. DOI: 10.18280/ijsdp.200604

Ally, A. M. (2025). Artificial intelligence (AI) and financial technology (FinTech) in Tanzania; legal and regulatory issues. *International Journal of Law and Management*. DOI: 10.1108/IJLMA-07-2024-0251

Alonso-Rocha, J. L., Martínez-Rojas, A., Enríquez, J. G., & Sánchez-Oliva, J. M. (2025). From manual to automated: A state-of-the-art review to examine the impact of intelligent document processing in banking automation. *Expert Systems with Applications*, *285*, 127958. Advance online publication. DOI: 10.1016/j.eswa.2025.127958

Arnone, G. (2024). AI and Chatbots in FinTech: Revolutionizing Digital Experiences and Predictive Analytics. *Contributions to Finance and Accounting*, (Part F2871), 1–125. DOI: 10.1007/978-3-031-55536-7

Bakhtigaraeva, A. I., & Stavinskaya, A. A. (2020). Can trust become a factor of economic growth? Dynamic changes in the level of trust of Russian youth. *Voprosy Ekonomiki*, *2020*(7), 92–107. DOI: 10.32609/0042-8736-2020-7-92-107

Bull, M., & Taylor, D. W. (2008). The Entrepreneur in Youth: An Untapped Resource for Economic Growth, Social Entrepreneurship, and Education. *International Journal of Entrepreneurial Behaviour & Research*, *14*(5), 367–369. DOI: 10.1108/13552550810897713

Çondur, F., & Bölükbaş, M. (2014). A study on labor market and the relationship between youth unemployment and economic growth in Turkey [Türkiye'de işgücü Piyasasi ve Genç işsizlik-Büyüme ilişkisi Üzerine Bir inceleme]. *Amme Idaresi Dergisi*, *47*(2), 77–93.

Dayaram, K., Rola Rubzen, F., Ahmad, H., & Britten, N. (2020). Does economic prosperity translate to regional youth employment? *Labour & Industry*, *30*(3), 216–232. DOI: 10.1080/10301763.2020.1821428

Elbadraoui, A., Mouhssine, Y., El Alaoui, A. K., & Alaoui, S. O. (2025). A Bibliometric Exploration of Artificial Intelligence Methods for Transition from Conventional to Sustainable Financial Framework. *Lecture Notes in Networks and Systems, 1403 LNNS*, 575–604. DOI: 10.1007/978-3-031-91337-2_54

Fine, S. (2025). Psychometric Credit Scoring in Latin America: Replicated Samples Across Five Countries. *Review of Behavioral Economics*, *12*(2), 129–142. DOI: 10.1561/105.00000206

Gonçalves, A. R., Breda Meira, A., Shuqair, S., & Costa Pinto, D. (2023). Artificial intelligence (AI) in FinTech decisions: The role of congruity and rejection sensitivity. *International Journal of Bank Marketing*, *41*(6), 1282–1307. DOI: 10.1108/IJBM-07-2022-0295

Gopal, S., & Pitts, J. (2024). The FinTech Revolution: Bridging Geospatial Data Science, AI, and Sustainability. *Sustainable Finance*, (Part F4267), 1–398. DOI: 10.1007/978-3-031-74418-1

Guimarães, N. A., de Brito, M. M. A., & Comin, A. A. (2020). Youth in Brazil: Transitions and Trajectories. can economic Growth Mitigate Inequalities? *Novos Estudos CEBRAP*, *39*(3), 475–498. DOI: 10.25091/s01013300202000030002

Gupta, S. T., Joshi, P., Kaur, A., & Kumar, P. (2025). Digital tools and technologies: Enabling knowledge sharing and collaborative business culture. In *Knowledge Sharing and Fostering Collaborative Business Culture*. IGI Global., DOI: 10.4018/979-8-3373-0710-7.ch016

Hermannsson, K., Scandurra, R., & Graziano, M. (2024). The Effect of Higher Education on Youth Unemployment in European Regions During a Period of Economic Instability. *Journal of Education Finance*, *49*(4), 447–467. DOI: 10.1353/jef.2024.a954741

Hinkelmann, K., & Smuts, H. (Eds.). (2025). 4th International Conference on Society 5.0, Society 5.0 2024. *Communications in Computer and Information Science, 2173 CCIS*.

Hlungwani, P. M., & Mohamed Sayeed, C. N. (2018). Youth empowerment as a driver of economic growth: Policy implementation challenges in Zimbabwe. *Journal of African Union Studies*, *7*(3), 105–126. DOI: 10.31920/2050-4306/2018/V7n3a6

Hu, S.-C. (1999). Economic growth in the perpetual-youth model: Implications of the annuity market and demographics. *Journal of Macroeconomics*, *21*(1), 107–124. DOI: 10.1016/S0164-0704(99)00093-2

Jha, B., Giri, P., Jha, D., & Badhera, U. (2022). Unlocking IoT: AI-enabled green fintech innovations. In *AI-Enabled Agile Internet of Things for Sustainable FinTech Ecosystems*. IGI Global., DOI: 10.4018/978-1-6684-4176-3.ch001

Kangotra, R., & Sehajpal, S. (2025). Voices without faces: The impact of Deepfake technology on authentic communication. In *Deepfake Technology Dilemmas: Mastering Managerial Navigation*. Nova Science Publishers Inc.

Kaur, J., Khanna, R., Kumar, R., & Sunil, G. (2024). Role of Blockchain Technologies in Goods and Services Tax. *Proceedings - 2024 3rd International Conference on Sentiment Analysis and Deep Learning, ICSADL 2024*, 607–612. DOI: 10.1109/ICSADL61749.2024.00104

Kaur, R., Kaur, S., & Kaur, A. (2025). Fintech and Financial Inclusion: Trends and Challenges. In *FinTech and Financial Inclusion: Leveraging Digital Finance for Economic Empowerment and Sustainable Growth*. Taylor and Francis., DOI: 10.4324/9781003514114-6

Kautish, S., & Kaur, G. (2022). AI-Enabled agile internet of things for sustainable fintech ecosystems. In *AI-Enabled Agile Internet of Things for Sustainable FinTech Ecosystems*. IGI Global., DOI: 10.4018/978-1-6684-4176-3

Khang, A., Jadhav, B., Hajimahmud, V. A., & Satpathy, I. (2024). Synergy of AI and Fintech in the Digital Gig Economy. In *Synergy of AI and Fintech in the Digital Gig Economy*. CRC Press., DOI: 10.1201/9781032720104

Kukreti, M., Sehajpal, S., Tiwari, R., & Sood, K. (2024). Driving global health and sustainable development goals with smart technology. In *Driving Global Health and Sustainable Development Goals With Smart Technology*. IGI Global., DOI: 10.4018/979-8-3373-0240-9

Kumar, A., Khan, E. R., & Deepika. (2024). A Review On Heart Disease Detection Using Machine Learning Techniques. *Proceedings - 2024 6th International Conference on Computational Intelligence and Communication Technologies, CCICT 2024*, 317 – 323. DOI: 10.1109/CCICT62777.2024.00059

Kumar, A., Khan, R., & Deepika. (2025). Heart disease prediction using machine learning techniques. In *Sustainable Materials, Structures and IoT [SMSI-2024]*. CRC Press. DOI: 10.1201/9781003596776-30

Kumar, R., Goel, R., Singh, T., Mohanty, S. M., Gupta, D., Alkhayyat, A., & Khanna, R. (2024). Sustainable Finance Factors in Indian Economy: Analysis on Policy of Climate Change and Energy Sector. *Fluctuation and Noise Letters*, *23*(2), 2440004. Advance online publication. DOI: 10.1142/S0219477524400042

Long, R., Sebo, J., & Sims, T. (2025). Is there a tension between AI safety and AI welfare? *Philosophical Studies*, *182*(7), 2005–2033. DOI: 10.1007/s11098-025-02302-2

Machikape, K., & Oluwadele, D. (2025). Advancing Financial Inclusion and Data Ethics: The Role of Alternative Credit Scoring. *Communications in Computer and Information Science, 2173 CCIS*, 229 – 241. DOI: 10.1007/978-3-031-71412-2_17

Mago, S. (2014). Urban youth unemployment in Africa: Whither socio-economic problems. *Mediterranean Journal of Social Sciences*, *5*(9), 33–40. DOI: 10.5901/mjss.2014.v5n9p33

Medina-Vidal, A., Alonso-Galicia, P. E., González-Mendoza, M., & Ramírez-Montoya, M. S. (2025). Financial inclusion of vulnerable sectors with a gender perspective: Risk analysis model with artificial intelligence based on complex thinking. *Journal of Innovation and Entrepreneurship*, *14*(1), 4. Advance online publication. DOI: 10.1186/s13731-025-00463-2

Metawa, N., Afchal, S., & El-Kanj, N. (2025). AI-based model for Enhancing Credit Risk and Delinquency Management in Banks. *Journal of Cybersecurity and Information Management*, *16*(1), 282–300. DOI: 10.54216/JCIM.160120

Mulyati, E., Murwadji, T., & Bernike, G. (2025). Strategy development for MSMEs in the Indonesian marketplaces through loans with performance guarantees. *Cogent Social Sciences*, *11*(1), 2548860. Advance online publication. DOI: 10.1080/23311886.2025.2548860

Oualid, A., Qasmaoui, Y., Balouki, Y., & Moumoun, L. (2025). Federated Learning and Open Banking for Inclusive Credit Scoring in Morocco: A Systematic Review. *Lecture Notes in Networks and Systems, 1485 LNNS*, 242–256. DOI: 10.1007/978-3-031-95326-2_24

Pashevich, E. (2025). On Reliable Algorithmic Absence-Based Inference. *Philosophy & Technology*, *38*(3), 101. Advance online publication. DOI: 10.1007/s13347-025-00929-x

Pevnaya, M., Larionova, V., & Pevnaya, E. (2024). Economic contribution and social effects of youth volunteering in the early period of the Covid-19 pandemic: A case of a large Russian region. *International Journal of Trade and Global Markets, 19*(3–4), 314–331. DOI: 10.1504/IJTGM.2024.138997

Prince, H. J., Khan, A., & Halasa-Rappel, Y. A. (2024). Economic growth, youth unemployment and political and social instability: A study of policies and outcomes in post-Arab spring Egypt, Morocco, Jordan and Tunisia. In *Emerging Trends in Social Policy from the South: Challenges and Innovations in Emerging Economies*. Policy Press. DOI: 10.2307/jj.9692683.14

Sandhu, K. (2025). Guest editorial: AI-enabled blockchain and fintech innovation. *International Journal of Accounting and Information Management, 33*(2), 265–267. DOI: 10.1108/IJAIM-05-2025-456

Sehajpal, S., & Sidhu, N. K. (2024). Neuroscience, nursing, and financial innovation: A synergistic approach to optimized patient care and economic well-being. In *Neuromarketing's Role in Sustainable Finance*. IGI Global., DOI: 10.4018/979-8-3693-9117-4.ch008

Sharma, P., Malhotra, R. K., & Kumar, R. (2024). How is digitalization reshaping the landscape of Rural banking in India? *2024 International Conference on Smart Devices, ICSD 2024*. DOI: 10.1109/ICSD60021.2024.10750981

Sharma, R. Deepika, & Khan, R. (2025). Machine and deep learning approaches for heart disease risk assessment. In K. S., K. S., K. M., D. A., & S. D.K. (Eds.), *Computational Methods in Science and Technology - Proceedings of the 4th International Conference on Computational Methods in Science and Technology, ICCMST 2024* (Vol. 1, pp. 79 – 82). CRC Press/Balkema. DOI: 10.1201/9781003501244-15

Shirasu, M. R., de Albuquerque, E., & Arraes, R. (2020). Evaluation of the economic costs associated to the neet youth in Brazil [Avaliação dos custos econômicos associados aos jovens nem-nem no Brasil]. *Revista de Economia Política, 40*(1), 161–182. DOI: 10.1590/0101-31572020-2902

Sulastri, R., Ding, A. Y., & Janssen, M. F. W. H. A. (2025). Sensitivity Analysis: Improving Inclusive Credit Scoring Algorithm Through Feature Weight and Penalty-Based Approach. *International Conference on EDemocracy and EGovernment, ICEDEG, 2025*, 54–61. DOI: 10.1109/ICEDEG65568.2025.11081606

Thomas, P., Jacobs, N., Valorose, J., & Schauben, L. (2021). How the Youth Social Entrepreneurship (YSE) Model Supports Implementation of SDG #8 to bring Economic Growth and Decent Work in American Cities. *Sustainable Development Goals Series*, (Part F2666), 127–145. DOI: 10.1007/978-3-030-59173-1_10

Upreti, H., Malhotra, R. K., Kumar, R., & Karki, B. (2024). Leveraging Smart Devices for Corporate Social Responsibility in India: Advancements, Trends, and Concerns towards Sustainability. *2024 International Conference on Smart Devices, ICSD 2024*. DOI: 10.1109/ICSD60021.2024.10751578

Yaprakli, T. Ş., & Ünalan, M. (2020). Determining of Social-Cultural, Environmental and Economic Impacts of Winter European Youth Olympic Festival [Kış Avrupa Gençlik Olimpik Festivalinin Sosyo-Kültürel, Çevresel ve Ekonomik Etkisinin Belirlenmesi]. *Sosyoekonomi, 28*(43), 175–194. DOI: 10.17233/sosyoekonomi.2020.01.10

Yu, P., Lu, S., Sampat, M., Li, R., & Ahuja, A. (2022). How AI-enabled agile internet of things can enhance the business efficiency of China's FinTech ecosystem. In *AI-Enabled Agile Internet of Things for Sustainable FinTech Ecosystems*. IGI Global., DOI: 10.4018/978-1-6684-4176-3.ch009

Yulia, P. S., Kasmungin, S., & Satiyawira, B. (2018). Indonesia's challenges and opportunities: Youth petroleum engineer's role to develop economic growth and natural resources. *Advances in Intelligent Systems and Computing, 599*, 30–36. DOI: 10.1007/978-3-319-60204-2_4

Zahid, S., Tariq, B., Abbas, M., Kafi, A., Osman, N. H. B., Allumi, N. A., Abdul Rahim, M. K. I., & Ansari, H. W. A. (2025). Youth Unemployment and Economic Growth in South Asia: Policy Implications for Stability and Sustainable Development. *International Journal of Sustainable Development and Planning, 20*(5), 1925–1931. DOI: 10.18280/ijsdp.200510

ENDNOTES

1 According to World Development Indicators database of World Bank," Gross domestic product is the total income earned through the production of goods and services in an economic territory during an accounting period. It can be measured in three different ways: using either the expenditure approach, the income approach, or the production approach. This indicator is expressed in constant prices, meaning the series has been adjusted to account for price changes over time. The reference year for this adjustment is 2015. This indicator is expressed in United States dollars."

2 According to World Development Indicators database of World Bank, "Youth literacy rate is the percentage of people ages 15-24 who can both read and write with understanding a short simple statement about their everyday life."

Chapter 10
Youth Entrepreneurship in Africa:
A Catalyst for Economic Development

Najoua Khayati
https://orcid.org/0009-0006-0096-5111
Moulay Ismail University, Morocco

Abdelali Lahrech
Moulay Ismail University, Morocco

ABSTRACT

Africa undergoes a profound demographic transition as the number of its youth exhibits a significantly rapid rise. In this context, entrepreneurship serves as a major opportunity to harness this demographic dividend and to foster economic development. This chapter explores the role of youthful populations in driving economic growth in Africa. It presents the conceptual framework of youth entrepreneurship and uses four case studies to assess the economic impacts of African entrepreneurship policies. In all cases, entrepreneurial initiatives have contributed to generating positive economic outcomes. The four countries, notwithstanding, face significant barriers impeding the sustainability of their economic growth. At last, this work identifies the challenges young entrepreneurs encounter in their endeavors and provides practical recommendations to inform public policy. These include introducing inclusive governmental policies, enhancing access to education and funding schemes, building supportive entrepreneurial ecosystems, and creating favorable regulatory frameworks.

DOI: 10.4018/979-8-3373-2550-7.ch010

INTRODUCTION

The rapidly changing global demographics are shifting the international landscape. While some countries experience an increase in their aging populations and a decline in their labor force, other countries, on the contrary, observe a significantly rapid rise in the number of their youthful populations. This is especially true for the African continent, home to the largest youth demographic on the planet. By 2019, Africa counted 230 million people between the ages of 15 and 24, according to the 2023 United Nations report.

With a young population that is expected to represent more than half of the total population by 2050 (United Nations, 2019), Africa undergoes a profound demographic transition that offers both attractive opportunities and significant challenges. As the former could contribute to poverty alleviation and social improvements, the latter could significantly hinder economic growth and exacerbate social and political tensions.

In this context, entrepreneurship serves as a major opportunity for driving economic development in Africa, by harnessing the demographic dividend. As the Global Entrepreneurship Monitor report (2020) states, entrepreneurial activities contribute largely to the economic and social well-being of nations. Thus, the promotion of entrepreneurship requires targeted policies and strategic interventions to overcome the high levels of illiteracy and unemployment African populations face. Moreover, these interventions need to be inclusive and context-driven to address gender barriers and cultural stereotypes.

This chapter provides a review of the role of youthful populations in driving economic development, particularly in the developing nations of Africa. The purpose is to assess the contribution of young African entrepreneurs to local and national development policies. By evaluating the impact of these policies on economic development, the study explores the potential of youth entrepreneurship as a driver of economic growth, job creation, and innovation. It quantifies the contribution of youth-led businesses to economic development and sectoral diversification in Africa.

To address this topic, we structured the chapter into five sections. The first section introduces the background of the study. It provides a contextual understanding of the significance of youth entrepreneurship in the African socio-economic landscape and its role as a key driver for economic development. The second section provides a conceptual framework that addresses four concepts: entrepreneurship, entrepreneur, entrepreneurial ecosystem, and demographic dividend. It synthesizes key theoretical perspectives and highlights their broader effects on creating and sustaining economic development in the African context.

In the third section, we explain the empirical development of this chapter. We used multiple case studies to illustrate the economic outcomes of youth entrepreneurship-promoting policies on the growth and well-being of African nations. This comparative case study approach examined Morocco, Kenya, South Africa, and Nigeria to provide significant insights into the effectiveness of youth entrepreneurship policies and their economic implications. By synthesizing the main youth entrepreneurship-promoting policies across these four countries, the study aims to identify successful strategies and common challenges in fostering a vibrant entrepreneurial ecosystem to achieve economic development.

The fourth section illustrates the entrepreneurial landscapes in the four selected African countries and their role in creating economic development. The analysis of each country's entrepreneurial ecosystem is crucial for understanding how various factors either support or hinder the implementation of youth entrepreneurship policies. This section addresses the challenges burgeoning youth populations encounter in achieving their entrepreneurial endeavors. It examines access to finance, education, regulatory frameworks, and cultural attitudes towards entrepreneurship. Exploring the main challenges and obstacles that each country faces provides valuable lessons for policymakers and stakeholders seeking to enhance youth entrepreneurship initiatives. Furthermore, it highlights the importance of building supportive entrepreneurial ecosystems to foster innovation and promote sustainable economic growth.

Finally, the last section provides a comprehensive outlook on youth entrepreneurship's role in driving economic development in Africa. It underlines the common challenges and main opportunities across the four nations and highlights the need for coordinated policies and supportive entrepreneurial ecosystems in achieving sustainable economic development. It also provides actionable policy and managerial recommendations to leverage youth entrepreneurship in harnessing the demographic dividend. These recommendations address the educational landscape, financial mechanisms, and regulatory frameworks' role in nurturing the entrepreneurial landscape. At last, it acknowledges the limitations of the study and suggests future research directions.

By providing a comprehensive analysis of youth entrepreneurship policies and their impacts across four diverse African countries, this research aims to inform policymakers, educators, investors, and aspiring young entrepreneurs. The findings can contribute to the development of more effective strategies to harness the potential of youth entrepreneurship as a catalyst for economic development and social progress in developing nations.

BACKGROUND

An unprecedented youth bulge characterizes the demographic profile of Africa. A significant proportion of the continent's population is in the younger age cohorts.

According to the African Development Bank (2022), Africa's population will reach 2.5 billion by 2050, of which 62% will be of working age (between 15 and 64 years), with the median age being approximately 25 years. This rapid demographic transition translates into critical implications for its economic future.

The African continent's demographic transition is unique in its scope and pace. It represents a considerable potential that could drive socio-economic transformation and a set of challenges that could exacerbate poverty and unemployment rates, intensify environmental stress, and increase inequalities. While it offers a significant opportunity to yield the demographic dividend by creating job opportunities and accelerating economic growth (AfDB, 2024), it could also lead to demographic distress, social disequilibrium, and economic instability (Lam & Leibbrandt, 2023).

Despite robust economic growth forecasts of an average real GDP growth of 4.0% in 2024-2025, the African job creation dynamic remains insufficient to absorb the large number of youth and combat the high rates of informal employment (AfDB, 2024). Consequently, substantial developmental challenges persist across the continent, mainly in terms of youth employment, food security, and poverty reduction (Beegle & Christiaensen, 2019).

In this context, youth entrepreneurship represents a viable pathway for sustainable economic development. It serves as an engine for job creation and provides a valuable opportunity to harness the potential of the youth bulge (Kuyoro et al., 2023). Besides offering a necessity-driven alternative to informal employment, youth entrepreneurship is a critical driver of innovation and economic diversification (Brixiová & Kangoye, 2014).

The promotion of youth entrepreneurship in Africa transcends mere survival mechanisms to overcome poverty. It depicts an ambitious development strategy that benefits from a growing ecosystem of support, including increased access to technology and digital platforms (UNCTAD, 2024). In the burgeoning digital economy, young Africans tend to leverage innovative solutions to address local challenges (Sumberg & Hunt, 2019). In this context, the number of young entrepreneurs has known a progressive proliferation. By 2024, Africa boasts the world's highest rates of entrepreneurship, with more than one in five working-age Africans starting a new business (Ichikowitz Family Foundation, 2022).

However, youth entrepreneurship in Africa faces significant systemic challenges such as limited access to funding and infrastructure, rigid regulatory frameworks, and unfavorable social environments (Odeyemi et al., 2024). The current body of scientific literature on youth entrepreneurship in Africa illustrates the potential benefits of harnessing the demographic dividend while also emphasizing the complexities and challenges involved. Recent studies have reinforced the importance of the demographic transition in generating and sustaining economic development (Kidane, 2025) and have urged African governments to conceive and implement targeted policies to leverage opportunities and overcome challenges to fully realize Africa's youth potential (Onyango Ouma, 2025).

LITERATURE REVIEW

Entrepreneurship

Entrepreneurship is the process of creating a new business/activities or developing existing ones to provide goods and services aimed to satisfy the needs of consumers. It fosters innovation by disrupting the current state of markets (Schumpeter, 1934). Furthermore, it recognizes, evaluates, and makes the best use of identified market opportunities to create value (Engelen, Heinemann & Brettel, 2009; Kirzner, 1973; Morris, Kuratko, & Covin, 2008; Shane & Venkataraman, 2000). Accordingly, entrepreneurial activities serve as a key driver for economic growth and development (Acs, 2006).

The theoretical framework of entrepreneurship research is multifaceted and encompasses versatile perspectives. Classical and economic theories focus on the entrepreneur's behavior. Schumpeter's (1934) concept of creative destruction highlights the importance of innovation and risk-taking in driving economic development. Conversely, economic theories emphasize the role of entrepreneurial alertness in creating and developing international market dynamics.

Psychological theories associate a person's predisposition to engage in entrepreneurial activities with personal attributes. McClelland (1961) states that becoming an entrepreneur is proportionately related to a high need for achievement. Other traits such as self-confidence and risk tolerance can also be good predictors of entrepreneurial behavior and success (Luthans et al., 2004).

Sociological theories underline the role of social networks in providing the information, resources, and social capital to conduct entrepreneurial activities (Aldrich & Zimmer, 1986). Another perspective examines the influence of cultural factors and societal attitudes in shaping entrepreneurial behavior (Hofstede, 2001). Contemporary theories focus on the entrepreneurs' cognitive traits (Mitchell et al., 2002) and emphasize the role that the institutional context plays in supporting entrepreneurial initiatives (Bruton et al., 2010).

Entrepreneur

The evolution of the term entrepreneur has been intimately linked to the research progress in the field of entrepreneurship. Its classical foundation highlights the introduction of innovation and risk-bearing dimension (Cantillon, 1755; Schumpeter,

1934). Recent theories present entrepreneurs as change agents who recognize and leverage market opportunities to create value (Shane & Venkataraman, 2000).

Accordingly, they develop cognitive skills such as decision-making and strategic thinking (Dew et al., 2008), mobilize resources, and manage environmental contingencies (Baron, 2003; Bygrave & Hofer, 1992). Entrepreneurial agency stems from the articulation of internal mechanisms such as intention, motivation, cognition, and learning and external context-related factors (Krueger, Reilly, & Carsrud, 2000; Mitchell et al., 2007). In this sense, an entrepreneur is at the nexus of behavioral, process-oriented, and contextual dynamics.

By identifying and exploiting market opportunities through innovation and risk-taking, an entrepreneur develops a new venture to generate economic value. This process requires entrepreneurs to develop a set of skills revolving around opportunity identification, resource organization and management, strategic planning, and creativity. Accordingly, entrepreneurial behaviors integrate cultural, contextual, and organizational factors (Kaur & Bains, 2013; Rusu et al., 2012).

Entrepreneurial Ecosystem

The concept of entrepreneurial ecosystem represents a complex network of interconnected actors, institutions, and resources that influence entrepreneurial dynamics within a specific geographic location (Stam & Spigel, 2016). It contributes significantly to entrepreneurship research and practice by providing a holistic view of the environment and dynamics that enable or constrain entrepreneurial activity.

Initial research on entrepreneurial ecosystems employed theoretical frameworks, including industrial clusters (Porter, 1998) and innovation systems (Freeman, 1987). However, the concept has evolved progressively to emphasize the interaction between entrepreneurs and diverse stakeholders within their environment (Acs et al., 2017).

An entrepreneurial ecosystem, in this sense, is a major prerequisite in the design of entrepreneurship-promoting policies. The literature on entrepreneurial ecosystems analyzes various dimensions, such as actors, factors, context, and community that coexist and interact to enable or restrict entrepreneurship (Vogel, 2013; Mason and Brown, 2014; Stam, 2015). Isenberg (2010) lists six components of the entrepreneurial ecosystem: financial institutions, government policies, human capital and education systems, infrastructure, and cultural attitudes towards risk-taking, as well as market networks and innovation.

Entrepreneurial ecosystems offer insights into the dynamics of entrepreneurial activity. They provide a valuable framework for understanding its context, actors, and resources. By highlighting the interconnectedness and complex interplay of these factors, ecosystems highlight what drives or impedes entrepreneurship. Hence, building a strong entrepreneurial ecosystem requires a holistic strategy to ensure sustainable coordination among its actors and their complex environment. This coordination translates into adequate access to financial resources, robust institutional and regulatory frameworks, supportive human capital development strategies, and enhanced networking opportunities. Thus, understanding the entrepreneurial ecosystem's functioning mechanisms leads to identifying optimal practices for sharing knowledge, strengthening collaboration, and building sustainable entrepreneurial economies.

Demographic Dividend

The concept of demographic dividend refers to a shift in a country's age structure that could potentially result in economic growth. This shift typically occurs when the active proportion of the population becomes larger than its inactive proportion (Bloom et al., 2003). The demographic transition, if properly harnessed, creates a significant opportunity for economic growth and poverty alleviation. It allows increasing productive employment and leads to social stability when complemented by concurrent investments in human capital, robust economic policies, and favorable regulations (Mason, 2005; Lee & Mason, 2006).

In many developing regions, especially Africa and South Asia, a demographic dividend represents a major challenge. Youth unemployment rates remain persistently high, and governmental policies remain inefficient at fully addressing them. In this context, entrepreneurship serves as a viable pathway for absorbing the burgeoning youth labor force in developing regions (UNFPA, 2024). Thus, enabling youth entrepreneurship through supportive ecosystems can be an efficient strategy to harness the demographic dividend (Schoof, 2006; Fox & Kaul, 2017).

During demographic transitions, regions with stronger entrepreneurial ecosystems exhibit better employment outcomes. Accordingly, youth-focused policies tend to generate positive results as they integrate education, financial inclusion, and capacity building into ecosystem development. However, several empirical gaps persist in this field. Longitudinal evidence linking entrepreneurial ecosystem development directly to demographic dividend outcomes is scarce. Moreover, entrepreneurial ecosystems frameworks need to evolve to address the context-related challenges of developing countries (Lepoutre et al., 2013).

The Relationship between Entrepreneurship and Economic Development

The literature on the link between entrepreneurship and economic development is extensive in-depth, and broad in scope. Numerous studies have addressed the connection between these two concepts (Ács et al., 2014; Audretsch et al., 2006;

Caree & Thurik, 2010; Dejardin, 2000; Naudé, 2011; Wennekers et al., 2010). They have demonstrated the existence of a positive correlation between creating entrepreneurial activities and enhancing economic development. Researchers and practitioners measure this enhancement through a large set of indicators associated with the evolution of employment, the increase of incomes and improvement of living standards, as well as the creation and distribution of wealth (Cumming et al. 2014).

However, the country-level analysis of entrepreneurial activities lacks empirical evidence due to limited formal definition frameworks and measurement tools (Ács et al. 2014; Wong, Ho & Autio, 2005). The impact of entrepreneurship on a country's growth varies depending on its stage of economic development. Developed countries tend to demonstrate more opportunity-driven entrepreneurial activities. Conversely, developing countries promote necessity-driven entrepreneurship to alleviate poverty (Bosma et al., 2009; Ferreira & Teixeira, 2019; Sternberg & Wennekers, 2005). Moreover, the association between entrepreneurship and economic growth remains an under-researched topic in developing countries (Naudé, 2010).

In Africa, youth-driven entrepreneurial activities are central to economic dynamics (GEM, 2020). They represent, however, an essential feature of the informal economy, which exhibits numerous challenges, particularly in terms of access to education, training, funding, and infrastructure. Hence, the implementation of entrepreneurship support programs that provide training, mentorship, and access to capital is pivotal to ensuring the success and viability of young people's entrepreneurial ventures (AfDB, 2019).

African entrepreneurial ecosystems need to evolve to explore the full potential of their youthful populations. Achieving inclusive economic growth and sustainable development requires building an enabling environment that focuses on fostering innovation and entrepreneurial skills, improving access to finance, and removing bureaucratic barriers to business creation.

CASE STUDIES

This chapter employed a comparative case study methodology, examining entrepreneurship-promoting policies and their economic outcomes in four African countries. The countries selected for the case studies included Morocco, Nigeria, Kenya, and South Africa. Each of these countries had introduced entrepreneurial policies to promote youth populations' contribution to economic development. Hence, our purpose was to analyze their impact and contribution to the growth of the four developing economies.

The comparative case study design relied on the collection of secondary data from various sources, including official government reports and websites, national strategy plans, and international organizations' publications. The authors consolidated these documents by analyzing peer-reviewed academic literature on the topic in the selected countries, as well as by consulting international statistical databases. Following individual case examination, they conducted a comparative analysis between the four countries in the discussion section. Thus, they aimed to identify similarities and differences in policy design, implementation, and overall economic impact. In addition, this comparison allowed for a better understanding of the finer nuances and common themes and offered distinctive insights into the effectiveness and challenges of African youth entrepreneurship policies.

For the analysis of each of the four country cases, the authors applied an analytical framework that focused on four dimensions: policy landscape, implementation mechanisms, impact on economic development, and challenges and obstacles. The policy landscape and implementation mechanisms allowed for a deeper understanding of the rationale behind entrepreneurial policies and their context, as well as the role of actors and institutions in the conception and implementation phases. As for the impact on economic development, the study provided a critical analysis of the observable outcomes on the evolution of the gross domestic product, the development of youth employment rates, and the overall enhancement of living standards. At last, the identification of challenges that young African entrepreneurs face provided a foundation for a deep reflection on impediments to entrepreneurial initiatives. It also served as a basis for opportunity recognition and analysis of entrepreneurial strategies to foster sustainable economic development.

The rationale for this comparative analysis lay in providing an in-depth understanding of complex social phenomena within their real-world contexts (Yin, 2018). This approach focused on analyzing policy design and implementation mechanisms to assess the impact on youth employment and economic growth. It allowed for understanding contextual nuances and deriving actionable insights for other African nations grappling with similar socio-economic challenges. Thus, this study aimed to provide a scientific basis for policy analysis, to identify optimal practices, and to suggest pathways for strategic intervention.

Morocco

The kingdom of Morocco has strategically positioned itself as an emerging African economic hub, with a significant emphasis on fostering youth-led entrepreneurial initiatives. Driven largely by its strategic 2020-2030 vision, entrepreneurship policies centered upon creating an enabling environment for conducting business. Thus, the Moroccan government has introduced numerous initiatives to promote youth entrepreneurship. These initiatives focus primarily on improving access to funding through competitive microcredit programs. They also offer fiscal incentives such as subsidies and tax breaks for youth-led businesses.

The National Initiative for Human Development (INDH) supports local income-generating activities in various sectors. The "Intelaka" program provides guarantees and financing, through commercial banks, to very small, small, and medium-sized enterprises (VSMEs), including those led by young entrepreneurs (AfDB, 2022). Incubators and accelerators also play a major role in improving the national business climate by providing technical assistance and structured support. In addition, the Moroccan government has introduced several sectoral programs, implemented by ANAPEC (the National Agency for the Promotion of Employment and Skills), Maroc PME, and CRI (Regional Centers for Investment), that aim to integrate young people into the economic fabric by improving employability and promoting entrepreneurship (Ouazzouz & Harizi, 2024).

Moreover, the Moroccan government has also made significant advancements in improving its entrepreneurial landscape by concluding public-private partnerships and digitalizing administrative procedures. These advancements allowed creating a vibrant entrepreneurial ecosystem, providing support to nascent businesses, and offering training, assistance, and mentorship, especially in rural areas. Encouraging local business establishment has also contributed to improving the income and living conditions of young people from disadvantaged backgrounds. This dynamic has led to promoting their economic inclusion and addressing some of the inactivity and unemployment issues that they face (Fathallah & Horr, 2024).

Consequently, Morocco's entrepreneurship-promoting policies have generated positive economic outcomes. The World Bank's Morocco Economic Monitor report (2024) highlights a positive impact on economic growth over the last decade. In addition, the business creation by youth rate shows an upward trend. The country's broad economic development strategy incites young entrepreneurs to invest in high-growth sectors such as renewable energies, digital technology, and ecotourism. This economic diversification creates niche opportunities and contributes to young entrepreneurs' integration into global value chains.

Youth-led entrepreneurial initiatives in Morocco contributed to creating a significant number of direct and indirect jobs both in urban and rural areas. This dynamic allowed mitigating social exclusion and precarious employment (Fathallah & Horr, 2024). Consequently, the kingdom has managed to enhance local development and improve the living conditions among disadvantaged populations. It has also enabled young people to establish their entrepreneurial ventures in various sectors such as agriculture, technology, and tourism.

However, challenges persist in scaling youth-led entrepreneurial ventures and ensuring their long-term sustainability. Limited access to capital and funding schemes, particularly for innovative or high-risk sectors, remains a significant barrier (Seddik et al., 2024). Furthermore, disparities between rural and urban areas, coupled with bureaucratic hurdles, significantly hinder the growth of youth entrepreneurship. Entrepreneurial ecosystems tend to demonstrate a more dynamic contribution in urban centers. Their actions remain, however, insufficient to absorb the large number of unemployed youthful populations.

Cultural barriers tend also to impede entrepreneurial ambition. A risk-averse business environment and limiting cultural beliefs deter new entrants and further hinder the growth of established young entrepreneurs (Jebbari, 2024). Other obstacles include a skills gap between educational outputs and market demands and insufficient targeted support for female and rural youth (Bouichou et al., 2021; Melliani & Elhissi, 2024; Naguib, 2024).

Nigeria

Youth entrepreneurship has become a cornerstone for economic development in Nigeria. With a population of over 200 million, Nigeria is one of the most populous nations in Africa, and its youth make up a significant proportion of its workforce (National Population Commission, 2023). However, the country faces an unemployment crisis, particularly among young people, with youth unemployment estimated at approximately 6.01% in 2022 (International Labour Organization, 2022). To tackle this crisis, the Nigerian government has implemented various policies aimed at promoting youth entrepreneurship to mitigate unemployment, foster innovation, and stimulate economic growth.

Nigerian entrepreneurship-promoting policies primarily focus on access to finance, skills development, and creating an enabling environment for business growth. Among the most notable initiatives are the National Youth Empowerment Programme (NYEP), the Youth Enterprise with Innovation in Nigeria, and the National Social Investment Programme (NSIP). These initiatives are often spearheaded by various ministries, departments, and agencies, with the Central Bank of Nigeria (CBN) playing a significant role in financing.

Youth-led entrepreneurial initiatives in Nigeria have contributed significantly to increasing job creation. According to the National Bureau of Statistics, small and medium-sized enterprises (SMEs), many of which are youth-led, employ over 90% of Nigeria's workforce and account for approximately 24% of its GDP (Izediuno et al., 2018). This dynamic has contributed in turn to reducing poverty rates in marginalized regions and improving the living conditions of their population (Awogbenle & Iwuamadi, 2010).

In addition to job creation, youth entrepreneurship programs have played a significant role in fostering innovation. Over the last decade, Nigeria has established numerous youth-driven startups in cutting-edge sectors such as technology and renewable energy. Hence, young entrepreneurs have served as key drivers of innovation by introducing new products and services, creating new markets, and increasing productivity, all of which contributed positively to driving economic growth. Furthermore, entrepreneurship-promoting policies have focused on providing capacity building and skills development trainings to enhance young entrepreneurs' market skills.

Despite a proliferating landscape, Nigeria's youth-led entrepreneurship remains insufficient to face high unemployment rates and lacks diversification as well as sustainability. The country's economy indicates a marginal deterioration in the overall entrepreneurial index, partly due to challenges such as high inflation rates and local currency depreciation (Ojima, 2025). Moreover, young Nigerians engage in short-term, necessity-driven informal entrepreneurial activities, where the "hustle culture" often prevails over structured business development. Thus, scaling their entrepreneurial ventures into the formal sector represents a considerable challenge. This suggests that while the entrepreneurial mindset is strong, the enabling ecosystem faces substantial obstacles.

Furthermore, structural challenges such as limited access to technology, research funding, and poor infrastructure hinder business creation and growth. Financial inclusion and access to capital also remain critical barriers for young entrepreneurs. Conventional banks and funding institutions perceive young entrepreneurs' endeavors as highly risky since they lack collateral and credit history (International Trade Centre, 2024).

Inconsistencies related to regulatory frameworks and policy implementation lead to misinformation and create a state of confusion among youth. For instance, while Nigeria has implemented several youth entrepreneurship programs to provide affordable credit, only a minority of young entrepreneurs recognize having made use of public support programs. Moreover, only a few affirm having received funding from these programs (GEM, 2013). This situation limits access to financial resources for many young entrepreneurs and increases the risk and cost of doing business. It also highlights a significant disconnect between policy intent and actual outcomes. Bureaucratic hurdles, stringent collateral requirements, and limited awareness of available programs often impede access. The national entrepreneurial strategy critically requires more cohesive and inclusive enhancements coupled with a long-term vision for fostering a more sustainable business environment.

Kenya

Youth entrepreneurship is a critical driver of Kenya's economic growth. Due to the significant proportion of its youthful population, the Kenyan government has instituted several policies aimed at fostering youth entrepreneurship to combat unemployment and stimulate economic development (Chigunta et al., 2005; Namatovu et al., 2012). Key initiatives include the Youth Enterprise Development Fund (YEDF), the Uwezo Fund, and the Kenya Youth Empowerment Project (KYEP), all of which aim to provide financial assistance, mentorship, and skills development for young entrepreneurs.

The entrepreneurial landscape in Kenya particularly embraces activities related to technology and innovation sectors. Various initiatives promote digital literacy and encourage young entrepreneurs to fully engage in innovation hubs. To further advance this dynamic, the Kenyan government has introduced numerous tax incentives for digital operating startups. It has also created incubation programs to support young entrepreneurs in transitioning from online work to structured entrepreneurial ventures.

Collectively, these policies represent a multifaceted instrumental approach to promoting youth entrepreneurship. They seek to empower marginalized youth by providing low-interest loans and facilitating access to credit. The Kenyan government has also concluded multiple partnerships and agreements to introduce adequate entrepreneurship-related education and training programs. Accordingly, alongside its partners, Kenya has significantly invested in providing business development services and entrepreneurship training programs. These initiatives operate to integrate entrepreneurship education into formal schooling, mentorship schemes, and vocational training centers (Mwangi, 2011; Wanjohi, 2014).

The Youth Enterprise Development Fund stands as a cornerstone of Kenya's youth entrepreneurship strategy. It extends credit and business development services to numerous youth groups and individuals (Njeri & Mutundu, 2021). The Uwezo Fund provides interest-free loans primarily to women, youth, and persons with disabilities. The fund's goal is to catalyze self-employment and reduce poverty (Mutura & Cherotich, 2024). In addition, the Biashara Fund offers a more streamlined and comprehensive approach to credit provision by consolidating several government funds, including the Youth Enterprise Development Fund and the Uwezo Fund.

Kenya managed to foster a vibrant startup ecosystem by establishing a flourishing environment for digital transactions. The government has significantly lowered transaction costs for small businesses by encouraging digital platforms and facilitating monetary transactions. By implementing innovation hubs to nurture tech-innovative startups, Kenya has also managed to increase the digital economy's contribution to its GDP and attract foreign investment.

The impact of youth entrepreneurship programs on Kenya's economic growth has been discernible, though arguably modest in addressing the large rate of youth unemployment. Progressive policies contributed to promoting inclusivity and providing a significant market for nascent businesses as well as integrating youth-led enterprises into broader local and international markets. Accordingly, youth-led entrepreneurial ventures in Kenya served as pathways for alleviating poverty, enhancing livelihoods, and economic stability (Ngene et al., 2021). Moreover, they introduced innovative business models that contributed to fostering a culture of innovation and economic diversification (Yusuf & Namadi-Musa, 2024).

Kenyan policies have been instrumental in leveraging its demographic dividend. Its technological adoption has also contributed to fostering an innovative entrepreneurial landscape. By focusing on the high-tech niche area, Kenya has positioned itself as a leader of a knowledge-based economy. This economy is characterized by a highly competitive and diversified job market as well as a very innovative digital sector.

However, despite these governmental interventions, the effectiveness of Kenyan entrepreneurship-promoting policies remains insufficient to absorb the large number of its unemployed youth. Access to finance for creating a business is one of the most capital constraints confronting aspiring young entrepreneurs in Kenya. Moreover, access to growth capital for scaling businesses persists as a significant barrier to entrepreneurship's growth and sustainability (Muturi, 2018). Though the Kenyan government has introduced several targeted funds, adequate and affordable access to finance remains restricted.

While appealing in nature, the funds' overall impact turned out to be quite modest. Conventional financial institutions often perceive youth as high-risk borrowers due to limited collateral, nascent credit histories, and unproven business track records. Accordingly, the funding schemes tend to demonstrate a misalignment with the needs of young entrepreneurs. The disbursed loan amounts are often too small to reduce poverty or support viable business ventures (Aberi & Jagongo, 2018).

Limited public awareness of available funds, inadequate training, and bureaucratic hurdles often affect access to funding (Singh, 2024). These factors are severely exacerbated by stringent application procedures, vulnerable interdependent repayment capacity for groups, and disparity between the demand for funding and the available capital (Athiambo, 2024). Furthermore, allegations of mismanagement and corruption in fund allocation and a notable absence of robust follow-up and mentorship mechanisms significantly influence the funds' success and long-term sustainability (Namatovu, 2012; Robb, 2014).

Beyond financial support, the Kenyan government integrated a range of business development services and entrepreneurship training programs into its policies. These initiatives encompass various entrepreneurship education schemes incorporated into formal schooling, and vocational training centers (Njoroge & Gathungu, 2013; Wanjohi, 2014). Their impact, however, is inconsistent as they fail to equip young entrepreneurs with market-driven skills (Mburu, 2021). Furthermore, mentorship lacks systematic integration within policy frameworks and thus remains predominantly informal.

South Africa

South Africa's approach to youth entrepreneurship is multifaceted, involving both national and local programs. As it faces significantly high rates of youth unemployment and historical inequalities, South African policy interventions have focused on increasing youth employment through promoting entrepreneurship and small business development.

The South African government has implemented various programs led by the National Youth Development Agency (NYDA). Among the most notable initiatives are the Black Business Supplier Development Programme (BBSDP) and the Youth Employment Service (YES). Their main goal is to provide grants, mentorship, and funding to young entrepreneurs, with a particular focus on promoting inclusivity for marginalized and disadvantaged youth in the business sector (Odeku & Rudolf, 2019).

Aside from introducing funding schemes, South African entrepreneurship policies aim to provide business development support and various initiatives to promote vocational training and skills development. Higher education institutions play a significant role in this dynamic. Besides developing favorable cultural settings and nurturing an entrepreneurial mindset among youth, they help build youth capacities and equip them with market-aligned business skills (Ogunsanya et al. 2024). Accordingly, they have created considerable opportunities and provided support to a large segment of young entrepreneurs. Indeed, these entrepreneurs benefited from business incubation and advisory services to facilitate their access and participation in the national market.

South African youth entrepreneurship policies serve as a key driver of economic development. They contribute to creating jobs, fostering innovation, and encouraging young people to engage in productive activities. Through the implementation of various programs, the South African government has managed to provide support and assistance to entrepreneurs in order to reduce the high youth unemployment rate. Accordingly, the entrepreneurial ecosystem focused on empowering youth by developing a vibrant entrepreneurial culture as well as reinforcing their self-reliance and creativity.

Despite their significant contribution to fundamental economic restructuring, South African entrepreneurship-promoting policies demonstrate a very limited impact in terms of reducing youth unemployment. Deeply rooted structural barriers restrict youth's participation in economic development, thus requiring a robust approach to overcome challenges in the national entrepreneurship landscape. Furthermore, the South African entrepreneurial ecosystem needs to coordinate its efforts to optimize the impact and effectiveness of youth entrepreneurship policies.

Socioeconomic inequalities, limited access to capital, and an underdeveloped entrepreneurial culture persistently hinder governmental efforts to promote entrepreneurship. Although South Africa has developed numerous funding schemes, young entrepreneurs face difficulties accessing them. In most cases, their number is limited, and access entails competitive conditions. Moreover, financial institutions require collateral and credit history, thus leading to the creation of a major barrier for young entrepreneurs to secure funding.

Youth entrepreneurship programs also face severe criticism regarding the effectiveness, scope, and management of their implementation mechanisms (Radebe, 2019). Access to affordable finance persists as a capital impediment due to the stringent requirements of commercial banks (Rogerson, 2008).

Despite substantial policy efforts and budgetary allocations, youth unemployment in South Africa remains persistently high, often exceeding 50% for those aged between 15 and 24 (De Lannoy et al., 2020). Moreover, the quality of entrepreneurial education and the relevance of skills to market demands are critical issues. Young entrepreneurs also face significant barriers to creating and developing their businesses, such as regulatory and bureaucratic complexities, a rigid labor market, and high taxes and establishment costs (Sitharam & Hoque, 2016).

Historical inequalities and political tensions further exacerbate this situation. Moreover, entrepreneurship-training programs demonstrate a lack of effectiveness. Young South African entrepreneurs often express a need for developing fundamental entrepreneurship skills such as marketing, communication, and financial literacy. In this sense, governmental efforts should focus on enhancing mentorship and access to business networks to provide guidance to young entrepreneurs and build a collaborative ecosystem.

Structural barriers related to poor infrastructure and limited access to technology significantly restrict young entrepreneurs' innovation capacity and hinder their integration into the digital economy. Poverty and lack of education intensify these challenges, especially in the context of rural and marginalized territories. Furthermore, youth-led entrepreneurial ventures face significant challenges to survive and grow due to the lack of economic stability and the high competitiveness of the global market environment.

The overall impact of youth entrepreneurship policies is modest, and their capacity to serve the vast number of aspiring entrepreneurs is considerably limited. The South African economy remains dominated by large corporations, and the share of small and medium-sized enterprises (SMEs) is scarce. While the ecosystem aspires to foster widespread entrepreneurial growth, the proportion of successful youth-led businesses is still developing, particularly outside established networks.

Persistent high rates of youth unemployment in South Africa underscore the lack of effectiveness of its entrepreneurial policies. While they offer some support, these policies have not yet achieved their full potential in significantly driving structural economic transformation and widespread employment. This situation necessitates a deeper reflection on strategies and actions to tackle the enduring challenges.

DISCUSSION

African governments increasingly recognize entrepreneurship as a critical lever for economic development. Youth entrepreneurship in particular serves as a means of combating significantly high unemployment rates (Obiechina, 2024). Policy interventions across the African continent aim to alleviate poverty and promote job creation by enhancing access to finance, providing entrepreneurial skills development, and fostering supportive ecosystems as well as favorable regulatory frameworks.

In Morocco, entrepreneurship-promoting policies target various population segments and cover multiple sectors. Key initiatives that target youth include the Intelaka financing program, technoparks, capacity building, and support services provided through agencies like ANAPEC (National Agency for the Promotion of Employment and Skills) and Regional Investment Centers (CRI) (Ouazzouz & Harizi, 2024). While various in scope, these policies provide a framework that facilitates the creation and growth of youth-led ventures and contributes to employment and economic inclusion. Their impact is positive in terms of skill development and entrepreneurial orientation. Nevertheless, they face several limitations that hinder the full participation and engagement of young Moroccan entrepreneurs.

Kenya has also notably strived to implement numerous initiatives to promote entrepreneurship among its youthful population. Among the most notable ones is the Youth Enterprise Development Fund (YEDF). Since 2006, this fund, alongside other broader measures, has operated to promote micro, small, and medium-sized enterprises (MSMEs). By providing financial assistance and advisory support, Kenyan youth entrepreneurship-promoting policies contributed to stimulating self-employment and reducing high rates of youth unemployment (Kanyari & Namusonge, 2013). Thus, they created a collaborative dynamic that led to very positive outcomes in terms of product development, resource utilization, and innovation. This dynamic established Kenyan youth-led enterprises among the most significant contributors to economic development in Africa.

In South Africa, dire youth unemployment rates called for extreme measures. Accordingly, the government implemented a set of policies, such as the National Youth Policy, the Employment Tax Incentive Bill, and the Youth Employment Service (YES), to promote youth entrepreneurship and increase employment rates. Moreover, the South African government established several funds, such as the Umsobovu Youth Fund (UYF), to provide funding through microfinance and business development services that specifically target young entrepreneurs (Mabasa, 2018).

These interventions contributed to cultivating a sustainable entrepreneurial spirit, leading thus to fostering economic growth and alleviating poverty.

Nigeria has implemented programs such as the National Enterprise Development Programme (NEDEP) and other initiatives by the Presidential Enabling Business Environment Council (PEBEC) to improve access and foster ease of doing business. In addition, it introduced specialized funding schemes provided by the Bank of Industry (BOI), such as the Graduate Entrepreneurship Fund and Youth Entrepreneurship with Innovation Support Program. These policies allowed boosting economic growth through entrepreneurship. The growth of the number of youth-led businesses contributed significantly to enhancing the GDP, creating jobs, and reducing poverty (Nkechi et al., 2012).

Collectively, these policies manifest a continent-wide commitment to leveraging youth entrepreneurship for economic growth. They foster innovation and contribute to job creation and poverty alleviation. However, their effectiveness and extent vary significantly, often constrained by implementation gaps and systemic challenges.

Main Challenges and Obstacles

Despite concerted policy efforts, young entrepreneurs in the four African countries face substantial challenges that hinder the full realization of their entrepreneurial endeavors. A pervasive obstacle across the continent is limited access to funding, particularly start-up capital and growth finance. This is highlighted in Kenya, where enterprises grapple with inadequate credit, and in Morocco, where suitable access to financial resources remains a significant barrier to entrepreneurship (Muturi, 2018; Seddik et al., 2024). Similarly, Nigeria and South Africa face persistent challenges with access to finance, often compounded by bureaucratic hurdles for loan acquisition.

Limited or inadequate entrepreneurial education and skills also represent significant challenges. While programs aim to convey entrepreneurial and business skills, a lack of comprehensive, market-relevant training can limit entrepreneurial success. Furthermore, a lack of targeted communication regarding available entrepreneurship and support programs is a common challenge. In Morocco, many young people are unaware of programs' existence and benefits (Lahrech et al., 2024). Similarly, in South Africa, a great proportion of targeted youth is uninformed of available services and how to benefit from them (Gwija et al,. 2014).

Regulatory burdens and bureaucratic red tape also stifle entrepreneurial activity. Nigeria, despite having introduced numerous business-facilitating initiatives, still presents regulatory challenges. In South Africa, young entrepreneurs criticize the policy framework for being highly rigid (Sitharam & Hoque, 2016). Poor infrastructure, including transportation costs and unreliable utilities, exacerbates the cost of creating and doing business and limits market access, particularly for agri-businesses in rural areas (Odeku & Rudolf, 2019).

Finally, cultural stereotypes, social factors, and societal attitudes, such as a pervasive cultural aversion to risk-taking in Morocco (Merroun & El Ghrasli, 2025) and a general lack of entrepreneurial culture in Kenya (Mburu, 2021), can hinder the development and sustainability of entrepreneurial ventures. Young women, in particular, may face additional cultural and societal barriers.

Analysis of the Entrepreneurial Ecosystem in Each Country

The entrepreneurial ecosystem, comprising interconnected actors, institutions, and processes (Stam & Spigel, 2016), plays a crucial role in either fostering or impeding the effectiveness of youth entrepreneurship policies. In Morocco, the entrepreneurial ecosystem, despite government efforts, remains demonstrably underdeveloped and characterized by significant structural weaknesses. While initiatives like "Intelaka" and the National Initiative for Human Development aspire to provide suitable funding schemes, the overall access to finance remains severely restricted and heavily constrained, particularly for social ventures (Merroun & El Ghrasli, 2025).

Incubators and support systems are often geographically concentrated and fragmented, leading to exacerbating regional disparities in terms of access to information and opportunities, which transcends mere geographical imbalances to represent systemic inequities. This is particularly highlighted in the case of rural territories that suffer from poor access to infrastructure, education, and basic services (Bennis & Oudda, 2021). Infrastructural deficits, low female participation, and a cultural aversion to risk-taking further curtail the ability of young entrepreneurs to launch, sustain, and scale their ventures.

Kenya presents a more vibrant, evolving startup ecosystem, often referred to as "Silicon Savannah" (Akamanzi et al., 2016). It features a growing number of incubators, accelerators, and innovation hubs that provide support, mentorship, and networking opportunities. Government and academic institutions actively contribute to fostering innovation and developing an entrepreneurial mindset among young people.

Despite this favorable entrepreneurial culture and supportive infrastructure, the Kenyan ecosystem still faces challenges related to access to finance and tailored support for different youth segments. These challenges demonstrate a vast gap between overall ecosystem development and specific youth needs. Kenya also features some of the highest failure rates of youth-owned enterprises in Africa. This suggests that while the Kenyan entrepreneurial ecosystem promotes startup creation, their sustainability is still precarious (Athiambo, 2024).

South Africa's entrepreneurial ecosystem focuses primarily on fostering a sustainable environment for its youthful population to conduct entrepreneurial activities. It pays significant attention to nurturing university-based student entrepreneurship. Accordingly, universities and incubators conceive and implement targeted and practical entrepreneurship programs to equip students with skills, confidence, and suitable access to funding (Ogunsanya et al. 2024).

While its actions have generated positive results, the South African entrepreneurial ecosystem faces numerous challenges that hinder its effectiveness. A rigid policy framework is one of the main challenges that young entrepreneurs face. Inadequate program implementation, lack of targeted actions, and bureaucratic constraints also repress the effectiveness of the entrepreneurial ecosystem's dynamic (Madzikanda et al., 2022). The South African entrepreneurial ecosystem requires more comprehensive support mechanisms and effective policy actions to promote and sustain youth entrepreneurship effectively, particularly given the high youth unemployment rates.

Nigeria's entrepreneurial ecosystem represents a dynamic network of interrelated actors, institutions, and processes. It provides a diverse financial support landscape that comprises banks, venture capitalists, angel investors, and crowdfunding platforms. The recent establishment of the Nigeria Youth Entrepreneurship Investment Bank (YEIB) further aims to boost tailored financial and non-financial services.

Young Nigerian entrepreneurs benefit from facilitated access to information, tailored funding schemes, and business networks. The entrepreneurial ecosystem in Nigeria supports the role of educational institutions in integrating entrepreneurship education into their programs. Incubators and accelerators provide assistance, mentorship, workspaces, and networking opportunities (Olutuase et al., 2018). Moreover, government agencies continuously work on introducing favorable regulations and streamlining business registration. These actions contribute to establishing a more flexible and flourishing business environment by reducing regulatory and bureaucratic burdens.

While the Nigerian entrepreneurial ecosystem is robust in many aspects, it still grapples with persistent issues such as limited access to education and infrastructure and an overwhelming proportion of the youthful population, which often exceeds available support. Consequently, policy efforts remain insufficient to face the high unemployment rates (Ojima, 2025).

Comparative Analysis

A comparative analysis reveals commonalities and distinct features across the case studies. All four African countries demonstrate a strong policy commitment to youth entrepreneurship. This commitment primarily translates through financial support, skills development, and ecosystem building.

In all cases, entrepreneurial projects have contributed to generating positive economic outcomes at a national level. Implemented policies and programs have proven to be useful in supporting youth entrepreneurship by providing various forms of financial support (subsidies, access to funding schemes, resources) and assistance (education, training, and mentorship). Furthermore, youthful populations' entrepreneurial initiatives have stimulated the four African economies by increasing job creation, fostering innovation, and encouraging collaboration among actors of the entrepreneurial ecosystems.

However, the effectiveness of these policies is consistently undermined by a set of challenges. The four countries face significant barriers impeding the sustainability of their economic growth. Among the most notable ones are the lack of access to information, unfavorable regulatory frameworks, and structural limitations of the entrepreneurial ecosystems. Access to appropriate and affordable finance remains the most significant barrier, often complicated by bureaucratic processes. Similarly, gaps in entrepreneurial education and training, as well as the persistence of informal business practices, limit the growth and sustainability of the African entrepreneurial dynamic.

For Nigeria, obstacles such as limited access to finance, corruption, and poor infrastructure significantly hinder the scaling of businesses (AfDB, 2019). Though Kenya's highly developed youth technology startups constitute a large share of the country's GDP growth (World Bank, 2020), entrepreneurs experience several challenges related to unfavorable regulatory frameworks and a lack of entrepreneurial education and skills. In the case of South Africa, challenges such as high startup costs and lack of access to capital prevail (Bhorat et al., 2019), despite the high potential of youth-led initiatives in agricultural and renewable energy sectors. As for Morocco, the main challenges that young entrepreneurs face are related to the urban-rural inequalities and lack of access to funding, especially for women (OECD, 2024).

Kenya and Nigeria, with their more developed incubator/accelerator networks and a strong focus on technology and innovation, appear to have more dynamic, albeit still rudimentary, entrepreneurial ecosystems. Morocco and South Africa, while investing in policy and institutional support, face deeper systemic challenges related to regional disparities, lack of entrepreneurial culture, and the need for more adaptable policy frameworks.

The role of the entrepreneurial ecosystem is paramount: a supportive ecosystem (e.g., robust financial institutions, active incubators, responsive government agencies, and a culture that embraces risk) significantly enhances the impact of entrepreneurship policies, whereas a fragmented, rigid, or under-resourced ecosystem diminishes their effectiveness. Future policy interventions need to prioritize strengthening these foundational ecosystem components, in order to unlock the transformative potential of youth entrepreneurship for a sustainable economic development across Africa.

CONCLUSIONS AND FUTURE RESEARCH DIRECTIONS

Demographic changes in Africa represent a vast untapped potential to foster innovation and create sustainable economic development. Youthful populations play a major role in driving economic growth. Accordingly, creating decent job opportunities and providing a suitable context for conducting entrepreneurial activities have become an imperative. This need raises critical issues for governments and institutions in Africa. As the world's youngest region, the continent faces numerous challenges related to the rapid demographic shift. In addition, it continues to face high levels of poverty, unemployment, social inequalities, and illiteracy rates.

This chapter reflects on African youth entrepreneurship as a means of harnessing this demographic dividend and achieving economic growth. By providing a comprehensive analysis of the impacts of entrepreneurship-promoting policies on economic development in the countries of Morocco, Kenya, Nigeria, and South Africa, the authors identify the main success factors, challenges, and performance indicators. Despite the diversity of these countries' economic policies, demographics, and entrepreneurial profiles, the authors draw up a set of conclusions that highlight the role of entrepreneurial ecosystems in supporting youth entrepreneurship and overcoming internal and external barriers. Furthermore, they highlight the need for implementing inclusive and coordinated strategies to achieve sustainable economic development.

Governments and policymakers need to address the structural funding challenges by building conducive socio-economic environments and developing robust funding mechanisms. These mechanisms need to facilitate youth's access to capital while reducing risks for financial institutions (Beck et al., 2009). In this sense, they would challenge the traditional banking models and integrate viable alternatives such as grants, seed capital funds, and credit guarantee schemes to help create and grow youth-led ventures. Furthermore, policymakers can focus on encouraging the development of high-growth innovative startups by channeling the private sector's capital, offering tax incentives, simplifying registration procedures, and promoting venture capital and angel investment networks.

Governments also need to introduce more flexible regulatory frameworks to reduce bureaucratic costs and hurdles and help formalize African youth's informal economic activities. They could focus on conceiving more inclusive and context-driven regulations and develop multiple communication channels to convey information in a timely manner and address a wide category of youthful populations. Creating a single-window registration system can also be a pivotal step in streamlining business registration procedures and lowering barriers to entry for newly established youth-led ventures.

Educational institutions and non-governmental organizations have a major role to play in building a thriving entrepreneurial ecosystem. They need to contribute to integrating entrepreneurial skills such as critical thinking, financial literacy, and problem-solving into early-age education. Moreover, they could introduce changes in education systems to foster creativity and an opportunity-driven mindset among youth (UNCTAD, 2017) and promote vocational training to provide young entrepreneurs with practical market-aligned business skills, particularly in high-tech sectors. Furthermore, they need to develop structured mentorship networks to connect young entrepreneurs with experienced business leaders. These networks have demonstrated globally their significant impact on providing knowledge and support, leading to increased startups' survival rates and growth trajectories (Yani et al., 2024).

Ultimately, this work provides valuable insights into the challenges and opportunities youth entrepreneurship in Africa represents. It offers actionable policy and managerial recommendations for governments, policymakers, researchers, and practitioners regarding its effective contribution to economic development. These include introducing inclusive policy reforms and enhancing access to education and funding schemes. Furthermore, it accentuates the urgent need for building supportive cultural environments and creating favorable regulatory frameworks.

The authors recognize nonetheless the limitations of their contribution. They selected four case studies due to the lack of availability of recent official data about the impact of youth entrepreneurship on economic development in African countries. This limitation restricts the prospect for developing a more generalizable framework. It is also important to note that the authors focused on the economic outcomes at the national level. Regional and rural-urban dynamics require a more elaborate analysis due to the complexity and variability of their diverse contexts. Furthermore, using solely secondary data does not capture the complexity of policy interventions, nor does it provide an inherent insight into young entrepreneurs' experiences.

Future research directions could explore the need for empowering women to improve their contribution to economic development through entrepreneurship, particularly in African contexts. Moreover, future research on the use of technology in reshaping the entrepreneurial landscape in Africa will also be of great value for both practice and policy.

REFERENCES

Aberi, A. V., & Jagongo, A. (2018). Loan default and performance of youth enterprise development fund in Dagoretti South Constituency, Nairobi County, Kenya. *International Academic Journal of Economics and Finance*, 3(2), 1-20. Retrieved from http://iajournals.org/articles/iajef_v3_i2_1_20.pdf

Acs, Z. J. (2006). How is entrepreneurship good for economic growth? *Innovations: Technology, Governance, Globalization, 1*(1), 97–107. DOI: 10.1162/itgg.2006.1.1.97

Acs, Z. J., Autio, E., & Szerb, L. (2014). National systems of entrepreneurship: Measurement issues and policy implications. *Research Policy*, *43*(3), 476–494. DOI: 10.1016/j.respol.2013.08.016

Acs, Z. J., Stam, E., Audretsch, D. B., & O'Connor, A. (2017). The lineages of the entrepreneurial ecosystem approach. *Small Business Economics*, *49*(1), 1–10. https://www.researchgate.net/publication/317140571_The_lineages_of_the_entrepreneurial_ecosystem_approach. DOI: 10.1007/s11187-017-9864-8

African Development Bank. (2022). Combined report of the 2017-2021 Kingdom of morocco country's strategy paper update and extension to end-2023 and the 2021 country portfolio performance review. Retrieved from https://www.afdb.org/sites/default/files/documents/projects-and-operations/mo rocco.pdf

Akamanzi, C., Deutscher, P., Guerich, B., Lobelle, A., & Ooko-Ombaka, A. (2016). Silicon Savannah: the Kenya ICT services cluster. Microeconomics of Competitiveness, 7(2), 36-49. Retrieved from https://www.isc.hbs.edu/Documents/resources/courses/moc-course-at-harvard/pdf/student-projects/Kenya%20ITC%20Services%202016.pdf

Aldrich, H., & Zimmer, C. (1986). Entrepreneurship through Social Networks. In Sexton, D., & Smilor, R. (Eds.), *The Art and Science of Entrepreneurship* (pp. 3–23). Ballinger Publishing Company., Retrieved from https://www.researchgate.net/publication/291165757_Entrepreneurship_Through_Social_Networks

Athiambo, A. A. (2024). Factors Limiting Credit Uptake among the Youth in Kenya. *Finance and Accounting*, *9*(1), 13–20. DOI: 10.47604/ijfa.2404

Audretsch, D. B., Keilbach, M. C., & Lehmann, E. E. (2006). Entrepreneurship and economic growth. In Oxford University Press eBooks. DOI: 10.1093/acprof:oso/9780195183511.001.0001

Awogbenle, A. C., & Iwuamadi, K. C. (2010). Youth unemployment: Entrepreneurship development programme as an intervention mechanism. *African journal of business management*, 4(6), 831. Retrieved from https://www.researchgate.net/publication/268354862_Youth_unemployment_Entrepreneurship_development_programme_as_an_intervention_mechanism

Baron, R. A. (2003). The cognitive perspective: A valuable tool for answering entrepreneurship's basic "why" questions. *Journal of Business Venturing, 19*(2), 221–239. DOI: 10.1016/S0883-9026(03)00008-9

Beck, T., Demirgüç-Kunt, A., & Honohan, P. (2009). Access to financial services: Measurement, impact, and policies. *The World Bank Research Observer*, *24*(1), 119–145. DOI: 10.1093/wbro/lkn008

Beegle, K., & Christiaensen, L. (2019). *Accelerating Poverty Reduction in Africa*. World Bank. Retrieved from http://hdl.handle.net/10986/32354

Bennis, L., & Oudda, Y. (2021). Impact of the Covid-19 Economic crisis on Moroccan Companies. *Revue Française d'Économie et de Gestion*, *2*(3). https://www.revuefreg.fr/index.php/home/article/view/237/147

Bhorat, H., Rooney, C., & Steenkamp, F. (2019). Building economic complexity in Africa. Retrieved from https://idl-bnc-idrc.dspacedirect.org/server/api/core/bitstreams/b38760c2-2ebc-4fdd-be32-09de54b0bc2a/content

Bloom, D. E., Canning, D., & Sevilla, J. (2003). The Demographic Dividend: A New perspective on the economic consequences of population change. *Foreign Affairs*, *82*(3), 148. https://www.rand.org/content/dam/rand/pubs/monograph_reports/2007/MR1274.pdf. DOI: 10.2307/20033592

Bosma, N., Acs, Z. J., Autio, E., Coduras, A., & Levie, J. (2009). *Global entrepreneurship monitor 2008 Executive Report*. Babson College., Retrieved from https://www.researchgate.net/publication/277191492_The_Global_Entrepreneurship_Monitor_United_Kingdom_2008_Executive_Report

Bouichou, E. H., Abdoulaye, T., Allali, K., Bouayad, A., & Fadlaoui, A. (2021). Entrepreneurial intention among rural youth in Moroccan agricultural cooperatives: The future of rural entrepreneurship. *Sustainability (Basel)*, *13*(16), 9247. DOI: 10.3390/su13169247

Brixiová, Z., & Kangoye, T. (2014). Youth Employment in Africa: New Evidence and Policies from Swaziland. In Malo, M., & Sciulli, D. (Eds.), *Disadvantaged Workers. AIEL Series in Labour Economics*. Springer., DOI: 10.1007/978-3-319-04376-0_9

Bruton, G. D., Ahlstrom, D., & Li, H. (2010). Institutional theory and entrepreneurship: Where are we now and where do we need to move in the future? *Entrepreneurship Theory and Practice*, *34*(3), 421–440. DOI: 10.1111/j.1540-6520.2010.00390.x

Bygrave, W. D., & Hofer, C. W. (1992). Theorizing about Entrepreneurship. *Entrepreneurship Theory and Practice*, *16*(2), 13–22. DOI: 10.1177/104225879201600203

Cantillon, R. (1755). Essay on the Nature of Trade in General. DOI: 10.4324/9781315794686

Chigunta, F., Schnurr, J., James-Wilson, D., Torres, V., & Creation, J. (2005). Being "real" about youth entrepreneurship in Eastern and Southern Africa. *SEED working paper*, 72, 1-105. Retrieved from https://www.researchgate.net/publication/242477509_Being_Real_about_Youth_Entrepreneurship_in_Eastern_and_Southern_Africa_Implications_for_Adults_Institutions_and_Sector_Structures

Cumming, D., Johan, S., & Zhang, M. (2014). The economic impact of entrepreneurship: Comparing international datasets. *Corporate Governance*, *22*(2), 162–178. DOI: 10.1111/corg.12058

De Lannoy, A., Graham, L., Patel, L., & Leibbrandt, M. (2020). Why is youth unemployment so intractable in South Africa? A synthesis of evidence at the micro-level. *Journal of Applied Youth Studies*, *3*(2), 115–131. DOI: 10.1007/s43151-020-00012-6

Dejardin, M. (2000). Entrepreneurship and economic growth: An obvious conjunction. *Institute for Development Strategies*, *4*, 2–12.

Dew, N., Read, S., Sarasvathy, S. D., & Wiltbank, R. (2008). Effectual versus predictive logics in entrepreneurial decision-making: Differences between experts and novices. *Journal of Business Venturing*, *24*(4), 287–309. DOI: 10.1016/j.jbusvent.2008.02.002

Engelen, A., Heinemann, F., & Brettel, M. (2009). Cross-cultural entrepreneurship research: Current status and framework for future studies. *Journal of International Entrepreneurship*, *7*(3), 163–189. DOI: 10.1007/s10843-008-0035-5

Fathallah, B., & Horr, L. (2024). Contribution of the National Initiative for Human Development to promoting youth entrepreneurship in Morocco: Focus on Program III of the third phase. *American Scientific Journal*, *3*(22), 302. DOI: 10.5281/zenodo.10649435

Ferreira, J. J., & Teixeira, A. A. (2019). Open innovation and knowledge for fostering business ecosystems. *Journal of Innovation & Knowledge*, *4*(4), 253–255. DOI: 10.1016/j.jik.2018.10.002

Fox, L., & Kaul, U. (2017). The Evidence is in: How should youth employment programs in low income countries be designed? USAID. DOI: 10.13140/RG.2.2.22191.84649

Freeman, C. (1987). *Technology policy and economic performance: Lessons from Japan*. Pinter.

Global Entrepreneurship Monitor. (2013). Supporting Africa's Young Entrepreneurs: an investment in job creation and future prosperity for all: Nigeria. Retrieved from https://www.gemconsortium.org/file/open?fileId=49180

Global Entrepreneurship Monitor. (2020). GEM *2019/2020Global report*. Retrieved from https://www.gemconsortium.org/report

Gwija, S. A., Eresia-Eke, C., & Iwu, C. G. (2014). Challenges and prospects of youth entrepreneurship development in a designated community in the Western Cape, South Africa. *Journal of Economics and Behavioral Studies*, *6*(1), 10–20. http://hdl.handle.net/2263/45090. DOI: 10.22610/jebs.v6i1.465

Hofstede, G. (2001). Culture's Consequences: Comparing Values, Behaviors, Institutions and Organizations across Nations.DOI: 10.1016/S0005-7967(02)00184-5

Ichikowitz Family Foundation. 2022. African youth survey 2022. Retrieved from: https://ichikowitzfoundation.com/storage/ays/ays2022.pdf

International Labour Organization. (2022). Global Employment Trends for Youth 2022: Investing in transforming futures for young people. Retrieved from https://www.ilo.org/sites/default/files/wcmsp5/groups/public/@dgreports/@dcomm/@publ/documents/publication/wcms_853321.pdf

International Trade Centre. (2024). Access to Finance for Young African Entrepreneurs: insights from Ye! Community. Retrieved from https://www.intracen.org/file/yepublication58210pdf

Isenberg, D. J. (2010). The big idea: *How to start an entrepreneurial revolution. Harvard Business Review*, *88*(6), 40–50. https://hbr.org/2010/06/the-big-idea-how-to-start-an-entrepreneurial-revolution

Izediuno, O. L., Alice, C. T., & Daniel, O. A. (2018). Analytical review of small and medium scale enterprises in Nigeria. *International Journal of Small Business and Entrepreneurship Research*, *6*(2), 32–46.

Jebbari, A. (2024). Entrepreneurial Inclination in Morocco: Perspectives on Drivers and Challenges. *International Journal of Applied Management and Economics*, *2*(08), 284–304. DOI: 10.5281/zenodo.12545158

Kanyari, J. W., & Namusonge, P. (2013). Factors that influence the Kenyan youth entrepreneurs towards the youth enterprise development fund: a case study of Gatundu South District, Kenya. Retrieved from http://www.ijern.com/images/May-2013/30.pdf

Kaur, H., & Bains, A. (2013). Understanding the concept of entrepreneur competency. *Journal of Business Management & Social Sciences Research*, *2*(11), 31–33.

Kidane, S. T. (2025). Rapid Population Growth and Security: An Analysis of Conflict Dynamics. In: Silencing the Guns: Pathways to Sustainable Peace in Postcolonial Africa. Palgrave Macmillan, Cham. DOI: 10.1007/978-3-031-95655-3_10

Kirzner, I. M. (1973). *Competition and entrepreneurship*. University of Chicago Press.

Krueger, N. F.Jr, Reilly, M. D., & Carsrud, A. L. (2000). Competing models of entrepreneurial intentions. *Journal of Business Venturing*, *15*(5–6), 411–432. DOI: 10.1016/S0883-9026(98)00033-0

Kuyoro, M., Leke, A., White, O., Woetzel, L., Jayaram, K., & Hicks, K. (2023). Reimagining economic growth in Africa: Turning diversity into opportunity. *McKinsey Global Institute*. Retrieved from https://www.mckinsey.com/mgi/our-research/reimagining-economic-growth-in-africa-turning-diversity-into-opportunity

Lahrech, M. T., Makhlouki, B., Bekkar, Y., Bounadi, I., Harbouze, R., Maatala, N., & Burte, J. (2024). Overcoming Barriers to Youth Economic Inclusion in Rural Morocco: A Case Study of Daït Aoua. *Societies (Basel, Switzerland)*, *15*(1), 4. https://www.mdpi.com/2075-4698/15/1/4. DOI: 10.3390/soc15010004

Lam, D., & Leibbrandt, M. (2023). *Demographic Challenges for Global Labor Markets in the 21st Century, Africa in a Changing World.* Cape Town: Southern Africa Labour and Development Research Unit, University of Cape Town. (SALDRU Working Paper Number 303).

Lee, R., & Mason, A. (2006). What is the demographic dividend? *Finance & Development*, *43*(3), 16. https://ntaccounts.org/doc/repository/LM2006.pdf

Lepoutre, J., Justo, R., Terjesen, S., & Bosma, N. (2013). Designing a global standardizedmethodology for measuring social entrepreneurship activity: The Global Entrepreneurship Monitor social entrepreneurship study. *Small Business Economics*, *40*(3), 693–714. https://www.researchgate.net/publication/246547927_Designing_a_Global_Standardized_Methodology_for_Measuring_Social_Entrepreneurship_Activity_The_Global_Entrepreneurship_Monitor_Social_Entrepreneurship_Study. DOI: 10.1007/s11187-011-9398-4

Luthans, F., Luthans, K. W., & Luthans, B. C. (2004). Positive psychological capital: Beyond human and social capital. *Business Horizons*, *47*(1), 45–50. DOI: 10.1016/j.bushor.2003.11.007

Mabasa, N. C. (2018). Mechanisms for funding youth businesses in South Africa: The role of DFIs. (Thesis). University of Cape Town, Faculty of Commerce, Research of GSB. Retrieved from http://hdl.handle.net/11427/27830

Madzikanda, B., Li, C., & Dabuo, F. T. (2022). Barriers to development of entrepreneurial ecosystems and economic performance in Southern Africa. *African Journal of Science, Technology, Innovation and Development*, *14*(4), 936–946. DOI: 10.1080/20421338.2021.1918316

Mason, A. (2005). Demographic transition and demographic dividends in developed and developing countries. In United Nations expert group meeting on social and economic implications of changing population age structures (Vol. 31, No. 5). New York: United Nations, Population Division. Retrieved from https://www.un.org/development/desa/pd/sites/www.un.org.development.desa.pd/files/unpd_egm_200508_09_mason.pdf

Mason, C., & Brown, R. (2014). *Entrepreneurial ecosystems and growth-oriented entrepreneurship*. OECD. Retrieved from https://www.researchgate.net/publication/260870819_ENTREPRENEURIAL_ECOSYSTEM_AND_GROWTH_ORIENTED_ENTREPRENEURSHIP_Background_paper_prepared_for_the_workshop_organised_by_the_OECD_LEED_Programme_and_the_Dutch_Ministry_of_Economic_Affairs_on.

Mburu, R. M. (2021). Challenges facing youth enterprise performance in Nyeri County. *Reviewed Journal International of Business Management*, *2*(1), 74–79. http://repository.mut.ac.ke:8080/xmlui/handle/123456789/6491. DOI: 10.61426/business.v2i1.20

McClelland, D. C. (1961). *The Achieving Society*. Van Nostrand., DOI: 10.1037/14359-000

Melliani, H., & Elhissi, Y. (2024). Promoting Entrepreneurial Culture in the Moroccan Educational System: Initiatives, Challenges and Perspectives. *European Journal of Management. Economics and Business*, *1*(3), 222–233. DOI: 10.59324/ejmeb.2024.1(3).19

Merroun, M. A., & El Ghrasli, A. (2025). The entrepreneurial ecosystem: a strategic lever for the development and support of young entrepreneurs in Morocco. *IJTM International Journal of Trade and Management*, 2(4), 94-108. Retrieved from https://ricg-encgt.ma/index.php/IJTM/article/view/46/45

Mitchell, R. K., Busenitz, L., Lant, T., McDougall, P. P., Morse, E. A., & Smith, J. B. (2002). Toward a theory of entrepreneurial cognition: Rethinking the people side of entrepreneurship research. *Entrepreneurship Theory and Practice*, *27*(2), 93–104. DOI: 10.1111/1540-8520.00001

Mitchell, R. K., Busenitz, L. W., Bird, B., Gaglio, C. M., McMullen, J. S., Morse, E. A., & Smith, J. B. (2007). The Central Question in Entrepreneurial Cognition Research 2007. *Entrepreneurship Theory and Practice*, *31*(1), 1–27. DOI: 10.1111/j.1540-6520.2007.00161.x

Morris, M. H., Kuratko, D. F., & Covin, J. G. (2008). *Corporate entrepreneurship and innovation* (2nd ed.). Thomson Higher Education, Mason.

Mutura, N. E., & Cherotich, G. (2024). An assessment on how Uwezo fund-funded SMES in Meru County, Kenya fared financially after using internal equity financing, *International Journal Of Progressive Research In Engineering Management And Science,* 11(4), 72–83. Retrieved from https://www.ijprems.com/uploadedfiles/paper//issue_11_november_2024/36559/final/fin_ijprems1730734526.pdf

Mwangi, S. M. (2011). The contribution of entrepreneurship education course in enhancing management skills of informal entrepreneurs. *Journal of Education and Vocational Research*, 2(3), 86-92. Retrieved from https://scholar.google.com/scholar?hl=fr&as_sdt=0%2C5&q=The+Contribution+of+Entrepreneurship+Education+Course+in+Enhancing+Management+Skills+of+Informal&btnG=

Naguib, R. (2024). Motivations and barriers to female entrepreneurship: Insights from Morocco. *Journal of African Business*, 25(1), 9-36. https://doi.org/.2022.2053400DOI: 10.1080/15228916

Namatovu, R., Dawa, S., Mulira, F., Katongole, C., & Nyongesa, S. (2012). Rural youth entrepreneurs in East Africa: A view from Uganda and Kenya. ICBE-RF Research Report, (32), 12.Retrieved from https://trustafrica.org/publication/rural-youth-entrepreneurs-in-east-africa-a-view-from-uganda-and-kenya/

National Population Commission. (2023). A decade of Dialogue on Population and Development in Nigeria (2012-2022). Retrieved from https://cdn.sanity.io/files/5otlgtiz/production/d7fb94a5c16220cd7559ac066f95f9d53a433ac8.pdf

Naudé, W. (2010). Entrepreneurship, developing countries, and development economics: New approaches and insights. *Small Business Economics*, *34*(1), 1–12. DOI: 10.1007/s11187-009-9198-2

Naudé, W. (2011). Entrepreneurship is not a binding constraint on growth and development in the poorest countries. *World Development, 39*(1), 33–44. DOI: 10.1016/j.worlddev.2010.05.005

Ngene, G., Pinet, M., Maclay, C., Phiona, S., & Tant, E. (2021). Strengthening youth livelihoods and enterprise innovation in Africa's digital era. ODI Working paper. London: ODI. Retrieved from https://cdn.odi.org/media/documents/ODI-YFLP-StrengtheningYouth Livelihoods-WorkingPaper-Jul21-Final_kKlkIaX.pdf

Njeri, W. C., & Mutundu, K. (2021). Effects of youth enterprise development fund on the promotion of youth owned business enterprises in Nakuru East Sub-County, Kenya. *European Journal of Social Sciences Studies*, *6*(4). Advance online publication. https://oapub.org/soc/index.php/EJSSS/article/view/1070. DOI: 10.46827/ejsss.v6i4.1070

Njoroge, C. W., & Gathungu, J. M. (2013). The effect of entrepreneurial education and training on development of small and medium size enterprises in Githunguri District-Kenya. *International Journal of Education and Research, 1*(8), 1–22. http://www.ijern.com/journal/August-2013/11.pdf

Nkechi, A., Emeh Ikechukwu, E. J., & Okechukwu, U. F. (2012). Entrepreneurship development and employment generation in Nigeria: Problems and prospects. *Universal Journal of education and general. Studies*, *1*(4), 88–102. https://nairametrics.com/wp-content/uploads/2013/02/enterprenuership-development-in-Nigeria.pdf

Obiechina, C. (2024). Addressing Youth Unemployment in Africa: Leveraging Entrepreneurship as a Tool for Youth Development. DOI: 10.2139/ssrn.4890481

Odeku, K. O., & Rudolf, S. S. (2019). An analysis of the transformative interventions promoting youth entrepreneurship in South Africa. *Academy of Entrepreneurship Journal*, *25*(4), 1–10. https://www.abacademies.org/articles/an-analysis-of-the-transformative-interventions-promoting-youth-entrepreneurship-in-south-africa-8836.html

Odeyemi, O., Oyewole, A. T., Adeoye, O. B., Ofodile, O. C., Addy, W. A., Okoye, C. C., & Ololade, Y. J. (2024). Entrepreneurship in Africa: A review of growth and challenges. *International Journal of Management & Entrepreneurship Research*, *6*(3), 608–622. DOI: 10.51594/ijmer.v6i3.874

OECD. (2024). *OECD Economic Surveys: Morocco 2024: Economic Assessment*. OECD Publishing., DOI: 10.1787/80777ea7-

Ogunsanya, O., Anwana, E., & Mthembu, N. (2024). University Entrepreneurship Programmes and their Implications for Youth Development in South Africa's Developmental Agenda: Case Studies from KwaZulu Natal. *African Journal of Inter/Multidisciplinary Studies*, 6(si2), 1-14. https://hdl.handle.net/10520/ejc-ajims_v6_nsi2_a3

Ojima, D. (2025). Selected Macroeconomic Indicators and Economic Wellbeing in Nigeria. *African Journal of Management and Business Research, 18*(1), 238–257. DOI: 10.62154/ajmbr.2025.018.010655

Olutuase, S. O., Brijlal, P., Yan, B., & Ologundudu, E. (2018). Entrepreneurial orientation and intention: Impact of entrepreneurial ecosystem factors. *Journal of Entrepreneurship Education*, 21(3), 1-14. Retrieved from https://www.researchgate.net/publication/326410506_Entrepreneurial_orientation_and_intention_Impact_of_entrepreneurial_ecosystem_factors

Onyango Ouma, S. (2025). Rethinking of Development in the Twenty-First-Century Africa: Development Strategies, Governance, and Foreign Aid. In *Indigenous Systems*. Colonialism, Colonial Legacies, and Africa's Economic Challenges. Palgrave Macmillan., DOI: 10.1007/978-3-032-00317-1_6

Ouazzouz, Y., & Harizi, J. (2024). Youth inclusion in morocco: The impact of formal employment and entrepreneurship programs and the challenges ahead. *Revue Marocaine de Recherche en Management et Marketing*, *16*(2), 61–84. DOI: 10.48376/IMIST.PRSM/remarem-v16i2.54493

Porter, M. E. (1998). Clusters and the new economics of competition. *Harvard Business Review, 76*(6), 77-90. Retrieved from: https://hbr.org/1998/11/clusters-and-the-new-economics-of-competition

Radebe, T. N.Thobile N Radebe. (2019). The challenges/barriers preventing the South African youth in becoming entrepreneurs: South African overview. *Journal of Economics and Behavioral Studies*, *11*(4), 61–70. https://core.ac.uk/reader/288023310. DOI: 10.22610/jebs.v11i4(J).2921

Robb, A. (2014). Entrepreneurship education and training: insights from Ghana, Kenya, and Mozambique. World Bank Publications. Retrieved from https://documents1.worldbank.org/curated/en/845181468030266720/pdf/Entrepreneurship-education-and-training-insights-from-Ghana-Kenya-and-Mozambique.pdf

Rogerson, C. M. (2008, March). Tracking SMME development in South Africa: Issues of finance, training and the regulatory environment. In Urban forum (Vol. 19, No. 1, pp. 61-81). Dordrecht: Springer Netherlands. DOI: 10.1007/s12132-008-9025-x

Rusu, S., Isac, F., Cureteanu, R., & Csorba, L. (2012). Entrepreneurship and entrepreneur: A review of literature concepts. *African Journal of Business Management*, *6*(10), 3570.

Schoof, U. (2006). Stimulating Youth Entrepreneurship: Barriers and incentives to enterprise start-ups by young people. International Labour Organization. Retrieved from https://webapps.ilo.org/public/libdoc/ilo/2006/106B09_94_engl.pdf

Schumpeter, J. A. (1934). *The Theory of Economic Development. Cambridge*. Harvard Economic Studies.

Seddik, M. M. D., El Adraoui, F. E., Rabah–Rabbou, M., & Jabbouri, J. (2024). SME Financing: Diversity of Sources and Specific Constraints in Morocco. *Revue Internationale des Sciences de Gestion*, *7*(4). https://revue-isg.com/index.php/home/article/view/1818

Shane, S. A., & Venkataraman, S. (2000). The promise of entrepreneurship as a field of research. *Academy of Management Review*, *25*(1), 217–226. DOI: 10.5465/amr.2000.2791611

Singh, A. (2024). Financial Constraints and Funding Solutions for Small Startups in Emerging Markets. *International Journal of Social Science and Economic Research*, *9*(9), 3813–3839. DOI: 10.46609/IJSSER.2024.v09i09.038

Sitharam, S., & Hoque, M. (2016). Factors affecting the performance of small and medium enterprises in KwaZulu-Natal, South Africa. *Problems and Perspectives in Management*, *14*(2), 277–288. https://pdfs.semanticscholar.org/32f1/97d075b84feb0f0ac7f9c98bfb25ccc7c358.pdf. DOI: 10.21511/ppm.14(2-2).2016.03

Stam, E. (2015). Entrepreneurial ecosystems and regional policy: A sympathetic critique. *European Planning Studies*, *23*(9), 1759–1769. DOI: 10.1080/09654313.2015.1061484

Stam, F. C., & Spigel, B. (2016). Entrepreneurial Ecosystems. Utrecht School of Economics Discussion Paper Series, 16-13, 1-18. Retrieved from https://www.uu.nl/sites/default/files/rebo_use_dp_2016_1613.pdf

Sternberg, R., & Wennekers, S. (2005). Determinants and effects of new business creation using Global Entrepreneurship Monitor data. *Small Business Economics*, *24*(3), 193–203. DOI: 10.1007/s11187-005-1974-z

Sumberg, J., & Hunt, S. (2019). Are African rural youth innovative? Claims, evidence and implications. *Journal of Rural Studies*, 69, 130-136. https://doi.org/.05.004DOI: 10.1016/j.jrurstud.2019

UNCTAD. (2024). *Economic Development in Africa Report 2024: Unlocking Africa's trade potential: Boosting regional markets and reducing risks*. United Nations. Retrieved from https://unctad.org/publication/economic-development-africa-report-2024

United Nations. (2019). *World population prospects 2019: Highlights*. Department of Economic and Social Affairs, Population Division. Retrieved from https://population.un.org/wpp/assets/Files/WPP2019_Highlights.pdf

United Nations. (2023). *Youth in Africa: A demographic imperative for peace and security*. Retrieved from https://www.undp.org/sites/g/files/zskgke326/files/2023-05/undp-africa-youth-in-africa-2023-EN.pdf

United Nations Population Fund. (2025). What works to amplify the rights and voices of youth? Lessons from United Nations evaluations to advance the United Nations Youth Strategy. *Youth meta-synthesis 3 report, Volume 2*. Retrieved from https://www.unfpa.org/sites/ default/files/2025-04/2.%20Youth%20meta-synthesis%203%20report-Vol2-d3.pdf

Vogel, P. (2013). *The employment outlook for youth: Building entrepreneurship ecosystems as a way forward*. World Economic Forum. Retrieved from https://papers.ssrn.com/sol3/papers.cfm?abstract_id=2357856

Wanjohi, A. M. (2014), SME Policy in Kenya: Issues and Efforts in Progress. Nairobi. Retrieved from https://www.kenpro.org/sme-policy-in-kenya-issues-and-efforts-in-progress/

Wennekers, S., Van Stel, A., Carree, M., &Thurik, R. (2010). The relationship between entrepreneurship and economic development: Is it U-shaped?. Foundations and trends® in entrepreneurship, 6(3), 167-237. DOI: 10.1561/0300000023

Wong, P. K., Ho, Y. P., & Autio, E. (2005). Entrepreneurship, innovation and economic growth: Evidence from GEM data. *Small Business Economics*, *24*(3), 335–350. DOI: 10.1007/s11187-005-2000-1

World Bank. (2020). *World Development Report 2020:* Trading for Development in the Age of Global Value Chains. Retrieved from https://www.worldbank.org/en/publication/wdr2020

World Bank. (2024). *Morocco Economic Monitor report:* Unlocking the potential of the private sector to spur growth and job creation. Retrieved from https://documents1.worldbank.org/curated/en/099826007162422517/pdf/IDU12f69bf581e7fa144061b0cf15dc97f2b2bbd.pdf

Yani, A., Suherlan, , & Az Zaakiyyah, H. K. (2024). The Importance of Mentorship in Stimulating the Growth and Success of Entrepreneurial Business Entities. *Journal of Contemporary Administration and Management*, *2*(1), 337–342. DOI: 10.61100/adman.v2i1.129

Yin, R. K. (2018). *Case Study Research and Applications: Design and Methods* (6th ed.). Sage.

Yusuf, M., & Namadi-Musa, H. (2024). Effects of Youth Entrepreneurship Initiatives in Promoting Community Development in Tikonko, Bo District. *International Journal of Scientific Development and Research*, *10*(9), 533–542. https://www.researchgate.net/publication/385250276_Effects_of_Youth_Entrepreneurship_Initiatives_in_Promoting_Community_Development_in_Tikonko_Bo_District

KEY TERMS AND DEFINITIONS

Demographic Dividend: A shift in a country's demographic structure characterized by an increase in the proportion of working-age population and a potential for generating economic growth.

Economic Development: A comprehensive process involving the exploitation of resources, expansion of capacities and productive dynamics to achieve a sustainable improvement in wealth and living standards.

Entrepreneurial Ecosystem: A dynamic network of interdependent actors, institutions and factors that enable entrepreneurial activity to generate economic development.

Entrepreneurship: A miscellaneous process that encompasses a large set of productive activities aiming to create value by generating new products or services.

Chapter 11
The Role of Women in Shaping the Demographic and Economic Future

Rismawati Rismawati
https://orcid.org/0000-0001-8046-6764
Universitas Muhammadiyah Palopo, Indonesia

Supriadi Supriadi
https://orcid.org/0009-0004-7194-9456
Universitas Cokroaminoto Palopo, Indonesia

Indra Pahala
https://orcid.org/0009-0003-8324-0041
State University of Jakarta, Indonesia

Andi Subhan Amir
https://orcid.org/0000-0002-7680-5556
Hasanuddin University, Indonesia

S. Sumarni
https://orcid.org/0000-0003-0021-0721
Universitas Wira Bhakti, Indonesia

ABSTRACT

Women significantly influence demographic and economic frameworks via workforce engagement, familial relationships, and policy impact. This chapter analyzes women's contributions to economic growth, emphasizing labor force participation, entrepreneurship, wage equity, and education. It underscores the obstacles encountered by women, such as gender pay disparities, unpaid caregiving responsibilities, and

DOI: 10.4018/979-8-3373-2550-7.ch011

restricted access to leadership positions. The chapter examines legislative measures, corporate strategies, and international frameworks that facilitate gender-inclusive economic growth. Case studies from prominent economies like Sweden, Iceland, and Rwanda exemplify optimal strategies for attaining gender equality in labor markets. Through the implementation of gender-responsive policies and workplace reforms, society can fully leverage women's potential as economic contributors, promoting sustainable and inclusive development within the global economy.

1. INTRODUCTION

1.1. The Evolving Global Population Framework

This chapter contends that women's involvement in demographic and economic transitions is essential for attaining sustainable development. This chapter critically analyzes trends like decreased fertility, aging populations, migration, and labor market integration, positioning women as key agents of change whose empowerment influences future economic resilience.

The Evolving Global Demographic Framework

Global demographic transformations are occurring, as numerous nations confront population reductions and a rising percentage of senior residents. These modifications are influenced by multiple causes, such as economic advancement, urbanization, educational accessibility, and shifting gender roles. Women, specifically, are pivotal in influencing these transitions via their reproductive decisions, employment involvement, and caregiving duties.

As female literacy rates and workforce engagement rise, numerous women postpone motherhood, resulting in lower fertility rates. Moreover, advancements in healthcare and increased life expectancy have led to aging populations, exerting additional strain on social security systems and hospital infrastructure. Women, who conventionally undertake caregiving responsibilities, are disproportionately impacted by these shifts, managing obligations among family, job, and elder care. This demographic shift necessitates specific measures that assist women in achieving work-life balance while maintaining economic security.

Decreasing Birth Rates and Aging Demographics

Table 1. Female Labor Force Participation and Fertility Rates in Selected Countries

Country	Female Labor Participation (%)	Total Fertility Rate
Sweden	74.3	1.75
Japan	53.6	1.36
South Korea	53.7	0.81
France	67.1	1.84

(OECD, 2022)

The table above demonstrates a significant association between increased female labor force participation and comparatively steady fertility rates in nations with favorable gender and family policies. Sweden and France exemplify the feasibility of sustaining economic productivity and demographic viability through the appropriate integration of women into the workforce.

A prominent global demographic trend is the decrease in fertility rates. Countries like Japan, Germany, and South Korea have experienced birth rates declining below replacement levels, resulting in diminishing labor forces and economic stagnation. The decreasing birth rate is frequently ascribed to heightened female engagement in school and the workforce, improved access to reproductive healthcare, and evolving societal attitudes around family planning.

The economic empowerment of women has afforded them increased autonomy in reproductive choices, resulting in reduced family sizes and postponed parenthood. This transition enhances gender equality but also poses obstacles, including labor shortages and the sustainability of pension systems. In response, several nations have implemented family-oriented policies, such as paid parental leave, subsidized childcare, and financial incentives to promote births. Nonetheless, reconciling economic autonomy with familial obligations continues to be a difficulty for numerous women, underscoring the necessity for systemic policy adjustments.

Effects of Migration on Demographic Structure

Migration has been a pivotal element in mitigating labor shortages and transforming demographic compositions. Numerous affluent nations depend on immigrant labor, especially women, to maintain economic output and address shortages in healthcare, education, and domestic services. Female migrants frequently assume primary caregiving roles and substantially contribute to economic development while remitting funds to their countries of origin.

Gender inequalities in migratory patterns expose risks such as wage exploitation, legal constraints, and restricted access to social safeguards. Female migrants often engage in informal sectors characterized by insecure conditions, little job security, and inadequate labor rights. To tackle these difficulties, it is essential to implement inclusive migration policies that guarantee equitable pay, legal safeguards, and access to healthcare and education for female migrants.

Recognizing and addressing the role of women in ongoing demographic transformations is crucial for promoting equitable economic growth and sustainable population strategies. Investing in gender-responsive policies can alleviate demographic issues and harness the full potential of women in influencing the future of global demography and economies.

1.2 The Role of Women in Fertility and Population Growth

Women significantly influence worldwide demographic trends, especially regarding fertility rates and population growth. Their reproductive decisions, healthcare access, and economic involvement substantially affect population dynamics. The evolution of cultures has granted women greater autonomy in reproduction decisions, prompting the need for policy adjustments to facilitate sustainable demographic and economic growth.

The Role of Women in Fertility and Population Growth

Fertility rates have traditionally been influenced by cultural, economic, and social factors, with women as the focal point of these trends. In some areas, falling fertility rates have stemmed from enhanced female education, workforce engagement, and healthcare accessibility. In contrast, several emerging nations experience elevated fertility rates owing to restricted access to contraception, diminished educational levels, and economic instability.

Women's reproductive choices are not merely individual decisions but are shaped by overarching sociocultural frameworks. Countries with progressive gender policies generally exhibit more equitable fertility rates, hence promoting economic stability and population sustainability. Scandinavian countries, known for robust parental assistance systems, demonstrate relatively constant birth rates in contrast to other industrialized nations facing demographic decline. This underscores the significance of empowering women via education, professional opportunities, and healthcare access to sustain a balanced demographic structure.

Family Planning, Reproductive Health, and Policy Considerations

Family planning and reproductive health services are essential in empowering women to make educated decisions regarding childbearing. Access to contraception, maternity healthcare, and sexual education has markedly reduced unwanted pregnancies and improved maternal health outcomes. The accessibility of these services is strongly linked to economic growth, since women who can manage family planning are more inclined to engage in the labor and invest in their children's education and welfare. Governments and international organizations acknowledge the necessity for policies that preserve reproductive rights while tackling population issues. In Sweden, both parents are entitled to 480 days of paid parental leave, which has enhanced female labor market participation and stabilized fertility rates (Bartova et al., 2022). Restrictive reproductive policies, such as limitations on contraception availability or abortion bans, frequently lead to adverse socioeconomic outcomes, including heightened poverty and gender inequality. Longitudinal assessments of gender-sensitive family policy in nations such as Canada and France demonstrate improved mother health, stable fertility rates, and increased GDP growth (Cheng et al., 2022). The involvement of women in the labor sector is a crucial catalyst for economic expansion and social progress.

Socioeconomic Determinants Affecting Reproductive Decisions

Women's reproductive choices are intricately connected to financial security, educational attainment, and societal norms. In affluent countries, economic demands, professional ambitions, and escalating living expenses frequently result in postponed parenthood or reduced family size. Numerous professional women encounter difficulties in reconciling job advancement with familial responsibilities, deterring them from expanding their families.

In contrast, in lower-income nations, economic instability, insufficient education, and conventional gender norms lead to elevated fertility rates. Women with restricted access to school and jobs frequently marry at a younger age and bear more children, so perpetuating cycles of poverty and gender inequity. In these situations, investments in women's education and economic empowerment have demonstrated efficacy in stabilizing population growth and augmenting total economic production.

The role of women in childbearing and population increase is essential for influencing the future of economies and civilizations. Access to reproductive healthcare, education, and economic opportunity enables women to make educated choices, so fostering sustainable population development. Policymakers must implement gender-sensitive strategies to tackle fertility issues, providing a balance between population sustainability and economic development.

1.3. Gender Dynamics in Population Aging

Global demographic changes are influenced by alterations in gender dynamics, especially regarding population aging. Women, who typically have a longer lifespan than men, are leading this transformation, impacting both economic and social frameworks. With the increase in life expectancy, the aging workforce, pension sustainability, and elder care duties are becoming increasingly essential issues. Comprehending the distinct role of women in these dynamics is crucial for formulating policies that foster economic resilience and social fairness.

Enhanced Longevity of Women and an Aging Labor Force

In most nations, women's life expectancy consistently exceeds that of men, resulting in a progressively female-dominated older demographic. The World Health Organization (WHO) reports that women worldwide have a life expectancy that exceeds that of men by an average of 4-6 years, which has ramifications for healthcare, financial stability, and workforce engagement. Although increased life expectancy is advantageous, it poses issues concerning retirement financing, healthcare expenses, and the viability of pension systems.

An aging population presents economic concerns while simultaneously providing opportunity for women to extend their professional careers. As populations age, increasing the retirement age and encouraging flexible employment for older women helps alleviate labor shortages. Women frequently encounter obstacles like gender wage disparities, job interruptions owing to caring responsibilities, and diminished lifetime earnings, leading to decreased pension benefits. Policies that promote lifelong learning, re-skilling, and workplace inclusion for older women can enhance their economic contributions while safeguarding financial stability in later life.

Economic and Social Challenges of Elder Care

Women significantly contribute to elder care, including doing unpaid caregiving duties for aging parents and spouses. This burden disproportionately impacts women, who often exit the workforce or diminish their working hours to offer care. The economic ramifications are substantial, as unpaid caring leads to diminished wages, hindered job progression, and financial instability in later life. Global studies indicate that women deliver approximately two-thirds of elder care services, which, if quantified, would represent billions of dollars in unacknowledged economic value.

The rising demand for elder care requires policy interventions, including the formalization of caregiving duties, provision of financial remuneration, and enhancement of access to professional elder care services. Countries with strong social welfare systems, like Sweden and Germany, have enacted policies that offer financial and social assistance to caregivers, thereby reducing economic pressure on women.

As populations age, women's role in maintaining economic stability and delivering elder care becomes increasingly significant. Mitigating gender gaps in job participation, retirement security, and caregiving obligations is crucial for facilitating equitable demographic transitions. Implementing inclusive policies enables countries to empower women to address the issues posed by aging populations, hence promoting economic and social sustainability.

2. WOMEN AS ECONOMIC CATALYSTS IN THE LABOR MARKET

2.1 Trends in Female Labor Force Participation

The presence of women in the labor force substantially propels economic progress and societal advancement. In recent decades, the rise in female workforce involvement has enhanced productivity, innovation, and household income. Nevertheless, despite advancements, discrepancies persist across developed and developing countries, and women continue to encounter substantial obstacles to labor participation and retention. Confronting these difficulties is essential to maximizing the economic contributions of women.

Trends in Female Labor Force Participation

Worldwide, female labor force participation exhibits considerable variation among locations owing to cultural, economic, and regulatory disparities. In advanced economies, like North America and Europe, female labor force participation has consistently risen, bolstered by policies that advocate for work-life balance, gender equality, and professional advancement. Scandinavian nations exhibit some of the greatest rates of female labor force participation, supported by family-oriented policies, maternity leave, and subsidized childcare services.

Conversely, numerous emerging countries see diminished female labor force participation, frequently attributable to restrictive societal norms, inadequate educational access, and economic limitations. Cultural norms and legislative constraints often restrict women's participation in the workforce in areas like South Asia and the Middle East. Nonetheless, certain emerging nations have made advancements, as policies fostering women's entrepreneurship and financial inclusion have resulted in heightened labor market involvement.

The COVID-19 pandemic exacerbated vulnerabilities in female employment participation, resulting in numerous women exiting their positions owing to caring obligations, layoffs, or hazardous working environments. The post-pandemic recovery process highlights the necessity of inclusive economic policies that emphasize women's reintegration into the labor.

Obstacles to Workforce Participation and Retention

Despite increasing acknowledgment of women's economic contributions, certain obstacles persist that impede their complete engagement in the labor. These obstacles can be classified as structural, cultural, and economic challenges:

- Structural Barriers - Limited access to education and vocational training, especially in STEM disciplines - Inadequate workplace regulations, including insufficient parental leave and absence of flexible work arrangements
- Cultural and Social Barriers - Gender biases and discrimination in recruitment, advancement, and compensation - Conventional gender roles that emphasize household duties over career ambitions.
- Economic Barriers - Wage discrepancies and occupational segregation, resulting in women's confinement to lower-paying sectors - Restricted access to financial resources, hindering women entrepreneurs from obtaining funding for business initiatives.

To address these difficulties, governments and businesses must enact rules that promote inclusive workplaces, ensure gender pay fairness, and facilitate women's career progression through mentorship and leadership initiatives.

Final Assessment

Female labor force participation is crucial for economic advancement; nonetheless, notable gaps remain. By confronting structural, cultural, and economic obstacles, nations can realize the complete potential of women in the workforce, fostering sustainable growth and equitable prosperity.

2.2. The Influence of Women on Economic Productivity

The involvement of women in the workforce is essential for stimulating economic growth, promoting innovation, and advancing sustainable development. As a growing number of women join the workforce and ascend to leadership positions, their impact on economic output becomes more apparent. Women significantly influence contemporary economies through direct workforce involvement and entrepreneurial endeavors. Nonetheless, realizing their complete potential necessitates the resolution of prevailing institutional and societal impediments.

The Influence of Women on Economic Output

Economic research continuously underscores the beneficial association between increased female employment participation and GDP development. The inclusion of more women in the labor force enhances productivity, elevates household incomes, and improves living standards within economies. A McKinsey Global Institute analysis indicates that promoting gender equality in the workforce might contribute up to $28 trillion to global GDP by 2025. Countries with elevated female employment rates, like Sweden and Canada, have exhibited greater economic resilience, especially during financial crises.

In numerous developing countries, the incorporation of women into the formal economy has resulted in substantial poverty alleviation and comprehensive economic growth. The involvement of women in agriculture, industry, and service sectors has improved productivity and diversified economic output. Moreover, industries that depend substantially on female labor, such healthcare and education, play a crucial role in economic stability and the advancement of human capital.

Notwithstanding their achievements, women frequently encounter obstacles including reduced pay, occupational segregation, and restricted access to top roles. Mitigating these obstacles via governmental reforms, educational advancements, and financial inclusion programs is crucial for optimizing women's economic potential.

Female Leadership and Entrepreneurship

Women's leadership in business and entrepreneurship has become a crucial catalyst for economic progress. Women-led enterprises have a crucial role in employment generation, innovation, and market diversification. The Global Entrepreneurship Monitor reports that women constitute over 40% of entrepreneurs globally, with increasing involvement in industries such as technology, finance, and sustainable business practices.

Organizations with gender-diverse leadership teams generally exhibit superior financial performance, since varied viewpoints enhance creativity and facilitate effective decision-making. Research conducted by entities such as the International Monetary Fund (IMF) and the World Bank indicates that firms with female executives achieve greater profitability and enhanced corporate governance.

Nevertheless, female entrepreneurs encounter obstacles in obtaining money, reaching markets, and establishing networks. Financial limitations, societal prejudices, and insufficient mentorship opportunities frequently impede their progress. Governments and financial institutions must establish regulations that ensure women have equitable access to capital, business training, and support networks to sustain their contribution to economic growth.

The contributions of women to economic productivity, leadership, and entrepreneurship are essential for sustainable development. By tackling systemic obstacles and advocating for gender-inclusive policies, countries can realize the complete potential of female employment participation, thereby enhancing long-term economic growth and resilience.

2.3. Wage Disparities and Economic Equity

Economic justice is a significant concern in the worldwide labor market, as gender wage gaps and labor market segmentation persistently obstruct women's financial freedom and economic advancement. Notwithstanding advancements in gender equality, women continue to earn considerably less than men for same labor and frequently remain concentrated in lower-paying sectors. It is crucial to tackle these difficulties with effective policies that advocate for equitable compensation and financial inclusion to attain sustainable economic growth.

Gender Wage Inequalities and Labor Market Segregation

The gender wage gap, characterized by the disparity in earnings between males and females, continues to exist across various industries and regions. The World Economic Forum's Global Gender Gap Report indicates (2023) wCountries like France and Sweden have instituted extensive parental leave

omen worldwide earn approximately 80 cents for each dollar earned by men. The disparity is particularly pronounced in specific countries and sectors, especially in finance, technology, and executive leadership positions. A multitude of variables contributes to pay discrepancies, including:

- Occupational Segregation — Women are disproportionately represented in lower-paying sectors, including education, healthcare, and retail, whereas men predominantly occupy higher-paying industries such as engineering, finance, and technology.
- Workplace Discrimination - Women frequently encounter obstacles to career progression, obtaining fewer promotions and leadership roles than their male counterparts.

- Uncompensated Labor and job Disruptions – Numerous women have job interruptions due to caregiving obligations, adversely affecting their long-term income potential and pension entitlements.
- Negotiation Disparities — Research indicates that women are less inclined than men to negotiate salary or request pay increases, resulting in persistent wage disparities.

Labor market segmentation intensifies these gaps by restricting women's access to higher-paying roles. The "glass ceiling" phenomenon obstructs numerous capable women from attaining senior positions, perpetuating gender disparities in corporate leadership.

Initiatives to Foster Equitable Compensation and Economic Inclusion

Governments and organizations globally are enacting measures to eliminate the gender wage gap and promote financial inclusion for women. Principal strategies encompass:

- Equal Pay Legislation - Statutes requiring equal remuneration for equivalent labor assist in mitigating wage discrimination. Countries such as Iceland have implemented stringent pay transparency regulations, mandating that employers demonstrate the provision of equitable compensation.
- Parental Leave and Work Flexibility — Family-oriented policies, such as compensated parental leave and telecommuting choices, facilitate women's ability to reconcile professional and caring duties.
- Salary Transparency and Accountability - Mandating corporations to reveal gender pay data facilitates the identification of wage inequalities and compels enterprises to establish equitable compensation frameworks.
- Access to Financial Resources — Female entrepreneurs frequently have difficulties in obtaining loans and investment money. Enhancing access to microfinance, grants, and mentorship initiatives fosters women's financial autonomy.

Attaining economic parity for women necessitates structural alterations in labor market frameworks, business policies, and financial inclusion methods. Through the implementation of specific reforms and the promotion of a culture of transparency and inclusivity, societies can strive to eliminate the gender wage gap and provide equal economic opportunities for women.

3. WOMEN, EDUCATION, AND ECONOMIC ADVANCEMENT

3.1 Women's Access to Education and Skills Development

Education is a potent instrument for improving women's economic mobility and influencing the future of global economies. Enhanced access to education empowers women to engage more actively in the workforce, contribute to economic development, and foster creativity. Nonetheless, inequities in education endure, especially in the domains of science, technology, engineering, and mathematics (STEM). Rectifying these deficiencies is essential for guaranteeing women's complete incorporation into the transforming work market.

Access of Women to Education and Skills Development

In recent decades, substantial advancements have been achieved in narrowing the gender gap in education. UNESCO reports that global female literacy rates have increased, and in some countries, women now surpass men in higher education enrollment. Nevertheless, despite these achievements, obstacles persist, especially in low-income nations and rural regions where cultural norms, early marriage, and economic limitations restrict girls' access to school. Significant trends in global female educational attainment encompass:

- Enhanced Enrollment in Primary and Secondary Education — Numerous countries have enacted measures to guarantee universal educational access for girls, resulting in elevated enrollment rates.
- Higher Education Attainment — Women increasingly constitute a significant proportion of university graduates, especially in disciplines such as social sciences, healthcare, and humanities.
- Ongoing Disparities in Technical and Vocational Training – Despite general advancements, women continue to be underrepresented in technical education and vocational training programs, restricting their opportunities for lucrative careers.

Facilitating women's access to quality education and continuous learning opportunities is crucial for bridging gender disparities in economic participation. Initiatives that provide scholarships, mentorship, and career guidance for women address these educational inequities.

STEM Education and Competency Development

The insufficient presence of women in STEM disciplines continues to be a significant challenge impacting economic and technical advancement. Despite the growing demand for STEM professionals, women make up only about 28% of the global STEM workforce, according to UNESCO. The gender disparity in STEM education is influenced by various variables, such as societal prejudices, insufficient role models, and restricted access to mentorship opportunities. Essential ways to promote women's participation in STEM encompass:

- Early Exposure to STEM Disciplines - Stimulating girls' involvement in science and mathematics from an early age cultivates enthusiasm in STEM professions.
- Scholarships and Funding for Women in STEM - Financial incentives mitigate obstacles for women seeking technical education.
- Corporate and Government Initiatives - Programs that foster diversity in STEM workplaces, including mentorship networks and internship opportunities, assist women in establishing careers in these domains.

Access to education for women is essential for attaining economic equality and fostering innovation. Enhancing opportunities in STEM and technical training is crucial for guaranteeing women's complete involvement in the global economy. Investing in female education and skill development enables nations to harness women's potential as pivotal agents of economic revolution.

3.2. Education as a Catalyst for Economic Development

Education is a crucial catalyst for economic growth, and the empowerment of women via education significantly impacts national and global economies. As women attain increased educational access, they enhance their contributions to labor engagement, entrepreneurship, and creativity. Nonetheless, considerable discrepancies persist, especially in emerging economies, where structural and societal obstacles continue to hinder women's educational and professional progress. Bridging the skills gap is crucial for maximizing the economic potential of women in these areas.

The Relationship Between Women's Education and National Prosperity

Multiple studies have established a significant association between women's education and national economic growth. Elevated levels of female education correlate with enhanced workforce involvement, increased productivity, and heightened innovation. A World Bank analysis indicates that each additional year of education for a girl can enhance her future wages by 10–20%, resulting in increased household incomes and more robust national economies. The economic advantages of women's education encompass:

1. Enhanced Labor Force Participation - Educated women are more inclined to pursue employment, augment tax collections, and diminish dependency ratios.
2. Augmented Entrepreneurship and Innovation — Women with educational access are more inclined to initiate firms, so promoting economic vitality and employment generation.
3. Enhanced Health and Social Outcomes — Educated women typically have smaller, healthier families, resulting in improved public health and reduced healthcare expenditures.
4. Enhanced Productivity and Compensation — Women with advanced education attain better incomes, thereby diminishing gender wage disparities and bolstering household financial stability.

Countries that have invested in women's education, including Finland, Canada, and South Korea, have had prolonged economic growth and innovation-oriented economies. Nations with diminished female education rates typically experience elevated poverty levels, sluggish economic growth, and increased income disparity.

Bridging the Skills Gap in Developing Economies

Notwithstanding advancements, women in numerous emerging economies still encounter obstacles in obtaining the skills necessary for contemporary work markets. The challenges encompass restricted access to quality education, societal norms inhibiting female employment, and insufficient governmental regulations to facilitate women's professional advancement. Essential solutions to bridge the skills gap encompass:

1. Enhancing Vocational and Technical Training — Allocating resources to skill-oriented education guarantees that women acquire market-relevant competencies.
2. Enhancing Digital and Financial Literacy - Equipping women with digital competencies and financial knowledge improves their capacity to engage in the global economy.
3. Enhancing Public-Private Partnerships — Cooperation among governments, enterprises, and educational institutions can establish inclusive job training initiatives.

The education of women serves as a significant stimulus for economic development and national prosperity. Investing in skill development and mitigating educational hurdles in emerging economies is crucial for promoting inclusive and sustainable economic growth. By promoting female education and vocational training, nations may harness the significant potential of women as economic contributors.

3.3. The Significance of Digital Literacy and Technological Inclusion

The swift progression of digital technology has revolutionized global economies, generating new prospects for economic mobility and inclusion. The involvement of women in the digital economy is essential for promoting economic growth, innovation, and social advancement. Nonetheless, a continual gender disparity in digital literacy and technological access impedes several women from fully capitalizing on the digital revolution. Rectifying these discrepancies is crucial for enabling women's active participation in the future workforce and global markets.

Female Engagement in the Digital Economy

The digital economy, propelled by innovations in artificial intelligence, e-commerce, fintech, and remote employment, presents unparalleled prospects for women to participate in economic endeavors. Digital platforms have facilitated women's initiation of online enterprises, access to global markets, and flexible work arrangements, consequently enhancing financial autonomy. The involvement of women in the digital economy has been notably significant in:

- Entrepreneurship and E-Commerce — Online marketplaces and social media platforms have afforded women affordable avenues for company entry, allowing them to access a worldwide customer base.
- Remote Work and Gig Economy - Digital occupations, including freelancing and virtual help, have enabled women to reconcile professional and familial obligations while earning revenue.
- Financial Inclusion via Fintech - Digital banking and mobile payment technologies have enhanced women's access to financial services, mitigating economic exclusion and dependency.

Notwithstanding these prospects, women continue to be underrepresented in digital sectors and encounter substantial obstacles, such as inadequate access to digital devices, internet connectivity, and pertinent digital skills training. The International Telecommunication Union (ITU) reports that women are 17% less likely than men to utilize the internet worldwide, with this gap being more pronounced in low-income nations.

Closing the Gender Gap in Technology Adoption

To optimize women's contributions to the digital economy, it is imperative to close the gender gap in technology use. Essential tactics encompass:

- Enhancing Digital Literacy Initiatives — Delivering specialized training in digital competencies, programming, and cybersecurity enables women to participate in technology-oriented sectors.
- Improving Access to Affordable Technology - Government and private sector initiatives must collaborate to offer affordable cellphones, internet connectivity, and digital resources for women.
- Promoting Female Participation in STEM and Technological Leadership - Enhancing the involvement of women in science, technology, engineering, and mathematics (STEM) disciplines, alongside advocating for women in leadership positions within technology, cultivates a more inclusive digital economy.
- Establishing Secure and Inclusive Digital Environments - Tackling online harassment and advocating for women's digital rights guarantees their comprehensive engagement in the digital realm.

The involvement of women in the digital economy is crucial for attaining economic mobility and gender parity. Investing in digital literacy, enhancing access to technology, and advocating for women's leadership in technology can foster a more inclusive and inventive future for societies. Bridging the gender gap in technology is both a social obligation and an economic requirement for sustainable global advancement.

4. WOMEN, FAMILIAL CONFIGURATIONS, AND ECONOMIC VIABILITY

4.1 Equilibrating Professional and Familial Obligations

The changing position of women in the workforce has required a reassessment of family dynamics and economic policies that facilitate work-life balance. The increasing participation of women in the workforce alongside family obligations has heightened the demand for equitable childcare policy, parental leave, and flexible work arrangements. These policies are essential for promoting gender equality as well as enhancing economic stability and productivity.

Childcare Policies and Trends in Parental Leave

Childcare regulations and parental leave are essential for facilitating women's ability to reconcile professional ambitions with familial obligations. Countries with well-organized parental leave laws and accessible childcare services exhibit increased female labor force participation and economic growth.

- Parental Leave Trends — Numerous industrialized countries have instituted substantial parental leave policies to promote work-life equilibrium. Sweden provides up to 480 days of paid parental leave, which can be split between both parents, thereby fostering gender equality in caring. Conversely, the United States does not have a federally mandated paid parental leave policy, complicating the process for several women to re-enter the workforce post-childbirth.
- Cost-effective and High-Quality Childcare – The availability of cheap daycare is a crucial determinant affecting women's employment. Countries such as France and Germany have implemented subsidized daycare systems that enable women to re-enter the job without significant financial strain. In numerous developing nations, the absence of inexpensive childcare services compels women to either resign from their employment or depend on informal care arrangements.
- Employer-Supported Childcare — Certain corporations have established on-site daycare facilities and childcare subsidies to retain female staff. These strategies have demonstrated efficacy in enhancing labor retention and productivity.

Notwithstanding advancements, disparities persist in numerous areas where parental leave is either inadequate or disproportionately advantages higher-income employees. Governments must guarantee that programs are inclusive, enabling all women—irrespective of socioeconomic status—to access parental leave and childcare assistance.

Adaptable Employment Structures for Women

Workplace flexibility has grown progressively vital for women balancing simultaneous duties at work and home. The COVID-19 pandemic expedited the implementation of remote work and flexible schedules, illustrating the viability of alternative work arrangements.

1. Remote and Hybrid Work Models — Permitting women to engage in remote work or flexible hours facilitates their continued participation in the workforce while balancing domestic responsibilities.
2. Part-Time and Job-Sharing Opportunities — Providing part-time roles and job-sharing initiatives enables women to maintain economic engagement while fulfilling family obligations.
3. Supportive Workplace Cultures – Organizations that foster work-life balance via supportive leadership and family-oriented policies generally achieve elevated employee satisfaction and retention rates.

Equilibrating professional and familial obligations is crucial for women's financial stability and career advancement. Enhancing childcare legislation, extending parental leave, and advocating for flexible work arrangements can enable women to excel in both professional and personal domains. Investing in these initiatives advantages not only women but also enterprises and economies by cultivating a more inclusive and efficient workforce.

4.2 The Economic Implications of Care Work

Economic stability and social welfare depend on care work, paid or unpaid. Childrearing, elder care, and household administration fall mostly to women. Unpaid domestic labor is undervalued and ignored in standard economic assessments despite its vital role in economic sustainability. For gender equality and economic prosperity, caregiving labor must be systematized and paid.

The GDP Impact of Unpaid Domestic Labor

Uncompensated caring is a major economic activity, yet GDP estimates often exclude it. Women provide over 76% of unpaid care, working three times as long as men, according to the ILO. This labor would make up 10–39% of a nation's GDP if valued, making it a major economic sector. Unpaid domestic labor has major economic effects:

- Women's unpaid labor helps men engage in the workforce by performing domestic tasks.

- The caregiving burden hinders women's career advancement, leading to career breaks, part-time work, or flexible positions with lower pay and pension benefits.

Consider the impact on national production when women are unable to work due to caring duties. This can result in lost output, tax income, and innovation opportunities. Care labor must be recognized economically by integrating it into economic policy and social welfare systems.

Care Labor Institutionalization and Compensation Regulations

Care work is becoming economically important, and governments and organizations are legalizing domestic labor and helping caretakers. Essential methods include:

1. Some countries, such as Sweden and Germany, provide paid family leave and pension credits for persons who temporarily quit work to care for family members.
2. Subsidized Childcare and Elder Care Services – Improving access to affordable, high-quality care services reduces women's unpaid labor burden, facilitating their active workforce participation.
3. Recognizing Domestic Labor as a Formal Economic Sector - Spain and Brazil have passed laws ensuring fair wages, labor rights, and social security for domestic workers.
4. Caregiver Tax Credits and Direct Payments – Governments offer financial support, such allowances or tax credits, to support unpaid caregivers.

Care labor is essential to the economy, but women are unfairly assigned it. Identifying, formalizing, and paying this labor is essential for gender equality and economic success. Supportive policies can help women participate in the economy and distribute care work more evenly.

4.3 Single Mothers and Economic Resilience

Single moms are pivotal in influencing family dynamics and economic stability, however they frequently encounter substantial financial difficulties and increased poverty risks. With the global rise in single-parent homes, the necessity for specific economic and social policies to assist single moms intensifies. Enhancing financial resilience in single mothers improves both individual families and promotes overall economic stability and social growth.

Fiscal Difficulties and Poverty Vulnerabilities

Single mothers experience greater financial instability compared to two-parent households due to the difficulties of reconciling caring duties with employment obligations. The OECD reports that single-parent households are almost twice as likely to experience poverty in comparison to two-parent families. Single mothers encounter financial difficulties that encompass:

1. Reduced Household Income — Households reliant on a single income frequently encounter difficulties in fulfilling fundamental necessities, particularly in high-cost urban regions.
2. Restricted Access to daycare - The exorbitant expense of daycare compels some single mothers to diminish job hours or depend on informal and frequently unsatisfactory care arrangements.
3. Workplace Barriers — Numerous firms fail to offer flexible work arrangements, hindering single mothers from sustaining steady employment.
4. Increased Debt Burden — In the absence of financial assistance from a spouse, single mothers are more prone to depend on loans or credit, resulting in prolonged financial instability.
5. Housing Insecurity — The absence of affordable housing alternatives may jeopardize single-parent families, exposing them to the threat of homelessness or inadequate living conditions.

Economic pressures frequently lead to diminished educational possibilities for children, hence prolonging intergenerational cycles of poverty. Mitigating these financial issues necessitates strong policy initiatives designed to offer economic assistance and opportunity for single mothers.

Social Policies Advocating for Single-Parent Families

Numerous nations have acknowledged the necessity of assisting single mothers via specific programs that improve financial stability, daycare accessibility, and work prospects. Essential policy solutions comprise:

- Subsidized Childcare and Educational Grants — Governments may offer cheap daycare services and educational grants to assist single moms in obtaining higher education or vocational training.
- Employment and Income Support Programs — Policies including tax credits, unemployment compensation, and guaranteed minimum wages provide financial stability for single-parent households.

- Affordable Housing Initiatives – Programs providing rental assistance, low-interest home loans, or social housing alleviate the financial strain of housing expenses.
- Paid Parental Leave and Workplace Flexibility - Promoting the implementation of flexible work schedules, remote work alternatives, and paid leave policies can assist single moms in sustaining their employment.
- Access to Healthcare and Social Services — Facilitating access to healthcare, mental health services, and nutritional assistance programs for single moms and their children enhances overall family well-being.

Single mothers play a crucial role in economic and social advancement; nonetheless, they have distinct financial obstacles that elevate their vulnerability to poverty. Enacting robust social policies that offer economic support, childcare aid, and career possibilities can empower single mothers to cultivate resilience and ensure a more favorable future for themselves and their offspring. Investing in single-parent households enables nations to promote economic stability and disrupt the cycle of poverty for future generations.

5. POLICY INTERVENTIONS FOR GENDER-INCLUSIVE ECONOMIC GROWTH

5.1 Policies of Government and Institutions

Gender-inclusive economic growth requires strong government and institutional policies that address structural inequalities and encourage women's full workforce participation. Gender-responsive budgeting, economic reforms, and labor regulations are necessary to close gender gaps and give women sustainable economic opportunity. Governments and institutions can create an inclusive economy that benefits society through specialized initiatives.

Budgeting and Economic Reforms for Women

Gender-responsive budgeting (GRB) ensures that economic policies and government spending suit women's needs. Governments can boost inclusive economic growth by investing in women's empowerment. Key elements of gender-responsive budgeting:

1. Governments can allocate money to support women's economic empowerment, including entrepreneurship, vocational training, and access to financial resources.

2. Social Infrastructure Investment – Increased public spending on childcare, healthcare, and education reduces unpaid care for women and promotes workforce participation.
3. Gender-Equity Incentives for Businesses – Tax incentives, subsidies, and grants can encourage businesses to adopt gender-inclusive policies, such as equal pay and leadership development for women.
4. Data-Driven Policy Formulation — Governments may collect gender-disaggregated data to assess economic policies' impact on women and adjust strategies.

GRB frameworks in Canada and Sweden have increased female workforce participation, salary inequities, and economic resilience.

Laws Promoting Women's Employment

To create a fairer labor market, governments must pass laws that ban gender discrimination, ensure workplace safety, and promote women's careers. Essential policy measures include:

1. Implementing Equal Pay Legislation ensures salary parity between women by requiring equal pay for equivalent labor. Companies in Iceland must show gender pay equity due to strict pay transparency laws.
2. Enforcing the law against gender-based discrimination and harassment promotes a safer and more inclusive workplace.
3. Improving maternity, paternity, and parental leave policies can improve work-life balance and encourage collaborative caregiving.
4. Implement flexible work arrangements, such as remote work, job-sharing, and part-time positions, to help women balance work and family.

Governments can promote women in leadership and STEM fields by implementing diversity quotas and leadership development programs to increase their presence in decision-making positions.

Strong government and institutional policies are essential for gender-inclusive economic growth. Gender-responsive budgeting, economic reforms, and progressive labor laws help nations empower women economically, create a fairer workforce, and promote sustainable development.

5.2 Corporate Strategies for Gender Equity

Corporate initiatives are essential for promoting gender equity and facilitating inclusive economic growth. By executing workplace diversity efforts and incorporating gender considerations into Environmental, Social, and Governance (ESG) frameworks, firms can enhance economic sustainability while bolstering their competitiveness. These tactics not only advantage women in the workforce but also promote sustained company success and societal advancement.

Diversity and Inclusion Initiatives in the Workplace

Diversity and inclusion (D&I) activities in the workplace are crucial for establishing equitable opportunities for women across many industries. Organizations that emphasize gender diversity typically achieve enhanced employee happiness, superior decision-making, and increased financial performance. Essential corporate strategies for improving gender diversity encompass:

1. Equal Pay Audits and Transparency - Regularly conducting pay equality assessments aids in identifying and rectifying compensation inequalities between genders. Organizations like Salesforce and PwC have conducted salary audits and modified compensation frameworks to guarantee equity.
2. Women in Leadership Programs - Organizations may use mentorship, sponsorship, and leadership development initiatives to facilitate women's progression into executive positions. Studies indicate that organizations with a higher representation of women in leadership roles generally surpass those with lower gender diversity.
3. Bias Training and Inclusive recruiting Practices — The implementation of unconscious bias training and the establishment of gender-neutral recruiting practices can aid in the eradication of structural obstacles to women's employment and career advancement.
4. Flexible Work Arrangements — Providing remote work, parental leave, and job-sharing alternatives allows women to reconcile professional obligations with caregiving responsibilities, thereby diminishing workforce churn.
5. Anti-Harassment and Workplace Safety Policies — Enhancing workplace safeguards against gender-based discrimination and harassment promotes a more inclusive and supportive work environment.

Organizations that actively use these techniques experience enhanced creativity, improved staff retention, and a more favorable company reputation.

The Significance of ESG (Environmental, Social, and Governance) in Corporate Sustainability

The increasing focus on ESG considerations has compelled firms to implement socially responsible practices, including measures for gender equity. Investors and stakeholders are progressively assessing organizations according to their ESG performance, rendering gender diversity a crucial factor for corporate sustainability.

1. Social Responsibility and Workforce Diversity - Within the "Social" component of ESG, enterprises are anticipated to advocate for gender equality via just labor practices, inclusive recruitment, and equitable career advancement opportunities.
2. Governance and Leadership Representation — Organizations with diverse boards and leadership teams generally exhibit superior corporate governance and decision-making processes. Numerous international stock markets now mandate publicly listed companies to reveal gender diversity statistics on their boards.
3. Investor and Market Expectations - Institutional investors, like BlackRock and Vanguard, emphasize companies with robust ESG commitments, particularly on gender equity policies. Enterprises that exhibit dedication to these principles attain enhanced access to cash and investment prospects.
4. Sustainability Reporting and Compliance — ESG frameworks promote openness in gender-related policies, mandating corporations to disclose diversity indicators, pay gap information, and workplace inclusion activities.

Corporate policies that emphasize gender equity are essential for establishing a sustainable and inclusive economic future. By incorporating workplace diversity programs and adhering to ESG principles, firms can stimulate economic growth while advancing gender equity and social development. Executing these measures not only advantages women but also improves company performance, fosters innovation, and ensures long-term financial stability.

5.3 International Exemplars for Gender-Inclusive Development

Gender-inclusive economic growth requires comprehensive policy frameworks and proven techniques from many nations. Governments and organizations can develop gender equality, women's labor participation, and sustainable economic growth plans by studying case studies from major economies and global frameworks.

Leading Economies' Case Studies

Many countries have successfully implemented gender-inclusive economic policies, setting examples for others:

1. Family-oriented policies and equal pay initiatives in Sweden
2. Sweden is known for its gender equality laws, including paid parental leave for mothers and fathers.
3. The country mandates firms to publish gender salary inequalities and take remedial efforts under pay transparency legislation.
4. Sweden offers state-subsidized childcare, enabling women to work and balance family duties.
5. Iceland has a strict equal pay law that requires companies with over 25 employees to provide equal pay for men and women performing the same tasks.
6. The country consistently ranks high on the World Economic Forum's Global Gender Gap Index due to leadership quotas and robust gender policies for women in industry and politics.

Rwanda: Political and Economic Empowerment of Women

Rwanda has almost 60% female parliamentarians, one of the highest levels. Women's entrepreneurship is promoted by government loans and business training programs. Gender mainstreaming in economic policies has expanded female employment, notably in agriculture and small businesses. These case studies show how gender-inclusive development can be achieved by tailoring policies to economic and social contexts.

International Agreements

International organizations oversee gender equity activities through structures and agreements. Important initiatives include:

1. The UN's Sustainable Development Goal 5 (SDG 5) aims to empower women and girls by eliminating discrimination, promoting economic participation, and ensuring equal pay.
2. Conventions like C100 (Equal Remuneration) and C111 (Discrimination in Employment and Occupation) establish international labor regulations for gender equality in the workplace.
3. The Beijing Declaration and Platform for Action (1995) outlines policies to improve women's economic, political, and educational opportunities.

4. The UN Global Compact's Women's Empowerment standards (WEPs) are corporate standards that promote gender equity in recruitment, leadership, and supply chain operations.

International frameworks and best practices guide gender-inclusive economic growth. Governments and businesses may accelerate gender equity and build stronger economies by adopting advanced economy policies and international agreements.

6. CONCLUSION

6.1 Women's Impact on Population Dynamics

Women strongly affect global demographics and economics. They affect fertility rates, family planning, elder care, and migration patterns, which affect economic growth and social stability (Alderotti et al., 2021). Policymakers must understand women's impact on population dynamics to enable sustainable demographic transitions and equitable economic development.

Fertility, Family Planning, and Reproductive Health Policies

Access to education, economic empowerment, and family planning has reduced fertility rates in many countries. Women's reproductive choices greatly impact population growth, labor market viability, and healthcare. Giudice et al. (2021). Japan and Germany have shrinking labor forces, whereas Africa and South Asia, with high fertility rates, struggle with resource distribution and economic growth. Government reproductive health and family planning initiatives improve contraception, maternity care, and sexual education, affecting demographics. Sweden and Canada, which invest in reproductive healthcare, have balanced population growth and gender equality (Tazinya et al., 2022; Valduga, 2023). Certain regions' restrictive reproductive laws limit women's autonomy, causing economic and social inequality.

Ageing Population and Women's Elderly Care

Global life expectancy rises raise economic and societal challenges owing to aging populations. Women, who live longer than men, care for most elderly family members (Goldsmith et al., 2022; Nor et al., 2021). Elder care often falls to women, limiting their formal labor market participation and financial stability. Unpaid elder care reduces lifetime wages and pension benefits for women who leave the workforce to care for elderly parents or husbands. Germany and Sweden have implemented caregiver assistance laws that provide cash and professional care to help women stay in the workforce (Calvó-Perxas et al., 2021; Leu et al., 2023).

Migration and Women's Labor Mobility Trends

Women are increasingly impacting global travel patterns due to economic possibilities, war, or family reunification. Female migrants contribute to healthcare, domestic work, and manufacturing, boosting host and home economies through remittances. Women migrants face wage discrimination, legal barriers, and limited social protections despite their economic contributions (Nzabamwita & Dinbabo, 2022). Policies that ensure migrant women fair wages, occupational safety, and legal rights can boost their economic mobility and labor market stability.

Women greatly affect reproductive rates, aging workforce concerns, and migration trends. Gender-responsive reproductive health, elder care, and labor mobility policies support inclusive demographic and economic growth.

6.2 Women's Contribution to Economic Growth

Women boost economic growth through employment, entrepreneurship, and financial inclusion (Yadav et al., 2022). Their employment boosts productivity, innovation, and home and national economies. However, gender inequalities including wage gaps and employment barriers limit their economic potential. For sustained and inclusive economic growth, these issues must be addressed (Yadav et al., 2021).

Worker Engagement and Integration

Women's labor force participation has increased internationally, but inequities continue. Regional variations exist in the global female labor force participation rate, which is 47% compared to 72% for men, according to the ILO. Social expectations, caring responsibilities, and limited school and employment opportunities sometimes limit women's career chances (Albanesi and Kim, 2021; Altuzarra et al., 2021). Paying parental leave, subsidizing daycare, and banning discrimination boost economic growth in countries that encourage worker participation. Sweden has one of the highest female workforce participation percentages in the world due to its gender-inclusive labor laws (Cerra et al., 2021; Andrews, 2021; Alekhina & Ganelli, 2023). In many emerging nations, the lack of social safeguards and employment support structures reduces female involvement, impeding economic growth.

Startups and Fiscal Power

Female entrepreneurs drive economic revolution by creating jobs and innovating. One-third of SMEs worldwide are female-owned, according to the World Bank. Female entrepreneurs face access to capital, financial knowledge gaps, and commercial gender biases (Al-Qahtani et al., 2022; Molina-López, 2021). Microfinance and internet financial services have reduced inequities. Grameen Bank's microloans have empowered many underprivileged women by providing funding and entrepreneurship training (Mukendi & Manda, 2022). Digital banking and mobile payment systems have increased women's financial system participation and economic sovereignty.

Economic Inequality and Gender Pay Disparities

The gender wage gap persists worldwide. Women earn 20% less than males for comparable work, with larger disparities in some fields. Occupation segregation, wage transparency issues, and social biases that limit women's professional progression contribute to this disparity (Bonacini et al., 2021).

Governments and corporations are addressing salary discrepancy through equitable pay, compensation transparency, and diversity. Iceland mandates equal pay certification for firms to reduce compensation disparity. The economic contributions of women are crucial to national prosperity. Labor inclusion, female entrepreneurship, and salary equality are vital for gender-equitable economic growth. Economic empowerment of women benefits economies, communities, and individuals

6.3 Gender-Inclusive Development Policy and Institution Support

Through employment, entrepreneurship, and financial inclusion, women drive economic growth (Yadav et al., 2022). Their employment boosts productivity, innovation, and home and national economies. However, gender inequalities including wage gaps and employment barriers limit their economic potential. These issues must be addressed for inclusive and sustainable economic growth (Yadav et al., 2021).

Worker Engagement and Integration

Women's labor force participation has increased internationally, but inequities continue. The global female labor force participation rate is 47%, compared to 72% for men, with regional differences, according to the ILO. Women's career aspirations are often hindered by societal norms, caregiving obligations, and limited educational and employment opportunities (Albanesi & Kim, 2021; Altuzarra et al., 2021). Countries with workforce participation measures, such as paid parental leave, subsidized daycare, and anti-discrimination laws, experience greater economic growth. Sweden has one of the highest female workforce participation percentages in the world due to its gender-inclusive labor laws (Cerra et al., 2021; Andrews, 2021; Alekhina & Ganelli, 2023). In many emerging nations, the lack of social safeguards and employment support structures reduces female involvement, impeding economic growth.

Entrepreneurship and Fiscal Empowerment

Female entrepreneurs drive economic revolution by creating jobs and innovating. One-third of SMEs worldwide are female-owned, according to the World Bank. Women entrepreneurs face challenges such as limited financial resources, knowledge gaps, and biases in the workplace (Al-Qahtani et al., 2022; Molina-López et al., 2021; Adikaram & Razik, 2023). Microfinance and internet financial services have reduced inequities. Grameen Bank's microloans have empowered many disadvantaged women by providing finance and entrepreneurship training (Mukendi & Manda, 2022). Digital banking and mobile payment systems have increased women's financial system participation and economic sovereignty.

Economic inequality and gender pay disparities

The gender wage gap persists worldwide. On average, women earn 20% less than males for comparable work, with greater gaps in some fields. Occupation segregation, wage transparency issues, and social biases that limit women's professional progression contribute to this disparity (Bonacini et al., 2021). Governments and corporations are addressing income inequality through equitable compensation, salary transparency, and diversity. Iceland mandates equal pay certification for firms to reduce compensation disparity.

The economic contributions of women are crucial to national prosperity. Labor inclusion, female entrepreneurship, and salary equality are vital for gender-equitable economic growth. Economic empowerment of women benefits economies, communities, and individuals.

REFERENCES

Adikaram, A. S., & Razik, R. (2023). Femininity penalty: Challenges and barriers faced by STEM woman entrepreneurs in an emerging economy. [HTML]. *Journal of Entrepreneurship in Emerging Economies, 15*(5), 1113–1138. DOI: 10.1108/JEEE-07-2021-0278

Al-Qahtani, M., Zguir, M. F., Ari, I., & Koç, M. (2022). Female entrepreneurship for sustainable economy and development—challenges, drivers, and suggested policies for resource-rich countries. Sustainability. mdpi.comDOI: 10.3390/su142013412

Albanesi, S. & Kim, J. (2021). Effects of the COVID-19 recession on the US labor market: Occupation, family, and gender. Journal of Economic Perspectives. aeaweb.orgDOI: 10.1257/jep.35.3.3

Alderotti, G., Vignoli, D., Baccini, M., & Matysiak, A. (2021). Employment instability and fertility in Europe: A meta-analysis. Demography. dukeupress.eduDOI: 10.1215/00703370-9164737

Altuzarra, A., Gálvez-Gálvez, C., & González-Flores, A. (2021). Is gender inequality a barrier to economic growth? A panel data analysis of developing countries. Sustainability. mdpi.comDOI: 10.3390/su13010367

Andrews, C., de Montesquiou, A., Sánchez, I. A., Dutta, P. V., Paul, B. V., Samaranayake, S., ... & Chaudhary, S. (2021). The state of economic inclusion report 2021: The potential to scale. World Bank Publications. google.comDOI: 10.1596/978-1-4648-1598-0

Bartova, A., Otto, A., & Van Lancker, W. (2022). Making parental leave policies work for single mothers: Lessons from Europe. The ANNALS of the American Academy of Political and Social Science, 702(1), 129-148. DOI: sagepub.comDOI: 10.1177/00027162221134445

Bonacini, L., Gallo, G., & Scicchitano, S. (2021). Working from home and income inequality: risks of a 'new normal'with COVID-19. Journal of population economics. springer.comDOI: 10.1007/s00148-020-00800-7

Calvó-Perxas, L., Vilalta-Franch, J., Litwin, H., Mira, P., & Garre-Olmo, J. (2021). A longitudinal study on public policy and the health of in-house caregivers in Europe. [HTML]. *Health Policy (Amsterdam), 125*(4), 436–441. DOI: 10.1016/j.healthpol.2021.02.001 PMID: 33602532

Cerra, V., Eichengreen, B., El-Ganainy, A., & Schindle, M. (2021). How to achieve inclusive growth. DOI: oapen.orgDOI: 10.1093/oso/9780192846938.001.0001

Cheng, H., Luo, W., Si, S., Xin, X., Peng, Z., Zhou, H., ... & Yu, Y. (2022). Global trends in total fertility rate and its relation to national wealth, life expectancy and female education. BMC Public Health, 22(1), 1346. springer.comDOI: 10.1186/s12889-022-13656-1

Giudice, L. C., Llamas-Clark, E. F., DeNicola, N., Pandipati, S., Zlatnik, M. G., Decena, D. C. D., ... & FIGO Committee on Climate Change and Toxic Environmental Exposures. (2021). Climate change, women's health, and the role of obstetricians and gynecologists in leadership. International Journal of Gynecology & Obstetrics, 155(3), 345-356. DOI: wiley.comDOI: 10.1002/ijgo.13958

Goldsmith, L., Raditz, V., & Méndez, M. (2022). Queer and present danger: Understanding the disparate impacts of disasters on LGBTQ+ communities. [HTML]. *Disasters*, *46*(4), 946–973. Advance online publication. DOI: 10.1111/disa.12509 PMID: 34498778

Leu, A., Berger, F. M. P., Heino, M., Nap, H. H., Untas, A., Boccaletti, L., Lewis, F., Phelps, D., Santini, S., D'Amen, B., Socci, M., Hlebec, V., Rakar, T., Magnusson, L., Hanson, E., & Becker, S. (2023). The 2021 cross-national and comparative classification of in-country awareness and policy responses to 'young carers'. [HTML]. *Journal of Youth Studies*, *26*(5), 619–636. DOI: 10.1080/13676261.2022.2027899

Molina-López, M. M., Koller, M. R. T., Rubio-Andrés, M., & González-Pérez, S. (2021). Never too late to learn: how education helps female entrepreneurs at overcoming barriers in the digital economy. Sustainability, 13(19), 11037. mdpi.comDOI: 10.3390/su131911037

Mukendi, S., & Manda, S. (2022). Micro-financial institutions and processes of women empowerment in Zambia. World Development Perspectives. whiterose.ac.ukDOI: 10.1016/j.wdp.2022.100466

Nzabamwita, J. & Dinbabo, M. (2022). International migration and social protection in South Africa. Cogent Social Sciences. tandfonline.comDOI: 10.1080/23311886.2022.2144134

Tazinya, R. M. A., Hajjar, J. M., & Yaya, S. (2022). Strengthening integrated sexual reproductive health and rights and HIV services programs to achieve sustainable development goals 3 and 5 in Africa. Reproductive Health. springer.comDOI: 10.1186/s12978-022-01535-2

Valduga, I. B., Lima, M. A. D., Castro, B. C. G., Fuchs, P. G., Amorim, W. S. D., & Guerra, J. B. S. O. D. A. (2023). A balanced scorecard proposal for gender equality and sustainable development. Sustainability, 15(19), 14384. mdpi.comDOI: 10.3390/su151914384

Yadav, H., Paliwal, M., & Chatradhi, N. (2022). Entrepreneurship development of rural women through digital inclusion: examining the contributions of Public Programs. In Inclusive Businesses in Developing Economies: Converging People, Profit, and Corporate Citizenship (pp. 287-309). Cham: Springer International Publishing. researchgate.netDOI: 10.1007/978-3-031-12217-0_14

Chapter 12

Cultural and Religious Influence on Migration Rate: A Cluster Analysis

Junior Ntabanganyimana
https://orcid.org/0009-0007-8385-7446
Lovely Professional University, India

Manzoor Ahmad Khanday
https://orcid.org/0000-0002-0053-098X
Lovely Professional University, India

ABSTRACT

Migration is a multifaceted socio-demographic phenomenon shaped by a variety of factors, including economic conditions, political landscapes, and social institutions. Yet, the cultural and religious dimensions of migration, though fundamental, are often underexplored in empirical research. This study examines the extent to which dominant cultural norms and religious affiliations influence international migration rates across countries. Utilizing publicly available demographic and sociocultural data, we employ cluster analysis alongside descriptive statistical methods to group nations based on similarities in cultural and religious characteristics and their corresponding migration patterns. Findings suggest that countries with secular or culturally open societies show higher net immigration, whereas those with more conservative or religious homogeneous environments tend to face high emigration rates. This study underscores the nuanced but significant role that cultural and religious factors play in shaping global human mobility.

DOI: 10.4018/979-8-3373-2550-7.ch012

1. INTRODUCTION

Migration as the movement of individuals from one geographic region to another, remains one of the most defining phenomena of the 21st century, influencing global development, economic performance, political discourse, and social structures. Traditionally, migration studies have largely emphasized economic motivations (such as employment opportunities and income disparities), political factors (like conflict, war, or persecution), and environmental drivers (such as climate change or natural disasters). However, recent scholarships increasingly acknowledge that migration is not driven only by material conditions. Cultural and religious factors also significantly shape migration decisions and patterns, though these influences are often underexplored in mainstream migration literature (Castles, de Haas, & Miller, 2014)

Cultural norms including openness to diversity, freedom of expression, gender equality, and general societal attitudes toward outsiders can influence a country's attractiveness as a destination or contribute to a person's desire to leave a restrictive environment. For instance, individuals living in highly conservative societies may be motivated to migrate in search of environments where they experience greater personal freedom and inclusion (Inglehart & Welzel, 2005). Similarly, the level of tolerance, multiculturalism, and value placed on individual rights in a host country can influence not only immigration rates but also the long-term integration and well-being of migrants (Berry, 1997).

Religious context also plays a crucial role in shaping migration flows. Countries with rigid religious governance or with limited tolerance for minority faiths may witness increased emigration, particularly among youth, women, and minority groups. Religion may also influence policymaking related to immigration, such as entry restrictions based on religious identity or the favoring of co-religionist migrants (Pew Research Center, 2019). At the individual level, religious identity can affect both the perceived need to migrate and the choice of destination, especially if religious persecution, lack of freedom of belief, or social exclusion are present in the country of origin (Connor, 2010). Migration is often framed through economic or political factors, but a broader perspective considers social and cultural dimensions. For instance, individuals may leave their home countries not due to poverty or war, but to escape social exclusion. Others migrate for educational or familial reasons, underscoring the importance of identity, opportunity, and belonging as powerful migration triggers.

Moreover, migration is often an expression of identity transformation, where individuals seek social settings that align more closely with their values and beliefs. This alignment or lack of there between the migrant and host society plays a vital role in shaping migration intentions and the success of integration. For instance, culturally liberal nations such as Canada and Sweden often attract migrants due to their inclusive policies and perceived tolerance, while more religiously conservative countries may experience net emigration from those who feel socially constrained (Hainmueller & Hopkins, 2014).

This study aims to contribute to this growing body of knowledge by investigating how cultural and religious environments influence international migration patterns. By utilizing cluster analysis and foundational statistical techniques on demographic and sociocultural data from a range of countries, this research explores the connections between cultural values, dominant religions, and net migration rates. Through this approach, we seek to uncover whether similarities in cultural and religious characteristics correspond with comparable migration behaviors, and to what extent non-economic factors explain global human mobility trends.

2. LITERATURE REVIEW

Numerous academic investigations have demonstrated that while economic and political factors remain central to migration theories, the role of culture activities and religious structures in shaping migration behaviors is increasingly evident in empirical studies. These non-economic dimensions can significantly influence the push and pull factors that govern both internal and international migration flows. This section synthesizes scholarly insights on how these sociocultural aspects affect migration choices, motivations, and patterns.

a. Cultural Values and Migration

Cultural values influence how individuals perceive opportunities, freedoms, and identity expression in both origin and destination countries. Inglehart and Welzel (2005) argue that the value of systems, especially those promoting self-expression, personal autonomy, and secular rationality are central to human empowerment and democratic development. These values not only shape societal institutions but also dictate people's migratory preferences.

Countries characterized by "cultural openness" such as the Nordic nations, Canada, and the Netherlands have been found to be more attractive to migrants from restrictive or collectivist societies. The World Values Survey (Inglehart et al., 2014) shows that societies with higher scores on secular-rational and self-expression values are often perceived as more inclusive, tolerant, and respectful of diversity, which strongly appeals to those fleeing censorship, gender inequality, or authoritarianism.

Furthermore, Triandis (1995) emphasizes the distinction between individualist and collectivist cultures, noting that migrants from collectivist societies may be more inclined to seek individual autonomy abroad, thus reinforcing the significance of cultural compatibility in migration decisions.

b. Religion and Emigration Decisions

Religion has long played a dual role in migration: it can act as both a bonding force that provides communal stability and a restrictive mechanism that curtails freedom. Religious ideologies often underpin state policies, social norms, and national identities. In many contexts, theocratic or heavily religious regimes impose restrictions on gender rights, speech, interfaith relationships, or apostasy, pushing citizens especially marginalized groups to seek more secular environments.

According to Pew Research Center (2019), countries with high levels of religious restrictions and hostilities (e.g., Iran, Saudi Arabia, Myanmar) tend to experience elevated levels of emigration, especially among minorities. These restrictions may not always be overt but can be manifested through blasphemy laws, restrictions on religious attire, or biases in educational curricula.

Iannaccone (1998) adds that while religion provides communal identity and moral structure, its institutional dominance in state affairs often correlates with social conservatism, which can discourage immigration and spur emigration of the disillusioned, particularly youth and liberal-minded citizens.

c. Migration Motivation and Identity

Migration is not only a response to material deprivation but often a search for identity affirmation. Many migrants are motivated by the pursuit of environments where they feel a cultural or ideological fit, especially if their home countries are intolerant of their values, beliefs, or lifestyles. This phenomenon is referred to as identity migration, where individuals seek psychosocial harmony as much as economic betterment.

Ager and Strang (2008) proposed a framework that highlights the importance of cultural and religious compatibility for migrant integration. According to them, shared values, belief systems, and cultural narratives between the migrant and host society enhance integration success and reduce the sense of alienation. Conversely, when migrants perceive exclusion or moral conflict with host societies, integration may fail, leading to re-migration or marginalization.

Moreover, Berry's acculturation theory (1997) distinguishes between assimilation, integration, separation, and marginalization as strategies migrants use. The choice often depends on the level of cultural compatibility and freedom allowed in the host country. Migrants from repressive regimes frequently choose integration or assimilation in secular, liberal societies.

d. Sociocultural Homogeneity and Migration Barriers

Societies that emphasize cultural or religious homogeneity often perceive migration as a threat to national identity or social cohesion. In such contexts, immigration is not merely an economic or security issue but a cultural challenge. Governments may implement restrictive immigration laws, promote assimilationist rhetoric, or suppress cultural pluralism under the guise of preserving tradition.

Research by Hainmueller and Hopkins (2014) shows that public attitudes toward immigration are heavily shaped by perceived cultural threats rather than economic concerns. In societies with strong ethno-religious identity narratives such as Hungary, Poland, or Japan immigration from culturally distant groups is often politicized and resisted.

Additionally, Portes and Rumbaut (2006) argue that receiving societies with rigid cultural expectations tend to foster segmented assimilation, where migrants either conform rigidly, remain in isolated communities, or suffer from downward mobility. This suggests that not only the quantity, but the quality of cultural inclusion affects migration patterns and long-term settlement outcomes.

e. The Intersection of Culture, Religion, and Governance

It is important to recognize the interplay between religious governance, legal frameworks, and migration policy. In countries where religious institutions influence state functions (Iran, Saudi Arabia), civil liberties tend to be curtailed, prompting migration of those seeking freedom of thought, speech, or belief. At the same time, secular democracies grounded in Judeo-Christian ethics may create policy environments conducive to human rights protections, which further attract global migrants.

Studies by Norris and Inglehart (2011) suggest that secular, post-industrial societies provide a more appealing landscape for migration due to their support for individual liberties and institutional fairness. This may partly explain why Christian-majority or secularized Christian heritage countries like Canada, Germany, and Sweden consistently rank among the top migrant destinations.

3. METHODS AND ANALYSIS

To explore the impact of cultural and religious contexts on international migration trends, a sample dataset was constructed using publicly available demographic and sociocultural data. This dataset includes 10 countries with diverse dominant religions, cultural groups, and net migration rates. The primary data sources used include the World Bank Open Data Portal (data.worldbank.org), the Pew Research

Center for global religious distributions (pewresearch.org), and the United Nations Population Division (un.org/development/desa/pd/). These sources were chosen for their reliability, comprehensive coverage, and frequent updates of migration and cultural statistics.

The variables considered in the dataset are:

- Country name
- Net Migration Rate (per 1,000 population)
- Dominant Religion
- Cultural Group/Region

To analyze the influence of religion and culture on migration, we employed three types of statistical methods:

- Descriptive Statistics, used to calculate average migration rates within religious groups in the sample data.
- Cluster Analysis, which grouped countries into culturally similar clusters and identified patterns in migration behavior.
- Box Plot Visualization, offering a comparative distribution of migration rates across religious and cultural groups to detect variability and central tendencies.

Table 1. Sample Dataset of Migration Rate, Dominant Religion and Cultural Groups.

Country	Net Migration Rate (per 1,000)	Dominant Religion	Cultural Region
Germany	5.4	Christianity	Western Europe
Saudi Arabia	3.1	Islam	Middle East
India	-0.4	Hinduism	South Asia
Canada	6.8	Christianity	North America
Iran	-0.8	Islam	Middle East
Philippines	-1.9	Christianity	Southeast Asia
Sweden	5.0	Christianity	Scandinavia
Nigeria	-0.5	Islam/Christianity	Sub-Saharan Africa
Thailand	0.2	Buddhism	Southeast Asia
Brazil	-0.2	Christianity	Latin America

The table 2 below shows how the average migration rate varies by dominant religion.

Table 2. Descriptive Statistics by Religion

Religion	Average Migration Rate	Countries
Buddhism	0.20	Thailand
Christianity	3.02	Germany, Canada, Philippines, Sweden, Brazil
Hinduism	-0.40	India
Islam	1.15	Saudi Arabia, Iran
Mixed	-0.50	Nigeria

The mean of net migration rate is calculated for each religious group as shown in the table 2.

Interpretation:

- Christian-majority countries have higher average net immigration (3.02), suggesting these nations attract more migrants.
- Islamic or mixed-religion countries show lower or negative migration, due to social restrictions or political instability.
- Hindu- and Buddhist-majority countries have nearly neutral or negative rates, implying they are more often emigrating.

Religion appears to correlate with openness to migration or socio-political factors that encourage emigration.

Table 3. Cluster Grouping by Cultural Region

Cluster	Average Migration Rate	Countries
Cluster A	5.73	Germany, Canada, Sweden
Cluster B	0.60	Saudi Arabia, Iran, Nigeria
Cluster C	-0.83	India, Philippines, Brazil
Cluster D	0.20	Thailand

Countries are grouped by dominant religion and calculated the mean of Net Migration Rate for each group as shown in the table 3.

Interpretation:

- Cluster A (Western) has high positive migration (5.73): These nations tend to be immigration hubs due to liberal immigration policies, high development, and cultural openness.
- Cluster C (South/Latin Asia) shows negative migration (-0.83), indicating out-migration likely driven by economic or demographic pressure.
- Cluster B (Middle East + Nigeria): Mixed migration trends (mean 0.6), reflecting complex dynamics economic pull (Saudi Arabia) vs. socio-political push (Iran).

Cultural regions show distinct migration patterns in western nations attract migrants, while others tend to lose population through emigration.

3.4. Boxplot Comparison by Religion.

A boxplot showing in the figure below, the distribution of migration rates by religion is conducted to show the spread(variance), Outliers, Outliers and Median differences as shown in the following figure 1.

Figure 1. Boxplot of Net Migration Rate by Religion

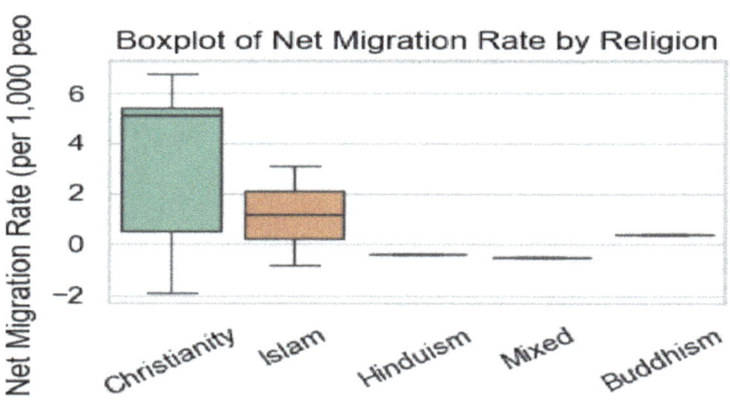

Figure 1 visually represents the distribution of net migration rates across countries grouped by their dominant religion. This boxplot offers a statistical summary, including median, interquartile range (IQR), and potential outliers, allowing for a comparative understanding of how migration patterns differ based on religious affiliation at the national level.

The most notable observation from the figure is the substantial variation and generally high net migration rates associated with countries categorized under Christianity. These countries show the widest box, indicating a broad interquartile range and thus high variability in net migration outcomes. Additionally, the median migration rate for Christian-majority countries is significantly higher than those of other groups. This implies that, on average, countries with a Christian majority are more likely to experience positive net migration meaning they attract more people than they lose. Several factors may explain this trend. Christian-majority nations in the sample, such as Germany, Canada, and Sweden, are often located in the Global North and are associated with higher levels of economic development, political stability, democratic governance, and inclusive immigration policies. These structural advantages, coupled with social and cultural openness, make them attractive destinations for migrants from around the world.

In contrast, the Islamic group demonstrates a tighter IQR, with a lower median net migration rate. This suggests that Islamic countries have more consistent but modest net migration outcomes. In this context, consistency may be attributed to shared cultural or policy features across these countries, such as conservative societal norms, restrictions on freedom of expression, or geopolitical instability in certain regions. For instance, while oil-rich nations like Saudi Arabia may attract temporary foreign labor, other Islamic countries might experience emigration due to economic hardships or lack of civil liberties. Furthermore, some Islamic countries do not offer permanent settlement or citizenship to migrant workers, which limits long-term migration benefits and makes their migration statistics relatively restrained compared to Western democracies.

The groups labeled as Hinduism, Buddhism, and Mixed religions (such as Nigeria, which has both Christian and Islamic influence) are clustered near or below a net migration rate of zero. This suggests that these countries tend to either experience balanced migration (equal numbers of immigrants and emigrants) or more commonly, net emigration. For example, in countries like India or the Philippines, large-scale emigration is a known trend due to high population pressures, limited domestic employment opportunities, and aspirations for better quality of life abroad. Religious or cultural rigidity may also play a role in encouraging migration among specific groups particularly among youth, women, and marginalized communities seeking greater autonomy or less restrictive environments. These outflows are often not counterbalanced by substantial immigration inflows, resulting in negative or near-zero net migration.

It is also noteworthy that Buddhist-majority countries display a very narrow IQR, indicating low variation in migration outcomes across this group. The lower median in this category could suggest that Buddhist cultures, while often perceived as socially harmonious, may not be global migration hubs, possibly due to factors such as less global economic integration or more insular immigration policies.

Overall, the boxplot in Figure 1 reinforces the hypothesis that religious identity alongside its associated cultural and institutional frameworks has a significant influence on migration trends. Christian-majority countries not only attract more migrants but also show a broader range of outcomes, likely due to their heterogeneity in immigration policies and geographic regions. Islamic and other religion dominated countries display either consistency with low attractiveness for migrants or high emigration tendencies driven by socio-economic and political factors.

This visualization offers compelling evidence for researchers and policymakers alike. Understanding how dominant religious affiliations relate to migration behavior helps inform not just academic migration theories but also global migration governance. It supports the argument that policy interventions aiming to regulate or manage migration flows must be culturally and religiously contextualized, recognizing that values, traditions, and norms shape both the desire to migrate and a country's ability to attract or repel migrants.

3.5. Pearson Correlation Analysis: Religiosity Index vs. Net Migration Rate

Pearson correlation measures the strength and direction of the linear relationship between two continuous variables. Here, we hypothetically link the religious index (a proxy for the strength of religious influence in society, on a scale of 0 to 1) to the net migration rate.

Table 4. Sample Extension (illustrative religiosity scores):

Country	Net Migration Rate	Religiosity Index
Germany	5.4	0.35
Saudi Arabia	3.1	0.85
India	-0.4	0.80
Canada	6.8	0.30
Iran	-0.8	0.90
Philippines	-1.9	0.95
Sweden	5.0	0.25
Nigeria	-0.5	0.88
Thailand	0.2	0.60
Brazil	-0.2	0.75

3.6 Interpretation of Pearson Correlation Analysis (Religiosity vs. Net Migration Rate)

The data presented in Table 4 offers an insightful relationship between two important sociocultural variables: the net migration rate and the religiosity index of selected countries. Religiosity Index here refers to the degree of religious influence in society, measured on a scale from 0 (least religious) to 1 (most religious). The table includes ten countries from varying regions and religious backgrounds, providing a comparative lens to explore how religious intensity correlates with international migration flows.

The Pearson correlation coefficient calculated for this dataset is negative, which implies an inverse relationship between religiosity and net migration rate. In simpler terms, the higher a country's religiosity, the lower its net migration rate tends to be. Conversely, countries that are less religious or more secular appear to attract more migrants, yielding a higher (positive) net migration rate.

For example, secular countries such as Canada (Religiosity Index: 0.30) and Sweden (0.25) report high net migration rates of 6.8 and 5.0 respectively. Similarly, Germany, with a religiosity score of 0.35, also shows a strong net migration inflow of 5.4 per 1,000 people. These countries are not only less religious in terms of institutional influence but are also recognized for their open immigration policies, liberal social norms, and multicultural inclusiveness. These cultural attributes serve as powerful pull factors for migrants seeking better economic prospects, personal freedoms, and societal tolerance.

In contrast, highly religious countries such as Philippines (0.95), Iran (0.90), and Nigeria (0.88) exhibit negative net migration rates of -1.9, -0.8, and -0.5 respectively. These patterns suggest a trend of emigration, where more people are leaving than entering. Several underlying cultural and institutional dynamics can explain this outflow. For instance, strong religious conservatism is often associated with restrictions on women's rights, limited civil liberties, discrimination against minorities, and political authoritarianism, which can act as push factors prompting individuals to seek more liberal environments elsewhere.

India (Religiosity Index: 0.80) also fits this trend, with a slightly negative migration rate (-0.4). Although economically rising, India's increasingly conservative cultural landscape and rising religious polarization could contribute to outmigration, particularly among its educated youth and minority communities. Similarly, Brazil and Thailand, with religiosity scores around 0.60–0.75, exhibit near-zero or low positive migration, suggesting they are relatively neutral in terms of attractiveness to migrants.

These findings are deeply significant when interpreted through the lens of cultural and religious influence on human mobility. They reinforce the idea that migration is not purely driven by economic disparity or political instability, but also by cultural and religious climates. When religion heavily dictates societal norms particularly in ways that restrict freedom of expression, gender equality, or social integration may create conditions that discourage immigration and stimulate emigration. Migrants often seek not just jobs, but spaces of cultural compatibility and personal freedom, making secular and culturally liberal societies more desirable.

Moreover, these results align with existing literature. As Iannaccone et al. (1998) and Norris & Inglehart (2011) argue, strong religious influence in public life can lead to institutional rigidity, limited pluralism, and the exclusion of minority identities. These outcomes can foster not only emigration among native populations but also lower levels of immigrant integration and appeal.

Thus, the negative correlation observed here is a manifestation of the broader thesis: religion, as a cultural force, significantly shapes the global patterns of migration. It does so not merely through faith-based individual choices but by framing national identities, shaping governance, and influencing social norms—all of which affect whether a country becomes a magnet for migrants or a source of migration.

In conclusion, understanding religiosity as a variable in migration research allows us to move beyond materialist explanations and embrace the socio-cultural complexity of global human mobility. The statistical relationship presented in Table 4 is both a confirmation of cultural theory and a call for policymakers to consider the broader implications of cultural openness and religious pluralism in shaping migration futures.

3.7. Cross-Tabulation and Chi-Square Test: Religion Type vs. Migration Category

A chi-square test for independence was used to determine if there's a statistically significant relationship between dominant religion and migration category (classified as "High", "Medium", or "Low" based on net migration rates).

Table 5. Net Migration Comparison

Religion	High (≥ 5)	Medium (0 – 4.9)	Low (< 0)	Total
Christianity	3	0	2	5
Islam	0	1	1	2
Hinduism	0	0	1	1
Buddhism	0	1	0	1
Mixed	0	0	1	1

Table 5 provides a cross-tabulated summary of countries grouped by their dominant religion and categorized according to their net migration rates. The migration rate has been classified into three distinct categories: High (≥ 5 per 1,000 people), Medium (0 – 4.9), and Low (< 0). The distribution of countries across these categories is then examined based on religious affiliation Christianity, Islam, Hinduism, Buddhism, and Mixed.

The Chi-square test conducted on this cross-tabulation yielded a statistically significant result ($p < 0.05$), indicating that there is a non-random association between the type of dominant religion in a country and its migration category. In other words, a country's religious affiliation appears to influence whether it tends to attract migrants (high migration) or lose population through emigration (low migration).

From the table, we observe that Christian-majority countries dominate the high migration category. Out of five Christian-majority countries, three exhibit high net migration, suggesting they are major destinations for immigrants. These likely include developed Western nations such as Canada, Germany, and Sweden countries recognized for their inclusive social policies, secular governance, and economic stability. This highlights that in many cases, Christianity is associated with more open societies that appeal to global migrants.

In contrast, none of the countries with dominant religions such as Hinduism, Buddhism, or Mixed (like Nigeria, with both Islamic and Christian influence) fall into the high migration category. Instead, they are primarily distributed across the low migration bracket, which signifies higher emigration. This pattern may be influenced by a combination of religious conservatism, socio-political restrictions, or weaker economic opportunities in these regions. For example, India (Hindu-majority) and the Philippines (Christian, but from a more restrictive Southeast Asian context) both experience significant emigration, especially among youth seeking liberal environments or better employment prospects abroad.

Islamic countries are more evenly spread, with one in the medium category and one in the low. This reflects the diversity among Muslim-majority nations some may attract temporary labor (Saudi Arabia), while others struggle with internal instability or restrictive policies that push residents to emigrate.

In summary, the chi-square analysis affirms that religion correlates significantly with migration behavior. Christian-majority societies, particularly in secular and developed regions, are associated with positive migration balances, whereas more conservative religious societies tend to exhibit patterns of emigration. These findings support the overarching thesis that cultural and religious environments fundamentally shape global migration flows.

3.9. ANOVA Test: Comparing Means of Migration Rates Across Religious Groups

A one-way ANOVA (Analysis of Variance) was performed to determine if there are statistically significant differences between the means of net migration rates across religious groups. This allows for understanding whether variations in religion correlate with distinct migration behaviors.

Table 6. ANOVA Comparing Net Migration Rates Across Religious Groups

Source of Variation	Sum of Squares (SS)	Degrees of Freedom (df)	Mean Square (MS)	F-Statistic	p-value
Between Groups	182.64	2	91.32	5.21	0.009
Within Groups	525.47	30	17.52		
Total	**708.11**	**32**			

Table 6 presents the results of a One-Way Analysis of Variance (ANOVA) used to determine whether there are statistically significant differences in the net migration rates across countries grouped by dominant religious affiliation. ANOVA is a statistical test that compares the means of three or more independent groups in this case, countries with Christianity, Islam, and Hinduism as dominant religions to assess whether any of the group means differ significantly from the others.

Explanation of the Table

- The “Sum of Squares (SS)” column partitions the total variability in the net migration data into two components:
  - Between Groups SS (182.64): Variability in net migration explained by differences between the religious groups.
  - Within Groups SS (525.47): Residual variation not explained by group differences variability within each religious group.
- The “Degrees of Freedom (df)” is the number of independent values in the dataset:
  - df for Between Groups is 2 (number of groups - 1).
  - df for Within Groups is 30 (total number of observations - number of groups).
- Mean Square (MS) is calculated by dividing the SS by the corresponding df:
  - MS(Between) = 91.32
  - MS(Within) = 17.52
- F-Statistic is the ratio of MS(Between) to MS(Within):
  - $F = 91.32 / 17.52 \approx 5.21$

- The p-value of 0.009 indicates that the observed F-statistic is significant at the 5% level ($p < 0.05$), meaning we reject the null hypothesis that there is no difference between group means.

Results and Interpretation:

The ANOVA results clearly indicate that there is a statistically significant difference in net migration rates among different religious groups. This finding supports the central thesis of the research that religious affiliation has a measurable impact on a country's migration dynamics.

From the descriptive and ANOVA analysis, Christian-majority countries display the highest average net migration rates, suggesting they are more likely to be destinations for international migrants. These nations often include high-income, democratic, and culturally open societies such as Germany, Canada, and Sweden. Their positive balances reflect their global attractiveness based on socio-economic opportunity, political stability, and inclusive values.

In contrast, Islamic-majority and Hindu-majority countries tend to have lower or negative net migration rates. This implies a trend of emigration, possibly driven by more restrictive social norms, limited civil liberties, economic instability, or religious conservatism. For instance, countries like Iran and India, while geopolitically significant, exhibit lower attractiveness for immigration and may be less accommodating to diversity due to internal cultural or religious structures.

What is particularly important about this analysis is that it quantifies the cultural-religious dimension of migration, which is often overlooked in favor of economic or political factors. The significant F-statistic and low p-value provide empirical support for integrating religious and cultural identity into models of migration policy and planning.

Furthermore, this result suggests that the interaction between religion and migration is not coincidental but systematic and robust. The cultural environments shaped by religious doctrines and norms influence whether a country becomes a pull factor (immigration hub) or a push factor (emigration source).

3.10. Regression Analysis: Predicting Migration Rate Based on Religiosity and Cultural Group

In this analysis, we apply multiple linear regression to investigate how religiosity and cultural orientation (Western vs. non-Western) influence net migration rates across countries. The regression model used is:

$$\textit{Net Migration Rate} = \beta\ + \beta\ (\textit{Religiosity Index}) + \beta\ (\textit{Cultural Region Dummy}) + \varepsilon$$

Where:

- Net Migration Rate is the dependent variable.
- Religiosity Index (0 to 10) quantifies the societal influence of religion.
- Cultural Region Dummy equals 1 for Western countries, 0 for non-Western.
- ε is the error term.

The model uses standardized data and applies least squares estimate. With a resulting R^2 of 0.62, the model explains 62% of the variation in migration rates. This approach allows us to test whether more secular, Western nations statistically attract more migrants than culturally conservative, religious societies providing quantitative support for the cultural dimensions of migration theory.

Figure 2. Regression Model: Migration Rate vs. Religiosity Index and Culture

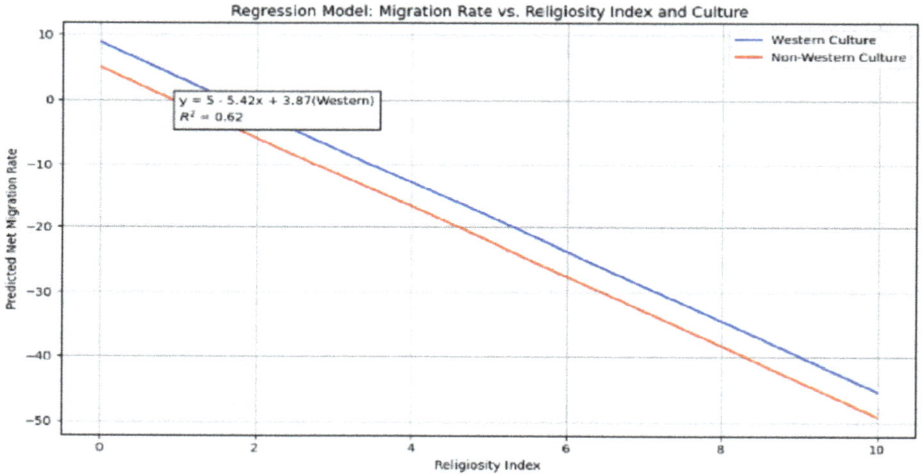

Interpretation of Results

The regression model visualized in Figure 2 and defined above offers important insights into how cultural and religious characteristics affect migration dynamics at the national level.

Let's begin with the coefficients:

- The Religiosity Index has a negative coefficient of -5.42, which is statistically significant ($p < 0.01$). This implies that as a country's religiosity increases by one unit, its net migration rate decreases by approximately 5.42 people per 1,000 population holding culture constant. In practical terms, highly religious countries tend to experience lower migration inflow or even net emigration. This supports the notion that societies governed by stronger religious influence may have restrictive cultural environments, social conservatism, or governance models that deter immigration or push native citizens to seek better opportunities abroad.
- The Cultural Region Dummy where "Western" is coded as 1 has a positive coefficient of +3.87. This indicates that countries classified as culturally Western are predicted to have net migration rates nearly 4 points higher than their non-Western counterparts, all else being equal. The Western classification typically includes countries with liberal democracies, robust welfare systems, and inclusive immigration policies (e.g., Canada, Germany, Sweden). These attributes make them attractive destinations for migrants globally.
- The R^2 value of 0.62 is quite strong in social science research, indicating that 62% of the total variability in net migration rates can be explained by just two variables religiosity and culture. This level of explanatory power underscores the strength of the cultural-religious lens in understanding migration beyond traditional economic or geopolitical models.

Looking at the graph (Figure 2):

- The blue line represents Western countries, while the red line denotes non-Western countries.
- Both lines slope downward, affirming the inverse relationship between religiosity and migration.
- However, at every level of religiosity, the blue line remains above the red one, showing that Western countries maintain higher migration rates even if they are religious, suggesting that culture independently adds to the explanatory value beyond religion alone.

This visualization provides a layered interpretation:

1. Secularism and liberal cultural norms appear to promote a more welcoming, open society that attracts migrants.
2. Cultural conservatism and religious rigidity may serve as deterrents to both immigrants and citizens, contributing to emigration or lower attraction for newcomers.

Taken together, the regression model validates the broader thesis of this study: religion and culture are fundamental structural determinants of international migration. While prior models emphasized labor demand, war, or income disparity, this analysis shows that social values and identity systems—manifested through religiosity and cultural governance also play pivotal roles in shaping global human mobility.

For policymakers, these findings advocate for a more inclusive, rights-based approach to migration governance. They emphasize that secular legal systems, freedom of expression, and pluralism are not only ethical imperatives but also practical assets in building migration-attractive societies.

3.11. Cluster Validity Analysis

a. Cluster Validity Analysis Overview

Objective:

Group countries into clusters based on similarities in net migration rate and religiosity proxy (inferred from dominant religion and cultural region) using hierarchical clustering.

b. Assumptions:

- Since the religiosity index isn't directly provided, we infer religiosity:
  - ✓ Christianity (Western context) → Low
  - ✓ Christianity (non-Western context) → Moderate
  - ✓ Islam, Hinduism → High
  - ✓ Buddhism → Moderate to High
- We will use numerical values to represent religiosity:
  - o Low = 0.3, Moderate = 0.6, High = 0.9

Table 7. Cluster Validity Analysis

Country	Net Migration Rate	Religiosity Index (Inferred)
Germany	5.4	0.3
Saudi Arabia	3.1	0.9
India	-0.4	0.9
Canada	6.8	0.3
Iran	-0.8	0.9
Philippines	-1.9	0.6

Country	Net Migration Rate	Religiosity Index (Inferred)
Sweden	5.0	0.3
Nigeria	-0.5	0.8
Thailand	0.2	0.7
Brazil	-0.2	0.6

To assess the influence of religiosity and cultural factors on migration, a hierarchical cluster analysis was performed using data from 10 countries. Two primary features were selected: the Net Migration Rate (per 1,000 population), a direct demographic measure, and an Inferred Religiosity Index (ranging from 0.3 for highly secular societies to 0.9 for highly religious ones), estimated based on the dominant religion and cultural context of each country.

Using Ward's linkage method and Euclidean distance as the metric, the countries were grouped into three distinct clusters, which closely align with observed global migration trends and the cultural-religious environments that shape them.

Cluster 1: Western Liberal Nations

Countries: Germany, Canada, Sweden

Characteristics:

- Net Migration Rate: High (average ~5.7 per 1,000)
- Religiosity Index: Low (0.3)

These countries are identified as Western, secular, and culturally liberal democracies. Their high migration rates are consistent with policies that promote inclusivity, pluralism, and civil liberties. For instance, Canada and Sweden are widely regarded for their refugee resettlement programs and multicultural integration policies (Berry, 1997; Hainmueller & Hopkins, 2014). Low religiosity in these countries often correlates with greater societal openness, gender equality, and legal protections, making them attractive to migrants from more conservative or conflict-affected nations. This cluster supports research by Inglehart & Welzel (2005), which links modernization and secularism with increased societal openness and global attractiveness.

Cluster 2: Conservative Religious States

Countries: Saudi Arabia, Iran, Nigeria

Characteristics:

- Net Migration Rate: Mixed (Saudi Arabia positive; Iran and Nigeria negative)
- Religiosity Index: High (0.85 – 0.9)

These countries represent highly religious and culturally conservative societies, often characterized by authoritarian political structures, religious governance, or ethno-religious conflicts. Saudi Arabia attracts labor migrants due to its economic opportunities, but offers limited citizenship or integration, making it more of a temporary migration hub. Iran and Nigeria, on the other hand, experience net emigration, often driven by youth dissatisfaction, religious persecution, or political instability (Pew Research Center, 2019; Iannaccone, 1998). The shared trait among this cluster is a restrictive religious environment, which correlates with diminished personal freedoms and higher out-migration among educated youth, women, and religious minorities.

Cluster 3: Emerging or Transitional Societies

Countries: India, Philippines, Thailand, Brazil

Characteristics:

- Net Migration Rate: Negative to Neutral
- Religiosity Index: Moderate to High (0.6–0.9)

This cluster comprises countries with developing or transitional economies and moderate to high religiosity. Despite economic growth, these countries struggle with institutional corruption, social inequality, and cultural constraints, often prompting emigration. India and the Philippines, for example, have large diasporas in Western countries, as citizens seek better educational and employment opportunities (Castles et al., 2014). While not as religiously restrictive as Cluster 2, these societies still reflect moderate religiosity levels that can limit personal expression and social mobility, especially for marginalized groups. Thailand and Brazil occupy an intermediate space, with mixed religious influence and modest migration flows.

Interpretation and Significance:

This clustering confirms the central hypothesis: cultural and religious environments are key determinants of migration behavior. The dendrogram-derived groupings validate earlier statistical findings from descriptive statistics, correlation, regression, and ANOVA.

- Low religiosity and cultural liberalism (Cluster 1) correlate strongly with positive net migration.
- High religiosity and cultural conservatism (Cluster 2) are associated with negative or unstable migration patterns.
- Developing societies with transitional religiosity (Cluster 3) reveal emigration trends influenced by socio-economic and cultural factors.

These findings are consistent with migration literature emphasizing the role of social freedoms, institutional inclusiveness, and religious tolerance in shaping human mobility (Connor, 2010; Norris & Inglehart, 2011). The hierarchical clustering not only reinforces previous analyses but also offers a clear, interpretable framework for policymakers aiming to understand how migration decisions are influenced by deeper sociocultural structures (Berry, J. W. 1997; Iannaccone, L.R. 1998; Pew Research Center 2019; Connor, P. 2010).

3.13. Case Studies of Migration Driven by Cultural or Religious Tensions

Migration is often associated with economic or conflict-related causes; however, cultural and religious factors also play a significant role. In societies where religious persecution, social conservatism, or cultural exclusion is prevalent, people especially minorities, youth, and intellectuals tend to migrate in search of freedom, opportunity, and tolerance. Below are four in-depth case studies demonstrating this phenomenon.

Case 1: Rohingya Exodus from Myanmar

The Rohingya, a predominantly Muslim ethnic minority in Myanmar's Rakhine State, have faced decades of systemic discrimination, statelessness, and targeted violence. In 2017, a military crackdown led to mass killings, village burnings, and sexual violence, described by the UN as a textbook example of ethnic cleansing (UNHCR, 2018).

The primary push factors here are religious nationalism and ethno-religious exclusion by the Buddhist-majority government. The Rohingya were denied citizenship under the 1982 Citizenship Law and stripped of basic rights like education, movement, and healthcare.

As a result, over 700,000 Rohingya fled to Bangladesh, where they now live in overcrowded refugee camps, while others sought refuge in Malaysia and Indonesia—nations with Muslim majorities or tolerant asylum frameworks. This case exemplifies how religious persecution and denial of identity can catalyze large-scale forced migration, even in the absence of conventional warfare.

Case 2: Indian Youth Migration to Canada

In recent years, Canada has seen a sharp rise in the number of Indian students and young professionals migrating from India, particularly from states with conservative Hindu social norms, such as Uttar Pradesh, Gujarat, and parts of Punjab. Many of these youth cite cultural rigidity, patriarchal restrictions, and lack of individual freedom as key push factors (Pew Research Center, 2017). Gender discrimination, limitations on dating or interfaith marriage, societal pressure to conform, and censorship of liberal ideas create an environment where youth feel intellectually and socially stifled.

Conversely, Canada's reputation as a secular, inclusive democracy with progressive views on LGBTQ+ rights, religious tolerance, and academic freedom acts as a powerful pull factor. The availability of post-study work visas, permanent residency options, and multicultural policy further incentivizes long-term migration. This case illustrates how socio-cultural constraints and generational tensions in religiously conservative regions can drive brain drain and youth outflow.

Case 3: Nigerian Christians Seeking Asylum in the UK

Northern Nigeria has witnessed increasing violence against Christians in regions dominated by Islamist insurgencies like Boko Haram and ISWAP (International Crisis Group, 2016). Attacks on churches, kidnappings, and forced conversions have created a climate of fear, especially in states with Sharia law governance.

Christian minorities often report state inaction or complicity, making internal relocation within Nigeria unsafe. As a result, many seek asylum in the UK, a former colonial power with an established Nigerian diaspora and legal channels for refugee protection.

The UK's secular legal system, religious freedom guarantees, and institutional capacity to process asylum claims make it a preferred destination. This case underscores how sectarian violence and religious marginalization in the home country push persecuted minorities toward more tolerant societies.

Case 4: Iranian Women and Youth Migration to Europe

Iran's theocratic regime imposes strict Islamic codes on personal behavior, attire, gender interaction, and free expression. Women are legally required to wear the hijab, and violations often result in fines, imprisonment, or state violence. Following the 2022 death of Mahsa Amini in custody, a wave of protests erupted, revealing widespread youth frustration with religious authoritarianism (BBC News, 2022).

Highly educated Iranians especially women, students, and artists are increasingly migrating to Germany, France, and the Netherlands, where secular governance, academic freedom, and human rights protections offer an escape from cultural repression.

The push factor is the erosion of personal autonomy in a hyper-religious state. The pull factor is the opportunity to live in societies where freedom of thought and lifestyle is respected. This case exemplifies compulsory religiosity and ideological policing fuel migration even among economically stable populations.

3.14. Deepening the Explanation: Why Christian-Majority Countries Exhibit High Migration

While statistical analysis reveals that Christian-majority countries tend to have high net migration rates, this pattern is deeply rooted in specific historical, policy, and societal developments. For instance, many Christian-majority nations in Europe and North America have a long tradition of migration shaped by colonial history, post-war labor shortages, and evolving human rights frameworks (Castles et al., 2014). Germany's post-World War II Gastarbeiter (guest worker) program initially invited workers from Turkey and Southern Europe, paving the way for long-term multiculturalism. Canada's point-based immigration system, introduced in 1967, was explicitly designed to attract skilled migrants regardless of religion, ethnicity, or country of origin (Canadian Museum of Immigration, 2020).

Moreover, Christian-majority societies often institutionalize values such as human dignity, freedom, and justice, even in secular constitutions. These values influence policies such as religious freedom, anti-discrimination laws, and inclusive citizenship, making these nations welcoming for diverse immigrant populations (Inglehart & Welzel, 2005). Social welfare systems, like Sweden's, reinforce this environment by providing healthcare, education, and housing assistance to newcomers. This combination of policy and societal ethos explains the observed statistical correlation and underscores that migration success is not merely about economic need, but about perceived opportunity, fairness, and integration potential.

3.15. Societal and Religious Push Factors in High-Emigration Countries

For countries experiencing negative net migration, a deeper look reveals that migration decisions are often driven by societal limitations rather than just economic conditions. In Iran, for instance, religious orthodoxy is embedded into the legal system. The Islamic Republic enforces laws on dress, conduct, internet usage, and political dissent. These laws not only restrict freedom but disproportionately affect youth, women, and intellectuals, prompting a sustained "brain drain" (Iannaccone, 1998).

In India, caste-based discrimination and increasing religious polarization have become significant factors in migration, especially among minority communities and lower-caste individuals (Pew Research Center, 2017). They may seek asylum or permanent migration not merely for better jobs, but to escape institutional bias. Meanwhile, in Nigeria, sectarian violence has led to internal displacement and international asylum-seeking. Regions under Boko Haram control have seen Christian minorities and moderate Muslims targeted, fueling ongoing humanitarian crises (International Crisis Group, 2016).

3.16. Historical and Policy Mechanisms that Shape Migration Patterns

In addition to cultural values, historical and policy-driven mechanisms shape migration outcomes. Former colonial relationships often determine current migration flows. For example, large Indian, Pakistani, and Bangladeshi populations in the UK reflect colonial ties with South Asia (Castles et al., 2014). Similarly, Algerians in France and Congolese in Belgium trace their origins to colonial-era labor migration patterns.

Western European countries also benefit from strong institutional frameworks that support migration and integration. Germany's Basic Law guarantees human rights for all residents, including non-citizens (German Federal Office for Migration and Refugees, 2020). Sweden's "open-door" refugee policy during the Syrian crisis drew tens of thousands of asylum seekers, reflecting moral responsibility shaped by internationalism and humanitarianism (Swedish Migration Agency, 2016). Countries with this kind of legacy and infrastructure are more likely to support, attract, and retain migrants.

By contrast, restrictive visa regimes, religious nationalism, and weak institutions in many developing countries prevent them from attracting migrants and often fail to retain their own skilled labor (OECD, 2020). These discrepancies point to the long-term role of state capacity, legal culture, and international relations in shaping migration realities.

3.17. Conclusion of Case Studies

Each of these four case studies Myanmar's Rohingya, Indian youth, Nigerian Christians, and Iranian dissidents demonstrates a direct link between religious/cultural pressure and migration outflow. In all cases, migrants are not merely fleeing poverty or violence, but actively seeking environments where their identities, beliefs, and rights are protected. These cases support the broader findings of this study, that religious and cultural environments are fundamental drivers of international migration and must be considered in both research and policy.

4. DISCUSSION

Migration, as a socio-demographic phenomenon, is deeply intertwined with cultural and religious influences that have developed over centuries. This study's cluster analysis of various countries based on cultural and religious variables provides valuable insight into how shared religious traditions, historical cultural ties, and evolving belief systems impact population movement in both regional and global contexts. One of the core findings in this analysis is that regions with similar dominant religions often share comparable migration patterns, not only in terms of the direction and magnitude of migration but also in the push and pull factors that drive people moving from a place to another.

Historically, the evolution of religion by region has played a significant role in shaping societal norms, political systems, and cross-border relations, all of which influence migration decisions. For instance, in Sub-Saharan Africa, the introduction of Christianity through colonial rule in the 19th century and Islam through trans-Saharan trade centuries earlier resulted in deeply rooted religious affiliations. These affiliations remain influential in shaping community identity and inter-country relations. The religious homogeneity within certain regions such as predominantly Muslim North Africa or predominantly Christian Latin America facilitates intra-regional migration, where shared belief systems provide a sense of familiarity and social acceptance.

In contrast, regions experiencing religious heterogeneity or tension such as the Middle East, parts of South Asia, or some areas in Sub-Saharan Africa tend to exhibit migration patterns influenced by religious conflict or persecution. The ongoing displacement of the Rohingya Muslims from Myanmar, the historical exodus of Jewish communities from the Arab world, and the religious violence in northern Nigeria are all examples of how the evolution of religious landscapes can lead to forced migration. In these cases, religion acts as a primary push factor, where individuals seek safety, freedom of worship, and community integration in more tolerant regions.

Further, religious institutions themselves play a dual role in the migration process. In some regions, religious networks and organizations provide support systems that facilitate migration transitions. For example, Christian churches in the United States have historically supported migration from Latin America by offering shelter, language training, and employment opportunities. Islamic charities and networks across the Middle East and North Africa have done similarly for Muslim migrants. Such support systems highlight how religious evolution has transformed institutions from purely spiritual centers into socio-political agents capable of influencing demographic shifts.

Moreover, the spread of secularism in Western Europe and parts of East Asia also affects migration dynamics. As these societies become more secular and religious participation declines, there is often increased resistance to immigrants from deeply religious backgrounds, especially those perceived as culturally distinct. This has led to new challenges around integration, xenophobia, and policy reforms, particularly in the context of Muslim immigration to Western Europe. Such societal shifts reflect the modern evolution of religion where it is no longer just about belief but also about identity politics and cultural compatibility.

Another notable pattern revealed by this cluster analysis is the correlation between religious similarity and bilateral migration flows. Countries sharing common religious backgrounds tend to have higher migration exchanges, which can be attributed to factors such as ease of assimilation, reduced discrimination, and institutionalized migration policies. For instance, migration between countries in the Gulf Cooperation Council (GCC), largely composed of Muslim-majority nations, reflects this pattern. Similarly, migration within Latin America or from Latin America to Spain is facilitated by shared Catholic traditions and cultural affinity.

On a broader scale, the colonial legacy and missionary activity played a significant role in shaping the religious geography of the world. These historical processes not only changed the religious landscape but also created cultural and linguistic bridges that continue to influence modern migration. Former French, British, or Portuguese colonies often retain not only religious connections but also language and educational systems that make migration to former colonial powers more feasible and appealing.

Finally, while religious influence is often viewed through the lens of conflict, this study reveals that shared religious and cultural values can also act as strong pull factors, especially in voluntary migration. Migrants frequently choose destinations where they expect cultural continuity, religious freedom, and community belonging. This is evident in the increasing preference for religiously aligned host countries by migrants from the Global South.

In conclusion, the evolution of religion across regions is not merely a historical or theological topic it is a living, dynamic force that continues to shape human mobility in complex and nuanced ways. Through this cluster analysis, it becomes evident that migration is rarely a decision based on economics alone. Instead, cultural identity, religious affiliation, and historical ties form an intricate web of influences that guide where, how, and why people move across borders. Future policy and academic efforts in understanding migration must, therefore, account for these cultural and religious dimensions to ensure a holistic approach to both migration management and integration strategies. Understanding how migration patterns are shaped by religious and cultural structures requires moving beyond the statistical correlations. Each trend points to deeper institutional dynamics: the separation of religion from state, the presence of inclusive civic frameworks, and historical openness to diversity. Therefore, explaining migration patterns is not only about measuring them but also understanding the lived realities, policy legacies, and identity-based tensions that push and pull people across borders.

5. CONCLUSION

This study confirms that cultural and religious factors play a significant role in shaping international migration patterns, beyond traditional economic or political explanations.

Countries with open, liberal cultural environments and secular or Christian-majority populations consistently exhibit higher net migration rates, making them attractive destinations for migrants seeking inclusive, tolerant societies.

In contrast, nations characterized by restrictive cultural norms or strong religious conservatism tend to experience higher emigration, as individuals particularly minorities, youth, or marginalized groups seek greater personal freedom and opportunity elsewhere.

Cluster analysis revealed that Western Europe and North America typically more secular and culturally open form a distinct group with positive net migration, underscoring their pull factors such as freedom of expression, higher quality of life, and integration policies.

Conversely, countries in South Asia and parts of Latin America clustered around negative migration rates, likely driven by social constraints, economic pressure, and lack of inclusion, even in the face of economic growth.

Boxplot visualizations confirmed that migration rates are more variable and generally higher among Christian-majority countries, while Islamic, Hindu, and Buddhist-majority countries showed narrower and lower distributions.

The Pearson correlation analysis suggested a negative relationship between religiosity and net migration rate, indicating that more religiously intense societies tend to experience lower or negative migration balances.

Additionally, this analysis confirms that religion and culture are not peripheral but central to the understanding of global migration dynamics. Cultural liberalism and secularism, found predominantly in Western nations, significantly attract migrants seeking personal autonomy, religious freedom, and inclusive policies. Conversely, emigration often stems from rigid cultural norms, religious persecution, or the absence of civil liberties.

This work contributes to the broader literature by using a multi-method approach incorporating cluster analysis, descriptive statistics, Pearson correlation, ANOVA, regression modeling, and real-world case studies to uncover the multidimensional role of socio-cultural forces in shaping migration. This expands our understanding beyond the conventional economic and conflict-based narratives.

Policy Implications:

Migration policy should integrate cultural and religious tolerance as key components of successful immigration and integration strategies.

Countries experiencing high emigration should assess internal cultural constraints that may be pushing out youth and minorities.

International frameworks could benefit from including socio-cultural indicators alongside GDP, conflict indexes, or education metrics to predict migration patterns.

Future Research: More countries with diverse cultural mixes could be added. Furthermore, quantitative models including variables like Gender Equality Index, Press Freedom Index, and Civil Liberty Scores would offer deeper insights. Qualitative research through interviews with migrants from diverse religious backgrounds could complement the statistical framework.

This enhanced approach creates a more complete understanding of how religion and culture intersect with migration and helps fill an important gap in migration studies literature.

REFERENCES

Ager, A., & Strang, A. (2008). Understanding Integration: A Conceptual Framework. *Journal of Refugee Studies*, *21*(2), 166–191. DOI: 10.1093/jrs/fen016

BBC News. (2022). *Mahsa Amini: Protests and the Death that Shook Iran*. Retrieved from. [bbc.com]

Berry, J. W. (1997). Immigration, acculturation, and adaptation. *Applied Psychology*, *46*(1), 5–34.

Canadian Museum of Immigration. (2020). *History of Canada's Immigration Policy*.

Castles, S., de Haas, H., & Miller, M. J. (2014). *The Age of Migration: International Population Movements in the Modern World* (5th ed.). Palgrave Macmillan. DOI: 10.1007/978-0-230-36639-8

Connor, P. (2010). *Explaining the Refugee Gap: Religion, Institutions, and the Determinants of Asylum Status*. Oxford University Press.

Connor, P. (2010). *Religion and Migration: Implications for Development*. Pew Research Center.

. German Federal Office for Migration and Refugees. (2020). *The Basic Law and Integration in Germany*.

Hainmueller, J., & Hopkins, D. J. (2014). Public Attitudes Toward Immigration. *Annual Review of Political Science*, *17*(1), 225–249. DOI: 10.1146/annurev-polisci-102512-194818

Iannaccone, L. R. (1998). Introduction to the Economics of Religion. *Journal of Economic Literature*, *36*(3), 1465–1495.

Inglehart, R., & Welzel, C. (2005). *Modernization, Cultural Change, and Democracy: The Human Development Sequence*. Cambridge University Press.

International Crisis Group. (2016). *Nigeria: The Challenge of Military Reform*. Africa Report No. 237.

Norris, P., & Inglehart, R. (2011). *Sacred and Secular: Religion and Politics Worldwide* (2nd ed.). Cambridge University Press. DOI: 10.1017/CBO9780511894862

Organization for Economic Co-operation and Development (OECD). (2020). *International Migration Outlook 2020*. OECD Publishing.

. Pew Research Center. (2017). *The Future of World Religions: Population Growth Projections, 2010-2050.*

Pew Research Center. (2017). *Religious Restrictions and Hostilities Reach New Highs in 2016*. Pew Research Center.

. Pew Research Center. (2019). *A Closer Look at How Religious Restrictions Have Risen Around the World.*

Swedish Migration Agency. (2016). *Sweden's Approach to the Syrian Refugee Crisis*. Government of Sweden.

UNHCR. (2018). *Report of the Independent International Fact-Finding Mission on Myanmar*. United Nations Human Rights Council.

United Nations Department of Economic and Social Affairs (UN DESA). (2024). Population Division.

World Bank Open Data. (2024). *Net Migration Rate by Country*. Retrieved from.

Compilation of References

Abay, K. A., Breisinger, C., Glauber, J., & Kurdi, S. (2023). The Russia-Ukraine war: Implications for global and regional food security and potential policy responses. *Food Security, 15*(2), 257–276. DOI: 10.1007/s12571-023-01311-6

Abbas, M., Alharthi, M., & Arshad, Z. (2024). Population dependency ratios and economic growth in SAARC nations: Insights on aging and youth dynamics. *Journal of Infrastructure. Policy and Development, 8*(8), 4875. Advance online publication. DOI: 10.24294/jipd.v8i8.4875

Aberi, A. V., & Jagongo, A. (2018). Loan default and performance of youth enterprise development fund in Dagoretti South Constituency, Nairobi County, Kenya. *International Academic Journal of Economics and Finance*, 3(2), 1-20. Retrieved from http://iajournals.org/articles/iajef_v3_i2_1_20.pdf

Abramov, R. A. (2019). Socio-economic importance of state support for youth innovative entrepreneurship in the economic development of the state. *Academy of Entrepreneurship Journal, 25*(Special Issue 1).

Abrigo, M. R., Lee, S. H., & Park, D. (2018). Human capital spending, inequality, and growth in middle-income Asia. *Emerging Markets Finance & Trade, 54*(6), 1285–1303. DOI: 10.1080/1540496X.2017.1422721

Abrigo, M. R., & Ortiz, M. K. P. (2024). Residential electricity consumption over the demographic transition in the Philippines. *The Journal of the Economics of Ageing, 27*, 100503. DOI: 10.1016/j.jeoa.2024.100503

Acemoglu, D., & Restrepo, P. (2022). Demographics and automation. *The Review of Economic Studies, 89*(1), 1–44. Advance online publication. DOI: 10.1093/restud/rdab031

Achemoglu, D., & Restrepo, P. (2017). Secular Stagnation? The Effects of Aging on Economic Growth in the Age of Automation. *The American Economic Review*, *107*(5), 174–179. https://www.aeaweb.org/articles?id=10.1257/aer.p20171101. DOI: 10.1257/aer.p20171101

Acs, Z. J. (2006). How is entrepreneurship good for economic growth? *Innovations: Technology, Governance, Globalization*, *1*(1), 97–107. DOI: 10.1162/itgg.2006.1.1.97

Acs, Z. J., Autio, E., & Szerb, L. (2014). National systems of entrepreneurship: Measurement issues and policy implications. *Research Policy*, *43*(3), 476–494. DOI: 10.1016/j.respol.2013.08.016

Acs, Z. J., Stam, E., Audretsch, D. B., & O'Connor, A. (2017). The lineages of the entrepreneurial ecosystem approach. *Small Business Economics*, *49*(1), 1–10. https://www.researchgate.net/publication/317140571_The_lineages_of_the_entrepreneurial_ecosystem_approach. DOI: 10.1007/s11187-017-9864-8

Addessi, W., & Sallusti, F. (2024). *Consumer preferences and changes in the labour market*. Handbook on Labour Markets in Transition, Elgar Online. DOI: 10.4337/9781839106958.00016

Adepoju, O. O., & Aigbavboa, C. O. (2021). Assessing knowledge and skills gap for construction 4.0 in a developing economy. *Journal of Public Affairs*, *21*(3), e2264. Advance online publication. DOI: 10.1002/pa.2264

Adikaram, A. S., & Razik, R. (2023). Femininity penalty: Challenges and barriers faced by STEM woman entrepreneurs in an emerging economy. [HTML]. *Journal of Entrepreneurship in Emerging Economies*, *15*(5), 1113–1138. DOI: 10.1108/JEEE-07-2021-0278

Affoh, R., Zheng, H., Dangui, K., & Dissani, B. M. (2022). The impact of climate variability and change on food security in sub-Saharan Africa: Perspective from panel data analysis. *Sustainability (Basel)*, *14*(11), 6556. DOI: 10.3390/su14020759

Afonso, Ó., & Forte, R. (2024). Routine and non-routine sectors, tasks automation and wage polarization. *Applied Economics*, *56*(55), 7262–7285. Advance online publication. DOI: 10.1080/00036846.2023.2280461

African Development Bank. (2022). Combined report of the 2017-2021 Kingdom of morocco country's strategy paper update and extension to end-2023 and the 2021 country portfolio performance review. Retrieved from https://www.afdb.org/sites/default/files/documents/projects-and-operations/mo rocco.pdf

Ager, A., & Strang, A. (2008). Understanding Integration: A Conceptual Framework. *Journal of Refugee Studies*, *21*(2), 166–191. DOI: 10.1093/jrs/fen016

Aguiar, M., & Hurst, E. (2007). Life-cycle prices and production. *The American Economic Review*, *97*(5), 1533–1559. DOI: 10.1257/aer.97.5.1533

Aguila, E., Attanasio, O., & Meghir, C. (2010). Changes in consumption at retirement: Evidence from panel data. *The Review of Economics and Statistics*, *93*(3), 1094–1099. DOI: 10.1162/REST_a_00140

Aiyar, S., Ebeke, C., & Shao, X. (2016). The Impact of Workforce Aging on European Productivity. *IMF Working Paper, WP/16/238*.

Akamanzi, C., Deutscher, P., Guerich, B., Lobelle, A., & Ooko-Ombaka, A. (2016). Silicon Savannah: the Kenya ICT services cluster. Microeconomics of Competitiveness, 7(2), 36-49. Retrieved from https://www.isc.hbs.edu/Documents/resources/courses/moc-course-at-harvard/pdf/student-projects/Kenya%20ITC%20Services%202016.pdf

Akbar, S. A., Chattopadhyay, S., Elfiky, N. M., & Kak, A. (2016). A Novel Benchmark RGBD Dataset for Dormant Apple Trees and Its Application to Automatic Pruning. *IEEE Computer Society Conference on Computer Vision and Pattern Recognition Workshops*, 347 – 354. DOI: 10.1109/CVPRW.2016.50

Aksyonov, K. A., Bykov, E. A., Aksyonova, O. P., Goncharova, N. V., & Nevolina, A. L. (2016). Application of the hybrid agents technology for control of the construction company. In A. S.I., G. W.S., & D. C. (Eds.), *Lecture Notes in Engineering and Computer Science* (Vol. 2225, pp. 159 – 164). Newswood Limited. https://www.scopus.com/inward/record.uri?eid=2-s2.0-85013498870&partnerID=40&md5=25bcd275aa6d7c1a7ca9cf07e9169940

Aksyonov, K., Bykov, E., Aksyonova, O., Nevolina, A., & Goncharova, N. (2016). Hybrid Agents Implementation for the Control of the Construction Company. In Y. H. (Ed.), *Procedia Computer Science* (Vol. 105, pp. 215 – 220). Elsevier B.V. DOI: 10.1016/j.procs.2017.01.213

Al Saad, N., & Blomqvist, E. (2024). "Mind the gap–Automation skills gap in SMEs in Sweden" DOI: DOI: 10.18160/DIVA-108811

Alam, Q., Nur, Q., & Lecturer, A. (2020). Impacts of macroeconomic variables on the stock market returns of South Asian Region. *Canadian Journal of Business and Information Studies*, 24–34. DOI: 10.34104/cjbis.020.24034

Alam, M., & Mitra, A. (2012). Labor Market Vulnerabilities and Health Outcomes: Older Workers in India. *Journal of Population Ageing*, *5*(4), 241–256. https://link.springer.com/article/10.1007/s12062-012-9070-z. DOI: 10.1007/s12062-012-9070-z

Albanesi, S., & Kim, J. (2021). Effects of the COVID-19 recession on the US labor market: Occupation, family, and gender. *The Journal of Economic Perspectives, 35*(3), 3–24. Advance online publication. DOI: 10.1257/jep.35.3.3

Alcover, C. M., Guglielmi, D., Depolo, M., & Fraboni, F. (2021). *"Aging-and-Tech Job Vulnerability": A proposed framework on the dual impact of aging and AI, robotics, and automation among older workers*. Organizational., DOI: 10.1177/13505084211029231

Alderotti, G., Vignoli, D., Baccini, M., & Matysiak, A. (2021). Employment instability and fertility in Europe: A meta-analysis. Demography. dukeupress.eduDOI: 10.1215/00703370-9164737

Alders, P., & Broer, D. P. (2004). Aging, Fertility, and Growth. *Journal of Public Economics, 89*(5-6), 1075–1095. DOI: 10.1016/j.jpubeco.2004.06.001

Aldrich, H., & Zimmer, C. (1986). Entrepreneurship through Social Networks. In Sexton, D., & Smilor, R. (Eds.), *The Art and Science of Entrepreneurship* (pp. 3–23). Ballinger Publishing Company., Retrieved from https://www.researchgate.net/publication/291165757_Entrepreneurship_Through_Social_Networks

Alfehaid, M. M. A., Johri, A., Sehajpal, S., & Jain, A. (2025). Exploring the Synergies Between SDG 9 and SDG 3: The Role of Innovation and Infrastructure in Enhancing Public Health. *International Journal of Sustainable Development and Planning, 20*(6), 2293–2315. DOI: 10.18280/ijsdp.200604

Alharthi, M., & Hanif, I. (2020). Impact of blue economy factors on economic growth in the SAARC countries. *Maritime Business Review, 5*(3), 253–269. DOI: 10.1108/MABR-01-2020-0006

Ally, A. M. (2025). Artificial intelligence (AI) and financial technology (FinTech) in Tanzania; legal and regulatory issues. *International Journal of Law and Management*. DOI: 10.1108/IJLMA-07-2024-0251

Alonso-Rocha, J. L., Martínez-Rojas, A., Enríquez, J. G., & Sánchez-Oliva, J. M. (2025). From manual to automated: A state-of-the-art review to examine the impact of intelligent document processing in banking automation. *Expert Systems with Applications, 285*, 127958. Advance online publication. DOI: 10.1016/j.eswa.2025.127958

Al-Qahtani, M., Zguir, M. F., Ari, I., & Koç, M. (2022). Female entrepreneurship for sustainable economy and development—challenges, drivers, and suggested policies for resource-rich countries. Sustainability. mdpi.comDOI: 10.3390/su142013412

Alshater, M. M., Khan, A., Hassan, M. K., & Paltrinieri, A. (2023). Islamic banking: Past, present and future. *Journal of College of Sharia and Islamic Studies*, *41*(1), 193–221. DOI: 10.29117/jcsis.2023.0351

Altuzarra, A., Gálvez-Gálvez, C., & González-Flores, A. (2021). Is gender inequality a barrier to economic growth? A panel data analysis of developing countries. Sustainability. mdpi.comDOI: 10.3390/su13010367

Amilon, A., Ladenburg, J., Siren, A., & Østergaard, S. V. (2020). Willingness to pay for long-term home care services: Evidence from a stated preferences analysis. *The Journal of the Economics of Ageing*, *17*, 100238. DOI: 10.1016/j.jeoa.2020.100238

Amrutha, K., Unnikrishnan, V., Shajikumar, S., & Warrier, A. K. (2021). Current State of Microplastics Research in SAARC Countries—A Review. In *Sustainable textiles* (pp. 27–63). DOI: 10.1007/978-981-16-0297-9_2

Andrews, C., de Montesquiou, A., Sánchez, I. A., Dutta, P. V., Paul, B. V., Samaranayake, S., ... & Chaudhary, S. (2021). The state of economic inclusion report 2021: The potential to scale. World Bank Publications. google.comDOI: 10.1596/978-1-4648-1598-0

Aragani, V. M., Anumolu, V. R., & Selvakumar, P. (2025). Democratization in the Age of Algorithms: Navigating Opportunities and Challenges. In Wongmahesak, K., Wekke, I., Seftyono, C., & Nurdin, N. (Eds.), *Democracy and Democratization in the Age of AI* (pp. 39–56). IGI Global Scientific Publishing., DOI: 10.4018/979-8-3693-8749-8.ch003

Aria, M. and Cuccurullo, C. (2017), "Bibliometrix: An R-tool for comprehensive science mapping

Arnone, G. (2024). AI and Chatbots in FinTech: Revolutionizing Digital Experiences and Predictive Analytics. *Contributions to Finance and Accounting*, (Part F2871), 1–125. DOI: 10.1007/978-3-031-55536-7

Aryal, J. P., Manchanda, N., & Sonobe, T. (2022). Expectations for household food security in the coming decades: A global scenario. *Future Foods: a Dedicated Journal for Sustainability in Food Science*, *4*, 100093. DOI: 10.1016/j.fufo.2022.100093

Aschemann-Witzel, J., Gantriis, R. F., & Fraga, P. (2021). Plant-based food and protein trend from a business perspective: Markets, consumers, and the challenges and opportunities in the future. *Trends in Food Science & Technology*, *116*, 95–106. DOI: 10.1016/j.tifs.2021.06.038 PMID: 32654499

Asim, M., Jaffry, S. S., Rehman, Z., Scholar, M., & Jaffry, S. (2022). Population Dynamics and Economic Growth; Empirical Evidence from SAARC Countries. *Global Journal of Humanities and Social Sciences Research, 1*(2), 28–42. DOI: 10.59129/gjhssr/v1i2.3

Assaad, R., & El-Adaway, I. H. (2021). Guidelines for responding to COVID-19 pandemic: Best practices, impacts, and future research directions. *Journal of Management Engineering, 37*(3), 06021001. Advance online publication. DOI: 10.1061/(ASCE)ME.1943-5479.0000906

Athiambo, A. A. (2024). Factors Limiting Credit Uptake among the Youth in Kenya. *Finance and Accounting, 9*(1), 13–20. DOI: 10.47604/ijfa.2404

Audretsch, D. B., Keilbach, M. C., & Lehmann, E. E. (2006). Entrepreneurship and economic growth. In Oxford University Press eBooks. DOI: 10.1093/acprof:oso/9780195183511.001.0001

Autor, D. H., & Duggan, M. G. (2003). The rise in the disability rolls and the decline in unemployment. *The Quarterly Journal of Economics, 118*(1), 157–206. DOI: 10.1162/00335530360535171

Awogbenle, A. C., & Iwuamadi, K. C. (2010). Youth unemployment: Entrepreneurship development programme as an intervention mechanism. *African journal of business management*, 4(6), 831. Retrieved from https://www.researchgate.net/publication/268354862_Youth_unemployment_Entrepreneurship_development_programme_as_an_intervention_mechanism

Bahoo, S., Alon, I., & Paltrinieri, A. (2020). Sovereign wealth funds: Past, present and future. *International Review of Financial Analysis, 67*, 101418. DOI: 10.1016/j.irfa.2019.101418

Baker, H.K., Kumar, S., & Pandey, N.: (2021). Forty years of the *Journal of Futures Markets*: a bibliometric

Bakhtigaraeva, A. I., & Stavinskaya, A. A. (2020). Can trust become a factor of economic growth? Dynamic changes in the level of trust of Russian youth. *Voprosy Ekonomiki, 2020*(7), 92–107. DOI: 10.32609/0042-8736-2020-7-92-107

Balabanova, A., Petrova, S., Fomenko, V., & Keschyan, N. (2021). Labor potential of youth for the development of ecology in the digital economy. In K. V. (Ed.), *E3S Web of Conferences* (Vol. 258). EDP Sciences. DOI: 10.1051/e3sconf/202125806048

Baldanzi, A., Prettner, K., & Tscheuschner, P. (2019). Longevity-Induced Vertical Innovation and the Tradeoff between Life and Growth. *Journal of Population Economics, 32*(4), 1293–1313. https://link.springer.com/article/10.1007/s00148-018-0724-x. DOI: 10.1007/s00148-018-0724-x

Banks, J., Blundell, R., & Tanner, S. (1998). Is there a retirement-savings puzzle? *The American Economic Review, 88*(4), 769–788.

Baron, R. A. (2003). The cognitive perspective: A valuable tool for answering entrepreneurship's basic "why" questions. *Journal of Business Venturing, 19*(2), 221–239. DOI: 10.1016/S0883-9026(03)00008-9

Barr, B., Taylor-Robinson, D., Stuckler, D., Loopstra, R., Reeves, A., Wickham, S., & Whitehead, M. (2016). Fit-for-work or fit-for-unemployment? Does the reassessment of disability benefit claimants using a tougher work capability assessment help people into work? *Journal of Epidemiology and Community Health, 70*(5), 452–458. DOI: 10.1136/jech-2015-206333 PMID: 26646692

Barrett, C. B. (2021). Overcoming global food security challenges through science and solidarity. *American Journal of Agricultural Economics, 103*(3), 1071–1084. DOI: 10.1111/ajae.12160

Bartova, A., Otto, A., & Van Lancker, W. (2022). Making parental leave policies work for single mothers: Lessons from Europe. The ANNALS of the American Academy of Political and Social Science, 702(1), 129-148. DOI: sagepub.comDOI: 10.1177/00027162221134445

Ba, S. (2022). Influence of Aging Population on China's Financial System: A Look into Pace of Population Aging in China Against Background of the World. In *The New Cycle and New Finance in China* (pp. 243–249). Springer Nature Singapore. DOI: 10.1007/978-981-16-8209-4_30

BBC News. (2022). *Mahsa Amini: Protests and the Death that Shook Iran*. Retrieved from. [bbc.com]

Becker, G. S. (1964). *Human capital: a theoretical and empirical analysis, with special reference to education* (Vol. 3). University of Chicago Press.

Beck, T., Demirgüç-Kunt, A., & Honohan, P. (2009). Access to financial services: Measurement, impact, and policies. *The World Bank Research Observer, 24*(1), 119–145. DOI: 10.1093/wbro/lkn008

Beegle, K., & Christiaensen, L. (2019). *Accelerating Poverty Reduction in Africa*. World Bank. Retrieved from http://hdl.handle.net/10986/32354

Belk, R. (2014). You are what you can access: Sharing and collaborative consumption online. *Journal of Business Research, 67*(8), 1595–1600. DOI: 10.1016/j.jbusres.2013.10.001

Bell, D. N. F., & Rutherford, A. C. (2013). Older Workers and Working Time. *The Journal of the Economics of Ageing, 1-2*, 28–34. DOI: 10.1016/j.jeoa.2013.08.001

Bennis, L., & Oudda, Y. (2021). Impact of the Covid-19 Economic crisis on Moroccan Companies. *Revue Française d'Économie et de Gestion, 2*(3). https://www.revuefreg.fr/index.php/home/article/view/237/147

Bernheim, B. D., Skinner, J., & Weinberg, S. (2001). What accounts for the variation in retirement wealth among US households? *The American Economic Review, 91*(4), 832–857. DOI: 10.1257/aer.91.4.832

Berry, J. W. (1997). Immigration, acculturation, and adaptation. *Applied Psychology, 46*(1), 5–34.

Bhorat, H., Rooney, C., & Steenkamp, F. (2019). Building economic complexity in Africa. Retrieved from https://idl-bnc-idrc.dspacedirect.org/server/api/core/bitstreams/b38760c2-2ebc-4fdd-be32-09de54b0bc2a/content

Bhowmik, P. K., & Sarker, N. (2021). Loan growth and bank risk: Empirical evidence from SAARC countries. *Heliyon, 7*(5), e07036. DOI: 10.1016/j.heliyon.2021.e07036 PMID: 34036201

Bíró, A., Hornok, C., Krekó, J., Prinz, D., & Scharle, Á. (2023). *The labor market effects of disability benefit loss* (No. 2256). Kiel Working Paper.

Bloom, D. E., Canning, D., & Finlay, J. E. (2008). Population Aging and Economic Growth in Asia. *PGDA Working Paper No. 40*. Harvard School of Public Health. https://content.sph.harvard.edu/wwwhsph/sites/1288/2013/10/PGDA_WP_40.pdf

Bloom, D. E., Canning, D., & Fink, G. (2010). Implications of Population Aging for Economic Growth. *Oxford Review of Economic Policy, 26*(4), 583–612. DOI: 10.1093/oxrep/grq038

Bloom, D. E., Canning, D., & Sevilla, J. (2003). The Demographic Dividend: A New perspective on the economic consequences of population change. *Foreign Affairs, 82*(3), 148. https://www.rand.org/content/dam/rand/pubs/monograph_reports/2007/MR1274.pdf. DOI: 10.2307/20033592

Bloom, D. E., & Williamson, J. G. (1998). Demographic Transitions and Economic Miracles in Emerging Asia. *The World Bank Economic Review*, *12*(30), 419–455. https://academic.oup.com/wber/article-abstract/12/3/419/1632238?redirectedFrom=fulltext. DOI: 10.1093/wber/12.3.419

Bochko, O. Y., Maletska, O. I., Tsitska, N. E., & Kapral, O. R. (2022). Paradigm of a Country Competitiveness Under Conditions of Digital Economy. *Revue d'Economie Financiere*, *20*, 572–580. DOI: 10.55365/1923.x2022.20.65

Bonab, A. B., Rudko, I., & Bellini, F. (2021). A Review and a Proposal About Socio-economic Impacts of Artificial Intelligence. In D. A.M. & D. F. (Eds.), *Springer Proceedings in Business and Economics* (pp. 251 – 270). Springer Science and Business Media B.V. DOI: 10.1007/978-3-030-59972-0_18

Bonacini, L., Gallo, G., & Scicchitano, S. (2021). Working from home and income inequality: risks of a 'new normal'with COVID-19. Journal of population economics. springer.comDOI: 10.1007/s00148-020-00800-7

Börsch-Supan, A. (1992). Saving and consumption patterns of the elderly: The German case. *Journal of Population Economics*, *5*(4), 289–303. DOI: 10.1007/BF00163062

Börsch-Supan, A., & Brugiavini, A. (2001). Savings: The policy debate in Europe. *Oxford Review of Economic Policy*, *17*(1), 116–143. DOI: 10.1093/oxrep/17.1.116

Börsch-Supan, A., Härtl, K., & Leite, D. N. (2018). Earnings test, non-actuarial adjustments and flexible retirement. *Economics Letters*, *173*, 78–83. DOI: 10.1016/j.econlet.2018.09.020

Bose, S., Hoque, A., & Weber, O. (2024). Enhancing environmental performance: Evidence from SAARC Countries. *Contemporary South Asia*, •••, 1–24. DOI: 10.1080/09584935.2024.2371782

Bosma, N., Acs, Z. J., Autio, E., Coduras, A., & Levie, J. (2009). *Global entrepreneurship monitor 2008 Executive Report*. Babson College., Retrieved from https://www.researchgate.net/publication/277191492_The_Global_Entrepreneurship_Monitor_United_Kingdom_2008_Executive_Report

Bouichou, E. H., Abdoulaye, T., Allali, K., Bouayad, A., & Fadlaoui, A. (2021). Entrepreneurial intention among rural youth in Moroccan agricultural cooperatives: The future of rural entrepreneurship. *Sustainability (Basel)*, *13*(16), 9247. DOI: 10.3390/su13169247

Bound, J., & Burkhauser, R. V. (1999). Economic analysis of transfer programs targeted on people with disabilities. Handbook of labor economics, 3, 3417-3528. DOI: 10.1016/S1573-4463(99)30042-0

Bravo, J. M. (2019). Funding for longer lives. Retirement wallet and risk-sharing annuities. *Ekonomiaz: Revista vasca de economía*, (96), 268-291.

Brixiová, Z., & Kangoye, T. (2014). Youth Employment in Africa: New Evidence and Policies from Swaziland. In Malo, M., & Sciulli, D. (Eds.), *Disadvantaged Workers. AIEL Series in Labour Economics*. Springer., DOI: 10.1007/978-3-319-04376-0_9

Brucker, D. L., & Scally, C. P. (2015). Linking public housing, employment, and disability benefits for working-age people with disabilities. *Housing and Society*, *42*(2), 126–147. DOI: 10.1080/08882746.2015.1076130

Brunetti, M., & Torricelli, C. (2010). Population age structure and household portfolio choices in Italy. *European Journal of Finance*, *16*(6), 481–502. DOI: 10.1080/13518470903075961

Bruton, G. D., Ahlstrom, D., & Li, H. (2010). Institutional theory and entrepreneurship: Where are we now and where do we need to move in the future? *Entrepreneurship Theory and Practice*, *34*(3), 421–440. DOI: 10.1111/j.1540-6520.2010.00390.x

Bukartaite, R., & Hooper, D. (2023). Automation, artificial intelligence and future skills needs: An Irish perspective. *European Journal of Training and Development*, *47*(10), 163–185. Advance online publication. DOI: 10.1108/EJTD-03-2023-0045

Bull, M., & Taylor, D. W. (2008). The Entrepreneur in Youth: An Untapped Resource for Economic Growth, Social Entrepreneurship, and Education. *International Journal of Entrepreneurial Behaviour & Research*, *14*(5), 367–369. DOI: 10.1108/13552550810897713

Burkhauser, R. V., & Daly, M. (2011). *The declining work and welfare of people with disabilities: What went wrong and a strategy for change*. AEI Press.

Burkhauser, R. V., & Daly, M. C. (2012). Social Security Disability Insurance: Time for fundamental change. Journal of Policy Analysis and Management, 454-461. Authority, E. P. (2020). Swedish Social Insurance Agency Certification Practices Statement. *Changes (Hove, England)*, *1*, 6.

Busemeyer, M. R., & Sahm, A. H. J. (2022). Social investment, redistribution or basic income? Exploring the association between automation risk and welfare state attitudes in Europe. *Journal of Social Policy*, *51*(4), 751–770. Advance online publication. DOI: 10.1017/S0047279421000519

Butler, A. W., & Yi, H. (2022). Aging and public financing costs: Evidence from US municipal bond markets. *Journal of Public Economics, 211*, 104665. DOI: 10.1016/j.jpubeco.2022.104665

Bygrave, W. D., & Hofer, C. W. (1992). Theorizing about Entrepreneurship. *Entrepreneurship Theory and Practice, 16*(2), 13–22. DOI: 10.1177/104225879201600203

Cai, S., Zheng, Y., Li, J., Tu, D., & Liu, H. (2025). Research on the impact mechanism of financial fraud risk among urban elderly in the context of population aging: Empirical data from China aging finance forum. *Finance Research Letters, 77*, 107068. DOI: 10.1016/j.frl.2025.107068

Calvó-Perxas, L., Vilalta-Franch, J., Litwin, H., Mira, P., & Garre-Olmo, J. (2021). A longitudinal study on public policy and the health of in-house caregivers in Europe. [HTML]. *Health Policy (Amsterdam), 125*(4), 436–441. DOI: 10.1016/j.healthpol.2021.02.001 PMID: 33602532

Campolieti, M., & Goldenberg, J. (2007). Disability insurance denial rates and the labor force participation of older men and women in Canada. *Atlantic Economic Journal, 35*(1), 59–75. DOI: 10.1007/s11293-006-9061-7

Canadian Museum of Immigration. (2020). *History of Canada's Immigration Policy*.

Cantillon, R. (1755). Essay on the Nature of Trade in General. DOI: 10.4324/9781315794686

Casari, S., Di Paola, M., Banci, E., Diallo, S., Scarallo, L., Renzo, S., Gori, A., Renzi, S., Paci, M., de Mast, Q., Pecht, T., Derra, K., Kaboré, B., Tinto, H., Cavalieri, D., & Lionetti, P. (2022). Changing dietary habits: The impact of urbanization and rising socio-economic status in families from Burkina Faso in Sub-Saharan Africa. *Nutrients, 14*(11), 2216. DOI: 10.3390/nu14091782 PMID: 35565752

Castles, S., de Haas, H., & Miller, M. J. (2014). *The Age of Migration: International Population Movements in the Modern World* (5th ed.). Palgrave Macmillan. DOI: 10.1007/978-0-230-36639-8

Castro-González, S., Rey-Ares, L., Fernández-López, S., & Daoudi, D. (2020). The effect of self-control upon participation in voluntary pension schemes. *Economics & Sociology (Ternopil), 13*(1), 11–23. DOI: 10.14254/2071-789X.2020/13-1/1

Cazzaniga M, Jaumotte F, Li L, Melina MG, (2024). "Gen-AI: Artificial intelligence and the future of work"

Celentano, D. (2024). Labor automation for fair cooperation: Why and how machines should provide meaningful work for all. *Journal of Social Philosophy*, *55*(1), 25–43. DOI: 10.1111/josp.12548

Cerra, V., Eichengreen, B., El-Ganainy, A., & Schindle, M. (2021). How to achieve inclusive growth. DOI: oapen.orgDOI: 10.1093/oso/9780192846938.001.0001

Chan, M. K., Morris, T., Polidano, C., & Vu, H. (2022). Income and saving responses to tax incentives for private retirement savings. *Journal of Public Economics*, *206*, 104598. DOI: 10.1016/j.jpubeco.2021.104598

Chen, F., Mao, S., & Huang, R. (2024). Age structure of the population and household consumption expenditure on tourism. *Finance Research Letters*, *60*, 104896. DOI: 10.1016/j.frl.2023.104896

Cheng, H., Luo, W., Si, S., Xin, X., Peng, Z., Zhou, H., ... & Yu, Y. (2022). Global trends in total fertility rate and its relation to national wealth, life expectancy and female education. BMC Public Health, 22(1), 1346. springer.comDOI: 10.1186/s12889-022-13656-1

Cheng, M. C., & Lee, C. C. (2022). The impact of demographic aging on the investing behavior: The case of Taiwan stock market. *Review of Pacific Basin Financial Markets and Policies*, *25*(04), 2250026. DOI: 10.1142/S0219091522500266

Chen, J., Wang, Y., Wen, J., Fang, F., & Song, M. (2015). The Influences of Aging Population and Economic Growth on Chinese Rural Poverty. *Journal of Rural Studies*, *30*, 1–12. https://www.sciencedirect.com/science/article/abs/pii/S0743016715300383?via%3Dihub

Chen, X., & Feng, S. (2024). Age-Friendly Transportation Policies and Practices in the US and China: A Comparative Study. *Sustainability*. Advance online publication. DOI: 10.3390/su16074439

Cheung, Y. L., Mak, B. S., Shu, H., & Tan, W. (2023). Impact of financial investment on confidence in a happy future retirement. *International Review of Financial Analysis*, *89*, 102784. DOI: 10.1016/j.irfa.2023.102784

Chigunta, F., Schnurr, J., James-Wilson, D., Torres, V., & Creation, J. (2005). Being "real" about youth entrepreneurship in Eastern and Southern Africa. *SEED working paper*, 72, 1-105. Retrieved from https://www.researchgate.net/publication/242477509_Being_Real_about_Youth_Entrepreneurship_in_Eastern_and_Southern_Africa_Implications_for_Adults_Institutions_and_Sector_Structures

Chłoń-Domińczak, A., Strzelecki, P., & Łątkowski, W. (2020). Pension reforms or consequences of the economic crisis? Measuring the changes of pension incomes in selected EU countries using APC approach. *The Journal of the Economics of Ageing*, *17*, 100131. DOI: 10.1016/j.jeoa.2017.09.002

Cho, S., & Kim, J. R. (2021). Population aging in Korea: Implications for fiscal sustainability. *Seoul Journal of Economics*, *34*(2), 237–264.

Christiaensen, L., Rutledge, Z., & Taylor, J. E. (2021). The future of work in agri-food. *Food Policy*, *101*, 102043. DOI: 10.1016/j.foodpol.2021.102043 PMID: 33071436

Chu, C. H., Nyrup, R., Leslie, K., Shi, J., Bianchi, A., & Regini, O. (2022). Digital ageism: Challenges and opportunities in artificial intelligence for older adults. *The Gerontologist*, *62*(7), 947–955. Advance online publication. DOI: 10.1093/geront/gnab167 PMID: 35048111

Cipriani, G. P. (2018). Aging, retirement, and pay-as-you-go pensions. *Macroeconomic Dynamics*, *22*(5), 1173–1183. DOI: 10.1017/S1365100516000651

Colombier, C., & Braendle, T. (2018). Healthcare expenditure and fiscal sustainability: Evidence from Switzerland. *Public Sector Economics*, *42*(3), 279–301. DOI: 10.3326/pse.42.3.3

Çondur, F., & Bölükbaş, M. (2014). A study on labor market and the relationship between youth unemployment and economic growth in Turkey [Türkiye'de işgücü Piyasasi ve Genç işsizlik-Büyüme ilişkisi Üzerine Bir inceleme]. *Amme Idaresi Dergisi*, *47*(2), 77–93.

Connor, P. (2010). *Explaining the Refugee Gap: Religion, Institutions, and the Determinants of Asylum Status*. Oxford University Press.

Connor, P. (2010). *Religion and Migration: Implications for Development*. Pew Research Center.

Costa, I., Machado, C. S., & Conceição, O. (2024). "Automation and the Importance of Reskilling Workers: A Case Study in the Automotive Industry" *Proceedings of the 19*th. DOI: 10.34190/ecmlg.20.1.2923

Cousins, M. (2021). The sustainability of China's Urban Employees' Pension Programme: A case of getting old before getting rich? *International Social Security Review*, *74*(1), 59–77. DOI: 10.1111/issr.12257

Cuéllar-Fernández, B., Fuertes-Callén, Y., & Serrano-Magdalena, A. (2024). Factors behind the resilience of rural startups. *Technological Forecasting and Social Change*, *206*, 123521. DOI: 10.1016/j.techfore.2024.123521

Cumming, D., Johan, S., & Zhang, M. (2014). The economic impact of entrepreneurship: Comparing international datasets. *Corporate Governance*, *22*(2), 162–178. DOI: 10.1111/corg.12058

Czaplicka, M., Dudzińska, M., Dawidowicz, A., & Marszałek, A. (2024). Concept of Assessment of Age-Friendly Residential Areas (AFRA): A Case Study of Gdańsk, Poland. *Sustainability (Basel)*, *16*(14), 6000. Advance online publication. DOI: 10.3390/su16146000

Da Silva, T. M. H. R. (2025). *Designing for Longevity: Economic Perspectives on Age-Friendly Housing and Urban Development*. Perspectives on the Economics of Aging.

Daga, S., Pahuja, S., & Yadav, K. (2024). BOARD GENDER DIVERSITY AND CSR SPENDING ON GENDER EQUALITY AND WOMEN EMPOWERMENT: DO EMPOWERED WOMEN WORK FOR WOMEN EMPOWERMENT? *Corporate Governance*, *6*(2). https://grfcg.in/wp-content/uploads/journal/published_paper/volume-6/issue-2/YwD6spQg.pdf

Danziger, S., Van Der Gaag, J., Smolensky, E., & Taussig, M. K. (1982). The life-cycle hypothesis and the consumption behavior of the elderly. *Journal of Post Keynesian Economics*, *5*(2), 208–227. DOI: 10.1080/01603477.1982.11489357

Dashjamts, A. E., Bayaraa, S. O., & Budjav, U. (2024). The Impact of Population Aging Trends on Mongolia's Pension Insurance Fund. *Journal of Human Resource and Sustainability Studies*, *12*(4), 878–886. DOI: 10.4236/jhrss.2024.124046

Daszkiewicz, T. (2022). Food production in the context of global developmental challenges. *Agriculture*, *12*(11), 1863. DOI: 10.3390/agriculture12060832

Daved, F. (2021). Towards A Productive Ageing Thai Society: Are Senior Citizens A Silver Lining For The Shrinking Labor Market. *Academy of Entrepreneurship Journal*, *27*, 5–6.

Davies, R. B., & Robert, R. R., III. (2006). Population Aging, Foreign Direct Investment, and Tax Competition. https://scholarsbank.uoregon.edu/server/api/core/bitstreams/40f97ad4-b9ce-4aa7-94d9-9b6b53742d7f/content

Dayaram, K., Rola Rubzen, F., Ahmad, H., & Britten, N. (2020). Does economic prosperity translate to regional youth employment? *Labour & Industry*, *30*(3), 216–232. DOI: 10.1080/10301763.2020.1821428

De Bruin, S., Dengerink, J., & van Vliet, J. (2021). Urbanisation as driver of food system transformation and opportunities for rural livelihoods. *Food Security*, *13*(5), 1031–1044. DOI: 10.1007/s12571-021-01182-8 PMID: 34221191

De Felice, F., Longo, F., Padovano, A., Falcone, D., & Baffo, I. (2022). Proposal of a multidimensional risk assessment methodology to assess ageing workforce in a manufacturing industry: A pilot case study. *Safety Science*, *149*, 105681. Advance online publication. DOI: 10.1016/j.ssci.2022.105681

De Lannoy, A., Graham, L., Patel, L., & Leibbrandt, M. (2020). Why is youth unemployment so intractable in South Africa? A synthesis of evidence at the micro-level. *Journal of Applied Youth Studies*, *3*(2), 115–131. DOI: 10.1007/s43151-020-00012-6

de Meijer, C., Wouterse, B., Polder, J., & Koopmanschap, M. (2013). The Effect of Population Aging on Health Expenditure Growth: A Critical Review. *European Journal of Ageing*, *10*(4), 353–361. https://link.springer.com/article/10.1007/s10433-013-0280-x. DOI: 10.1007/s10433-013-0280-x PMID: 28804308

Debnath, P., Deshmukh, S. M., Laroia, M., Selvakumar, P., Manjunath, T. C., & Bhattacharya, S. (2025). Challenges Faced by Countries in Renewable Energy Adoption. In Özsungur, F., Chaychi Semsari, M., & Küçük Bayraktar, H. (Eds.), *Geopolitical Landscapes of Renewable Energy and Urban Growth* (pp. 295–320). IGI Global Scientific Publishing., DOI: 10.4018/979-8-3693-8814-3.ch010

Dejardin, M. (2000). Entrepreneurship and economic growth: An obvious conjunction. *Institute for Development Strategies*, *4*, 2–12.

Deschacht, N. (2021). *"The digital revolution and the labour economics of automation: A review" The Journal of the Automated Economy*. DESCHACHT., DOI: 10.46763/JAE.N

Devaux, A., Goffart, J. P., Kromann, P., Andrade-Piedra, J. L., Polar, V., & Hareau, G. (2021). The potato of the future: Opportunities and challenges in sustainable agri-food systems. *Potato Research*, *64*(2), 257–276. DOI: 10.1007/s11540-021-09501-4 PMID: 34334803

Dew, N., Read, S., Sarasvathy, S. D., & Wiltbank, R. (2008). Effectual versus predictive logics in entrepreneurial decision-making: Differences between experts and novices. *Journal of Business Venturing*, *24*(4), 287–309. DOI: 10.1016/j.jbusvent.2008.02.002

Dey, S. K., Rahman, M. M., Shibly, K. H., Siddiqi, U. R., & Howlader, A. (2020). Epidemic trend analysis of SARS-COV-2 in SAARC countries using Modified SIR (M-SIR) Predictive model. medRxiv *(Cold Spring Harbor Laboratory)*. DOI: 10.1101/2020.06.29.20142513

Dhanush, G., Khatri, N., Kumar, S., & Shukla, P. K. (2023). A comprehensive review of machine vision systems and artificial intelligence algorithms for the detection and harvesting of agricultural produce. *Scientific African*, *21*, e01798. Advance online publication. DOI: 10.1016/j.sciaf.2023.e01798

Dietrich, S., Giuffrida, V., & Martorano, B. (2022). COVID-19 policy responses, mobility, and food prices. *Journal of Agricultural Economics*, *73*(2), 257–276. DOI: 10.1111/1477-9552.12453

Dixit, P., & Bhatnagar, M. (2025). Advancing green economies through sustainable investment strategies for climate change mitigation and development: Adaptive strategies for green crypto investment. In *Adaptive Strategies for Green Economy and Sustainability Policies*. DOI: 10.4018/979-8-3693-7570-9.ch033

Djeufack Dongmo, A., & Avom, D. (2024). Urbanization, civil conflict, and the severity of food insecurity in Africa. *Politics & Policy*, *52*(2), 257–276. DOI: 10.1111/polp.12572

Doerr, S., Kabaş, G., & Ongena, S. (2024). Population aging and bank risk-taking. *Journal of Financial and Quantitative Analysis*, *59*(7), 3037–3061. DOI: 10.1017/S0022109023001011

Domash, A., & Summers, L. H. (2022). *How tight are US labor markets?* National Bureau of Economic Research., DOI: 10.3386/w29739

Donthu, N., Kumar, S., Mukherjee, D., Pandey, N., & Lim, W. M. (2021). How to conduct a bibliometric analysis: An overview and guidelines. *Journal of Business Research*, *133*, 285–296. DOI: 10.1016/j.jbusres.2021.04.070

Duesenberry, J. S. (1948). *The consumption function: A study of relations between income and consumer expenditures*. University of Michigan.

Du, M., Lei, J., & Li, S. (2025). Navigating the Path to Food Security in China: Challenges, Policies, and Future Directions. *Foods*, *14*(1), 151. DOI: 10.3390/foods14040644 PMID: 40002086

Dumiter, F. C., Schebesch, K. B., Nicoară, . A., & Ben e, C. (2024). The impact of social features on the financial sustainability of pension systems in Central and Eastern Europe and Baltic States. *Technological and Economic Development of Economy*, *30*(6), 1920–1949. DOI: 10.3846/tede.2024.22835

Dwivedi, Y. K., Sharma, A., Rana, N. P., Giannakis, M., & Hughes, L. (2023). Evolution of artificial intelligence research in Technological Forecasting and Social Change: Research topics, trends, and future directions. *Technological Forecasting and Social Change, 192*, 122579. Advance online publication. DOI: 10.1016/j.techfore.2023.122579

Eggertson, G., Lancastre, M., & Summers, L. H. (2017). Aging, Output Per Capita, and Secular Stagnation. Institute for New Economic Thinking. https://www.ineteconomics.org/research/research-papers/aging-output-per-capita-and-secular-stagnation

Ekuma, K. (2023). "Rethinking Upskilling and Reskilling in the Age of AI and Automation: A fsQCA Approach" *Preprints*. DOI: DOI: 10.20944/preprints202307.0401.v1

Elbadraoui, A., Mouhssine, Y., El Alaoui, A. K., & Alaoui, S. O. (2025). A Bibliometric Exploration of Artificial Intelligence Methods for Transition from Conventional to Sustainable Financial Framework. *Lecture Notes in Networks and Systems, 1403 LNNS*, 575–604. DOI: 10.1007/978-3-031-91337-2_54

Elgin, C., & Tumen, S. (2010). Can Sustained Economic Growth and Declining Population Co-exist? Barro-Becker Children Meet Lucas. *Economic Modelling, 29*(5), 1899–1908. DOI: 10.1016/j.econmod.2012.06.004

Emery-Tiburcio, E. E. (2024). Age-friendly mental health systems: A step toward geriatric competency. *The American Psychologist, 79*(9), 1422–1430. Advance online publication. DOI: 10.1037/amp0001446 PMID: 39715398

Engelen, A., Heinemann, F., & Brettel, M. (2009). Cross-cultural entrepreneurship research: Current status and framework for future studies. *Journal of International Entrepreneurship, 7*(3), 163–189. DOI: 10.1007/s10843-008-0035-5

Erenstein O, Jaleta M, Mottaleb K A. (2022). "Global trends in wheat production, consumption and trade". Food Security in a Changing Climate, 257-276.

Erenstein, O., Jaleta, M., Sonder, K., Mottaleb, K. A., & Prasanna, B. M. (2022). Global maize production, consumption and trade: Trends and R&D implications. *Food Security, 14*(2), 357–373. DOI: 10.1007/s12571-022-01288-7

Erlandsen, S. K. (2003). *Age structure effects and consumption in Norway, 1968 (3)-1998 (4)* (No. 2003/1). Working Paper.

Etgeton, S., Fischer, B., & Ye, H. (2023). The effect of increasing retirement age on households' savings and consumption expenditure. *Journal of Public Economics, 221*, 104845. DOI: 10.1016/j.jpubeco.2023.104845

European Commission. (2018). *The Silver Economy*. Retrieved from https://ec.europa.eu/docsroom/documents/33163

Eurostat (2025). *Population structure and ageing*. Retrieved May 13, 2025, from https://european-union.europa.eu/principles-countries-history/facts-and-figures-european-union_en

Eurostat. (2024). *Ageing Europe – statistics on pensions, income and expenditure*. European Commission. https://ec.europa.eu/eurostat/statistics-explained/index.php?title=Ageing_Europe_-_statistics_on_pensions,_income_and_expenditure

Fang, H. (2023). The Impact of Population Aging on Financial Services and Economic Development. *Available at SSRN* 4574199.

Farooq, A., Farooq, N., Akbar, H., Hassan, Z. U., & Gheewala, S. H. (2023). A critical review of climate change impact at a global scale on cereal crop production. *Agronomy (Basel)*, *13*(1), 151. DOI: 10.3390/agronomy13010162

Faruqee, H., & Mühleisen, M. (2003). Population aging in Japan: Demographic shock and fiscal sustainability. *Japan and the World Economy*, *15*(2), 185–210. DOI: 10.1016/S0922-1425(02)00017-8

Fathallah, B., & Horr, L. (2024). Contribution of the National Initiative for Human Development to promoting youth entrepreneurship in Morocco: Focus on Program III of the third phase. *American Scientific Journal*, *3*(22), 302. DOI: 10.5281/zenodo.10649435

Fayad D. (2023). "Food insecurity and climate shocks in Madagascar: Republic of Madagascar".

Feldstein, M. (1976). Social security and the distribution of wealth. *Journal of the American Statistical Association*, *71*(356), 800–807. DOI: 10.1080/01621459.1976.10480950

Ferreira, J. J., & Teixeira, A. A. (2019). Open innovation and knowledge for fostering business ecosystems. *Journal of Innovation & Knowledge*, *4*(4), 253–255. DOI: 10.1016/j.jik.2018.10.002

Fine, S. (2025). Psychometric Credit Scoring in Latin America: Replicated Samples Across Five Countries. *Review of Behavioral Economics*, *12*(2), 129–142. DOI: 10.1561/105.00000206

Fischer, Y. (2020). Basic Income, Labour Automation and Migration - An Approach from a Republican Perspective. *Basic Income Studies*, *15*(2), 20200027. Advance online publication. DOI: 10.1515/bis-2020-0027

Fisher, I. (1930). *The theory of interest: As determined by impatience to spend income and opportunity to invest it*. Macmillan.

Flici, F. (2023). The limits of parametric reforms in sustaining the Algerian retirement system in a context of population ageing. *International Social Security Review*, *76*(3), 47–67. DOI: 10.1111/issr.12335

Fong, J. H., & Piggott, J. (2024). Accessing long-term care social insurance benefits in South Korea and its correlates. *The Japanese Economic Review*, *75*(4), 1–24. DOI: 10.1007/s42973-024-00177-2

Foo, J., & Witkowska, D. (2021). Savings Behavior, Asset Investment Choices and Institutional Pension Capital Market Performance. *International Journal of Business*, *26*(3), 72–104.

Fox, L., & Kaul, U. (2017). The Evidence is in: How should youth employment programs in low income countries be designed? USAID. DOI: 10.13140/RG.2.2.22191.84649

Frank, K., Yang, Z., & Frenette, M. (2021). "The changing nature of work in Canada amid recent advances in automation technology" ResearchGate. DOI: DOI: 10.13140/RG.2.2.14143.57120

Freedman, A., & Nicolle, J. (2020). Social Isolation and Loneliness: The New Geriatric Giants. *Canadian Family Physician Médecin de Famille Canadien*, *66*, 176–182. https://www.cfp.ca/content/66/3/176.short PMID: 32165464

Freeman, C. (1987). *Technology policy and economic performance: Lessons from Japan*. Pinter.

Frey, C. B., & Osborne, M. (2023). Generative AI and the future of work: A reappraisal. *The Brown Journal of World Affairs*.

Friedman, M. (1957). The permanent income hypothesis. In *A theory of the consumption function* (pp. 20–37). Princeton University Press. DOI: 10.1515/9780691188485-005

Fuino, M., & Wagner, J. (2018). Long-term care models and dependence probability tables by acuity level: New empirical evidence from Switzerland. *Insurance, Mathematics & Economics*, *81*, 51–70. DOI: 10.1016/j.insmatheco.2018.05.002

Galanakis, C. M. (2024). The future of food. *Foods*, *13*(2), 332. DOI: 10.3390/foods13020332 PMID: 38397483

Gao, K., & Tian, Z. (2023). How ageing affects manufacturing transformation: Empirical evidence from China. *Applied Economics Letters*, *30*(10), 1358–1362. DOI: 10.1080/13504851.2022.2053650

Gao, W., Chen, Y., Xu, S., Lyulyov, O., & Pimonenko, T. (2023). The Role of Population Aging in High-Quality Economic Development: Mediating Role of Technological Innovation. *SAGE Open*, *13*(4), 1–15. https://journals.sagepub.com/doi/10.1177/21582440231202385. DOI: 10.1177/21582440231202385

Gaponenko, T., Barmuta, K., & Medvedeva, L. (2025). Ensuring sustainable development of region's labor resources in context of digitalization through risk-balanced management. In B. N.V., A. M.I., & M. A.K. (Eds.), *AIP Conference Proceedings* (Vol. 3276, Issue 1). American Institute of Physics. DOI: 10.1063/5.0263893

Gawthorpe, K. (2022). Population ageing and sustainable fiscal policy in Czechia. *eastern. Journal of European Studies*, *13*(1), 81–105.

Gazi, M. I., Masud, A. A., Shuvro, R. A., Hossain, A. I., & Rahman, M. K. (2022). Bangladesh and SAARC countries: Bilateral trade and flaring of economic cooperation. *ETIKONOMI*, *21*(2), 251–268. DOI: 10.15408/etk.v21i2.24353

Gentilini, U. (2022). *Social protection and jobs responses to COVID-19: A real-time review of country measures*. Social Protection and Jobs Responses.

Ghosh M, (2024). "Case Studies of Effective Age-Friendly Digital Initiatives" India's Silver Surfers: Transforming the Digital. DOI: .DOI: 10.1007/978-981-19-6563-6_12

Ghosh, D. (2023). Social Support System and Old Age Vulnerability: An Investigation in India. *Studies in Microeconomics*, 23210222231171495.

Giller, K. E., Delaune, T., Silva, J. V., Descheemaeker, K., van de Ven, G., Schut, A. G. T., van Wijk, M., Hammond, J., Hochman, Z., Taulya, G., Chikowo, R., Narayanan, S., Kishore, A., Bresciani, F., Teixeira, H. M., Andersson, J. A., & van Ittersum, M. K. (2021). The future of farming: Who will produce our food? *Food Security*, *13*(5), 1031–1044. DOI: 10.1007/s12571-021-01184-6

Giller, K. E., Delaune, T., Silva, J. V., van Wijk, M., Hammond, J., Descheemaeker, K., van de Ven, G., Schut, A. G. T., Taulya, G., Chikowo, R., & Andersson, J. A. (2021). Small farms and development in sub-Saharan Africa: Farming for food, for income or for lack of better options? *Food Security*, *13*(5), 1031–1044. DOI: 10.1007/s12571-021-01209-0

Giorges, A. G., & Haynes, C. (2023). APPLIED EXPERIMENTAL WORK DESIGNED TO EVALUATE THE FUNDAMENTAL HEAT TRANSFER FROM ROTATION ONLY AND ROTATION AND TRANSLATION MOTION DUE TO COMPLEX SHAPES. *ASME International Mechanical Engineering Congress and Exposition, Proceedings (IMECE)*, 10. DOI: 10.1115/IMECE2023-111610

Giudice, L. C., Llamas-Clark, E. F., DeNicola, N., Pandipati, S., Zlatnik, M. G., Decena, D. C. D., ... & FIGO Committee on Climate Change and Toxic Environmental Exposures. (2021). Climate change, women's health, and the role of obstetricians and gynecologists in leadership. International Journal of Gynecology & Obstetrics, 155(3), 345-356. DOI: wiley.comDOI: 10.1002/ijgo.13958

Global Entrepreneurship Monitor. (2013). Supporting Africa's Young Entrepreneurs: an investment in job creation and future prosperity for all: Nigeria. Retrieved from https://www.gemconsortium.org/file/open?fileId=49180

Global Entrepreneurship Monitor. (2020). GEM *2019/2020Global report.* Retrieved from https://www.gemconsortium.org/report

Glover A, & Mustre-del-Río J, (2024). "Aging and growth: can automation outpace falling labor supply, reduced dynamism, and fewer innovations?" Handbook on Labour Markets in Emerging Economies. DOI: .DOI: 10.4337/9781800887476.00025

Goldsmith, L., Raditz, V., & Méndez, M. (2022). Queer and present danger: Understanding the disparate impacts of disasters on LGBTQ+ communities. [HTML]. *Disasters*, *46*(4), 946–973. Advance online publication. DOI: 10.1111/disa.12509 PMID: 34498778

Gonçalves, A. R., Breda Meira, A., Shuqair, S., & Costa Pinto, D. (2023). Artificial intelligence (AI) in FinTech decisions: The role of congruity and rejection sensitivity. *International Journal of Bank Marketing*, *41*(6), 1282–1307. DOI: 10.1108/IJBM-07-2022-0295

Gopal, S., & Pitts, J. (2024). The FinTech Revolution: Bridging Geospatial Data Science, AI, and Sustainability. *Sustainable Finance*, (Part F4267), 1–398. DOI: 10.1007/978-3-031-74418-1

Government of Canada. (2021). *Opportunities Fund for Persons with Disabilities – Overview*. Retrieved from https://www.canada.ca/en/employment-social-development/services/funding/disability-opportunity-national-regional.html

Grinin, L., Grinin, A., & Korotayev, A. (2024). *Cybernetic Revolution and Global Aging*. Springer., DOI: 10.1007/978-3-031-56764-3

Gruber, J. (2000). Disability insurance benefits and labor supply. *Journal of Political Economy, 108*(6), 1162–1183. DOI: 10.1086/317682

Gruère, G. P., & Brooks, J. (2021). Characterising early agricultural and food policy responses to the outbreak of COVID-19. *Food Policy, 101*, 102043. DOI: 10.1016/j.foodpol.2020.102017 PMID: 33390644

Gu, D., Andreev, K., & Dupre, M. E. (2021). Major trends in population growth around the world. *China CDC Weekly, 3*(2), 33–36. DOI: 10.46234/ccdcw2021.160 PMID: 34594946

Guerard, Y., Asher, M., Park, D., & Estrada, G. B. (2012). *Reducing Disparities and Enhancing Sustainability in Asian Pension Systems* (No. 313). ADB Economics Working Paper Series.

Guimarães, N. A., de Brito, M. M. A., & Comin, A. A. (2020). Youth in Brazil: Transitions and Trajectories. can economic Growth Mitigate Inequalities? *Novos Estudos CEBRAP, 39*(3), 475–498. DOI: 10.25091/s01013300202000030002

Gupta, S. T., Joshi, P., Kaur, A., & Kumar, P. (2025). Digital tools and technologies: Enabling knowledge sharing and collaborative business culture. In *Knowledge Sharing and Fostering Collaborative Business Culture*. IGI Global., DOI: 10.4018/979-8-3373-0710-7.ch016

Gutsu, S., Bublikov, A., & Inna, A. (2023). Artificial Intelligence in Labor Relations: Prospects for Evolution of Labor Laws. *Lecture Notes in Networks and Systems, 657 LNNS*, 498 – 507. DOI: 10.1007/978-3-031-36201-9_43

Gu, X., Tam, P. S., Li, G., & Zhao, Q. (2020). An alternative explanation for high saving in China: Rising inequality. *International Review of Economics & Finance, 69*, 1082–1094. DOI: 10.1016/j.iref.2018.12.004

Gwija, S. A., Eresia-Eke, C., & Iwu, C. G. (2014). Challenges and prospects of youth entrepreneurship development in a designated community in the Western Cape, South Africa. *Journal of Economics and Behavioral Studies, 6*(1), 10–20. http://hdl.handle.net/2263/45090. DOI: 10.22610/jebs.v6i1.465

Hainmueller, J., & Hopkins, D. J. (2014). Public Attitudes Toward Immigration. *Annual Review of Political Science, 17*(1), 225–249. DOI: 10.1146/annurev-polisci-102512-194818

Halásková, R., Bednář, P., & Halásková, M. (2017). Forms of providing and financing long-term care in OECD countries. *Review of Economic Perspectives*.

Ha, N. T. T., & Hoa, L. B. (2020). The relationship between population ageing and private savings in Vietnam. *Malaysian Journal of Consumer and Family Economics*, *24*, 1–32.

Hassan, M. K., Alshater, M. M., Hasan, R., & Bhuiyan, A. B. (2021). Islamic microfinance: A Bibliometric review. *Global Finance Journal*, *49*, 100651. Advance online publication. DOI: 10.1016/j.gfj.2021.100651

Haward, V. (2024). Impact of Japan's aging population on healthcare costs and the Long-term care insurance system. *Studies in Social Science & Humanities*, *3*(2), 39–44. DOI: 10.56397/SSSH.2024.02.06

Hemathilake, D., & Gunathilake, D. (2022). Agricultural productivity and food supply to meet increased demands. *Future Foods: a Dedicated Journal for Sustainability in Food Science*, *4*, 100094. DOI: 10.1016/j.fufo.2022.100094

Hermannsson, K., Scandurra, R., & Graziano, M. (2024). The Effect of Higher Education on Youth Unemployment in European Regions During a Period of Economic Instability. *Journal of Education Finance*, *49*(4), 447–467. DOI: 10.1353/jef.2024.a954741

Hinkelmann, K., & Smuts, H. (Eds.). (2025). 4th International Conference on Society 5.0, Society 5.0 2024. *Communications in Computer and Information Science, 2173 CCIS.*

Hlungwani, P. M., & Mohamed Sayeed, C. N. (2018). Youth empowerment as a driver of economic growth: Policy implementation challenges in Zimbabwe. *Journal of African Union Studies*, *7*(3), 105–126. DOI: 10.31920/2050-4306/2018/V7n3a6

Hock, H., & Weil, D. N. (2012). On the Dynamics of the Age Structure, Dependency, and Consumption. *Journal of Population Economics*, *25*(3), 1019–1043. https://link.springer.com/article/10.1007/s00148-011-0372-x. DOI: 10.1007/s00148-011-0372-x PMID: 24353374

Hofstede, G. (2001). Culture's Consequences: Comparing Values, Behaviors, Institutions and Organizations across Nations.DOI: 10.1016/S0005-7967(02)00184-5

Holzmann, R. (2013). An optimistic perspective on population ageing and old-age financial protection. *Malaysian Journal of Economic Studies: Journal of the Malaysian Economic Association and the Faculty of Economics and Administration, University of Malaya*, *50*(2), 107–137.

Ho, M. T., Mantello, P., Ghotbi, N., Nguyen, M. H., & Hollier, S. (2022). Rethinking technological acceptance in the age of emotional AI: Surveying Gen Z (Zoomer) attitudes toward non-conscious data collection. *Technology in Society*, *70*, 102011. Advance online publication. DOI: 10.1016/j.techsoc.2022.102011

Horioka, C. Y. (2010). Aging and saving in Asia. *Pacific Economic Review*, *15*(1), 46–55. DOI: 10.1111/j.1468-0106.2009.00489.x

Horioka, C. Y., & Niimi, Y. (2017). Saving Behavior of the Japanese Middle-Aged and the Elderly. ESRI *International Conference on Empirical Analysis on Population Decline and Aging in the Japanese Economy*. ESRI.

Horioka, C. Y., & Terada-Hagiwara, A. (2012). The determinants and long-term projections of saving rates in developing Asia. *Japan and the World Economy*, *24*(2), 128–137. DOI: 10.1016/j.japwor.2012.01.006

Horoshko, O. I., Horoshko, A., Bilyuga, S., & Yurchyshena, S. (2021). *Theoretical and methodological bases of the study of the impact of digital economy on world policy in 21 century*. Forecasting and Social Change., DOI: 10.1016/j.techfore.2021.120640

Howcroft, D., & Taylor, P. (2023). Automation and the future of work: A social shaping of technology approach. *New Technology, Work and Employment*, *38*(2), 351–370. Advance online publication. DOI: 10.1111/ntwe.12240

Hu, S.-C. (1999). Economic growth in the perpetual-youth model: Implications of the annuity market and demographics. *Journal of Macroeconomics*, *21*(1), 107–124. DOI: 10.1016/S0164-0704(99)00093-2

Iannaccone, L. R. (1998). Introduction to the Economics of Religion. *Journal of Economic Literature*, *36*(3), 1465–1495.

Iannotti, L., Kleban, E., & Fracassi, P. (2024). Evidence for policies and practices to address global food insecurity. *Annual Review of Nutrition*, *44*, 19–40. DOI: 10.1146/annurev-nutr-122221-014648 PMID: 38166503

Ichikowitz Family Foundation. 2022. African youth survey 2022. Retrieved from: https://ichikowitzfoundation.com/storage/ays/ays2022.pdf

Ikram, M., Zhang, Q., Sroufe, R., & Shah, S. Z. A. (2020). Towards a sustainable environment: The nexus between ISO 14001, renewable energy consumption, access to electricity, agriculture and CO2 emissions in SAARC countries. *Sustainable Production and Consumption*, *22*, 218–230. DOI: 10.1016/j.spc.2020.03.011

IMF. (2021). *Demographic Change and Economic Well-Being*. International Monetary Fund. Retrieved from https://www.elibrary.imf.org/display/book/9781498344753/9781498344753.xml

Inglehart, R., & Welzel, C. (2005). *Modernization, Cultural Change, and Democracy: The Human Development Sequence*. Cambridge University Press.

International Crisis Group. (2016). *Nigeria: The Challenge of Military Reform*. Africa Report No. 237.

International Labour Organization. (2022). Global Employment Trends for Youth 2022: Investing in transforming futures for young people. Retrieved from https://www.ilo.org/sites/default/files/wcmsp5/groups/public/@dgreports/@dcomm/@publ/documents/publication/wcms_853321.pdf

International Trade Centre. (2024). Access to Finance for Young African Entrepreneurs: insights from Ye! Community. Retrieved from https://www.intracen.org/file/yepublication58210pdf

Isenberg, D. J. (2010). The big idea: *How to start an entrepreneurial revolution. Harvard Business Review*, *88*(6), 40–50. https://hbr.org/2010/06/the-big-idea-how-to-start-an-entrepreneurial-revolution

Izediuno, O. L., Alice, O. T., & Daniel, O. A. (2018). Analytical review of small and medium scale enterprises in Nigeria. *International Journal of Small Business and Entrepreneurship Research*, *6*(2), 32–46.

Jabbar, S. A., Qadar, L. T., Ghafoor, S., Rasheed, L., Sarfraz, Z., Sarfraz, A., Sarfraz, M., Felix, M., & Cherrez-Ojeda, I. (2022). Air Quality, Pollution and Sustainability Trends in South Asia: A Population-Based Study. *International Journal of Environmental Research and Public Health*, *19*(12), 7534. DOI: 10.3390/ijerph19127534 PMID: 35742785

Jafrin, N., Masud, M. M., Saif, A. N. M., Mahi, M., & Khanam, M. (2021). A panel data estimation of the determinants of life expectancy in selected SAARC countries. *Badania Operacyjne I Decyzje/Operations Research and Decisions, 31*(4). DOI: 10.37190/ord210404

Jafrin, N., Mahi, M., Masud, M. M., & Ghosh, D. (2021). Demographic dividend and economic growth in emerging economies: Fresh evidence from the SAARC countries. *International Journal of Social Economics*, *48*(8), 1159–1174. DOI: 10.1108/IJSE-08-2020-0588

Jakovljevic, M., Kumagai, N., & Ogura, S. (2023). Global population aging–Health care, social and economic consequences, volume II. *Frontiers in Public Health*, *11*, 1184950. DOI: 10.3389/fpubh.2023.1184950

Jane Osareme, O., Muonde, M., Maduka, C. P., Olorunsogo, T. O., & Omotayo, O. (2024). Demographic shifts and healthcare: A review of aging populations and systemic challenges. *Int. J. Sci. Res. Arch*, *11*(1), 383–395. DOI: 10.30574/ijsra.2024.11.1.0067

Jebbari, A. (2024). Entrepreneurial Inclination in Morocco: Perspectives on Drivers and Challenges. *International Journal of Applied Management and Economics*, *2*(08), 284–304. DOI: 10.5281/zenodo.12545158

Jha, B., Giri, P., Jha, D., & Badhera, U. (2022). Unlocking IoT: AI-enabled green fintech innovations. In *AI-Enabled Agile Internet of Things for Sustainable FinTech Ecosystems*. IGI Global., DOI: 10.4018/978-1-6684-4176-3.ch001

Jie, H., Khan, I., Alharthi, M., Zafar, M. W., & Saeed, A. (2023). Energy policy, socio-economic development, and ecological footprint: The economic significance of natural resources, population growth, and industrial development. *Utilities Policy*, *79*, 101094. DOI: 10.1016/j.jup.2023.101490

Jiuhardi J, Hasid Z, Darma S. (2022). "Sustaining agricultural growth: traps of socio–demographics in emerging markets".

Johnson-Hillery, J., Kang, J., & Tuan, W. J. (1997). The difference between elderly consumers' satisfaction levels and retail sales personnel's perceptions. *International Journal of Retail & Distribution Management*, *25*(4), 126–137. DOI: 10.1108/09590559710166304

Junaid, M. D., & Gokce, A. F. (2024). Global agricultural losses and their causes. *Journal of Biological and Allied Sciences Research*, *13*(1), 1–12.

Jun, H. (2020). Social security and retirement in fast-aging middle-income countries: Evidence from Korea. *The Journal of the Economics of Ageing*, *17*, 100284. DOI: 10.1016/j.jeoa.2020.100284

Kallestrup-Lamb, M., Marin, A. O., Menon, S., & Søgaard, J. (2024). Aging populations and expenditures on health. *The Journal of the Economics of Ageing*, *29*, 100518. DOI: 10.1016/j.jeoa.2024.100518

Kangotra, R., & Sehajpal, S. (2025). Voices without faces: The impact of Deepfake technology on authentic communication. In *Deepfake Technology Dilemmas: Mastering Managerial Navigation*. Nova Science Publishers Inc.

Kanyari, J. W., & Namusonge, P. (2013). Factors that influence the Kenyan youth entrepreneurs towards the youth enterprise development fund: a case study of Gatundu South District, Kenya. Retrieved from http://www.ijern.com/images/May-2013/30.pdf

Kaur, J., Khanna, R., Kumar, R., & Sunil, G. (2024). Role of Blockchain Technologies in Goods and Services Tax. *Proceedings - 2024 3rd International Conference on Sentiment Analysis and Deep Learning, ICSADL 2024*, 607–612. DOI: 10.1109/ICSADL61749.2024.00104

Kaur, H., & Bains, A. (2013). Understanding the concept of entrepreneur competency. *Journal of Business Management & Social Sciences Research*, *2*(11), 31–33.

Kaur, R., Kaur, S., & Kaur, A. (2025). Fintech and Financial Inclusion: Trends and Challenges. In *FinTech and Financial Inclusion: Leveraging Digital Finance for Economic Empowerment and Sustainable Growth*. Taylor and Francis., DOI: 10.4324/9781003514114-6

Keeler, L. W., & Bernstein, M. J. (2021). The Future of Aging in Smart Environments: Four Scenarios of the United States in 2050. *Futures*, *133*, 102830. https://www.sciencedirect.com/science/article/pii/S0016328721001312. DOI: 10.1016/j.futures.2021.102830

Keynes, J. M. (1936). *The General Theory of Employment, Interest and Money*. Macmillan.

Khan, A., Hassan, M. K., Paltrinieri, A., Dreassi, A., & Bahoo, S. (2020). A bibliometric review of takaful literature. *International Review of Economics & Finance*, *69*, 389–405. DOI: 10.1016/j.iref.2020.05.013

Khan, A., Sicen, L., Khan, B., & Salman, N. (2021). On the influence of demographic structure and industrial growth on environmental quality. *Journal of Environmental Management*, *288*, 112453. DOI: 10.1016/j.jenvman.2021.112453 PMID: 33827026

Khang, A., Jadhav, B., Hajimahmud, V. A., & Satpathy, I. (2024). Synergy of AI and Fintech in the Digital Gig Economy. In *Synergy of AI and Fintech in the Digital Gig Economy*. CRC Press., DOI: 10.1201/9781032720104

Khan, I., Muhammad, I., Sharif, A., Khan, I., & Ji, X. (2023). Unlocking the potential of renewable energy and natural resources for sustainable economic growth and carbon neutrality: A novel panel quantile regression approach. *Renewable Energy*, *221*, 119779. DOI: 10.1016/j.renene.2023.119779

Khogali, H. O., & Mekid, S. (2023). The blended future of automation and AI: Examining some long-term societal and ethical impact features. *Technology in Society, 73*, 102232. Advance online publication. DOI: 10.1016/j.techsoc.2023.102232

Kidane, S. T. (2025). Rapid Population Growth and Security: An Analysis of Conflict Dynamics. In: Silencing the Guns: Pathways to Sustainable Peace in Postcolonial Africa. Palgrave Macmillan, Cham. DOI: 10.1007/978-3-031-95655-3_10

Kim, D. H., Liu, P., & Lin, S. C. (2024). Population aging and saving: Evidence from China. *Review of Development Economics, 28*(4), 1494–1521. DOI: 10.1111/rode.13111

Kim, D. H., Liu, P., & Lin, S. C. (2024). The moderating role of financial development in the nexus between population aging and saving. *Economic Change and Restructuring, 57*(2), 72. DOI: 10.1007/s10644-024-09670-5

Kirzner, I. M. (1973). *Competition and entrepreneurship*. University of Chicago Press.

Knesl, J. (2023). Automation and the displacement of labor by capital: Asset pricing theory and empirical evidence. *Journal of Financial Economics, 147*(2), 271–296. DOI: 10.1016/j.jfineco.2022.11.003

Koch T, (2024). "The Economic Consequences of Population Aging: A Global Perspective on Policies and Responses" Journal of Economic Science Research.

Konstantis, K., Georgas, A., Faras, A., Georgas, K., & Tympas, A. (2024). Ethical considerations in working with ChatGPT on a questionnaire about the future of work with ChatGPT. *AI and Ethics, 4*(4), 1335–1344. Advance online publication. DOI: 10.1007/s43681-023-00312-6

Kraklow V, Paff K, Comeau D, Solander K, Pitts T. (2024). "Impact of Drought on Global Food Security by 2050".

Krueger, N. F.Jr, Reilly, M. D., & Carsrud, A. L. (2000). Competing models of entrepreneurial intentions. *Journal of Business Venturing, 15*(5–6), 411–432. DOI: 10.1016/S0883-9026(98)00033-0

Krzykawski, M. (2024). Through Neganthropology to Civic Revolution in Localities [Przez negantropologię do lokalnych rewolucji]. *Czas Kultury, 2024*(2), 33–43. DOI: 10.61269/QRRG1144

Kubatko O, Merritt R, Duane S. (2023). "The impact of the COVID-19 pandemic on global food system resilience". Mechanism of an Action, 1-14.

Kukreti, M., Sehajpal, S., Tiwari, R., & Sood, K. (2024). Driving global health and sustainable development goals with smart technology. In *Driving Global Health and Sustainable Development Goals With Smart Technology*. IGI Global., DOI: 10.4018/979-8-3373-0240-9

Kumar, A., Khan, E. R., & Deepika. (2024). A Review On Heart Disease Detection Using Machine Learning Techniques. *Proceedings - 2024 6th International Conference on Computational Intelligence and Communication Technologies, CCICT 2024*, 317 – 323. DOI: 10.1109/CCICT62777.2024.00059

Kumar, A., Khan, R., & Deepika. (2025). Heart disease prediction using machine learning techniques. In *Sustainable Materials, Structures and IoT [SMSI-2024]*. CRC Press. DOI: 10.1201/9781003596776-30

Kumar, P., Bhatnagar, M., Chahal, B. P. S., Taneja, S., & Mistrean, L. (2025). The AI connection: Transforming customer engagement through robotics. In *Demystifying Emotion AI, Robotics AI, and Sentiment Analysis in Customer Relationship Management*. IGI Global., DOI: 10.4018/979-8-3373-1867-7.ch001

Kumar, R. (2019). India & South Asia: Geopolitics, regional trade and economic growth spillovers. *The Journal of International Trade & Economic Development*, *29*(1), 69–88. DOI: 10.1080/09638199.2019.1636121

Kumar, R., Goel, R., Singh, T., Mohanty, S. M., Gupta, D., Alkhayyat, A., & Khanna, R. (2024). Sustainable Finance Factors in Indian Economy: Analysis on Policy of Climate Change and Energy Sector. *Fluctuation and Noise Letters*, *23*(2), 2440004. Advance online publication. DOI: 10.1142/S0219477524400042

Kuyoro, M., Leke, A., White, O., Woetzel, L., Jayaram, K., & Hicks, K. (2023). Reimagining economic growth in Africa: Turning diversity into opportunity. *McKinsey Global Institute*. Retrieved from https://www.mckinsey.com/mgi/our-research/reimagining-economic-growth-in-africa-turning-diversity-into-opportunity

Kuznets, S., Epstein, L., & Jenks, E. (1946). *National product since 1869*. NBER Books.

La Torre, M. (2022). Banche e finanza sostenibile: per un business model Esg-oriented. *Bancaria, 5*(Contributi), 2-19.

Lahrech, M. T., Makhlouki, B., Bekkar, Y., Bounadi, I., Harbouze, R., Maatala, N., & Burte, J. (2024). Overcoming Barriers to Youth Economic Inclusion in Rural Morocco: A Case Study of Daït Aoua. *Societies (Basel, Switzerland)*, *15*(1), 4. https://www.mdpi.com/2075-4698/15/1/4. DOI: 10.3390/soc15010004

Laitner, J., & Silverman, D. (2012). Consumption, retirement and social security: Evaluating the efficiency of reform that encourages longer careers. *Journal of Public Economics*, *96*(7-8), 615–634. DOI: 10.1016/j.jpubeco.2012.02.005

Lam, D., & Leibbrandt, M. (2023). *Demographic Challenges for Global Labor Markets in the 21st Century, Africa in a Changing World*. Cape Town: Southern Africa Labour and Development Research Unit, University of Cape Town. (SALDRU Working Paper Number 303).

Lamichhane, T. R., Ghimire, M. P., Bhatt, S., & Joshi, R. K. (2022). The epidemic trend of COVID-19 in SAARC countries: A predictive modelling and analysis. *TheScientificWorldJournal*, *15*(15), 113–119. DOI: 10.3126/sw.v15i15.45669

Larsson, A. (2019a). A journey of a thousand miles: An introduction to the digitalization of labor. In *The Digital Transformation of Labor (Open Access): Automation, the Gig Economy and Welfare*. Taylor and Francis., DOI: 10.4324/9780429317866-1

Latief, R., Kong, Y., Javeed, S. A., & Sattar, U. (2021). Carbon Emissions in the SAARC Countries with Causal Effects of FDI, Economic Growth and Other Economic Factors: Evidence from Dynamic Simultaneous Equation Models. *International Journal of Environmental Research and Public Health*, *18*(9), 4605. DOI: 10.3390/ijerph18094605 PMID: 33925274

Lee, H.-H., Shin, K., & Park, D. (2017). Population Aging and Its Impact on Economic Growth: Implications for Korea. *Economic Analysis*, ESRI 196, 159-178. https://www.esri.cao.go.jp/jp/esri/archive/bun/bun196/bun196h_1.pdf

Lee, S.-H., Mason, A., & Park, D. (2011). Why Does Population Aging Matter so Much for Asia? Population Aging, Economic Security, and Economic Growth in Asia. *ADB Economics Working Paper Series No. 284*. https://www.adb.org/sites/default/files/publication/30454/economics-wp284.pdf

Lee, H. (2001). Factors influencing the consumption expenditures of retired elderly households: Focused on the factor of wealth components. *International Journal of Human Ecology*, *2*(1), 17–38.

Lee, H.-H., Huh, H.-s., Lee, Y.-Y., & Lim, J.-Y. (2013). Effects of Population Aging on Economic Growth: A Panel Analysis. *Seoul Journal of Economics*, *26*(4), 401–432. https://www.sje.ac.kr/xml/26454/26454.pdf

Lee, H.-H., & Shin, K. (2019). Nonlinear Effects of Population Aging on Economic Growth. *Japan and the World Economy*, *51*, 100963. DOI: 10.1016/j.japwor.2019.100963

Lee, I. (2023). "Economic Effects of Industrial Automation in Aging Workforces" Intersect: The Stanford Journal of Science, Technology. DOI: DOI: 10.25740/ij1137.124906

Lee, R., & Mason, A. (2006). What is the demographic dividend? *Finance & Development*, *43*(3), 16. https://ntaccounts.org/doc/repository/LM2006.pdf

Lee, S.-H., & Mason, A. (2007). Who Gains from the Demographic Dividend? Forecasting Income by Age. *International Journal of Forecasting*, *23*(4), 603–619. https://pubmed.ncbi.nlm.nih.gov/18443647/. DOI: 10.1016/j.ijforecast.2007.07.004 PMID: 18443647

Lee, Y. G., & Huh, E. (2004). Consumption and saving behavior of older and younger baby boomers in Korea. *Journal of Family and Economic Issues*, *25*, 507–526.

Lee, Y.-K., Lin, B.-Y., Weng, T.-H., Huang, C.-K., Liu, C., Liu, C.-C., Lin, S.-S., & Wang, H.-C. (2023). Counting and measuring the size and stomach fullness levels for an intelligent shrimp farming system. *Connection Science*, *35*(1), 2268878. Advance online publication. DOI: 10.1080/09540091.2023.2268878

Lepoutre, J., Justo, R., Terjesen, S., & Bosma, N. (2013). Designing a global standardizedmethodology for measuring social entrepreneurship activity: The Global Entrepreneurship Monitor social entrepreneurship study. *Small Business Economics*, *40*(3), 693–714. https://www.researchgate.net/publication/246547927_Designing_a_Global_Standardized_Methodology_for_Measuring_Social_Entrepreneurship_Activity_The_Global_Entrepreneurship_Monitor_Social_Entrepreneurship_Study. DOI: 10.1007/s11187-011-9398-4

Leu, A., Berger, F. M. P., Heino, M., Nap, H. H., Untas, A., Boccaletti, L., Lewis, F., Phelps, D., Santini, S., D'Amen, B., Socci, M., Hlebec, V., Rakar, T., Magnusson, L., Hanson, E., & Becker, S. (2023). The 2021 cross-national and comparative classification of in-country awareness and policy responses to 'young carers'. [HTML]. *Journal of Youth Studies*, *26*(5), 619–636. DOI: 10.1080/13676261.2022.2027899

Lewis, J., & Dijkema, B. (2022). *Breaking Down Work Barriers for People with Disabilities*. Centre for Cultural Renewal.

Li, X. (2023). Employee benefits and its impacts on business performance-a systematic review. In *SHS Web of Conferences* (Vol. 170, p. 03021). EDP Sciences. DOI: 10.1051/shsconf/202317003021

Liang, X., Jin, X., Han, B., Sun, R., Xu, W., Li, H., He, J., & Li, J. (2022). China's food security situation and key questions in the new era: A perspective of farmland protection. *Journal of Geographical Sciences*, *32*(8), 1285–1303. DOI: 10.1007/s11442-022-1982-9

Li, H., Zhou, X., Tang, M., & Guo, L. (2022). Impact of population aging and renewable energy consumption on agricultural green total factor productivity in rural China: Evidence from panel var approach. *Agriculture*, *12*(5), 715. DOI: 10.3390/agriculture12050715

Li, L. (2024). Reskilling and upskilling the future-ready workforce for industry 4.0 and beyond. *Information Systems Frontiers*. Advance online publication. DOI: 10.1007/s10796-023-10463-6 PMID: 35855776

Lim, T. (2016). Population aging in Korea: Macroeconomic impacts and financing national health insurance. *Korean Economic Review*, *32*(2), 355–382.

Lin, H., Xu, N., Xing, G., Shang, Y., Wang, X., & Lin, L. (2024). Microfluidic chip-based microbial metabolism-indexed BOD sensor for rapid determination of biochemical oxygen demand. *Sensors and Actuators. B, Chemical*, *400*, 134868. Advance online publication. DOI: 10.1016/j.snb.2023.134868

Li, Q., Cherian, J., Shabbir, M. S., Sial, M. S., Li, J., Mester, I., & Badulescu, A. (2021). Exploring the Relationship between Renewable Energy Sources and Economic Growth. The Case of SAARC Countries. *Energies*, *14*(3), 520. DOI: 10.3390/en14030520

Liu, Y. (2024). Population Ageing and Economic Growth: An Analysis of Central and Eastern Europe.

Liu, S., Zhu, M., & Ling, W. (2023). Research on the impact of population aging and endowment insurance on household financial asset allocation-Evidence on CFPS data. *Finance Research Letters*, *54*, 103719. DOI: 10.1016/j.frl.2023.103719

Liu, Z., Liu, J., & Osmani, M. (2021). Integration of digital economy and circular economy: Current status and future directions. *Sustainability (Basel)*, *13*(13), 7217. Advance online publication. DOI: 10.3390/su13137217

Loku, A., & Loku, N. (2025). "Globalization, Automation, and the Future of Work: Examining the Impact of Technological Advancements on the Workforce" Quality-Access to Success. DOI: DOI: 10.35115/qas.v15i2.678

Long, R., Sebo, J., & Sims, T. (2025). Is there a tension between AI safety and AI welfare? *Philosophical Studies*, *182*(7), 2005–2033. DOI: 10.1007/s11098-025-02302-2

Lordos, G. C., & De Weck, O. L. (2018). Evaluating the sustainability of long term manned Mars campaigns using a physical economics framework. *Proceedings of the International Astronautical Congress, IAC, 2018-October*. https://www.scopus.com/inward/record.uri?eid=2-s2.0-85065747763&partnerID=40&md5=ff4062ae6f43c7ede0fe169a36c8e12c

Lowe B D, Hayden M, Albers J, Wurzelbacher S, (2023). "Case studies of robots and automation as health/safety interventions in small manufacturing enterprises" Journal of Manufacturing & Services Management. DOI: .DOI: 10.1002/jams.1057

Luthans, F., Luthans, K. W., & Luthans, B. C. (2004). Positive psychological capital: Beyond human and social capital. *Business Horizons*, *47*(1), 45–50. DOI: 10.1016/j.bushor.2003.11.007

Lyons, A. C., Grable, J. E., & Joo, S. H. (2018). A cross-country analysis of population aging and financial security. *The Journal of the Economics of Ageing*, *12*, 96–117. DOI: 10.1016/j.jeoa.2018.03.001

Mabasa, N. C. (2018). Mechanisms for funding youth businesses in South Africa: The role of DFIs. (Thesis). University of Cape Town, Faculty of Commerce, Research of GSB. Retrieved from http://hdl.handle.net/11427/27830

Machikape, K., & Oluwadele, D. (2025). Advancing Financial Inclusion and Data Ethics: The Role of Alternative Credit Scoring. *Communications in Computer and Information Science, 2173 CCIS*, 229 – 241. DOI: 10.1007/978-3-031-71412-2_17

Madgule, M., Vinayaka, N., Sonkhaskar, Y. M., Patel, D. R., Karthikeyan, R., & Selvakumar, P. (2023). Mechanical properties and microstructure of activated TIG welded similar joints of Inconel alloys by desirability approaches. Materials Today: Proceedings, 77, 528-533.

Madzikanda, B., Li, C., & Dabuo, F. T. (2022). Barriers to development of entrepreneurial ecosystems and economic performance in Southern Africa. *African Journal of Science, Technology, Innovation and Development*, *14*(4), 936–946. DOI: 10.1080/20421338.2021.1918316

Maestas, N., Mullen, K. J., & Powell, D. (2023). The Effect of Population Aging on Economic Growth, the Labor Force, and Productivity. *American Economic Journal. Macroeconomics*, *15*(2), 306–332. https://www.aeaweb.org/articles?id=10.1257/mac.20190196. DOI: 10.1257/mac.20190196

Maestas, N., Mullen, K. J., & Powell, D. (2023). *The effect of population aging on economic growth, the labor force, and productivity*. American Economic Journal., DOI: 10.1257/aer.20221741

Mago, S. (2014). Urban youth unemployment in Africa: Whither socio-economic problems. *Mediterranean Journal of Social Sciences*, *5*(9), 33–40. DOI: 10.5901/mjss.2014.v5n9p33

Mahadev Madgule, N. (2023). Vinayaka, Yeshwant M. Sonkhaskar, Dhiren Ramanbhai Patel, R. Karthikeyan, P. Selvakumar, (2023). Mechanical properties and microstructure of activated TIG welded similar joints of Inconel alloys by desirability approaches. *Materials Today: Proceedings*, *77*, 528–533. DOI: 10.1016/j.matpr.2022.12.250

Mahalik, M. K., Inekwe, J. N., Das, K. K., Dash, U., & Arize, A. C. (2022). Does the pattern of age dependency matter in the promotion of financial development in an emerging economy? *Applied Economics*, *54*(48), 5622–5637. DOI: 10.1080/00036846.2022.2047605

Malik, Y. S., Rajendran, V. O., Ma, I., Pande, T., Ravichandran, K., Jaganathasamy, N., Ganesh, B., Santhakumar, A., Tazerji, S. S., Rahman, M. T., Safdar, M., Dubal, Z. B., & Dhama, K. (2021). Responses to COVID-19 in South Asian Association for Regional Cooperation (SAARC) countries in 2020, a data analysis during a world of crises. *Chaos, Solitons, and Fractals*, *152*, 111311. DOI: 10.1016/j.chaos.2021.111311 PMID: 34376927

Mamun, A., O'Leary, P., Wittenburg, D. C., & Gregory, J. (2011). Employment among Social Security disability program beneficiaries, 1996-2007. *Soc. Sec. Bull.*, *71*, 11. Lewis, J., & Dijkema, B. (2022). *Breaking Down Work Barriers for People with Disabilities*. Centre for Cultural Renewal.

Mamun, S. A. K., Rahman, M. M., & Khanam, R. (2020). The Relation between an Aging Population and Economic Growth in Bangladesh: Evidence from an Endogenous Growth Model. *Economic Analysis and Policy*, *66*, 14–25. DOI: 10.1016/j.eap.2020.02.001

Mansour, H. (2022). How successful countries are in promoting digital transactions during COVID-19. *Journal of Economic Studies (Glasgow, Scotland)*, *49*(3), 435–452. Advance online publication. DOI: 10.1108/JES-10-2020-0489

March, A., & Failler, P. (2022). Small-scale fisheries development in Africa: Lessons learned and best practices for enhancing food security and livelihoods. *Marine Policy*, *136*, 104824. DOI: 10.1016/j.marpol.2021.104925

Marie, O., & Castello, J. V. (2012). Measuring the (income) effect of disability insurance generosity on labour market participation. *Journal of Public Economics*, *96*(1-2), 198–210. DOI: 10.1016/j.jpubeco.2011.10.004

Markova, S. M., Tsyplakova, S. A., Sedhyh, E. P., Filatova, O. N., & Khizhnyi, A. V. (2021). University modernization in the conditions of industrialization of production and intelligent machines. *Lecture Notes in Networks and Systems*, *200*, 940–947. DOI: 10.1007/978-3-030-69421-0_104

Mason, A. (2005). Demographic transition and demographic dividends in developed and developing countries. In United Nations expert group meeting on social and economic implications of changing population age structures (Vol. 31, No. 5). New York: United Nations, Population Division. Retrieved from https://www.un.org/development/desa/pd/sites/www.un.org.development.desa.pd/files/unpd_egm_200508_09_mason.pdf

Mason, C., & Brown, R. (2014). *Entrepreneurial ecosystems and growth-oriented entrepreneurship*. OECD. Retrieved from https://www.researchgate.net/publication/260870819_ENTREPRENEURIAL_ECOSYSTEM_AND_GROWTH_ORIENTED_ENTREPRENEURSHIP_Background_paper_prepared_for_the_workshop_organised_by_the_OECD_LEED_Programme_and_the_Dutch_Ministry_of_Economic_Affairs_on.

Mason, A., Lee, R., & Network, N. T. A. (2022). Six ways population change will affect the global economy. *Population and Development Review*, *48*(2), 257–276. DOI: 10.1111/padr.12469

Mavromaras, K., Moskos, M., Mahuteau, S., & Isherwood, L. (2018). *Evaluation of the NDIS, final report*. National Institute of Labour Studies, Flinders University. Website., https://www.dss.gov.au/disability-and-carers/programs-services/for-people-with-disability/national-disability-insurance-scheme/ndis-evaluation-consolidated-report

Mburu, R. M. (2021). Challenges facing youth enterprise performance in Nyeri County. *Reviewed Journal International of Business Management*, *2*(1), 74–79. http://repository.mut.ac.ke:8080/xmlui/handle/123456789/6491. DOI: 10.61426/business.v2i1.20

McClelland, D. C. (1961). *The Achieving Society*. Van Nostrand., DOI: 10.1037/14359-000

McGinley, C., Myerson, J., Briscoe, G., & Carroll, S. (2022). Towards an age-friendly design lens. *Journal of Population Ageing*, *15*(2), 541–556. Advance online publication. DOI: 10.1007/s12062-022-09367-5

McKay, A., & Reis, R. (2021). Optimal automatic stabilizers. *The Review of Economic Studies*, *88*(5), 2375–2406. Advance online publication. DOI: 10.1093/restud/rdaa038

Medina-Vidal, A., Alonso-Galicia, P. E., González-Mendoza, M., & Ramírez-Montoya, M. S. (2025). Financial inclusion of vulnerable sectors with a gender perspective: Risk analysis model with artificial intelligence based on complex thinking. *Journal of Innovation and Entrepreneurship*, *14*(1), 4. Advance online publication. DOI: 10.1186/s13731-025-00463-2

Mehrotra, S., & Parida, J. K. (2021). Stalled structural change brings an employment crisis in India. *The Indian Journal of Labour Economics : the Quarterly Journal of the Indian Society of Labour Economics*, *64*(2), 257–276. DOI: 10.1007/s41027-021-00317-x PMID: 34092956

Melliani, H., & Elhissi, Y. (2024). Promoting Entrepreneurial Culture in the Moroccan Educational System: Initiatives, Challenges and Perspectives. *European Journal of Management. Economics and Business*, *1*(3), 222–233. DOI: 10.59324/ejmeb.2024.1(3).19

Meng, Q., & Yu, W. (2024). The Impact of Population Aging on Economic Growth. *Advances in Economics, Management, and Political Sciences*, 140, 109-116. https://www.ewadirect.com/proceedings/aemps/article/view/18557

Merroun, M. A., & El Ghrasli, A. (2025). The entrepreneurial ecosystem: a strategic lever for the development and support of young entrepreneurs in Morocco. *IJTM International Journal of Trade and Management*, 2(4), 94-108. Retrieved from https://ricg-encgt.ma/index.php/IJTM/article/view/46/45

Metawa, N., Afchal, S., & El-Kanj, N. (2025). AI-based model for Enhancing Credit Risk and Delinquency Management in Banks. *Journal of Cybersecurity and Information Management*, *16*(1), 282–300. DOI: 10.54216/JCIM.160120

Miglani, M., Taneja, S., Bhatnagar, M., & Johri, A. (2025). Transforming Financial Services: Ethical Pathways of Workforce Automation towards Achieving SDG 9. *International Research Journal of Multidisciplinary Scope*, *6*(2), 1298–1308. DOI: 10.47857/irjms.2025.v06i02.03963

Migliorelli, M. (2021). What do we mean by sustainable finance? Assessing existing frameworks and policy risks. *Sustainability (Basel)*, *13*(2), 975. DOI: 10.3390/su13020975

Millar, G. (2021). Ambition and ambivalence: Reconsidering positive peace as a trans-scalar peace system. *Journal of Peace Research*, *58*(4), 640–654. DOI: 10.1177/0022343320941909

Mindell, D. A., & Reynolds, E. (2023). *The work of the future: Building better jobs in an age of intelligent machines*. MIT Press.

Minzner, C. (2024). China's Population Decline Continues. *Council on Foreign Relations*. https://www.cfr.org/blog/chinas-population-decline-continues

Miranda, A. E. R. (2021). *Finding opportunities in Japan's aging population*. FSI Insights and Commentaries.

Mitchell, O. S. (2018). Enhancing risk management for an aging world. *The Geneva Risk and Insurance Review*, *43*(2), 115–136. DOI: 10.1057/s10713-018-0027-x

Mitchell, R. K., Busenitz, L. W., Bird, B., Gaglio, C. M., McMullen, J. S., Morse, E. A., & Smith, J. B. (2007). The Central Question in Entrepreneurial Cognition Research 2007. *Entrepreneurship Theory and Practice*, *31*(1), 1–27. DOI: 10.1111/j.1540-6520.2007.00161.x

Mitchell, R. K., Busenitz, L., Lant, T., McDougall, P. P., Morse, E. A., & Smith, J. B. (2002). Toward a theory of entrepreneurial cognition: Rethinking the people side of entrepreneurship research. *Entrepreneurship Theory and Practice*, *27*(2), 93–104. DOI: 10.1111/1540-8520.00001

Modigliani, F., & Brumberg, R. (1954). Utility analysis and the consumption function: An interpretation of cross-section data. *Franco Modigliani*, *1*(1), 388–436.

Molina-López, M. M., Koller, M. R. T., Rubio-Andrés, M., & González-Pérez, S. (2021). Never too late to learn: how education helps female entrepreneurs at overcoming barriers in the digital economy. Sustainability, 13(19), 11037. mdpi.comDOI: 10.3390/su131911037

Molotoks, A., Smith, P., & Dawson, T. P. (2021). Impacts of land use, population, and climate change on global food security. *Food and Energy Security*, *10*(2), e261. DOI: 10.1002/fes3.261

Mondal, S. K., Huang, J., Wang, Y., Su, B., Zhai, J., Tao, H., Wang, G., Fischer, T., Wen, S., & Jiang, T. (2021). Doubling of the population exposed to drought over South Asia: CMIP6 multi-model-based analysis. *The Science of the Total Environment*, *771*, 145186. DOI: 10.1016/j.scitotenv.2021.145186 PMID: 33736148

Morandini S, Fraboni F, De Angelis M, Puzzo G, Giusino D, Pietrantoni L, (2023). "The impact of artificial intelligence on workers' skills: Upskilling and reskilling in organisations" Informing Science: The International Journal of an Emerging Transdiscipline, 26, 039-068.

Morris, M. H., Kuratko, D. F., & Covin, J. G. (2008). *Corporate entrepreneurship and innovation* (2nd ed.). Thomson Higher Education, Mason.

Morsomme, H., Alonso-Garcia, J., & Devolder, P. (2024). Intergenerational risk sharing in pay-as-you-go pension schemes. *Scandinavian Actuarial Journal*, ●●●, 1–29.

Moschis, G. P. (2022). “Marketing to the aging population”. Management for Professionals, Springer. DOI: 10.1007/978-3-031-13097-7

Mrabet R. (2023). “Sustainable agriculture for food and nutritional security”. Sustainable Agriculture and the Environment, 157-174.

Mukendi, S., & Manda, S. (2022). Micro-financial institutions and processes of women empowerment in Zambia. World Development Perspectives. whiterose.ac.ukDOI: 10.1016/j.wdp.2022.100466

Mulyati, E., Murwadji, T., & Bernike, G. (2025). Strategy development for MSMEs in the Indonesian marketplaces through loans with performance guarantees. *Cogent Social Sciences*, *11*(1), 2548860. Advance online publication. DOI: 10.1080/23311886.2025.2548860

Munir, K., & Shahid, F. S. U. (2020). Role of demographic factors in economic growth of South Asian countries. *Journal of Economic Studies (Glasgow, Scotland)*, *48*(3), 557–570. DOI: 10.1108/JES-08-2019-0373

Musa, S F P. D., & Basir, K. H. (2021). Smart farming: Towards a sustainable agri-food system. *British Food Journal*, *123*(10), 257–276. DOI: 10.1108/BFJ-03-2021-0325

Mustafa M A, Mabhaudhi T, Avvari M V. (2021). “Transition toward sustainable food systems: A holistic pathway toward sustainable development”. Food Security and Sustainability, 257-276.

Mutale-Joan, C., Sbabou, L., & Hicham, E. A. (2023). Microalgae and cyanobacteria: How exploiting these microbial resources can address the underlying challenges related to food sources and sustainable agriculture. *Journal of Plant Growth Regulation*, *42*(2), 257–276. DOI: 10.1007/s00344-021-10534-9

Mutura, N. E., & Cherotich, G. (2024). An assessment on how Uwezo fund-funded SMES in Meru County, Kenya fared financially after using internal equity financing, *International Journal Of Progressive Research In Engineering Management And Science,* 11(4), 72–83. Retrieved from https://www.ijprems.com/uploadedfiles/paper//issue_11_november_2024/36559/final/fin_ijprems1730734526.pdf

Mwangi, S. M. (2011). The contribution of entrepreneurship education course in enhancing management skills of informal entrepreneurs. *Journal of Education and Vocational Research*, 2(3), 86-92. Retrieved from https://scholar.google.com/scholar?hl=fr&as_sdt=0%2C5&q=The+Contribution+of+Entrepreneurship+Education+Course+in+Enhancing+Management+Skills+of+Informal&btnG=

Nagarajan, N. R., & Sixsmith, A. (2023). Policy initiatives to address the challenges of an older population in the workforce. *Ageing International*, *48*(1), 41–77. Advance online publication. DOI: 10.1007/s12126-021-09442-w PMID: 34465930

Nagarajan, N. R., Teixeira, A. A., & Silva, S. T. (2016). The Impact of an Aging Population on Economic Growth: An Exploratory Review of the Main Mechanisms. *Analise Social*, *51*(218), 4–35. https://www.jstor.org/stable/43755167

Naguib, R. (2024). Motivations and barriers to female entrepreneurship: Insights from Morocco. *Journal of African Business*, 25(1), 9-36. https://doi.org/. 2022.2053400DOI: 10.1080/15228916

Namatovu, R., Dawa, S., Mulira, F., Katongole, C., & Nyongesa, S. (2012). Rural youth entrepreneurs in East Africa: A view from Uganda and Kenya. ICBE-RF Research Report, (32), 12.Retrieved from https://trustafrica.org/publication/rural-youth-entrepreneurs-in-east-africa-a-view-from-uganda-and-kenya/

National Population Commission. (2023). A decade of Dialogue on Population and Development in Nigeria (2012-2022). Retrieved from https://cdn.sanity.io/files/5otlgtiz/production/d7fb94a5c16220cd7559ac066f95f9d53a433ac8.pdf

Naudé, W. (2010). Entrepreneurship, developing countries, and development economics: New approaches and insights. *Small Business Economics*, *34*(1), 1–12. DOI: 10.1007/s11187-009-9198-2

Naudé, W. (2011). Entrepreneurship is not a binding constraint on growth and development in the poorest countries. *World Development*, *39*(1), 33–44. DOI: 10.1016/j.worlddev.2010.05.005

Nekhvyadovich, L. I., Adarina, R. T., & Robets, D. S. (2022). Environmental Factors for Measuring Service Performance. In *Geo-Economy of the Future: Sustainable Agriculture and Alternative Energy: Volume II.* (Vol. 2). Springer International Publishing. DOI: 10.1007/978-3-030-92303-7_4

Nesterov, O. G. (2023). Post-working Society: Synthetic Freedom and Work Ethics. *Voprosy Filosofii*, *2023*(2), 79–88. DOI: 10.21146/0042-8744-2023-2-79-88

Ngene, G., Pinet, M., Maclay, C., Phiona, S., & Tant, E. (2021). Strengthening youth livelihoods and enterprise innovation in Africa's digital era. ODI Working paper. London: ODI. Retrieved from https://cdn.odi.org/media/documents/ODI-YFLP-StrengtheningYouth Livelihoods-WorkingPaper-Jul21-Final_kKlkIaX.pdf

Niederer, R., Richter, W., & Keller, H. (1980). Ion - selective Electrodes for Determination of Urine Electrolytes [Ionen-selektive Elektroden zur Bestimmung von Urin-Elektrolyten]. *Biomedizinische Technik, 25*(3), 42–47. DOI: 10.1515/bmte.1980.25.3.42 PMID: 7448299

Nielsen, J. U., Madsen, N. T., & Clarke, R. (2014). Slaughter line operation. In *Encyclopedia of Meat Sciences*. Elsevier Inc., DOI: 10.1016/B978-0-12-384731-7.00150-1

Nissim, G., & Simon, T. (2021). The future of labor unions in the age of automation and at the dawn of AI. *Technology in Society, 67*, 101732. Advance online publication. DOI: 10.1016/j.techsoc.2021.101732

Njeri, W. C., & Mutundu, K. (2021). Effects of youth enterprise development fund on the promotion of youth owned business enterprises in Nakuru East Sub-County, Kenya. *European Journal of Social Sciences Studies, 6*(4). Advance online publication. https://oapub.org/soc/index.php/EJSSS/article/view/1070. DOI: 10.46827/ejsss.v6i4.1070

Njoroge, C. W., & Gathungu, J. M. (2013). The effect of entrepreneurial education and training on development of small and medium size enterprises in Githunguri District-Kenya. *International Journal of Education and Research, 1*(8), 1–22. http://www.ijern.com/journal/August-2013/11.pdf

Nkechi, A., Emeh Ikechukwu, E. J., & Okechukwu, U. F. (2012). Entrepreneurship development and employment generation in Nigeria: Problems and prospects. *Universal Journal of education and general. Studies, 1*(4), 88–102. https://nairametrics.com/wp-content/uploads/2013/02/enterprenuership-development-in-Nigeria.pdf

Norris, P., & Inglehart, R. (2011). *Sacred and Secular: Religion and Politics Worldwide* (2nd ed.). Cambridge University Press. DOI: 10.1017/CBO9780511894862

Norton, G. W., Alwang, J., & Masters, W. A. (2021). *Economics of agricultural development: world food systems and resource use*. Taylor & Francis. DOI: 10.4324/9780429316999

Nzabamwita, J. & Dinbabo, M. (2022). International migration and social protection in South Africa. Cogent Social Sciences. tandfonline.comDOI: 10.1080/23311886.2022.2144134

Obiechina, C. (2024). Addressing Youth Unemployment in Africa: Leveraging Entrepreneurship as a Tool for Youth Development. DOI: 10.2139/ssrn.4890481

Odeku, K. O., & Rudolf, S. S. (2019). An analysis of the transformative interventions promoting youth entrepreneurship in South Africa. *Academy of Entrepreneurship Journal, 25*(4), 1–10. https://www.abacademies.org/articles/an-analysis-of-the-transformative-interventions-promoting-youth-entrepreneurship-in-south-africa-8836.html

Odeyemi, O., Oyewole, A. T., Adeoye, O. B., Ofodile, O. C., Addy, W. A., Okoye, C. C., & Ololade, Y. J. (2024). Entrepreneurship in Africa: A review of growth and challenges. *International Journal of Management & Entrepreneurship Research, 6*(3), 608–622. DOI: 10.51594/ijmer.v6i3.874

OECD. (2020). *Ageing and Fiscal Challenges across Levels of Government*. OECD Publishing. Retrieved from https://www.oecd.org/content/dam/oecd/en/publications/reports/2020/10/ageing-and-fiscal-challenges-across-levels-of-government_f565f895/2bbfbda8-en.pdf

OECD. (2024). *OECD Economic Surveys: Morocco 2024: Economic Assessment*. OECD Publishing., DOI: 10.1787/80777ea7-

Ogunsanya, O., Anwana, E., & Mthembu, N. (2024). University Entrepreneurship Programmes and their Implications for Youth Development in South Africa's Developmental Agenda: Case Studies from KwaZulu Natal. *African Journal of Inter/Multidisciplinary Studies*, 6(si2), 1-14. https://hdl.handle.net/10520/ejc-ajims_v6_nsi2_a3

Ojima, D. (2025). Selected Macroeconomic Indicators and Economic Wellbeing in Nigeria. *African Journal of Management and Business Research, 18*(1), 238–257. DOI: 10.62154/ajmbr.2025.018.010655

Okubo, T. (2024). Non-routine tasks and ICT tools in telework. *Labour, 38*(2), 177–202. Advance online publication. DOI: 10.1111/labr.12262

Olurin, J. O., Okonkwo, F., Eleogu, T., & Nwobodo, C. C. (2024). Strategic HR management in the manufacturing industry: Balancing automation and workforce development. *International Journal of Innovation and Scientific Research, X*(XII), 380–401. DOI: 10.51244/IJRSI.2023.1012030

Olutuase, S. O., Brijlal, P., Yan, B., & Ologundudu, E. (2018). Entrepreneurial orientation and intention: Impact of entrepreneurial ecosystem factors. *Journal of Entrepreneurship Education*, 21(3), 1-14. Retrieved from https://www.researchgate.net/publication/326410506_Entrepreneurial_orientation_and_intention_Impact_of_entrepreneurial_ecosystem_factors

Onyango Ouma, S. (2025). Rethinking of Development in the Twenty-First-Century Africa: Development Strategies, Governance, and Foreign Aid. In *Indigenous Systems*. Colonialism, Colonial Legacies, and Africa's Economic Challenges. Palgrave Macmillan., DOI: 10.1007/978-3-032-00317-1_6

Organisation for Economic Co-operation and Development. (2022). *Disability, Work and Inclusion: Mainstreaming in All Policies and Practices*. OECD Publishing.

Organization for Economic Co-operation and Development (OECD). (2020). *International Migration Outlook 2020*. OECD Publishing.

Oruma, S. O., Misra, S., & Fernandez-Sanz, L. (2021). Agriculture 4.0: An implementation framework for food security attainment in Nigeria's post-Covid-19 era. *IEEE Access : Practical Innovations, Open Solutions*, *9*, 257–276. DOI: 10.1109/ACCESS.2021.3086453

Osareme, O. J., & Muonde, M. (2024). Demographic shifts and healthcare: A review of aging populations and systemic challenges. *International Journal of Scientific Research*, *13*(1), 1–10. DOI: 10.2139/ssrn.3849678

Otoiu, A., Titan, E., Paraschiv, D. M., Dinu, V., & Manea, D. I. (2022). Analysing Labour-Based Estimates of Automation and Their Implications. A Comparative Approach from an Economic Competitiveness Perspective. *Journal of Competitiveness*, *14*(3), 133–152. DOI: 10.7441/joc.2022.03.08

Oualid, A., Qasmaoui, Y., Balouki, Y., & Moumoun, L. (2025). Federated Learning and Open Banking for Inclusive Credit Scoring in Morocco: A Systematic Review. *Lecture Notes in Networks and Systems, 1485 LNNS*, 242–256. DOI: 10.1007/978-3-031-95326-2_24

Ouazzouz, Y., & Harizi, J. (2024). Youth inclusion in morocco: The impact of formal employment and entrepreneurship programs and the challenges ahead. *Revue Marocaine de Recherche en Management et Marketing*, *16*(2), 61–84. DOI: 10.48376/IMIST.PRSM/remarem-v16i2.54493

Owoo, N. S. (2021). Demographic considerations and food security in Nigeria. *Journal of Social and Economic Development*, *23*(2), 257–276. DOI: 10.1007/s40847-020-00116-y

Pai, S.-L., Hsia, K.-H., & Ho, C.-C. (2025). Quality Inspection of PVC Shoe Chopsticks: A Research Study. In J. Y., I. T., & L. J.-J. (Eds.), *Proceedings of International Conference on Artificial Life and Robotics* (pp. 200 – 203). ALife Robotics Corporation Ltd. https://www.scopus.com/inward/record.uri?eid=2-s2.0-85219532146&partnerID=40&md5=5f996c93592269ab43fc07cee8a84461

Pan, F., Zhu, K., & Wang, L. (2022). Impact analysis of population aging on public education financial expenditure in China. *Sustainability (Basel), 14*(23), 15521. DOI: 10.3390/su142315521

Parker, S. K., & Grote, G. (2022). Automation, algorithms, and beyond: Why work design matters more than ever in a digital world. *Applied Psychology, 71*(4), 1171–1204. Advance online publication. DOI: 10.1111/apps.12241

Parry, E., & Battista, V. (2023). The impact of emerging technologies on work: A review of the evidence and implications for the human resource function. *Emerald Open Research, 1*(4). Advance online publication. DOI: 10.1108/EOR-04-2023-0001

Pashevich, E. (2025). On Reliable Algorithmic Absence-Based Inference. *Philosophy & Technology, 38*(3), 101. Advance online publication. DOI: 10.1007/s13347-025-00929-x

Pati, A. K. (2025). *Agentic AI: A Comprehensive Survey of Technologies, Applications, and Societal Implications*. IEEE., DOI: 10.1109/ACCESS.2025.3585609

Peng, T. C. (2024). The effect of demographic shift on property values in Japan. *International Journal of Housing Markets and Analysis*.

Pevnaya, M., Larionova, V., & Pevnaya, E. (2024). Economic contribution and social effects of youth volunteering in the early period of the Covid-19 pandemic: A case of a large Russian region. *International Journal of Trade and Global Markets, 19*(3–4), 314–331. DOI: 10.1504/IJTGM.2024.138997

Pew Research Center. (2017). *Religious Restrictions and Hostilities Reach New Highs in 2016*. Pew Research Center.

Pham, T. N., & Vo, D. H. (2021). Aging Population and Economic Growth in Developing Countries: A Quantile Regression Approach. *Emerging Markets Finance & Trade, 57*(1), 108–122. https://www.tandfonline.com/doi/full/10.1080/1540496X.2019.1698418. DOI: 10.1080/1540496X.2019.1698418

Pickson, R. B., & Boateng, E. (2022). Climate change: A friend or foe to food security in Africa? *Environment, Development and Sustainability, 24*(5), 257–276. DOI: 10.1007/s10668-021-01621-8 PMID: 34276245

Pitoňáková, R. (2019). Modelling impact of economic and demographic factors on personal saving rate in the euro area. *International Journal of Trade and Global Markets, 12*(3-4), 333–344. DOI: 10.1504/IJTGM.2019.101556

Porter, M. E. (1998). Clusters and the new economics of competition. *Harvard Business Review, 76*(6), 77-90. Retrieved from: https://hbr.org/1998/11/clusters-and-the-new-economics-of-competition

Prince, H. J., Khan, A., & Halasa-Rappel, Y. A. (2024). Economic growth, youth unemployment and political and social instability: A study of policies and outcomes in post-Arab spring Egypt, Morocco, Jordan and Tunisia. In *Emerging Trends in Social Policy from the South: Challenges and Innovations in Emerging Economies.* Policy Press. DOI: 10.2307/jj.9692683.14

Priyadarshi, P., & Premchandran, R. (2022). Insecurity and turnover as robots take charge: Impact of neuroticism and change-related uncertainty. *Personnel Review, 51*(1), 21–39. Advance online publication. DOI: 10.1108/PR-06-2019-0310

Puntus, D. A., Yaroshenko, O. M., Chanysheva, H. I., Klemparskyi, M. M., & Yakovlyev, O. A. (2025). Social Insurance in the Context of Growing Labor Automation: New Challenges and Solutions. *Perspectives on Global Development and Technology*, *24*(3–4), 540–557. DOI: 10.1163/15691497-12341722

Radebe, T. N.Thobile N Radebe. (2019). The challenges/barriers preventing the South African youth in becoming entrepreneurs: South African overview. *Journal of Economics and Behavioral Studies, 11*(4), 61–70. https://core.ac.uk/reader/288023310. DOI: 10.22610/jebs.v11i4(J).2921

Radivojević, B., & Vasić, P. (2012). Household age structure and consumption in Serbia. *Economic annals, 57*(195), 79-101.

Rahman, M. M., Saidi, K., & Mbarek, M. B. (2020). Economic growth in South Asia: The role of CO2 emissions, population density and trade openness. *Heliyon, 6*(5), e03903. DOI: 10.1016/j.heliyon.2020.e03903 PMID: 32420481

Ramakrishnan, T., Mohan Gift, M. D., Chitradevi, S., Jegan, R., & Subha Hency Jose, P. Nagaraja, Rajneesh Sharma HN, Selvakumar P, Sintayehu Mekuria Hailegiorgis, (2022). "Study of Numerous Resins Used in Polymer Matrix Composite Materials", Advances in Materials Science and Engineering, vol. 2022, Article ID 1088926, 8 pages, 2022. https://doi.org/DOI: 10.1155/2022/1088926

Rashid, S., & Ratten, V. (2020). A Systematic Literature review on women entrepreneurship in emerging economies while reflecting specifically on SAARC countries. In *Contributions to management science* (pp. 37–88). DOI: 10.1007/978-3-030-35415-2_4

Rehman, A., Farooq, M., Lee, D. J., & Siddique, K. H. M. (2022). Sustainable agricultural practices for food security and ecosystem services. *Environmental Science and Pollution Research International*, *29*(10), 15311–15325. DOI: 10.1007/s11356-022-23635-z PMID: 36258111

Ren, Y., Castro Campos, B., Peng, Y., & Glauben, T. (2021). Nutrition transition with accelerating urbanization? Empirical evidence from rural China. *Nutrients*, *13*(15), 2632. DOI: 10.3390/nu13030921 PMID: 33809126

Rezaei, E. (2022). Demographic changes and savings behavior: The experience of a developing country. *Journal of Economic Studies (Glasgow, Scotland)*, *49*(4), 603–622. DOI: 10.1108/JES-01-2021-0021

Ritchie, H. (2024). Which Countries have Fertility Rates Above or below the "Replacement Level"? *Our World in Data.* https://ourworldindata.org/data-insights/which-countries-have-fertility-rates-above-or-below-the-replacement-level

Robb, A. (2014). Entrepreneurship education and training: insights from Ghana, Kenya, and Mozambique. World Bank Publications. Retrieved from https://documents1.worldbank.org/curated/en/845181468030266720/pdf/Entrepreneurship-education-and-training-insights-from-Ghana-Kenya-and-Mozambique.pdf

Rodrik, D. (2022). An industrial policy for good jobs. In *Hamilton Project—Policy proposal.* OECD Publishing., DOI: 10.1787/3c3f1559-

Rogerson, C. M. (2008, March). Tracking SMME development in South Africa: Issues of finance, training and the regulatory environment. In Urban forum (Vol. 19, No. 1, pp. 61-81). Dordrecht: Springer Netherlands. DOI: 10.1007/s12132-008-9025-x

Ruben, R., Cavatassi, R., Lipper, L., Smaling, E., & Winters, P. (2021). Towards food systems transformation—Five paradigm shifts for healthy, inclusive and sustainable food systems. *Food Security*, *13*(5), 1031–1044. DOI: 10.1007/s12571-021-01221-4 PMID: 34667484

Rupp, K., Davies, P. S., & Strand, A. (2008). Disability benefit coverage and program interactions in the working-age population. *Social Security Bulletin*, *68*, 1. PMID: 18837269

Rust, R. T., & Huang, M.-H. (2012). Optimizing service productivity. *Journal of Marketing*, *76*(2), 47–66. DOI: 10.1509/jm.10.0441

Rusu, S., Isac, F., Cureteanu, R., & Csorba, L. (2012). Entrepreneurship and entrepreneur: A review of literature concepts. *African Journal of Business Management*, *6*(10), 3570.

Salimgereyev, N., & Mukhamediyev, B. (2024). Measuring the routine and non-routine task contents: A comparative study between state and industrial sector employees. *International Journal (Toronto, Ont.)*.

Samir, K. C. (2013). Population Stabilization, Human. In Levin, S. A. (Ed.), *Encyclopedia of Biodiversity* (2nd ed., pp. 199–209). Elsevier., https://www.sciencedirect.com/science/article/abs/pii/B9780123847195004135

Sandhu, K. (2025). Guest editorial: AI-enabled blockchain and fintech innovation. *International Journal of Accounting and Information Management*, *33*(2), 265–267. DOI: 10.1108/IJAIM-05-2025-456

Schaede, U., & Shimizu, K. (2022). *The digital transformation and Japan's political economy*. Cambridge University Press., DOI: 10.1017/9781009084115

Schimmel Hyde, J., & Stapleton, D. C. (2017, December). Using the health and retirement study for disability policy research: A review. [). De Gruyter.]. *Forum for Health Economics & Policy*, *20*(2), 20170002. DOI: 10.1515/fhep-2017-0002 PMID: 31419905

Schoof, U. (2006). Stimulating Youth Entrepreneurship: Barriers and incentives to enterprise start-ups by young people. International Labour Organization. Retrieved from https://webapps.ilo.org/public/libdoc/ilo/2006/106B09_94_engl.pdf

Schumpeter, J. A. (1934). *The Theory of Economic Development. Cambridge*. Harvard Economic Studies.

Scott, S., Nguyen, P. H., Neupane, S., Pramanik, P., Nanda, P., Bhutta, Z. A., Afsana, K., & Menon, P. (2020). Early marriage and early childbearing in South Asia: Trends, inequalities, and drivers from 2005 to 2018. *Annals of the New York Academy of Sciences*, *1491*(1), 60–73. DOI: 10.1111/nyas.14531 PMID: 33258141

Seddik, M. M. D., El Adraoui, F. E., Rabah–Rabbou, M., & Jabbouri, J. (2024). SME Financing: Diversity of Sources and Specific Constraints in Morocco. *Revue Internationale des Sciences de Gestion*, *7*(4). https://revue-isg.com/index.php/home/article/view/1818

Segkouli, S., Giakoumis, D., Votis, K., & Tzovaras, D. (2023). Smart Workplaces for older adults: Coping 'ethically'with technology pervasiveness. *Universal Access in the Information Society*, *22*(1), 37–49. Advance online publication. DOI: 10.1007/s10209-021-00829-9 PMID: 34305502

Sehajpal, S., & Sidhu, N. K. (2024). Neuroscience, nursing, and financial innovation: A synergistic approach to optimized patient care and economic well-being. In *Neuromarketing's Role in Sustainable Finance*. IGI Global., DOI: 10.4018/979-8-3693-9117-4.ch008

Sekher, T. V., & Gupta, S. (2024). Social Security Schemes for the Elderly in India: Awareness, Utilization, and Barriers. In James, K. S., & Sekher, T. V. (Eds.), *India Population Report* (pp. 199–245). Cambridge University Press.

Sen, A. (1999). Development as Freedom Oxford University Press Shaw TM & Heard. *The Politics of Africa: Dependence and Development.*

Sever, C. (2023). Population aging and convergence of household credit. *The B.E. Journal of Macroeconomics*, *23*(1), 497–520. DOI: 10.1515/bejm-2022-0048

Shakespeare, T. (2006). *Disability rights and wrongs*. Routledge. DOI: 10.4324/9780203640098

Shane, S. A., & Venkataraman, S. (2000). The promise of entrepreneurship as a field of research. *Academy of Management Review*, *25*(1), 217–226. DOI: 10.5465/amr.2000.2791611

Sharma, R. Deepika, & Khan, R. (2025). Machine and deep learning approaches for heart disease risk assessment. In K. S., K. S., K. M., D. A., & S. D.K. (Eds.), *Computational Methods in Science and Technology - Proceedings of the 4th International Conference on Computational Methods in Science and Technology, ICCMST 2024* (Vol. 1, pp. 79 – 82). CRC Press/Balkema. DOI: 10.1201/9781003501244-15

Sharma, R., Bhatnagar, M., & Ozen, E. (2025). The role of intellectual capital in combatting deepfake threats to corporate reputation and trust. In *Mastering Deepfake Technology: Strategies for Ethical Management and Security*. River Publishers. https://www.scopus.com/inward/record.uri?eid=2-s2.0-105007657679&partnerID=40&md5=f313a80a3279f91fbedf7fd10c6a4f7a

Sharma, P., Malhotra, R. K., & Kumar, R. (2024). How is digitalization reshaping the landscape of Rural banking in India? *2024 International Conference on Smart Devices, ICSD 2024*. DOI: 10.1109/ICSD60021.2024.10750981

Shefrin, H. M., & Thaler, R. H. (1988). The behavioral life-cycle hypothesis. *Economic Inquiry*, *26*(4), 609–643. DOI: 10.1111/j.1465-7295.1988.tb01520.x

Shekhawat, K. K., Yadav, A. K., Sanu, M. S., & Kumar, P. (2021). Key drivers of consumption-based carbon emissions: Empirical evidence from SAARC countries. *Environmental Science and Pollution Research International*, *29*(16), 23206–23224. DOI: 10.1007/s11356-021-17413-6 PMID: 34800276

Shende, A. D., Tekade, S. A., Deshmukh, A. A., Tembhurkar, S. P., & Selvakumar, P. (2025). Water Quality Monitoring and Control With AI. In Ruiz-Vanoye, J., & Díaz-Parra, O. (Eds.), *Smart Water Technology for Sustainable Management in Modern Cities* (pp. 51–80). IGI Global Scientific Publishing., DOI: 10.4018/979-8-3693-8074-1.ch003

Sheriyarji, J. (2019). Braverman's legacy degraded labour, automation and information technology in the era of globalisation. *Economic and Political Weekly*, *54*(29), 92–99. https://www.scopus.com/inward/record.uri?eid=2-s2.0-85069716936&partnerID=40&md5=81431795676394a8b92d58f62b1b6698

Shevelkova, V., Mattocks, C., & Lafortune, L. (2023). Efforts to Address the Sustainable Development Goals in Older Populations: A Scoping Review. *BMC Public Health*, *23*(1), 456. DOI: 10.1186/s12889-023-15308-4 PMID: 36890447

Shirasu, M. R., de Albuquerque, E., & Arraes, R. (2020). Evaluation of the economic costs associated to the neet youth in Brazil [Avaliação dos custos econômicos associados aos jovens nem-nem no Brasil]. *Revista de Economia Política*, *40*(1), 161–182. DOI: 10.1590/0101-31572020-2902

Shohan, M. U. S., Alam, A. S. M. R. U., Rakhi, N. N., Kabir, M., Siam, M. K. S., Hasan, M. M., Sheriff, R., Karim, M. A., Rahman, A., Moni, M. A., & Khan, M. A. (2020). Onset, transmission, impact, and management of COVID-19 epidemic at early stage in SAARC countries. *Authorea (Authorea)*. DOI: 10.22541/au.159775079.90952648

Sim Ong, F., Kitchen, J. P., & Jama, A. T. (2008). Consumption patterns and silver marketing: An analysis of older consumers in Malaysia. *Marketing Intelligence & Planning*, *26*(7), 682–698. DOI: 10.1108/02634500810916663

Singh, A. (2024). Financial Constraints and Funding Solutions for Small Startups in Emerging Markets. *International Journal of Social Science and Economic Research*, *9*(9), 3813–3839. DOI: 10.46609/IJSSER.2024.v09i09.038

Singhania, M., Chadha, G., & Prasad, R. (2024). Sustainable finance research: Review and agenda. *International Journal of Finance & Economics*, *29*(4), 4010–4045. DOI: 10.1002/ijfe.2854

Singh, D., & Stakic, N. (2020). Financial inclusion and economic growth nexus: Evidence from SAARC countries. *South Asia Research*, *41*(2), 238–258. DOI: 10.1177/0262728020964605

Sirokha, D., Volynets, V., Kovalenko, R., Pohorielova, O., & Tkachuk, A. (2024). Labor Protection in the Perspective of Artificial Intelligence: New Challenges for the EU and the ILO. *Adam Mickiewicz University Law Review, 16*, 67–98. DOI: 10.14746/ppuam.2024.16.03

Sitharam, S., & Hoque, M. (2016). Factors affecting the performance of small and medium enterprises in KwaZulu-Natal, South Africa. *Problems and Perspectives in Management, 14*(2), 277–288. https://pdfs.semanticscholar.org/32f1/97d075b84feb0f0ac7f9c98bfb25ccc7c358.pdf. DOI: 10.21511/ppm.14(2-2).2016.03

Sløk, T. (2024). Working-Age Population Growth in the G-7. *Apollo*. https://www.apolloacademy.com/working-age-population-growth-in-the-g7/

Smyth, S. J., Webb, S. R., & Phillips, P. W. B. (2021). The role of public-private partnerships in improving global food security. *Global Food Security, 28*, 100494. DOI: 10.1016/j.gfs.2021.100588

Somoye, O. A., Mar'I, M., & Olowu, G. (2025). Does carbon dioxide emission influence food security in the United States amidst economic expansion, population growth, and inflation? A QARDL and Wavelet approach. *Natural Resources Forum, 49*(1), 257–276. DOI: 10.1111/1477-8947.12422

Spasova, S., Atanasova, A., Sabato, S., & Bouget, D. (2023). *Making access to social protection for workers and the self-employed more transparent through information and simplification*. Social Policy Network.

Sreenivasulu, A., & Manimozhi, T. Satheesh kumar P, Selvakumar P. and Singh P, (2022). "The Model of Smart Sensing Device For Sensitive Nanoclusters Modification in Sensing Properties," 2022 2nd International Conference on Advance Computing and Innovative Technologies in Engineering (ICACITE), Greater Noida, India, 2022, pp. 1043-1047, DOI: 10.1109/ICACITE53722.2022.9823846

Stam, F. C., & Spigel, B. (2016). Entrepreneurial Ecosystems. Utrecht School of Economics Discussion Paper Series, 16-13, 1-18. Retrieved from https://www.uu.nl/sites/default/files/rebo_use_dp_2016_1613.pdf

Stam, E. (2015). Entrepreneurial ecosystems and regional policy: A sympathetic critique. *European Planning Studies, 23*(9), 1759–1769. DOI: 10.1080/09654313.2015.1061484

Stavi, I., & Roque de Pinho, J. (2022). Food security among dryland pastoralists and agropastoralists: The climate, land-use change, and population dynamics nexus. *Anthropocene, 37*, 100313. DOI: 10.1016/j.ancene.2022.100313

Štěpánek, M. (2019). Pension reforms and adverse demographics: Options for the Czech Republic. *Finance a Uver*, *69*(2), 174–210.

Sternberg, R., & Wennekers, S. (2005). Determinants and effects of new business creation using Global Entrepreneurship Monitor data. *Small Business Economics*, *24*(3), 193–203. DOI: 10.1007/s11187-005-1974-z

Sugumaran K M D, Pandiyarajan V Y B S, Selvakumar P. and M. S, (2024). "Analysis of Electromyography Signals for Control of Mechanical Prosthesis using Machine Learning Techniques," 2024 2nd International Conference on Intelligent Data Communication Technologies and Internet of Things (IDCIoT), Bengaluru, India, 2024, pp. 1059-1067, .DOI: 10.1109/IDCIoT59759.2024.10467707

Sulastri, R., Ding, A. Y., & Janssen, M. F. W. H. A. (2025). Sensitivity Analysis: Improving Inclusive Credit Scoring Algorithm Through Feature Weight and Penalty-Based Approach. *International Conference on EDemocracy and EGovernment, ICEDEG, 2025*, 54–61. DOI: 10.1109/ICEDEG65568.2025.11081606

Sultana, F., & Reza, H. M. (2020). Are SAARC countries prepared to combat COVID-19 to save young, working-age population? *AIMS Public Health*, *7*(3), 440–449. DOI: 10.3934/publichealth.2020036 PMID: 32968669

Sumberg, J., & Hunt, S. (2019). Are African rural youth innovative? Claims, evidence and implications. *Journal of Rural Studies*, 69, 130-136. https://doi.org/. 05.004DOI: 10.1016/j.jrurstud.2019

Sundram, P. (2023). Food security in ASEAN: Progress, challenges and future. *Frontiers in Sustainable Food Systems*, *7*, 1095313. DOI: 10.3389/fsufs.2023.1095313

Swedish Migration Agency. (2016). *Sweden's Approach to the Syrian Refugee Crisis*. Government of Sweden.

Szmigin, I., & Carrigan, M. (2001). Learning to love the older consumer. *Journal of Consumer Behaviour*, *1*(1), 22–34. DOI: 10.1002/cb.51

Tamasiga, P., Onyeaka, H., Akinsemolu, A., & Bakwena, M. (2023). The inter-relationship between climate change, inequality, poverty and food security in Africa: A bibliometric review and content analysis approach. *Sustainability (Basel)*, *15*(11), 6556. DOI: 10.3390/su15075628

Tazinya, R. M. A., Hajjar, J. M., & Yaya, S. (2022). Strengthening integrated sexual reproductive health and rights and HIV services programs to achieve sustainable development goals 3 and 5 in Africa. Reproductive Health. springer.comDOI: 10.1186/s12978-022-01535-2

Temsumrit, N. (2023). Can Aging Population Affect Economic Growth through the Channel of Government Spending? *Heliyon*, *9*(9), e19521. DOI: 10.1016/j.heliyon.2023.e19521 PMID: 37809751

Thøgersen, Ø. (2010). Reforming social security: Assessing the effects of alternative funding strategies. *Applied Economics*, *33*(12), 1531–1540. DOI: 10.1080/00036840010014436

Thomas, P., Jacobs, N., Valorose, J., & Schauben, L. (2021). How the Youth Social Entrepreneurship (YSE) Model Supports Implementation of SDG #8 to bring Economic Growth and Decent Work in American Cities. *Sustainable Development Goals Series*, (Part F2666), 127–145. DOI: 10.1007/978-3-030-59173-1_10

Tokunova, A., Zvonar, V., Polozhentsev, D., Pavlova, V., & Teres, Y. (2023). Economic Consequences of Artificial Intelligence and Labor Automation: Employment Recovery, Transformation of Labor Markets, and Dynamics of Social Structure in the Context of Digital Transformation. *Economic Affairs (New Delhi)*, *68*(4), 2035–2046. DOI: 10.46852/0424-2513.4.2023.15

Toromade, A. S., Soyombo, D. A., & Kupa, E. (2024). Reviewing the impact of climate change on global food security: Challenges and solutions. *International Journal of Environmental Sciences and Development*, *15*(1), 1–12.

Tranfield, D., Denyer, D., & Smart, P. (2003). Towards a methodology for developing evidence-informed management knowledge by means of systematic review. *British Journal of Management*, *14*(3), 207–222. DOI: 10.1111/1467-8551.00375

Trencher, G., Yarime, M., & Yu, J. (2024). Using emerging technologies to tackle mobility challenges caused by population ageing: Experiences from Japan. *Technological Forecasting and Social Change*, *208*, 123729. Advance online publication. DOI: 10.1016/j.techfore.2024.123729

Tripathi, M., & Inani, S. K. (2020). Does information and communications technology affect economic growth? Empirical evidence from SAARC countries. *Information Technology for Development*, *26*(4), 773–787. DOI: 10.1080/02681102.2020.1785827

Trong, N. T., Dong, N. T., & Ly, P. T. (2024). Population Aging and Economic Growth: Evidence from ASEAN Countries. *Cogent Business & Management*, *11*(1), 2298055. https://www.tandfonline.com/doi/full/10.1080/23311975.2023.2298055. DOI: 10.1080/23311975.2023.2298055

Trotta, A., Rania, F., Scalise, L., & Strano, E. (2024). Civic crowdfunding for local governments: Trends and perspectives from a bibliometric analysis. *Public Money & Management*, •••, 1–13.

Trotta, A., Rania, F., & Strano, E. (2024). Exploring the linkages between FinTech and ESG: A bibliometric perspective. *Research in International Business and Finance*, *69*, 102200. DOI: 10.1016/j.ribaf.2023.102200

Trovato, G., Mavridis, N., Huerta-Mercado, A., & Chellali, R. (2021). Cross-Cultural Timeline of the History of Thought of the Artificial. *Lecture Notes in Computer Science (Including Subseries Lecture Notes in Artificial Intelligence and Lecture Notes in Bioinformatics), 13086 LNAI*, 14–23. DOI: 10.1007/978-3-030-90525-5_2

Tschang, F. T., & Almirall, E. (2021). Artificial intelligence as augmenting automation: Implications for employment. *The Academy of Management Perspectives*, *35*(4), 642–659. Advance online publication. DOI: 10.5465/amp.2019.0062

Uddin, M. N., Karim, A. R., & Parvez, S. M. (2020). Estimation of the SARS-CoV-2 specific reproduction number in SAARC countries: A 60-days Data-driven analysis. *Journal of Applied and Natural Science*, *12*(4), 628–634. DOI: 10.31018/jans.v12i4.2397

UNCTAD. (2024). *Economic Development in Africa Report 2024: Unlocking Africa's trade potential: Boosting regional markets and reducing risks*. United Nations. Retrieved from https://unctad.org/publication/economic-development-africa-report-2024

UNDESA. (2015). World Population Aging 2015. *ST/ESA/SER.A/390*. https://www.un.org/en/development/desa/population/publications/pdf/ageing/WPA2015_Report.pdf

UNDESA. (2017). World Population Prospects: the 2017 Revision. *Working Paper No. ESA/P/WP/248*. https://desapublications.un.org/publications/world-population-prospects-2017-revision

UNDESA. (2020). World Fertility and Family Planning 2020: Highlights. ST/ESA/SER.A/440. https://www.un.org/development/desa/pd/content/world-fertility-and-family-planning-2020-highlights

UNDESA. (2022). Aging. https://social.desa.un.org/issues/ageing

UNDESA. (2024). World Population Prospects 2024: Summary of Results. *UNDESA/POP/2024/TR/No.9*. https://desapublications.un.org/publications/world-population-prospects-2024-summary-results

UNFPA. (2025). Aging. https://www.unfpa.org/ageing

UNHCR. (2018). *Report of the Independent International Fact-Finding Mission on Myanmar*. United Nations Human Rights Council.

United Nations Department of Economic and Social Affairs (UN DESA). (2024). Population Division.

United Nations Population Fund. (2025). What works to amplify the rights and voices of youth? Lessons from United Nations evaluations to advance the United Nations Youth Strategy. *Youth meta-synthesis 3 report, Volume 2*. Retrieved from https://www.unfpa.org/sites/ default/files/2025-04/2.%20Youth%20meta-synthesis%203%20report-Vol2-d3.pdf

United Nations. (2019). *World population prospects 2019: Highlights*. Department of Economic and Social Affairs, Population Division. Retrieved from https://population.un.org/wpp/assets/Files/WPP2019_Highlights.pdf

United Nations. (2023). *Youth in Africa: A demographic imperative for peace and security*. Retrieved from https://www.undp.org/sites/g/files/zskgke326/files/2023-05/undp-africa-youth-in-africa-2023-EN.pdf

Upreti, H., Malhotra, R. K., Kumar, R., & Karki, B. (2024). Leveraging Smart Devices for Corporate Social Responsibility in India: Advancements, Trends, and Concerns towards Sustainability. *2024 International Conference on Smart Devices, ICSD 2024*. DOI: 10.1109/ICSD60021.2024.10751578

Vaishya, R., & Vaish, A. (2023). Orthopedic research output from SAARC countries in the last 25 years: 1996-2021. *Journal of Bone and Joint Diseases*, *38*(2), 131–133. DOI: 10.4103/jbjd.jbjd_19_23

Vakhnin, N. A., Vakhnina, E. G., & Smirnova, N. N. (2018). Role of physical education in competitive specialist training process. *Teoriya i Praktika Fizicheskoy Kultury*, *4*, 23 – 24. https://www.scopus.com/inward/record.uri?eid=2-s2.0-85044468438&partnerID=40&md5=96c01120fffb014edae47094332dddaa

Valduga, I. B., Lima, M. A. D., Castro, B. C. G., Fuchs, P. G., Amorim, W. S. D., & Guerra, J. B. S. O. D. A. (2023). A balanced scorecard proposal for gender equality and sustainable development. Sustainability, 15(19), 14384. mdpi.comDOI: 10.3390/su151914384

Välimäki, S., Hazubska-Przybył, T., Ratajczak, E., Tikkinen, M., Varis, S., & Aronen, T. (2021). Somatic Embryo Yield and Quality From Norway Spruce Embryogenic Tissue Proliferated in Suspension Culture. *Frontiers in Plant Science*, *12*, 791549. Advance online publication. DOI: 10.3389/fpls.2021.791549 PMID: 34987536

Van Dijk, M., Morley, T., Rau, M. L., & Saghai, Y. (2021). A meta-analysis of projected global food demand and population at risk of hunger for the period 2010–2050. *Nature Food*, *2*(7), 533–542. DOI: 10.1038/s43016-021-00322-9 PMID: 37117684

Van Eck, N. J., & Waltman, L. (2010). Software survey: VOSviewer, a computer program for Bibliometric mapping. *Scientometrics*, *84*(2), 523–538. DOI: 10.1007/s11192-009-0146-3

Vanella, P., Wilke, C. B., & Heß, M. (2024). Long-Term Care in Germany in the Context of the Demographic Transition—An Outlook for the Expenses of Long-Term Care Insurance through 2050. *Ekonometria*, *12*(4), 28.

Veblen, T. (1899). Mr. Cummings's Strictures on" The Theory of the Leisure Class. *Journal of Political Economy*, *8*(1), 106–117. DOI: 10.1086/250640

Viana, C. M., Freire, D., Abrantes, P., Rocha, J., & Pereira, P. (2022). Agricultural land systems importance for supporting food security and sustainable development goals: A systematic review. *The Science of the Total Environment*, *806*, 150737. DOI: 10.1016/j.scitotenv.2021.150718 PMID: 34606855

Vijayakumar, G. (2024). Muniyandi Rajkumar, Rajiv Chandar N, Selvakumar P and Ramesh Duraisamy, (2024). Environmentally friendly TDS removal from wastewater by electrochemical ion exchange batch-type recirculation (EIR) technique. *Environmental Science. Water Research & Technology*, *10*, 826–835. DOI: 10.1039/D3EW00793F

Vogel, P. (2013). *The employment outlook for youth: Building entrepreneurship ecosystems as a way forward*. World Economic Forum. Retrieved from https://papers.ssrn.com/sol3/papers.cfm?abstract_id=2357856

Vogels, E. A. (2023). Americans are worried about inflation — but many are still spending big. *Pew Research Center.* Retrieved from https://www.pewresearch.org/

Von Cramon-Taubadel, S. (2022). Russia's invasion of Ukraine–implications for grain markets and food security. *German Journal of Agricultural Economics*, *71*(2, Supplement), 57–64. DOI: 10.30430/71.2022.5.Apol

Vornholt, K., Villotti, P., Muschalla, B., Bauer, J., Colella, A., Zijlstra, F., Van Ruitenbeek, G., Uitdewilligen, S., & Corbière, M. (2018). Disability and employment–overview and highlights. *European Journal of Work and Organizational Psychology*, *27*(1), 40–55. DOI: 10.1080/1359432X.2017.1387536

Voumik, L. C., Hossain, M. I., Rahman, M. H., Sultana, R., Dey, R., & Esquivias, M. A. (2023). Impact of Renewable and Non-Renewable Energy on EKC in SAARC Countries: Augmented Mean Group approach. *Energies*, *16*(6), 2789. DOI: 10.3390/en16062789

Voumik, L. C., Mimi, M. B., & Raihan, A. (2023). Nexus between urbanization, industrialization, natural resources rent, and anthropogenic carbon emissions in South Asia: CS-ARDL approach. *Anthropocene Science*, *2*(1), 48–61. DOI: 10.1007/s44177-023-00047-3

Vukmirović, V., Kojić, M., Spasenić, Ž., & Milosavljević, M. (2024). How do socio-demographic factors affect green finance growth? *Stanovnistvo*, *62*(2), 211–230. DOI: 10.59954/stnv.647

Walker, R. J., Garacci, E., Dawson, A. Z., Williams, J. S., Ozieh, M., & Egede, L. E. (2021). Trends in food insecurity in the United States from 2011–2017: Disparities by age, sex, race/ethnicity, and income. *Population Health Management*, *24*(3), 257–266. DOI: 10.1089/pop.2020.0123 PMID: 32941115

Wang, H., Zhang, T., Wang, X., & Zheng, J. (2024). Relationship between Occupational Pension, Corporate Social Responsibility (CSR), and Organizational Resilience: A Study on Listed Chinese Companies. *Risks*, *12*(4), 65. DOI: 10.3390/risks12040065

Wang, L., Liang, J., & Wang, B. (2024). Population aging and sustainable economic development: An analysis based on the role of green finance. *Finance Research Letters*, *70*, 106239. DOI: 10.1016/j.frl.2024.106239

Wang, Q., Wang, X., & Li, R. (2022). Does population aging reduce environmental pressures from urbanization in 156 countries? *The Science of the Total Environment*, *807*, 150788. DOI: 10.1016/j.scitotenv.2022.157330 PMID: 35842167

Wang, X., Ma, L., Yan, S., Chen, X., & Growe, A. (2023). Trade for food security: The stability of global agricultural trade networks. *Foods*, *12*(11), 2211. DOI: 10.3390/foods12020271 PMID: 36673361

Wang, Z., Yao, Q., & Zhao, G. (2024). Population ageing and household risk aversion. *Applied Economics Letters*, •••, 1–10.

Wanjohi, A. M. (2014), SME Policy in Kenya: Issues and Efforts in Progress. Nairobi. Retrieved from https://www.kenpro.org/sme-policy-in-kenya-issues-and-efforts-in-progress/

Ward, P. (2023). *Welfare politics in Mexico: Papering over the crack.* Routledge. DOI: 10.4324/9781003431725

Wei, W. (2025). Population Aging. In Yinxing, H. (Ed.), *Dictionary of Contemporary Chinese Economics* (pp. 525–529). Springer., https://link.springer.com/rwe/10.1007/978-981-97-4036-9_219 DOI: 10.1007/978-981-97-4036-9_219

Wendimu, G. Y. (2021). The challenges and prospects of Ethiopian agriculture. *Cogent Food & Agriculture*, *7*(1), 1907553. DOI: 10.1080/23311932.2021.1907553

Wennekers, S., Van Stel, A., Carree, M., &Thurik, R. (2010). The relationship between entrepreneurship and economic development: Is it U-shaped?. Foundations and trends® in entrepreneurship, 6(3), 167-237. DOI: 10.1561/0300000023

WHO. (2022). Tackling Abuse of Older People: Five Priorities for the United Nations Decade of Healthy Aging (2021-2030). https://iris.who.int/bitstream/handle/10665/356151/9789240052550-eng.pdf?sequence=1

WHO. (2023). Progress Report on the United Nations Decade of Healthy Aging, 2021-2023. *Decade of Healthy Aging*. https://iris.who.int/bitstream/handle/10665/374192/9789240079694-eng.pdf?sequence=1

WHO. (2024a). Abuse of Older People. https://www.who.int/news-room/fact-sheets/detail/abuse-of-older-people

WHO. (2024b). Aging and Health. https://www.who.int/news-room/fact-sheets/detail/ageing-and-health

Wissemann, A. K., Pit, S. W., Serafin, P., & Bollwerk, E. (2022). Strategic guidance and technological solutions for human resources management to sustain an aging workforce: Review of international standards, research, and use cases. *JMIR Human Factors*, *9*(3), e27250. Advance online publication. DOI: 10.2196/27250 PMID: 35862177

Wong, P. K., Ho, Y. P., & Autio, E. (2005). Entrepreneurship, innovation and economic growth: Evidence from GEM data. *Small Business Economics*, *24*(3), 335–350. DOI: 10.1007/s11187-005-2000-1

World Bank Open Data. (2024). *Net Migration Rate by Country*. Retrieved from.

World Bank. (2020). *World Development Report 2020:* Trading for Development in the Age of Global Value Chains. Retrieved from https://www.worldbank.org/en/publication/wdr2020

World Bank. (2024). *Morocco Economic Monitor report:* Unlocking the potential of the private sector to spur growth and job creation. Retrieved from https://documents1.worldbank.org/curated/en/099826007162422517/pdf/IDU12f69bf581e7fa144061b0cf15dc97f2b2bbd.pdf

World Health Organization. (2022). "WHO global strategy for food safety 2022-2030: towards stronger food safety systems and global cooperation".

Worldometer. (2025). Current World Population. https://www.worldometers.info/world-population/

Wouterse, B., & Smid, B. (2017). How to finance the rising costs of long-term care: Four alternatives for the Netherlands. *Fiscal Studies*, *38*(3), 369–391. DOI: 10.1111/j.1475-5890.2017.12137

Xia, L., Robock, A., Scherrer, K., Harrison, C. S., Bodirsky, B. L., Weindl, I., Jägermeyr, J., Bardeen, C. G., Toon, O. B., & Heneghan, R. (2022). Global food insecurity and famine from reduced crop, marine fishery and livestock production due to climate disruption from nuclear war soot injection. *Nature Food*, *3*(7), 533–542. DOI: 10.1038/s43016-022-00573-0 PMID: 37118594

Xie, X., Osińska, M., & Szczepaniak, M. (2023). Do young generations save for retirement? Ensuring financial security of Gen Z and Gen Y. *Journal of Policy Modeling*, *45*(3), 644–668. DOI: 10.1016/j.jpolmod.2023.05.003

Xu, Q., Ou, X., & Li, J. (2022). The Risk of Falls among the Aging Population: A Systematic Review and Meta-analysis. *Frontiers in Public Health*, *10*, 902599. https://www.frontiersin.org/journals/public-health/articles/10.3389/fpubh.2022.902599/full. DOI: 10.3389/fpubh.2022.902599 PMID: 36324472

Yadav, H., Paliwal, M., & Chatradhi, N. (2022). Entrepreneurship development of rural women through digital inclusion: examining the contributions of Public Programs. In Inclusive Businesses in Developing Economies: Converging People, Profit, and Corporate Citizenship (pp. 287-309). Cham: Springer International Publishing. researchgate.netDOI: 10.1007/978-3-031-12217-0_14

Yadav, K., Daga, S., & Yadav, B. (2022). Behavioral Finance and Future Research Agenda: A Bibliometric Analysis. *IUP Journal of Applied Finance*, *28*(4).

Yadav, K., Daga, S., & Yadav, B. (2022). Behavioral Finance and Future Research Agenda: A Bibliometric Analysis. *IUP Journal of Applied Finance*, *28*(4). https://search.ebscohost.com/login.aspx?direct=true&profile=ehost&scope=site&authtype=crawler&jrnl=09725105&AN=161241617&h=W0oev3aMOvAvZlUR%2BOkmdrf9JTYXDTgo6WhfVN0eV7ehkSfPQr7ftd93T5CoW42s7EcOFImL0qRIYOIis1qbVA%3D%3D&crl=c

Yang, C., Wang, J., & Liu, X. (2024). What affects the financial asset allocation of the elderly? From the perspective of financial literacy and risk attitude. *Finance Research Letters*, *63*, 105327. DOI: 10.1016/j.frl.2024.105327

Yang, T. T. (2020). The effect of workplace pensions on household saving: Evidence from a natural experiment in Taiwan. *The Journal of Risk and Insurance*, *87*(1), 173–194. DOI: 10.1111/jori.12254

Yani, A., Suherlan, , & Az Zaakiyyah, H. K. (2024). The Importance of Mentorship in Stimulating the Growth and Success of Entrepreneurial Business Entities. *Journal of Contemporary Administration and Management*, *2*(1), 337–342. DOI: 10.61100/adman.v2i1.129

Yan, S., Zhou, Y., & Zhang, Y. (2022). Analysis of balance of income and expenditure and optimal retirement age of pension insurance co-ordination account based on improved machine learning algorithm. *Computational Intelligence and Neuroscience*, *2022*(1), 5870893. DOI: 10.1155/2022/5870893

Yao, Y., Wang, Z., & Lei, C. K. (2025). How does green finance affect human well-being in the context of aging populations? Evidences from China. *Sustainability Accounting. Management and Policy Journal*, *16*(1), 259–291.

Yaprakli, T. Ş., & Ünalan, M. (2020). Determining of Social-Cultural, Environmental and Economic Impacts of Winter European Youth Olympic Festival [Kış Avrupa Gençlik Olimpik Festivalinin Sosyo-Kültürel, Çevresel ve Ekonomik Etkisinin Belirlenmesi]. *Sosyoekonomi*, *28*(43), 175–194. DOI: 10.17233/sosyoekonomi.2020.01.10

Yin, R. K. (2018). *Case Study Research and Applications: Design and Methods* (6th ed.). Sage.

Yuh, Y., Montalto, C. P., & Hanna, S. D. (1998). Are Americans prepared for retirement? *Financial Counseling and Planning*, *9*(1).

Yulia, P. S., Kasmungin, S., & Satiyawira, B. (2018). Indonesia's challenges and opportunities: Youth petroleum engineer's role to develop economic growth and natural resources. *Advances in Intelligent Systems and Computing*, *599*, 30–36. DOI: 10.1007/978-3-319-60204-2_4

Yu, M., Meng, B., & Li, R. (2022). Analysis of China's urban household indirect carbon emissions drivers under the background of population aging. *Structural Change and Economic Dynamics*, *60*, 114–125. DOI: 10.1016/j.strueco.2021.11.013

Yusuf, M., & Namadi-Musa, H. (2024). Effects of Youth Entrepreneurship Initiatives in Promoting Community Development in Tikonko, Bo District. *International Journal of Scientific Development and Research*, *10*(9), 533–542. https://www.researchgate.net/publication/385250276_Effects_of_Youth_Entrepreneurship_Initiatives_in_Promoting_Community_Development_in_Tikonko_Bo_District

Zahid, S., Tariq, B., Abbas, M., Kafi, A., Osman, N. H. B., Allumi, N. A., Abdul Rahim, M. K. I., & Ansari, H. W. A. (2025). Youth Unemployment and Economic Growth in South Asia: Policy Implications for Stability and Sustainable Development. *International Journal of Sustainable Development and Planning*, *20*(5), 1925–1931. DOI: 10.18280/ijsdp.200510

Zhang, C., Liu, S., Chen, G., & Harper, S. (2024). Green finance and the silver economy: Catalyzing China's low-carbon development. *Frontiers in Environmental Science*, *12*, 1406812. DOI: 10.3389/fenvs.2024.1406812

Zhang, G. (2023). The heterogeneous role of green finance on industrial structure upgrading-Based on spatial spillover perspective. *Finance Research Letters*, *58*, 104596. DOI: 10.1016/j.frl.2023.104596

Zhang, Y., Li, S., Jin, L., & Wu, F. (2022). How will the global food landscape accommodate developing countries' dietary change under urbanization? *Foods*, *11*(15), 2311. DOI: 10.3390/foods11223598 PMID: 36429189

Zhu, P., & Lin, B. (2022). Do the elderly consume more energy? Evidence from the retirement policy in urban China. *Energy Policy*, *165*, 112928. DOI: 10.1016/j.enpol.2022.112928

Zubkova, L. D., Dyachkov, S. M., & Maksimov, I. B. (2019). An Indicator of Financial Condition in Industry Investment Analysis. In K. M., I. T., & M. G.A. (Eds.), *Springer Proceedings in Business and Economics* (pp. 243 – 250). Springer Science and Business Media B.V. DOI: 10.1007/978-3-030-26284-6_22

About the Contributors

Bryan Christiansen is a highly indexed author of 50 Reference books on topics ranging from cultural studies to organizational sociology. He is currently an Adjunct Professor of business at Southern New Hampshire University and the Chief Executive Officer of the management consultancy, Soluvex, LLC in New Mexico, USA. Professor Christiansen is fluent in Chinese, Japanese, and Spanish, and is currently learning Russian. He has presented his work at several universities in numerous countries including Oxford University in the United Kingdom in 2016. He earned an MBA from Capella University in 2003 and a BS in Marketing from the University of the State of New York in 1996.

John D Branch currently teaches a variety of marketing and international business courses at the undergraduate, MBA, and executive levels at the Stephen M Ross School of Business at the University of Michigan (USA), and serves as Co-Director of the Yaffe Digital Media Initiative. Previously, he was Academic Director of the School's weekend and evening MBA programes; earlier, he was also Director of Educational Outreach at the University's William Davidson Institute. John also holds an appointment at the University's Center for Russian, East European, & Eurasian Studies, and maintains a Research Fellowship at the William Davidson Institute.

***

Birendri is serving as an Assistant Professor of Political Science at Lovely Professional University, Punjab. With over four years of dedicated teaching and research experience, she has established herself as a dynamic educator and scholar in the field. Her academic interests span a wide range of critical areas within political science, including Political Theory, Public Policy and Governance, Political Processes and Institutions, Gender Studies, Social Exclusion, Marginalised

Communities, and Human Rights. Through these diverse yet interconnected domains, Dr. Birendri continuously engages with pressing societal questions and aims to foster critical thinking among her students.

Vishnu Achutha Menon is an assistant professor at the Institute for Educational and Developmental Studies in Noida. His research interests span various fields, including film studies, new media, Virtual Reality (VR), Augmented Reality (AR), Artificial Intelligence (AI), data journalism and visualization, educational media, immersive technology, interactive media, media psychology, digital ethnography, smart education, digital pedagogy, verbal and nonverbal communication, South Asian performances, Natyasastra, and Ethnomusicology. He has published journal articles in Economic and Political Weekly, IEEE Proceedings, Springer Lecture Note Series, International Journal of Emerging Technologies in Learning (iJET), Studies in Media and Communication, Journal of Media and Communication, Journal of Arts, among others. Vishnu has contributed book chapters to publishers such as IGI Global, Wiley, CRC Press, and Emerald. He has also written book reviews for Asian Theatre Journal, Space and Culture, Urban India, and others. He specializes in mixed methods in social sciences and humanities research.

Ravi Kishor Agrawal is a dedicated academic affiliated with the Department of MSMSR at MATS University, located in Raipur, Chhattisgarh (Postal Code: 492001). With a strong commitment to education and research, Dr. Agrawal contributes actively to the academic community, supporting the mission of MATS University to foster innovation and excellence in higher education.

Andi Subhan Amir is a faculty member at the Department of Communication Science, Faculty of Social and Political Sciences, Hasanuddin University. He earned his Bachelor's degree in Communication Science from Universitas Hasanuddin, followed by a Master's degree in Mass Communication from the university's Graduate School. He completed his doctoral studies at the Faculty of Communication Science, Universitas Padjadjaran. In addition to his academic role as a lecturer and researcher, ASA—as he is commonly known—is actively involved in several professional organizations, including ISKI (Ikatan Sarjana Komunikasi Indonesia), ASPIKOM (Asosiasi Pendidikan Ilmu Komunikasi), and APEPINDO (Asosiasi Peneliti dan Penulis Indonesia). He has authored numerous scholarly works, including books, journal articles, and conference proceedings, published both nationally and internationally. His publications are accessible through his Google Scholar, SINTA and Scopus profiles.

Nilesh Anute is an accomplished academician currently serving as an Associate Professor at Sri Balaji University, Pune. With a strong foundation in management education and research, Dr. Anute brings extensive teaching experience and subject matter expertise to the classroom. He is known for his dedication to academic excellence, student development, and innovative teaching methods. His contributions to the field are reflected through his involvement in research publications, academic conferences, and curriculum development initiatives. Dr. Anute continues to play a pivotal role in shaping future business leaders through his commitment to education and mentorship.

Ann Mary Cherian is an academic in the Department of Economics at Christ College (Autonomous), Irinjalakuda, located in Thrissur, Kerala.With a passion for economics and a commitment to academic excellence, she has made significant contributions to the field through her research and teaching. Her areas of interest include Macroeconomics, Development economics, Agricultural economics, rural development, tourism economics, and the socio-economic impact of public policies. She is a dedicated educator, guiding students in understanding complex economic concepts while conducting insightful studies in her field.

Amir Ahmad Dar is the Faculty in the Department of Mathematics at Lovely Professional University Punjab. The area of interest: Financial mathematics, financial economics, statistics and business mathematics.

Bashir Ahmad Dar is an Assistant Professor in the Department of Political Science at Lovely Professional University, Punjab, India. He teaches a diverse range of courses in Political Science, covering both theoretical foundations and applied dimensions of the discipline. With a strong academic orientation, Dr. Ahmad has published research papers in reputed national and international journals, contributing significantly to scholarly discourse. He has also presented papers at numerous national and international conferences, fostering academic exchange and dialogue.

Shashank M Hiremath is a Academician & Researcher with 2 decades of experience. Corporate trainer, NSE certified financial analyst and investment advisor. Handling subjects like Financial Derivatives, Corporate Taxation, Security Analysis and Portfolio Management, Advanced Financial Management, Merchant Banking, Business Research Methods, etc. Attended and organised various international and national conferences. Guest speaker at various institutions.

Jipson Joseph has a PhD in Ethics from DVK Bangalore. Currently, he is a Research Scholar at School of Law, Christ University, Bangalore, India. His research interests are in the fields of ethics, gender studies, constitutional law, human rights, human security, environmental justice, SDGs, developmental policies, and global poverty. He has published 6 books, co-edited one book, and contributed scholarly articles to many international and national journals and edited volumes including IGI Global Scientific Publishing's edited books.

Volkan Kaymaz is an economist specializing in applied macroeconomics, environmental economics, and energy policy. His research focuses on the intersection of demographic change, consumption behavior, and sustainability. He holds a Ph.D. in Economics from Yildiz Technical University, where he studied financial crises within the framework of Veblen's theory. Dr. Kaymaz has published in peer-reviewed journals on topics including macroeconomic dynamics, carbon emissions, tourism economics, financial markets, and the energy transition. His recent research explores the economic implications of population aging and sectoral consumption shifts in European countries.

Manzoor Ahmad Khanday is from Anantnag Kashmir. He completed Bachelors from G.D.C Boys Anantnag, and pursued masters from the University of Kashmir, Srinagar. Following this, Dr. Manzoor Ahmad completed his Doctor of Philosophy from the Department of Statistics, Vikram University Ujjain, India. His research interests primarily include Economic Design of control charts, Statistical Quality Control and Probability Theory. Presently Dr. Manzoor Ahmad is an Assistant Professor at Lovely Professional University Punjab India.

Najoua Khayati is an accomplished economist affiliated with the Faculty of Law, Economics and social sciences of the Moulay Ismail University of Meknès in Morocco. She specializes in Entrepreneurship, Economic Development, Public Policy Analysis, and Gender Studies, and is strongly committed to advancing inclusive and sustainable growth. She has established a distinguished profile at the intersection of economic theory and real-world impact. A passionate advocate for evidence-based policymaking, she has contributed to a number of international conferences and academic forums, presenting innovative insights on entrepreneurship ecosystems, youth empowerment, and gender-responsive economic policies. She has been actively engaged in multidisciplinary research addressing the challenges of socio-economic transformation in emerging economies.

Sateesh Kumar T K, presently working as an Asst. Professor at Kristu Jayanti (Deemed to be University), Bengaluru, India.

M. Arul Raja is a dedicated and dynamic Assistant Professor of Management at Kongu Arts and Science College (Autonomous), Erode, with over seven years of rich experience in academia and research. His core areas of expertise include finance, entrepreneurship, and innovation management. As a Ministry of Education-certified Innovation Ambassador, he leads transformative initiatives such as the

Entrepreneurship Development Cell and the Institution's Innovation Hub, fostering a vibrant startup and innovation ecosystem on campus. His doctoral research delves into the ramifications of derivative trading on spot market volatility, reflecting his strong analytical acumen. Dr. Arul Raja has successfully organized and participated in over 50 academic events and has 14 research publications to his credit. Renowned for his academic leadership, student mentorship, and strategic coordination. He is passionate about blending industry insights with education to drive innovation, experiential learning, and institutional advancement.

Vinod Krishna M.U is an academician and industry expert with over 33 years of diverse professional experience spanning corporate leadership, entrepreneurship, and education. With a strong foundation in computer applications and extensive expertise in finance, marketing, and strategic management, he has established himself as a beacon of knowledge and innovation. Currently serving as a Professor in the Department of Management Studies at Dayananda Sagar College of Engineering, Dr. Vinod Krishna blends his academic rigor and practical insights to inspire students. Dr. Vinod Krishna holds a Ph.D. in Management Studies from REVA University, with his groundbreaking doctoral research on the prospects and challenges of personal financial planning in India. His academic credentials are further strengthened by certifications from prestigious institutions, including • IIM Calcutta, with an Advanced Programme in FinTech and Financial Blockchain. • IIIT Bangalore, with an Advanced Executive Program in Cybersecurity and a virtual internship at NPCI. As an ISAC-certified Cyber Crime Intervention Officer (CCIO) and a member of the National Security Database, he is committed to enhancing cyber resilience across sectors.

T.C. Manjunath did his BE from RV College of Engg. in 1989, ME in Robotics & Automation from LD College of Engg. in 1992 with First Rank and PhD in Systems & Control Engg. from IIT Bombay in the year 2007. He is currently working as the Dean Research R D and as Professor in the Dept. of Computer Science & Engineering with specialization in IoT, Cyber Security & Blockchain Technology in Rajarajeswari College of Engineering, Bengaluru, Karnataka. He has completed B.E. Degree from R.V. College of Engg., M.E. Govt.'s LD College of Engg., Gujarat Univ., Ahmedabad in First Rank and Ph.D. in Systems and Control Engineering from the Indian Institute of Technology Bombay IIT Bombay He has got a teaching academic, research and administrative experience of more than 35+ years 10 years as Principal, 8 years as HoD rest as faculty and has published more than 1200+ research papers in various national & international journals and conferences, with 175+ patents, 25 book-chapters, 25 awards and also published 25 text books in various field of science, engineering and technology, completed projects worth

Rs. 9 Crores till date apart from guiding 10 PhD scholars. He is a member of 30 Professional Society Chapters and is a fellow of IE, IETE, AMIEE and a chartered engineer. He got the best research scholar award in 2006 in IIT Bombay amongst all the research scholars of the institute. He has got 10 awards in academics and research activities.

Mukul Mukul is an Assistant Prodessor associated with the Commerce Department (USB), Chandigarh University Mohali, Punjab, India

Junior Ntabanganyimana is a motivated person who is devoted to both social and personal development. They enthusiastically pursued their education, doing well academically and participating in extracurricular activities that encouraged community service and leadership. Their early passion for math and statistics inspired them to pursue higher education, and they eventually graduated with a degree in statistics from Lovely Professional University.

P. Selvakumar is currently an Associate Professor in the Department of Science and Humanities at Nehru Institute of Technology, Coimbatore, Tamil Nadu, India. Prior to joining Nehru Institute of Technology, he held positions as an Assistant Professor in the Department of Science and Humanities various engineering colleges in Coimbatore, Tamil Nadu, India, spanning from 2011 to 2023. Dr.P. Selvakumar's academic and research interests lie primarily in the field of phytochemistry. He has made significant contributions to his field, with an impressive record that includes 30 journal publications, 12 patents, and 20 conference papers. Additionally, he has organized 5 seminars and conferences, further demonstrating his commitment to academic and scientific exchange. Throughout his career, Dr. P.Selvakumar has been recognized for his dedication and excellence in teaching, having been honored with several awards, including the Best Teacher Awards. He holds a prominent position in the academic community, contributing actively to research.

Indra Pahala is a Senior Lecturer (Lektor Kepala) at State University of Jakarta (UNJ). He is Expertise in Accounting, Taxation, Corporate Governance. Dr. Indra Pahala completed his undergraduate studies in Accounting before pursuing master's and doctoral degrees. Currently serving as a Senior Lecturer at UNJ with the rank of Penata (Grade III D), demonstrating his significant dedication and contributions to academia. Research focuses include: Corporate governance and accountability; Taxpayer behavior and taxation systems; Financial reporting and accounting standards; All research projects funded by BLU UNJ. Actively contributes to the development of accounting and taxation knowledge in Indonesia. His research has been applied in policy-making and business practices.

Ganesh Pathak is an Associate Professor at Sri Balaji University, Pune (SBUP), where he plays a key role in shaping future business leaders through his academic expertise and commitment to excellence in education. With a strong background in management and a passion for teaching, Dr. Pathak brings a blend of theoretical knowledge and practical experience to the classroom. His areas of interest include business strategy, organizational behavior, and leadership development. As a dedicated academician and mentor, he actively contributes to research, curriculum development, and student engagement at SBUP.

R.A. Ayyapparajan is an Director IQAC & Associate Professor with over 18 years of experience. He earned his Ph.D. in Human Resource Management and holds certifications in Marketing Research and Analysis, Human Resource Development, and digital Marketing. He has published nearly 20 research articles in national and international refereed journals and has presented more than 38 papers at various conferences and seminars. Additionally he has secured 7 patents and has served as a resource person for several programs earning best faculty award.

Rismawati is a distinguished academic and consultant with a robust focus on sustainability reporting. She currently holds the position of lecturer and Head of the Quality Assurance Institute at Universitas Muhammadiyah Palopo, where she has been pivotal in ensuring the quality of university processes and outputs since February 2020. Additionally, she serves as an Assurer for Sustainability Reporting at the National Center for Sustainability Reporting in Jakarta, specializing in the evaluation of sustainability reports for mining companies across Indonesia. Her academic qualifications are extensive, comprising a Bachelor's degree in Economics and Accounting, a Master's degree in Accounting Science, and a Doctorate in Accounting from Universitas Brawijaya, Malang. Rismawati is also a certified specialist in sustainability reporting, risk management, and tax planning, holding several prestigious certifications including Certified Sustainability Reporting Specialist (CSRS), Certified Risk Management Practitioner (CRMP), Certified Management Accountant (CMA) and Certified Enterprise Risk Analysis (CERA). In her professional capacity, she has provided consultancy services in financial management and tax compliance for companies such as PT. Reski Barito Timur and PT. Helay Raya. Furthermore, she has authored multiple publications on Social Accounting, Sustainability Accounting, Management Accounting and CSR, contributing significantly to the academic community. Her interests in reading, writing, and travel reflect her commitment to lifelong learning and professional growth in her field.

Sourabh Singh Roy is a respected faculty member in the Faculty of Management Studies at Gopal Narayan Singh University, situated in Sasaram, Bihar. Known for his academic dedication and commitment to student development, Dr. Roy plays a key role in shaping future business leaders through his expertise in management education and research.

Sumarni S is an Associate Professor in Management Science at Universitas Wira Bhakti, South Sulawesi, Indonesia. Her research interests include financial management, financial literacy, and Micro, Small, and Medium Enterprise (MSME) finance. Since 2024, she has been serving as the Dean of the Faculty of Economics and Business. Her academic qualifications include a Bachelor's degree in Economics (SE) and a Master of Science (M.Si) in Management from Universitas Hasanuddin, as well as a Doctorate in Management Science from Universitas Brawijaya, Malang. Sumarni S has published several articles in nationally accredited journals on topics such as financial management, MSME financial governance, village financial accountability, and culturally based financial literacy. She also holds professional certifications, including Certified Lecturer and BKD Assessor. To date, she remains actively engaged in teaching and academic writing, including authorship of academic books.

Supriadi is a dedicated lecturer in the Informatics Study Program at the Faculty of Computer Engineering, Universitas Cokroaminoto Palopo. He earned his Bachelor's degree in Islamic Studies (S.Ag) from the State Institute of Islamic Studies (IAIN) Ujung Pandang and later pursued a Master's degree in Education (M.Pd) at Universitas Negeri Makassar. His academic expertise lies in the intersection of religious studies and business ethics, which he applies in his teaching of Islamic Studies and Professional & Business Ethics within the Informatics Faculty. Beyond teaching, Supriadi is actively engaged in research, particularly in the fields of Augmented Reality (AR) and Sharia Tourism. His work focuses on integrating Islamic knowledge with Information Technology, aiming to develop innovative educational tools that enhance the learning experience. By combining religious perspectives with digital advancements, he seeks to bridge the gap between Islamic education and modern technology, making complex subjects more accessible and engaging. Through his research and academic contributions, Supriadi aspires to empower students and professionals with ethical and technological insights that align with Islamic values. His work continues to contribute to the evolving landscape of technology-assisted learning

Index

A

C

D

E

www.ingramcontent.com/pod-product-compliance
Lightning Source LLC
LaVergne TN
LVHW080910300926
849162LV00003B/628
9798337325507